THE
EFFECTIVE
OFFICE

A Handbook of

Modern Office Management

LIONEL G. TITMAN

CASSELL

To Ana.
Esalsts.

First published 1990 by **Cassell Educational Limited**
Villiers House, 41/47 Strand, London WC2N 5JE

© Cassell Educational Limited 1990

British Library Cataloguing in Publication Data

Titman, Lionel G.
The effective office.
1. Offices.   Management
I. Title
651.3

ISBN 0–304–31676–8

Printed and bound in Great Britain by
Dotesios Printers Ltd, Trowbridge, Wiltshire

THE EFFECTIVE OFFICE

A Handbook of
Modern Office Management

CONTENTS

THE AUTHOR

Lionel Titman was born in London, England. For personal reasons, he emigrated to Yugoslavia. He now lives in Ljubljana (the capital of the Republic of Slovenija) with his wife, who is a manager with a large commercial firm. His early career was with several major firms (the National Westminster Bank, Unilever, J. Sainsbury, Trust House Forte) working in both managerial and advisory roles.

He has worked as a management consultant in Australia, Bahrain, Brazil, Denmark, France, Great Britain, Greece, Hungary, Iran, Ireland, Italy, Spain, Switzerland, the United States of America, the United Arab Emirates and Yugoslavia. Clients worked for include the Greek Ministry of Finance, the Royal Commission on the Press, Rank Xerox, Bank of America, Arthur Anderson, BP Chemicals, a millionaire entrepreneur, trade unions, a night club, the London Clinic and some thirty financial institutions.

He is also a writer, speaker and broadcaster on management subjects and was the originator of several management techniques, including Office Group Capability, Corporate Trunking and Customer Latent Profiling. He was co-author of *Company Organization: Theory and Practice*, a book that has been translated into Polish, Italian and Danish. He is an ex-examiner of the Institute of Management Services, and an ex-Member of the Council of the Institute of Administrative Management. He is a Fellow of both Institutes as well as of the Institute of Management Consultants.

Lionel Titman started his consultancy career with Research and Marketing Ltd. He then joined PA Consultants, where he worked for a number of years. He was then appointed Director of Consulting, Lombardy Management and Personnel Services. After a spell as Managing Director of Berkeley Lion, he moved to Yugoslavia. He is now Chairman of Harvard Consultants Ltd – a group of specially selected independent senior management consultants operating internationally.

I

Introduction

Either dance well or leave the ballroom.
Greek proverb

He wanted to do well, simply for doing-well's sake, to acquit himself
decently of a job.   **Saul Bellow, *Looking for Mr Green* (1951)**

The French regard it as an art and do it with style. The Americans write extensive instruction manuals about it, and dislike paying too much for it. The British rarely talk about it, and often seem to prefer the amateur to the professional approach. When experts give advice about it, they tend to place too much emphasis on the technique to be used. 'It' is effective administration.

This book is devoted to improving offices. It is intended for everybody who has the same aim, everybody who knows that office work (like all else in life) can be done either well or badly. For all those who know that 90 per cent of office ills are self-inflicted. During the night of 10/11 November, 1918, Marshall Foch dictated to clerk M. Henri Deledicq the terms of the armistice that was to end the 1914–18 war. At 5.10 a.m. the war leaders signed the armistice in a railway carriage at Rethondes. There was something about the armistice that none of the leaders noticed. Clerk Deledicq had put some of the carbon papers in the wrong way round, so much of the armistice was unreadable unless one had a mirror and read the back of the paper. Many offices have daily occurrences of the Rethondes syndrome.

It should not be thought that any miracle technique ensures effortless and overnight success. Admittedly, this book does contain a number of techniques. But technique is not enough. During a tour of the West Indies, the English cricket captain was seen to be wearing an unusual T-shirt. Unusual because on it was written the word, 'TECHNIQUE'. The talisman failed – on that tour England lost every single test match. In management there is no magic wand, no talisman. Technique is not enough. What matters is how well the technique is applied.

There is also a tendency to discard a new technique if it fails the test of effortless, overnight success. On an early morning Glasgow shuttle flight two managers were reading their *Financial Times*. Suddenly one turned to the other and said, 'Do you remember Management by Objectives?' 'Ah, yes,' said the second nostalgically, 'Did you ever have Quality Circles?' 'No, we missed that,' said the first, then brightened up, 'but we had Marginal Costing.' It was difficult not to intervene indignantly. But we sank back into our seats and stayed silent. Searchers for the Holy Grail are not easily dissuaded.

Since techniques have been somewhat slighted, it might seem strange to find so many chapters devoted to describing techniques. The answer is that only those techniques that can really help office effectiveness are included. So there is nothing on such areas as Merit Rating or Job Grading. There is nothing inherently wrong with such approaches but they are not sharp enough for our purpose (on the other hand Organization

Development is included although it does not get a good press nowadays). Our purpose is attaining effective offices.

An effective office is one in which what should happen, does happen. It has about it an atmosphere – an atmosphere of confidence, certainty and smoothness. It gives an excellent level of service to outsiders and to the rest of the organization, and it knows it, while at the same time instinctively searching for improvement all the time. Such offices exist, as do their opposites. Every organization has a choice – to have effective offices or to have a shambles.

The other characteristic of the effective office is that it is lean. Fat cats move slowly and are not outstandingly good at their task of catching mice. On the other hand, slimming by sudden starvation is not the only alternative. A better route is to attain slimness and then to stay fit by constantly watching the scales. The importance of white-collar productivity is growing in importance, and will continue to do so. That is the view of a panel of 200 chief executives from 14 European countries representing 15 industries.

This panel of European chief executives was surveyed by Booz-Allen & Hamilton Inc. for the *Wall Street Journal*.[1] The panel assessed the growing priority of white-collar productivity with the following result:

	Important	Very Important
1979	37%	19%
1984	38%	52%
1989	24%	67%

It is also interesting to see where these chief executives thought that efforts at productivity improvement were most likely to focus in the coming years. Number one target was middle management. Now, the imminent demise of middle management has been widely predicted periodically for the past quarter of a century and more. First it was because of the increasing use of statistical tools, then because of new forms of organization structure. Then it was going to be because of computers, then advanced office technology, and now office automation. It has not happened yet, but perhaps it will at last, though it may be because the number of middle managers has grown so much that they are very visible, and so their value is being more closely looked at.

The panel of chief executives put the targets for white-collar productivity improvement in the following order:

1 Middle managers.
2 Sales and marketing.
3 Clerks and secretaries.
4 Operations.
5 Design and engineering.
6 Financial staff.

In many organizations that list will add up to a sizeable number of people and a major programme of improvement, especially as the survey revealed the opinion that improving staff productivity will make a major difference to companies' competitive success in the future.

Office costs do have the trait of going up rather than down. This characteristic can be observed in a number of ways:

- costs act as a ratchet. They go up a notch ('Let's give everybody colour monitors') much more easily than down a notch;
- all capital expenditure brings in its wake increased revenue expenditure; a simple fact known to everybody who has ever been in house-owner mode, but one which escapes the same person when in covetous-employee mode;
- 'what comes down must go up' – the motto of many people who have had to face cost reductions and do their best to restore the status quo;
- cutting budgets is not saving money. Cutting spending is;
- buying new technology does not guarantee cost reduction.

Attitudes on the last point have changed. During the late 1970s and early 1980s there was a widespread feeling that there was no need to justify buying advanced office technology. It was so obviously such a good thing that cost savings were not needed. A common analogy that was used was to ask whether it was necessary to justify the telephone. This attitude crumbled away for several reasons.

First, as advanced technology became more widespread it lost its aura of arcane mystery. Second, it was realized that while buying hardware and software could be cheap, buying the wrong items could be expensive. Third, the lack of normal restraints led to some aggravating excesses. Fourth, the introduction of advanced technology failed to realize the anticipated leap in productivity in too many cases for comfort. The advent of advanced technology was likened to the Industrial Revolution. Some people referred to it as the Second Industrial Revolution – even in whimsical mood calling it 'IR^2'.

Perhaps people have forgotten how great a change the Industrial Revolution brought about. Not just the vast network of railways, canals and roads, but the difference to living standards. Beforehand, buying an overcoat was the equivalent of our buying a new car now. But – 'between, say, the 1750s and the 1830s the mechanization of spinning in Britain had increased productivity in that sector alone by a factor of 300 to 400'.[2] Not by 300–400 per cent, but by a factor of 300–400. Today, as management consultants, we are usually hard-pressed to increase office productivity using advanced technology by as little as 50 per cent.

Productivity is not just a matter of better use of capital or staff; it is the better use of all inputs, which includes capital *and* staff. This is known as Total Factor Productivity (TFP). But even using this all-embracing definition, new technology has not helped OECD countries to improve productivity to the sort of level seen during the Industrial Revolution. In fact, in some years OECD productivity has actually gone down. One report states that in service industries (such as finance, insurance and business services) 'that should benefit the most from advances in computerisation and communications, there has been little or no sign of improved TFP growth in recent years, surprising as it may seem'.[3]

This is no Luddite attack on advanced office technology. It is a plea for a realization that installing a few small office computers is no quick fix for solving low productivity. What is needed is the effective use of advanced technology – what is known as the management of technology. Nor is the effective use of advanced technology a mere

3

dream for the future such as one used to read in magazine articles at one time. Some clients are already using advanced technology so well that it almost causes one to stand back in admiration. Strangely enough, the staff who work in such offices are not equally impressed. They just regard it as natural and obvious – some will even tell one how it could all be further improved. Moreover, they are nearly always right.

It is suggested that a start to using new office technology well is to understand a little about it. Here there is a gap to which many managers refer: books tend to be written either at a vaguely insulting cat-sat-on-the-mat level or at an advanced jargon-filled level which is not what people need. Part B of this book (Technology Enlacement) addresses this difficulty by discussing equipment and software but in a volume such as this it is not possible to go into too much detail about technological matters.

The phrase 'advanced office technology' (AOT) has been used several times. This fact reveals a linguistic shortcoming. There is no word or phrase which describes to people's satisfaction the set of machines used in offices that employ a measure of electronic components. 'Office equipment' somehow implies items like staplers and guillotines. 'Office machinery' is not bad but sounds unexciting and slightly old-fashioned. 'Office automation' should be reserved for the real thing, which is computer-based procedures with little human or paper interruption. That still leaves the phrase 'information technology'.

The trouble with 'information technology' is two-fold. First, there is little agreement on its definition – one Australian source suggests that it includes cave drawings.[4] Second, it sounds rather like harking back to the idea that was once espoused that all office work consists of processing information. So we are left with AOT (Advanced Office Technology) which is not very much better – some of the items included can hardly be thought of as being 'advanced' any longer.

The attainment of the effective office cannot be left to the development of new equipment, no matter how ingenious this may be. The ultimate path to greater effectiveness has to remain that of managers working with the staff. For this reason, a number of what have been called 'management tools' have been brought together in Part C. This includes such areas as organization structure, effecting change, levels of service as well as management accounting and management information systems.

It also includes a chapter on assessing the performance of managers. This is based on the approach of EPR (Executive Performance Review), which is particularly applicable to the work of middle managers. This is an area which has been largely untouched in practice, although many people appreciate that it can be a major source of ineffectiveness. The remarks of the panel of chief executives already referred to supports the contention that the time is right for action.

A long-standing, basic, and necessary part of attaining an effective office is the improvement of procedures and methods. The approaches are covered in Part D (Method Design). We have worked in a number of offices that are automated or 'paperless'. Occasionally this involved the actual equipment. Much more commonly, however, the problems are what they have always been – systems or personnel. Even the details of the problems have changed very little. This odd fact is either reassuring or disturbing depending on one's point of view. It has even been suggested that the whole gamut of advanced technology is a complete circle. Many multinational banks have spent deeply on the installation of technology-based international systems for the movement of funds and data. Many of them followed similar approaches. Having done this, they found themselves back where they started – competitive advantage depended on the quality of the staff, and the systems.

A basic quandary of office life, which has faced managers since at least the time of the ancient Egyptians, is the question of staff numbers. A balance has to be found for the quantity of work to be done and the number of staff required to do it. Too few staff leads to backlogs. Too many staff leads to lack of concentration and high costs. Solving this quandary is a reasonably straightforward affair if one uses some form of work quantification.

Youth sees everything as new, old age sees everything as a repeating cycle. If this aphorism is true, then many of us are in an advanced stage of senility. Office work quantification was popular during the 1960s, seemed to retreat during the 1970s and then became strongly advocated during the middle and late 1980s. The result is that there are some industrial sectors (such as multinational banking) where most of the participants seem to have a form of work quantification. The main approaches, as well as ways of dealing with problem areas, are given in Part E.

This structure would omit some useful information, and so these other areas have been collected together in the final two parts (F and G). This covers a number of items such as security and taxonomy as well as a glossary and an appendix of collated data. The shape of the book is therefore:

Part	Subject matter
A	Basics
B	Technology enlacement
C	Managerial tools
D	Method design
E	Work quantification
F	Support techniques
G	Final notes

References

1 'Executives emphasize improving productivity of white-collar staff', *Wall Street Journal*, 20 July, 1984.
2 Kennedy, P., *The Rise and Fall of the Great Powers*, New York: Random House, 1987.
3 'Productivity and economic performance', *OECD Observer*, No. 151, p. 27, April/May 1988.
4 Behan, K. and Holmes, D., *Understanding Information Technology*, Sydney: Prentice-Hall, 1986.

Basics

2

Approaches and Techniques

What sets us against one another is not our aims – they all come to
the same thing, but our methods, which are the fruit of our varied
reasoning.   Saint-Exupéry, *Wind, Sand and Stars* (1939)

I do not know how we got into this tunnel. I cannot explain it. But
look at it this way. We are travelling along a track; therefore this
tunnel leads somewhere. We have no cause to believe that anything
is wrong with this tunnel except, of course, that it seems to have no
end.   F. Dürrenmatt, *The Tunnel* (1961)

There is no one single route, one single technique, that is applicable to every occasion
when the aim is to attain the effective office. To many people this fact is so obvious that
it is hardly worth stating. But it is certainly not obvious to everybody. A few people stick
blindly to one technique, using it repeatedly no matter what the circumstances.
Whether this is due to a misplaced sense of loyalty or to sheer ignorance is unclear.
Even worse are the magazine articles that describe a new 'technique' that is a sure-fire
answer to all admin situations. Since the new technique can be fully described in under
a thousand words, it is also obviously incredibly easy to install.

These universalist wonder cures are known as 'slicing the melon' or 'cutting the
cone'. This is because if one slices a melon or cuts a cone at a different angle, one gets a
different shape. Of course, a slice (to pursue the metaphor) is not the whole.

It is said that there are basically five ways to increase profitability and that the right
one depends on circumstances. The five ways are:

- increase sales;
- raise the selling price;
- reduce costs;
- change the service/product mix;
- improve asset exploitation.

In a similar way, there are five basic ways to increase office effectiveness. These five
ways can, between them, impact all five ways of increasing profits – not only reducing
costs.

Five basic approaches

The five basic routes to improving office effectiveness are:

- using a quick fix;
- curing a specific sickness;
- overhauling the office admin;
- changing the culture;
- carrying out a complete, rounded investigation.

■ USING A QUICK FIX

The primary quick fix is issuing a directive that all costs are to be reduced by a pre-set amount, say 20 per cent. The advantage of this quick fix is that, provided it is pursued with sufficient vigour, then real savings are made and are made at the desired level. The disadvantage is that reductions are indiscriminate: they fall on the efficient and the inefficient equally. They also cut equally those services that are vital and those that are not needed. A better quick fix is that of stopping a current service or disbanding a department. Savings are quick –but it is important to choose an area that really is not needed.

A

A noted exponent of low office costs and quick fixing was Henry Ford. By 1919, a third of all cars sold in America were Fords though the office staff numbered just 1,074[1]. A year later, in 1920, there was a down-turn in the market. Ford cut the office staff from 1,074 to 528, closed the telecommunications office, sold off the excess furniture and disposed of the majority of telephones ('Only a comparatively few men in any organization need telephones'). Even the office pencil sharpeners went – staff had to bring their own knives. By 1923 the market had recovered (Ford made two million cars) but Henry Ford still disliked having too many office staff; he fired all the accounting staff.

By modern standards, the 1919 Ford office staff of 1,074 for a third of the market seems extremely modest. Some seventy years later, General Motors had about a third of the American market,[2] making some four million cars. But they had 123,000 office staff.

The other type of quick fix (the special techniques) are not worth considering in detail since these techniques disappear so quickly. Few people, for example, are still persevering with Pound-a-Day or PIP. The quick fix does have its place – but it should be recognized for what it is. It is of use in emergencies. But it is not a route that can be recommended for long-term health or for a robust effective office. It is dealt with in more detail in chapter 4, The Quick Fix and Beyond.

■ CURING SPECIFIC DISEASES

In ordinary conversation, we sometimes talk of a 'healthy business'. This is not easy to define. To say that it means freedom from disease is to beg the question, as we then have to define 'disease'. In medicine, disease can be divided into three types – infectious, genetic and environmental. The same division can be used when referring to ills in the office.

An infectious illness is one that spreads from person to person; an obvious example is low morale. A genetic illness is one that is passed from generation to generation, such as an inadequate organization structure. An environmental illness is one in which an organization finds itself at odds with the market or with the larger environment.

7

This description of the ills of an office is more than just an interesting metaphor. While it is always dangerous to argue by analogy, the splitting of ills in this way has led to some observed similarities between human illness and office ills:

- using a quick-fix technique will only help an infectious illness. It will not help a genetic or environmental one. In this, it is akin to taking an aspirin or antibiotic;
- curing one type of ill will not, of itself, cure one of the other types. Something extra has to be added to do that. For example, improving the Management Information System (MIS) will not, of itself, improve office productivity;
- in treating a disease, it is important to tackle the real cause and not just the symptoms.

Table 2.1 is an explanatory table of the concept of diseases.

In both the office and medical senses there is a widespread (though fortunately localized) tendency to blame environmental conditions for more illness than should be. For example, in the late 1980s there came the news that 16,000 seals had died in the North Sea. A group of people called 'environmentalists' claimed that this was due to chemical pollution. The evidence seemed to make this unlikely. The onset was rapid, deaths were highest among large puppying groups and low near major industrial centres, and common seals were affected rather than grey seals – all pointers to a viral cause. Even when the guilty virus was identified (belonging to the same family as canine distemper[3] people remained unconvinced. In the same way, it is remarkable how office staff will often blame 'them', or the government, or the customers for some ill that has befallen them. Blaming the environment for one's ills is highly popular with some people – it gives one somebody else to blame and means that one does not have to

Table 2.1   Office diseases

Type:	Infectious	Genetic	Environmental
Human ills:	Smallpox	Haemophilia	Frostbite
Office ills:	Low morale	Ineffective MIS	Continual change in government policy, laws
	High sickness/ absenteeism	Poor structure Inappropriate culture	Industry terms-of-trade
	Substandard productivity	Inadequate equipment or procedures	Image in the market-place
	Low levels of service		
Notes:	Fitness can be improved via improved leadership. Management development may inoculate to some degree	Sufferer may realize that something is amiss but be unable to identify the real causes of the illness	Management may accept both causes *and* the effects as being inescapable – or just rely on a form of insulation

change one's own attitudes. However, if the customer is continually being blamed, then the office is likely to be very diseased indeed.

Another analogy is the phantom disease. In this, a disease is postulated that does not exist. In the late 1980s, again, some of the more popular newspapers published photographs of 'diseased' trees. The cause of the distress was said by some people to be 'acid rain'. This continued for some time until eventually an arboriculturist had to reply. It was pointed out,[4] first, that trees had always had a finite life and all eventually died and, second, that the published photographs were of healthy trees showing the die-back that happened every year. The commonest phantom disease in office life is to blame the computer for continuing faults that it does not possess.

The main problem with both phantom diseases and blaming the environment is that people will not be convinced of their falsity by mere logic – just showing that it cannot be true is rarely enough. One will have to show the falseness repeatedly, or side-step what is to blame and get on with curing the real problem. Sometimes one may have to make a small show of treating the symptoms whilst in reality tackling the basic disease.

In the medical world the distinction between infectious, genetic and environmental diseases is becoming blurred.[5] For example, it is even possible that Alzheimer's disease can be predisposed by genetic (on chromosome 21) as well as environmental (aluminium) factors. In the same way, it is now being realized that some offices have a mixture of disease factors. This has led to the evolution of approaches like the Seven Tracks (see chapter 4).

If an otherwise healthy office is suffering from an ill that can be recognized and isolated, then the treatment is straightforward. One treats just the disease. There is no point in taking excessive time, treating ills that do not exist. We would not think much of a doctor who, though we just had influenza, insisted on giving us tablets against scurvy 'just in case'. In the same way, if the procedures are wrong in an office then one uses method design (Part D). If there is a need for mechanization, then one may decide on the introduction of some office technology (Part B). The use of other extraneous techniques such as Organization Development (chapter 19) may, in such cases, be a waste of time. The rule is the usual one – horses for courses.

■ OVERHAULING THE OFFICE ADMIN

There are times when the problem is more than a local ill which can be tackled by means of a single technique such as some method design or office technology. In such cases it may be necessary to look at the administration with a wider perspective, even sometimes in its entirety.

To do this one needs to have a logical framework containing a number of techniques. This 'basket' of techniques needs to remain in balance. It also needs to reflect the needs of the situation. This means that there cannot be a single basket that is always right for every circumstance. Three such baskets are described below – one of these should fit most situations. If it is felt that none of them is quite right for a particular circumstance, then it is not impossible to create a basket oneself by using a selection of techniques.

Office Group Capability (OGC)

This is the main approach to tackling office admin in a logical and coherent fashion. It is particularly appropriate to medium and large offices. Most of the components within

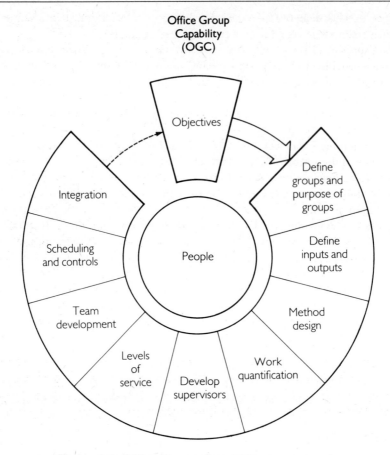

Figure 2.1 Office Group Capability components

it are covered in detail in other parts of the book. The diagram in Figure 2.1 shows the make-up of OGC. The separate parts of OGC are:

- objectives. These may have to be considered at different levels. They may be related back to the overall corporate strategy, or they may be part of a plan (such as automation);
- define the groups and purpose of the groups. The basis of OGC is the working group – a cohesive team of people who know their purpose, who are good at it, and who know that they are good at it. Part of knowing their responsibility is achieved by defining the group inputs and outputs. Groups and group working are covered in chapter 8;
- method design. The aim of the method design stage is to ensure that the systems and procedures are effective. Where appropriate this includes the introduction or extension of advanced office technology (see Part B and Part D);
- work quantification. Having completed the method design, the next stage is to quantify or measure the workloads using one of the approaches described in Part E;
- develop supervisors. The effectiveness of OGC is increased if the group supervision

is effective. It is unfortunately true that in many offices a supervisor is merely the 'senior person present', without any training in managerial skills;

- levels of service. There are two aspects to this stage. One is the concept of excellence of service provided to both customers and to the rest of the organization. The other aspect is the definition of service provisions, such as deadlines (see chapter 22 for a description of levels of service);
- team development. A group does not necessarily become a cohesive team, nor do groups work well together by accident. It is therefore necessary at this stage to give matters a helping hand (chapters 5, 8 and 19);
- scheduling and controls. By this time the workload, the procedures and the deadlines have all been defined. It is thus time to devise the scheduling of throughput, and to install a form of management controls so that the group knows how well it is doing (chapter 40);
- integration. Having ensured that each group is effective and that it is working with other groups, it is necessary that the overall procedures are working well. This is done by inspecting the overall situation, and checking whether any fine-tuning is needed to attain overall effectiveness;
- people. At the centre of the OGC diagram, the word 'people' appears. This is because people are at the heart of successful OGC. The OGC diagram shows that it is a mixture of the two components of an effective office: people-orientation and task-orientation. People remain at the centre.

Office Group Capability is applicable in many situations and has been used successfully in different organizations in different countries. None of the component techniques is difficult. It does, however, need an analyst or consultant who can handle the two types of aspect: both task and people orientation.

Overhead Cost Reduction (OCR)

The name of this approach is not particularly descriptive. It is sometimes called Overhead Value Analysis. Just to compound the confusion, Overhead Value Analysis is also the name given to a single technique (described in chapter 26). When used as a 'basket' descriptor, most of the components follow the lines described in detail in the same chapter. To avoid repeating the same information here, the stages are given in outline only below.

Overhead Cost Reduction can be used in most offices (it seems to be quite widely used in Australia). It is particularly useful when the primary aim is cost reduction, when the offices involved give a service to the rest of the enterprise rather than to customers, or when one is concerned with a number of branch offices (e.g. an international organization having a number of overseas offices). The stages of a study are:

- a functional analysis of the work performed;
- user interviews to obtain the users' perception of services;
- an effectiveness study based on an inter-office comparison. This may use ratios, work quantification and/or a comparison with known standards for the industry or type of service;
- a computer analysis of the data so far collected;
- method design to improve procedures. In international branch offices this often concentrates on eliminating local practices;

11

- organization structure study to decide reporting lines, and to decide the degree of decentralization. This will often be done by studying the scope for using tele-communications;
- setting standards for staffing levels. This will be based on work quantification, ratios or on industry standards.

These components are covered in chapter 26, Part D, and Part E.

Corporate Trunking

This approach is particularly effective when an organization wishes to tackle the two up-to-date problems of developing middle management and introducing office auto-mation. This dual problem is facing many organizations, and is not easy to tackle. Corporate Trunking addresses the special problem of top management wishing to get involved without participating in day-to-day details. Figure 2.2 is a diagram of Corporate Trunking. The diagram shows the continuing involvement of corporate senior management in the 'trunk' on the left-hand side (hence the name) while the continuing studies are shown as branches on the right-hand side. The stages of Corporate Trunking are:

- a top-level Task Force is set up, from the board and senior managers. A meeting of this Task Force and the consultants is held at which the overall study is described, the timetable set and a date for the next meeting agreed;
- the first stage consists of an 'Organizational Analysis', and an enquiry into the management information needs. The Organizational Analysis divides the offices into broad functional groups and collects details of their main activities. The approximate cost of each functional group is calculated. The probability of automat-ing each functional group is decided together with the selected route. Costs (current, automation, and future) and ratios are calculated;
- half-way through this first stage, a seminar is held. This covers a discussion on office automation and its likely impact on staff, specialists and middle managers. A short session on an office technology area (a spreadsheet) is normally included;
- three-quarters of the way through the first stage, details are distributed showing the details of costs, ratios and comparisons;
- at the end of the first stage, a whole-day meeting is held. This covers the findings of the first stage, costs, ratios and likely route(s) for office automation. If the spread-sheet was used at the initial meeting, then it is used here as an aid. Agreements are reached on any organizational changes, strategy for the rest of the studies, and probable routes for automation;
- the second stage is now carried out, depending on the agreements reached. This stage finalizes the plans for introducing office automation, completes the analysis of information needs and controls, and prepares for the management development of middle managers;
- at the end of this stage a further meeting is held with the Task Force. At this meeting, agreement is finalized on the details of the office automation and management information needs. Immediately after this meeting, there is a seminar on how it is proposed to improve the performance of middle management;
- the third stage now proceeds. This is likely to take place while awaiting delivery of automation equipment. It consists of staff development, management development

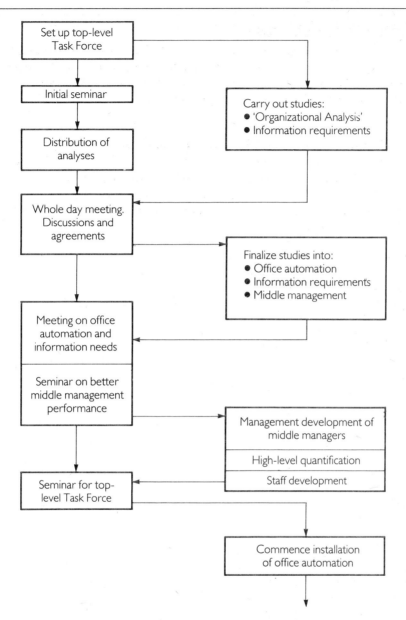

Figure 2.2 Corporate Trunking

of middle managers, and training. It will also normally include a form of work quantification (using high-level standards) followed by setting up controls;
- a final seminar is held for the Task Force on the overall study, prior to the commencement of the installation of the office automation and management information system.

Components of Corporate Trunking are to be found in Part B, chapter 17, chapter 21, Part E and chapter 40.

■ CHANGING THE CULTURE

There are times when even one of these baskets of techniques is not enough, because there is something basically inappropriate with the management style, the atmosphere, the beliefs, or the 'way things are done and run' in an organization. When this is the situation, it is necessary to alter the culture, to develop the organization itself. This is discussed in chapters 3 and 19.

■ CARRYING OUT A COMPLETE INVESTIGATION

There are times when an organization is in a thoroughly unhealthy state. Strangely enough, this is often the time when it attempts to improve itself by using a quick fix – which of course is not the right treatment. The right treatment is that of the Seven Tracks. These are discussed in chapter 4 (The Quick Fix and Beyond), which in turn leads to a large part of the book.

References

1 Lacey, R., *Ford*, London: Heinemann, 1986.
2 *The Economist*, 28 November, 1987, p. 72.
3 *The Guardian Weekly*, Vol. 139, No. 24, 11 December, 1988, p. 2, and Vol. 140, No. 2, 8 January, 1989, p. 3.
4 *The Guardian Weekly*, Vol. 140, No. 1, 1 January, 1989, p. 20.
5 *The Economist*, 12 September, 1987, p. 89.

3

Culture and Management

To almost all men the state of things under which they have been
used to live seems to be the necessary state of things.
Thomas Macaulay, *Southey's Colloquies*, 1830

When I hear the word culture, I reach for my gun.
attrib. Hermann Goering[1]

We speak readily about the variation between cultures of different countries – about how Britain is different from Turkey, how the USA is different from Chile. We even recognize that there can be variations within a single country, though one may have to know a country quite well to appreciate these. To a Briton, Liverpool is not like London. To an American, Berkeley is different from Boston.

The concept of organizational culture runs parallel to this common perception. Just as countries are different, so are organizations. And in similar sorts of ways. In both countries and organizations, there are things that one just does not do if one wishes to get on, so to speak. Culture covers acceptable behaviour, attitudes, beliefs, appearance, value judgements, status, tribal groupings, myths adhered to. These components of culture apply to both countries and organizations.

Some people dislike the use of the concept of organizational culture, preferring to use a simpler word such as 'atmosphere'. But culture is much wider than atmosphere, though certainly atmosphere is a component. There are many definitions of culture as used in concerns, but one of the most attractive is also one of the simplest. It is 'the way we do things around here, and our beliefs'.

Manifestations of culture

Among writers, there is a considerable variation in emphasis as to what is important in cultural differences. The following is a composite list:

1 The basic philosophy that guides the organization in its attitudes to employees and to customers/the public. Some organizations have an actual 'corporate philosophy' printed. These can be an accurate summation of how the enterprise thinks – or they can be quite meaningless pieces of public relations.
2 The dominant aims. These can be a high level of service (IBM) or product innovation (3M), for example.
3 Behaviour of staff. This includes how they act towards one another, how they defer to seniors, how they dress, what meetings are like and so on.
4 Physical surroundings. Offices vary from the sybaritic to the imitation slum.
5 Unspoken rules. New staff getting to grips with these are said to be 'learning the ropes' – a phrase that may be unconsciously most apposite.
6 Myths related. This is a favourite topic for writers, just as anthropologists are fascinated by the myths that are passed on from one generation to another in tribes.

15

In companies they are often stories about a founder that become parables for expected attitudes – though one well-known writer, Edgar Schein, prefers to reserve the word 'culture' for the deeper level of basic assumptions and beliefs that are shared by an organization and that operate unconsciously.[2] Schein also puts forward a reason that he believes is the cause for an organization having a specific culture. He believes that it is a response to previous problems of survival. The responses come to be taken for granted because they solved the problems repeatedly and reliably. And from this, the culture arises.

The differences can be illustrated by two chimerical enterprises, called Technol and Pyramid. Technol has open-plan offices with modish furniture, the staff are informally dressed, status symbols are so rare that it is not easy to see who are seniors. Individual creativity and accountability are rated highly, though so too is wide consensus before decisions are formulated. There is little sense of a boss handing down decisions and action plans. The organization structure is fluid. Staff see themselves as a cohesive group, almost family-like.

Pyramid is very different. Offices are separate and doors are normally closed. Staff are formally dressed. Status symbols are clear – such as the different dining rooms for seniors. Staff tend to wait until asked before venturing opinions, accepting decisions from above and implementing them. The organization is printed and a framed copy is in reception. Staff see themselves as loyal to their manager and dedicated to getting the work done.

These archetypes are not unfamiliar. The first point that has to be made is that neither type is automatically and infallibly more effective than the other – though both would regard themselves as being superior to the other.

The second point is that ways of improving effectiveness should be used in a different fashion in the two organizations – and may well have different outcomes. Take for example the introduction of advanced office technology. At Technol, a committee might be set up that would take soundings from the staff and try to get their agreement on a common approach. At Pyramid, the committee would study the technical aspects of possible equipment solutions, sound out the management, and issue a report that would be the foundation of the new scheme.

Neither approach will necessarily lead to failure or success. This is a good thing since it means that any organization can make itself more effective, irrespective of the dominant culture. In spite of this, many people will prefer one approach to the other. This is probably because we all have different backgrounds and personalities.

This leads to another inescapable fact. It might be thought that as staff with varying backgrounds and personalities change employers, so gradually all organizations would become similar – along the lines of the analogy of mixing warm and cold water. Anybody who has worked for several organizations knows that this does not happen. Every separate organization is different, with its own atmosphere and culture. The fact is that every organization is to a large extent self-selecting. First, people tend to apply to organizations that have the reputation of being the sort of place that they approve of. Second, when they get there, they will tend to leave if they do not like it. Third, there is a very strong tendency for people to act as the organization expects them to – even if this means hiding their true inclinations.

A person may move from Pyramid to Technol. This person's manager puts forward (for discussion, so the manager thinks) a way of improving effectiveness. To this, the ex-

Pyramid subordinate agrees fully. Not because the idea looks good but because experience has taught the importance of saving a boss any embarrassment. Any other reaction would be unthinkable. The new improvement goes in – and fails.

If the puzzled manager asks the subordinate about this, the subordinate may reply that he/she would have done something different. The manager may well then ask why the subordinate did not say so earlier. Now the subordinate is really in a cleft stick. Any normal reply will inevitably do the one thing that has to be avoided – embarrassing the boss. At this stage, communications have broken down because of a difference of priorities. To the ex-Pyramid subordinate, not embarrassing the boss is more important than expressing a helpful opinion. To the Technol manager, the opposite is true. Both hold their beliefs to be self-evident.

A management consultant, or anyone else trying to make our two companies more effective, has to work within the over-riding culture. First, in the selection of suitable approaches. Technol might benefit from sharpening the decision-making process and better time management. Pyramid might benefit from improving their staff-handling abilities and increasing creativity potentialities. Second, in the selection of approach, Technol would need many discussions; Pyramid would tend to accept the word of an expert – though that expert must be right.

There is one aspect of culture that may or may not be present in Technol or Pyramid or any other organization: the ability to change and to improve. As one works in different organizations, there is one cultural aspect that stands out above all else: the ability or lack of it to attain improvements. In some offices, change and improvement are a natural way of life. In others, both are a frightening prospect and to be resisted. Many people (such as Schein) take a quasi-psychoanalytical approach: to be able to improve a situation, it is necessary first to understand the underlying culture. Some years ago, Lewin[3] expressed it somewhat differently. Only when attempting to change a system does one really understand it.

Leadership

Few aspects of management have led to more writing and discussion than the nature and impact of leadership. Here we are concerned with the impact of leadership on culture, rather than its wider implications. Leaders seem to have the ability to get people to do well. As Abraham Zaleznik put it,[4] 'Leaders with brilliant ideas and the capacity to inspire thought and action in others are the main generators of energy. The effects of their personality induce a contagion to perform that is considerably stronger in directing organizations than depersonalized systems.'

This was written a long time ago, but is reinforced by the well-known work on achieving excellence by Peters and Waterman: 'Associated with almost every excellent company was a strong leader (or two) who seemed to have a lot to do with making the company excellent in the first place.'[5] The mechanisms that founders and key leaders can be seen to use include:

- formal statements of philosophy such as a 'charter';
- explicit reward systems and criteria for promotion;
- physical design of buildings and offices; status symbols;
- teaching and coaching given;

- stories, parables and 'myths' about people and events;
- certain items that leaders pay particular attention to, place emphasis upon, and/or measure and control;
- how leaders react to crises and important incidents;
- systems and procedures used; the organization structure;
- personnel policies; criteria used for staff recruitment, selection, promotion, retirement and 'excommunication'.[6]

The impact of key leaders and founders on the fortunes of an enterprise can be crucial. Examples often put forward include Thomas Watson (IBM), Konosuke Matsushita (Matsushita–National Panasonic/Technics) and Richard Branson (Virgin Records). Of course, though a key leader can give an organization a strong and easily recognizable culture, he or she cannot guarantee success over the long term. Some notable leaders have either been strongly attacked or have overseen the fall as well as the rise of a firm. Thus Geneen of ITT has been called 'Mr Theory X'[7] and Lawrence of Braniff has been blamed for the fall of the airline because of his personality.[8]

Much of the research suggests that leaders and managers can be described by one of two parameters: being task-centered or people-centered. The characteristics of the task-centered style are: autocratic, restrictive, task-oriented, socially distant, directive and structuring. The characteristics of the people-centered style are: democratic, permissive, people-oriented, participative and considerate.[9] Which is better, orientation towards the work or the people? The answer is that it depends on what one means by 'better'. It appears that most of the characteristics of task-orientation are correlated with productivity (though not autocratic and restrictive behaviour) but depress staff satisfaction and group cohesion (though structuring helps). On the other hand, the style of people-orientation does not appear to be correlated (either positively or negatively) with productivity. It is, however, correlated with staff satisfaction and group cohesiveness.[10] These results can be summarized somewhat crudely in a table thus:

	Productivity	Satisfaction/ Cohesiveness
Task-centered:		
Autocratic	Bad	Bad
Restrictive	Bad	Bad
Work orientation	Good	Bad
Socially distant	Good	Bad
Directive	Good	Bad
Work structuring	Good	Good
People-centered:	Neutral	Good

So it would appear that leaders should try to avoid being either too autocratic or restrictive but should structure the work to be done. Other studies suggest (perhaps less definitely) that the task-centered approach works well if the situation is either very good or very bad, but that the people-centered approach works well for average situations.

This does, of course, presuppose that a leader or manager can to some extent change approaches. Some people would say that this is tantamount to changing one's personality. Even if this is asking rather a lot, it certainly appears that one should temper or curb any extremes of approach – to make the approach suit the situation.

It may be objected that this is not exactly earth-shattering. Most people feel that if an organization is faced with a critical situation, then knuckling down to the work comes first. And many of us have experienced the founder of an enterprise who was superb in the initial stages but who became a liability later on.

A target culture

There is no one right culture that is appropriate for all cases. That suitable for the Pentagon would not be right for Hewlett-Packard when Bill Hewlett moved out of his garage. This may also seem somewhat obvious, but every few years some new concept of culture gains ground and one finds organizations everywhere trying to install it, quite irrespective of its suitability.

We believe, however, that there are certain aspects of culture that are worth cultivating in virtually all circumstances. These can be characterized respectively as distinction, pride in success, helpfulness and sharpness.

■ DISTINCTION

An enterprise should have a distinctive aim and sense of direction, so that everybody knows where they are going rather than being aimlessly opportunistic. Some firms make this almost a sense of mission:

'IBM means service' – IBM

'No surprises' – Holiday Inns

'Never knowingly undersold' – John Lewis

'Never kill a new product idea' – 3M

■ PRIDE IN SUCCESS

People like to work for a success. They enjoy being proud to be associated with something that is good. This can be the entire enterprise, or their department, or even just their section. This fact has been observed on a number of occasions and, where observed, it is a matter of agreement among all staff. Yet there are some organizations where it verges on being a taboo subject. Pride appears to be regarded as a small step up from pornography; something absolutely alien. It is not. It is desirable. It is an asset – not merely to the organization itself but even more, to the staff. One should be able to be proud of the excellence of the work that is done in one's office.

■ HELPFULNESS

When training staff that deal with the public, we ask them to be selfish for a while – and to think of being nice to the public as being an investment for the future. We tell them that if they are pleasant to the public, then a high percentage of people will be pleasant in return, and that will give them a nicer life. It is true of course. The same approach of helpfulness also works within an organization. If section A is pleasant to section B, then there is a high probability that section B will be helpful in return – possibly at a time that matters.

■ SHARPNESS

'Sharpness' is used as a combination of effectiveness, efficiency, productivity, continuous improvement – a feeling among the staff that the systems and procedures are robust, that they (the staff) can always improve them, and that the staff are working more smartly than the competition.

These, then, are the components of our target culture: distinction, pride in success, helpfulness and sharpness. Given these, we are well on the way to achieving an effective office.

References

1 An incorrect attribution, presumably for wartime propaganda purposes. The real author was a German playwright, Jonathon Green. As so often happens, the actual quotation is less impressive: 'When I hear the word culture I release the safety catch on my Browning'.
2 Schein, E. H., *Organizational Culture and Leadership*, San Francisco: Jossey-Bass, 1985.
3 Lewin, K., 'Group decision and social change', in Swanson, G. E. *et al.* (eds), *Readings in Social Psychology*, New York: Holt, Rinehart & Winston, 1952.
4 Zaleznik, A., *Leadership in Administration*, New York: Harper & Row, 1957.
5 Peters, T. J. and Waterman, R. H., *In Search of Excellence*, New York: Harper & Row, 1982.
6 Schein, E. H., 'The role of the founder in creating organizational culture', *Organizational Dynamics*, Summer 1983, p. 22.
7 Pascale, R. T. and Athos, A. G., *The Art of Japanese Management*, New York: Simon & Schuster, 1981.
8 Harris, B., 'The man who killed Braniff', *Texas Monthly*, July 1982.
9 Hampton, D. R., *Management*, New York: McGraw-Hill, 1986.
10 Stogdill, R. M., *Handbook of Leadership*, New York: Free Press, 1974; and Bass, B. M., *Stogdill's Handbook of Leadership*, New York: Free Press, 1981.

Further reading

Bower, M., *The Will to Manage*, New York: McGraw-Hill, 1966.
Jenkins, K. *et al.*, *Improving Management in Government: The Next Steps*, London: Her Majesty's Stationery Office, 1988.
Prior, P. J., *Leadership Is Not a Bowler Hat*, David & Charles, 1982.

4

The Quick Fix and Beyond

Light boats sail swift, though greater hulks draw deep.

Shakespeare, *Troilus and Cressida* (1602)

Do nothing hastily but catching of fleas.

Thomas Fuller, *Gnomologia* (1732)

A group of entrepreneurs and managers went to Japan, and there listened to a series of speeches from leading industrialists. One of these was from Konosuke Matsushita, the president of Matsushita Electric (which includes National Panasonic, Technics and Qasar). The eponymous Matsushita is well known for having a distinctive culture and clear strategic aims. It is not strongly innovative (it leaves that to firms like Sony) but comes into the market with inexpensive goods of a reasonable quality.

At the time of the visit, president Matsushita was an alert eighty-eight years of age. After his speech, he answered questions and the session went something like this:[1]

Question: 'Mr. Matsushita, does your company have long-term goals?'
Answer: 'Yes.'
Question: 'How long are your long-term goals?'
Answer: 'Two hundred and fifty years.'
Question: 'What do you need to carry them out?'
Answer: 'Patience.'

Patience is a virtue that few people allow to be an ingredient of success – it sounds too much like sloth. (We do nevertheless expect surgeons to be able to combine patience with speed and accuracy, especially when we are the patient.)

It has already been said that there is a need for a target culture and agreement about goals. These do not have to be complex or fanciful. For example, IBM has three aspects of culture:

- outstandingly good level of service;
- the pursuit of excellence; and
- respect for the individual.

It also has four basic goals:

- growth at least equivalent to that of the rest of the electronics industry;
- to be among the industry's lowest-cost producers;
- to sell optimal technology;
- to sustain high profitability.

Thus Matsushita and IBM both have easily recognizable identities. This of itself does not guarantee success in the long term but it certainly appears to help. At least both organizations have thought through where they are going. For such organizations, the definition of the effective office is that the office has to aid the organization to achieve its goals.

21

For many years, it has been said that marketing strategy offers three basic routes to success. One can:

- be cheap (low cost);
- be distinctive (offer something unique);
- be selective (find a niche).

Of course in many organizations (e.g. banking) the office *is* the organization, in which case the three routes are descriptive. However, in all offices similar considerations apply. All offices can:

- be cheap (ultra-low cost);
- be distinctive (offer a specialized service to the rest of the organization);
- be selective (offer services in open competition with external services).

None of this, however, exonerates the office from its primary duty: offering a good level of service at an optimum cost.

So getting the office right can take time – planning, ensuring that it serves the overall organizational objectives, reducing costs, making the administration smooth. It also takes effort. This can lead people (for real or imaginary reasons) to take short cuts to making offices effective – the quick fix.

Types of quick fix

The main types of quick fix that one comes across in offices are known, somewhat colloquially, as:

- the Quick Cut;
- the Band-Aid;
- the Magic Formula; and
- VDU Management.

■ THE QUICK CUT

A common 'technique' for reducing office costs is to issue a directive that all costs are to be cut by say 15 per cent within two months. This usually translates into redundancies. Now, there are times when such action is defensible – when, for example, the organization finds itself in a battle for sheer survival. Some newly appointed chief executives may feel that such action is warranted if they find the organization in a parlous state.

Less defensible was the approach of one entrepreneur who, on taking over another firm always had one inviolable rule: sack 40 per cent of the office staff and run the company with the remaining 60 per cent. Not surprisingly, this could lead to difficulties which could take a long time to rectify.

Even less defensible is the commonest manifestation of the Quick Cut. This occurs when an organization finds the office staff numbers out of line with falling turnover. Management know that turnover is falling but wait, Micawber-like, for something good to happen to restore the firm's fortunes. When the Good Lord fails to provide a miracle, the inevitable follows: major office redundancies. This scenario has been observed so often that it appears that there is a danger of its becoming accepted as normal, even inevitable.

22

What should happen, of course, is that staff numbers should be kept more closely in line with requirements all the time. The judicious use of work quantification and management controls make this a much less difficult task than otherwise. Alternatively, an organization may use other approaches for short-term problems. This is not just pious theory. During the 1970s, the electronics industry hit a sticky patch. The response of Hewlett-Packard was the 'nine-day fortnight': staff took a 10 per cent cut in pay and worked 10 per cent fewer hours. This enabled Hewlett-Packard to maintain their full complement of staff while other electronic companies were sacking people. So the Quick Cut is sometimes necessary – but not as often as it erupts.

■ THE BAND-AID

The American term 'Band-Aid' is used rather than the European equivalents Hansaplast or Elastoplast not because it only happens in the USA but because it was first so described by American writers. It is an apt phrase. Band-Aiding is covering up the wound quickly but it does not cure any sickness that may be present – just the superficial symptoms (to avoid any possible litigation it should be pointed out that the real Band-Aid is, of course, a wonderful product).

One person describes the Band-Aid style of management as being a reactive style which[2] 'responds to each problem in the organization as if it were an isolated phenomenon. Instead of preventing fires, it's always fighting fires. Because it favours the quick fix over the long-term solution, it may not be fixing the right thing at all'.

It has to be said that some organizations have been observed where the Band-Aid approach was the everyday, normal (and only) approach used. Working in such clients as a consultant, one is reminded of the traditional Chinese curse, 'May you live in interesting times.' A colleague has told me that he can always quickly recognize a Band-Aid company. The managers all seem prematurely grey, eat sandwich lunches at their desks; nobody can describe the current systems and procedures. And costs stay stubbornly high no matter how fast people work.

More tangible examples of a Band-Aid office are:

- a few lines of undocumented code are added to software, as a quick effort at rectification;
- new forms are hastily drawn by hand, and supplies are photocopied before distribution to waiting staff;
- changes in procedures are announced verbally to staff who are fortunate in being in the office at the time.

The most disappointing aspect of Band-Aid offices is that some of the managers fondly imagine that they will one day achieve effectiveness, if only they apply enough of it.

■ THE MAGIC FORMULA

Every few years a new technique appears that looks like the answer to the quick-fixers' prayers. It is usually based on some genuine research that looks at management in a new way and is published in a widely advertised book. Follow-ups and explanations appear in journals and magazines. Seminars are held. Somewhere, groups of managers or academics leave their employers to set up consultancies.

Soon, companies in various industries are adopting the new technique in the vague expectation that it will make problems disappear. Slowly, people discover that it is neither as sure-fire or as easy as had been hoped, and it gradually falls into disuse. One can be fairly confident that the days of a technique are numbered when it starts being referred to by politicians at press interviews.

It has to be admitted that management consultants are not immune from the Magic Formula syndrome. One author[3] referred to it as the 'seagull' approach: 'It was, according to the industry joke, the seagull model of consulting. You flew out from Boston, made a couple of circles around the client's head, dropped a strategy on him, and flew back.' As we keep telling people – there is no magic wand in management. We tend to agree with Andy Grove when he said,[4] 'Most of managing is like driving down a bumpy road that's full of potholes. You have to get around the potholes . . . forget all the fads and slogans. They are the mind-altering drugs of management, and they don't do you any good.'

■ VDU MANAGEMENT

The advent of 'information technology' offered a new tool to the determined advocates of the quick fix. If it was true that all office work was information, then it seemed to follow that management of office work was also just a matter of information. Moreover, information (and lots of it) was readily available by switching on one's monitor (or VDU). This opened up the prospect of being able to manage without ever leaving one's desk or even opening one's door – an obvious time saver. At last, science had developed the ultimate quick fix.

Now it is true that technology can save time, it can make management more effective, it can give us better information. But it is an aid to management, not a facile substitute. Printouts are not management. Electronic mail is not supervision.

The quick fix, then, in any of its forms, is no strategy for attaining the 'Effective Office'. There are times in the life of every office when matters have to be fixed quickly – the danger lies in its becoming the accepted means of management.

Past the quick fix – the Seven Tracks

If the quick fix is not the right route to attaining the 'Effective Office', what should be done instead? In a sense, the whole of this book is devoted to showing how to avoid the dangers of the quick fix. However, a more structured system is that afforded by the Seven Tracks approach. This is a seven-fold attack on ineffective organizations. A detailed description (slightly different from the one used here) appears in a recommended book by Ralph Kilmann.[5] The seven tracks are:

- the Culture Track;
- the Management Skills Track;
- the Organization Structure Track;
- the Group Track;
- the Team-building Track;
- the Systems and Procedures Track; and
- the Reward System Track.

■ THE CULTURE TRACK

The importance of an organization's culture has already been emphasized in chapter 2. Two extracts may help to encapsulate what was said. The first explains what is meant by culture:[6] 'Culture ... is a pattern of beliefs and expectations shared by the organization's members. These beliefs and expectations produce norms that power-fully shape the behaviour of individuals and groups in the organization.' On the other hand, yesterday's successful culture may not be right for today and tomorrow:[7] 'People in an organization frequently follow norms that have long outlived their usefulness.'

We also believe that the chief executive and top managers set the tone for an organization. As E. W. Spencer, Chairman of Honeywell Inc., put it (ref. 5, p. 99): 'The Chief Executive's tone, his integrity, his standards, his way of dealing with people, his focussing on things that are important or not important can have a profound impact on the rest of the organization. What I am saying is that the way the chief executive and senior managers of the company conduct themselves as individuals has a more profound impact on how other people in the company conduct *themselves* than anything else that happens.'

■ THE MANAGEMENT SKILLS TRACK

Management is difficult and complex – which is what makes it so interesting and enjoyable. The skills needed to be a good manager are many and varied. Indeed, they are so many and varied that there is a marked lack of agreement as to their nature, or their definition. For our purposes, we will assume that they can be summarized as being:

- technical skills;
- communication skills;
- problem-solving skills;
- interpersonal and social skills;
- administrative skills.

The particular mix of these skills that is required depends on the position held and the place in the hierarchy.

Technical skills include a knowledge of the industry, its place in the environment, a knowledge about production/marketing/finance and a reasonable level of numeracy. Communication skills include the ability to transfer information, concepts and feelings to and from people. Problem-solving skills are just what they sound like: the skill at solving problems, which can occur in any area. Interpersonal and social skills are concerned with the interaction with other people, whether they are considered one's superior, equal or subordinate. Administrative skills concern those parts of the manager's job that are not about problems or people.

This list would be considered by many people to be somewhat truncated and missing a number of important items. However, it is long enough to show why many of us realize that we would never achieve 100 per cent in any examination of managerial skills. That does not mean that one should not try to improve oneself continuously – nor that any of the skills are disposable.

One skill that does not fall easily into the above list is that of getting out of one's office and finding out what is really happening at the coal face. This is something that many of us have long believed in. Some research that was started in 1979 into what differentiated successful companies from the unsuccessful found that one factor was the habit of executives of getting close to the 'sharp end' of the operations. This was written up in the series of books on 'excellence' that began to be published in the early 1980s. It even led to the development of a technique. This was given the mildly odd name of 'MBWA' (Management By Wandering About). One can only hope that this will not

25

lead to the approach becoming a fad to be discarded with the passage of time.

It may seem odd to refer to such a simple thing as 'MBWA' as a skill. Well, it is – to do it properly, that is. MBWA can take four forms, only one of which is the skilled form. One form is the ceremonial. This is exemplified by something known to anybody who has been in the army: the Canteen Inspection. Once a month a junior officer, accompanied by the Regimental Sergeant Major, would visit the canteen. The soldiers would put down their knives and forks and sit to attention. The junior officer would enquire if everything was all right. The troops would reply in unison, 'Yes – Sir' (they had been trained to put a gap between the two words by silently counting 'one'). The whole affair was over quickly, to the satisfaction of everybody concerned. It was just a ceremony. Even the oldest soldiers could not remember anybody actually complaining about the food. Such an unspeakable act would have been bad manners – a slur on the regiment.

A second form of 'MBWA' is the one that causes some staff to be suspicious of the whole approach – that of what amounts to spying on the staff. The third form is somewhat similar in its effect – that used as a form of increasing discipline. This is the fate of MBWA when practised by the 'meddling and meddlesome' school of management. Such managers will wander around looking for something to complain about.

It is the fourth form of MBWA that takes skill: the creative form. In this form, it becomes a means of solving problems, improving service, being innovative and attaining effectiveness. It is done by observing and listening – above all by listening: listening to the frontline staff, to suppliers and to customers.[8]

■ THE ORGANIZATION STRUCTURE TRACK

'Many organizations are reshaping and reorganizing departments to find ways of accomplishing work more effectively . . . Making a transition from one organizational structure to another can be a period of intense creativity and progress or it can be one of disruption, anxiety, and low productivity'.[9] Pointers to achieving the former rather than the latter are given in chapter 18.

■ THE GROUP TRACK

The group is the basic molecule of both organization structure and of getting the work done in offices. The nature of the group and group working is covered in chapter 8.

■ THE TEAM-BUILDING TRACK

Team building is getting people to work together. This has to be achieved at two levels. The first level is team building within each group. The second level is getting individual groups to work together. In a sense, if the culture is right, then team building is reasonably straightforward. If the culture is poor, then team building is an uphill task and can even be a negative influence – people can be a good team but be working for bad ends.

Aspects of team building include:

- agreement on aims and objectives of the group;
- achievement of a sense of direction and high morale;
- removal of obstacles to performing effectively;
- utilizing the skills and experience of group members;

- installing good channels of information for all types of information, and good decision-making facilities;
- achieving good methods of problem solving;
- demonstrating clearly the interaction of the group with other groups, and between individuals.

Perhaps the biggest hindrance to team building is one that is seldom mentioned: the disrupter, a person who seems to disagree with everybody and everything. There are three alternatives:

- learn to live with the disruptive troublemaker (he or she can be a hard worker or possess other redeeming features);
- ameliorate the disruption by individual counselling;
- remove the disruptive troublemaker from the scene.

■ THE SYSTEMS AND PROCEDURES TRACK

No office can be effective unless the methods of working are right. This is a major subject and so is dealt with in detail in Part D of the book (Method Design).

■ THE REWARD SYSTEMS TRACK

Staff perform work for the organization. In return, the organization gives rewards depending on what it regards as important. Thus one organization may promote people on the basis of seniority because (implicitly or explicitly) it values length of service above other attributes such as innovation or hard work. Another organization may give higher salaries to line managers than to staff managers because it values the frontline staff more than the back-office people. But, whether it means to or not, every organization sends signals to every person working there about what it values most.

A good way to change the signals, therefore, is to change the rewards system. Rewards come in many forms, including salaries, bonuses, promotion, praise, opportunities, fringe benefits – and the chance to do interesting and challenging work. If one wants an effective office, then one rewards effectiveness in all of its many forms.

References

1 Mackay, H., *Swim with the Sharks*, New York: William Morrow, 1988.
2 Boyle, R. J., 'Designing the energetic organization', *Management Review*, August 1983, p. 20.
3 Kiechel, W., 'Corporate strategists', *Fortune*, 27 December, 1982, p. 34.
4 Grove, A., *One-on-one with Andy Grove*, New York: Penguin, 1988.
5 Kilmann, R. H., *Beyond the Quick Fix*, San Francisco: Jossey-Bass, 1984.
6 Schwartz, H. and Davis, S. M., 'Matching corporate culture and business strategy', *Organizational Dynamics*, Summer 1981, p. 30.
7 Allen, R. F. and Dyer, F., 'A tool for tapping the organizational unconscious', *Personnel Journal*, March 1980, p. 192.
8 Peters, T. J. and Austin, N., *A Passion for Excellence*, New York: Random House, 1985.
9 Kaplan, J.H. and Kaplan, E. E., 'Organizational restructuring: how managers can actively assist in shaping a firm's new architecture', *Management Review*, January 1984, p. 15.

5

Behavioural and People Aspects

People are what they are
Because they have come out of what was.
        Carl Sandburg, *The People. Yes* (1936)

I must believe in the Apostolic Succession, there being no other way
of accounting for the descent of the Bishop of Exeter from Judas
Iscariot.   The Rev. Sydney Smith (1771–1845)

It is widely agreed that people are at the centre of every organization and every form of endeavour. Unfortunately, as with most things on which there is wide agreement, when one turns to specifics and details the widespread agreement evaporates somewhat. There is the initial problem of deciding which direction one should follow. Should one follow the theories of motivation (ignoring the secondary question of 'which one?')? Or should one use the ideas about behaviour? Or should one instead concentrate on those aspects that together make up Human Resource Management? Alternatively, should one utilize a theory of psychotherapy?

A second problem is, in practice, even thornier: *how* is it to be used? This is a problem that does not affect other areas of management to the same extent. If there is an agreed body of knowledge about marketing, then it is installed and run by a marketing department. But who is to install and run an agreed body of knowledge about people? Certainly not the personnel department in most organizations that one sees. Traditionally, the personnel department is an administrative function. It is responsible for collecting statistics, hiring lower-level staff, administering salary policies and conducting exit interviews when staff leave.

Although some personnel managers hanker after a more active role, the nearest many of them get to the front line is when there is an incipient dispute with a trade union. They are then supposed to sweet-talk the union leader, because of an assumed knowledge and ability to handle people – an ability that remains fallow most of the time. To rectify this situation, some organizations have renamed the personnel function as the Human Resource Management Group. Of course, merely changing the name changes nothing.

Human Resource Management (HRM)

HRM departments usually address the areas of attracting new employees, staff development, motivation, and the effective use of people's capabilities. This can be done by focussing on three aspects: human resource flow, reward systems and work systems.

■ HUMAN RESOURCE FLOW

This is the flow of staff into, through, and eventually out of the organization. This includes staff recruitment, selection, induction, training, development and exit interviews. It also covers career planning, performance assessment, counselling and establishing/maintaining policies for promotion. This basket of responsibilities can become administrative, even bureaucratic. Alternatively it can be an important component of the human relations factor. It depends on the organization and the person in charge of the personnel department which it is.

■ REWARD SYSTEMS

Examples of rewards covered are:

Cash salary, overtime, bonus, incentives, commission, profit-sharing, relocation/foreign payments, study, children's education, home telephone, use of own car.

Near-cash subsidized canteen, cheap/free car parking, transport, car, cheap/free goods, creche, private medicine, use internal professionals, keep external earnings, pension.

Amenities office (location, style, furnishings), rest room, sports club, cloakroom facilities, surgery, hairdresser.

Perquisites time off, chauffeur, medical checks, use of Lodge.

Recognition praise, public recognition, accelerated promotion.

The theory of reward systems is straightforward: they are a cost-effective way of improving staff commitment, quality of work, morale, costs and a feeling of equity. In practice, they can be a minefield causing resentment and divisiveness. Sometimes they owe more to habit and history rather than to effectiveness. Often, perquisites are related to rank alone. A millionaire British cabinet minister used to take delight in flying economy class on short journeys while his senior civil servants were in first class.

Even salaries can cause problems. Take the example of high-flyers. Their line manager will want to pay them well, both to keep them and because high salaries reflect well on him. The HRM manager will want to pay them within scale to avoid problems elsewhere. The chief executive wants to have good staff, but at the lowest cost possible. Result – disagreement.

■ WORK SYSTEMS

This includes such aspects as job design, reporting systems, responsibility definitions, job definitions and specifications, performance evaluation systems. Responsibility for these aspects varies widely between organizations. In some cases they are part of the remit of the HRM group. Elsewhere responsibility can be more fragmented. Variability also occurs in how the work systems are handled. Like the human resource flow, they can be regarded as administrative or human relations in orientation.

Motivation and human needs

In modern industrial society, work is a major part of our lives. The glib answer to the question 'why work?' would be that one works to earn money. But this is not the whole answer. Two-thirds of a sample of Britons said that they would continue to work even in the absence of any financial need,[1] and it is common for people who are unemployed or retired to say that they miss more than just the money. There are a number of benefits of having a job, such as:

- money (and what one can get with money);
- social contact;
- status in society;
- a sense of achievement;
- a structure to one's time;
- activity, variety.

The impact of these benefits and their importance will vary considerably from person to person. Some people need to work and have a deep sense of unease if they are not working. Many management consultants, for example, find it very hard to retire (this is not, of course, to imply any moral superiority). Other people would genuinely prefer to stay at home watching television rather than going out to work, even when this meant a much lower standard of living. Some people are very strongly motivated by money, pursuing it with great determination. But others are certainly not, as shown by the large number of people who willingly undertake charitable and socially useful work even when this reduces their personal income. So everybody is different.

This brings us to a central problem of theories of motivation and the needs of people. First, since everybody is different, it is not easy to postulate a general theory of motivation which will apply meaningfully to the whole population. Second, any theory is likely to be of limited value in predicting behaviour. Third, managers would prefer to have available an approved universal approach rather than be told that they have to take the time to treat everybody separately.

The arguments about human nature have been going on for a long time. Reading about the competing theories about motivation, one is irresistibly reminded of the competition between Augustine and Chrysostom in the Roman Catholic church during the fourth century.[2] Chrysostom was not good at politics and was too other-worldly (he even tried to build a hospital for lepers outside the city wall at Constantinople). Augustine was a firm believer in the basic sinfulness of mankind and the power of the big battalions; he 'wrote the only full justification, in the history of the early church, of the right of the state to suppress non-Catholics'.[3] The fact that Augustine and his ideas won and became part of the beliefs of the church has clearly not ended discussion or debate.

The logic of motivation rests on a series of assumptions and ideas:

- people have certain needs;
- these needs make people act in particular ways;
- if an organization can harness these needs at the right time and the right place, it can influence the way that people act at work;
- if people are to act in a way that an organization wishes, then there has to be an integration of people's needs and the objectives, aims and wishes of the organization.

Each of these points could be (and have been) subjected to lengthy discussions. For our purposes it is preferable to consider their implications. First, we have to try to understand people, their needs and their motivations. Second, people will naturally gravitate to those organizations that have reputations that line up with their own outlook on life. Third, it should be accepted that there is a wide variety of individual mixtures of needs. Fourth, people's needs are not constant. This is partly because

30

people change; they mature, regress, and incidents in their personal life will affect them. Partly it is because circumstances change; if cast away on a desert island where the only food is poisonous snakes one might alternate between searching for the snakes as food and hiding from them for survival.

If we accept that people differ in their personal needs then clearly the most effective incentives are wholly personal and in some way related to the individual concerned. In most organizations, however, this is hardly a practical proposition. What can be done is to formulate policies to appeal to the most common or most strongly felt, and then train managers to allow informally for the individual mixtures of motives of their staff. A common problem for many theories of motivation is that they have to be based (implicitly or explicitly) on an assumption that certain motives are prevalent.

A further difficulty in looking at motivation is that most individuals themselves have only an incomplete realization of their motives. Freud believed strongly in the concept of unconscious motivation, stressing the underlying motives of self-preservation and pleasure seeking. Adler, the one-time associate of Freud, stressed the motive of power seeking. At a different conceptual level, we might refer to the motives of:

Survival	Security	Achievement	Personal growth
Self-esteem	Pride	Power	Competence
Prestige	Belonging	Acceptability	Ego protection

Most of us, at one time or another, are likely to possess a number of these motives. This list, or any other, is unlikely to be complete. Even so, to expect our colleagues and superiors to make allowances for all of them is expecting a lot. One author[4] gave a list of 14,000 instincts – one of which was 'to eat apples from one's own orchard'; this is rarely encountered in company incentive schemes.

What can, however, be done is to cater for a wide spectrum of human needs when designing an organization structure, a package of incentives or employment conditions, and when carrying out organization (and management) development. An appreciation of the place of motivation should also help us in dealing with colleagues.

■ MOTIVATORS, HYGIENIC FACTORS AND EXPECTANCY

Clearly, then, the ability of people's needs to stimulate behaviour will fluctuate. It will fluctuate with time, circumstances, personal development and non-work incidents in a person's life (someone who is newly married is likely to find cash a very strong motivator). Some theories of motivation go further. They claim that as we satisfy one need, it ceases to motivate and we then move on to another need. This new need will motivate us until that too is satisfied. We then move on to another need.

One such theory that was widely commented upon at one time was the 'Hierarchy of Needs', developed by the American psychologist Abraham Maslow.[5] This suggested that people were motivated by five types of need: physiological (e.g. hunger), safety, love (social), esteem and self-actualization (realizing one's potential). It also suggested that these needs were arrayed in a hierarchy. Moreover, it postulated that the higher needs could only emerge after the primary, physiological needs had been satisfied – after which the primary needs could no longer motivate behaviour. At the time, a number of managers felt that the theory gave them an insight into motivation. It was discarded, however, mainly because attempts at testing it were unsatisfactory.[6]

Some authors have proposed changing Maslow's listing slightly while still maintaining the idea that the needs could motivate in a sequence. For example, Alderfer combined esteem and self-actualization into 'growth', dropped safety, and renamed physiological needs 'existence' and love 'relatedness'.[7] Porter added 'autonomy' between esteem and self-actualization in Maslow's list.[8]

David McClelland took a more 'realpolitik' approach. Apart from the primary needs (physiological and survival), McClelland put the emphasis on three secondary, or socially acquired, needs. These are:

- *power*. 'The goal of power motivation is to feel powerful';[9]
- *affiliation*. People with a high affiliation need try hard to get along with others and enjoy the company of other people.
- *achievement*. Those with a need for achievement set themselves fairly difficult tasks, strive to reach them, use feedback, and want recognition for success. The need for achievement was jargonized to n-Ach.

There have been a number of research studies into McClelland's concept. Some of these show that there seems to be a correlation between the three named needs and success at certain types of job. 'Power' is allied with production managers in offices, factories and product development. 'Affiliation' with those managers whose jobs needed co-ordination between departments. 'Achievement' was allied with entrepreneurs, presidents of R & D corporations, and certain types of selling job.

Another author whose work has been commented upon widely is Frederick Herzberg. Herzberg is best known for his Motivation/Hygiene theory. This is concerned with those factors that improve satisfaction with the job (rather than, say, those that improve productivity). The theory postulates that factors causing satisfaction ('satisfiers') are those which arise from the intrinsic content of the job – factors such as responsibility and challenge. The factors that cause dissatisfaction ('hygiene factors' or 'dissatisfiers') are those that are extrinsic to the job itself – things like supervision and pay. The theory holds that the hygienic factors are not motivators, but their removal will cause a loss of satisfaction. Thus a well-furnished office will not motivate people directly, but moving people from a good office to a poor one will cause dissatisfaction.

The motivation/hygiene theory originated from interviews with 203 accountants and engineers. They were asked to recall and describe specific situations when they felt particularly good or particularly bad about their jobs. Studies which copied the original study largely gave similar results. In spite of this (and in spite of the frequent references to the idea in books), the theory has attracted a lot of criticism. One criticism strikes at the heart of the theory. What sort of response would one expect if one asked people what made them feel exceptionally good or bad about their job? Surely, say the critics, one will feel good about those aspects for which one feels personally responsible (such as achievement). Similarly, one would feel bad about those things for which others are responsible (such as pay or relations with the supervisor).

Some theories about motivation concentrate on the needs of people, such as security and self-esteem. These are known as 'content' theories. Others concentrate on the psychological processes of motivation. These are known as 'process' theories. One of the process theories is Expectancy Theory.

People will strive for a goal if they value the goal. But that may not be enough: they must also have a reasonable expectation that they will reach the goal. One may wish fervently to be a world-famous brain surgeon but, if the chances look small, one may not expend a lot of effort on becoming one. Expectancy theory states that the motivation

(M) is a function of the expectation (E) of reaching a goal by acting in a particular way, multiplied by the worthwhileness or value (V) of the result to the individual. This can be expressed as:

$$M = f(E \times V).$$

A demonstration of this is the motivating power of promotion prospects – would this make somebody work hard? Firstly it depends on whether the individual finds promotion desirable. It can also depend on how hard one would have to work (if it entailed considerable overtime, then a single parent might be dissuaded). Then it depends on whether the individual feels that hard work is likely to lead to promotion; if promotion appears to the individual to be the result of length of service rather than working hard, then the motivation decreases.

One of the disadvantages of the Hierarchy of Needs, and similar theories, was the implication that most people's needs are similar. One of the advantages of expectancy (and similar) theories is that they assume that everybody is different. People have different needs and goals and their perceptions of these will vary over time.

In formal terms, expectancy-valency theory proposes that the effort that people will put into a task will depend on:

- *expectancy*. This is the belief of people about whether effort is expected to lead to better performance;
- *instrumentality*. This is the belief that better performance is expected to lead to desired outcomes (these outcomes can be either direct or indirect);
- *valency*. This is how attractive these outcomes are likely to be to the individual.

As an example, let us consider somebody who is considering writing a book of short stories. 'Expectancy' concerns belief that if a lot of effort were expended, it would be possible to write good material. 'Instrumentality' concerns the belief that if one writes good stories, the desired outcomes will be achieved. The direct outcome would be the actual publication of the book; the indirect outcomes would be that the writer would become famous or rich. 'Valency' concerns how attractive the outcomes (direct and indirect) would be to the writer.

Since expectancy theories appear to be relevant, it is worth considering some of the practical implications:

1 Do not expect rewards to affect everybody equally: it is often suggested that about 10–15 per cent of people are ambitious and will really strive for promotion, while about the same percentage would actually try to avoid promotion.
2 Ensure that desired behaviour is rewarded (do not link pay to years of service instead of good performance, unless you would rather have people stay with you than work well).
3 Ensure that the relationship between good performance and reward is clear, known to all, and maintained (do not increase the pay of, or promote, people who are friends of their manager but who do not perform well – unless the aim is to get everybody to pretend to be friends of the manager and one does not care about good performance of the work).
4 Design jobs and roles so that people can satisfy their wants through their work, remembering that not everybody wants the same thing (some people want job enrichment, others will not. Some may want security. After a cutback in the City of

33

London, some financial experts[10] offered to accept lower salaries in return for a three-year contract of employment).

5 Ensure that the system treats people fairly (good and poor performers should see clearly that good performers get a larger share of the rewards).

6 Ensure that rewards for major performance achievements are not trivial, in the eyes of the staff. When somebody lands a major contract that saves the firm from bankruptcy, check first before rewarding the person with a signed photo of the chief executive sent through the mail.

It may be felt that one could arrive at these points without the benefit of any expectancy theory. This does not, of course, mean that the theories are incorrect – espousers would claim the contrary.

References

1 Warr, P. D., 'A national study of non-financial employment commitment', *Journal of Occupational Psychology*, Vol. 55, No. 4, 1982, p. 297.

2 See, for example, 'The politics of Paradise', *New York Review*, Vol. XXXV, No. 8, 12 May, 1988, p. 28; and Pagels, E., *Adam, Eve, and the Serpent*, New York: Random House, 1988.

3 Brown, P., *Augustine of Hippo*, Berkeley: University of California Press, 1967.

4 See Porter, L. W. *et al.*, *Behaviour in Organizations*, New York: McGraw-Hill, p. 40, 1975.

5 Maslow, A. H., 'A theory of human motivation', *Psychological Review*, Vol. 50, 1943, p. 370; and Maslow, A. H., *Motivation and Personality*, New York: Harper & Bros., 1954.

6 See, for example, chapter 19 of this book; Hampton, D. R., *Management*, New York: McGraw-Hill, 1986, pp. 412–420; and Robertson, I. T. and Smith, M., *Motivation and Job Design*, Institute of Personnel Management, 1985, pp. 20–25.

7 Alderfer, C. P., *Existence, Relatedness and Growth: Human Needs in Organizational Settings*, New York: Free Press, 1972.

8 Porter, L. W., *Organizational Patterns of Managerial Job Attitudes*, New York: American Foundation for Management Research, 1964.

9 McClelland, D. C., *Power: The Inner Experience*, New York: Irvington, 1975.

10 'You 'orrible little market-maker you', *The Economist*, Vol. 309, No. 7581, 17 December, 1988, p. 82.

6

Selling and Persuading

Dogs bark at a person they do not know.

Heraclitus, *Fragments* (c. 500 BC).

'I am an Englishman and require instant attention to the damage
done to my solar topee' is far better than any equivocation that may
be meant well but will gain little respect.

Guide to the Native Languages of Africa,
by 'A Gentleman of Experience' (1890).

A

The well-known irregular verb that goes:

> *I persuade*
> *You sell*
> *He orders*

may demonstrate the reservation that some people feel towards attempts at persuasion. A few people even feel that it is too close to manipulation to be honest, and reject any overt methods of persuasion. However, persuasion is all around us. There are the obvious examples of advertising, politicians and newspaper leader columns.

Closer to home are the attempts at persuasion that we all attempt when we converse with friends and acquaintances. In fact the whole art of conversation would be greatly diminished if we stopped trying to show how our ideas are correct; in other words trying to persuade people that our beliefs are right. These beliefs are varied: how to bring up babies, that the referee at last Saturday's match had defective eyesight, that Rembrandt was a better salesman than Jeffrey Archer; or that the Sales Department should all learn spreadsheet analysis to save staff.

So we all use persuasion. In fact, if analysts or consultants try to avoid persuasion completely then life will be somewhat difficult since none of their ideas will ever get listened to or used. What can, however, be objectionable are certain types or extremes of persuasion.

Types of persuasion

■ EMOTION

Persuading by means of emotion is very common because it can be effective, is superficially easy, some people like doing it, and there are plenty of emotions to choose from. In skilled hands it can be a powerful route. It is said that Harold Macmillan, when Prime Minister, reduced a trade union delegation to tears with an impassioned account of the slaughter at Passchendaele.

However, emotion is a double-sided device. When it fails, it may make the situation worse than it was before. It can be too obvious, too transparent, too reminiscent of the 'always be sincere, whether you mean it or not' school. Even when it is a success, it can make the unpersuaded antagonistic. The American 'television evangelists' have, over the years, been remarkably successful at getting people to donate large sums of money running into hundreds of millions of dollars. The donors were persuaded to give money by the use of emotion, often guilt. However, although the process was highly successful, the unconvinced found it distasteful.

Analysts and consultants rarely use emotion as a basis for persuasion. This is partly because of the downside possibilities but also, we suspect, because most of us are temperamentally not suited to it.

■ POWER

Power comes in many forms. There is the sheer naked power that turns any persuasion into an order. A story (presumably apocryphal) concerns Napoleon Bonaparte whose troops had, in 1799, captured 1,200 Turks at Jaffa. Napoleon was not in the best of health at the time, having a bad cough. Asked about the captives, he gave a cough and exclaimed, 'Ma sacré toux!' (My wretched cough). Unfortunately for the captured Turks, this was understood as 'Massacrez tous!' (Massacre them all).

Words are always an uncertain measure of the power behind a suggestion. At a rather different level from the Napoleon example, a manager may want somebody to work late at the office. The manager may say, 'You'll have to work late tonight' or, alternatively, 'Would you mind working late tonight?'. In practice, the two phrases may hide exactly the same amount of power held by the manager and offer the same amount of freedom to refuse.

Analysts rarely use power as a means of persuasion – mainly for the simple reason that they rarely have any real power; what little they have is carefully reserved for emergencies.

■ PEER PRESSURE

Pressure from one's colleagues and equals is a most potent source of persuasion. This often works in the favour of analysts and consultants; if a proposition is clearly to the benefit and wishes of the majority then waverers are likely to come round. There are times when one meets an individual who appears to have a positive need to defy the wishes of the group. How one handles this depends on circumstances.

If there is enough time, the rest of the group will often effect a change. If time is short, one has to try to find a face-saving formula for the individual concerned. In this situation, we will sometimes talk to the individual privately, discuss the reservations, try to answer them (e.g. special one-to-one tuition) and then ask the individual to give the proposed change a trial. When one does this, one should return to the individual after the change has been installed and discuss it openly, showing that the person's opinions matter.

■ TRICKERY

In the 1930s some salesmen were supposed to persuade pharmacists to allow them to put up metal plaques in the shops to advertise their products. As pharmacies were often made of finely figured mahogany (as they still are in many places in Austria), this prospect was highly unattractive. The thought of making screw holes in the mahogany would make the pharmacist shudder, and permission would be refused.

The determined salesman would then use some trickery to get the pharmacist to leave the shop (e.g. for a glass of water to relieve a sudden feeling of faintness on the part of the salesman). With the pharmacist out of the way, the salesman would quickly screw his metal plaque up, using screws with heads that could not be unscrewed. The salesman had, of course, made sure that he had a signed order before starting the charade.

This example shows both the attraction and the drawback of trickery as a route to persuasion. The superficial attraction is that it seems to work. The drawback is that it only works once, at most.

■ TRUST

There are times when a manager says that since the manager trusts you, the proposal is accepted. Over the years, we have developed a rule about this situation. If the matter is relatively minor, then the statement is accepted graciously as a compliment. But if the matter involves a major change then we reply, 'That's all very well. But just because I'm infallible doesn't mean that I can't make a mistake.' An attempt is then made to involve the manager in a discussion on the proposal, with the aim of getting some suggestion that will improve the proposal in some way. Of course, this approach does bring with it the danger that during the discussion the manager will suddenly realize that the proposal is not so attractive after all.

Other analysts and consultants may disagree with our approach, and feel that if one has acceptance it is better to take it and run. This is something that people must make up their own minds about. Our feeling is that trust between client and consultant is a good thing (and is not as rare as is sometimes thought). It is not, therefore, something that can be abused.

■ SAPIENTIAL AUTHORITY

This ponderous phrase means the sort of authority that comes from having knowledge, from being an expert. It is not therefore the same as trust. Trust comes from the manager or client and is an expression of that person's evaluation of the consultant's characteristics. Sapiential authority emanates from the consultant and is a reflection of experience and knowledge rather than personality.

Sapiential authority can be a highly useful asset and may well be one of the things that the client is paying for. But if it is used as a short cut to persuasion, then it may be resented and be counter-productive. If phrases like 'blinding with science' are being used, then the line has been overstepped.

■ FACTUAL PERSUASION/RATIONAL PERSUASION

Marshalling and presenting the facts is the basis for most of the persuading undertaken by analysts and consultants. This may sound an ineffective route, but a straight recitation can be greatly strengthened by the use of a few extra modifications which are described below. Factual persuasion is usually referred to by the more impressive-sounding phrase, 'rational persuasion'.

Rational persuasion has a number of advantages. The main one usually cited is that it is neutral in its effect on a client: neither success or failure in its use will cause any emotional reaction in the mind of the client. We sometimes suspect that this is a euphemism for saying that it is more dignified. Be that as it may, it is an advantage. Another advantage is that if one is going to base one's case on rationality, then it follows that the proposal itself is likely to be the rational course of action.

37

There are three main stages in rational persuasion:

- exploration (of the ground to be covered);
- exposition (on one's ideas);
- examination (of how well one did).

Exploration

Unless one is a particularly talented persuader who can extemporize at will, it remains true that half of persuasion is preparation. The steps for this preparation involve exploring a number of aspects:

1 Define the objective and the primary means. It is easy to confuse these. For example, one may wish to persuade a group of key punch staff to work late each night next week. But in reality this may be the means, not the true objective, which is to eliminate the backlog. One has to decide what it is that one is going to try to achieve, and the reason for this.

2 List alternative means that one might find acceptable to achieve one's objectives. There are two reasons for this. First, one may decide that the primary means is unlikely to be acceptable. Second, if, during the actual persuasion activity, one finds things going poorly it may be necessary to put forward an alternative proposition.

3 List the likely and possible objectives of the listener. It is always possible that the means and the objectives are fine for the persuader but offer the listener nothing. In this case, why should the listener agree? To explore this, one has to put oneself in the shoes of the listener and think the whole proposition through. What would the other person like to see happen and what does the listener want not to happen? These two aspects are sometimes referred to as 'wants' and 'not wants'. For example, our key punch staff may want more cash, but not want to lose five evenings.

4 Decide on an 'acceptable proposition' – this is one that meets the aims of both the persuader and the listener. It may be that one sticks to one's original primary means as the basis for this. Or one may move away slightly to one that still satisfies one's objective but which stands a better chance of acceptance. In our example, one might decide to propose weekend working to the key punch staff, instead of overtime working.

5 Marshal the facts. Most of the facts will already be known to one, but extra background information is often the clincher in persuasion. It is almost impossible to have too much background knowledge, even though one knows from experience that most of it will not be used. This has two advantages: first, it does wonders for one's self-confidence; second, it enables one to answer any objection on a purely factual basis. In our example of key punching, one might like to know why the backlog arose, the history of overtime working, the actual hours that need to be worked.

6 Analyse one's case through the eyes of the listener. What are the benefits and the disadvantages to the listener? If you were the listener, would you be persuaded? Are there any weak links in the reasoning?

7 Prepare the presentation. Perhaps the hardest aspect of this is to ensure that one has enough time to prepare adequately. It is common to find that time is pressing most just at this juncture. Rules to follow are:

- pare the facts down. You cannot use everything you know;
- keep the proposition simple, and easy to understand;

- keep the emphasis on the benefits, not the means. This is particularly true if the means involve technical matters – one can get lost in complexities;
- do not use too many visual aids or too-bulky handouts;
- use concrete examples, not abstractions;
- prepare your answers to possible awkward questions;
- prepare and rehearse the opening sentences;
- memorize the extra background information and statistics.

If the matter is important, then time spent on a full rehearsal will improve confidence and improve impact.

Exposition

To improve the percentage of successful presentations, the rules that one should try to follow are:

- remember that first impressions are disproportionately important. So – be obviously organized and well-prepared, be well turned out, appear confident, avoid off-putting mannerisms and deliver the opening sentences as rehearsed (only better);
- keep the 'antennae' active, to be aware of reaction;
- try to establish some common ground that all can agree on;
- try to avoid a monologue by getting some two-way communication but not so much that the thread of the logic is lost;
- do not turn the exposition into a contest which the persuader is going to win and the listener(s) lose. Show respect for the listener and the listener's opinions. Avoid sarcasm and rhetorical questions that invite a 'no' response. Do not over-sell or steamroller points raised. The listener should feel 'I agreed' and not 'I was sold';
- if the proposition is something that you want to be accepted, then start by emphasizing the advantages before considering the disadvantages. If you want something to be rejected, then start with the disadvantages before moving on to the advantages;
- when agreement is reached, move on to agree action for implementation;
- if a proposition looks like failing, then try to get a deferral before a final decision is made (this must be done before a definite 'no' is made). If it is obvious that the proposition is going to be accepted, then cut the exposition short without being abrupt. By going on, one can only unpersuade.

Perhaps the most important rule is to be natural. Consciously donning an alien style may lead to a transparent insincerity.

Of course, not every presentation follows the same pattern; not even the successful ones. We were once asked to look at two departments and suggest improvements. Our studies showed that neither department was any longer fulfilling any useful function and we felt that both should be disbanded. Attempts to raise the prospect informally with the client were remarkably unsuccessful. Each time we tried, the reply was the same: 'We don't want to influence you in your decisions.'

The day of the presentation arrived – to the general manager and two senior managers. We had already decided that, since we believed it, we would recommend disbanding the two departments. The presentation was listened to without any feedback. Attempts to get some were politely refused: 'You just carry on.' At the end, we were asked to leave the room, without even a smile.

Later we were told, 'We agree about disbanding the departments. I suppose we knew it before but did not want to face it.' And then: 'We have had enough of paying management consultants so that they can tell us what they think we want to hear.'

Examination

After the exposition, analyse your performance:

- did you achieve your objectives?
- what went well and what could have been done better?
- what lessons can be learnt?
- what will you do differently and better next time?

By carrying out this post-exposition examination, one can look forward to becoming ever better.

Finally, let us consider the Coffee Pot Syndrome. An enjoyable drink of coffee depends on two conditions:

- there should be no skin from the milk in it;
- it should not contain any coarse coffee grounds.

For the past two centuries or so, two types of jug have been in use: one for the milk and one for the coffee. They look like this:

Milk   Coffee

Inspection of the two jugs will show that the milk jug is so designed that the skin from the milk shoots into the cup as soon as it is used. Similarly, the coffee jug is so designed that the grounds are quickly transferred from the bottom of the jug into a cup. Now, demonstrating this fact to people will not make them change the habits of a lifetime. In other words:

It's not enough just to be right.
You have to persuade people to change.

7

Interviews and Meetings

When two men communicate with each other by word of mouth, there is a two-fold hazard in that communication.

Sam Ervin, at the Watergate hearings, 1973

It is terrible to speak well and be wrong.

Sophocles, *Electra* (c. 416 BC)

There are many types of meetings and interviews. Interviews can vary from a policeman interrogating a suspect to a plumber trying to get a householder to explain what has gone wrong with the kitchen sink. Meetings can vary from a United Nations session on world peace to a Parent–Teacher Association meeting to raise funds for new kit for the school synchronized swimming team.

Meetings and interviews are all around us. They must occupy a large part of our existence. It is strange, then, that so few people ever receive any training in doing them tolerably well. Even stranger is the fact that often no training is received by people whose life-work is rooted in meetings and interviews: people such as systems designers, O & M staff and technology analysts. The work of such people depends absolutely on the fact-finding interview and the explanatory meeting.

The communication process

Take the simple phrase, 'This cupboard is locked' and consider what it means. It may mean that a piece of furniture with doors, in which things are stored, has been fastened with a device in such a way that it cannot be opened without utilizing another device known as a key. In fact, the phrase is rarely used in this factual sense without some added (hidden) information. As a piece of information, the phrase is so trivial that it would rarely be said.

If the phrase were used in a detective novel, then one could assume that it is a clue to the identity of the murderer. If it were used by a politician, it is probable that it is being used as a metaphor. If a manager utters the phrase at eleven o'clock in the morning, then it is likely to be an implied rebuke: somebody has not unlocked the door and should have done.

If a phrase as simple as 'the cupboard is locked' can carry these additional overtones, then more complex concepts are even more loaded. For example, we sometimes say that we do not know what the word 'profit' means. 'Profit' is such a slippery word, with many meanings depending on the circumstances, that it is often necessary to have it explained. One problem is that both speaker and listener are adamantly positive about any piece of information. Years ago, a violinist took the name 'Alfredo Campoli'. After a radio broadcast, the announcer said, 'Alfredo Campoli has just played part of Mendelssohn's violin concerto.' A few days later the BBC were somewhat surprised to receive an angry letter from a listener, complaining indignantly about the discourtesy of the announcer. The listener wanted to know why the BBC dared to let their employee say, 'I'm afraid old Campoli ...'. So the communication process is often pictured as:

This is expanded for the situation at interviews and meetings to the diagram shown in Figure 7.1.

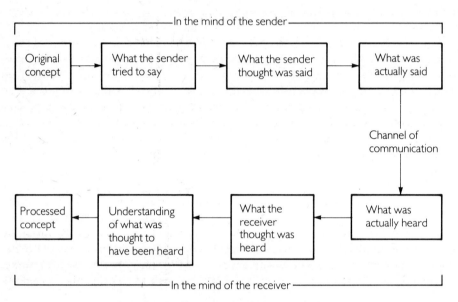

Figure 7.1 The communication process

Barriers to communication

Figure 7.1 shows that there are plenty of opportunities for communication to break down. In practice, these barriers take well-known forms.

■ THE WORDS USED

The words used have to suit the situation. Take auto-diallers. If one were explaining these to bank foreign exchange staff, one would point out how they give one easy access to other banks to take a forward Deutschmark position by just touching the monitor screen. To hackers, an auto-dialler is a means of breaking into a network, so they may like to know that[1] 'line seizure detect is ... simply a question of reading the phone line voltage; other conditions can be detected with simple tone decoder modules on the 567 chip'.

Though every office has its own language and jargon which one has to learn to use, office concepts are not well communicated by using complex language. 'Eschotological epidemislogists, eschew epididymical epidermes' lacks the impact of 'stop scratching yourself'.

As a language, English is particularly rich. With its three-fold basis (rooted in Celtic, Germanic and Romance languages) and its wide borrowings, it is capable of great subtlety and fine shades of meaning. Of the world's 2,700 languages, English probably has the largest vocabulary. The *Oxford English Dictionary* lists some 500,000 words. In comparison, it is often said that German has only 185,000 while French has to manage with fewer than 100,000. This is a boon for the 350 million people for whom English is the mother tongue (it is said that 40 per cent of the world's trade is conducted in English).

It can also be a curse. The large vocabulary gives plenty of scope for hiding meanings or talking a lot without saying anything. One manager we know is highly educated, being a qualified barrister, chartered secretary and actuary – he is also a nice person about whom nobody says anything unpleasant. Except for one weakness. One can go to a meeting with him for three hours, and understand every single sentence he says, as isolated sentences. But people will come out of these long meetings muttering, 'What was he trying to say to us?' Just to make matters worse, he was the manager of the Systems and Procedures Office.

■ THE WAY WORDS ARE USED

Conversation analysts have demonstrated how much information is communicated in non-verbal ways. For example, in a smooth conversation, both sides pick up cues which show when it is their turn to speak and for how long. This sets up a sort of rhythm for the conversation.[2] If this rhythm is missing, then the conversation becomes uncomfortable. There can be embarrassing pauses with both sides waiting for the other one to continue. The analyst may start asking long, involved questions which prompt only yes or no as the response.

The analyst may feel incorrectly that the staff member lacks clarity of argument. There are three main reasons for this. First, if the interviewee does not know the reason for a question, then the response can include a lot of information that the analyst considers irrelevant. For example, the analyst may say, 'How are you?' just as a social lubricant. The expected answer is, 'Fine, thanks'. But if the interviewee thinks that the analyst is studying office conditions, a long description of aches and pains may result. (In such a situation, we were once regaled with a description of how photocopiers caused the teeth to go black and were a source of influenza and catarrh.)

Second, people may emphasize, list and order their points in a way that is unfamiliar to the analyst. Third, the interviewee may use tone, pitch and metre in a different way from the analyst. This can happen, for example, in an inter-ethnic exchange between a person whose mother tongue is English and a bilingual Asian whose primary influence was a North Indian language. In such exchanges, both sides may experience difficulty in associating what was said previously with what is being said now. They can also find it difficult to understand emphasis and contrast.[3]

■ EMOTIONS

Interviews, even more than meetings, are likely to be burdened by the emotions that both sides bring to the conversation. The analyst may be under time pressure, and hence harassed (this will appear to the interviewee as either lack of interest or discourtesy). The analyst may have cut himself shaving or snagged her blouse, before coming to the office. The analyst may even be nervous. Unthinkable? Not so – but a definite problem for both sides.

Similarly, the interviewee may bring emotions to the conversation which act as a barrier to good communications. Like the analyst's, these emotions can be varied: a need to show off, over-deference, nervousness. Each has to be handled carefully.

Some commentators make much of the emotional factor, especially on the part of the interviewee. In response, we can only say that in our experience it rarely causes a real difficulty – perhaps once every four or five years. These have included two cases of extreme general nervousness, two instances of being 'tired and emotional', one case of (unknown) recent bereavement. There was also one person who over-compensated by being an obsessive practical joker.

■ HIDDEN MESSAGES

Many conversations have hidden messages:

(a) *The hidden agenda*. The analyst may switch from topic to topic without signalling the change, or showing how each topic fits in with the overall line of questioning. If the analyst is not explicit about the topic, then it may be difficult for the interviewee to speak relevantly. Another type of hidden agenda is when one or more people are conversing with a hidden 'win–lose' objective. When this objective is recognized, it often pushes other participants into the same objective. Especially ineffective is the situation when one person thinks, 'Smith made me look small at the last meeting so I must get my own back this time.'

(b) *Directness or indirectness*. Conversation has been categorized[4] as being positive (friendly, part of the team, showing solidarity) or negative (unemotional, staying private, showing deference). The analyst may assume that the conversation will be the 'solidarity' type while the interviewee may think that it should be formal. The hidden message is that the analyst may appear overbearing and inquisitive; the interviewee may appear unhelpful or devious.

(c) *Hidden signals*. The importance of 'prosody' in talk has already been mentioned (rhythm, intonation, emphasis, pauses, pitch). However it is possible that attempts at 'talk management' can backfire, to the discomfiture of participants. For example, some people will make encouraging noises to get interviewees to elaborate, repeat a word with a rising inflection; or agree with something said and then look away – to show that it is the analyst's turn to speak. This is fine if all parties share the same conventions, but not otherwise. For example, Erickson and Shultz[2] record that people from white and black cultures have different ways of demonstrating attention or turn-taking. The repetition of a response with a rising inflection may be taken as signals to elaborate, as agreement (and hence no need to elaborate), or as utter disbelief and disagreement. Hidden messages can be misinterpreted just as easily as spoken ones.

■ RULES AND CONVENTIONS

Every conversation has certain unspoken 'rules' or conventions. These are only useful, of course, if all participants abide by the same conventions. At a game of football, if one side is using Gaelic football rules while the other is playing to American football rules, then the resulting game is unlikely to satisfy anybody. Though, like a badly conducted interview, it might provide a brief period of amusement to any onlookers.

Some of the unspoken conventions for interviews are:

1 As the philosopher Paul Grice[5] put it, there are four maxims for conversational co-operation: you should be truthful, you should be relevant, you must say enough but not too much, and you must be clear.
2 Interviewees are expected to tell the truth on factual matters, but are not expected to show themselves in a bad light.
3 It is the analyst's job to create a relaxed atmosphere, but the interviewee is expected to respond by helping.
4 The analyst should not cause embarrassment by prying into private matters.
5 The analyst can control the interview, but the interviewee can (not too frequently) take the initiative and elaborate.
6 Analysts do not have to show agreement or give much feedback – it is an interview and not an informal conversation.
7 The analyst must not betray a confidence, but the interviewee must not disclose something that puts the analyst in an invidious position (e.g. anything illegal).

It should be pointed out that these are social conventions, and not rules to be followed for success. These follow.

Rules for interviewing

The rules for good interviewing have appeared many times in magazines, books and seminars. Since, however, they are important, they are repeated here.

1 *Always, but always, plan for an interview.* Sometimes, this process can be quite lengthy – such as when one has to learn about a previously unknown aspect of the business, or read job descriptions or one's existing notes. One must know the objective of the interview, and know what facts have to be covered. To ensure that these facts are indeed covered one can use a checklist or a form of reminder.

If one is interviewing many people on the same largely factual matters (such as a records management study) then one can often benefit from a pre-printed form. This makes analysis more accurate and easier, without necessarily inhibiting spontaneity. The use of 'memory cards' can be useful. These are *aides-mémoire* on 15 × 10 cm cards. Examples are given in chapters 33 and 34. Another example (this time for use when talking to a supervisor) is the following:

Initial talk with supervisor
1 Explain study, terms of reference.
2 Discuss section office layout.
3 Pinpoint who does which task.
4 Establish who should be interviewed for each task.
5 Ask about absences (e.g. holidays), interruptions (e.g. training), inconveniences (e.g. peaks, deadlines).
6 Discuss overview of section's jobs, tasks.
7 Discuss problems within the section.
8 Ask for introduction to first job-holder.

2 *Arrange the interview.* If the study is not known about by the staff, then naturally it will first be necessary to publicize it. Of course, this should have been done once the study had been agreed but there are times when it is forgotten or done too superficially. It is then best to arrange for introductions, going generally down the hierarchy. Thus the chief executive will introduce one to any directors whom one has not met. These directors will then introduce one to senior managers, these senior managers to other managers, and these managers to the supervisors. One's aim is not to work in anybody's area of responsibility without their knowledge.

The interview then has to be arranged as to place and time. It is usually best to have the interview at the person's place of work. This is largely because it is much easier to explain something when all the necessary paraphernalia is to hand. Open-plan offices are no problem because everybody is used to working there; noisy offices can be a nuisance, though few are so noisy that conversation is impossible. The worst situation is probably that of continual interruptions – in that case, it may be a good plan to try to borrow the manager's office.

The times for interviews are obvious: not when it's inconvenient, not during meal-breaks or after working hours (unless the culture favours out-of-hours interviews). The main problem with timing interviews is the question of scheduling. On may be faced with the need to complete a certain number of interviews in a set time. In practice, this usually means doing slightly too many interviews each day and then completing the analysis during the evenings.

3 *First impressions.* Some people get a trifle excited about first impressions, feeling that trying to make a good first impression is somehow dishonest. The comment, 'People must take me as I am' still causes one's heart to sink slightly. One is tempted to reply, 'You mean, an inconsiderate grumpy isolate who refuses to use soap?' However, such a riposte is best avoided since it tends to lead to a long philosophical discussion.

Like it or not, first impressions do count. On meeting the surgeon who is going to cut one up, one does not want to see a scruffy mumbler with dank unwashed hair, swaying slightly from snorting cocaine. Such a person may be a genius with the scalpel but we would still like to meet a formally dressed smoothie – who is also a genius with a scalpel.

The second half of the first impression is the opening remarks. Here it must be remembered that the interviewee may not really take in the first comments, either because of uncertainty or thinking about whether the analyst is sitting comfortably – so the tone matters. 'How do y'do, Alice isn't it, I just thought we'd have a little chat' can sound intolerably supercilious and élitist. It is also untrue.

'Good morning, my name's Jonathon Fortescue-Smithington of Over-global Management Consultancies, representing Advanced Technology Interface Division. My specialism is ergonometric strategies with special reference to network facilities and operational visual interfaces' may not be untrue – but it may make the interviewee wonder how to remember all that. On the whole we prefer the banal opening, said pleasantly:

Analyst: Good morning. Thank you for seeing me.
Interviewee: Not at all. Please sit down.
Analyst: Thanks. Would you mind if I take my coat off? It's rather cold outside today, and . . .

And so on. In Western industrial countries, this will probably take about a minute, by which time the participants are likely to be reasonably relaxed and feeling in a positive frame of mind. The banal start must not be prolonged or the interviewee may think that the analyst is a waffler or ill-prepared. (In some countries, it is only polite to prolong the small talk and one may have to drink a formal cup of coffee or tea – a rather pleasant convention.)

4 *Conducting the interview.* Discussions about how to conduct interviews often tend to a moralizing or sermonizing tone – perhaps because we all know how we really ought to behave but tend to forget in the heat of the moment. Some points that should be remembered are:

(a) A rapport should be established by 'active listening'. This requires paying attention to the talker and trying to understand what is being said. Beware of 'yes, but' interruptions. 'Yes, but' does not usually mean 'I understand/agree'. It usually means 'You've had your turn so it's mine now.'
(b) Give occasional feedback. Not just to be polite but to check that one has grasped the facts.
(c) Take notes. This must be done openly, preferably in such a manner that the interviewee could actually read them if he/she really wanted to.
(d) 'Open' questions are those inviting the interviewee to give an expansive answer. 'Closed' questions are those that imply a specific and shorter response. For some topics, what is know as the 'Funnel sequence' is useful. In this, one starts off with an open question, and then follows it with a series of closed ones. For example, 'Tell me about your time in Buenos Aires.' 'What services does our office there provide?' 'Is their forex department like ours here?'
(e) Mentally cross-check the answers, especially to the well-known cloudy ones • such as, 'What is it that you do?' There are five possible answers to this question:
   • the formal job description;
   • the theoretically possible;
   • that originally intended;
   • that hoped for or aspired to;
   • the work actually actually performed.
   We once got the first four from the same person, at the first four interviews. The colleagues of the manager concerned told us the fifth – with some enjoyment, it has to be admitted.
(f) One must behave properly towards the interviewee. What does 'properly' mean? It can be summed up in a simple slogan that we use constantly:

> **Courtesy with tenacity**

There is much to be said for straight, old-fashioned courtesy in one's interviewing. At the same time, one has to remember that the objective is to obtain facts and so some tenacity is called for in pursuing this aim.

(g) Conclude the interview. This will often involve a degree of recapitulation, depending on the degree of complexity of the matters discussed. One has to ensure that one has copies of all relevant material. Give the interviewee your

47

internal phone number so that any further thoughts can be communicated. Ask whether you can return if you find that you need elaboration. Finally, thank the interviewee for the time and help given.

Meetings

Research shows that meetings account for a large part of the life of managers, so they are important. They also loom large in the life of analysts and consultants, to whom they may well be even more important. Not so much because of the amount of time that they occupy as the fact that, individually, a lot hangs on them. A consultant may be meeting a large number of staff to explain some recommendations, or a group of trade union delegates to explain a technique, or a few managers to defend certain findings. Whatever the reason (and there are many types of such meetings), one aspect is a constant: the consultant only has one chance to get it right.

Since meetings are so often a means of communication, many of the points already made apply as much to meetings as to interviews. However, running a successful meeting does require attention to some specific points.

■ PLAN THE MEETING

The first aspect of this is to decide why the meeting is taking place (alternatives may be preferable sometimes). Having decided that a meeting is the best route, the next point is to decide the objectives and who should participate. Objectives, again? Yes, it is true that management consultants are always referring to the need for objectives. One manager complained, 'Consultants say "what are our objectives?" the way the rest of us say "Good morning".' This may or may not be true. It does not prevent the need to state or to recapitulate them. Not only should one decide on the meeting's objectives, a consultancy team should decide on their own objectives. It is then possible, after the meeting, to see if one reached these objectives (and, if not, what has to be done to retrieve the situation).

Decisions about who should attend a meeting are usually straightforward. Text-books sometimes state that only those people with something important to contribute should be invited. This, of course, is rubbish. Just try *not* inviting a trade union general secretary or a company's managing director to a meeting that they consider they should attend. If there is a valid reason for some people not attending a meeting that they would expect to, then a brief explanation is called for. Finally, the people attending have to be notified about the details of the meeting.

■ PREPARATION

The preparation for the meeting has one important output: the agenda. Many agendas contain few words and fewer thoughts. We have all seen an agenda that goes: 1. Last month's sales. 2. New product budget. 3. AOB. Such agendas have often been prepared by a secretary copying out the agenda for the last meeting. Much preferable is:

> 2. New product budget.
> To discuss the budget implications of postponing the introduction of the new Miracle Jelly. To decide how much, if any, of this has to be transferred to development of the new Miracle Trifle. To decide who should recalculate the Miracle Trifle costings and by when.

The improvement enables the participants to prepare for the meeting. It also enables the meeting 'chair' to run the meeting, and to avoid the over-pursuit of irrelevant side issues.

■ RUNNING THE MEETING

The person chairing the meeting can make an enormous difference. If skilled, the meeting can be so effective that it is a pleasure. If unskilled, then the meeting can be insufferably frustrating. This person has to ensure that decisions are made, consensus reached, contributions made, the point kept to, and be able to summarize effectively and accurately, all with a display of urbane goodwill.

Research suggests that effective discussions need the presence of two types of person: one dedicated to getting the work done and the other effective at keeping the group acting as a team (in the jargon 'task leadership' and 'social leadership'). The same research suggests that overall it is better for the person chairing the meeting to be a 'social leader' even if this means having somebody else to act as task leader.

■ RECORDING THE MEETING

Good minutes of a meeting have been described as 'what people wish that they had said if only they had been paying attention'. In fact, good minutes should be a précis of the main points made. Even more, they must record what decisions were made and what actions must result, by whom and by when.

How to ruin a meeting

1 Send out the notices of the meeting either a month or a few hours in advance (with luck, this will reduce the number of people who attend).
2 Arrange for all telephone calls to be transferred to the meeting room (otherwise people might think that the meeting is important, or miss the pleasure of joining in the telephone calls).
3 Encourage private conversations between individual participants.
4 Encourage the garrulous to keep on talking as long as they want (the silent, weak types must learn to stand up for themselves – especially if they have something relevant to say).
5 Make sure that on every topic the most senior speak first and then work down the hierarchy (this prevents wasting time on considering alternatives which the inexperienced might suggest).
6 Do not bother with the agenda (if anything is really important, it can be reserved for the final 'Any Other Business' item).
7 Hold the meeting in the most cramped, unsuitable conditions that can be found (this will save everybody time as the meeting will not take too long).
8 Remember that meetings are only a sop to industrial democracy or some such trendy sociological theory (real chief executives issue orders).

References

1 Cornwall, H., *The Hacker's Handbook*, London: Century Communications, 1985.
2 Erickson, F. and Shultz, J., *The Counsellor as Gatekeeper: Social Interaction in Interviews*, London: Academic Press, 1982.

3 Gumperz, J., *Discourse Strategies*, and Gumperz, J. (ed.), *Language and Social Identity*, both Cambridge: Cambridge University Press, 1982.
4 Brown, P. and Levinson, S., 'Universals in language usage: politeness phenomena', in Goody, E., *Questions and Politeness: Strategies in Social Interaction*, Cambridge: Cambridge University Press, 1978.
5 Grice, P., 'Logic and conversation', in Cole, P. and Morgan, J. (eds), *Syntax and Semantics*, Vol. 3, *Speech Acts*, London: Academic Press, 1975.

Further reading

Armstrong, M., *How to Be an Even Better Manager*, London: Kogan Page, 1988.
Jay, A., *How to Run a Meeting*, London: Visual Arts, 1976 (written in conjunction with the film, 'Meetings, Bloody Meetings').
Lord, G. A., *Know What I Mean?*, Maidenhead: McGraw-Hill, 1984.
Roberts, C., *The Interview Game*, London: BBC Enterprises, 1985.
The 3M Meeting Management Team, *How to Run Better Business Meetings*, New York: McGraw-Hill, 1984.
Turner, S., *Thorsons' Guide to Making Business Presentations*, Wellingborough: Thorsons, 1986.

8

Groups and Group Working

No man is an Island, entire of itself; every man is a piece of the Continent...

John Donne, *Devotions* (1624)

Infinitely often it is clear that we appreciate, even respect – not a multitude – but ten people gathered in a room.

Giacomo Leopardi, *Pensieri* (1837)

Few of us can truthfully claim never to have been members of a group. Most of us start life as members of a family, going on to be members of a school. While there, we are likely to have been members of a class, an interest group, a gang, a clique of friends, a 'house'. We may have been members of a school team that tried to prove superiority to teams from other schools – at football, athletics, debating, chess. As adults, we find society replete with other 'societies' set up to share a common interest in hobbies, sport, consumerism, religion, politics, skills, and so on. At work, we find ourselves members of still more interlocking groups.

Since most of us have such an extensive knowledge of being in groups, it is perhaps remarkable how often groups do not work well. With all that experience around, one might expect groups to be almost perfect. In fact, the ability to get groups working well is often a highly prized facility, as in the case of successful football team managers. When one looks at such managers one discerns a wide variety of approaches. Some appear to base their work on consensus while others border on the dictatorial. Some are ebullient extroverts while others are so quiet they seem to be introverted. Even more, success can be transient. Last year's success can become this year's flop. Success with one team can melt away upon transfer to another team. Clearly, then, managing groups is a complex affair. A few simple rules that guarantee success have so far eluded investigators.

When we turn to experts for their advice, we meet another problem. Historically, psychologists have concentrated on the individual rather than on groups. Orthodox Freudians have tended to put the emphasis on the interaction with the family (though people like Eric Hickson have tried to free us from the straitjacket of ignoring society and other environmental considerations). On the other hand, social scientists have historically tended to concentrate on the activities of groups as though the group were an indivisible entity. This compartmentalization largely continued until as late as the 1960s.

Management consultants who specialize in human resources have thus had to draw their thinking from two mainstream sources. This matters since an office group has two basic types of interaction. First, there is the interaction between separate groups (e.g. the computer department and accounts staff). Second, there are the relationships inside each group, including those between a leader (formal or informal) and the other members.

A second form of compartmentalism has occurred in Organization Development

(OD). OD practitioners may refer to group activities by using two descriptive words, 'content' and 'process'. 'Content' is what goes on within the group (the work that is done). 'Process' is how the group behaves (e.g. how it solves problems). Practitioners of OD have traditionally concentrated on 'process' aspects and only looked at 'content' in so far as 'the content is a function of the process'.[1] Some years ago a survey found that 80 per cent of OD practitioners used process skills more than any other.[2]

For our purposes, however, the traditional Freudian and OD approaches may not be enough. There are two important reasons for this. First, the actual work may be of great concern to us, both because it affects effectiveness and because it can affect the relationships of the group. Second, we are not only concerned with problem solving. We are continually looking for improvements, and this does not necessarily mean that there is always a problem to solve. (The claim that absolutely everything that happens in an office has to be regarded as a problem we would regard as a form of solipsism.)

Creating groups

We are fortunate that in the majority of cases the question, 'How should we group office activities?' has a fairly obvious answer. We tend to put together those people that are at a similar point in the work flow (e.g. the stores office), or those people with similar skills whose work interacts (e.g. personnel department). Of course, there is no reason why any split is sacrosanct, provided we can see some logic in a new split.

At one time it was anticipated that advanced office technology would radically change the way that groups would be set up. A few proponents of 'information technology' assumed that all office work was information, that technology would de-skill most office work, and that communications technology would enable people to be situated randomly. In reply, it has to be said that those automated and paperless offices in which we have worked have not changed in this respect. They are still grouped in 'natural' formations. There are two probable reasons for this. First, it is easier for managers and staff to think along quasi-traditional lines (a restraint that by its nature may diminish over the years). Second, the advent of new office technology has definitely not removed the need for staff to be skilled. Some skills may have gone, some new ones have been acquired, but many skills are as vital as ever. Two obvious examples are answering queries from the public and customers, and maintaining good product knowledge.

There are occasions when the correct grouping of people is not obvious. A colleague (who started life as a psychologist) had to study the bus service in a large city. The buses had a poor reputation for service and timekeeping, and it was decided that matters would be improved by creating more effective work groups. The question was – what was the best grouping? This city still had two-person crewing, a driver and a conductor. The first experiment (building on the 'natural' group of the two-person crew) failed to make much improvement. Thinking that one reason for this was that this grouping was too small, further experiments were carried out. One tried to build on the working shift, another the local garage out of which the crews worked.

These experiments failed to improve matters very much. So finally an experiment was carried out in which the people who were working on the same route were brought together. This grouping was the one that the members felt was right. There was a commonality of tasks and problems. The same destinations, the same peaks, the same roadworks gave a shared experience. The same sights ('Have you seen that new hotel?') gave a basis for mutual conversations. Such things may seem trivial to those who did not experience them, but they are part of human experience and satisfaction. Anyway, this grouping was clearly the correct one as shown by the considerable improvement in the bus service.

Group development

Groups develop. Or, to be more accurate, they can develop. There are times when a group seems to get stuck at a particular point in its development. The stages and the characteristics of each stage can be postulated as follows:

1 *Group creation.* A new group can be created for many reasons such as a reorganization, bringing together particular skills, a response to market changes and so on. In a new group, the members are likely to be concentrating on their own personal needs, which will vary widely. Some will be concerned with their territory, others will be trying to attain or affirm their role, some will be jockeying for influence while others will be trying to make friendships, and some will take refuge in working hard. One characteristic of new groups is a relative willingness to accept somebody (such as a manager) to lead the group. At times this becomes even stronger so that it becomes an unspoken expectation that a manager will direct operations, and know what should be done.

2 *Group linking.* Provided that the group was not created for discreditable reasons, it is not uncommon for a group to go through a stage of elation or a self-congratulatory period. During this stage, once linkages of common interest or amity have been forged, the group may become idealized in members' minds. As such, members will often want to defend it. So people will want (and value) harmony within the group, and attack any members who deviate or do not 'follow the party line' (new political parties tend to stay at this stage for a lengthy period).

3 *Group performance.* At this stage the group will concentrate on the task(s) in hand and, if successful at this, find pleasure in performing the work effectively. Teamwork, work-sharing and helping one another may then become accepted norms of behaviour. Members who exhibit a tendency not to toe the party line will be tolerated provided that they are good team members in other ways and/or are ultra-expert. Managers are accepted as part of the team provided they help the group in its relationships with outsiders. One of the problems of having constantly shifting project teams in organization structures is moving a group into this stage and out of the second stage.

4 *Group co-operation.* Performing well within the group is not enough. Effectiveness is only reached if separate groups co-operate with one another. This is something that groups would like to achieve but may not be able to if there are obstructions in the way. The commonest obstruction is where the groups see their objectives in paro-chial terms, or even as being in opposition. A common example is where quality control staff are seen by operating staff as being the opposition. This can result in hostility or 'side-stepping'. Thus in an advertising agency the film unit would side-step the quality control staff by over-running so that there was insufficient time for

reshooting (and then appealing to top management that the campaign was being held up). In practice, the intergroup co-operation stage is the most difficult to maintain over the long term. The reason for this is that there are so many occurrences that can upset it – anything from inequality between groups in pay rises to changes in the market causing strains. The best defence is the maintenance of an effective and supportive culture.

5 *Group stagnation.* One of the well-known penalties of success is that it can actually inhibit change and flexibility. This happens because the success is ascribed to having done things right. Logically, then, further success will follow if the same things are continued. This leads to inflexibility, a lack of willingness to change, and thence over-defensiveness to preserve the group as it is against all-comers. The same end result can arise from failure, when people may feel that change can only make matters worse. Ineffectiveness will occur, as may 'balkanization'.

Table 8.1 summarizes these stages. The aim has to be to move fairly rapidly to the third stage and then to build up to the fourth stage, without spilling over into the fifth stage. Moving back from the fifth stage to the fourth stage is not an easy or fast transition.

Table 8.1   Stages of group development

Group stage	Example characteristics	Examples of means of effecting movement between stages	
(i) Creation	Leader dependency	Clarity of objectives and aims Previous preparation, planning	↓
(ii) Linking	Friendliness	Good systems and procedures Effective leadership	↓
(iii) Performance	Confidence	Team-building, problem solving Striving for excellence	↓
(iv) Co-operation	Team-working	Lack of leadership Inattention to culture	↓
(v) Stagnation	Truculence	Organization development Major change (e.g. splitting up the group)	↓

The manager as facilitator

Managers are expected to possess an apparently ever-widening range of abilities, so that one hesitates to produce yet another long list of desirable attributes in the group environment. Instead, perhaps it is better to quote Dyer[3], who said that the need is for 'managers who are able to pull together people of diverse backgrounds, personalities, training, and experience and weld them into an effective working group'.

The ways in which managers who are effective leaders do this was well put by Katz and Kahn[4] when they said that effective leaders:

- plan and supervise, rather than spend all their time on day-to-day work (the old problem of the 'senior person who is present');
- delegate work, and help people with new tasks rather than supervising too closely;
- are truly available to listen to and talk to group members;
- encourage group solidarity and a sense of pride.

At the same time, group members make certain demands on the manager. Just as senior management expect a manager to have influence on the group so the group expects the manager to have influence on senior management, as well as sideways on managers of other groups. This influence on behalf of the group is expected to be exercised in a number of ways. The manager is expected to defend the group's 'rights' (such as pay differentials, office space, coffee breaks) and to be a channel of information about what is going on. The manager is also expected to negotiate with other groups if there is any conflict.

To satisfy these demands by the group, the manager needs to have a degree of self-confidence and a healthy relationship with the group, with senior managers and with other managers. As in other relationships, healthy does not mean authoritarian or subservient. It implies an openness and an ability to discuss differences in an honest and solution-seeking manner, rather than bottling up resentments.

Self-governing work groups

In autonomous work groups, managers and supervisors are dispensed with. Instead, staff are divided into small work groups each of which are given specific tasks and targets. The staff themselves decide how the tasks are to be carried out and how the targets are to be met (in some cases, the staff themselves set the targets). Supporters of this approach can quote anecdotal and some experimental evidence on their behalf. The basic problem is that few organizations would be willing to carry out a controlled experiment – though it has to be admitted that few management theories are tested in this way either.

One of the few experiments was carried out in Norway by the Institute for Industrial Social Research in Trondheim. This arose out of interest by the Federation of Trade Unions and the Employers' Federation. The project extended over four years and was carried out in four firms.[5] The results were not conclusive, though absenteeism seems to have been reduced. Success appears to have needed improved training and higher pay. Our own views on autonomous work groups are:

- they are likely to be applicable in small rather than large firms;
- they only address some (lower) managerial functions. Integration of others is not

55

easy. An example is the facilitator role mentioned above (in one experiment, people took turns at being what was called a 'contact man');

● group tasks need to be discrete in the sense that interaction with other groups can go against the spirit of the concept. This can be difficult in those offices that are complex and that rely on advanced technology.

We feel, therefore, that the case for autonomous groups remains unproven. Although we have worked where it has been the approach, it is not easy to predict where it would be the best system.

Team building

A common approach to the question of team building is to put forward ways of solving difficulties encountered by groups, and this is certainly an important aspect. Dyer[3] suggests that a problem group can be recognized by the following symptoms:

● a too-dominant leader;
● warring cliques;
● unequal workloads and inequitable sharing of resources;
● rigidity of procedures and group beliefs;
● a lack of creativity in tackling problems; and
● a feeling of defensiveness.

To this we would add low productivity and a lack of co-operation with other groups. Different consultants have different ways of approaching team-building, but the stages are usually:

1 *Gaining acceptance.* Logic tells one that it is unlikely that people will reveal their innermost thoughts and feelings at a first meeting. They have to get to know one first. To gain acceptance, we like to carry out an initial fact-finding study with a number of face-to-face interviews. The sort of facts one tries to acquire are rather like those in method design (see Part D). This has the added advantage that the consultant gets to understand the work of the group.

2 *Group discussions.* A number of discussions are held with the staff. For these, the group is divided into sets of about five and these sets are usually kept constant for some time. At these discussions, problems are put forward by the staff and discussed (this may need some structuring by the consultant by looking at various parts of the work flow successively). These discussions are kept at a reasonably low emotional level, with a touch of good humour. They are not just 'gripe sessions' – the aim is to find approaches to tackling the problems. These discussions need sensitivity by the consultant. Some guidance is needed without being heavy-handed, the work of the department must not be overly interrupted, people must not feel that it's all talk and no action but action must not be precipitate. During the discussions, the consultant is also trying to answer some questions:

● do the staff have a feeling for group objectives and aims?
● are procedural difficulties (e.g. bottlenecks) frustrating?
● are the group wasting their time on unwanted activities?
● are problems 'solved' only to reappear?
● what are the real unspoken dissatisfiers?

3 *Consolidation.* These discussions can go on for some time. They may have to while the real underlying problems are uncovered. But this can lead to a feeling among the staff that nothing is happening. So some actual improvements must be made before the discussions are complete. Often these are improvements that the consultant can make (such as agreeing new deadlines with another group). In other cases, a few action groups are set up. These are small sub-groups, who have the task of seeking solutions to some of the problems that have been raised. It is common for some of these solutions to be implemented before the discussion stage is complete.

4 *Deriving solutions.* During the discussions, the consultant is seeking the real underlying causes of the difficulties and also deriving solutions. The implementation of these solutions is quite likely to take the consultant outside the boundaries of the group. An example would be if any of the managers themselves have inadequacies which need attention. To tackle some of the other problems, the previously formed action groups are upgraded with the task of developing solutions. Any other problems are tackled by the consultant, depending on their nature.

5 *Action plans.* In conjunction with the action groups, plans for implementing the solutions are set out. This is easy to say but will involve the consultant in strenuous talks with senior managers to ensure that implementation is not hindered.

6 *Reinforcers.* As well as discussions and problem solving, it is necessary to change attitudes (see chapter 19). Different consultants have non-emotional ways of reinforcing this. Some use a form of Training Groups.[6] Others use a series of seminars (we favour these). Some use 'games' such as the Egg Drop Exercise used by Vector Management Systems.

7 *Monitoring.* Feedback has to be obtained by the consultant so that improvement can be certified and measured. Here it is necessary to discount any Hawthorne-type improvements – those due to the fact that the problems are being looked at by the consultant. This means returning to the group at a future date to ensure that improvement has been maintained.

Team building through problem solving is a reactive approach. The pro-active approach is via the overall culture. At the risk of appearing repetitive, this can be summarized as:

- ensure that people know the objectives and aims of the organization, and are committed to them;
- provide effective leadership;
- make the customer the dominant factor;
- strive for superior service;
- pursue constant innovation, and flexibility for change;
- make full use of the capabilities of all staff.

Groups are not just the basic constituent of every organization structure. They are also the immediate surroundings of all the staff. As such, the working group can be of paramount importance in people's working life. Not surprisingly, therefore, we sometimes have to make considerable efforts at getting them right.

References

1 Harvey, D. F. and Brown, D. R., *An Experiential Approach to Organization Development*, Englewood Cliffs: Prentice-Hall, 1988.
2 Burke, W. W. *et al.*, 'Improve your OD Project's chances for success', *Training and Development Journal*, September 1984, p. 67.
3 Dyer, W. G., *Team Building: Issues and Alternatives*, Reading: Addison-Wesley, 1977.
4 Katz, D. and Kahn, R. L., 'Human organization and worker motivation', in Tripp, L. R. (ed.), *Industrial Productivity*, Wisconsin: Industrial Relations Research Associates, 1951.
5 Thorsrud, E. and Emery, F., *Mot en ny bedriftsorganisasjon*, Oslo: Johan Grundt Tanum Forlag, 1969.
6 Schein, E. H., *Organizational Culture and Leadership*, San Francisco: Jossey-Bass, 1985.

Further reading

Hare, A., *Handbook of Small Group Research*, New York: Free Press, 1976.
O'Brien, D., 'The quality of management and the role of technology', *Management Services*, Vol. 33, No. 1, January, 1989, p. 53.
Pages, M., *The Emotional Life of Groups*, Paris: Dunod, 1968.
Wells, L., 'The group-as-a-whole: a systemic socio-analytic perspective on interpersonal and group relations', in Alderfer, C. P. *et al.*, (eds), *Advances in Experiential Social Processes*, New York: Wiley, 1980.

9

Departments and Assignments

In the field of observation, chance favours only the prepared minds.
Louis Pasteur (1888)

All excellence is equally difficult.
Thornton Wilder (interview), *Writers at Work* (1958)

Many organizations have internal departments whose function is the improvement of the effectiveness of the offices. Such departments can have a bewilderingly large variety of titles, for example Management Services, Systems & Procedures, O & M, Staff Inspection, CIR, ADP Advisory, Systems Audit, Internal Consultants, to name just a few. In one enterprise, the staff were part of the personnel department, because 'the job of a personnel department is to reduce staff costs'.

For the purposes of this chapter, such departments will be referred to as the 'AM Department' (for Admin Management). This will probably satisfy nobody, but has the advantage of not carrying the burden of hidden implications. All AM Departments face the same problems at some stage in their existence:

- gaining acceptance by other line and staff departments;
- following a defined programme of work;
- having an acceptable position in the organization structure;
- self-improvement; and
- proving the value of their existence.

None of these problems has facile solutions, except perhaps the final one. No AM department should be so introspective that it suffers the fate that was observed in one case. A well-known international company disbanded its O & M department and declared the staff redundant. This was done 'to cut costs'. Such departments are not killed off by management – they commit suicide.

The department

■ SETTING UP

A new AM Department can arise through several routes:

- spinning off a new group of people with particular areas of expertise from an existing department, such as Internal Audit or Computer Department;
- bringing in an experienced person from outside to head and build a new department;
- giving the job of heading and building a new department to an insider 'product champion'. This route often follows a successful in-house cost-cutting exercise;
- using a consultancy assignment whereby the external consultants set up a new department (and train selected internal staff), as part of an assignment.

Being thoroughly biased and prejudiced, we favour the final alternative as being the preferred one. In practice, this route has in many instances resulted in new AM departments with high morale and a sense of purpose.

■ ORGANIZATIONAL PLACING

Where should AM departments be in the organization structure? To whom should they report? Discussions on these points have been proceeding for at least the last forty years, though inconclusively. Most members of AM departments are quite sure of the answer: they should report to the chief executive, since only this will give them adequate status and ensure that their recommendations are acted upon.

Unfortunately, in most organizations this is not really practical. The chief executive is governed by 'span of control' considerations as much as the rest of us. The place of AM departments is usually governed by the particular circumstances of the concern, especially as every other specialism (such as Facilities Management, Public Relations, Design, Product Development, the Library and the Surgery) all have the same aspiration of reporting to the chief executive and being autonomous.

Even more problematical is the situation where an organization has a number of subsidiaries. In this situation, members of the main AM department may be attached to the subsidiary, they may stay central and visit the other companies, or the subsidiaries may have their own mini-AM departments. From observation (though no proof is offered) the third of these is the least satisfactory. The question of centralizing the AM department or not should usually be settled by following the example of the rest of the concern.

One important point that has to be made is that status cannot be conferred and maintained by organizational placement. The quality and type of work of the AM department, as perceived by the rest of the organization, can be a much more potent source of status. One of the items for which we receive many requests is a copy of a description of AM departments as seen by others. By way of explanation it should be pointed out that in charting office systems it is common to use six symbols (these are shown in chapter 24):

Departments can 'resemble' each of the six symbols in the eyes of the rest of the organization thus:

a forward-looking group of people;

those people who hold us all up;

a bunch of square pegs in round holes;

always hoping for inspiration and help from above;

the Bermuda Triangle of management: 'If any good ideas go into that department, they disappear without trace';

 (worst of all) a millstone around everyone's neck.

■ TECHNIQUES COVERED

A

The question of which areas an AM department should cover overlaps to some extent the matter of organizational placing. A number of analyses have been made to show which areas are commonly covered. This is usually found to be along the following lines:

- method design and work quantification;
- computers;
- statistics and Operational Research;
- systems analysis;
- project networks.[1]

For any new department being set up, the areas covered in this book will provide an indication of the techniques that should be known and used. However, a reservation has to be made about organization structure studies. In practice, in-house staff are rarely asked to undertake such work except at a relatively low level. One important point that has to be settled is whether or not an AM department has the responsibility for the advanced office technology in the organization. Our own view is that it should, but it is a view that is not universally shared.

We believe that 'advanced office technology' has been around so long that it is no longer reasonable to think of it as being separate from the whole gamut of improving office effectiveness. A simple example is the payroll. A method-design study of payroll will have to consider a number of possible alternatives including:

- centralization or decentralization;
- manual preparation (such as multi-part forms);
- bureaux (generalized or specialized);
- in-house mainframe computer;
- network/distributed processing;
- small office computers (package or custom software).

Other studies are similar; one cannot improve methods without considering the three general alternatives of manual, machine or technology. So splitting off advanced office technology into a separate department is both artificial and ineffective. It really is time that we stopped treating 'new' technology with wide-eyed wonder; it is just a tool which we can use for improving effectiveness. If AM staff do not understand it (in fact most of them do), then they have to learn enough to be able to use it to improve effectiveness.

■ THE STAFF

Reading some of the published lists of desirable attributes of AM staff is enough to make the archangel Gabriel himself quail at the prospect of applying for a position. No such list is offered here. When interviewing prospective staff we tend to prefer using a questionnaire (along the lines of the well-known Kostick PAPI inventory) as the basis for a discussion. We prefer people who have become accustomed to success as opposed to those fearing more failures. There is one type of applicant who rarely gets on to our shortlist. This is the person who tells of a series of AM studies resulting in superb reports – none of which was accepted by management, owing to the shortcomings of the management.

Fundamental to the type of staff in an AM department is the basic decision of its role. Some organizations like a department consisting of experienced professionals who will have spent some years in AM work. Other concerns use it as a training ground for high-flyers who will move on to managerial positions after two to three years in the department. Those departments that combine both types of staff often have about them a vitality that is refreshing.

In Britain, the 'professional' type of staff should be encouraged to study for the examinations of one of the two main institutes: either the Institute of Administrative Management or the Institute of Management Services. Our experience of both institutes is that the examinations are run by people who care about them and who make considerable efforts. Concerns that use the AM department as a training ground for future managers often find that such people mature well in such an environment. Such a process also reveals those who are 'accommodators' – people who become diffident about change from fear of upsetting managers with whom they will have to work in the future.

The head of the AM department must understand the techniques that the department utilizes, but does not have to possess great practical expertise in them. What is definitely needed, though, is somebody with good social and communication skills.

■ DEPARTMENTAL DATABASE

AM departments slowly build up their own databases, which are likely to include:

- organizational details (structures, numbers, etc.);
- systems (paperwork, methods, regulations, guard books);
- equipment and layouts;
- past studies, and details of standard times;
- training material, books and magazines, external contacts.

All of this can assist new studies. As always, the most important aspect is creating a balance. The database must not become a monster of a bureaucracy by people being paranoiac about keeping every detail up to date. On the other hand it must not fall into disuse and disrepute because staff can never find anything.

A typical aspect is the use of magazines. AM departments usually receive a number of these, especially if one includes the free ones. Very occasionally one comes across a department that keeps all the back copies. These are usually to be found stacked, by years, in a cupboard somewhere. Of course, they are rarely looked at; even if one can remember an article, it is very difficult to recall when it was printed. Sometimes even the exact year eludes one. In theory one could record all the articles in a database on a small computer but, mercifully, few departments have that much spare time.

An alternative is to use a 'tear-sheet' system. In this, one only keeps the last two copies of each magazine (mainly for the advertisements). Before discarding a magazine, any important material is torn out and filed in one of two ways: one for 'techniques' and the other for equipment and machinery. (A system suitable for the equipment and machinery is shown in chapter 16.) Once a year one can fillet the files by throwing away virtually everything that is more than three years old.

■ ANNUAL REPORT

Once a year, the AM department should produce a report for senior and middle management. In a way, the main aim of this report is defensive – to show what a fantastic job the department is doing, as proved by the vast savings that it has made. But the report must never read defensively. It should be bright, easy to read, attractive to look at – and short. The report should describe briefly each study undertaken during the year, taking one or two paragraphs only for each study. The report must also state briefly the cost of the department compared with the savings.

This savings:cost aspect is important. If an AM department costs more than it saves, then it is almost inevitable that management will at some stage wonder why the department exists (and if it does not, then it should). Many departments (e.g. the one at British Rail) show an impressive multiple for their savings:cost ratio.

Of course, some people may object to this approach, saying that some studies are undertaken for management even though both sides know that they will not show a return. This can be true. But the number of such studies should not be so high that in any year costs exceed the savings. If they do then this fact may be hiding a deeper malaise. It may be that managers are being pressured to 'find some work for the AM people to do', or that the department is insufficiently skilled or trusted to do worthwhile work. The possibility that any enterprise is so efficient that no further improvement is possible is not a situation that has yet been encountered.

One item that sometimes causes query is when a study results in a large saving which will continue for many years. In theory, a department could then show a high return for a decade without doing any work. The approach that is recommended for such a situation is very simple. In the first year, 100 per cent of the savings are claimed. In year 2, two-thirds are claimed. In year 3, one-third is claimed. In years 4 and later, none is claimed.

Some organizations take an even more rigorous approach: they charge user departments directly for studies undertaken. This means treating the AM department as internal consultants. It also means preparing an operating budget for the department, to decide fee rates. Such a budget must include allowances for utilization, 'selling', etc.[2]

The assignment

An assignment starts with what is known as a 'Survey Report'. This is a proposal for a study prepared by the department and submitted to management. To write a survey report, it is necessary to collect data about the problem area and analyse it to identify the main issues involved. It is then necessary to decide how to tackle the study, plan the study and calculate the resources and inputs that will be needed. The survey report itself will cover:

- a brief description of the current situation;
- details of the proposed study together with time plan;
- a comparison of the benefits and costs of the study.

Some organizations also like to have formal Terms of Reference which are agreed by management and distributed before the study proceeds.

The structure of the study itself will naturally depend to some extent on the nature of the particular assignment. Some detailed examples are given elsewhere in the book (e.g. chapter 18). In general terms, the study is likely to follow a pattern:

1 The person who wrote the Survey Report briefs the analyst(s) who will carry out the study. The overall approach, objectives and the programme of work/timetable are agreed.
2 The analyst(s) absorb the survey report and any relevant background information that the department possesses. Any relevant documentation (e.g. manuals) is obtained from the client department and absorbed.
3 The analyst opens a study file and starts a Study Diary. The latter is just a daily record of the main events of the study (usually just one sentence a day). The former is just a folder divided into five: statics (names, phone numbers), working papers, special notes, reports/correspondence and start-up material (survey report plus background and the terms of reference).
4 The trade union is contacted and the study is discussed (this is usually fairly brief since management will already have discussed it with them).
5 Introductions are carried out.
6 If the study is to be performed some way away from the AM department's office, arrangements for accommodation and facilities are made.
7 Analyst(s) collect any further background information (e.g. current organization structure, staff numbers, services provided, outline procedures, office layout, main items of equipment).
8 A short-term study plan is detailed and agreed with senior AM staff.
9 If appropriate, appreciation talks are prepared and delivered to staff.
10 Detailed fact finding is carried out in the client department (or in the first department if several are involved). This will usually involve a detailed look at the systems and procedures used, the paperwork involved, equipment and machinery used, interaction with other people, deadlines, timetables.
11 Any problems such as bottlenecks, oppressive deadlines, sharp work peaks are discussed – anything that the staff consider to be problems.
12 Full details of volumes, frequencies, cycles and trends are obtained. These are nearly always very important, even vital, in a study.
13 If the study may result in any staff reductions, a stop is put temporarily on new staff engagement.
14 The collected facts are examined critically and systematically; the new systems and procedures are developed (along the lines of the mnemonic 'ICICLES' as detailed mainly in Part D).
15 The proposals are discussed thoroughly with a senior AM member or the head of the department. Further discussions are held with the management of the client department, the staff and the trade union representatives.
16 The delivery of any new forms, equipment and software is arranged. Timely and correct delivery must be ensured.

17 If appropriate, the new office layout should be installed.

18 Staff and supervision should be trained thoroughly in the improved systems and procedures. Improvements should be installed.

19 Work quantification (see Part E) is started. Work values are established, and agreed with the AM manager, client manager, staff and trade union representative.

20 Any new forms needed for work quantification/management controls are prepared, ordered and obtained.

21 Details of new control procedures based on the results of the work quantification studies are finalized, and explained fully to supervisors and managers. New controls are installed.

22 Staff are trained to use the new work values. Work values are installed as standard practice. Staff are helped to achieve correct level of performance. The transfer of any excess staff is arranged.

23 A review of staff job grading, where appropriate, is arranged.

24 New organization structures within the department are developed, as appropriate. They must be discussed with staff and management. New groupings are installed, and staff assisted to achieve new groupings.

25 The original Terms of Reference are rechecked, as are problems raised by staff in item (11). It must be ensured that all Terms of Reference have been fulfilled and action taken on staff problems.

26 The assignment is finalized. This is likely to involve completion of certain documentation, such as:

- Standard Procedure Instructions ('SPIs'), utilizing algorithms where appropriate. (The terminology of the documentation – such as SPI – will vary from organization to organization, but should be self-explanatory);
- an Operating Manual for the work values and controls;
- a Savings Report for the entire assignment, presented to management;
- new organization structure and supervisory job descriptions, as appropriate.

A de-briefing session will then be held within the AM department.

■ FACING SUB-PERFECTION

Occasionally, just occasionally, an assignment falls short of one's standard of excellence. The way we handle this situation is important – mainly for ourselves, which may be why this is such a taboo subject. A 'bad' assignment can result in considerable pressure. One feels that one has lost face greatly in the eyes of staff and management. One's colleagues may be unsympathetic; they may even feel let down. One dreads the next Annual Assessment when the whole sorry story will be dissected again. Perhaps the most pressure comes from the next assignment: one knows that two 'bad' assignments in a row can be an irrecoverable disaster. The worst thing that can happen is that one starts expecting failure instead of expecting success.

Every individual has to learn how to handle failure in life. A few people seem to be able to shrug it off as unimportant (though we suspect that this is either a facade or a form of self-deception). The rest of us feel affected and have to do something about it. What this action is depends on the individual, and we certainly do not propose that there is any magic formula. However, an approach that may be useful is to convince oneself that a failure is not a failure but just a temporary set-back that one can plan to retrieve. In chess, one may lose a queen but still win the game. And if one loses this game, one can still win the next three. Goethe used chess as a metaphor when he said:

> *Daring ideas are like chessmen moving forward;*
> *they may be beaten, but they may start a winning game.*

An example of what we mean is provided by Schumann's Symphony 'No. 4'. Schumann wrote a symphony – his Symphony No. 2 in D minor. To say that this was not received well would be an understatement. It was withdrawn and disappeared from view for ten years. Schumann reworked it. It was then reissued as Symphony No. 4. Result – applause. In the same way, if an assignment does not go well one can be determined that one will return at some time and retrieve it. 'Don't get despondent, get back.'

A few people have to face in their lives a disaster so major that it could affect the whole of their professional careers. Even then one has to fight back, even if one has to seek success in a second career. One person who had to face this was Sir Brian Urquhart. He was chief intelligence officer of the British Airborne Corps in 1944 prior to the disastrous paratroop action at Arnhem – the story of which was told in the book *A Bridge Too Far* by Cornelius Ryan. From his intelligence gathering, Urquhart became increasingly concerned about the forthcoming action. He repeated his fears so much that eventually he was sent home on 'sick leave' in disgrace, being told that if he did not then he would be court-martialled for refusing orders. His fears were realized when 17,000 casualties were suffered, all for nothing.

Looking back at the events, Sir Brian says that one young officer could not hope to change a plan approved by the President of the United States, the Prime Minister of Britain and all the military top brass. Against that, rational arguments could not prevail. 'Once a group of powerful people have made up their minds on something, it develops a life and momentum of its own that is almost impervious to reason or argument.'[3] The Arnhem tragedy had a deep effect on Urquhart's life. Before, he had been optimistic, trusting and self-confident. After, he was doubtful, mistrustful and 'deeply skeptical about the behavior of leaders'. Nevertheless, after leaving the army he did succeed in life, becoming an exemplary and widely respected Under-Secretary-General of the United Nations.

References

1 Bentley, T. J. (ed.), *The Management Services Handbook*, London: Holt, Rinehart & Winston, 1984.
2 ILO, *Management Consulting*, Geneva: International Labour Office, 1977.
3 Urquhart, Sir B., 'The last disaster of the war', *The New York Review of Books*, Vol. 34, No. 14, 24 September, 1987, p. 27.

Further reading

Ruston, A. and Ram, R., *Effective Assignment Skills and Strategies*, London: HMSO, 1987.

10

Creativity

Think before you speak is criticism's motto; speak before you think creation's.   E. M. Forster, *Two Cheers for Democracy* (1951)

Man is, above all, he who creates.
                              Saint-Exupéry, *The Wisdom of the Sands* (1948)

Logical and creative thought

Many of us have a dichotomous attitude towards creativity. We expect those responsible for corporate planning and marketing strategies to be creative. At the same time we want such planning to obey a logical, non-creative, format. Perhaps this is a product of our upbringing.

Children are very creative. One has only to watch them at play or talking unselfconsciously in television shows. However, society soon teaches children that they must think logically. Too much imagination can lead to chastisement. Education, by and large, continues this process. By the time most of us reach the age of twenty-five, we know that logic is an admirable trait.

So it is. But in reaching this stage, too many of us lose the ability to be truly creative. This is unfortunate since so much depends upon creativity. When Einstein was asked how he thought of his General Theory of Relativity, he replied that it was like writing poetry. Unravelling the mystery of the DNA double helix depended on imagination. So does thinking of the best way to use an intricate piece of microcomputer software.

Table 10.1 shows the differences between logical and creative thought. Two questions (from one of Martin Gardner's books)[1] help to demonstrate the difference.

Table 10.1   Logical versus creative thought

	Logical thought	Creative thought
Other names	Convergent or vertical thinking	Divergent or lateral thinking
Basis	Deduction	Imagination
How many answers?	Usually one – sometimes a few	Can be many
Can result be shown to be correct?	Yes, it can be 'proved' to be correct	No, not in the sense of being 'right'
Would other people get the same result?	Yes – if they work the 'correct' way	Probably not. New answers may be achieved

The first is a straightforward question in logical deduction:

> Boris gave a hotel clerk 30 roubles for his room for the night. Later, the clerk realized that the charge should have been 10 roubles less. He sent Ivan to Boris's room with the 10 roubles. Ivan, being dishonest, gave only 6 to Boris, keeping the other 4 for himself. Now, Boris has paid 24 roubles for his room and Ivan has got 4. That accounts for 28 roubles. What has happened to the other 2?

The second question needs imagination:

> Can you think of three ways in which a barometer can be used to discover the height of a very tall building?

(Answers to questions are at the end of the chapter.)

Being creative

Some people do retain their ability to be creative. As Anna Freud once said, 'Creative minds have always been known to survive any kind of bad training'.[2] Others can improve their creativity through the process of:

- understanding the stages they go through when thinking and the barriers to creative thought;
- learning at least one of the techniques which help creative thinking (e.g. brainstorming);
- practising the technique.

Being able to think creatively is of considerable value in many situations:

- designing new organization structures;
- modifying and adapting any techniques in all areas of management;
- improving methods, systems and procedures;
- making the best use of work quantification;
- problem solving in administration, production, personnel, business strategy, etc.;
- in marketing (segmentation, new product development, sales approaches, advertising, etc.).

In fact many people claim that the ability to think creatively is one of the components of being a good leader and manager. It is also of major assistance to other specialists such as computer programmers. In commercial life, most commonly met problems need the use of both types of thinking: logical and creative. One analyses the known facts, and then casts around for other possibilities or other approaches. These possibilities are considered, selecting the most promising. Then one reflects further, eventually selecting an idea that seems particularly promising. This is inspected to see whether it is robust.

Barriers to creative thinking

There are a number of barriers to thinking creatively though not all the barriers are present all the time. But we need to realize what barriers we may encounter. In this way we can recognize them, face them, and then escape from them.

■ TiME

The first barrier is that we may be under time pressure or under stress. In these conditions most of us find it difficult to come up with creative ideas. This is the problem often expressed as, 'It's very difficult to think of ways to drain the swamp when you're up to your neck in alligators.' Of course, stress can sometimes be a spur. The advertising executive who is told to think up a new campaign by morning or lose his job will normally be able to produce one. Rembrandt could produce a masterpiece even when under considerable commercial pressure – but we are not all in his class. The basic barrier remains. Most of us cannot be at our most creative when under stress or pressure of time.

■ A DOMINANT IDEA

Sometimes a tune comes into one's head which is difficult to get rid of. In the same way, we can get an idea into our head which we cannot dislodge. It dominates our thinking, preventing us from having any other ideas. A useful habit in this situation is to write the idea down fully on a piece of paper, with as much detail as one can muster. It is usually then much easier to go on to other ideas with the barrier removed.

■ PREVIOUS EXPERIENCE

Our experience can be a boon if our aim is to carry out a task quickly. It can be a curse if we are trying to think of a way of doing it differently (even though a new way might be even quicker). Slicing cucumbers for sandwiches for a party is not difficult. Thinking of a better method may be. But the method used by a chef in a busy restaurant is not only different – it is also definitely faster, and the result looks better. Another, perhaps more convincing, example is as follows:

> Shown below is a pattern of seven dots. Join all seven with 3 straight lines without taking the pen off the paper.

Similar to that one is the following:

> Shown below is a pattern of nine dots. Join all nine with 4 straight lines without taking the pen off the paper.

The strange fact is that most people have difficulty in doing this without quite a lot of thought. The reason for saying that this is strange? Most people, again, when presented with this puzzle will admit to having seen it before. But the experience of doing the first half of the puzzle makes it much harder to do the second half.

69

■ ESTABLISHING A PATTERN

Seeking a pattern is often an indispensable aid in logical thinking. But it can become a barrier when trying to think creatively. Once a pattern is seen, it can inhibit another pattern from being accepted. Many IQ tests include questions that can only be solved by finding the right pattern.

A demonstration of this effect is as follows. Below are printed the first five letters of the alphabet in a pattern:

$$\underline{\text{A} \qquad\qquad \text{E}}$$
$$\text{B} \quad \text{C} \quad \text{D}$$

The question is –where does the next letter of the alphabet go? Above or below the line? What is your reason for choosing that answer? What would you say to somebody who chose the opposite answer?

When this question is put to a group of people, some will say that the F should go above the line while others will vote for below the line. The reason is that both are possible. If you see that vowels go above and consonants below, then F goes below. If you see that letters with a curve go below and those composed of straight lines go above, then F goes above. But in fact there are other patterns. Some people see 1 above, 3 below, 1 above, 3 below. Others see 1 above, 3 below, 5 above, 7 below. And so on.

■ CONFORMITY

Behaviour expected of one by colleagues, friends or the culture (either stated or imagined) can hinder one's mind from exploring unusual paths. Giving the expected response can be a sort of knee-jerk reaction in some groups. The best weapon against this barrier is to face it, on a personal level. Group pressure may still be too strong. In this case, the group has to be persuaded to set aside a session or period. During this time, the group has to suspend its norms. It is helpful to represent this time period as a novelty, at first. Later, the time period can be extended, either subtly or openly. Eventually, in this way, the barrier will be lifted sufficiently to enable creativity to bloom.

A similar barrier is the fear of appearing foolish. Few of us relish being thought a fool. This can create diffidence in putting forward unusual ideas. The way to escape from this barrier is the same as from conformity.

■ LACK OF EFFORT

It can take effort to challenge the obvious. It can be easier to say 'no' than to think about fresh ideas. Some plodding reactionaries among us may even take refuge in the Automatic No. This is not a modern phenomenon. In the Dark Ages, Saint Benedict instructed 'managers' in monasteries to listen to the ideas of even the most junior staff.[3]

■ STAYING TOO NARROW

It is possible to take a very narrow view of a problem: to keep on hammering away at one small point, head on. This can become semi-obsessional. The way to escape from this barrier is to enlarge the problem area, to shift attention to other avenues, to come at the problem from another viewpoint. Houdini, the escapologist-conjuror, would for publicity challenge the police to lock him up in a cell. His approach was not to say, 'How on earth do I escape from this cell?' He asked himself other questions. Could he somehow get a copy of the cell key? Was there a way out through the window or the walls? Could he pick the lock with a piece of wire? Was the ceiling secure? Could he disguise himself and change places with a visitor? Could he pick the warder's pocket? Could he trick the prison authorities in some way?

Houdini's success rate proves how skilful and creative he was. The major stage effects of all conjurors, like Houdini, rely on the same premise: set a seemingly impossible problem before the audience; solve it creatively.

■ EVALUATING TOO QUICKLY

This is the well-known attitude of saying quickly that an idea will not work. It is impractical. It has already been tried and failed. It is ridiculous. Other examples are given in chapter 46. In 1939, it was suggested to the US navy that their fleet might be vulnerable to aeroplane attacks. To this idea US Rear Admiral Woodward responded, 'As far as sinking a ship with a bomb is concerned, you just can't do it.' The attack at Pearl Harbor a short time later showed that he had evaluated too quickly.

These, then, are barriers to creativity. If they are recognized, faced and dealt with then they can be removed, surmounted or gone round. Escape from them is the result.

Stages of creative thought

When considering the stages of creative thought, it is easy to become rather obtuse, even philosophical. For our purposes, however, a simplistic model will suffice. It is based on the mnemonic 'AWARE':

A – ANTICIPATION. Get as many facts as possible that are likely to be useful. At this stage, be logical rather than creative. State the problem carefully. Then restate the basic problem in other ways.

W – WORK. Think of possible solutions to the problem. At this stage, frustration is common – including the well-known 'it's on the tip of my tongue'. Some experts in this field maintain that a measure of frustration is beneficial. It can be followed, after a while, by high-quality ideas.

A – ALLOW TO FERMENT. When we have a problem, we often say that we will sleep on it. And it works. Our subconscious mind seems to come into its own. A fallow period gives time to see, remember or even hear about an item that can be incorporated. For example, we may be trying to think of an idea for a fancy costume for a child to wear to a party. Then we see a drama on TV and remember an old curtain that would make a grand cloak.

R – RECOGNITION. This is the sudden flash of realization that an answer is to hand. It is what psychologists call 'Aha'. It is what caused Archimedes to jump out of his bath and go running through the streets shouting 'Eureka'. His enthusiasm is understandable. It is a very satisfying moment.

E – EXAMINATION. This is inspecting the various ideas that have been produced. Which ones may lead to solutions? Is a favoured idea really the best? What are the possible snags? Are they feasible? At this stage logical thinking has to take over again.

Rules for creative thinking

Creative thinking (such as brainstorming) can be performed formally or informally. It can be performed by a group of colleagues, or by a group on a course. However it is being performed, there are four rules that are in widespread use. Practitioners use them faithfully:

> **NO EVALUATION**
>
> **DRIFT AROUND**
>
> **ENORMITY**
>
> **KIDNAP**

NO EVALUATION – during a brainstorming session, this rule reigns supreme. Nobody may say anything against another person's ideas. No comments, no criticisms, no evaluation. 'Never say never'.

DRIFT AROUND – ideas should cover a wide spectrum. Free association is encouraged. So are sudden jumps. So are outlandish ideas.

ENORMITY – as many ideas as possible are required. When introduced to brainstorming a group may think that, say, 25 new ideas would be quite good. In fact, 100 may not be enough.

KIDNAP – in most countries, it is thought to be rather impolite to plagiarize, to steal another person's ideas. In creative thinking, it is positively encouraged. People 'kidnap' one another's ideas. They build on them, use them, improve them, improvise on them, combine them and use them as a starting point for a whole new set of ideas.

Brainstorming

Brainstorming was originated in the 1930s by Alex Osborn, but the best-known name for those who use brainstorming is that of Geoffrey Rawlinson. His ideas are pervasive and he has probably performed more brainstorming sessions throughout the world than anybody else. Brainstorming is a way of getting many ideas from a group of people in a relatively short time.

■ BEFORE THE SESSION

A brainstorming session will normally be set up in response to the existence of a problem that seems suitable for the technique. The person who is going to be chairman will do some preparatory work. He will discuss it briefly so that everyone knows what the real problem is.

A group of people will be invited to the session. With fewer than six people it is difficult to maintain momentum. More than about fifteen may lead to some group members being passengers. The majority should have previous experience of the technique. Staff of widely varying seniority should never be mixed.

Supplies of large pieces of paper should be obtained, plus some drafting tape to stick them on the wall. Flip-chart paper is ideal. Also required are some felt-tipped pens to write on the paper in large enough letters for the group to be able to read.

If it is a training session, then some subjects for brainstorming are needed (examples are given below).

■ DURING THE SESSION

If it is a training session, then an explanation of the technique is given. This is normally based on the material in this chapter. Sometime during this introduction, trainees are told:

> 'Please take a piece of paper. Now carefully write down as many good uses of this paperclip as you can think of, and be prepared to read out your list to your colleagues.'

The wording is important: as can be seen, it includes several of the barriers. The object does not have to be a paperclip; other suitable objects can be a leather belt, a shoelace, a plastic bag or a metal ashtray. To people who are used to these sessions, the result of the above request is perennially surprising. Respondents will indicate that they have thought of five or six uses. Only two is not uncommon. Eight or more is rare. Afterwards, the introduction is continued. Strong emphasis is placed on the four rules for creative thinking.

A Brainstorming session proper starts with a statement of the problem. This is discussed briefly and restated in different words. One of these restatements is then turned round so that it is in the form of, 'In how many ways . . . ?'

There then follows what is known as the 'warm-up' session. This is analogous to the limbering-up of an athlete before a race. A subject is chosen – this is usually an item from the list given above for the training session. Alternatively it can be something similar such as a stale loaf of bread, a half-brick, an identity bracelet, a palm leaf – any of these can be utilized with a 'how many uses . . .' motif. Experienced practitioners tend to find such motifs insufficiently moving. For them, it is better to choose 'in how many ways could . . .' – the XYZ party improve its chances at the next election; one travel to Paris free; improve a disco, etc. The subject matter can be trivial; the aim is to get everybody into the right frame of mind.

Experts differ on the role of the chairman. Some think that his role should be rather passive, just writing the ideas on the large sheets of paper. Others think that he should be more like a TV competition show host, encouraging ideas and having them written up by an assistant. Since both methods seem to work in the hands of an experienced chairman, perhaps it depends on personality rather than approach.

After the warm-up session, the real session starts. The 'In how many ways . . .' statement is displayed. So are 'The Rules'. The chairman calls for ideas. These are written on one of the large sheets of paper, numbering them. They have to be written quickly, as the ideas come thick and fast. The chairman asks for more. He suggests some himself if the flood slackens. Some chairmen have their own devices. One will ask for 20 seconds' silence, before releasing a fresh rush of ideas; another will take an idea and ask for free associations. The result is that after about 20–35 minutes some 100–250 ideas will have been produced.

■ AFTER THE SESSION

After the brainstorming session it is time to move on to the evaluation stage. All ideas are scrutinized for winners. They are inspected to see if they have indeed answered the problem, or, more importantly, to see whether they can be turned or adapted.

Again, different chairmen have their own approaches. Some will select the most promising 30 per cent, analyse this group and from them select a third and so on. Others will try to get specific solutions thought through in detail. Others will carry out the evaluation separately from the brainstorming session.

Rawlinson himself suggests waiting for two days. During this time, all the ideas are typed and distributed to the participants. Each participant selects, say, 10 per cent for further study. The chairman then looks at the ones mentioned most often and refines them. He tests them against pre-set criteria to measure their suitability. He can then make them into specific proposals.

Brainstorming example

A law centre is a quasi-charitable organization that dispenses legal advice to those of very low income, free of charge. Its income arises from contributions from a number of sources including local authorities, concerned individuals, trade unions, trusts, charitable funds, etc. Law centres are always chronically short of money.

Problem   – Law centres do not have enough money.

Restatement – How to reduce costs?
             – How to increase contributions?
             – How to find new sources of funds?
             – How to reduce services?
             – How to raise funds?
             – How to get other bodies to take over the work?

Selected   – In how many ways can a law centre raise funds?

■ ANSWERS TO THE QUESTIONS

Boris and the hotel bill

Boris's 24 roubles have nothing to do with Ivan's 4. Boris has paid out 24 roubles. Of this Ivan has 4 and the hotel has 20. Boris got back 6 roubles which, added to the 24, accounts for the full 30 roubles that he paid in the first place.

Using a barometer

1 Tie a piece of string to the barometer, lower it from the top of the building to the street, pull it up, and measure the string.
2 Tie a piece of string to the barometer, lower it from the top of the building to the street, swing the barometer like a pendulum, calculate the length of the string from the formula using the time taken to swing.
3 Use the barometer to measure the barometric pressure at the top and bottom of the building. Use the formula of the relationship between height and pressure.
4 Drop the barometer from the roof and time how long it takes to hit the street. Use the formula for falling bodies.
5 Measure the length of the barometer. Put it against the wall of the building, mark its height on the wall. Move the barometer up the wall so that the bottom is against the mark and mark the top of the barometer. Repeat until the top of the building is reached. Multiply the number of marks by the length of the barometer.

6 Stand the barometer upright on the ground. Calculate the ratio of its shadow to its height. Apply this ratio to the length of the shadow cast by the building.

7 Offer the barometer to the building's maintenance man if he will tell you the height of the building.

Seven dots: **Nine dots:**

Uses of a paperclip

(These were the first twenty-five produced at a brainstorming session held in a government department).

Pipe cleaner	Typewriter cleaner	Tension reducer	Cuff-link
Tie clip	Nail cleaner	(fiddle with)	Knife for cutting Sellotape
Picture hook	Getting wax out of ear	Letter opener	Catapult missile
Screwdriver	Poking holes in paper	Ornament	Mobile
Zip fastener tag	Toy tow bar	Poker chips	Joining paper together
Picking locks	Broken bra strap	Daisy chain necklace	
Fuse wire	Fishing hook	Tooth-pick	

References

1 Gardner, Martin, *Mathematical Magic Show*, New York: Alfred A. Knopf (1977).

2 Freud, Anna, 1968, Annual Freud Lecture to the New York Psychoanalysts' Society.

3 The Rule of St Benedict (*c.* 530–540).

Further reading

de Bono, E., *Lateral Thinking for Management*, Maidenhead: McGraw-Hill UK, 1971.

Koestler, A., *The Act of Creation*, London: Hutchinson, 1964.

Osborn, A. F., *Applied Imagination*, New York: Charles Scribner's Sons, 1957.

Rawlinson, J. G., *Creative Thinking and Brainstorming*. Aldershot: Gower Press, 1981.

Technology Enlacement

11

Office Technology

No object is mysterious. The mystery is in your eye.
Elizabeth Bowen, *The House in Paris* (1935)

Technology made large populations possible; large populations now make technology indispensable.
J. W. Krutch, *Human Nature and the Human Condition* (1959)

For many of us, understanding advanced office technology is rather like knowing a big city that we live in. We are completely familiar with those areas that we see a lot. Those areas that we have read about repeatedly are not unfamiliar. But there are some areas that are completely unknown to us: if we found ourselves in such territories we would not know how to proceed. Quite often we are not sure how to get from one familiar area to another. Worst of all, there always seems to be some clever devil in the office who professes complete familiarity with those areas that we have never explored.

This part of the book gives a brief tourist's guide to technology. As such it will inevitably include information about areas that are familiar to some people (but, by the same token, will be fresh to others). It is not all-inclusive; for example it does not show how to write a computer program. Some examples concentrate on small office computers, to speed the discussion.

Pitfalls

Looking through a collection of magazines and books published over the last thirty years reveals a depressing catalogue of repetitive themes that should warn us of some of the pitfalls of technology:

Hype. Hype is usually defined as exaggerated claims and publicity. If anybody does not believe in miracles, then they should read some of the advertisements for computer equipment and programs. One program was so bad that it hurt one's eyes to look at it on the screen; it was advertised as, 'You've never seen graphics this good before.' At a time when most printers used the term 'NLQ' (Near Letter Quality) to denote a quality of output not far from fuzzy carbon paper, one manufacturer claimed its product had PLQ (Perfect Letter Quality): '... remarkable ... sets new standards in printer performance ... a whole new dimension of quality'. When *Byte* magazine tested the machine, it was awarded 3 out of 5 for print quality. There is also a tendency to call dustmen, Milieu Quality Control Managers – thus 'Environmental Preservation' accessories turned out to be desk fans and fan heaters. A conference 'To celebrate the

150th anniversary of Electronic Mail' was based on the anniversary of the patent for telegraphy. And, just as every cottage is charming to an estate agent, so all programs are 'user-friendly' to software houses. (If they are so user-friendly, why are there so many books explaining how to use them?) So if you see a program advertised as user-friendly, do not believe it; but if you see a magazine reviewer call a program user-hostile – believe it. Jim Manzi (President, Lotus Development) rightly said that the personal computer industry has a history of 'overpromising and underdelivering'.[1]

Compatibility. This is the bane of every analyst's life. Newcomers to office technology cannot understand why one cannot just link up a few pieces of equipment and start to use them. It is not only newcomers who are baffled. Technical magazines are full of queries from people who are presumably reasonably knowledgeable about computers. These are along the lines of, 'I have just replaced my old printer with an ABC printer. Why will this not work with my XYZ computer?' Or, 'The salesman assured me that the software would work with my XYZ computer. Since it will not, what are my rights?' One of the troubles is that you do not know until you unpack the equipment or program (and get to about page 20 of the manual) that you find you have made a mistake. There is still no legal obligation, for example, for a boxed program to state on the outside of the box what equipment it needs to run on – and you are not allowed to read the manual to find out until you have bought it. The rule is, ask a friend or colleague first. The second rule is to buy from a reputable outlet. This is not because they can necessarily give you proper advice, but they may at least give you a credit note if they misinformed you. Though, strangely enough, they may be breaking a contractual agreement by so doing (the law is about thirty-five years out of date in the field of office technology). When in doubt, remember the old computer joke:

B

> Q. What's the difference between a used-car salesman and a computer-program salesman?
> A. The used-car salesman knows it won't work.

Not to mention the old jibe about there being 'liars, damned liars and computer salesmen'. When buying a computer for personal use, one is likely to be buying a keyboard, some cables, a processor, a monitor, a printer, a program and some storage disks. The important thing to remember is that every single one of these items may not work with the others. So – check first with a friend or colleague who has the same combination as the one that you intend to buy.

Predictions. It is truly remarkable how bad people are at predicting future trends in office technology. One might expect such failure from, say, journalists on tabloid newspapers. But our bookshelves contain a number of examples from prestigious organizations of carefully researched reports that turned out to be utterly mistaken. The other side of this coin is that new equipment sometimes comes on to the market which looks very promising but which fails to succeed – not always for reasons that are obvious. For example, the Palo Alto Research Center (or 'PARC') have over the years had ideas that looked very promising but which did not have the impact that one would have expected. Another example is the IBM 3750 automatic telephone exchange, which was introduced in the 1970s (the 8750 model was not introduced until the 1980s). Perhaps the 3750 was ahead of its time; anyway it did not prove as successful as some of us expected. The moral for organizations is that they should go ahead and install what

77

they can justifiably feel is right, without taking too much notice of any predictions that are published.

Human problems. The problems in human terms of introducing office technology have been widely (one might say, vastly) written about by social scientists. A number of problems have been anticipated and commented upon. All that can be said in response is that the problems encountered in practice are almost always of a different nature. We return to this theme in chapter 15.

The best way to avoid most of these pitfalls is firstly, to learn something about office technology, and secondly to plan the introduction carefully.

The 'office technology revolution'

A cliché that still appears in the tabloid press talks of the 'accelerating rate of change' of office technology. Mathematically this would be surprising (the acceleration has been going on for so long that the speed of change should be approaching infinity by now). Historically it would also be surprising. The history of innovation follows a well-known pattern. A major innovation is followed by a lengthy period of consolidation – and we are now firmly in a typical period of consolidation and improvement. What the next innovation will be is anybody's guess. To get from the present computer speed of nanoseconds to attoseconds may have to wait until we can use the effect of a subatomic particle hitting a nucleus – and that appears unlikely until well into the twenty-first century. In this connection, the release of a new version of a piece of software does not count as a major innovation in the history of mankind.

The other cliché is how office technology has changed the world (tell that to a starving African). Consider this. 'We are living in exciting times. The new Industrial Revolution ... is having an impact on everyday life at least as great as that of its predecessor. Every one of us is benefiting from its results.' This rather Victorian-sounding message appeared in a respectable journal as recently as 1987. The falsity of likening the results achieved so far by office technology to that made by the Industrial Revolution has already been demonstrated.[2] Indeed, the 1980s were characterized by an actual drop in the productivity of information workers[3] which wiped out the improvement in productivity of the manufacturing sector. Not that this is surprising. American manufacturing productivity stayed fairly level from about 1900 to 1920 as manufacturers reorganized to exploit the production line. So it is distinctly possible that office productivity may start to improve once offices reorganize themselves in a sufficiently radical way.

There is, however, a long way to go. Study after study shows that organizations are not yet exploiting office technology fully. A study sponsored by Britain's Department of Trade and Industry and the Institute of Administrative Management was carried out by A. T. Kearney.[4] This suggested that new users were frequently choosing the wrong systems or buying unnecessary capability, and that some smaller companies were wasting up to 50 per cent of their money. A poll carried out by MORI for *The Economist* and Electronic Data Systems[5] elicited the comment from one investment banker that 'If the board really knew what went on they wouldn't sleep at night. They don't understand the very thin line between technical success and failure.' A study by the *Financial Times* in conjunction with Price Waterhouse[6] did, however, show that during the 1980s firms were progressively trying to put a figure on cost savings – in five years up from 40 per cent to 88 per cent of the companies asked. About the same time, a survey of 150 executives in the world's top banks[7] found that few of those interviewed 'could see any benefit from their huge spending on technology'. And a report by the British Institute of Management and Coopers & Lybrand[8] found that although 93 per cent of respondents had direct involvement with technology, training was so poor that managers 'discovered the capabilities of their system by trial and error'. The lesson is clear: new technology can bestow marvellous benefits but these benefits do not come automatically. Technology must be planned for, lined up with the organization's long-term plans, and costed. And the users must, *must*, be trained.

One final cliché that should be referred to is the assertion that we are now in the information age, that there are more 'information workers' now than other types such as manufacturing workers. In this connection, a graph is often shown along the lines of the one in Figure 11.1. It is not easy to estimate how many seminars one has attended at which this graph (or one very similar) is trotted out. It shows the percentage of the American work-force by types of occupation. As one writer typically put it, 'It was in 1957 that the United States passed from the industrial era to the information era.' The original of this graph appeared in a book by M. U. Porat[9] – though unfortunately Mr Porat is rarely given the credit by people who use his graph. The book was published in 1977, which means that most of the graphs one sees have been extrapolated by hand. Some people who have copied the original concept have been less rigorous in their treatment of the figures, which are admittedly very difficult to calculate. This can lead to some nonsenses unless one is very careful about the definition of an 'information worker'. Some analyses take a global approach so information workers will include priests, local authority pavement layers, lavatory attendants in government offices, and

B

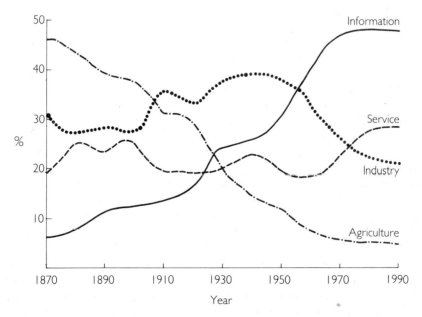

Figure 11.1 Percentage split of the American work-force

printers and publishers of pornography. Since priests are information workers, the Vatican City could claim to have led the world with Tibet a leading contender. So the concept of the 'Information Society' needs inspection as it can be somewhat meaningless.

A brief history

Although there was a degree of mechanization in offices in the second half of the nineteenth century, it was not until the middle of the twentieth century that the true basis of advanced technology appeared – the electronic computer.

The inventor was a professor at Iowa State University, Dr John V. Atanasoff. He started work on it in 1937 but first had to solve a number of theoretical considerations. These included modifying the standard algorithm for solving simultaneous equations so that only additions and subtractions were needed, adopting binary arithmetic, and inventing a storage system based on refreshing capacitors. Although a plaque at Iowa gives a date of 1939, we would prefer to take the completion date as 1942 (to include modifications). This was the ABC computer (an acronym for Atanasoff–Berry Computer).[10]

Atanasoff discussed the ABC computer with Dr John Mauchly, who, with Presper Eckert, developed a computer to compute artillery trajectory tables. This was the ENIAC (Electronic Numerical Integrator And Computer). Completed in 1946, it had taken only two and a half years to make. While the ABC proved that electronic computers could solve intricate mathematical equations accurately (to ten places of decimals), the ENIAC showed that they were fast (5,000 additions per minute). The ENIAC, however, used decimals instead of binary and was partly analogue.

The ENIAC was not completed by the time that World War II was over but provided Western armies with the basis for a computer which was known to its operators as the 'Predictor'. If a shell or missile is fired at a high-flying aircraft it will take some 30 seconds to gain the right altitude – by which time the aircraft is several kilometres away. The Predictor calculated where to fire so that the shell would meet the aircraft. The Predictor could thus work in three dimensions. It could also take into account a number of variables such as the age of the firing equipment, atmospheric pressures and wind speeds on the ground and where the aircraft was flying. By 1951 (when the writer started working on the Predictor) it had automated the entire process and had a plotter to show what was going on.

The ENIAC had a major disadvantage in that it used 18,000 electronic tubes/valves; even the Predictor had 10,000. It needed the invention of the transistor to solve this matter. Meanwhile, two computers both called 'Mark I' were being developed. One Mark I was developed by a Harvard professor, Howard Aiken. Sponsored by IBM and completed in 1944, in reality it was a number of electronic calculators joined up in series. The other Mark I was developed at Manchester University by Tom Kilburn and Fred Williams and first went into action in 1948. The big advance of this machine was its capacity to store programs. Kilburn had worked on the problem of computer storage[11] successfully and, in effect, the computer was built around the storage breakthrough. Later, Kilburn was responsible for developing the giant Atlas computer (prototype in 1960, first commercial machine delivered in 1964 by Ferranti).

Back in America, Mauchly and Eckert developed the UNIVAC I (Universal Automatic Computer) for Remington-Rand. This was installed in 1951 in the Bureau of the Census, who used it for twelve years. Commercial firms were now taking an interest: firms like Burroughs, Honeywell, RCA (Radio Corporation of America) and IBM (International Business Machines). By the end of the decade, they had been joined by firms like CDC (Control Data Corporation), NCR (National Cash Register) and GE (General Electric).

At the time, those of us who were working on computers anticipated that they would change the world (we are still waiting for some of our ideas to be fulfilled). Perhaps this was a reflection of the mad scientist Rotwang in the 1926 film *Metropolis* when he says, 'I have created a machine in the image of man that never tires or makes a mistake. Now we have no further use for living workers.' Anyway, commercial firms were less certain. IBM were not greatly impressed by Aiken's Mark I; they did not see how computers would replace punched card machines, which were selling well and which were less temperamental than even present-day computers. At the time, IBM were also doing quite well from their meat slicers, food scales and time clocks.

IBM introduced their first commercial computer in 1953. This was the IBM 701 and proved the temperamental nature of computers by timing an explosion for its press demonstration. Luckily, IBM were not too discouraged and introduced the IBM 650 in 1954. This was the breakthrough machine. Although IBM initially hoped to sell 50 of them, they actually sold over 1,000. Office computers had arrived.

B

The second generation of computers exploited the characteristics of the transistor. The German, Ferdinand Braun, had tried to use crystals to process signals but the nature of crystals was not fully understood – and so the electron tube/valve was invented. Years later Bell Laboratories needed a small but simple switching mechanism. The research cost hundreds of millions of dollars but in 1947 the transistor was born. At the time, it was dismissed by many Europeans, with some British researchers regarding it as 'a clever publicity stunt by Bell'.[12] The Europeans had changed their assessment by 1956 when William Shockley was awarded a Nobel Physics Prize for his work on the transistor. Shockley set up the Shockley Transistor Corporation. Disagreements led eight of his staff (whom he called the 'eight traitors') to leave. With money from the Fairchild Camera & Instrument Company they set up Fairchild Semiconductor, from which grew Silicon Valley.

The second generation of computers (from, say, 1959 to 1964) depended on the transistor. This meant that only those firms that could exploit semiconductors could impact the market. At the time it became common to refer to this as 'IBM v. The Bunch'. Bunch was an acronym for IBM's main competitors: Burroughs, Univac, NCR, CDC and Honeywell. This period also saw the emergence of several new computer languages to facilitate the writing of computer applications. Some of these are older than may be realized (though there is still a degree of disagreement about a few of these dates):

1955	FORTRAN	1968	Pascal
1959	COBOL	1968	APL
1960	LISP	1970	FORTH
1964	RPG	1970	Prolog
1964	PL/I	1972	C
1965	BASIC	1980	ADA

Then, in 1964 (7 April, to be pedantic), IBM struck again. They heralded the third generation of computers with the IBM 360. The new generation made older machines obsolete, and gave conversion headaches to thousands of firms that owned computers. What transistors were to the older machines, integrated circuits were to third generation equipment. These machines were much faster, which helped the introduction of multi-programming in which the computer can run more than one program simultaneously. These machines also offered, to the relief of many managers, the prospect of upgrading. Upgrading meant that firms could move up to a bigger machine (from the same vendor) without facing too much redesign of their information systems. Third-generation integrated circuits also gave rise to minicomputers. These were smaller machines, ideal for dedicated use in scientific and office work. The best-known name for years was DEC (Digital Equipment Corporation) whose PDP series acquired a considerable reputation among its users.

After the third generation came the fourth generation. Here we come across a semantic difficulty. Some people would date the fourth generation to about 1971 with the introduction of large-scale integration; that is, getting a lot of circuits on to one small area of board. Others reply that this was a very small evolutionary step compared with the introduction of the transistor and the integrated circuit. The truth is that the concept of generations became submerged by claims made by advertisers. A manufacturer in 1989 claimed to be offering a sixth-generation micro. Since it appeared to be a bog-standard machine and less advanced than the competition, this led to one commentator asking whether people were aware that the Japanese were secretly working on an eleventh generation machine.

So far as most office staff were concerned, however, the next big change was the introduction of the microcomputer. The first microprocessor arrived in March 1971. But it was not until 1978 that the office micro really took off. In that year two separate events combined fortuitously. Dan Bricklin and Robert Frankston formed Software Arts and in 1978 launched the first spreadsheet: VisiCalc. In the same year the microcomputer Apple II was launched. The two seemed made for one another and caught people's imagination. Soon, people were waiting to see what IBM would do. The answer was the IBM PC which arrived in 1980. This was technically conservative, perhaps even disappointing. But IBM had not forgotten how to sell: by the end of 1984 over two million had been sold.

There then followed a period of leapfrogging in which improved micros were launched by companies all eager to catch the attention of the public. These machines became faster, with more memory, better graphics and more capabilities. In 1984 came the Apple Macintosh (which was unusual in not having an 'operating system' as such), soon followed by the IBM PC AT. Then in 1987 (with improvements in each of the next few years) came the IBM PS/2.

References

1 Talking at the 1988 Microsoft CD-ROM Conference in Seattle.
2 'Executives emphasize improving productivity of white-collar staff', *Wall Street Journal*, 20 July, 1984.
3 Kennedy, P., *The Rise and Fall of the Great Powers*, New York: Random House, 1987 and *The Economist*, 13 December, 1986, p. 75.
4 *The Barriers and Opportunities from Information Technology – a Management Perspective*, A. T. Kearney, 1984.

5 *The Economist*, 31 October, 1987, p. 86.
6 *Financial Times*, 15 April, 1988; and *The Price Waterhouse IT Review 1988/89*.
7 *The Economist*, 11 June, 1988, p. 75.
8 *Financial Times*, 12 September, 1988; and *Managers and IT Competence*, British Institute of Management, 1988.
9 Porat, M. U., *The Information Economy*, Washington: Office of Telecommunications, US Department of Commerce, 1977.
10 Burks, A. R. and Burks, A. W., *The First Electronic Computer*, Ann Arbor: University of Michigan Press, 1988.
11 Kilburn, T., 'A storage system for use with binary computing machines', doctoral dissertation, Manchester University, 1947.
12 Queisser, H., *The Conquest of the Microchip*, Cambridge, Massachusetts: Harvard University Press, 1988.

B

Hardware

Any sufficiently advanced technology is indistinguishable from magic.
Arthur C. Clarke, *Profiles of the Future* (1962)

To err is human, but to really foul things up requires a computer.
Paul Ehrlich, *The Farmer's Almanac* (1978)

Booting up

The best way to learn about computers is to own one at home, finding out slowly what it can do and how it does it. This, of course, takes time and money. Also, it is not necessary to have a great depth of knowledge to operate office equipment or to participate in automating offices. Few of the millions of people throughout the world that use photocopiers either know or care how they work. Analysts or consultants working in this field do, however, need a measure of knowledge. How much knowledge is a matter of debate. In a sense, the more one knows the better. On the other hand, few of us will ever get to grips with the extreme detail so beloved by the fanatic hobbyists whose whole life seems to revolve around their computer. These fans are known as 'techies'.

Starting up a small office computer is called 'booting up' and means the process whereby the computer is prepared for actually doing some work. The word comes from the idea of 'dragging oneself up by one's bootstraps'. This is an apt phrase because the computer slowly heaves itself up by a series of small steps. When the computer is switched on, the boot ROM sends a small program to the CPU. A memory is a place where humans or computers retain information. A ROM is a Read Only Memory – a memory that one can look at and use but which resists attempts at changing it. So a boot ROM is the ROM used in booting up. A program (also known as software) is a series of small instructions that is the only way of telling a computer what to do. The CPU (the Central Processing Unit) is the heart of the computer and where most of the real work is done.

The boot program gets things under way by telling the disk drive controller to go and look at the disk drive. The disk drive is the mechanism that operates the disk, which holds information – information that stays there until one changes it, just like the cassette in a television video player. The disk contains the operating system (or OS). The OS is a program that manages or runs the computer and its bits and pieces. The OS is transferred to the RAM. The RAM (Random Access Memory) is not a disk; it consists of a number of electrical components which act as a memory. This means that when the computer is turned off, all the information that was in the RAM disappears, which is why one has to go through this transfer business every time one uses the computer. The RAM is much faster than a disk but is also more expensive.

A piece of information can be held anywhere in a RAM and as one works with the computer this information is continually changing. Since the OS is needed continuously until the machine is switched off, part of the RAM is reserved exclusively for its use. The rest of it is used as one wishes. A piece of information that is needed may be anywhere in the RAM so to find it the computer has to know where it is, its location being known as its 'address'. The main connections inside the computer are made by a group of wires known as the 'bus'. The bus transfers two main types of matter: the address lines carry the addresses of pieces of information, while the data lines carry the actual information itself.

Once the OS has been transferred to the RAM, it will continue to work until the computer is switched off. The OS operates the computer. It controls the data coming in and going out, and keeps track of what is where in the memory. So far, we have switched the computer on, put the special disc with the OS on into the disc drive, waited for the boot ROM to transfer the OS into RAM, and then removed the OS disc from the drive and stored it somewhere safely. 'Safely' means putting it somewhere ready for tomorrow when we have to go through the whole boring procedure again, and where one's colleagues or children cannot use it as a drip mat for a cup of coffee.

A way to improve matters is to install a 'hard card'. A hard card is a special type of disk that is mounted on a carrier (known as a 'card'). This is installed in the main box of the computer, so is well out of the way. The OS (as well as all the other software that one uses regularly) is kept on this hard disk, which also provides a lot of extra memory. To start a computer with a hard card which contains the OS, one switches on the computer and then hangs up one's coat. The rest is automatic and in about 30 seconds, the computer screen shows that it is ready for work. This is shown by what is known as the screen prompt. This may look like: C>. For most of us, to lack a hard card is a real deprivation. They are, however, expensive: about \$200 (even more in Britain and Austria, less in Hong Kong and Dubai).

B

The machine is now ready for work. Whatever application we wish to use it for (such as typing a letter or calculating a balance sheet) will need extra program(s). This will entail putting an applications software disc into the disk drive and telling the OS to transfer it to the RAM where the computer can use it. For many applications programs the OS will transfer only some of the contents of the disk to the RAM, to save filling up the RAM. It will then have to refer back to the disk for further material as it is needed. In such cases one will, of course, have to leave the disk in its drive ready for access as needed. If one has a hard card, then most of one's applications programs will be on it all ready. In this case one will not need to keep a disk in the disk drive.

The OS has loaded the program into the RAM. From there it will go into the CPU one step (or 'instruction') at a time for processing. To enable it to do this, a CPU has its own temporary memory ('registers'). These instructions are very small steps. An example might be 'Read the contents at RAM address 1876, add 100, and put the answer in register B until another instruction is received.' These steps may be small but a computer can carry out millions of them in a second. To keep everything in step, the computer has the equivalent of a ticking clock. A quartz wristwatch has a crystal which can oscillate at a much faster rate than the watch shows – the second hand does not move each time the crystal vibrates. Similarly, an atomic clock is based on movements of ammonia molecules (at a rate of 24 thousand million times a second). So two ways to speed up computers are, firstly, to increase the speed of the internal clock and, secondly, to get closer to ensuring that the computer carries out one instruction each time the clock ticks.

When micros were first introduced, they used clocks which ticked at just over 4 million times a second (4 MHz). Over the years this speed increased, soon reaching 20–25 MHz. This is particularly useful for those times when a specific task relies on speed, as for example when a complex high-definition graphics task is being displayed on a screen. But an increase in clock speed makes much less impact on ordinary run-of-the-mill work. A comparison is to take work that would need a year to complete using an 8 MHz machine. This can be expressed as saying that it would be completed on 31 December. The dates by which the same work would be completed using faster machines can be expressed[1] thus:

8 MHz – 31 December

12 MHz – 22 November

16 MHz – 4 November

20 MHz – 26 October

It should also be noted that there are other ways of increasing speed to complete work. Some of these are discussed later.

Some tasks slow down a computer's operation quite appreciably because they are individually time-consuming. One such is working with floating-point decimals. These are decimals that can be anywhere in a series of digits, rather than being in a fixed place (so they tend to be a common feature in calculations). One way to stop this loss in overall speed is to use a 'co-processor'. This is a secondary processor, in addition to the one in the CPU. An optional extra, it is another item that comes mounted on a card and can be installed in the main computer box. If the processor is specially meant for arithmetic, then it is called a math co-processor. In use, the OS shunts some work to the co-processor to get on with while the CPU does something else.

Information is entered into a computer from a disk, from another computer or from an input device. An example of an input device is a typewriter-style keyboard. Information is taken from a computer onto a disk, or another computer or an output device. An example of an output device is a printer. Input/output devices are connected to the computer through input/output ports (i/o ports). A port is a socket for a special plug – rather like the socket where one puts the lead from an aerial into the back of a television set. The OS works with the CPU which will send information to an i/o (input/output) controller on its way to the output device. There may be an i/o bus separate from the CPU bus – this is a simpler bus since there are fewer addresses to contend with and the information is passing more slowly. Information is passed between this i/o bus and the i/o devices.

This passage is either parallel or serial. To send a character (a number or alphabetical letter or symbol), it is necessary to send eight bits of data for each character. This can be done down one wire, a bit at a time until all eight bits have been sent – this is serial. Or it can be done by sending all eight bits at the same time down eight wires – this is parallel. Naturally, parallel is much faster than serial. If one has 16 wires, then 16 bits can be sent at nearly the same time. The information associated with the 8 bits of information is called a 'byte'. A thousand bytes is a kilobyte (Kbyte) while a million bytes is a megabyte (Mbyte). The word 'byte' is used a lot to describe sizes of memory. The RAM of a home computer is likely to be 640 Kbyte, while a hard card is likely to be between 20 and 100 Mbyte. To give a comparison, a one-page document will need 2–4 Kbyte.

The commonest input device is the keyboard. When a key is pressed on a keyboard it signals its position (horizontally and vertically) to a separate processor, the keyboard processor. This processor converts this position to a code which describes which key was pressed. It does this from a table that is kept in a small keyboard ROM. This code can then be sent to the CPU bus. The keyboard will also (like other devices such as a printer) have a small memory called a buffer memory. A buffer is a temporary memory. By holding some information it allows two parts of a computer that work at vastly different speeds to work together, without the faster part forever waiting for the slower one to catch up.

Figure 12.1 draws together much of the above material. Other names for the item called 'screen', which looks like a small television, are video, monitor, display or CRT.

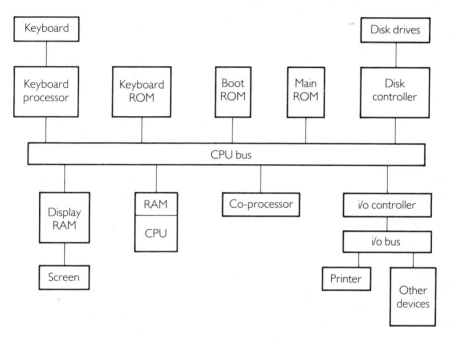

Figure 12.1 Schema of small computer

B

Input devices

The ideal input device would be:

● extremely accurate;
● fast;
● easy to use; and
● inexpensive.

There are no ideal input devices.

The commonest input device seen in offices is the typewriter-style keyboard. Although not expensive, it is excessively slow. Keys can, in theory, be pressed at a rate of 16/sec although in practice the rate is closer to 4/sec – while the computer is more accustomed to working at a rate a million times faster. So while the computer has to keep up a fair speed while operating the screen, to deal with the keyboard it uses a

87

special approach. At intervals, it languidly polls the keyboard to see if a key has been pressed since it last had a look (in this case, languidly means 100 times a second).

The output from the keyboard can be taken direct to the computer but because it is so slow, it is common to have an intermediate storage between the two. Types of such storage are:

- key-to-disk and magnetic tape. This is the system usually used for mainframe computers. Smaller equipment often uses floppy disks.
- key to punched paper tape. This is used for telex, numerically controlled machines and for some items of scientific equipment.
- key-to-paper. Used for point-of-sale machines, this is dying out as such equipment tends to be linked directly to a computer.
- key-to-memory. There are a number of hand-held devices which are in effect a store, from which data can be transferred (or 'downloaded') to a computer later. These devices are useful for any off-site uses such as stock-taking, activity sampling and sales records.

There are situations when a keyboard is connected almost directly with the computer. This is when it is important for the computer to be operating in real time. 'Real time' is the term used for any system in which the result of inputing data is virtually simultaneous with the act of generating the data. A common example is the airline reservation system. Other examples are warehouse inventory control and factory flow processes.

When the need is for direct entry of data to a computer, there are a number of devices available for use in different circumstances:

■ DOCUMENT SCANNERS/READERS

On the bottom of a cheque appear three pieces of information: the number of the cheque, the branch code and the customer's account number. This information is written with magnetic ink. When a cheque is passed through a reader this information is read into the computer. This system is known as MICR (Magnetic Ink Character Recognition). When the shape of the character is recognized rather than the magnetic properties, the system is OCR (Optical Character Recognition). OCR readers suitable for handwriting have yet to achieve sufficient speed, reliability and low cost to be widely used, but they are used to read print, typewritten material and specially formed alphabets.

Bar-mark readers are machines that detect the presence of a mark (not only bars) at a predetermined place on a document. Common uses are football pool coupons and market research questionnaires. They seem such a good idea that it seems surprising that they are not more widely used. One problem is that the documents have to be in good condition, without bad creases and staple holes. 'Scanner' is a term often reserved for a machine that scans a document (especially pictures) and stores the result in such a way that the picture can be reproduced later when required. Facsimile ('fax') machines work in a similar manner.

■ NON-ALPHANUMERIC DEVICES

It is not always necessary to be able to input full alphanumeric data. For such purposes, a number of devices are available, including:

Label scanners. The widely used bar codes seen in supermarkets and libraries can be read either by a wand or by passing the label over a scanning window. Bar codes are usually a set of vertical lines of varying thickness or a set of concentric circles. Since bar codes can be produced by a computer printer they can also be used for stock-taking and even for more esoteric purposes such as recording money from parking meters.

Digitizers. These devices are used for reading drawings (such as maps), converting the information into a digital form and then storing the result.

Cursor surrogates. The conventional cursor that is used on screens to define a position is too slow for some purposes, and several alternatives have been produced. One of these is the light pen. This is a wand that can be placed on a screen to pinpoint a position that one wishes to indicate to the computer. Similar is the touch screen. This is a screen that is sensitive to being touched by one's fingers. This is widely used where frequent telephone-based communications are made (such as in a bank dealing room). The screen is filled with the names or codes of contacts; by touching the contact name, the computer will automatically dial the correct number.

B

The mouse. A mouse is a small device that is pushed about on a table-top, the relative movement being fed to the computer. It can therefore be used to move an arrow around the screen or for building up drawings (though this has been described as being 'like drawing with a house brick'). The mouse can arouse quite strong feelings of warmth or hatred. The haters prefer trackballs or trackwheels.

Trackballs/trackwheels. These are small devices on which is a small ball or wheel that one moves with one's finger-tips. This movement gives directions to the computer. Users claim that they are faster, more responsive, more sophisticated, and much more accurate than the mouse. They do not require one to be ambidextrous in use and do not need valuable desk space. They are also more expensive than a mouse.

Even more expensive are a number of advanced devices. The DataGlove is a glove which contains optical fibres which detect the bending or moving of the user's joints. Currently, this is mainly used in the fields of high-end graphics, robotics and biomedicine. The DataSuit is similar but covers the whole body (it uses software called 'Body Electric' – from a Walt Whitman poem – and a language called Flex). Some devices rely on pressure and force-feedback technology.[2] These measure movement or pressure of the user. For example, a drawing stylus will respond to increased pressure by increasing the width of the line that is drawn. Then there is the 'joystring'. This is a hand grip shaped like a T that is kept in position by thin taut wires. As the user applies a twisting force to the T-grip, the forces are measured by sensors at the ends of the wires. Some devices that have not yet become fully commercial are those relying on eye-tracking and head-tracking. One field of devices that is on the edge of commercial use is workable real-time voice recognition. Ordinary voice recognition currently has a restricted vocabulary (less than 20,000 words), has to be 'trained' to recognize users' voices and is not cheap. Its most common use is in medical applications (e.g. for dictating X-ray results).

Less esoteric input devices are magnetic stripe plastic cards, such as those used on credit cards, and smart cards. Smart cards are plastic cards which have a microprocessor embedded in them. This enables them not only to input data but to interact with a computer.

One final point on input devices shows how difficult it can be to gain public acceptance. When bar codes started to appear widely in supermarkets they were condemned by some fundamentalist Christian sects as being the 'mark of the Devil' as described in the Bible.[3] Some supermarkets even found themselves the object of demonstrations.

Data storage

As we have seen, the main memory or storage actually inside a computer is the RAM. In a small computer this may be as small as 640 Kbytes. In the early days of computing, this would have been thought positively generous. Nowadays even some computer games need more than this. So some form of secondary storage is needed.

Subsidiary storage is used for:

- *transaction files*. These are details of the work done during the day, such as letters typed or entries to a ledger;
- *master files*. These show the current position of any records, such as all ledgers, stocks, assets, and names and addresses;
- *back-ups*. It is always possible for things to go wrong with a computer, and sometimes this can mean the loss of all the data. To reduce the problems that this causes it is necessary to copy the files periodically. It is then possible (though still tedious) to reconstruct the data. On a mainframe this is done at high speed onto what is known as streaming tape;
- *programs*. These are held in secondary storage ready to be read into main memory when not in use.

■ MAGNETIC TAPE (MAINFRAMES)

Computer magnetic tape is rather like the tape used in audio or video cassettes. Like them, it is read from or written to (play or record in audio) by passing over a magnetic head. The files on magnetic tape are held in a sequence from beginning to end; data cannot be accessed at random. So it is used for those applications that can be run in sequence (such as inventory) and back-up. Magnetic tape is usually 1.25 cm wide and about 725 m long. Along every centimetre of its length will be 2,500 bytes of data (though this can be as high as 8,000). The tape will go past the head at over 750 cm/sec. So, in theory, the transmission rate is 1,875,000 characters per second and one reel of tape can hold over 180 Mbytes. In practice these figures are not attained when running the tape. Firstly, some information has to be added to identify the material, etc. Secondly, and more importantly, the machine has to accelerate and slow down the tape each time a block of information is used.

Blocks are separated by a 1.25 cm blank length of tape to allow for the speeding up and slowing down. This is known as the inter-block gap (IBG). So a length of tape might look like this:

IBG	Data Record	IBG	Data Record	IBG	Data Record	IBG

However, many files take up less tape length than an IBG (so a tape would have more gaps than data). In such cases, a number of files are put together like this:

IBG	Data Record	Data Record	Data Record	IBG

On the other hand, some files are so large that they will need more than one reel of tape.

■ MAGNETIC DISKS

A magnetic disk is like a plate or record player disk covered with a metallic coating (such as cobalt) on which data is recorded. The advantage of the disk is that although data is recorded sequentially, it can be found again at random. This is done by spinning the disk at high speed and moving an access arm over the revolving disk. This access arm is like the arm on a record player, and on the end of the arm is a small read/write head. Data can be recorded on both surfaces of the disk. A mainframe computer will have several hard disks arranged in a pile with a space between them for the heads. Typically a disk pack, as multiple hard disks are called, will have 11 hard disks giving 20 surfaces and a capacity of 1,000 Mbytes. The hard disks in home or small office computers are usually rather more modest, having a capacity in the 20–100 Mbyte range, though if you want it you can get a 5.25 inch drive with a capacity of over a gigabyte.

B

■ FLOPPY DISKS

These are flexible disks and are still found in most small office computers. Their imminent demise is continually being forecast but the manufacturers remain secure in the knowledge of the large user base and relative cheapness of their product. Floppy disk sizes are still quoted in non-metric sizes, being available in sizes of 3, 3.5 and 5.25 inches. When a floppy is inserted into a disk drive, it is clamped at its centre by a pair of rings with the motor actually operating inside this ring. This motor only spins the disk when a read/write command is received. The conventional 5.25 inch disks had a capacity up to 1.2 Mbytes, while 3.5 inch disks tend to be 1.44 Mbytes. Higher capacities are possible but not all small computers can handle them. One of the problems of floppy disks is that manufacturers are not all as quality conscious as they might be. Tests that have been carried out on even well-known brands are disappointing.

■ OPTICAL DISKS

There are three streams of optical disks:

- CD-ROM (Compact Disk Read Only Memory);
- write-once. These are also known as OPROM (Optical Programmable Read Only Memory), non-erasable, and WORM (Write Once Read Many) disks;
- erasable optical disks.

All use a small laser to make and read small pits that represent data.

Compact disks (CDs) were developed for audio purposes. They use a low-power laser to record and read information. CD-ROMs work in a similar manner, storing data in a way that can be read by a computer – though this needs a special drive and associated software. CDs are 130 mm in diameter and 1.5 mm thick with a single spiral track nearly 5 km long. They are made of light plastic that flows easily in fabrication and has good optical properties (e.g. Makrolon). A single CD-ROM has a capacity of 660 Mbytes (say, 150,000 pages) and can be thought of as a sort of computer equivalent of microfilm. One buys a CD complete with the information on it, such as an encyclopedia or 'books in print' or the *Oxford English Dictionary* (the *OED* – on two disks). An early entrant was a most useful aid to word processing, produced by Microsoft. This contained *Roget's Thesaurus*, the *World Almanac* and *Book of Facts*, a dictionary, a spelling checker, a manual of style, *Bartlett's Familiar Quotations*, the US zip code directory and *Business Information Sources* – all on one disk. A disadvantage of this disk was that it was not compatible with all word processing software. The great advantage of such data on a CD is the ability to cross-refer entries. For example, one could obtain all the references to Shakespeare in the *OED*.

In general terms, the CD-ROM has several advantages compared with other storage methods. It contains a lot of information in a reasonably small space. Unlike most hard disks, it is removable from the drive, which aids security (though it also aids pilfering). Access to data is random. Data is effectively in a database and so is accessible. The reading head is not so close to the surface that it will easily crash down onto it (which it can on hard disks). For manufacturers, the CD-ROM is attractive. It is difficult to copy, the contents are easy to copyright, and manufacturing costs are low – about $1–2 each (though, as with software, this advantage is rarely passed on to the buyer).

The main disadvantage of the CD-ROM is its read-only property. It cannot be used to record the user's data, which is the way most computer applications need to work. It also has a slower access time than hard disks (though this is being improved all the time). Data transfer rates for the early CDs were about 1.2 Mbytes/sec compared with the then rate for hard disks of 5 Mbytes/sec. The other factor that held back CD-ROM use was a lack of standardization and compatibility. A group of manufacturers got together and called themselves the High Sierra Group (HSG) with the aim of standardization, which is why now one sees CD-ROMs referred to as HSG-format. Another problem was the manufacture of CDs. The thin aluminium layer must be intact and fully reflective, free from aluminium oxide rusting. The quality of manufacturing is much more important with CD-ROMs than with audio CDs. It was estimated that as many as 5 per cent of audio CDs could be defective. The industry were very secretive about such figures – usually blaming 'other manufacturers' or the disk drives.

Write-once optical disks (often called WORM – Write Once Read Many) do enable one to record data onto the optical disk. But only once. When the data has been written on the disk it is there for good. Apart from this WORMS are very much like CD-ROMS, with the same advantages and disadvantages. One difference is that the data is formatted like a hard or floppy disk; it does not use the single long spiral of the CD-ROM. This, of course, means that a WORM is not usable on a standard CD-ROM reader. About 97 per cent of WORMS are the usual 130 mm size, like CDs, with capacities typically in the range of 250–800 Mbytes. The remaining 3 per cent are special sizes (such as 30 and 36 cm) holding several gigabytes.

Erasable optical disks can be used repeatedly, like hard/floppy disks and magnetic tape. To do this, they use a different approach from CD-ROMs. A spot of the ferromagnetic layer is heated above its Curie point – the point at which it becomes paramagnetic. This spot is magnetized in a direction that is maintained when it cools.

When being read, this spot polarizes the laser beam (known as a Kerr rotation) and this polarization is detected thus showing a 'bit' of data. To erase the bit of data, the process is repeated with the spot being magnetized in the original, opposite, direction. The first erasable was introduced in 1987, used a standard 130 mm size, and had a capacity of 211 Mbytes. By 1988, capacity had increased to 650 Mbytes and thence soon reached the gigabyte range.

■ PAPER

Paper can be used for storage. One system is the printed data strip (Softstrip). This consists of very small black rectangles printed in a strip 16 mm wide and 24 cm long. Each strip could hold up to 5.5 Kbytes and eight strips could be printed on one A4 page. The reader scans one strip in 30 seconds. Unless this scan speed can be increased by a quantum amount, it is difficult to see it becoming a dominant system, being reserved for special applications.

'Digital Paper' is a strip of thin plastic film coated with a dye that is sensitive to infrared light. Lasers burn data into and read from this strip. A reel of digital paper is the same size as magnetic tape (1.25 cm by 800 m). This has a capacity of 600 gigabytes, though improvements in laser technology could double this. A Canadian company (Creo) took this ICI invention to produce a digital paper strip 35 mm wide by 500 m long[4] – with a capacity of 1 terabyte (1,000 million bytes).

■ CACHES, RAM DISKS AND SPEED-UPS

A cache is a method of speeding up the transfer of data. This is done by using a portion of the fast static RAM for some of the data that will be normally read from a disk. When the disk-cache program realizes that data that is needed is in this reserved portion of RAM, it takes it from there rather than getting it from the disk. Transfer to and from a RAM is faster than using a disk so the process is speeded up. Caching is useful for slow disks (i.e. floppies) and for data that is going to be used repeatedly or in quick succession (such as spreadsheets). The idea behind caching is straightforward; the practice can be less so. Memory caching needs a program and these vary widely: one advertiser claimed that caching would increase the computer's internal clock from 16 MHz to 23 MHz, which is nonsense. It cannot affect the clock. One must also be careful when changing floppy disks in cache mode – do this at the wrong time and data cached from one disk may be written back to another.

A RAM disk is similar in some ways. Part of the RAM is made to act as though it were a separate disk. The OS believes that it is dealing with a disk and neither knows nor cares that it is not. Of course, being RAM, when the computer is turned off the 'disk' disappears. In use, the RAM disk is much faster than a floppy. Some RAM disk products are just a piece of software; others come complete with some extra memory on a board that is added to the computer.

'Speed-ups' are more properly known as accelerator boards. These come in four types:

● accelerators;
● co-processors;
● replacement boards; and
● clock enhancers.

Accelerators are basically faster microprocessors. To use them, one removes the

93

original microprocessor and replaces it with a new, faster one that will normally use a cache to help matters along. This means that only the components on the new card operate at the faster speed. So, although the final speed-up is not so dramatic as it is in some other methods, this is a fairly safe procedure (assuming, of course, that one installs it correctly).

As already mentioned, a co-processor is an extra processor which gets on with time-consuming tasks while the rest of the computer gets on with something else. Co-processors usually come with an extra megabyte or more of memory. In the right circumstances, they can be very useful – though their complexity can lead to hardware and software incompatibilities.

Replacement boards replace most of the computer's system: the CPU, RAM, ROM, data bus, etc. In effect they upgrade the computer, usually to a faster or better one in the same range. In a similar fashion, clock enhancers work by removing the old clock and replacing it with a new clock (plus some other components) on a card. This sounds such an obvious improvement that it is superficially attractive. However, if a machine is meant to run at a particular speed, then all the components were selected to work at that speed. So speeding up the clock may result in a marginal chip failing. And the only way to find out the maximum speed is by trial and error.

It can thus be seen that there are different types of storage: solid state (RAM), hard disks, floppy disks, optical disks. Manufacturers of these different types are all constantly seeking to improve the competitive position of their products in terms of lower costs, more memory, faster access and transfer, and greater reliability.

Displays

The monitors that display work on a computer are of four main types:

- cathode ray tube (CRT);
- liquid crystal display (LCD);
- electroluminescence (EL); and
- gas-plasma display.

Other technologies – light-emitting diode, vacuum fluorescence and electro-phoretics – are relatively uncommon. For most of its history, monitor design has been television-driven. Manufacturers would make a better television and then transfer the improvements to computers.

The cathode ray tube has been around for most of this century and has successfully fought off later technologies in spite of obvious disadvantages: weight, size and fragility. Users would like to have high resolution – they would rather have a picture on their screen that looks more like a photograph than something built up from Lego bricks. However, high resolution needs a good (i.e. expensive) CRT, appropriate software and lots of memory. Resolution is measured by pixels, which are in effect the dots that build up to make a picture. Over the years, the standards that have been most widely used have increased the pixels used:

CGA (Colour Graphics Adapter)	320 × 200	(4 colours)
	640 × 200	(2 colours)
EGA (Enhanced Graphics Adapter)	640 × 350	(16 colours)
Monochrome text ('MDA')	640 × 350	
Monochrome graphics (Hercules)	720 × 348	
VGA (Video Graphics Array)	720 × 400	(text)
	320 × 200	(256 colours)
	640 × 480	(16 colours)

There is no way that one can get a reasonable picture on a CGA monitor; it can only produce Lego pictures. The fact that some people have become used to such pictures merely demonstrates how current computers have made us all lower our standards. A similar case is that of 'high definition' television. For years this was going to be 2,000 lines minimum. When the industry could not solve the bandwidth problems, the term was attached to 1,250 line television. There are high-definition monitors. The Mega-screen has 4,096 × 3,300 pixels, equivalent to about 300 dots per inch. Monitors used for 'desk-top publishing' and 'computer aided design' are in the 1,280 × 1,600 pixel area.

B

Printers

The problem of quality is even more pronounced when one considers printers. Here, most users have to trade four main factors off against one another: quality, cost, speed and reliability. The commonest type of printer is the dot matrix. In these, the print mechanism consists of a grid of small pins from which shapes can be made. These pins hit an inked ribbon, transferring the shape to the paper. The simplest printers had a (usable) grid of 9 pins by 9 pins. Once one got used to it, the output from such printers was on the edge of bearability. Matters could be improved by a number of devices such as printing everything twice (moving the impression slightly on the second pass), increasing the number of pins from 9 to 24, and changing the shape of the pins. Better quality is attained by using daisywheel printers, which are like ordinary daisywheel electric typewriters. These have the disadvantages of being slower, slightly more expensive, and not being able to print anything that is not a normal typewriter character. Laser printers fall between the two in terms of quality. They are fast, but more expensive and need more maintenance and repairs.

■ OTHER TYPES OF PRINTER INCLUDE:

- *matrix-line printers.* These consist of a row of dot matrix hammers about 8 mm apart in a horizontal row: 24 hammers for an A4 sheet. The hammers print the entire line of dots by moving slightly horizontally.
- *thermal transfer.* A thermal head heats a wax-ink ribbon and transfers the shape of the character in wax-ink to the paper. This is different from direct-thermal printing in which the heated head acts on specially treated paper to darken it.

95

- *ink-jet.* An ink-jet head produces small droplets of ink from a nozzle that are then propelled towards the paper. 'Continuous-jet' shoots out a stream of 50,000 drops a second. 'Drop-on-demand' forms droplets in response to specific commands while 'phase-change' printers eject liquefied ink pellets that are then solidified on the surface of the paper. Phase-change and drop-on-demand are combined in plastic-ink printing, which is particularly effective in colour printing.
- *page printers.* The early page printers (around the late 1970s) were laser printers with a resolution of only 300 dots/inch and a speed of 5–10 pages per minute. Later technologies were based on LEDs (light emitting diodes) and LCSs (liquid crystal shutters).

All printers have disadvantages, but the manufacturers are continually working to improve them. As with all computer components, the secret of commercial success is cost, speed, quality and reliability. It is rather like the success of the first Kodak camera in 1888, which proved such a success with the public. The advertisements by Kodak at the time showed that a photograph could be taken with just three simple actions.

References

1 *Personal Computing*, Vol. 12, No. 5, May 1988, p. 116.
2 *Byte*, Vol. 13, No. 9, September 1988, p. 288.
3 See Revelation 3:20, Revelation 13:17, and St John 5:11–13.
4 *Gulf News*, 2 April, 1988.

13

Software

If civilisation has risen from the Stone Age, it can rise again from the
Wastepaper Age.　　　Jacques Barzun, *The House of Intellect* (1959)

It is a capital mistake to theorise before one has data.
　　Sir Arthur Conan Doyle, *The Adventures of Sherlock Holmes* (1891)

Computer programs, or software, are the sets of instructions that make computers
work. So we must have them. This leads to a strange love-hate relationship between the
users and the people who write programs. This is particularly true of the relationship
between users and the sellers of ready-made programs ('packages'). On the one hand,
we are grateful that somebody else has taken the time and trouble to do something for
which we lack the time, patience and ability. On the other hand, we dislike the way in
which what is written is so often not exactly what we want. And we do not like the tricks
that get played on us – the hype, the mistakes, and having to buy software before
finding out what equipment is needed to run it.

B

Some problems start when one buys the software – because one does not buy it, in
fact. One only pays for a licence to use it, and that usage is restricted to one machine.
One is forbidden to use it on both of one's two computers, or to let one's spouse or
children use it on their machines. One piece of software insists on a payment of $1,500
before one's spouse can use it. It is as though one could only play a pop record on one hi-
fi or could not let one's children read a book. One typical program states, 'By opening
this package you indicate your acceptance of the Licence Agreement and your agreement to be bound by the terms contained in it.' This particular package had already
been opened by the retailer – a fact quite impossible to prove in a court of law. But the
biggest bane in a user's life is 'copy protection'.

Copy protection

Software sellers do not want their programs copied by another commercial organization that might then sell the same products at a much reduced price – a reasonable
stance. To prevent this, the sellers write some instructions into the program which
prevents it from running if it is copied. It is here that the problems start.

It has already been stated that the use of a hard disk is a vast improvement in using
small computers. To do this, it is necessary to copy the program from the floppy on
which it is 'sold'. Later, when one improves the organization of the hard disk, one will
want to copy the floppy again each time. Many programs are protected so fiercely that
this is impossible. Some programs do not even allow one to make a back-up copy. So
one just has to go through the boring time-wasting procedure of loading the program
anew every time it is used, while waiting for it to wear out. One magazine reviewer
found that the disks were so tightly fitted into their covers that damage would occur
within a few usages – and this was software that cost a week's salary.

The task of incorporating copy protection is sometimes given by sellers to temporary employees, such as students. In one such case one well-known program would, if copied, flash a message on to the screen informing the user that the program was about to 'trash' the user's data. Unfortunately, this could happen in normal operation, when nothing was being copied.

In another case, the program would not run after a certain date even though it was being sold after the expiry date. A visit from the authorities managed to convince the seller that selling a non-viable program was against the law. But not, apparently, that the seller had done anything wrong.

What can be done about copy protection? One suggestion is that 'you make your own arrangements for copying a program that you have paid for'.[1] It is possible to by-pass protection but this would be against the licence contract. Another suggestion comes from a reviewer talking about the Ashton-Tate 'FullWrite Professional': 'Ring up ... and go right the way down to starting to read out your credit card number – and then say "Oh, is it copy-protected, by the way?" And then, regretfully but firmly, cancel the order.'[2] In fact, the answer to copy protection is simple. Do not buy any copy-protected software. But beware: some advertisers do not admit that their goods are, in fact, copy-protected. To find out, ask friends or colleagues. Or subscribe to an American computer magazine. These magazines are nearly all against the practice and make suitable comments.

The basic protection for software sellers is copyright and patents. Sellers prefer copyright – it is easy to get and lasts for fifty years while a patent is only granted if it is demonstrably an improvement. However, copyrighting causes disputes between software firms, leading to complexities. As one author put it, referring to software, 'It is virtually the only one of man's creations that can be protected both by patents and by copyright. . . . The lawyers are rubbing their hands.'[3]

Types of software

Software that is used in offices can be of several different types:

- operating systems;
- environments;
- utilities;
- memory-residents;
- applications.

It should be noted that some people would regard memory-residents as being a form of applications software, while some others would use just two divisions: operating systems and applications. Another term that is sometimes used is 'productivity' software. This usually refers to a group of applications programs or utilities or even something else by those 'who, if they can't think of something else to call it, define their software as a "productivity tool" '.[4]

OPERATING SYSTEMS AND ENVIRONMENTS

The programs that a user wishes to operate on a computer do not run by themselves. First, there has to be within the computer a program that will run the computer. This program will organize the memory, send instructions to any peripheral devices and protect the memory from errors in the user's program. This program is the operating system (OS). Over the years there have been many well-known operating systems. These have included MULTICS, IBM's OS/360 and TENNEX; for small computers they have included CP/M, MS-DOS and OS/2. An OS for a single user with a single machine may consist of:

- *an executive*. This is a short program that loads a named program and gets everything started;
- *free storage allocation*. This is the allocation of spare memory that is not needed by a program or the OS;
- *a file system*. A disk organizes permanently stored data in 'files' and the file system tracks these and keeps them in order;
- *input-output streams*. These provide a convenient method of handling inputs and outputs with i/o devices;
- *error handling*. This protects the memory from some of the errors in a faulty program;
- *virtual memory management*. Virtual memory is a way of keeping part of the free storage in main memory and part on disk.

B

The operating systems associated with small computers differ from one another in their approach. Three small computer examples are MS-DOS, OS/2 (both from Microsoft) and Unix (from AT & T). DOS (Disk Operating System) became widely used on the original IBM PC machines, where it was known as PC-DOS. This wide availability led to an extremely large amount of software being written that would run with DOS. Users of DOS found that they could improve the use of their machines by learning a number of the special DOS commands.

OS/2 was associated with the second range of IBM personal computers, the PS/2 series, though parts of it could be used on the IBM PC AT. The standard OS/2[5],[6] is multi-tasking and needs at least 2 Mbytes of memory. Multi-tasking means that the computer is enabled to carry out several tasks simultaneously. This is not the same as multi-user, which means that several people can use the same processor at the same time. The extended version (OS/2 EE) of OS/2 added database and communications facilities, while Presentations Manager added graphics.

Unix has had a long and chequered life. Introduced to small computers from mainframe use at a time when peripherals were expensive, it had multi-tasking facilities. A number of variations followed, such as XENIX and A-UX (for the Apple Macintosh II). Unix has a special flavour of its own which users either like or not.

The Apple Macintosh was introduced without an operating system, as such. There was no layer between the user's software and the machine. Instead there were a number of packages to help the applications programmer to use the hardware (this may seem like splitting hairs to some people, but it did not at the time).

Some users find operating systems too lengthy to learn, or perhaps lacking some facilities that they would like to have. Such people can use 'environments'. These programs are a layer between the operating system and themselves. Examples are IBM's Environmental Manager, GEM and Windows, with the last two being widely used. Such environments tend to use pictorial representations of commands, such as the GEM picture of a rubbish bin to indicate 'erase file'.

■ UTILITIES AND MEMORY-RESIDENTS

'Utilities' is another word that is used with different meanings:

- software that transfers files of data between stores;
- small generally useful programs that help one to use the computer in a more powerful way;
- as a synonym for 'desk-top management'.

A desk-top manager is a program which contains some or all of the following:

- a calculator; this enables one to use the power of an office computer to imitate a cheap pocket calculator;
- a calendar and an alarm clock;
- a 'notepad' on which to type brief notes;
- a telephone and address list;
- a telephone dialler;
- an appointments diary;
- an elementary text editor, filing system and index card file;
- a list of things to do.

Whether one regards this package as an irresistible necessity or a ridiculous waste of time depends on temperament. It is possible to write a simple program for a 'to do' list in one line.[7]

Utilities, desk managers and other programs (such as a program to run a spreadsheet sideways) can be put into memory and left there in such a way that they only come into use when one wants to use them. After use, they stay quietly in the background. Such programs are memory-resident software, often known as TSRs (Terminate and Stay Resident). Although they use up some of the memory, they are attractive to some people who would feel deprived without them. But they are not without disadvantages, especially if one is tempted to use several of them. Under many operating systems (such as DOS), the TSRs fight one another, all trying to grab the same things. They can even lock up one's complete system. If one needs to free some memory then (under DOS) it is necessary to unload them in the exact reverse order to that in which they were loaded. Having several TSRs has been described as being 'as much fun as keeping tabs on a room full of kindergarten kids'. A firm that specializes in helping people with software problems reports that 75 per cent of their work ends up as being due to TSRs.

■ APPLICATIONS

The programs known as applications software would, in most people's definition, include such areas as:

Accounting/book-keeping	Marketing	Spreadsheet
Database management	Personnel	Graphics
Financial modelling	Production	Hypertext
Word processing	Statistics	etc.
Communications	Industry specials	

'Industry specials' includes both baskets of programs for a specific industry (such as lawyers), and software of importance to an industry (such as airline reservations and bank fund transfers).

The outline flow of computer data in an organization is likely to be:

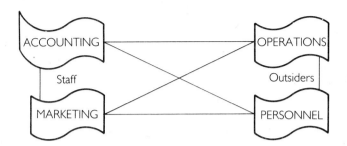

Within a function, such as accounting, the flow is likely to be:

B

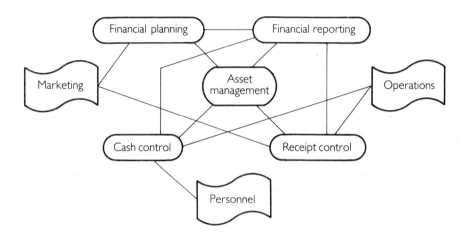

If the first level is 'area' and the second the blocks within the area, then the third level is the flow into and out of the blocks thus:

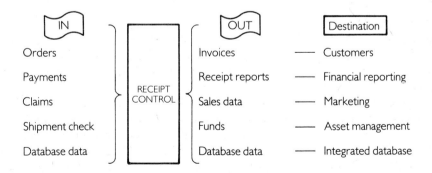

From this, it may be possible to glimpse the complexity of the data flow. In a basic 'suite' of programs for the accounting function alone, there will probably be forty-five such data flows even for a straightforward production process. To this must be added the flows for a particular industry and those which a particular organization considers prudent. So the totality of data flows within an organization is considerable.

This vast network of flows necessarily leads to certain considerations:

- an attempt to write the software from scratch for an entire organization would be an awesome and lengthy undertaking;
- changes to any part of the network of data will have a domino effect on other flows, all of which have to be investigated;
- it is easy to leave gaps between the individual programs – known as 'leaving gaps between the floorboards';
- changes and improvements inevitably tend to be 'bolt-ons' rather than making changes to the entire flow of data. It is not easy even for the human brain to wrap itself round the entire concept;
- considerable amounts of memory are needed. Except for small organizations, therefore, it is not feasible to use small office computers for the task. Even when this is done, it is difficult to achieve a satisfactory degree of integration.

Microcomputers are, however, useful for a number of specific applications and some of these are considered below.

Word processing

Without some additional software, it is not easy to use a small computer even to type a letter. Since the largest single use of small computers is as a super-typewriter, a considerable number of suitable programs have appeared on the market. There are three types of word processing installations:

- *dedicated machines*. These are small office computers that have just the one function of word processing. These are therefore of use in a small office where it is worth having a machine for the one task, perhaps having a separate machine for other tasks such as book-keeping. A common example is a small professional partnership such as a firm of lawyers;
- *general-purpose small computers* which have a word processing program as well as other software;
- centralized pools of typists who share a *central computer processor* to which are linked their individual keyboards and screens.

Studies suggest that the main saving of centralized pools arises from the act of centralization rather than the use of computerization. In operation, users employ the telephone to dictate their material to the pool where it is recorded ready for processing. This system was pioneered by Unilever in the 1950s and is worth considering by any organization that has more than six or seven typists.

The main advantage of word processing is the reduction in re-types. The original typing is stored in memory, so any alterations or errors can be effected and the result printed out automatically at speed. The main advantage of word processing by originators is that it enables one to 'think' and edit (change) ideas in a manner that is not possible at a typewriter. Book authors who use word processing would not wish to change to typewriters. However, the preparation of commercial reports in an office may be more efficient when dictated to a pool. The main disadvantage of centralized word processing occurs when the central processor stops operating, an event that is positively panic-producing.

Word processor software has three components:

- *the text editor.* This is the part that enables one to type and change the material;
- *the formatter.* This allows one to decide the appearance of the final document or other output;
- *the outputter.* This controls the printer or other output device.

All three components differ widely in sophistication and ease of use in different programs aimed at the three main market segments: corporate, professional and personal. Individual word processing programs for personal use each attract detractors and acclaimers. This is because users have so many different needs depending on what work is to be done and how users do it. Authors of technical books may like Nota Bene, while people who wish to 'personalize' their program may prefer Borland's Sprint. Two powerful programs are XyWrite and Q & A. Occasional users may want something more basic like Professional Write (which is not the same as FullWrite Professional). There are over sixty major alternatives to choose from so choosing is not easy. The usual advice is to choose a program that reflects the way that one works. This is not as easy as it sounds since programs differ from one another in quite subtle ways.

B

A group of computer management consultants had access to a number of programs that they could use, and were certainly not strangers to what computers could do for them. Their choice was unanimous: they all used a simple program in preference to a complex or powerful one. Though, of course, they were not spending all day at the word processor writing novels. So the choice has to remain a personal one.

Spreadsheets

A spreadsheet is a sheet of paper spread out and then filled with a table or matrix of rows and columns. Sacha gets 10 ECUs' pocket money a month but complains that this is not enough. Sacha's father suggests that a spreadsheet might help, so Sacha draws one (Table 13.1). If Table 13.1 were put onto a computer, it would be an 'electronic spreadsheet' – which was the name used in the early days. Sacha has called the rows 1, 2, 3, etc. and the columns A, B, C, and so on. This means that the box where a row and

Table 13.1 Example spreadsheet

	A	B	C	D	E	F
1		Jan	Feb	Mar	Apr	May
2						
3	Pocket money	10-00	10-00	10-00	10-00	10-00
4						
5	Comics	3-00	3-00	3-00	3-00	3-00
6	Albums	7-00		7-00	7-00	7-00
7	Presents		6-00	4-00		
8	Total costs	10-00	9-00	14-00	10-00	10-00
9						
10	Saving	Nil	+ 1	− 4	Nil	Nil

column meet (known as a 'cell') can be referred to by a code. Thus cell B10 is the anticipated saving in January. A cell can have in it:

- data (figures such as the pocket money in row 3);
- a label (words such as those in column A);
- a formula (thus 'B3 − B8' in cell B10).

In response to Sacha's request for more pocket money, Sacha's father suggests a 'what if' inspection of the spreadsheet. What if albums were bought on alternate months only? What if no comics were bought? Either alternative would balance the books.

Sacha's mother runs a company called 'Happicomp' which has a sales turnover of just over half a million. Based on last year's figures, it has been assumed that all revenues and costs increase by 5 per cent this year and next year. This does not look very exciting. Some elementary research suggests that sales could be increased by an extra 20 per cent if advertising were increased by 100 per cent and sales commissions were raised from 10 per cent to 12.5 per cent.

The question is whether this is worth doing. Making this sort of calculation by hand is long-winded and notoriously prone to calculation errors, especially if repeated. A computer spreadsheet shows the result in Table 13.2.

Table 13.2 Happicomp spreadsheet

	Last year	This year	Next year A	Next year B	Plus (%) B
Income					
Sales	523,000	549,000	576,000	659,000	20
Cost of sales					
Materials	204,000	214,000	225,000	269,600	20 + 5
Advertising	52,000	55,000	58,000	110,000	100
Logistics	21,000	22,000	23,000	27,700	20 + 5
Commissions	53,000	56,000	59,000	84,000	20 + 25
Overheads					
Staff	72,000	76,000	80,000	95,800	20 + 5
Legal/audit fees	5,000	5,300	5,600	6,700	20 + 5
Rent	30,000	31,000	33,000	43,400	'40'
Telephone	6,000	6,300	6,600	7,900	20 + 5
Depreciation	5,000	5,000	5,000	6,000	'20'
Miscellaneous	3,000	3,400	3,600	4,300	20 + 5
Total expenses	451,000	474,000	498,800	655,400	
Income less expenses	72,000	75,000	77,200	3,600	
Tax	31,000	32,000	33,200	1,500	
Net Profit	41,000	43,000	44,000	1,100	

Using a spreadsheet, it would be very easy to change any of the parameters in 'Next year B'. For example, what if the increase in sales were not 20 per cent but 33 per cent? The ease of answering such 'what-ifs' is a basic use of spreadsheets. It can also be a basic drawback: an over-optimistic sales director may be tempted to change the parameters until an answer is obtained that lines up with hopes. The other problem that can arise is that of putting an incorrect formula in a cell. This may not always be obvious with initial iterations.

The basic concept of the spreadsheet is very simple. Surprisingly, modern spread-sheets do not differ very much from the original model, VisiCalc. This simplicity should not blind one to spreadsheets' usefulness. By putting a small step in a calculation in successive cells, one can build up to some useful models. For example, in marketing a spreadsheet can be used for pricing, marginal profitability, sales productivity, media investment analysis, distribution, etc.[8]

Database management

A database can be compared to a set of index cards in a box that holds information on friends' names and addresses. When adding, deleting, changing or sorting this infor-mation one is 'managing' the database. A database management system is one that enables one to carry out these tasks of adding, deleting, changing, inspecting or sorting information and then printing the results in a format that one wishes.

If one were well organized one might hold the names and addresses of friends on pre-printed index cards. These index cards might look like this:

Last name:	Armstrong
First name:	Eddie
Street:	Rue Duquesnoy 5
Code:	1000
City:	Bruxelles

This type of record would be held in a computer database management system in a table thus:

Last name	First name	Street	Code	City	Ref
Armstrong	Eddie	Rue Duquesnoy 5	1000	Bruxelles	1
Beiderbecke	Louis	90 East 42nd Street	NY 10017	New York	2
Condon	Bix	Kuttelgasse 7	8001	Zurich	1

The fact that data is held in the form of a table helps to explain some of the terms used in a database management system (DBMS). The data held originally on one index card is known as a row or record. The different items (e.g. first name) originally on the index card are known as the columns or fields. Every column or field must have a field name (e.g. city). Each time the database is used, the computer has to be told which field name(s) to access.

When setting up a DBMS it is vital to think ahead to the likely uses for which it will be employed. Even a name and address database holds complications.

An early decision is the number of characters (bytes) that are to be allowed for each field. Most DBMSs keep the field length constant, so Condon and Beiderbecke take up the same amount of memory – the amount of room that has been allocated to 'Last name'. Since people do not want their databases to consist mainly of blank spaces and since DBMSs have a finite capacity, some limit has to be set. This can mean that some surnames will be shortened if the space allocated is too short. While Featherstonehaugh (17 characters) should be safe, there is somebody with a surname of 590 characters. A man with this name (who also has 26 first names) shortened it to the first 35 characters but then shortened it even more to Mr Wolfe + 585 Snr.[9] Names of towns can also be long. The official name for the capital of Thailand is Krungtep Mahanakhon – a reduction from the full name which has 167 characters.

DBMSs cannot discern context, which humans can. For example, most countries in the world have the postal code in front of the town name (e.g. 1025 Budapest). But Britain and America use the opposite convention. If one instructs a DBMS to start a letter 'Dear*Title*Last name' then one may send out a letter addressed to 'Dear Mr Saint George & the Dragon' unless some logical thought has been given to the DBMS usage. It is surprising how often one receives mail with errors in the address. This is usually due to sloppy DBMS work, though it can also be due to input errors that the computer cannot detect (*The Economist* sometimes sends the writer six copies of the same direct mail, each with the address slightly incorrect).

While it is necessary for carelessness to be avoided when setting up a DBMS, DBMSs are nevertheless very useful. One of their major advantages is the sheer size of the information that can be handled. Even on a home or small office computer, the limit is in the order of two billion records (or rows or index cards), while the number of tables that can be handled is only restricted by the amount of memory available. Keeping two billion index cards in order, and actually using them for anything useful, would be a daunting task.

A second major advantage of DBMSs is their ability to search for and find selected fields. For example, one might want to send advertising material to all customers living in Paris prior to a trip there by a sales team. With a manual system, this could be a major undertaking. With a DBMS, it is almost trivial – as well as being fast, automatic and accurate. The DBMS will utilize any field that one has set up. If one field is 'Credit limit' and another one is 'Current amount owed' then it is simple to send out chasing reminder letters to all customers who are over their limit. The computer is simply instructed to print out the letters addressed to all those with 'owing > limit'.

This leads to a third advantage of DBMSs. Their use is not, naturally, restricted to handling just names and addresses. One can use them for any purpose that can be expressed within their basic format. Examples are inventories, ledgers, personnel records, and invoicing. A small office can use a DBMS to write such applications quickly without the time and cost of specialized programming (especially as most main DBMSs contain their own 'language' to facilitate this). Larger offices may have to trade off this advantage against the speed of input and processing of custom-written software.

As with spreadsheets, different people have their own favourite DBMS software. Since it takes some time to learn and get to know a DBMS program, most people are disinclined to change the software that they use and are familiar with. Over the years, steady sellers for mainframes have been Adabas, Datacom, IDMS, IMS and DB2. For home and small office computers, the choice is complicated as manufacturers leapfrog one another with enhanced versions of their products. As a general rule, it is normally worthwhile buying the latest version of a program since it will represent a genuine improvement. The exception is the 'bells and whistles brigade'. These are the firms that provide pointless additions in the hope of attracting the attention of the ignorant or unwary. Some programs that are outside this group include dBase (good report generation), R:base (good for user-defined rules for data entry), Paradox (good all-round DBMS) and Foxbase + (fast).

Groupware

Office staff and managers do not work in isolation from one another. Success can only come from the multitude of their interactions. But computers and their software tend not merely to ignore this, they actually tend to isolate people. (Networks – see the next chapter – only share data, which falls very far short of group working.) Groupware is the generic term given to computer applications that seek to encourage group activities. Much groupware has arisen from the pioneering work done at ARC (Augmentation Research Centre) at Stanford Research International (SRI), starting in the 1960s.

B

Some 'groupware' is little better than teleconferencing, E-mail and conference boards. Other software is more promising for the future. Examples are COKES (office procedures), ForComment (group writing) and SuperSync (analysing group behaviour – popular with group-behaviour consultants). Only time will show whether real progress will be made, or if 'groupware' is debased by becoming an advertising slogan.[10]

The short history of computer software is already providing legends. It is said that dBase was invented by an engineer to help him with his football bets. Another legend is the large profits to be made from a successful product. As one commentator put it: 'Never in the history of capitalism have so many become so rich so young.'[11]

References

1 Sinclair, I., *The Amstrad PC Hard Disk Guide*, Oxford: Blackwell Scientific Publications, p. 58, 1988.
2 *Personal Computer World*, October 1988, p. 101.
3 *The Economist*, Vol. 310, No. 7585, 14 January 1989, p. 81.
4 Rash, W., 'Do productivity tools help productivity?', *Byte*, Vol. 13, No. 10, November 1988, p. 135.
5 Letwin, G., *Inside OS/2*, Redmond: Microsoft Press, 1988.
6 Iacobucci, E., *OS/2 Programmer's Guide*, Berkeley: Osborne/McGraw-Hill, 1988.
7 For computer buffs, the London *Evening Standard* ran this in Julian Allason's 'Micro File': 0 PRINT " (CLS) (24 down) RUN (ENTER)"; LIST 1–20; END.
8 West, A., *Spreadsheet Marketing*, Aldershot: Gower, 1987.
9 See the 12th and 34th editions of McWhirter, N. D., *The Guinness Book of Records*, London: Guinness Superlatives.
10 See, for example, Johansen, R., *Groupware*, New York: Free Press, 1988; Grief, I., *Computer-Supported Co-operative Work*, San Mateo: Morgan Kaufmann, 1988; and *Byte*, Vol. 13, No. 13, December 1988, pp. 242–282.
11 Computer software survey, *The Economist*, 30 January, 1988.

14
Telecommunications and Networks

Neither snow, nor rain, nor gloom of night stays these couriers from the swift completion of their appointed rounds.
Inscription on the New York General Post Office[1]

NETWORK. Anything reticulated or decussated, at equal distances, with interstices between the intersections.
Samuel Johnson, *Dictionary of the English Language* (1755)

The 'tele' part of telecommunications comes from the Greek word for 'far', and the ability to communicate over distances has long been a useful part of administration. In AD 750 Saffah defeated Marwan II and entered Damascus as the founder of the Abbasid ruling dynasty. The capital was moved from Damascus to the small village of Baghdad. Ministries ('divans') were set up, one of which was for communications. A line of semaphore towers was built covering nearly 5,000 km from Morocco to Baghdad, backed up by desert lighthouses and a pigeon-carrier service. The 'added value' of this system was that the local postmasters were employed as intelligence agents.[2]

A thousand years later, the British battle fleet at the 1805 battle of Trafalgar used the then recently invented system of signal flags. This gave it a considerable advantage as battle tactics could be communicated even after the battle had started. The opposition had to rely on tactics that had been decided before the battle had started. In 1878, just a few decades after the battle of Trafalgar, the first commercial telephone exchange was established. Thus two nineteenth-century inventions (the keyboard and the telephone) laid the foundations for the modern telecommunications industry.

By the end of the nineteenth century, the number of telephones in existence was approaching a million (now there are 700 million). In the 1880s and 1890s there was a rapid increase in offices and paperwork. Whether this increase resulted in the keyboard and the telephone, or if it was the other way round, is a matter of conjecture. The sheer number of telephones is a major strength, since it results in a vast network of communications. This network can be used for a range of services such as telex, facsimile and computer data transmission. However, there is a long way to go, especially internationally. People in Britain complain that it takes a week to get a new telephone installed. But in Yugoslavia a domestic request may have to wait four years while in India there are over 500,000 unfilled requests for telephones. In Iran, a manager may give one three or four different numbers for one to try to make contact. New York has more telephones than the whole of black Africa. For every 1,000 inhabitants Sweden has 900 telephones, while Portugal has only 200 and Ireland has 300 (India has 5). This international aspect of telecommunications is a major factor in one's thinking – of the 250 million telexes sent each year, over half are to another country. The other major factor is the fact that a basically simple concept (sending information from A to B) leads to so much confusion in people's minds.

Primary terminology

Much, if not the majority, of this confusion arises from the jargon used. No self-respecting technician talks of the telephone in the sense that the rest of us do. Instead, it will be referred to as the Public Switched Telephone Network (PSTN). The PSTN consists of the telephone handsets, which are connected by a 'local line' to the neighbourhood 'local exchange' and thence by 'trunk circuits' to the large 'trunk exchanges'. These telephone exchanges use switching equipment to connect individual subscribers to the PSTN.

Three related changes are taking place in the world's PSTNs. First, signals are being changed from analog to digital (the human voice is analog – a wave; digital is the rapid turning on and off of the energy). This is the same process that happened to audio recording – the wave that was made in a groove was replaced with digital recording and reproduction. Since most telephone traffic still consists of people talking to one another, this might seem a costly way to improve quality. But the main advantage is that it enables several voice and computer conversations to be mixed together and sent down the same channel. The other aspect of digitizing concerns the second change. The old mechanical switches in the telephone exchanges can be replaced by large computers – known as digital switching. These digital switches can be expanded and upgraded much easier than the old banks of mechanical switches. Developing a new digital switching computer from scratch is an expensive affair, so the vendors of current equipment (such as 5ESS and DMS–1) are hoping that they will enjoy sales for some years.

The third change in PSTNs is the replacement of copper wire with optical fibre. Optical fibre is finely drawn silica (glass) surrounded by a layer of similar material, the whole being about a tenth of a millimetre in diameter. Optical fibre transmits light faster than copper wire passes electrons, and it does so with less loss of signals. Even more, they can accommodate many more signals simultaneously. The exploitation of optical communications (which only started in the 1960s) has been closely tied in with the development of lasers. From the 1962 'semiconductor injection' laser to the 'distributed feedback' lasers of the 1980s. Optical fibres offer the possibility of large bandwidths – the range of frequencies that can be safely transmitted (technically, of the order of 20,000 gigahertz both ways down a fibre 4 mm across). But before the prospect of high-quality 3-D cable television comes about, further development is needed.

In particular, cheap optical switches will be needed. Without optical switches, it is necessary to convert optical signals into electronic ones, switch them towards their destination, and then reconvert them into their optical form. Switches using lithium niobate, or fibre memory loops, or indium-phosphide diode lasers have got partly there but a cheap commercial switch is still awaited.

Anything that a subscriber to a PSTN buys to attach to it, to make better use of it, is called Customer-premises Equipment (CPE). This includes such things as an answering machine, a fax, a telex or a modem. A modem (short for modulator-demodulator) is a way of transmitting data. The modem converts the digital data used by a computer into analog form for transmission, and back again when data is received. One can buy a modem on a card and just add it to the inside of a small computer, or buy a free-standing unit.

On the face of it, this seems like an ideal route to approach telecommunications. In practice, the path can be a rocky one. At every step things can go wrong. Firstly, the

B

modem may not be perfect – reading equipment comparative reviews is most disheartening. (The same applies to communications software of which there are eighty major products.) Secondly, one has to know how to set up the modem, which is more fiddly than setting up a new printer. One of the lesser settings is the speed of transmission and reception, which must be the same. Speed is expressed as bits of information per second (bps) or 'baud'. From a technical point of view bps is not the same as a baud (especially when considering data signalling rate) but many people and advertisers use the two terms interchangeably, so there is little point in arguing. Setting and transmitting depends on a standard set of commands. The main set of commands is the Hayes standard, or 'protocol', named for an early manufacturer of modems. One really needs to know these standards. For example, during transmission it is difficult to issue commands because anything one types on the keyboard is thought by the modem to be part of the message and so is just transmitted. So one learns to type '+++' in rapid succession, and then wait for one second. This gets the modem off-line so that one can issue a command.

There are such things as 'intelligent modems'. This term was applied to a modem that had certain facilities such as automatically dialling telephone numbers, and the ability to switch baud rates through software commands. Now, however, an 'intelligent modem' is usually taken to be one with its own microprocessor, so that one can send it commands in plain language. (Still not what most of us understand as being a good definition of intelligence, but never mind.) Baud rates vary widely, generally lying in the range of 300 to 115,200.

The next difficulty is the fact that transmission is not perfect, especially at higher baud rates. Errors can be due to 'impairment', caused by the imperfections that occur in the connecting lines, perhaps because of a poor connection, imperfections in the optical fibre, some dust in the exchange, and so on. In practice, the commonest cause is a fault in one of the telephone line amplifiers.

Other possible difficulties are legion. To give just one example, it can be difficult to log on to E-mail mailboxes which lock themselves if somebody makes three wrong attempts at entering the secret password. A hacker may know the number and have set his equipment to try to find your password, thus repeatedly locking the mailbox. One user has pointed out that the fact that one can eventually get through can be even more disturbing – this may be because the hacker has in fact managed to find out your 'secret' password. If all these potential difficulties cause one to despair somewhat of telecommunications, it should be pointed out that most communications are made successfully. On the other hand, one may agree with a writer specializing in high technology whose heartfelt cry was: 'Why is the technology so difficult to understand? Why is it so difficult to get a modem and communications software package successfully to dial a remote computer? Why, why, why?'[3]

Moving on to another area of terminology that causes confusion, one should consider the Videotex family of words. Videotex is a generic term for a family of services that makes available to users a set of computer-based information. This information is presented on screens or on television sets in the home (cheaper or older sets may need a special adapter). Two well-known examples of videotex are Teletext and Viewdata. Teletext is a way of showing information and crudely drawn pictures, usually on a television set. This information is sent out as a series of 'pages'; a page is one screenful. To refer to a page of information, one types a code on a keypad. For example, to see the weather forecast on the Yugoslav Teletekst system one looks at page 122, or at page 152 to see the latest currency rates. A problem with Teletext is that as the amount of information available increases, the number of pages has to increase and this increases the time taken to access a page. Even with as few as 200 pages, this can be 15–20 seconds on many systems (research shows that the maximum time that people are willing to wait for each page is about 12 seconds, and even that seems generous). Examples of teletext are Ceefax, Request and Oracle. Teletext is one area where cable television gives a far better service, provided an entire channel is dedicated to it.

Viewdata is different from teletext in that it is 'interactive' or two-way, so users can send information through it as well as receiving information. It is also, fortunately, faster in operation than most teletext systems and can handle a larger database. Originally, the link between the user and the provider of the service was the public telephone system, though now it may also be private lines, leased circuits, optical fibre linkages or cable television. Viewdata has been adapted for a number of purposes commercially, such as the travel agency business and car spares business. Perhaps the easiest way of looking at the relationship between the examples of videotex is thus:

B

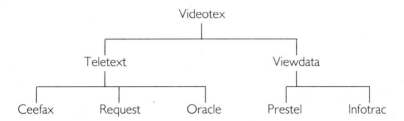

One commentator described videotex as 'computer time-sharing with enhanced graphics' – which shows either that some computer people have a sense of humour, or that standards are dropping. The graphics are not just inferior, they are appalling. This is because of the way that the pictures are built up. The screen is divided up into just 960 blocks (24 rows of 40). Each block can only be subdivided into a 2×3 sub-block for graphics (8×10 for text). Thus the pictures are bound to be very coarse, for speed of transmission. Actually, the graphics are not too bad if one stands 10 metres away and screws up one's eyes except that then one cannot read the text. The result is that graphics are tending to be dropped from the pages, leaving them with just text.

There are two other areas of possible confusion with videotex. One is that Prestel is the name of one of the viewdata services, but is also the name of a transmission standard used for many videotex systems. The second confusion is between teletext and teletex. As we have seen, teletext is the name for a family of receive-only videotex services. Teletex is completely different. It is a sort of superior telex, based on special non-telex machinery, though it can be connected to telex users. It is faster than telex (up to 40 times faster), and has more characters (lower case, as well as capitals, for example). Teletex started in Germany and was introduced to Britain in 1984. In time, it could replace telex for transmitting text. This was expected to happen within a few years of its introduction by some people. The fact that its take-up was so much slower than hoped did not surprise those of us who were the object of its advertising. One advertiser insisted on trying to blind one with science instead of emphasizing the practical advantages to users. Another manufacturer tried to ignore telex altogether and compared the system with sending letters.

On-line information services

None of us can keep our libraries or our reading of periodicals so current that we have all the information available that we could need. During a working day, we might want airline timetables and cheap ticket details, an inter-firm comparison, a look at an encyclopedia, and an investment analyst's report to help with a proposed strategy. This is just the sort of situation that can occupy a large part of one's day. The alternative is to use a database held somewhere on a large computer. If one has a modem and even a home computer, one can subscribe to an on-line information service. This is a database that is offered by a commercial organization. In use one can either just scan a regularly up-dated area of information, or one can hunt around the database looking for the facts that are wanted.

Some databases are specialized, dealing with just one area of knowledge though this will be in depth. There are over 5000 on-line databases covering about 400 specialist areas (from AIDS to coffee). However, it is not easy for the average person to get the most out of them. The databases use over 600 different systems, with different languages and searching techniques. For this reason the main use of specialized databases is by specialists in the particular area of knowledge. In practice, enquiries to such databases are not cheap.

Another group of information services is more general, though even these tend to have individual flavours by concentrating on a type of information. Different people have their own personal favourites. So computer people may like CompuServe, financial and management people will probably prefer the Dow-Jones services (which are good), while others may prefer a more general mix of services such as The Source. Most of these services charge a flat annual fee plus an hourly usage charge (one also has to pay for the time spent on the telephone, of course). Some of these services also offer an E-mail service.

■ E-MAIL

As late as 1980, the term 'electronic mail' was still being used as a generic term for a number of mailroom and messaging systems, including fax, telex and mailing and labelling machines. It is now reserved for messages that are read on a screen either from an intra-office network or, more commonly, from outside the office. The phrase is also often shortened to the term E-mail.

Vendors of E-mail services use a computer memory as a centralized 'letterbox'. Subscribers to the service compose a message on their screen. When ready they telephone the computer and send the message through their modem, quoting the code ('address') of the recipient. This recipient also has to be a subscriber (and have a modem and computer, of course). The message is held in the computer memory until the recipient, using a password, telephones the computer and downloads the messages (known as 'looking in the mailbox'). If desired, one can use the E-mail vendor to forward a message to a telex subscriber. One E-mail vendor offers to send messages anywhere in the country. This is achieved by a subscriber sending a message to the vendor who sends it by fax to a courier, who delivers it by motorbike (which sounds as though we have returned to the 'telegram').

E-mail has a number of advantages. If subscribers co-operate well with one another, it is fast. It enables peripatetic staff such as sales staff to receive messages each evening in their hotel bedroom. Messages can be sent to a large number of people very quickly and easily. An extension of this is for a person in an organization to poll a number of colleagues ('Does anyone know about this new way to make widgets?') and get helpful replies easily. Research suggests that E-mail can change office behaviour patterns. Not surprisingly, it can improve the productivity of dispersed software development teams. But it can reduce the productivity of some people, who become very 'chatty' or even addicted to its use. The system can be over-used for office gossip (and even obscenities and sexual harassment). It can also encourage isolates and lazy managers to spend too much time at their desks instead of getting out and working.

Apart from productivity questions, the main disadvantages of E-mail are not knowing when a recipient will read the message, and security. Both were combined in the case of the Duke of Edinburgh. He did not look at his E-mail for over a year and when he did it was found that a hacker had got there first. Security is always a problem on networks, of course. One concerned the electronic-mail program distributed with Berkeley Unix in 1985. A graduate student had inserted a 'trapdoor' in it by which a virus could be introduced. Although this was found by some researchers and 'shut', other Unix users did not bother. Not surprisingly, another graduate student used it and started a chain reaction. A computer sent the virus to all other computers on its mailing list. Since the first computer was on other computers' mailing list, it got the messages back, which it sent out again and so on. So soon everything seized solid.

B

■ FAX

Fax is also known as facsimile, telefax, and facsimile telegraphy. It was invented in 1842 by Alexander Bain, who used a pendulum which scanned the original. The pendulum was replaced with a photo-electric system, and commercial services using this system were available before 1910. In 1922 radio was used to send a fax from Europe to America. Faxes now operate by scanning the width of a piece of paper, detecting where the paper is blank and where marked, effectively moving down the paper and rescanning. These scans are 0.26 mm apart. The results of this scanning are transmitted over the telephone lines to a receiver. There the information is printed onto a piece of paper, thereby providing a copy of the contents of the original. Thus one gets a copy of the marks on the original, quite irrespective of what the markings were – they would be letters, numbers, drawings, anything.

Fax machines are referred to by their belonging to 'groups'. Each successive group represented an improvement on the previous models, the earliest ones being Group 1. The machines can 'talk down': a Group 2 machine can transmit to a Group 1, a Group 3 machine can transmit to machines in Groups 1 and 2. The speed of machines also increases with groups. Thus a Group 1 machine takes 6 minutes to transmit an A4 sheet of material (or 4 minutes with degradation of copy). Group 2 machines take 3 minutes. Group 3 machines take up to 1 minute. When telephone lines can handle a speed of 64,000 baud, Group 4 machines will manage it in about 5 seconds. Group 3 machines (the commonest) are usually capable of 9,600 baud, though some use 4,800 baud.

Although capable of a 9,600 baud rate, a Group 3 machine will slow down if it detects errors to as slow as 2,400 baud. This is good – except that some machines do not speed up again when the line interference stops (hence one pays more for transmission). Also, some terminals will 'confirm' a successful transmission after slowing down to 2,400 baud, even when data has in fact been lost (a fact which may be unknown to the recipient). If he knows that local lines are poor, an installation engineer may step down a 9,600 baud machine to 4,800 baud (this has been known in parts of north London and around Stansted). He is fairly safe in doing this (the buyer probably will not check) and it may save call-outs for maintenance calls.

Fax machines print out on thermal paper, or through xerographic or ink-jet printers. Thermal paper needs storing properly; the edges can 'bruise' and the sensitive side can be marked by friction (one uses this to test for sensitivity by rubbing with one's fingernail). Even within Group 3, paper sizes can vary, with the majority being 210 mm, 216 mm or 257 mm.

Like everything else, fax does have disadvantages. It cannot handle big volumes, compared with other transmission systems; a fast 20-second machine can only transmit about 1,000 pages in a day, even if one refuses to accept any incoming messages. It is not possible to get a complete directory of numbers since no compiler has any way of knowing if you have a fax, or have put a fax card in the back of your small computer, or are using a portable – the British Telecom directory is estimated to list 25–30 per cent of actual machines. Getting junk mail by post is bad enough but at least it can be thrown into the waste-basket unopened; getting junk mail by fax is more annoying, as it ties up the machine and costs the recipient for the thermal paper. Another disadvantage can be illustrated by a story. Your competitor has an eager young sales staff who are determined to beat you over a new contract. So they program their fax with your fax telephone number and send a bogus message to the customer apparently from you, as a result of which you lose the sale. If you ever find out about the fax and deny sending it, will the customer believe you with your telephone number on it?

■ LANs (LOCAL AREA NETWORKS)

The international public telephone system is the largest network in the world. More modest networks are known as WANs (wide area networks). A commercial WAN where a service is sold (such as the information services above) is a VAN (value added network), unless the service is data-oriented in which case it could be a VAD or VADS (value added data service). The other acronym in networks is LAN (local area network).

A LAN is typically contained within the offices of one organization and serves the needs of that organization alone; though it may reach out to other places such as a supplier. By definition, a LAN is private, not open to the public. A LAN connects together several small office computers (or workstations) with pieces of cable. A LAN allows one to move data (text, graphic images or voice) around between desk-top computers, workstations, a mainframe computer, other input/output devices (such as a printer) and even a data PABX. Thus a desk-top computer in a branch office might be connected to another desk-top with both sharing a large disk storage, with all being connected to the mainframe in a head office. Each component of a LAN might be a few metres apart up to a few kilometres. The advantage of a LAN is that it enables members to communicate with one another and to share a facility such as a database or a printer.

A LAN consists of pieces of hardware machinery plus

- a 'server' (software on a hard disk or hard card);
- the network 'interface' (usually on another card);
- transmission channel media (e.g. pieces of wire);
- a 'switching centre' (also known as a 'controller'), which co-ordinates and controls the network and the data flow.

There are three types of cabling ('transmission channel media') that can be used. One is 'twisted-pair wire' – the sort of wire that one uses for domestic purposes such as rigging up a front door bell. Twisted-pair is cheap, mechanically flexible (so will go round tight corners) and will transmit about 1 megabit/second – though it does not protect throughput from external EMI (electromagnetic interference). The second type of cabling is coaxial – the sort of cable ('coax') used to connect an aerial to a television set. Coax is more expensive than twisted pair, needs about 5 cm radius curves for turns but has a transmission rate about 10 times greater than twisted-pair. It is used for broadband transmissions such as video. The third type of cabling is optical fibre. This is thinner (about 3 mm) than coax but is currently still more expensive. Being a non-conductor, it is not affected by EMI nor does it radiate signals. It is popular with places like embassies which want security from snooping, and which may also use a relatively inexpensive system like 10Net.

LANs differ from one another in a number of ways:

B

1 *Shape.* It is common to describe a LAN layout shape as being a 'star', a 'ring' or a 'bus' (see Figure 14.1), though the differences are much more than a question of layout, and many LANs are a sort of mixture of the three. A star has individual computers all connected with a central switching centre, through which all data is routed. A ring LAN connects all the computers in a ring with data being passed from one to another (like the children's game of 'pass the parcel'); in turn each computer inspects the parcel of data and either uses it or passes it on. A bus LAN connects each computer to a single main cable, with the data going up the cable to a 'head-end retransmitter' which sends the data down the cable again.

2 *Categories.* LANs may be special-purpose (such as those used for factory robotics), proprietary (based on a single vendor's products) or the more common GP (general purpose, able to utilize applications software and hardware from a number of vendors). GP compatibility has been helped by a number of standards that have been agreed.

   LANs may also be categorized as being either baseband or broadband. Baseband uses ± voltage differences for the signals (something like telegraphy). Broadband is different in that it uses wave oscillations (something like television) to carry the signals.

3 *Sharing.* The members of a LAN have to share the one line for data transmission. Three methods of sharing (or 'arbitration') are token-passing ring, token-passing

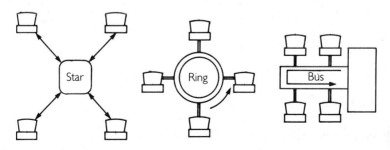

Figure 14.1 Star, ring and bus LANs

bus and CSMA (carrier-sensing multiple access). Standards for these have been set by what is known as the 802 Committee (part of the IEEE). In token-passing, a 'token' (or packet) is passed rapidly from member to member; a member can only transmit data if and when it has a token. When CSMA has collision detecting (CD) ability it becomes CSMA/CD, which is like a listening device. With CSMA/CD a member transmits a packet of data and listens for the echo from a receiver. If the echo is the same as the data sent out, then this shows that the message got through. If the echo is different, this means that another member tried to transmit at the same time and the two packets 'collided'. So, after a brief period, the transmission is repeated hoping for better luck. Generally, token passing is used in factories and CSMA/CD in offices.

LANs may sound complicated, and it is true that careful planning is needed. However, once they are in place and in use they need not be troublesome. A common error is installing a LAN when one is not needed and vice versa. For example, a LAN is often installed to share a laser printer on the grounds of cost and utilization. In such cases, a LAN may not be as good as a specialized printer or a printer server (a sort of buffer). On the other hand, a LAN may be ideal for investment analysts working on successive report drafts.

References

1 Loosely adapted from Herodotus, *The Histories*, (fifth century BC).
2 Wright, E., *History of the World: From Prehistory to the Renaissance*, Twickenham: Viscount Books, 1985.
3 Meeks, B. N., 'The wired society', *Byte*, Vol. 13, No. 8, August 1988, p. 138.

15

Automating Offices

The man whose life is devoted to paperwork has lost the initiative.
He is dealing with things that are brought to his notice, having ceased
to notice anything for himself.
C. Northcote Parkinson, *In-laws and Outlaws* (1962)

If [automation] keeps up, man will atrophy all his limbs but the push-
button finger. **Frank Lloyd Wright**, in *The New York Times* (1955)

The automated office is not attained by installing a few microcomputers, or hooking people up to an E-mail network. It goes much further than that. It is not easy to get agreement on what is meant by an automated office, but it is reasonably easy to recognize one when one works there. Most of the staff are seated in front of screens (terminals) that are connected to a mainframe computer or some form of network. They operate a keyboard (technology that may be over a century old, but we still do not have anything better). Paper is not abundant but it is not absent (what does tend to be absent is those 3 cm-thick files of computer print-out that one gets in other offices). Apart from this, the most noticeable feature is that the automated office seems just like an ordinary office. People discuss their work with their supervisor – in fact, they do most things that people in offices do. Perhaps one reason for this normality is that, since some automated offices were established by around 1980, there must be some people who have spent most or all of their working lives in automated offices.

Examples of automated offices

■ SALES OFFICE

Gillette made more money from selling blades than from his new-fangled razor. In the same way, one efficient photocopier manufacturer makes more money from selling paper than from the sales of photocopiers. The computer calculates when customers are likely to be getting low on paper stocks. This is done based on historical patterns and/or direct data (e.g. meter readings on rented equipment). The sales staff come to the office in the morning, switch on their screens, and don their lightweight earphones. The computer displays on the screen details of customers who should be contacted (e.g. types and quantities of paper usually ordered, names of contact, etc.). The number is dialled automatically and the salesperson discusses the order with the customer.

Quantities are keyed in for each 'line'. The computer can also handle any queries (e.g. stock situation on special lines). Once the order has been agreed, a single keystroke sets the rest of the process in train. The warehouse is notified, delivery runs produced, effective stocks reduced, delivery note/invoice printed, ledgers posted and the customer's history updated. The sales staff do not have to do any of this, and have meanwhile gone on to the next name on the list.

There are a number of advantages to this system. The firm sells at a cost far, far below that of a sales team making personal calls on the customers. The customers find it very convenient, and save the cost of order preparation. There is also what is known as 'added value' to the system. This is the fact that customers tend to stay with the seller rather than changing supplier. Society also gains: the system opens up opportunities to people from ethnic minorities and the physically disabled who might otherwise find it difficult to be successful in this area.

■ CONTRACT HOUSE IMPROVEMENTS

A large firm makes and sells house improvements such as double-glazing windows. This involves measuring the space for the window, preparing a contract and credit repayment details, tracking production, arranging installation dates with the customer, sending products to a depot, getting an external subcontractor to collect and install the windows, and carrying out post-installation checking. This could mean a lot of paper floating around the offices. In fact (apart from the contract), there is none. No piece of paper stays in the office for more than twenty-four hours. All information is either held on the computer (e.g. production progress) or is microfilmed (e.g. letters).

Any queries from customers (phone or letter) are answered with the help of the VDU and the microfilm reader. Ultimately it may be feasible to hold all information on a computer. This will probably have to await a technological change affecting markedly the speed/cost/quality comparison of the competing methods. The managers using the microfilm readers have acquired a remarkable facility. They flick through the letters on the reader, spending about 1.5 seconds on each letter. From this they appear able to follow the progress of even long and complex correspondence.

■ OTHER EXAMPLES

Several industries have examples of either automated offices or partially automated ones. Examples are banks (funds transfer), insurance (automobile), American newspapers (news prep) and airlines (reservations). Airline reservations are an interesting example. Just prior to automation, life was getting hectic in some of the largest offices. Some staff were reduced to using binoculars to see wall boards from their seats. Automation certainly effected large cost savings for airlines, but this is another example of 'added value' – an advantage (often unforeseen) over and above the cost saving of automation.

Added value

Two computer reservation systems (CRS) came to account for over 60 per cent of all terminals used by American travel agents.[1] An advantage of owning a large CRS is that it enables one to see quickly where people want to fly and how much they will pay. It transpired that the ability to fine tune fares and schedules was even more important for profits than maximizing seat occupancy rates; airlines had underestimated the effects of marginal pricing.

So 'added value' can be a major bonus of automating offices. However, this has led some analysts to concentrate on possible added value when trying to promote automation, even when (perhaps one should say, particularly when) cost savings prove elusive.

We are not in favour of justifying automation on added-value grounds (especially when these grounds are nebulous and unquantified) if automation is clearly not cost-effective. Some anticipated added values have proved an illusion while some of the most favourable have been serendipitous.

Automated offices and health

The widespread use of VDU screens in automated offices has led people to express concern about the effect that such screens (and other equipment) may have on the health of office staff. There has been considerable research in this area; indeed, few work environments have been the subject of as much research. The results of this research have not been entirely conclusive. Few harmful effects have been isolated but nagging doubts remain in many people's minds.

B

Screens were studied in depth in 1977 in America by the National Institute for Occupational Safety and Health (NIOSH). The NIOSH studied levels of emission of X-ray, ultraviolet, infra-red and radio frequencies, and found all were far below acceptable limits.[2] This is good news for those who watch television or play electronic games for hours on end. Nevertheless, some people (remembering problems with faulty microwave ovens) are still concerned about faulty screens. One group of people who can be affected adversely are those epileptics who can suffer from the visual effect of moving striped bars or patterns.[3] This effect has long been known about in industry, but it is possible that as many as 1 in every 30,000 people may be affected in this way by VDUs. If epileptics work on VDUs, possible epileptogenic effects can be reduced by their working only with small screens, by avoiding scrolling, and by turning down the brilliance and contrast controls.

Some of the problems that are associated with automated offices are, more strictly, attributes of all offices. Sedentary life needs certain precautions: proper seating, working surfaces at the correct height, good lighting and so on. Other problems are less easy to deal with. In one country, we were told by different people that electronic equipment caused teeth to blacken and gave one a tendency to have 'flu'. In Australia, we were told about 'RSI' (repetitive strain injury) which was caused by continual use of keyboards. Nobody else seemed to suffer from this until a few years later it was talked about in England (in the late 1980s it was prevalent in British newspaper offices). Does RSI exist? The sufferers are adamant that it does. But if it does, how can data prep staff do their 14,000 key depressions per hour, year in year out, without getting it? If it does not, why do tennis professionals suffer from the similar 'tennis elbow'? It is very difficult to be dogmatic one way or another. Some studies suggest that a contributory cause may be psychological in nature. It is true that even respected staff may feel that their pre-eminence is less certain if new skills have to be learnt, which could lead to a change in pre-eminence.[4] On the other hand, a researcher has pointed out that offices are on the whole good environments in which to work.[5] It is not always easy to fathom the human body. For example, organophosphate pesticides are held to be dangerous because they block the enzyme cholinesterase – but potatoes have high levels of solanine and chaconine, which do the same thing. Celery is even worse, containing psoralens, which are carconogenic when exposed to light (celery pickers often develop a rash on their arms).[6] But we have survived years of eating potatoes. In the face of the uncertain evidence, about all that can be said is:

- offices tend to be reasonably healthy environments;
- ergonometric considerations should be followed;
- keep an eye on any research studies;
- take all reasonable precautions.

Concerning the last point, some organizations have decided to limit the amount of time that can be spent working at a screen without a break to a maximum of four hours.

Problems of OA installation

The problems actually experienced by organizations that automate their offices are very different from those predicted by outsiders years ago. In particular, prognostications made by social scientists in the early 1970s now read strangely wide of the mark. Problems encountered in practice include:

- inadequate planning and investigation;
- technology (hardware and software);
- financial;
- human.

■ INADEQUATE PLANNING AND INVESTIGATION

Management consultants are notorious for wanting planning and setting of objectives. Perhaps sometimes they overdo this. But when automating offices, inadequate preparation really is tempting the fates to cause chaos.

■ TECHNOLOGY

'Techies' are fond of proclaiming that all the technology one needs already exists. This claim ignores certain facts:

- some manufacturers have distinct gaps in their product line, and will have to blur this fact when assembling a proposal;
- some manufacturers approach office automation by building on a particular mechanical strength (e.g. word processors or PABX) and this may not be the best approach for the organization;
- the use of networks brings other problem areas, especially if these extend outside the organization's own offices. These can include reliability, compatibility, service, back-up, and the major headache of security;
- counting software as part of technology, one has the usual problems of lack of robustness, hidden bugs, poor documentation, packages v. custom, gaps in suites, speed v. user-friendliness, and proper trails for control and audit.

■ FINANCIAL

Actual cost savings resulting from office automation have on occasions proved less than anticipated. This can be due to underestimating purchase and installation costs. It can also be due to using total or lifetime costs post-installation, but having omitted to do so during pre-installation enthusiasm. It is even possible for office automation to increase running costs. One organization had (pre-installation) 100 secretaries and 600 professionals and managers. After installation only 40 secretaries were needed but 900 others – partly resulting from managers doing work previously done by secretaries. This process is known as 'putting $60,000 bottoms onto $25,000 seats'.

■ HUMAN

Many successful office automation introductions have been achieved while avoiding some of the forecast troubles. This should not lead to complacency or carelessness. When automating offices, attention must be made to the same areas as with all change:

- hold consultations with the staff at all stages;
- ensure that, before making changes, the work that people do is fully known and understood;
- be aware of changes in personal pre-eminence;
- take care of ergonomic factors;
- ensure that staff are fully trained;
- check that changes will not put extra strain on the staff.

B

On the last point, an office supervisor was heard making the heartfelt plea, 'Please don't give us any more help from the computer – we have enough work already.' Automated offices do bring their own specific considerations. One is 'structured communications'. For example, staff in the field may be required to telephone in with data for inputting. This may entail relating strings of numbers interspersed with short set phrases. This process may need 'humanizing' to avoid conflict between field and office. In the same way, members of the public will in some proportion not be able to quote their 'reference number'. Another feature of automated offices is the question of checking outputs for reasonableness. Staff in a computer department can check mainframe output for reasonableness. This is not so easy when outputs are fed directly to screens on many staff desks. These staff have to be shown how to watch output for reasonableness without losing their faith in the overall system.

Strategies and tactics

The two best reasons for automating offices are:

- improving effectiveness (e.g. reducing costs);
- gaining a competitive edge.

There are a number of poor reasons. These include:

- installing automation because it is technologically possible (the technology-driven route to change);
- because present systems are in a mess (automating rubbish does not stop it from being rubbish);
- out of a cloudy desire to have a paperless office (in the wrong circumstances, a paperless office is as appropriate as the paperless toilet).

This means that in considering strategy, there are times when one has to think in terms of overall corporate strategy, while at other times it may be enough to consider the automation strategy in more isolation.

A complete corporate strategy approach is outside our present scope. It is, however, worth reminding ourselves of the steps involved. Using the mnemonic 'STRATOS', the steps are:

S – Set up the strategic team;
  State the objectives and resources;
  Set a time for completion;
T – Train the team;
R – Research the industry in which the organization competes;
  Research one's competitive advantages and disadvantages;
A – Analyse current and potential competitors;
T – Test the organization's competitive situation;
  Think through alternative routes to improvement;
O – Opt for the best alternative route to improvement;
  Optimize this best route;
  Organize an action plan;
S – Start the action plan.

The mnemonic used for a strategic approach to automating offices is 'PINPOINT':

P – Plan the plan;
I – Investigate the work (what is done and what should be done);
N – Nominate the alternatives;
P – Protect the organization;
O – Opt for the preferred alternative;
I – Inaugurate this alternative;
N – Navigate the installation;
T – Turbocharge the changes.

P – Plan the plan

Automating offices is not a quick matter. The process takes over a year in about 50 per cent of instances, while in the case of the other 50 per cent that take under a year, many wish that they had taken longer. A book that explores the experiences of users[7] puts planning this way: 'Plan carefully, plan thoroughly. The literature of office automation can't say it enough. Consultants preach it. Many a battle-scarred manager who 'brought OA in' knowingly confirms it.'

Although circumstances may vary such a plan, it is likely to cover the following aspects:

- setting up a strategic team. Apart from smaller offices, a team approach appears to be followed by most successful installations. This team is likely to include representatives from the various functions, a mix of generalists and specialists, and a generalist jack-of-all-trades as leader. External management consultants may also be involved (in about 30–40 per cent of cases);
- early agreement on the objectives of the team and a timetable;
- arrangements for training for those team members who need it;
- a statement on how people aspects will be handled;
- a brief description of how detailed the initial proposal will be (e.g. will it cover office layout, will it contain a short list of alternatives and possible suppliers?);
- an agreement on how the office automation must fit in with overall corporate strategy.

This last point should not be over-detailed or over-specific; more in the nature of signposts for the future.

I – Investigate the work

Investigating the work will normally follow the lines of the ICICLES approach (see chapter 23 for details). It is particularly important to cover the interfaces between departments, and between the organization and its customers. When moving from 'what is done' to 'what should be done' it is very easy to get bogged down, with the danger that individual functions may start to get territorial and overprotective. Luckily, the fairly low cost of computer memory means that it is possible to be reasonably indulgent about allowing functions to retain those extras that they would feel uncomfortable without.

N – Nominate the alternatives

B

In most instances, there are not just a few alternatives but there are different types of alternatives:

1 The first group of alternatives concerns the equipment and the software that is already in place (e.g. word processors and ledgers). The alternatives are likely to include leaving some areas unchanged, incorporating them into a new overall system, and replacing them completely or partially changed.

2 The second group of alternatives concerns the approach to implementation. This can be the 'big bang' (making all changes in one step), installing an initial stage while leaving future steps open, or planning all phases of the change but starting with just the initial phase. The methods of implementing can also vary between:

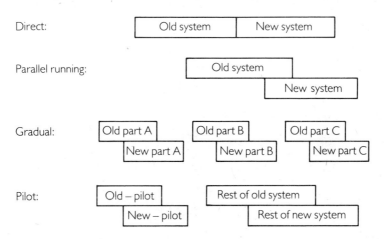

3 Hardware/software choice. There may be alternatives in the type of hardware to be used. For example, it may be possible either to base the automation on a mainframe with linked screens or to use smaller processors in individual functions. For software, there is nearly always the choice of using ready-made packages or having custom-made programs, or a mix of both.

4 Finally, there is the need to consider more than one supplier.

In practice, the alternatives are not as complex as this may make it appear. This is because the alternatives are to some degree intermixed. Thus, a particular supplier may make a proposal dependent upon a specific type of hardware, while a 'big-bang' installation is by definition usually a direct conversion (referred to as 'betting your company').

P – Protect the organization

It is clearly important that a new system will cover all the work done under the old system (e.g. setting reorder levels for raw material stocks). So some checking is called for: how much checking, and precisely when it is done depends on circumstances. Thus some checks may be indicated when looking at alternatives while others will wait until a specific alternative has been decided upon. 'Protection' is effected by:

- systems acuity; and
- systems affirmation.

Broadly, 'systems acuity' is concerned with making sure that the system is sharp. That is, the right degree of user friendliness/speed, the flexibility, and the capacity for upgrading and enhancements and enlarging. 'Systems affirmation' is making sure that a new system will fulfil the needs of users. This involves going through the old and new systems with users, ensuring that no sub-systems have been ignored.

O – Opt for the preferred alternative

Sometimes there is one alternative that is so outstandingly 'right' that it quickly gains agreement. At other times, there can be considerable division of opinion. It is at this stage that one of the biggest problems can arise. This is what is known as 'turf battles'. Office automation can change the delicate organizational relationship between functions or departments. If members of a group feel that their status or professionalism is in any way threatened, then they will fight to maintain the status quo. Resolution of this conflict may be a two-stage affair. First the study team will have to investigate the feelings aroused and see if a peaceful solution is possible. If not, it may be necessary for senior management to intervene.

I – Inaugurate the preferred alternative

Having decided on the preferred route, a supplier has to be selected. Vendors are neither devils nor angels. Their task is to persuade one to buy their product. The buyer's task is to obtain the right equipment at the best terms. The stages to a mutually satisfactory conclusion are:

- the buyer issues a formal request to potential vendors for them to prepare a proposal. This request will include some outline data, such as scope foreseen and an indication of volumes involved;
- the vendors carry out surveys of the situation and discuss the office workings with the buyer;
- the vendors submit their proposals for office automation. It is not unusual for these to suggest changes to the original buyer's concept. These proposals should be copied and distributed to a number of selected staff: a mix of senior managers, specialists and the original study team. These recipients should study the proposals individually before holding group discussions;

- the buyer asks two or three vendors for references and visits to two similar completed installations. The buyer also asks for a copy of the vendors' standard contract. The visits are completed and further discussions by the buyer's staff held;
- negotiations are held with the vendors' representatives on the proposed contract terms. Points that need clarification or amendment will depend on circumstances; these may be firmness of delivery date, length of maintenance guarantees and 'consequent damages' clauses (by which the vendor wishes to reduce liability to the cost of goods supplied). Since 1988 vendors' contracts tend to have contained a number of disclaimers, waivers and provisos which the buyer's lawyers may have to check;
- having reached agreement with a vendor on the installation, price, terms and conditions (and having had one's lawyer give the contract the green light), one can sign the contract. There may be times when a 'second-best' choice is indicated because of some difficulties with the 'first-best' terms and conditions. It has been observed that this can involve a definite exercise of will-power;
- preparations can now go ahead with the installation itself. This will include cabling installation, training of the staff, preparing the new office layout, building up new database(s), and transferring data.

The reason for mentioning the date 1988 above concerns a company called Geophysical Systems. This company went bankrupt in 1983. For this, it blamed its hardware and software. It took the vendor to court and five years later the court awarded it $48 million. This encouraged even more software companies to use the 'consequent damages' clauses referred to. Although the courts may give one some protection, this may not be so if a restrictive contract is signed: 'Businesses cannot claim that they were hoodwinked into signing away their right to legal redress.'[8]

N – Navigate the installation.

T – Turbocharge the changes.
} These aspects are covered in chapter 38.

Office automation is not confined to large offices; the benefits can be enjoyed by small offices as well. For example, a hop merchant firm had 7 directors and 17 staff. It acted for 100 brewers and 150 growers, covering 20 varieties of hop. A major problem occurred during a 10-week period each year, during which time all contracts were made, involving 100,000 entries in the books. Valuations, billing and delivery were all pressures, as were the continual risk of over- or under-commitment, the harvest and hop quotas. A medium-size office computer was installed with screens to work from. The result was a staff reduction of five people. The added value was a reduction in unsatisfied demand of 40 per cent.

References
1 'Happiness is a cheap seat', *The Economist*, Vol. 310, No. 7588, 4 February, 1989, p. 70.
2 Moss, C. E. *et al.*, *A Report on Electromagnetic Radiation Surveys of Video Display Terminals*, National Institute of Occupational Safety and Health, 1977.
3 Wilkins, A. J., *Epileptogenic Attributes of TV and VDUs*, presented at a seminar of the Ergonomics Society, 15 December, 1978.
4 Lawler, E., 'Control systems in organizations', *Handbook of Industrial and Organizational Psychology*, Chicago: Rand-McNally, 1976.

5 BBC World Service, 9 February, 1989.
6 Ames, B. (Chairman of the Biochemistry Department at the University of California at Berkeley) in a paper presented at the 1988 annual meeting of the American Society for the Advancement of Science.
7 Kleinschrod, W. A., *Strategies for Office Automation*, Willow Grove: Administrative Management Society Foundation, 1985.
8 'Suing for bugs', *The Economist*, Vol. 310, No. 7584, 7 January, 1989, p. 63.

16

Office Machinery

The moment man cast off his age-long belief in magic, Science
bestowed upon him the blessings of the Electric Current.
                              Jean Giraudoux, *The Enchanted* (1933)

Man is a tool-using animal. Nowhere do you find him without tools;
without tools he is nothing, with tools he is all.
                              Thomas Carlyle, *Sartor Resartus* (1834)

B

The widespread introduction of the computer brought with it two temptations. One was to think that all office work must be performed electronically. The second was to divide all office equipment into two streams, the first being 'information technology' and the other being boring old-fashioned stuff that was not worth learning about. This split was emphasized by the popular press and by certain politicians who could embarrass the pants off one by making speeches displaying an awe-inspiring ignorance.

This split of advanced technology/other equipment was even carried over into some books. These would be about administration but would have a chapter on semiconductor technology, apparently added as an afterthought, while the rest of the book would ignore electronics completely. The truth is that if we wish to perform a task, we should select the best method to do it – which will often be a mix of advanced technology and quill pens. This book is at least a partial advance in that it integrates old and new technology in many places. It does have a section on advanced technology so it is not completely integrated, and it would be nice if this could be the last non-integrated book about administration. After half a century, we should be able to take a more urbane view of electronics.

The other difficulty with office machinery is deciding how detailed one's knowledge about it should be. Most office staff have used a photocopier; one lays the original on a sheet of glass and presses a button. But how much more does an investigator need to know? In practice staff, employers and clients expect one to know quite a lot more, even to being able to recommend a specific shortlist of machines for a particular situation. One will also be expected to know the smart ways to use the equipment. It is even possible that one is expected to be able to repair it in an emergency (in such cases, one can plead pressure of work or claim that this would invalidate the guarantee).

Every new investigator is faced with this somewhat lengthy process of gaining knowledge and experience. There are several paths to this:

- take time to really know the equipment that is used in the offices around one. Talk to the staff who use it – they know the disadvantages, the reliability, the standard of servicing, the short-cuts, the smart tricks, and the 'if-onlys';
- take the free-issue monthly magazines that are published about office equipment (there are several of these). This will help to keep one up to date on currently available machines, though one has to learn to winnow out the advertising hype;
- talk to colleagues. Make contacts with other organizations: join (or start) a local group;

- join a professional institute such as the Institute of Administrative Management. Then join one or more of their specialist groups and go to the meetings;
- buy a few books (though look through them first to check if they will really help);
- persuade your employer to subscribe to a consumer magazine that deals with office machinery (in Britain there is *What to Buy for Business*.) Some people dislike their writing style, but it is worth ignoring this to gain the value of the publication which lies in the printing of users' experiences with specific machines. (Non-UK analysts will probably find the postal charges too steep to make a subscription worthwhile.)

One of the most valuable paths is to build up a 'library' or file of information about office machinery. Into this will go notes, cuttings, magazine articles, sales literature, contacts, etc. To get value from this collection, two things must be done. First, always write the date on each item ('4/1990'). Second, set the collection up in a logical format.

For a format to be logical, it needs to follow a clear shred-out. The first level of this could be:

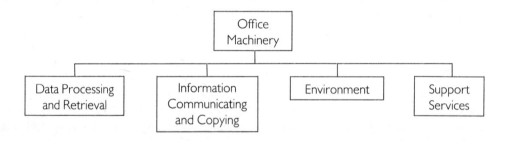

An example of a format that has been introduced into a number of organizations is given in Figures 16.1–16.4 (the items in lower-case can be varied depending on circumstances). This shred-out then provides the basis for a simple numbering system. For example, to hold the entire collection in forty parts, the numbering would be:

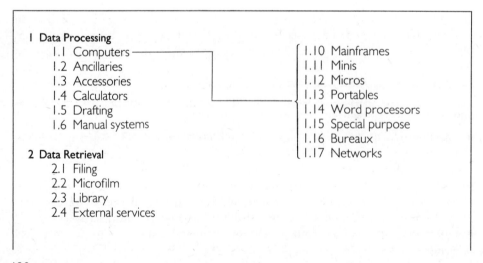

3 Information Communicating and Copying

Communicating
3.1 Physical
3.2 Pictorial
3.3 Data
3.4 Sound

Copying
3.6 Printing
3.7 Typing
3.8 Photocopying
3.9 Copy media

4 Environment – Building and Furniture
4.1 Power
4.2 Flooring
4.3 Partitions
4.4 Decorations
4.6 Furniture
4.7 Working surfaces

5 Environment – Other
5.1 Lighting and Heating
5.2 Sound
5.3 Air conditioning and Static
5.5 Commissariat
5.7 Maintenance
5.8 Office cleaning

6 Support Services – Security
6.1 Physical
6.2 Alarms
6.3 Fire
6.4 Protection

7 Support Services – Other
7.1 Stationery
7.2 Small equipment
7.3 Training
7.5 Medical
7.7 Mail room
7.8 Sports, etc.

B

This numbering can then be used in the refinement of a cross-index thus:

Acoustic screens	5.22
Acoustic couplers	1.22
Acoustic covers	5.23
Automated trolleys	3.13
Binding machines	7.56
.	
.	
.	
Flexible hours systems	6.15
Floppy disks	1.31

The files need keeping up to date, with details of new machines added and old ones discarded. This can be done by reading the magazines. Many manufacturers give advance details which tend to be printed well in advance of the actual advertising campaigns. Fortunately, examples of genuinely revolutionary new technology are rare and are signalled before their introduction. More common is incremental improvement in design.

Moreover, it does take a long time for new technology to reach the market place from the drawing board. The Xerox photocopier took fifteen years (from 1935 to 1950), though part of this delay was because no firm could be found to make and sell such a 'luxury' device. Fluorescent lighting took even longer – thirty years (from 1901 to 1934). A *Punch* cartoon in the 1920s showed the use of a video-telephone (which it was assumed would pre-date television because more people would want it first).

So one should not be afraid of technology and its onward march. Remember, canned food was invented and sold long before the can opener. One should also be wary of

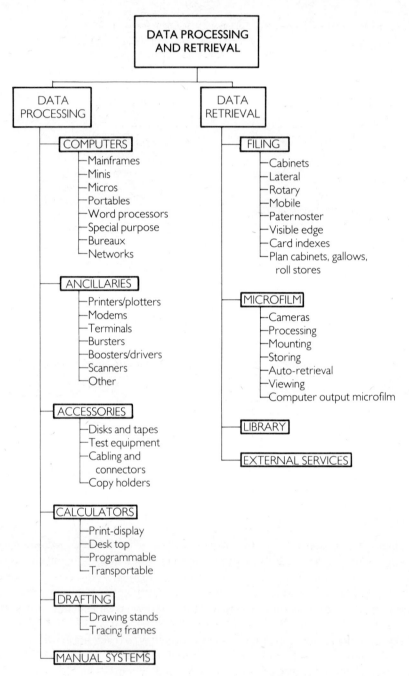

Figure 16.1 Office machinery – data processing and retrieval

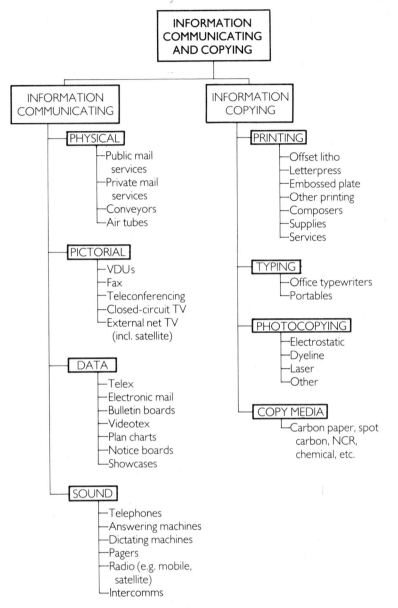

Figure 16.2 Office machinery – communicating and copying

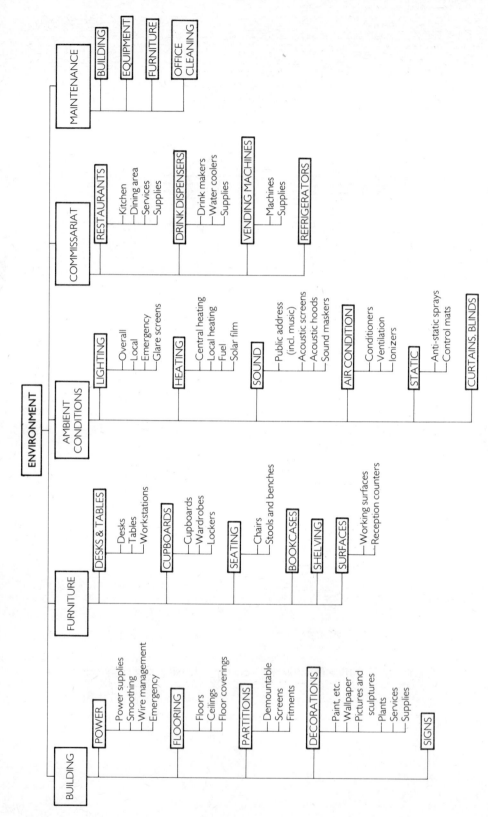

Figure 16.3 Office machinery – environment

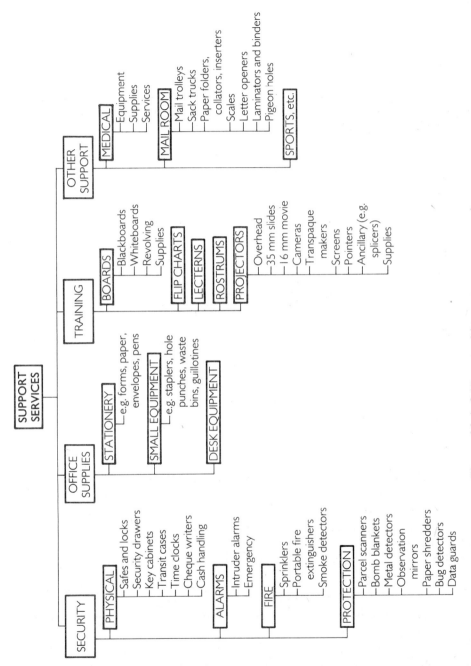

Figure 16.4 Office machinery – support services

B

133

using anything that is really new. Pioneers often have to pay the price of impulsiveness, which is why one sometimes sees on the walls of investigators the well-known notice that goes:

> **If it's new, it will let you down –**
> **If it works, it's obsolete.**

One must also watch new machines to make sure that they are actually advantageous. A new photocopier produced copies with enormous margins all round from an A4 original because it used a standard roll of paper instead of A4 sheets. When asked about this, the salesman said that this was a new unique feature – one could write one's comments in the 'generous' margins! And several manufacturers put coloured toner into an electrostatic copier and called the result a colour copier.

Details of many office machines are covered in the relevant parts of this book. Computers, etcs., are in this section (Part B); files and microfilm are in Filing and Finding (chapter 29); printing is in Forms and Paper (chapter 30). Some details of other machinery are included here, below.

Word processors ('1.14')

The early word processors were what would now be called automatic typewriters. Their main use was the utilization of standard paragraphs in letters, reports and contracts. In practical terms, people such as a lawyer or a sales manager would have a record of the standard paragraphs each of which would have a number. For correspondence, the writer would telephone the word processing pool and read out the numbers together with the name and address of the recipient. Such a system had considerable advantages over the previous shorthand-typing approach. It was not necessary to read the letters to check for typing errors. The whole process was quick. An organization knew that letters were well written because the standard paragraphs were vetted before loading.

As an example, Unilever in the 1950s used this type of system in the public relations field for replying to public enquiries for visits to their factories. It was only necessary to insert the person's name and the relevant dates. It was also possible to 'mail-merge'; that is, to send out standard letters to a list of people whose names and addresses were held separately.

Modern word processors can do a lot more than they could in the 1950s:

- editing. This is adding, removing, altering or moving the position of words, phrases, paragraphs or chunks of text at will;
- automatic numbering of pages, sections of text and paragraphs and their subsequent renumbering for revisions. Automatic collection and printing of footnotes and textual references;
- automatic indexing of key words so that the index will include cross-references as well as page numbers;
- right-hand justification of text; margin and top-and-tail adjustments; mixing single and double spacing; mixing of typefaces;

- searching the text for a string of characters and then replacing them with another (e.g. replacing all references to IT with Information Technology);
- checking spelling automatically from a dictionary (though check how this is done before purchase. With some one has to wait to the end before use; some keep on beeping until you agree with the dictionary even if you do not want to; some cause problems if one uses a word that is not in the set dictionary);
- preparing a table of contents from the main headings.

Modern word processors continue to have the ability to repeat standard pieces of text and to mail-merge.

Some machines are advertised as 'word processors' though they are not. These are usually typewriters with some electronics and a single-line display. This enables them to offer some facilities such as right-hand justification, display and correction before printing, memory, and typeface changes. These facilities are available in battery-powered portables, which can be useful to peripatetic investigators though their life is often very short (the machines', not the investigators').

When selecting a word processor system, a number of alternatives are available. Firstly, one has to decide what facilities are needed. Some word processors are particularly suitable for writing books and major reports, others for work involving the extensive use of scientific and mathematical symbols, others for general small office work. The answer is not to buy a system with absolutely every facility in the impression that one can just ignore the parts that one will not need. Complex systems take a long time to learn, which reduces staff flexibility to a degree that may be unacceptable in efficient offices.

It is also necessary to decide what type of configuration will be purchased. Some of the alternatives are:

- machinery that is dedicated to word processing or a general-purpose machine that can be used for word processing by the addition of suitable software;
- one or more completely self-contained machines that can be used without any additional machinery (known as 'stand-alone');
- some systems have several workstations (each one being a keyboard plus microprocessor plus storage with or without a display screen). These workstations all share a single printer. One of the processors controls the work going to the printer, switching from one keyboard to another, so it needs really first-rate programming. This type of system is known as a 'shared resource system';
- in the case of a typing pool or other departments with a heavy workload it is normal to use a single higher-capacity processor and storage to serve a number of keyboards plus screens. This is known as a 'shared logic system'. These systems may use one or more printers all controlled via the single central processor;
- where offices are dispersed and typing is not to be concentrated all in one pool, typists can have individual keyboards without screens. These keyboards can be intermittently connected to a central processor and printer(s). These systems ('linked logic') are useful where typing of correspondence and major reports is needed within the same keyboard workloads;
- linkages may be needed to other machinery. For example the word processing machines may be linked to a separate computer so that data can be transferred ('imported') or to a teletype machine for telex use. An international record company used this method to facilitate communications with its many overseas subsidiaries.

B

It is normal to have a mix of facilities within the one organization. There is no point in straining to put all one's work into a large typing pool if this leads to delays in despatching correspondence, creates chaos in the stores or brings the entire place to a halt when the main processor fails. Indeed, the skill of a good investigator working in a large organization often lies in creating the right mix more than in knowing precise details of a shared logic system. An international oil company had a Cray giant, an IBM computer, several linked systems, several shared logic systems, stand-alones, plus some manual typewriters. And it was pleased with the result.

Purchasing word processing equipment follows the usual rules for buying machinery, with some additional points of emphasis:

1 The precise systems and procedures that will be put into effect must be thought through carefully. Who will do what typing where? If a pool is to be set up, how and when will the work be collected and distributed? What level of service will be promised? What are the back-up facilities?

2 What is the true workload to be handled and what are the peaks? It is sad but true that the habit of some disorganized managers of keeping all their correspondence replies until 4.00 p.m. is not cured by word processing.

3 How will the input be prepared and what will the mix be between audio and hand-written drafts? If audio, will this be centralized over the telephone or decentralized via dictating machines? If centralized, will it be over the internal system (care with availability and loading) or over dedicated lines (expensive, especially if the pool location is constantly moved about).

4 What is the service like provided by the suppliers? This can be difficult to gauge. A large consultancy firm replaced its system with that of a brand leader. After a while, a fault developed in which envelopes were all addressed with the letter salutation (e.g. 'Dear Mr Smith') without any name and address. The supplier was, due to rapid expansion, overstretched and the people sent over a period of time to rectify the fault were unable to do so. It seemed an inordinate time before the firm could stop typing its envelopes manually.

5 How is the output to be typed/printed? One of the advantages claimed for word processors is the very high quality of output. This claim is rubbish. It all depends on the output machine. Some word processors use scant dot-matrix printers which make a mockery of the phrase 'near letter quality'. In fact, processors can be bought that use just about every type of printer or typewriter mechanism. The latter give good quality but are inevitably slow. Laser printers give good-quality output but need greater supplies and servicing and are difficult to substitute when they go wrong. If in doubt, go for good quality; users do not like poor-quality output, no matter what the reason.

The first step in a word processing study is to ask all typists to take an extra copy of everything they type, marking it with the time of day. It might be useful to ask for a lot of other information as well, but you probably will not get it over a period of time. These extra copies are collected each day and marked by the analyst with the date and name of department. For reasons of confidentiality, it is often necessary to promise to return the copies to the originators after the study. This promise should be given with good grace. Some managers may be worried about the introduction of word processing anyway because of a feared loss of confidentiality. As most investigators will know from experience, certain managers will greatly exaggerate the question of confidentiality;

however, this knowledge does not help to reduce the worry of the managers concerned. Where confidentiality is a real problem, it is often a good idea to introduce a stand-alone machine on which all confidential matter is prepared. This machine can then be located under the responsibility of a manager who is one level above that of the originators.

Having received the extra copies, the analyst inspects each one. He writes on each the work measurement time needed for typing it on a normal typewriter, by utilizing either one of the higher-level PMTS systems (see Part E) or by a simple line count. The copies are then divided into three piles:

- work which is definitely suitable for word processing (e.g. reports, standard form letters, work which would benefit from data importation or which includes simple calculations);
- work which could go onto a word processor with some advantage (e.g. lengthy letters to customers, oft-repeated correspondence);
- work which would benefit little if at all from being transferred onto a word processor (e.g. short internal memos, normal short letters).

B

By analysing the three work piles (workload, work cycles, peaks, nature of the work) and current staffing levels in the various departments, it is possible to calculate the type and numbers of word processors that are required. Word processing is normally faster than ordinary typing even in pure input terms (typing speeds are complex matters and have worried psychology researchers for half a century). Even larger savings can result from the fact that alterations and errors do not mean a retype. The total savings are a matter of considerable dispute, especially when quoted by suppliers. In our experience, the savings are in the range of 10–33 per cent, usually lying in the range of 15–20 per cent depending on circumstances. Claims much in excess of these figures should be treated with care.

One important point has to be made. Our experience, and that of other researchers, shows that the main savings result from setting up a pool rather than any other cause. It is the pool itself that really cuts costs. If therefore one's sole objective is to save money the answer is easy: set up a pool if one is considering eight or more typists/secretaries.

Physical document moves ('3.13')

The traditional method of moving documents about an office is for people to put them into an out tray from where they are removed by a messenger. The messenger takes them to the mailroom where they are sorted and then taken to the recipient. This process can be mechanized, though this mechanization is still the exception rather than the rule.

Conveyor belts that hold the documents upright (to handle different sizes) are found in offices where a number of staff work successively on a document while a customer is waiting for the finished product. They have been seen in large banks, in airline offices and in government offices dealing with legal documents. Their advantage is that they speed the processing. Their disadvantage is that they make office changes more difficult and that documents falling off the conveyor or getting stuck cause annoyance all round.

Pneumatic tubes use cylindrical carriers into which the documents are placed. The location is indicated on a dial on the carrier, after which the carrier is pushed into the tube. Compressed air pushes the carriers round the tube system. Some systems route all the carriers to a central point where they are redirected manually to the destination, while others use an automatic system for sending the carriers direct to the destination. One way of doing this is to fit the carrier with two reeds that vibrate. Different notes give combinations that correspond to the destinations. One such installation was seen where one of the reeds had failed. The carrier was merrily going round and round the system in a sort of endless loop. This amused the staff considerably, with some of the more adventurous pushing sticks into the tube to try to stop the lost carrier. Pneumatic tubes are fast. Their disadvantages are inflexibility, the difficulty of handling large material and cost (it is best if they can be installed when the building is being constructed except that at that stage one may not be able to predict the need or the best routes).

■ LIFTS

Small lifts are often used for sending documents vertically to and from the computer department and/or the central photocopying service. Some of them are an open endless conveyor (known as a 'pater noster'). Lifts are certainly time savers and can be very useful. However, like pneumatic tubes, they are better installed at the time of construction, otherwise the need to break through a series of reinforced concrete floors is an expensive and dusty business.

■ ELECTRIC TROLLEYS

Some offices are so large that they have led to the introduction of small electric trolleys. A few of these are little different from the trucks used in factories and warehouses, complete with a messenger on them. These can be useful if the sheer volume of material is massive or if the messengers have to travel between separate buildings. When used indoors, they give a sense of being unsafe though there is no proof of this. Some trolleys are automatic, travelling at about 1½ km/hour. They follow either a hidden metal wire or tape, or else a chemical applied to the floor covering (an ultraviolet emitter causes the chemical to fluoresce so that it can be detected by an optical sensor). These trolleys have never become widespread though Merrill Lynch, for example, had them at one time.

Conferencing ('3.23')

The problem of getting a number of people to travel to one place for a meeting is the usual reason given for the various conferencing methods. The main disadvantage of all conferencing methods is that they remove true personal face-to-face contact. The main methods are:

- audio;
- video – continuous;
- video – intermittent;
- computer – screen;
- computer – file-sharing.

Audio conferencing enables a number of people to talk to one another as a group via a telephone network. Participants utilize an ordinary telephone handset or, more conveniently, a hands-off amplifier attached to the telephone. This may not sound very exciting but a multinational bank uses it for 'meetings' between country managers within continents. These managers were positive about continuing the regular conferencing when asked.

Intermittent (or snapshot) video conferencing is like audio conferencing with the additional ability to transmit single frame video. Each picture takes about ten seconds to transmit and build up on the receiving screen, so it is normally used to transmit pictures of charts, documents or other graphics. The final result is less than overwhelming to most people.

Intermittent video demonstrates the problem of transmitting video: the volume of data involved. This needs either time or a wide bandwidth. This fact is still discernible with continuous video, which aims to give a picture almost as good as that seen on domestic TV receivers. This needs wideband transmission, a facility that few offices have because of cost. So an alternative has to be found. One is to transmit rather jerky pictures, one step up from intermittent video. Another alternative is for all the participants to go to a studio, but these studios only exist in major cities so can involve travel. The other alternatives are to hire a mobile studio or to set up full wide-band transmission – not cheap. Video conferencing is not widely used though it can be advantageous for public relations purposes.

B

Computer conferencing using shared screens and backed by audio facilities can be very useful when a group of managers wish to discuss financial matters. The data is shown on the screen and can be amended or processed by a computer as desired, followed by further discussion. Participants can save screen contents for their own use later.

File-sharing computer conferencing is less a true form of conferencing than like a superior form of a bulletin board. Contributions are usually made by respondents over a period of time, rather than simultaneously (though they can be made simultaneously, in which case it is still rather like a bulletin board). File-sharing conferencing facilities are often offered by value-added network systems so a variety of extra facilities may be on offer depending on the promoting company. An example is a report author 'discussing' the report with foreign colleagues.

Telex ('3.31')

Telex is a method of transmitting text over the telephone network. A unit consists of a keyboard for typing the message, a dial for making the telephone connection, a printer for receiving and recording the messages and a paper tape punch. This latter enables messages to be pre-typed and checked before transmitting at a speed that does not depend on the typing speed of the user.

Telex is old (introduced in 1932), it is slow (less than 100 words per minute) and it is noisy. Not surprisingly, its early demise and replacement by advanced technology has been long expected. But on and on it goes. This is because it works:

- it is simple to use;
- use of the 'call-back' code means that one knows that the message has got through (which is not always the case with fax or electronic mail);

- standards are agreed and implemented worldwide;
- above all, telex has a massive world-wide network which works.

This last point is important. Telex enables one to send a message to most major companies, hotels, airlines, government offices, banks, etc., in minutes at reasonable cost anywhere in the world. There are approximately 2,000,000 telex installations in 200 countries. This makes telex popular with PTTs – over 40 per cent of telexes are international and (from the UK) 80 per cent of duration.

Telex will be killed by better systems such as teletex in time. But its massive installed base will keep it going for a while yet.

Charting boards ('3.35')

The commonest charting/planning board found in offices is surely the simple one used to show when individual members of staff are going on their annual leave. Not only does this ensure that any overlapping of holiday dates is known in advance but it ensures that nobody forgets to take their holiday. This demonstrates the use of planning and charting boards: they provide a clear visual display and result in action being taken at the correct time.

Common types of board are:

- *simple plastic-covered sheets* that can be written or drawn on and changed. Examples are the holiday chart or office output charts when in competition with other offices;
- *perforated pegboards and panels and slotted panels* that take strips. Sample use: sales campaign progress;
- self-adhesive magnetic or plastic shapes. Sample use: office layouts or staff training;
- *card racks and pocket systems*. Sample use: production control.

Use of planning boards is limited only by the user's imagination. It is possible to go too far: a local government office was observed with a separate 'planning room' for management information. All four walls were covered with planning boards which were one person's full-time job to maintain. This room was shown off with pride – though not a single manager was seen ever going into the room.

Telephones ('3.41')

Most of us have something of a love-hate relationship with the telephone. On the one hand it is most annoying to be interrupted by a phone call just at the most inconvenient moment. On the other hand, it is most convenient to be able to phone other people – at moments which may be most inconvenient for them. Letters and telexes may stay unread for days, electronic mail may not be consulted for months, but the telephone is answered quickly and gives immediate feedback. Moreover, telephone conversations can transmit fine gradations of meaning, exchange information two-way and impart a measure of personality. This can be carried out between any two points in what has been called the biggest machine in the world.

This size can be deceptive. There are millions of telephones in the world, but most of them are concentrated in North America and Europe. Even there the penetration is uneven. The Swedes have virtually 100 phones for every 100 inhabitants. The Soviet Union had only 9 per 100 when it announced its giant expansion in the five-year plan in the 1980s (at the time Moscow had a waiting list for installations of 200,000 and it took four years to get one installed). Even this level was far above those attained in many parts of Africa and Asia where telephones are still very scarce.

This uneven spread may be emphasized by new technology rather than the opposite. Industrialized countries are updating their phone systems through digitalization and optical fibres. This will enable facilities to be introduced. This will be fine for medium-sized organizations that only communicate within narrow boundaries. The problem will still remain of what is known as the 'Burundi' factor. This is the fact that many countries will fall severely behind in this updating, thus making many enhancements internationally of less consequence.

When purchasing telephones for a small office, the two main measures are:

● *number of extensions* (the number of telephone handsets in the organization with direct access to the private exchange);
● *number of lines* (decided by the number of simultaneous calls in and out).

B

Things get noticeably more complicated as the size of organization increases. Most organizations above the very minimal size will have a PABX (private automatic branch exchange). This enables internal and outgoing calls to be made direct, with the caller dialling the desired number, needing a human operator for routing incoming calls only. Some private exchanges are very basic, only handling the telephone calls. Others are computers in effect and can offer a wide range of facilities, some of them having little to do with telephones as normally understood (e.g. listing, in conjunction with a metal-striped card, who has passed through specific doors).

A survey suggested that the life of a PABX is less than ten years, on average. This is not due to low reliability (though this has still to be watched) but to organizations availing themselves of updated facilities, whether because of digitalization, new manufacturers entering the market and offering new add-ons, or firms using their exchanges as part of their office mechanization. Large organizations have VDU screens attached to their exchanges showing the current situation such as loading (calls in and out). When considering the purchase of a PABX, one has to consider the level of traffic, the type of network to be used, reliability and the non-telephone aspects to be incorporated. This will involve a lot of planning. It can also involve a degree of knowledge of the equipment available, what it will do, and what one would like to do if only one knew what is possible. Major PABXs can benefit from the help of one of the specialist consultancies in this area. The price of buying the wrong PABX is rarely disaster, but it can certainly be a considerable sub-optimization which later makes one kick oneself.

Small and medium-size organizations that are not yet large enough for a sophisticated PABX might consider buying a key telephone system (KTS). This is a small electronic handset which can provide a number of facilities such as phones, extensions, networking and private circuits. KTS machines are sometimes known as SCRAP systems, from the authorization for Small Call Routing Apparatus. The life of a KTS should not be assumed as being longer than 5–10 years but this is long enough to see if the organization is growing sufficiently to warrant a full PABX.

When considering the purchase of a PABX, some of the possible additional areas to be taken into account include:

- *private networks*. These are lines between buildings, towns, etc. that are owned or leased by a firm and which are not part of the public network;
- *customer-premises equipment (CPE)*. This is anything that one buys and attaches to the network. Examples of CPE are fax, answering machines, modems and multiplexers;
- *value added networks (VAN)*. A VAN provider adds something to the basic service of transmission and switching and sells it to the telephone user. Examples are the databases available to subscribers, electronic mail and packet switching;
- *videotext systems* (which allow pictures and text to be sent along the phone lines).

Radiotelephones enable one to use the telephone without the need for a connecting wire. This is the principle for garden telephones and for cellular radio, which allows one to have a mobile telephone or fax in one's car.

The very ubiquitousness of the telephone can lead to difficulties. In Britain, an audio-conferencing service was abandoned after it was found to be resulting in children building up massive bills – and the offering of illegal sexual services. In the USA, the Federal Communications Commission tried to battle the dial-a-porn sellers without contravening the civil rights of citizens (one 16-year-old made 280 dial-a-porn calls after which he needed psychiatric treatment).[1]

Dictating machines ('3.43')

Early dictating machines were eponymously referred to as 'Dictaphones' – the Dictaphone was invented by Thomas Edison in 1877 as a sort of by-product of the gramophone. Later ones used a plastic belt but the recording medium is now normally magnetic, with a few using electronics (piano-wire steel was used from 1903, magnetic tape from 1927). The tape recorder was invented in 1899 and was called the 'telegraphone' since it was designed for use in recording telephone messages. Modern dictating machines are miniaturized tape recorders.

Dictating machines fall into several classes:

- office machines that normally use tape in a cassette that can be replayed on a machine for transcription by a typist;
- portable machines that are battery operated;
- machines used in a central typing/word processing pool and which can be accessed by users, normally via the internal telephone network.

Points to be kept in mind when purchasing dictating machines are:

- compatibility between an organization's machines;
- the quality of sound reproduction required;
- the length of recording times to be used;
- requirements for portability and mailing recordings for some, though probably not all, machines;
- servicing and reliability;
- the method of utilization (especially for pool use);
- the system used by the machines for separating and locating different items recorded.

When buying equipment, a major payback comes not from the equipment itself but from training users in the proper use of it. People like to think that they know by instinct how to use dictating machines – a belief that is strongly denied by the people who have to transcribe the results. Efforts should therefore always be made to persuade users to undertake some training; the ultimate persuasion may be to get users to listen to their output.

Pocket pagers ('3.44')

The term 'pocket pagers' or 'personal pagers' is reserved for personal contact by means of a receiver kept in the pocket and which is meant for a specific locality. It therefore excludes radio microphones (used for conferences), radiotelephones (used off site) and 'walkie-talkie' transceivers (also used off site).

Compared with most other technology used in the office, pocket pagers are quite new: the world's first was installed in 1956 in St Thomas's Hospital, London. There are two types of equipment. One is based on a radio transmitter, the other on an induction loop – a loop of wire that encircles the site and which carries the signals. In offices, the induction loop is the commoner, firstly because it is more secure, since radio cannot be prevented from being heard off-site, secondly because modern offices cause interference to and from radio waves.

When purchasing pocket pagers, the basic decision that has to be made is which style of pager would be the most appropriate:

- signal pagers are the simplest. In use they indicate to the recipient that there is a message or that contact is needed. This is indicated either by an audible bleep or (in noisy locations) a flashing light. In response, the person receiving the signal goes to the nearest internal telephone and calls the switchboard or a specific number;
- message pagers have a small window in which messages appear, such as 'phone dispensary' or 'visitor here';
- one-way speech pagers enable spoken messages to be sent to the recipient but do not permit spoken replies to be made;
- two-way speech pagers enable a conversation to be held over the equipment through a small microphone.

The other point that has to be considered is that of the battery power for the portable units. Some use long-life batteries; others use rechargeables, in which case arrangements have to be made for collecting the units, charging them overnight, and distributing them the next day. It is advisable to buy more units than one-per-person to allow for servicing and repairs, especially in high-need areas such as hospitals.

Printing machines ('3.6')

The main office printing method (offset litho) is covered in chapter 30, Forms and Paper. Other methods which may be met include:

- *spirit duplicating*. Rarely found in highly industrialized countries outside textbooks except in specialized circumstances. A master is typed or drawn using a 'transfer sheet' – rather like a piece of carbon paper using aniline dyes. Part of this dye is transferred at each pass onto special half-art paper (shiny paper). Run length is limited. Useful for its ability to print up to seven colours at each pass;

- *stencil duplicators*. So called because masters are a form of stencil cut into a thin plastic skin by a ribbonless typewriter or special tools. Some small offices still cling to this method but 'baby lithos' are almost always preferable. Stencil duplicators' history is well shown by one company – Gestetner. This company was founded in 1881. Seventy-five years later, the company had only one product – the stencil duplicator. But by the end of the 1950s, it had moved into the offset market as the sales of stencil machines tailed off;
- *addressing machines*. So called because originally they were widely used for printing addresses, etc. on invoices, letterheads and so on. The machines use embossed metal or plastic plates which impress details on the paper. The commonest use nowadays is with credit cards when impressing details onto a multi-part set. The original 'Addressograph' was invented by a J. C. Duncan of Sioux City, Iowa, in 1892;
- *letterpress*. So called because it uses relief (raised) letters made of metal which are then arranged to make words and hence text. Used in Europe since the fifteenth century, it now accounts for a quarter, say, of commercial printing at most; photographic-based systems are replacing it. Never recommended for office use.

When purchasing equipment to set up an in-house printing department, the following points should be kept in mind:

1 Skilled offset operators are a somewhat clannish, independent group. The best source is often to ask the machinery suppliers, especially the person who is actually responsible for physically setting up the machines at installation.
2 An alternative to using the skilled operator pool is to have junior office staff specially trained; however, the skilled operator can really achieve high levels of output (the machine never seems to stop).
3 It is important to decide what will be printed in-house. The more complex the work, the much more expensive the anciHary equipment becomes. There can be a temptation to buy expensive equipment for some special jobs that are not repeated very often.
4 In conurbations, the difference between commercial printers' prices and fully-costed in-house costs is usually quite low – in the 4–15 per cent area. This means that the cost justification for in-house departments will usually depend on the accounting conventions used for allocating overheads such as rent. The main justification for going in-house is often convenience, plus reduced stocks and turn-round time.
5 On the other hand, the break-even point between offset and photocopying is much lower than is generally realized. A well-organized in-house offset department can probably produce runs as short as 15–20 copies more cheaply than the office photocopier – and there are plenty of organizations that regularly use their photocopiers for that sort of run. There are even some offices where the word processor is used for short-run copying of this size.

Some organizations set up a reprographics centre to handle all copying, possibly located at a cheaper semi-suburban site. To be effective, this needs good organization of the work and a measure of self-discipline. Some firms find such self-discipline easy, others find it impossible.

One of the newer printing methods which has yet to make its mark in offices is 'remka'. This is a combination of stencil and silk-screen printing. It was invented by Polish samizdat distributors.[2]

Typewriters ('3.71')

Early typewriters were strange affairs to our eyes. Many only used capitals. Some had the paper feed under the machine, which then hid the paper from the user's view. Some had very ingenious systems of levers. But the typewriter did revolutionize the office.

The first patent for a typewriter was granted in England to H. Mill in 1714 but no details or drawing exist, so we do not know much about it except that it did not catch on. Two hundred years later, in 1829, an American patent was granted to W. Burt. This was not a great success either. The first commercially successful machine was evolved by C. Sholes and C. Glidden and was manufactured in 1873 by the Remington Firearms Company. The shift-key appeared in 1878. A portable was patented in 1892 by G. Blickensdorfer but it was not until 1909 that a commercial portable appeared. The electric typewriter was devised by J. Smathers in 1920. The first electric portable was introduced in 1957 by Smith Corona.

Machines now met in the office are:

B

- *manual.* These machines rely on the typists' fingers for their motive power. In large offices, they have been almost entirely replaced by electric machines – though a middle-aged temporary did once surprise us by insisting that we find a manual machine. They are still found in decentralized small offices such as stores and maintenance shops, where their use is infrequent. They have the ability to make up to eight copies at one typing, using thin carbon paper. In the Republic of Bosnia, a maintenance form needed twelve copies; when the typist was asked how this was possible, he proudly replied, 'German machine, but Bosnian finger.'
- *electric.* The electric typewriter may use individual characters each attached to a separate lever, but machines of this type have been largely replaced by daisywheel machines. These have the characters each mounted on the spokes of a printing wheel, which revolves to bring the desired character into position before being hit by a hammer.
- *electronic.* These machines have some facilities on a chip. Facilities usually include a memory to speed corrections or, if the memory is more than about 2 Kbytes, to print out a page of text. Many electronic machines have a small display window which allows the typist to change the text at will.
- *portable.* Portable machines may be manual, electric or electronic.

When purchasing typewriters, some points to keep in mind are:

1 What carriage width is needed? This depends on the size of paper that will be used. It should be remembered that the carriage length is greater than the width of paper that can be printed in many cases (to allow the printing head to move past the paper). Portables are usually restricted to a width of about 23 cm; non-portables are usually 28 cm wide. Others are 45 cm, 68 cm and even 90 cm wide.
2 Most office staff prefer a standardization on one machine. This has the advantage that all typed material will have a uniform appearance – so typists can help one another if there is a backlog.
3 Machines meant for domestic use will not stand up to continual office use. Buying them is a false economy.
4 Portable electronic machines are very useful for people working away from the office but their life is short. In many countries, consumables such as ribbons may be impossible to buy for a particular machine;

5 Italic typefaces may be acceptable for short letters but tend to be resented by readers of long reports.

6 The international standard for spacing is 10 or 12 characters per 25 mm horizontally, and 6/4½/3 lines per 25 mm vertically. Some machines (such as Japanese imports) differ from this. Too much variation will cause difficulties when typing pre-printed forms.

7 The display window on electronic machines is found to be very useful by most typists and even more so by originator-typists. Without it, a large memory is much less useful.

8 Daisywheels are interchangeable in the sense that the wheels can be changed. But there is too often a lack of standardization. Some manufacturers even use different wheels on different models of the same product line, which can be annoying, to put it mildly, especially as the range of prices of daisywheels is in the ratio of 5:1.

9 Most typewriters are known as 'Qwertyuiop' machines (from the first line of letters). Some machines, notably those from Germany, have a slightly different keyboard layout.

Why typewriters have their characters in the standard qwertyuiop configuration is something of a mystery. One myth is that it arose from the way printers arranged their type to print Bibles. The other myth is that an inefficient layout was deliberately chosen to slow typists down as the early machines could not cope with fast typists. Both myths seem equally unlikely.

Photocopiers ('3.8')

Photocopying machines are the best-known piece of machinery in the office, used by everybody, and so need the least introduction. Points to keep in mind when purchasing mainly concern marrying required facilities with those available, and trying to calculate how much the machinery will really cost.

The facilities on offer are almost endless as manufacturers jostle for position by offering new features. The basic ones that have to be considered when making a purchase are:

- *speed*. In general terms, the faster the machine the larger and more expensive it is. Speed thus becomes a function of workload. Big machines can achieve speeds of 100 copies/minute and up; medium-size machines clock up about 30/minute, while small machines do about 15/minute. Thus, as can be seen, photocopiers are rather slow as forms of machinery go. Surveys show that the average photocopier is used for 20 per cent of office time, which may come as a surprise to those who always seem to have to queue to get at one;

- *size of original*. The standard size of original is A4. To copy A3 means taking two copies and taping them together to make an A3 copy. For some reason, two such copies never match exactly. The alternative is to buy a machine that will copy an A3 original. (Lawyers use non-standard size paper and so need special machines.);

- *reduction and/or enlargement*. Reduction may be in a series of large steps ('memory zoom') and/or a large number of very small steps ('infinitely variable'). Reduction is very useful for charts, etc., though enlargement is much less often used. Machines offering both usually go from 50 per cent to 150 per cent copy ratios;

- *collator.* This goes on to the end of the machine and sorts the multi-copy work into sets. Useful for those machines on which multiple copies are made, instead of using an offset;
- *auto document feed.* This is useful for long runs if care is taken to remove paper clips and turn down dog-eared corners before use;
- *duplex.* This is the ability to copy onto both sides of the paper. Some machines do this at the end of the run; others can do it during the run (e.g. two pages of a book at the same time). Some machines seem to be particularly prone to static problems, which can cause the sheets to stick to one another;
- *dial copies.* The number of multi-copies required can be indicated at the start of the run. Unfortunately, some machines allow one to dial up to 99 copies which in the wrong hands is a positive nudge into inefficiency;
- *colour.* A colour photocopier should enable one to copy a colour photograph reasonably faithfully. Such machines are rare and of specialized utility. Some machines advertised as 'colour' merely enable one to copy in a colour other than black, such as yellow or turquoise. This, we feel, is a facility of dubious worth in normal circumstances;
- *exposure.* To copy coloured paper originals, it is useful to be able manually to override the automatic exposure;
- *editing.* This facility covers a number of features such as masking and centering of the image;
- *keys.* For allocating copy-making to departmental budgets, keys can be used. These are made such that the machine will not operate until an individual counter mechanism is inserted into a slot;
- *smart copiers.* Photocopying machines that can be linked automatically to other pieces of equipment, such as a fax, are called 'smart' copiers;
- *thick originals.* It is useful to be able to copy an open file or ledger or printout without having to disassemble them;
- *portability.* Some copiers are portable, mostly copying a strip 8 cm wide.

Large offices are easier to set up: they can use one large copier for bulk work, backed up by a number of smaller departmental machines.

When costing out machines, there are five aspects to be considered: cost of equipment, paper, toner, maintenance and spares. Most manufacturers offer a choice of purchase or rent (often by means of a meter charge per copy). Metering charges can become complicated. To forecast costs, one needs to have an idea of not only total workload per month but also the mix of copies per original.

Photocopying is one of the few pieces of office technology where people have become accustomed to, and expect, high quality. A high proportion of machines are capable of delivering high-quality output. Maintaining high quality over time is a function of care. Care means having somebody on the premises who understands the machine, having good maintenance and not abusing the machine. There are some countries in Eastern Europe where it is consistently almost impossible to obtain high-quality copies. This is partly a cultural difficulty ('if you can just read it, then it's OK') and also because of over-specialization – the person doing the copying is often a semi-automaton knowing nothing at all about the machine. This situation is slowly improving but one still tends to get copies of an interesting pale grey.

A few hints about photocopying:

B

1 Before using a new copier, polish the underside of the cover with silicon furniture polish and then treat it with anti-static. This helps to prevent toner build-up on the cover, makes it possible to keep it clean, and enables better positioning of originals for complex work.

2 Hunt around for copy paper. Not for the absolute cheapest, but for something cheaper than that provided by copier manufacturers. If users have become accustomed to '80 gsm' paper, try some 70 gsm paper of the same quality.

3 When looking at new machines, build up a personal test card and try it on the proposed machines. This test card is a piece of paper with a large variety of samples of possible originals. Stick on pieces of coloured paper with writing on them; write on it with different coloured pencils and ball-point pens, including blue. Remember that manufacturers' own test cards are always printed, so they will of course copy well.

4 When a selenium drum gets small marks on it, pull it out carefully and polish it very, very lightly with old-fashioned brass polish. This action makes the drum go 'blind' for a couple of minutes and so unusable. It recovers quickly, after which the copies will be much better. It must be *greatly* emphasized that only the lightest buffing action can be used – otherwise the drum will be ruined, which is expensive.

Mains supply smoothing ('4.12')

Large mainframe computers usually have a mains smoother incorporated with the original installation. Smaller equipment needs tend to be ignored. But if power dips too low for a ten thousandth of a second then theoretically a machine processing a million bits per second could lose 1,000 bits. This would be an odd event; more common is a spike, which is usually caused by switching on nearby electrical equipment. Culprits could be lifts, photocopiers, dishwashers, a computer, etc.

The simplest smoother is a mains filter and this is often used for microcomputers. This will smooth the power to an extent and filter out radio frequency interference. A useful example looks like (and can be used as) a mains extension lead. Typically, these will have four outlets, each rated at 3 amps giving a total of 12 amps.

Greater protection is afforded by a mains conditioner, which effectively isolates the equipment from the mains. Conditioners provide a stable voltage supply, filter out radio frequencies and spikes, and bridge a supply interruption for up to 20 milliseconds. Conditioners can be bought in ratings from 250 volt-amps (VA) and upwards. To find the rating needed, add up the total amperages needed by the equipment to be fed and multiply by the mains voltage.

Complete protection is given by uninterruptable power supply (UPS) systems. These provide a constant power supply that is stable. Supply interruptions are bridged by means of back-up batteries. 'On-line' UPS systems take the supply all the time from the batteries which are kept in a permanently charged state by the mains, and are thus truly uninterruptable. Off-line UPS systems bring the back-up batteries into operation only when an interruption in the mains supply is detected. Standard UPS systems will only bridge interruptions for five minutes to an hour. Systems handling longer breaks cost more.

Shredding machines ('6.45')

The main reason for buying shredders is security: to dispose of redundant documents in a way that prevents them from being easily readable by the unauthorized. The two main decisions that have to be made when purchasing shredders are:

- the degree of security required;
- whether to centralize or decentralize the shredding.

Most shredders cut the documents into 2 mm-wide strips. As this would not stop the really determined spy, some shredders incorporate a second action. This second action can be a second cut, punching holes or a whirl cut. Large 'shredders' grind the paper into dust. These machines are sometimes called 'disintegrators' and can handle floppy discs, coffee cups and soft drinks cans as well as paper. (Coffee cups and soft drink cans do not rank high as security risks – the facility means that all waste-basket material can be handled.)

B

Both centralization and decentralization bring into existence a weak link in the security chain. With centralization, secure material may be lost between the collection point and the centre, though it may make the purchase of a disintegrator worthwhile. Decentralization involves having a number of smaller machines distributed around the offices – and hence running the risk that people forget to shred secure material or even just not bothering.

Portable and small shredders will take 5–10 sheets of paper (70 gsm) at a time at a speed of about 25–35 metres per minute. Medium-size shredders will take up to 30 sheets thickness at a time at a speed of about 30–60 m/minute. Disintegrators usually have a hopper into which one keeps shovelling.

Dates of other machines

The office machine that can trace its history back furthest is probably the vending machine. Over 2,000 years ago there were holy water dispensers outside temples. Other dates are:

1694 Robert Grosvenor became a stationery single sourcer for the Bank of England.
1841 Dun & Bradstreet started the service of collecting and disseminating business information.
1899 The two Todd brothers invented a cheque writer (the company became the Burroughs Protectograph in 1959).
1878 Sir William Crookes invented the cathode ray tube, on which most VDU screens are based.
1964 Sharp Electronics introduced the first all-transistor electronic desk-top calculator.

References

1 *Wall Street Journal*, 9 December, 1987.
2 *The Economist*, 11 June, 1988, p. 96.

Managerial Tools

17

Assessing Managers' Performance

To lead means not only to decide general and specific policies but also to devise correct methods of work.   Mao Tsetung (1949)[1]

A business is about only two things – money and customers.
Theodore Levitt, HBR (1988)[2]

Although this chapter is one of the shorter ones in the book, for some organizations it will be the most important. Assessing managers and how good they are at their job causes many organizations lengthy headaches and a sense of dissatisfaction at the results. There are several reasons why this area is a problem. First, any form of measurement and assessment is bound to be difficult in such a subtle area as management. Second, managers themselves are a powerful pressure group that can find effective ways of deflecting or resisting unsatisfactory approaches.

The first of these two problems (measuring something subtle) is shown by some of the approaches used. Productivity is defined as comparing outputs with inputs. To measure the productivity of managers involves us at once in trying to define the output and the input. This can lead to the horror of measuring output by the number of reports produced and input by the hours worked or the capital expended. Such an approach ignores a basic fact of life: we do not pay managers just to be productive. We want them to be 'good managers'. And this leads us into the quagmire of defining good management. Specialist bookshops have shelf after shelf full of books that discuss the nature of management. Some will use the traditional definition of 'Organizing, Forecasting, Controlling, Commanding, Co-ordinating and Planning'.[3] Others will emphasize the role of leadership. Many unconsciously follow the economic cycle: the 1960s emphasis on working with one's colleagues as friends was replaced in the 1980s by the importance of assertiveness.

The second problem (the castration of measurement) is shown by the fate of so many approaches. Management By Objectives (MBO) started out as a very good approach. It focussed attention on setting specific targets by setting managers objectives that had to be attained. This was needed by many organizations that were coasting rudderless. However, MBO failed in many places for two main reasons. First, it could become bureaucratic – in some firms it resulted in massive amounts of paperwork and time spent. Second, some managers found ways to 'fix' it. They agreed simplistic objectives that they knew were easily attainable or which they knew were in the pipeline but which did not further the firm's true interests. For example, one manager agreed to improve his standard of dress during the next year, and he did indeed make an improvement on his previous rather scruffy look. However, the consultant knew something that senior management did not: the manager's wife had already convinced him of the need for a change and, with two new suits in his wardrobe, it was an easy option – one that deflected other possible options.

It is always easier to fail than to succeed when trying to assess the performance of managers. Some approaches (like MBO) become castrated. In the case of MBO it is difficult to know whether it contained within itself the germ from the start; certainly the basic concept was both valid and useful. Other approaches (such as Success Factor Analysis – SFA) turned out to be more attuned to a one-off exercise rather than to provide the basis for an on-going system. Many approaches relied upon a new definition of management, and defining management is never easy. One can become philosophical or one can quote aphorisms. Neither help one much in practical terms without a great deal of development and research.

On the other hand, many of us know that we have seen a good manager in action or one who has had a good year. We may not like the manager personally. The manager may seem to contradict every accepted tenet that we hold dear, may have obvious personality defects, may offend our sensibilities, may aggravate colleagues. But. But in private, we have to admit that this unattractive individual is a success, gets things done, and is a real asset for the organization.

What is needed, therefore, is a way of assessing managerial performance that:

- is suitable for organizations irrespective of size, culture required, industry or type;
- does not require previous agreement to a new definition of management;
- is sufficiently flexible so that it does not depend on the outside economy at any point in time;
- has a basic concept that is easy to understand;
- provides a basis for assessing managers, rewarding them, developing and improving them, as needed by the organization.

The technique described below is Executive Performance Review – EPR.

Scope of EPR

EPR covers middle and middle-senior management. Top management would be covered by a broader approach such as overall profitability or return on investment. Junior managers and supervisors would be covered by forms of work measurement plus simplified MBO. EPR does not measure the number of managers required nor their productivity; this would still be done by work measurement. EPR supports and does not replace management development and annual assessments and feedback.

■ EPR CONCEPTS

EPR is based on a double assessment of each manager. The manager is assessed by both his/her superiors and by his/her peers – that is, by the managers' colleagues at the same level in the hierarchy. This assessment is based on answering one basic question, namely, 'How good was the manager during the past year?'

This basic question completely ignores a manager's static attributes, such as the level of education or whether the manager is usually a co-operative type of person. It also ignores the fact that the manager did something fantastically good five years ago.

151

The emphasis is at a much more incisive level altogether: is the manager delivering results?

In one firm, a senior manager was overheard giving a middle manager a piece of advice: 'It doesn't matter if you fail on a project provided that you can give a good reason.' EPR, with its two-pronged assessment, prevents anybody from hiding by providing an excuse for failure.

The assessment is based on five factors, known as CARPO analysis. These factors are:

1 Controls.	**4** Progress.
2 Annual aims.	**5** Overall.
3 Retrospective aims.	

■ THE CARPO FACTORS

Controls

Management Controls vary widely depending on circumstances such as level of manager, the industry involved, the type of department, etc. A process department (such as a bank bulk clearing or credit card operation) will usually be based on measurements such as staffing levels and turnround times. A marketing department may have controls based on cost of sales and margins achieved.

Whatever the controls are, they are incorporated into EPR by asking the basic question: 'How well did the manager meet the management controls in the last year?' Some controls are constructed in such a way that it is a straightforward matter to convert them into an assessment just by using arithmetic.

If any major organization exists that does not have any form of management controls, then they should be installed, of course, quite irrespective of whether EPR is under consideration.

Annual aims

Under EPR, once a year each manager is set two to four specific aims for the next year. The nature of these aims will depend on what is important for the organization at the time rather than being intended to improve the manager personally. Indeed, it is common for the managers in a department to share one or more aims. These aims may be of the MBO type. Usually, they are on the lines of:

- reduce labour costs by 15 per cent;
- install successfully the new networking system;
- launch the new product line;
- reduce absenteeism by 40 per cent.

This means that it is often not enough to achieve an aim; for a good assessment it may be necessary to do it well. The basic assessment question is, 'How well did the manager achieve the annual aims?' The difficulty of the aims set will reflect the situation of the organization.

Retrospective aims

Retrospective aims are usually referred to as 'retros'. To be a good manager, it is not enough merely to achieve a few general objectives that were set during the previous year. A good manager reacts to the current situation and does something about it. It is important that managers know that they cannot coast along under the protection of thinking that they are meeting old objectives. They must be constantly helping the organization to meet its challenges.

To this end, once a year the organization sets one to three aims that would have been set as annual aims if only it had hindsight. Obviously, these are often slightly different from the actual annual aims. To set as an aim, 'reduce overtime by 30 per cent' would seem like trickery and bring the whole exercise into disrepute. Instead, retros are usually selected from a somewhat restricted list. Another way (which we prefer) is for the retros to be set about two-thirds of the way through the year. In organizations with really good communications, the retros seem to fall into place naturally, as managers know what is needed to keep the organization healthy. Sometimes, governments set the main retro by changing the law, which then has to be incorporated.

Progress

A year is a long time. A good manager will be running a better department today than a year ago. In what way it should be better will depend on circumstances. Examples are reduced or eliminated backlogs, better service to other departments or to the public, handling peaks better, higher morale, better use of new technology.

The 'progress' factor reflects one aspect of being a good manager. It also encourages communication with other managers (good news has to be shared for it to figure in assessments). This in turn helps an organization to feel that things are getting better all the time – which is also a desirable asset. Some managers may be tempted to spend too much time boasting about pseudo-events. But this is quickly recognized by other managers.

Overall

The overall factor is not a summary of the other factors. It is closer to what is known as the 'gestalt' impression. It answers the basic question, 'In general terms, how well did the manager do?' Inevitably there is a certain amount of a 'halo' effect; the rating given to the other factors influences the rating given to the overall factor. But it also introduces a large measure of justice into the whole scheme. A manager may have had a good year in ways not highlighted by the other factors. Conversely, a manager may score quite well on the other factors but have had a bad year – perhaps because of a series of small errors of judgement or outright mistakes.

■ USE OF THE FACTORS

As already stated, assessments are carried out by both superiors and equals of a manager. This inevitably involves some arithmetic. The five factors are each given a weighting. To some extent, these may vary depending on the organization: for example, a 'process' type of firm may want a higher weighting given to the 'Controls' factor while a young company may want to emphasize the 'Progress' factor. The 'standard' or unchanged weightings are:

Controls	25
Annual aims	15
Retrospectives	20
Progress	15
Overall	25
Total	100

The rating for each of the factors is a ten-point grading, thus:

1 – Exceptionally bad.
2 – Very poor.
3 – Poor.
4 – Below par.
5 – Average ($-$).
6 – Average ($+$).
7 – Good.
8 – Very good.
9 – Excellent.
10 – Exceptionally good.

It is normal for a manager's superiors to assess all five factors while the manager's equals miss out the first two (Controls and Annual aims). This is because the Controls assessment is not usually subjective (and may be straight arithmetic) and assessing the Annual aims involves the distribution of more paperwork. However, if an organization wishes to include all factors in both assessments then it can be done. It is also common for an organization to give different weightings to the assessments done by the superiors and the equals (with the former having a higher weighting). The advantage of this is that it takes some pressure from the manager's equals who are doing the grading. Some firms may prefer to give equal weightings if it wishes to present the EPR exercise as a democratic group scheme.

■ STARTING EPR

EPR is usually introduced to an organization with the aid of external management consultants. This is not necessary but it saves time, helps prevent mistakes and maintains momentum. The stages of a typical assignment are as follows:

1 Initial discussions are held with one or more members of the board of directors. At this meeting, the principles of EPR are explained. Then the consultant finds out where the organization is going, what is important to it and tries to gain a feel for the corporate culture. There is also some straightforward fact-finding: the organization structure, the nature of the management controls and how they are used, the nature of the annual assessments/feedback, the role of the Personnel department, etc. The consultant also tries to define what the organization hopes to get out of introducing EPR.

2 The assignment proper starts with meetings with senior managers. The practical implications of EPR are explained (senior managers are usually enthusiastic about EPR). The consultant then tries to get an impression about how the annual feedbacks and controls are regarded: some firms just go through the motions, others regard them as vital tools. These initial meetings are followed by meetings with the middle managers, who are the people who will be most affected.

These meetings with middle management are important. In some organizations they can be difficult. There are still some places where managerial promotion is regarded as a reward for past services rather than what it really is: a challenge. (One always wonders how such organizations survive.) In such places, some managers may have been looking forward to an easy time until retirement beckons so the idea of EPR is not then welcomed. In such a situation it is a truism to say that EPR should be preceded by

Organization Development or culture changing. It is also true that EPR is often an ideal follow-up to Organization Development.

3 The third stage is the building up of an EPR scheme suitable for the individual organization. All the necessary forms are prepared, weightings agreed and further meetings held.

4 A series of training seminars are held to explain how the scheme will operate in practice. There are four distinct seminars:
- since the Personnel department will normally be responsible for the annual analysis, this is explained to them (the analysis can be done manually but for a large firm a simple spreadsheet with report generation ability is preferable);
- senior managers are shown how to carry out the assessments and how to integrate them with the annual feedbacks;
- middle managers are shown how to carry out the assessments and how they will be used;
- one or more of the directors are shown how to prepare the annual 'tone notes'.

The 'tone notes' are a sort of report from the Board to the managers. They explain what was achieved in the past year and what the Board hopes to achieve in the next year. They thus explain the 'tone' of the current and future situation. They may be based on, though slightly different from, the chairman's report that accompanies the annual balance sheet. These tone notes provide the basis on which is built the aims used in the EPR assessments. This ensures in a very practical way that the organization actually pulls together in a single direction.

5 The next stage is to carry out a dry run. This is a complete practice for the real thing. It has two objectives: to ensure that people know what has to be done, and to ensure that the scheme is robust.

The timing of an EPR introduction can be important. The introduction may be at any time of the financial year and may not coincide with the previous timing of the annual feedbacks. It is therefore necessary to align the three components: tone notes, EPR assessments and annual assessments. This is not a problem but must not be overlooked. There may even be occasions when a firm prefers to combine the dry run with the first actual annual use of a scheme. Irrespective of timing, the consultants will give assistance during the first practical run of a scheme. Afterwards, the organization runs it on its own.

■ RUNNING EPR

The following stages are completed annually:
- the board of directors issue the 'tone notes' showing what was done last year and what is going to be important next year. In some firms (such as a decentralized multinational) these tone notes may be delegated to specified senior staff;
- on the basis of these tone notes, senior management set general annual aims and retros (if the retros were not set during the year). Some years there will be very important changes, such as the introduction of office automation over a large area. In such cases, departmental aims may be set direct at this stage;
- individual aims are now set. Depending on size, this will be done either by departmental leaders or the next higher rank of senior managers;

- next, the assessment forms are completed. Middle managers who are grading their equals also grade themselves;
- the results of the assessments are analysed;
- the annual feedbacks are carried out.

At these annual feedbacks, the following points are covered:

- a discussion on the manager's work during the past year, in the usual manner;
- a discussion on the assessments achieved by the individual;
- a comparison between the assessments and the manager's own grading marks;
- a discussion on the manager's personal annual aims for the forthcoming year;
- a discussion on how the manager can become even better.

This last stage will include any aspects of management development, including the proposal for the manager to attend training or other courses. As previously stated, attending a course is not an annual aim. This effectively shifts the emphasis; going on a course is not an improvement but going on a course may be a means of improvement which will be shown by gaining better assessments, i.e. becoming a better manager.

■ ADVANTAGES OF EPR

When properly run, EPR has many advantages, including:

1 It sharpens up the entire organization.
2 It involves the board and senior management in thinking about what the organization should be doing.
3 Changes of direction are helped, not hindered.
4 All managers are encouraged to work in the same direction.
5 Other approaches (Organization Development, Cultural Change, Management Development, Annual Feedbacks) are reinforced and made practical.
6 It improves the performance of middle managers.

The approach has few real disadvantages. It is of course a task that takes time but this is often less than poorer schemes that it replaces. It lacks the precision of techniques such as work measurement but then its objectives are different.

So EPR fills a gap that is felt by many organizations: how to assess and improve the performance of middle managers.

References

1 Mao Tsetung, 'Methods of work of Party Committees', 13 March, 1949, in *Selected Works*, Vol. IV quoted in *Quotations from Chairman Mao Tsetung*, Beijing: Foreign Language Press, 1966.
2 Theodore Levitt, Editorial, *Harvard Business Review*, Vol. 66, No. 5, p. 7, September–October 1988.
3 Henri Fayol, 'Administration industrielle et générale', first published March 1916 in the bulletin of the Société de l'Industrie Minérale. Translated as H. Fayol, *General and Industrial Management*, London: Pitman & Sons, 1949.

18

Organization Structure

A man's name, title, and rank are artificial and impermanent; they do nothing to reveal what he really is, even to himself.

J. Giraudoux, *Siegfried* (1928)

Superfluous branches
We lop away, that bearing boughs may live.

Shakespeare, *Richard II* (1596)

The Amadeus String Quartet were a group of four gifted musicians who played together for more than forty years. Even an 'organization' of four people needs administration, so the four split up the duties between themselves in a manner that seemed natural and which reflected individuals' abilities. The result was a structure that looks quite familiar to those working in a commercial environment:

String quartet	Commercial equivalent
1 Accounts and negotiations	Administration
2 Public relations	Marketing
3 Travel	Logistics
4 Rehearsals and programming	Production

Moses also had problems of organization. In his case the cause was overwork. He turned to a 'consultant' for advice – his father-in-law, Jethro, who said, 'I will give you counsel.' Jethro summed up the problem as he saw it: 'You will surely wear away ... for this thing is too heavy for you, you are not able to perform it yourself alone.' The answer was delegation and a formal structure with a set number of subordinates, or span of control. This answer was installed, as one can read in Exodus 18:

> And Moses chose able men out of all Israel, and made them heads over the people, rulers of thousands, rulers of fifties, and rulers of tens.

Exodus gives us a glimpse of the restructuring. For example, Moses chose as rulers 'able men, such as fear God, men of truth, hating covetousness'. This is good, but not really detailed enough to act as a formal textbook definition. Did Moses follow the Egyptian example and expect mangers to be technical experts first and good managers second? Did Moses regard skill at administration as highly as the Egyptians did? (The Egyptians commissioned a statue to Pepy II as a mark of his administrative ability.)[1]

So Exodus will not really serve as a textbook for us, stating rules which will apply to all problems that face us in dealing with organization structure. In fact, nowadays, there is a general rejection of the idea that any textbook can provide a pre-set answer to all situations. This has not always been so. In the last century, experts were more willing to provide cast-iron rules for organization structures. An example was the rule that the span of control should be 6. This meant that the hierarchy would go 1, 6, 36, 216, 1,296, 7,776 ... and so on. So if an organization had 1,296 people it should have five layers. This may be correct sometimes – but no   vays.

It is not enough, however, just to ignore the older theorists and to concentrate entirely on more modern writers. Most practitioners in organization structure are well steeped in the works of these early writers. They have read widely because the problems of structure have always been present and a breadth of knowledge aids understanding and is a definite aid to making better decisions. Moreover, structure is never a question of merely drawing a pretty organization chart. Anybody can do that. A good structure is one that is right for a particular organization at a particular time and in particular circumstances.

It is usual to allocate writers on structure to arbitrary divisions. The first of these is 'classical'. Since this may make them seem rather ancient, it should be pointed out that most writers falling into this group are those writing between the start of the Industrial Revolution and about 1940.

Classical approach

The Industrial Revolution placed considerable emphasis on machinery. People were fascinated by machines. At times it seemed as though machines were capable of anything, that they represented hope for the future and the final fruit of human intelligence. We should not dismiss such thoughts as outrageously naive; many people thought about computers in the 1950s and automation in the 1960s in the same way.

This way of thinking permeated society, perhaps reaching a peak around 1930. Politically it was one of the bases for the rise of ideas such as national socialism and fascism. It even spread to child upbringing. The Truby King Method laid down that a baby should be fed at 6 o'clock. No matter that it was crying at 5.55 or asleep at 6.00. Feeding time was 6 o'clock. The highest praise for an organization was that it ran 'like a well-oiled machine'. What more natural, then, than to regard the highest form of efficiency as being to make an organization as much like a machine as possible? For this reason the foundation of the classical approach is usually referred to as 'machine theory'.

This led writers to propose some ideas which now we would reject in most circumstances (though this definitely does not mean that all the classical ideas should be rejected). For example the strength of a machine, and hence an organization, lay in its ability to resist change rather than adapt.

One of the central themes of machine theory was the idea of specialization. Subdivision of jobs into small elements makes them easier to learn and quicker to achieve speed of performance. The question of specialization v. generalization is a basic problem when looking at organization structures. Following on from specialization was the concept of standardization. While standardization is usually very praiseworthy when considering production, it may not be the best way of considering such areas as R & D, management or structure (Moses is not right for all situations). Another aspect of standardization is the idea of 'uniformity of practices' – ensuring that outside contacts, negotiations, etc. are always carried out in the same way.

Many people believed that a natural consequence of these ideas was that they made centralization, rather then decentralization, the norm. The whole matter of centralization v. decentralization is another problem that has always been with us – certainly since the ancient Egyptians.

Human relations approach

The mechanistic approach to organizations concentrated on material objects: inputs, outputs, production methods. This emphasis brought a reaction. The human relations approach concentrated on people and their needs. Psychologists and sociologists tried to prescribe those conditions that would best make people co-operate with one another and with the organization.

Proponents of the human relations school of though pointed out the shortcomings of classical theory as they saw them. They based their comments on the undoubted diversity of human behaviour and motivation. This being so, it is not surprising that the human relations approach had difficulty in prescribing rules or guidelines which can act as a basis for setting up new structures. Unfortunately, the one idea that many proponents of this approach were agreed on was that decentralization was desirable.

The inability of the human relations school to be more specific about actual new structures in not completely negative. Much of their thinking has become embodied in current management practice, and we use their ideas as a backcloth upon which we can paint a new structure.

C

Systems approach

The systems approach had its foundation in the new ideas that arose from the development of cybernetics and (analogue) computers. One of these main ideas was the concept of 'feedback'. Feedback is the use of data output from one stage as input to another (usually earlier) stage. In cybernetics, feedback is a mechanism for control; a method of self-correction that ensures that results are those desired.

Feedback enables a system either to follow a desired path or to achieve a steady state (known as 'homeostasis'). Now that may sound rather like the classic approach. It is true that there is a danger that systems believers do indeed slip into a rigid, classical frame of mind, while at the same time denying the validity of the classical approach. This is something that one must be aware of when reading about organization structure.

Writers overcame this danger to some extent by adopting two extra concepts. One was the idea that organizations are not closed to the impact of the outside world but interact with it; they are 'open' systems – open to the environment. The second concept was that of 'equifinality'. This is the idea that organizations can reach the same finishing point even though they start from different points and follow different paths. For example, a firm can become brand leader by taking market share from the competition or by enlarging the whole market.

By adopting these two concepts, systems writers are in apparent direct competition with machine theory (though, as stated, because of the basis of systems theory, many writers do slip into a mechanistic way of thinking). The biggest difference is the consideration of an organization as an open rather than a closed entity. If we grant that a structure should aim to assist an organization in reaching its objectives, then it follows that we have to consider how the environment affects the realizing of these objectives. It may be felt that this is pretty obvious; nowadays nearly everybody admits that the market is paramount. But this has not always and in all places been realized. A firm's objectives may include growth, but growth is not assured merely by producing more if the market does not want more.

The analogy approach

Organization is an abstract thing. It is not always easy therefore to grasp, especially as the organization of a large concern is a most complex affair. It may thus be attractive to think of an organization as something else which is easier to grasp since it is familiar. The most common analogy is to say that an organization is like the human body (hence the use of the word 'corporate').

Other metaphors that are used include:

- the brain. Likening an organization to the human brain is popular with people who emphasize the importance of information and its processing. The brain as metaphor is also used to highlight the importance of decision making;
- political systems. Many writers on organizations ignore the matter of conflict and politics. In real life, as we all know this is not so. Some places seem to be in a constant state of ferment – though whether this is healthy or not is another matter. Treating an organization as a political system meets this head-on;
- a culture. The rise of Organization Development (OD) gave an impetus to thinking of organizations in anthropological terms. The logical extension of this was to consider them in purely cultural terms;
- power centres. This metaphor has been used by people who have been particularly concerned with very large multinational companies or large government departments. It is often useful in trying to understand what are known as unspoken objectives;
- an army. The use of armies as a metaphor for non-military concerns is a common one that reappears every few years. It may well be that there are lessons for management that can be appreciated by studying military affairs. It seems to us that it is more questionable to apply this to the field of structure since the objectives are not strictly comparable.

The main advantage of using metaphors in thinking about organization is that it can remove blockages in our conceptualization, making it easier to grasp some of the complexities. The danger is the common fallacy of arguing by analogy. There is nothing inherently wrong in saying that an organization is like a brain, but it is not the same as a brain. At some stage every such metaphor breaks down. The danger lies in pursuing the metaphor or analogy too far.

Writers on organization

It can be interesting to consider some of the very early writers. People such as the writer of Exodus, certain writers in Ancient Egypt,[2,3] China,[4,5] as well as Mencius[6] and Kautilya.[7] An interesting overview of early writers is given in a book by C. S. George.[8] However, it is felt that such writers give a backcloth rather than always helping us to deal with immediate problems of structure. We will therefore concentrate on more modern writers.

Karl von Clausewitz (1780–1831)

Clausewitz, a Prussian general, wrote extensively. He felt that his ideas applied to management in general, since business was a form of competition, as was war. Two of his beliefs affect us particularly. First, he emphasized the need for stating one's objectives and that careful planning should be based on the objective(s). Second, he was one of the early writers to emphasize that decisions have to be based on probability rather than certainty. Moreover, von Clausewitz pointed out that uncertainty was reduced by thorough analysis and planning. This was all in direct opposition to the concept of management by intuition that was prevalent at the time.[9]

Charles Babbage (1792–1871)

Babbage is perhaps best known to the layman for his work on early forms of 'computers' and for his attacks on the Royal Society. But his work in the field of management went much deeper than this, and was notable for being based on practical observations rather than on pure theory. These observations nevertheless led him to follow the conventional wisdom of the times, which was division of labour, and centralization. He did, however, emphasize that it was the actual production processes that should be centralized and not necessarily the entire concern.[10]

C

Frederick Winslow Taylor (1856–1917)

The epitaph on Taylor's grave includes the phrase 'The father of scientific management'. This is how people regard him, although it would be disputed by supporters of Henry Poor, Henry Towne and Henry Metcalf. Taylor pursued the logic of division of labour to the field of management itself. He split shop-floor management into eight areas with one person responsible for each area. This in turn meant that all workers had eight bosses (e.g. speed boss, discipline boss). This 'matrix' structure ran counter to the principle of 'one man, one boss' and so was heavily criticized at the time, though where Taylor himself installed the system it seems to have worked well enough.

Henri Fayol (1841–1925)

Fayol, like Taylor, was an engineer. For some of us, he was probably the best writer on management that we have. He had the ability to put forward principles, at the same time tempering them with common sense based on practical experience. For example, on division of labour he writes, 'Specialisation belongs to the natural order ... yet division of work has its limits which experience and a sense of proportion teach us may not be exceeded'. Division of work is the first of Fayol's fourteen principles of management. The second is authority and responsibility, about which he says, '... wheresoever authority is exercised responsibility arises'[11]

Some of Fayol's other principles were:

- unity of command – 'an employee should receive orders from one superior only'.
- unity of direction – 'one head and one plan for a group of activities having the same objectives'.
- general interest – 'the interest of one employee or group of employees should not prevail over that of the concern'.
- centralization – this, like division of labour, belonged to the natural order, but 'the question of centralization or decentralization is a simple matter of proportion, it is a matter of finding the optimum degree for the particular concern'.

- scalar chain (the hierarchy from the top to the bottom) – this should not preclude communications going direct from one person to another without going up and down the chain of command. Fayol called this direct communication a 'gang-plank'.

Fayol also emphasized the importance of fairness, stability of tenure, initiative and *esprit de corps*. It can be seen that the principles put forward by Fayol have stood the test of time better than most.

Mary Parker Follett (1868–1933)

Follett thought widely about management, presenting many of her ideas in papers and lectures (collected by Metcalf and Urwick in *Dynamic Administration, the Collected Papers of Mary Parker Follett*). Follett incorporated ideas from the field of psychology, and was one of the proponents of group authority and responsibility.

Follett looked at power and authority in a new manner. Power is simply the ability to make things happen, to initiate change. But it should be 'power with' others and not 'power over' people. Authority is power vested in individuals, not as individuals but as performers of functions. Therefore no manager should have 'more authority than goes with his function'.

Follett criticized the idea of one person controlling another, instead putting forward the idea of the 'law of the situation' – actions should depend on the situation. 'The head of the sales department does not give orders to the head of the production department, or vice versa. Each studies the market and the final decision is made as the market demands.' Orders should be the composite decision of those who give and those who receive them.

Follett also put forward four principles of co-ordination:

- co-ordination relates all the factors of the situation;
- there should be direct contact between the people whose activities need to be co-ordinated;
- co-ordination should start before policies have been completely formulated;
- co-ordination should be a continuing process.

Follett's thinking make her a pioneer of the human relations school. Other, and later, writers that used psychological insights in their writings include Douglas McGregor, Rensis Likert and Chris Argyris. It is not easy to summarize their writings as they affect actual structures and their formulation, since they concentrate on motivation and attitudes rather than formulating principles for constructing the structures. This is not to diminish their work in any way but it does mean that one should consult the actual works for exposition.

Peter F. Drucker

Drucker puts the emphasis on objectives and their definition as a basis for creating organizations. He recommends three aids to uncovering what structure will help an organization to attain its objectives:

- activities analysis – this should bring out what work has to be performed, what kinds of work belong together, and what emphasis is to be given to each activity. This is much more than merely listing functions such as marketing, production, finance, etc.;
- decisions analysis – the nature of decisions depends on four characteristics: how far

into the future the decision commits the firm, the impact on other functions, the number of qualitative factors (ethics, politics, etc.), and the rarity of the decision. The higher the 'score' on these factors, the higher up the hierarchy the decision should be taken;

- relations analysis – a manager's relationships should not only be thought of in terms of downwards relations. Recognition should also be made of the importance of 'the larger unit of which he is part', and of sideways relations which are always an important part of the job 'and may be the most important part'.

Drucker proposes three structural requirements. The first is that the criterion must be the attainment of the right objectives. The second is that it should have as few management levels as possible. Third, a structure must make possible the training and testing of future senior managers. Drucker is a believer in decentralization and promotes two specific types of decentralization. These he calls federal decentralization and functional decentralization.[12]

Gareth Morgan

Morgan has written widely and has the distinction of having lectured (to date) at over forty universities. Perhaps because of this his work is better known in academic circles than by managers. But in 1986 he published a book on structure that deserves to be widely read. This book[13] brings together the various topics of structure by metaphor. Morgan discusses thinking of organizations as (i.a.) brains, machines, organisms, cultures, political systems, 'psychic prisons', and instruments of domination. A second book by Morgan (published in 1989) is in the list of further reading at the end of this chapter.

Theoretical considerations

■ OBJECTIVES

Western management consultants always seem to want to talk about objectives; even worse, they want the objectives quantified. So goes a common, and true, complaint. (Some very successful Japanese managements take a completely different view of objectives.)[14] There are two reasons for this. First, it is a most fruitful action to discuss with top management their ideas about objectives. It enables both consultant and client to think about the concern in depth, to think about where it is going and how it should get there. Second, it helps to focus attention on shortcomings of the present structure and to decide some ways in which it should be changed.

It has to be admitted that the initial objectives usually turn out to be the same in most instances. These are survival, growth, profit, marketing and efficiency. It is when one starts to define (and to measure) the objectives that discussions become complex. Take survival for example. The introduction of quartz mechanisms made survival a most practical point for a number of Swiss watch manufacturers. Some of them responded by switching their definition of a watch. A Swiss watch was no longer just a way of accurately telling time. Patek Philippe advertised the 'exquisite pleasure of owning something very few others will ever experience'. Piaget claimed that their watches were 'More than a timepiece. An acquisition'. Swatch went the other way and made their watches a fashion accessory.

Another firm, Crown-Zellerbach, made paper and pulp. Realizing that their survival was threatened by a long-term shortage of timber; they established a function devoted to forest building, to provide raw materials in fifty years' time. Similarly, when looking at growth and profits one has to decide the relative importance of short-term and long-term considerations.

So defining objectives can not only reveal activities to be undertaken, it can also show the relative importance of such activities and the nature and type of important decisions that have to be undertaken. These key objectives, activities and decisions can provide a framework within which one can build a more detailed structure.

■ CENTRALIZATION AND DECENTRALIZATION

As has been indicated, over the centuries there have been many attempts to prove that both centralization and decentralization are desirable, correct or even a law of nature. Since the discussion continues it must be assumed that the proof offered by both sides has so far failed to convince everybody.

Our own view is that sometimes one is preferable, sometimes the other – though we would not go so far as some commentators who recommend that firms should switch between the two every fifteen years or so. To avoid the accusation of gross indecision on this matter, comments are as follows:

- offices and production units can be widely dispersed physically but can still be centralized in practice;
- complete decentralization is rarely desirable. The centre cannot abdicate its responsibilities. Decentralization has to be accompanied by proper information flow and a form of management control;
- decentralization is desirable when there is a need to remain flexible, to respond quickly to the market or the environment, to make local decisions quickly, or to increase job interest;
- centralization is desirable when there is a need to retain the economies of large-scale unit-operating, to prevent wasteful inter-unit competition, when bureaucracy is the correct style, or when middle management are for some reason incapable of making high-grade decisions locally;
- some functions should not be decentralized in most firms. For example, most firms should retain finance acquisition and internal audit at the centre. In most firms, it is also advisable to retain centrally the main personnel function and negotiations with trade unions, public relations and the formulation of house style, as well as the formulation of management controls/information flow systems.

No organization can be completely centralized or decentralized for ever. Complete centralization leads to a rigidity that ignores the environment, while complete decentralization leads eventually to anarchy. On the whole, the dangers of centralization exceed those of decentralization and, if for this reason alone, one should tend to a degree of decentralization. Moreover, a decentralized firm is more likely to respond to change.

■ SPECIALIZATION OR GENERALISM

Specialization does have certain specific advantages. Perhaps the greatest of these is the fact that it enables a higher level of skill to be attained, though of itself it does not guarantee increased efficiency. Our approach to the question of specialization is rather

164

different from that of other writers. We prefer to see groups of staff made responsible for a set of tasks. Within these groups the tasks of individuals will change slightly over time. These changes will depend on the individuals present.

When a new person joins a group, that person will tend to be specialized, either because he or she was taken on for their special skills or because of the initial need to learn how the firm does things. Over a period of time these new entrants will learn new tasks and skills – if they are capable of it and if they wish it. People with a large number of skills are known as generalists. In this way, working groups tend to minimize the problems of the specialist v. generalist argument. In general, too much specialism leads to boredom and too much generalism leads to a lack of skills.

■ GROUPING ACTIVITIES

The grouping of activities is the basis of organization structure. It has to be tackled in two routes which can be defined as top-down and bottom-up. The trick is in being able to do both at the same time. In other words, one has to split the main spheres of interest into a few large divisions at the same time as one allocates all the tasks performed to small groups. The main bases for the primary groupings are geographic/location, products, functions, customers, processes, and projects. In most cases one ends up with a mixture of these. The choice of which one to emphasize depends on a number of factors such as the type of industry and the immediate thrust of the overall marketing strategy.

C

■ FUNCTIONAL SPLIT

This division is reasonably self-explanatory. Most organizations use a form of functional split. (For small firms, it may be all that is needed.) For example, the top level of the CIA[15] is:

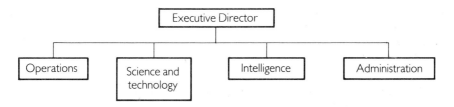

The main advantages for a functional split are that it tends to reduce duplication of tasks and that it exploits professional specialization such as accountants and salespeople. The disadvantages are that it complicates accountability, makes performance assessment harder, complicates co-ordination at the top, inhibits profit centre formation, encourages sectional interests pursuit and can lead to sectional empire-building. Functional splits are most appropriate for small firms, non-commercial organizations and mono-product enterprises with a stable and homogeneous market.

When looking bottom-up, there are a number of reasons why one might put a number of activities into a small functional group whether or not one is using function as the primary split. These reasons are:

- legal or audit requirements;
- to concentrate specialist knowledge, expertise, contacts or use of major equipment (e.g. a large single mainframe computer);

- viewed by top management as needed for strategic purposes;
- economies of scale; cost effectiveness;
- to provide functional independence; satisfy a security need;
- function seen as needing a distinctive management style;
- provision of a social service to the staff;
- to reduce duplication, overlap or to resolve conflict.

Most medium or large enterprises will have activities that meet these requirements, so it is common for firms to have at least one small functional group. But this does not mean that the entire enterprise should be organized along functional lines.

■ GEOGRAPHIC LOCATION

Using a regional basis for subsidiary groupings is common in, for example, sales departments, where it can be cost effective (reducing travel) and ensure responsiveness to customers' needs. It can also be used as a basis for the primary split. For example, international oil and banking firms often organize themselves along regional lines. The advantages of this are rapid collection of information and communication to where it is needed, and speedy and accurate response to the environment. Disadvantages are duplication of activities, a temptation for going native or local empire-building, and complexities of information flow/management control for the centre. An important factor is the degree of autonomy of the regional division.

An example of a primary split (from an international oil company) is:

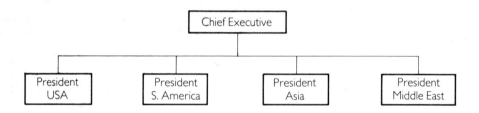

An example of activities grouping is the (partial) CIA Operations:

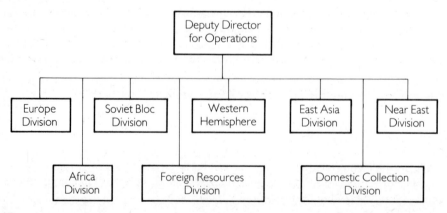

■ MARKET

Organizing by markets will in some enterprises mean the same thing as organizing by geography. In other cases it will be quite different. For example, it may be worthwhile having a separate division dealing only with the government or other important market segment. Other companies may split their sales division into retail/wholesale/large accounts. Some companies (e.g. clothing firms) have set up divisions dealing with the youth market complete with separate house style, name and advertising. The advantages and disadvantages of grouping by markets are the same as those as for grouping by geography.

■ PRODUCTS

Organizing by products does not make an enterprise product-oriented. In fact, some firms are driven to product-based organization because of market forces. Examples of this can be seen among firms making computers, photocopiers and other office equipment. Other firms are driven towards product organization because they make products that involve widely differing production processes. An example of this is ICI, who have separate divisions for paint, dyes, manmade fibres, drugs, metals, plastics and alkalis.

C

The advantage of product organization is that it utilizes specialized knowledge and/or production processes to the maximum. Also, each group of products receives proper attention in such areas as marketing, R & D and production. It also makes the formulation of profit centres much easier. The disadvantages are duplication, overlap and the complexities of co-ordination necessary for dealing with major accounts across product lines.

■ PROJECTS

Project organization can be indicated at two ends of the spectrum. It is used when a specific project accounts for a major part of an organization's resources (such as construction and aircraft). It is also used in those enterprises where there is a continual flow of new and relatively minor products (as in the case of some electronics firms).

In many cases project organization is typified by a continual formation, dissolution and re-formation of teams of managers, staff and specialists. This prospect will appear either attractive or the opposite to people, depending on their personalities. It does require a flexible and distinctive management style which not all managers can acquire naturally.

The advantages of project organization are clear project co-ordination, ease of identifying profit centres, closeness to the market, a natural team spirit attitude, and work that is interesting and challenging. The disadvantages are overall co-ordination, duplication, overlap, client co-ordination, a staff sense of insecurity, and practical problems of maintaining good records and files for future use. It is necessary to be very careful in allocating overhead costs of centrally provided functions such as personnel and computers.

■ PROCESS OR EQUIPMENT

Some concerns can with advantage organize themselves along process lines. It is rare for this to be a primary split but may be used for grouping activities within a division. Examples where this is common are steel (foundry/rolling/fabrications) and textiles (spinning/dyeing/weaving/fabrication). It tends to be used where there is a measure of vertical manufacturing integration, so that different processes have different needs. The advantages and disadvantages are similar to those for product organization.

■ SUBSIDIARY/PROFIT CENTRE

Some enterprises have within them widely differing types of 'industry'. For example one firm contains metal goods fabrication, automobile maintenance, building materials, a departmental store and import–export services. In some such cases the only logical organization appears to be along subsidiary-company/profit centre lines. The same approach is used when the centre regards itself as the holder of a portfolio of independent companies.

The main advantages of this are the ease of identifying profit centres and the utilization of specialist staff skills and knowledge. It will also normally bring the market and environment closer. The disadvantages can include the lack of top management involvement, incipient empire-building, the need for accuracy of overhead allocation, and the fact that staff identify themselves with individual units. There is also commonly a degree of argument about raising and allocating new finance.

■ OVERALL ASPECTS OF GROUPING

No matter how people are grouped, the same aspects need attention. These include co-ordination, management controls, overhead allocation, centralization, specialization, span of control, decision making, accountability – and objectives.

■ NOTES ON FAULT DIAGNOSIS

There are many reasons for undertaking a structural study: growth of the concern, change of personnel, change of corporate direction, new laws, poor results, changes in the market or environment, etc. Most structural studies involve fault diagnosis of the existing structure. Few faults can be discovered by merely studying the current organization chart, no matter how detailed this may be. Moreover, many faults are interwoven with other aspects such as a lack of agreed objectives, poor communications, ignoring market demands and so on. Therefore, in a way, one should find out as much as possible about the entire concern.

Time available is a constraint on how deeply one can delve, but some aspects are so basic that they cannot be left unconsidered. These will include:

- a discussion on corporate objectives;
- a consideration of the market and the environment;
- corporate image, policies, products, controls, traditions, processes, organization, size and ownership;
- style, capabilities and approach of management;
- skills, morale and attitudes of staff;
- type of industry and technology;
- personnel aspects including rules, motivating factors.

This partial list begins to look rather comprehensive and may lead to the objection that such matters are not necessary to the building up of a new organization chart. But a chart is only a picture (an incomplete picture at that) of some aspects of organization.

■ ANALYSTS ORGANIZATION CHART

An analyst will build up an organization chart for the analyst's own use. This is slightly different from the traditional one. It will show lines of authority and information flow as well as staff numbers. An example of part of an analyst's chart is shown in Figure 18.1. In this chart, certain symbols are used:

nominal authority and responsibility;   instructions given;

actual control and responsibility;   information commonly passed.

nominal *and* actual authority and responsibility;

The chart also shows numbers and grades of staff in individual sections or departments. These can then be related to the activities analysis.

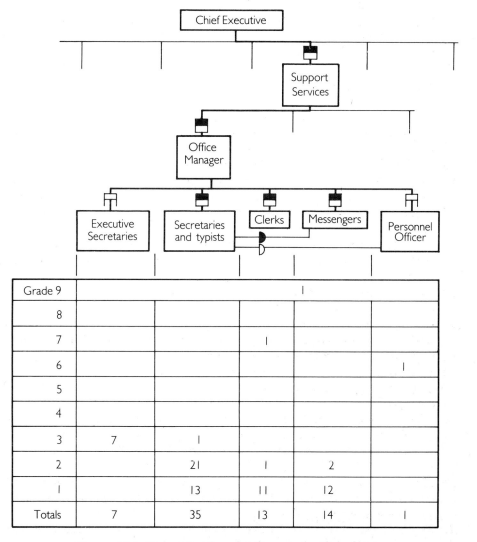

Grade 9				1		
8						
7			1			
6						1
5						
4						
3	7	1				
2		21	1	2		
1		13	11	12		
Totals	7	35	13	14		1

Figure 18.1 Example of analyst's organization chart

169

■ ASSIGNMENT SHAPE

The shape of a typical study of a medium-size enterprise is:

1 Initial meetings and discussions with senior management.

2 Obtain current organization charts, numbers, grades, job descriptions, names, last three balance sheets, industry notes.

3 Meet personnel manager for discussion on policies, etc.

4 Meet Marketing Director for discussion on market, environment, plan.

5 Prepare seminar (study details, discussion on structures, etc.).

6 Give seminars to middle and junior management.

7 Discuss market, production, industry, environment with external experts and relate to current situation.

8 Meet middle managers individually:
   - discuss seminar;
   - discuss how they see their jobs (aims, style, responsibilities, authority, communications);
   - structural and other problems;
   - future plans;
   - what they would like to see done;
   - who they work with (frequent basis, information to/from, functional groups dealt with) and general comments.

9 Meet junior managers, supervisors (use small groups of four if the firm is too large for individual meetings). Discuss as in item 8 above.

10 Analyse activities of concern by interviewing selected members of the staff.

11 Carry out initial analysis of situation by referring to meetings, charts, numbers, seminar comments, interviews, discussions with external experts and own notes.

12 Prepare for own reference a picture of the drawbacks of the current situation and structure.

13 If thought applicable, carry out attitude survey, draw up proximity matrix, draw up report matrix/information flow chart or any other aid that appears relevant.

14 Interview functional heads as in item 8 above.

15 Formulate main split of a proposed structure and reporting system.

16 Prepare initial report – thoughts, faults, main split, reasoning.

17 Discuss this report with top management.

18 Leave the report with top management for them to digest and discuss among themselves. Return for a second discussion with them.

19 Decide on grouping of activities within main split. Decide on how to treat functions and service departments (remember – everybody will want to report to the chief executive).

20 Allocate numbers to each department and section. State main tasks and functions of each. Describe communications and information flow. State reports, reporting mechanism. Write a few main job descriptions. Describe new responsibilities and changes.

21 List major changes to such basic factors as management style, interaction with the environment, marketing and corporate strategy, communications and information, together with reasoning.

22 Decide if any changes are so major that they will require special training or organization development for attitude improvements.

23 Prepare and draw up an action plan.
24 Discuss proposed changes and action plan with top management.
25 Prepare and submit report on proposals, including action plan.
26 Agree changes and plan.
27 Discuss proposals with middle management, supervision and staff.
28 Start action plan and implement.

■ FACTORS AFFECTING STRUCTURE

Some of the more visible factors that affect one's thinking about organization structure are given in Figure 18.2. A copy of this is sometimes used when discussing structure

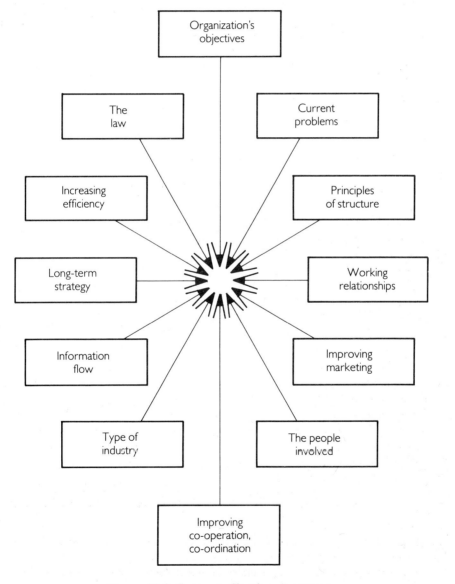

Figure 18.2 Factors affecting structure

with clients. It makes it easier for all concerned to visualize matters that may otherwise sound too abstract. One is also affected by certain principles of structure. These are less dogmatic than once they were and are given below.

Principles of organization structure

1 The basis of a structure must be the objectives of the organization. These objectives must be defined, known and agreed.
2 No organization is permanent. An organization must be aware of the necessity for change and review the structure periodically.
3 A structure must take account of the total environment in which it exists, take feedback from the environment and change as the environment changes.
4 The total organization should have only one head. This head has, and cannot abdicate, the ultimate responsibility for success.
5 The number of levels in the organization should be the minimum possible, consistent with effectiveness and personal workloads.
6 It follows from this that the number of people reporting to one person (span of control) should be kept optimally high.
7 The basic molecule of structure is the work group. Within a work group, individual responsibilities should be tailored to personal abilities and aspirations. The aim is to optimize personal growth and effectiveness.
8 Decentralization is normally preferable to centralization. A degree of co-ordination and control prevents unilateral activities that are incompatible with overall organizational objectives.
9 Activities, tasks and functions should be grouped according to skills, knowledge, homogeneity of purpose and simplicity of accountability.
10 Duplication and overlaps should be eliminated unless they increase effectiveness or can act as a spur to competitive behaviour.
11 Information flows, procedures and controls are more effective than job descriptions and organization charts in creating and maintaining a structure.
12 A structure is a balance, like all management. A balance between centralization v. decentralization, specialization v. generalization, control v. licence, stability v. change.

Maxims

1 It is not the boxes on an organization chart that define an organization; it is the white spaces between them.
2 No structure guarantees success or sound management. An enterprise is only as sound as the people in it.
3 Being sound today does not automatically mean being sound tomorrow.
4 Having good staff is not a perquisite of affluence but a prerequisite of success.
5 Somebody, somewhere is rejecting our ideas of structure and still being successful; probably by force of personality.

References

1 Bianchi, R. S., *Egyptian Treasures*, New York: Harry N. Abrams, 1978.
2 Erman, A., *The Literature of the Ancient Egyptians*, New York: E. P. Dutton, 1927.
3 Breasted, J. H., *Ancient Records of Egypt*, Chicago: University of Chicago Press, 1906.
4 Kuo-Cheng, W., *Ancient Chinese Political Theories*, Shanghai: Commercial Press, 1928.

5 Legg, J. (trans.), *The Chinese Classics*, Hong Kong: Hong Kong University Press, 1960.
6 Huan-Chang, C., *The Economic Principles of Confucius and His School*, New York: Columbia University Press, 1911.
7 Shamastray, R. (trans.), *Kautilya's Arthasutra*, Mysore: Sri Raghuveer, 1956.
8 George, C. S., *The History of Management Thought*, Englewood Cliffs: Prentice-Hall, 1972.
9 Clausewitz, K. von, *Principles of War*, Harrisburg: Military Service, 1832.
10 Babbage, C., *On the Economy of Machinery and Manufactures*, London: Charles Knight, 1832.
11 Fayol, H., *General and Industrial Management*, London: Pitman, 1949.
12 Drucker, P. F., *Practice of Management*, New York: Harper & Row, 1954.
13 Morgan, G., *Images of Organization*, Beverly Hills: Sage, 1986.
14 Ouchi, W., *Theory Z*, Reading, Massachusetts: Addison-Wesley, p. 33, 1981.
15 Ranelagh, J., *The Agency*, London: Sceptre, 1988.

Further reading

Barnes, M. C. *et al.*, *Company Organization – Theory and Practice*, London: Allen & Unwin, 1970.
Davis, S. M. and Lawrence, P. R., *Matrix*, Reading, Massachusetts: Addison-Wesley, 1977.
McGregor, D., *The Human Side of Enterprise*, New York: McGraw-Hill, 1960.
Mintzberg, H., *The Structuring of Organizations*, Englewood Cliffs: Prentice-Hall, 1979.
Morgan, G., *Creative Organization Theory*, Beverly Hills: Sage, 1989.
Pfeffer, J., *Organizations and Organization Theory*, Marshfield: Pitman, 1982.
Schein, E., *Organizational Culture and Leadership*, San Francisco: Jossey-Bass, 1985.
Trist, E. L. *et al.*, *Organizational Choice*, London: Tavistock, 1963.
Woodward, J., *Industrial Organization: Theory and Practice*, Oxford: Oxford University Press, 1965.
Zmud, R. W., *Information Systems in Organizations*, Glenview: Scott Foresman, 1983.

C

19

Organization Development and Managing Change

We cannot be satisfied with things as they are. We cannot be satisfied to drift, to rest on our oars, to glide over a sea whose depths are shaken by subterranean upheavals.

John Kennedy, campaign speech (1960)

After you've done a thing the same way for two years, look it over carefully. After five years, look at it with suspicion. And after ten years, throw it away and start all over.

A. E. Perlman, *The New York Times* (3 July 1958)

When discussing change, it is very easy to fall into circular traps. If asked, 'How do we change people's attitudes?', the answer is often to change the way that they do things: start working in teams, communicate more and do-as-you-would-be-done-to. How can one get people to change the way that they do things? The answer is to change attitudes. So we go round the circle.

It is the same with organizations. It is repeatedly said that organizations can change if they have the right culture. If they have a poor culture, then it should be changed. But if the culture is poor, then it resists change – including the change to a culture that will accept change such as a change in culture. And so on.

A number of other factors complicate matters further:

- it is easy to use the word 'change' as though it always had the same implications. From this assumption it is only a small step to providing one panacea – people resist change because of fear, either fear of the unknown or fear of failure. But this is not a universal cause. A group of people may be unwilling to work at night, not out of fear but because they do not like the idea. It is possible that extra cash might genuinely make many of them think that it is worthwhile. In dealing with people, there are few universals;

- it is still more difficult to define a number of other words satisfactorily – even when we all use the words. These are words like 'leadership', 'objectives' and 'culture'. Even 'Organization Development' and 'work measurement standards' can cause misunderstanding. This soon becomes clear to anybody who has to work through an interpreter. A Briton and an American mean different things by the words mission, objective, goal, target, aim. Others may have only one word for all of them;

- successful organizations (however defined) come in many styles: autocratic, democratic, chauvinist, stodgy, unfeeling. On the other hand, no matter what the style, it does seem to be very hard to stay successful for more than about fifteen years. One frequently reads a book that praises an organization as having an ideal culture and style. But by the time one reads it in paperback, the firm concerned is already bankrupt or has been taken over.

Since this may appear rather negative and unhopeful, the following are some points to act as a base.

Starting points

1 Improvement and change are always possible. They will usually need time, effort and determined willpower, but they are possible. Change may not always be attained, but it is always possible.

2 No matter how impossible a change appears to an organization, experience will have shown that bigger changes have been attained elsewhere.

3 Every person is different. We all know this, so there is no point in subscribing to a new theory that pretends otherwise.

4 Major changes should always be planned carefully. This ensures a smoother change, better timing, reduced costs and an ability to solve problems before they happen.

5 Contrary to popular opinion, the most difficult change is not the introduction of advanced office technology. The most difficult is to change the overall culture of an organization. The second most problematical changes are major changes of location, and new organization structures.

6 Change can be incremental or instantaneous ('big bang'). The disadvantage of incremental change is that momentum can be lost and the whole affair can get bogged down. The disadvantage of big-bang change is that any errors can be very difficult to retrieve.

7 Change can be installed immediately or after a period of time. Generally, immediate change is associated with a new chief executive or an emergency. Reflective change is associated with external management consultants.

8 Whether a major change should be incremental, big-bang, immediate or reflective depends on circumstances and the type of change. For example, moving a head office to another part of the country will be big-bang and reflective. Changing overseas representation can be incremental and immediate.

9 Any new 'technique' that promises easy and infallible change should be mistrusted. There are no magic wands in management.

There is no doubt that change is easy in some offices but a problem in others. Offices that have a history and an atmosphere of change are receptive to change. Offices that never seem to change are resistant to change. So if one can build up an atmosphere of improvement then further changes are much easier.

But changes must not appear to the staff to be change for the sake of change, or changes because management cannot get things right. Change must be associated with success, with improvement, with beating the competition. Staff in organizations are self-selecting. A firm may have an atmosphere of success and excitement, or it can have an atmosphere of stability and isolation. Staff who stay with one or the other type do so because they are happy in such an atmosphere. They also (whether management or staff) reinforce the atmosphere.

Two examples highlight this. An industrial engineer was offered a post in a new firm that would have opened up a completely new career for him. His colleagues envied him the potential prospects. But he refused the offer, giving as a reason the fact that it would have meant abandoning his garden. He did not like the idea of change.

In another firm, the consultant was studying the computer department. A systems designer was being asked about a procedure one Tuesday morning. Jokingly, she said, 'I may be wrong. I've been away since Wednesday and four days is a long time not to improve the system.' It was said in a way that showed that she liked the idea of a change having been made (actually, she was right; it had changed).

Change theories

There are many theories about change: the basis, the causes, the approach and the ways to effect it. Much of the theoretical work is rooted in the ideas of behavioural scientists. This fact is the cause of certain difficulties:

- behavioural scientists believe (sometimes passionately) in the truth of their own theories. This helps them greatly, because there is no doubt in our mind that believing in what one is doing gives one a strength in achieving success in effecting change (as in so much else). This messianic fervour is not easily communicable to people who are just reading a book;
- change theories themselves change as behavioural theories change. This can leave the layman, which most of us are, in some uncertainty and confusion;
- change theories very often reflect society in general. Thus theories that were easily acceptable in, say, the USA in the 1960s may appear crude, bourgeois or unfeeling in another country or at another time;
- managers may be totally unimpressed when confronted by a consultant who tries to explain why he is proposing a course of action, when this is based on a behavioural theory.

All this can mean that one is basing a proposal on a theory that can be alien, out of date and of most use to its originator. As an example, one can consider the Needs Hierarchy model. This was developed by Abraham Maslow in the 1960s and published in a book in 1970.[1] The theory held that people's needs were arranged in a hierarchy. When one type of need was satisfied, higher needs were activated. The hierarchy of needs put forward was (a) physiological, e.g. hunger; (b) safety – protection against threats and danger; (c) social, such as association, acceptance and friendship; (d) esteem, both of oneself and from others; and (e) self-actualization, or the need for continued self-development.

Maslow's theory was tested by the work of Hall and Nougaim in 1968,[2] which found little support for it. A further study by Wahba and Bridewell in 1979[3] commented that: 'Maslow's Need Hierarchy Theory has received little clear or consistent support from any available research findings. Some of Maslow's propositions are totally rejected....' If the theory was wounded in 1968 and, as some claim, killed in 1979 then the obituary could be said to have appeared in 1985. In a book published by the Institute of Personnel Management, there is the following comment on Maslow's hierarchy of needs and Herzberg's two-factor theory: 'Each of these theories has been subject to biting criticism ... there are two critical aspects of Maslow's theory: there are five categories of need and they are arranged in hierarchical order. Unfortunately, neither of these has received much empirical support.' This particular book[4] is recommended as a good introduction to many of the aspects of motivation.

The above remarks are not intended as an attack on Maslow's theory as such (it gives an interesting framework to a concept), but as an example of how an idea (and individual interpretation of it) can take root in some analysts' thinking. Although most technical books no longer use the Needs Hierarchy theory, some generalized books do.

There are even some training courses that still use it.

One final factor returns to haunt those who try to effect major change, whether they be 'company doctors' or a practising analyst. There are times when one is outstandingly successful at making such a change. This success may be so noteworthy that it is written about in the managerial literature or financial press. It is still possible to go to another organization to repeat the success – and to end up really struggling to make a change.

So there is no way of guaranteeing success in making a change. The message is clear though unwelcome to many managers. It is a message that we often repeat. In management there is no magic wand, no elixir of life, no guaranteed quick fix. One must beware of arguing by analogy, but it is somewhat like success at athletics. Every trainer has some pet theory to impart to athletes in his or her care. Using these theories, an athlete can achieve greatness. Another athlete can use the same approach and achieve much less. Success seems to crown a mixture of dedication, determination, fitness and a willing belief in oneself and in one's trainer.

However, the experienced consultant, like the trainer, brings certain advantages to a situation. Above all, the consultant is an outsider and can recognize and diagnose gross shortcomings. Previous experience helps to build expertise. It also helps the consultant's belief in values held and approaches to be employed.

Ultimately, we all have our own ideas of how people and organizations react to the need for change. These ideas will be based on our personalities, our philosophies, our experience and on our reading and learning. This varied background gives each of us an individual toolkit. The remarkable thing is that so many of these individual toolkits work in practice. People who want to introduce change may be company chairmen, counsellors, cabinet ministers, O & M staff, systems designers, management consultants and so on. All have been able to introduce changes in their professional career, even though each may hold widely differing ideas and theories of change. Perhaps one reason is the relevance of an aspect that is virtually ignored in the literature – namely, the personality of the person introducing the change.

Since so many of us have effected changes without a common set of beliefs or adherence to a single theory, it seems pointless to try overmuch to keep abreast of the latest fashionable change theory. For over three thousand years, managers have been worrying about the same things: motivation, centralization v. decentralization, and how to bring about major changes. It is statistically unlikely that a sure-fire answer will be found in the next ten years. Even more importantly, many of us find the concept of a sure-fire answer to be repugnant. It would somehow reduce the manipulation of our fellow humans to a purely mechanistic process.

The idea of a sure-fire change theory is also logically self-defeating. If there were a way of guaranteeing a change from condition A to condition B, then the same way could also be used to guarantee a change back again.

For managers to develop their own change theory which will work, they should:

- read about some of the ideas and theories that people have had about change and Organization Development. A start could be three books noted at the end of this chapter;[4–6]
- take on board those ideas that are compatible with their own values and beliefs;
- use these ideas and theories to build up an approach to effecting change;
- start to use this approach to effect small changes;

- give themselves feedback on how our ideas worked in practice. We have to be able to change our ideas about change;
- use the improved ideas on major changes.

Our own approach (which works for us and may not work for everybody else) is as follows.

Learn the background

The reason for an organization undertaking a study for a major change is usually seen as being one or more of:

- poor results (this may be poor profitability, low levels of service, inability to meet competition, etc.);
- underachievement by management;
- poor staff morale (e.g. bad labour relations);
- too much bureaucracy, and hence inflexibility;
- a major change in direction such as a merger or the introduction of office automation.

Knowing the apparent reason is a starting point. But it is not enough. One has to get to know the organization. Depending on circumstances, this may start in the usual consultancy manner: study the balance sheets, the organization charts, market share, trends and so on. The next stage is to get a feel for the culture of the organization. Is it stodgy, self-satisfied, paternalistic, aggressive, bureaucratic, customer-oriented, alert? Have management and unions taken to the trenches from where they are sniping at one another? Are the staff complete at odds with the organization? Is there interdepartmental infighting? And so on.

One gains this knowledge in a variety of ways. The main one has to be by talking to people. 'Talking to people' is a short phrase but a long phase. One is asking people to tell one their innermost feelings about the organization. Why should they? Only in the hope of future improvement. They certainly will not do so unless they trust one. This trust is not instantaneous; it has to be earned.

It is often necessary to talk to people outside the organization as well as to people within it, including customers, suppliers, the public and industry analysts. Not only can such discussions be revealing, they can often provide pointers to what changes are needed.

Focus on the landing-stage

Having uncovered where the organization is now, it is necessary to focus on where we want to go. In cases such as a merger this is reasonably obvious. In other cases this may not be so. In particular, one must beware of bringing to a situation a set of ready-made decisions. It is not true that stability, bureaucracy or paternalism are always out of place. For example, a nuclear power plant has a strongly bureaucratic approach to much of its work such as replacing fuel rods; a jet pilot has a checklist of over 100 items before a passenger plane takes off. In these instances bureaucracy is a virtue.

One of the most satisfactory situations occurs when the landing stage comes into focus as a result of discussions with people in the organization. When the consultant and the organization agree together in this way, then the change itself is likely to be that much easier.

Newton and the force field

In 1687 Sir Isaac Newton published his *Philosophiae Naturalis Principia Mathematica* and in it he postulated two laws of motion that can be paraphrased as follows:[7]

1 A body continues on its way unless acted on by a force.
2 Change is proportional to the strength of the force.

These laws may be used as an analogy for changing an organization. An organization will continue on its way unless acted upon by a force, and the force needed is proportional to the size of the change envisaged. It is not known who first used this analogy, but it was formalized by Kurt Lewin in 1974.[8] Lewin called the approach 'Force Field Analysis' (FFA). The idea behind force field analysis is that in any situation there are pressures (or 'forces') that are driving towards a change, and forces that act as restraints against change. To effect change, one increases those forces for it and/or decreases those forces against it. The stages of FFA are:

1 Carefully define the change desired.
2 Identify the forces for and against change. These forces can be technical or human, internal or external. The identification can arise out of discussions, group meetings or brainstorming.
3 Gauge the relative importance and strength of each force.
4 Create an action plan to increase the driving forces and to decrease the restraining forces.

To aid discussion and visualization, it is usual to draw a diagram. An example of a force diagram for a manager wishing to reduce weight is shown in Figure 19.1 overleaf. Another way of looking at this is the 'Gleicher formula'.[9] This is:

$$C = (ABD) > X$$

where C = change,
A = level of dissatisfaction with things as they are,
B = clarity of the 'landing stage',
D = practical first steps towards the landing stage,
X = the 'cost' of the change.

Thus, for a change to take place, it is necessary for A, B and D to be present and to be more than the cost of the change. The cost of the change here refers not so much to cash cost as intangible costs such as the upheaval discomforts. These costs are important. Much is made of people's 'fear of change', and it is true that we are all somewhat chary of the new. But the 'cost' is more complex than this.

In our experience, there are at least two other factors that are virtually ignored by the literature, are difficult to get people to talk about but which may be much greater obstacles to change on the personal level. The first is the fact that a major change will cause many people to worry about how their promotion prospects and paths have been affected. Some people may have felt that they could see a clear route for promotion before the change – but a major change may put everything back into the melting pot.

179

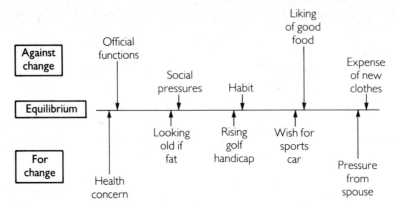

Figure 19.1 FFA diagram example

So a change can make some people feel that they have lost a year or two in their career development. It is hardly surprising in these circumstances if they fight the change.

A second obstacle can lie in the network of contacts that we all forge in an organization. Some of these contacts are links of friendship – these will survive a change although even here people can resent an increase in geographical distance from their friends and acquaintances. Other links are used by people in getting the work done and overcoming problems. In service organizations, these links can often benefit both the organization and the staff and so staff can dislike the thought of having to set up a new information and help network. Finally, some of these networks have a 'political' flavour and represent a system of favours owed and owing. A major change can cut these networks, leaving people unsure about the 'debts' and again facing them with the prospect of starting new networks.

Although the literature largely ignores these two obstacles, they can be the cause of really strong opposition from certain people to changes. If certain individuals are in strong opposition, it is well worth trying to find out if the cause lies here.

In using the Gleicher formula as a concept for effecting change, one tries to increase the factors A, B and D while reducing X. Factor A (dissatisfaction with the present) can be increased by:

- showing individuals that others share their wish for improvement;
- confronting people with facts uncovered;
- extrapolating trends into the future;
- describing the desirability of the proposed landing stage.

Factor B (clarity of the landing stage) can be increased by dealing in specifics rather than using generalized descriptions. One can use group discussions and explanatory seminars. One can have equipment demonstrations or arrange visits (e.g. a company moving its offices several hundred miles away arranged visits for staff and families to the new town).

Factor D (practical first steps) can be increased by setting out a detailed action plan, showing even extra detail for the initial stages. The first steps should be utterly non-technical and within people's previous experience. There are two aspects to clarity. One is summarized in the well-known phrase, 'Yes, but what do we do on Monday?' In other words, people want to understand actual, real, actions.

The other aspect is largely ignored in textbooks. This is the use of small steps. Most major changes can be atomized into a very large number of small steps that can be easily understood. They can also, if undertaken early, start a sense of momentum and, even more importantly, of success. For example, a firm was going to abandon a massive computer database and microfilm system at the same time as the filing system was overhauled. The consultant suggested a series of small initial steps. These included going through cupboards to throw away stocks of old forms, etc., and removing wrecked vehicles from a warehouse in preparation for a new archive.

Factor X (the cost of the change) can be decreased in many ways. These are of two types: cost to the work itself and cost to the lives of the individual people affected (and people that are far removed from the area of change can still see a cost to themselves). The cost to the work itself can be reduced by careful planning and explanations. The cost to individuals is a personal matter. It can be reduced to some extent by careful planning, detailed explanations, group discussions and seminars. But this will not be enough for everybody. Often, a number of personal one-to-one talks are required to find out individual costs and to try to reduce them.

The Gleicher formula is a concept rather than an arithmetic relationship. It is a very useful concept. At the very least, its use ensures that one does not forget the basic actions:

- collect basic facts and data;
- ensure that everyone understands where the end-point will be;
- ensure that the first practical steps are taken;
- take steps to reduce the 'cost' of the change.

The concept may not be sophisticated but it is useful, and recommended.

The importance of small steps

There are times when an organization undertaking a programme of change has to undertake some major improvements first. Examples are an overhaul of the marketing strategy, urgent production introduction or an immediate reform of the financial structure. The pressure of time and the nature of these improvements may be such that they are rather taken out of the type of change that we are considering.

Having set such improvements in train it is then necessary to turn attention to changing the culture (admittedly the standard textbooks put the process the other way round but perhaps the authors have never had to face bankers breathing down the necks of a client's management).

When one is looking at cultural change, the importance of small steps should never be overlooked. This was referred to above, together with an example, but is now repeated. Steps that may seem small to a consultant may not seem so small to the staff. If staff have despaired of ever seeing improvements, then a series of small changes can look like a breakthrough.

So it is often a good idea to atomize larger changes into small items that one is very likely to get adopted. It is even possible sometimes to go against a cardinal rule of consulting and install the changes oneself – or at any rate apparently to do so after talking it over with the chief executive. Of course, when one does this, one has to be right. But also, one has to broadcast news of achieving these successes.

■ FEEDBACK

News about these 'small step' successes has to be communicated to the staff. Not in the form of boasting, at all – that is counterproductive. But to show that change is not only possible, but has actually started. This feedback can be of considerable encouragement to the staff. It also gives a sense of that attribute that we keep emphasizing: momentum.

Resistance

No matter how skilled one may wish to think oneself, there will be times when one encounters resistance to change. The various approaches from which to select the most appropriate will depend on circumstances, and these are dealt with below.

1 *Education.* This approach is used when there is a large measure of misinformation (or a lack of information) among management and staff. It usually takes the form of seminars, training courses, group discussions or major feedback of the true facts. The advantage of this approach is that once people are in possession of information, they are likely to swing behind the change. The disadvantage is that it can take a long time.

2 *Participation.* A participatory approach is particularly appropriate where the consultant/initiator is aware that they do not or cannot have sufficient information themselves, or where others have considerable power to resist or disrupt change. The advantage of this approach is that the participants automatically 'own' the change process. The main disadvantages are that it takes a long time, and that a wrong decision by the participants is difficult to undo and is bad for morale.

3 *Facilitation.* This approach consists of arranging for people who further the change to be rewarded. These rewards include promotion, public acclaim and praise, going on desirable external courses and even monetary or quasi-monetary rewards. The main advantage of this approach is that, if carefully formulated, it works and works relatively quickly. The disadvantages are that it can cause resentment (or look like cynicism) to the unrewarded, and that it can be expensive if it fails.

4 *Negotiation.* This approach is useful if a group of people are clear losers in a change or are at loggerheads with another group. It is explained below in greater detail.

5 *Persuasion.* Trying to persuade people can be useful when other approaches will not work. The advantage of this approach is that it builds on the relationship between the initiator and the staff. The disadvantage is that if it fails it can increase resistance and make any other approach more difficult to try. There is also the possibility that people may feel that they are being manipulated.

6 *Coercion.* This approach can be countenanced when speed is vital and the coercer has more power than the objectors. A consultant is unlikely to have such power even if it would be helpful. The advantage of this approach is that it is fast and, by definition, likely to succeed. The main disadvantages are that genuine objections will be ignored, and that resentment may be caused which can surface later.

Negotiation

One of the approaches referred to above was 'negotiation'. An outsider such as a consultant can often arrange this to reduce conflict between departments; it is less easy for a member of an organization. The advantage of this approach is that (with practice) it can be remarkably effective.

A group of three people is selected from the two departments concerned. These six people, together with the consultant, meet in a room away from the main offices where they will not be disturbed. The meeting is held in a relaxed manner but is structured. To get things moving, the consultant starts by describing the work of the two departments in an unemotional manner. During this description, the consultant will touch on some of the difficulties of the work (e.g. skills and experience needed, deadlines, demands from the public, etc.).

The representatives from one department then are asked to say three things that are good about the other one, and vice versa. Sometimes, half jocularly, one group will say that there is nothing good about the other one. They must not be allowed to get away with this – one has to insist, otherwise the atmosphere can become unpleasant. After this, each group is asked to state three things that disappoint them about the other department.

At this stage, the consultant has to think on his or her feet because this exchange has to lead on to the main point of the discussions, which is to get each group to say what the other group could do to help them. This may be to produce output earlier, to reduce errors, to help out with peaks and so on. The consultant should have a reasonably good idea beforehand of what each group could in fact do to help the other, even if only to keep the meeting flowing.

The aim is to get each department to realize that they can actually help one another (if the work flow is 100 per cent one way, then an offer of help at peak periods can be valuable). Even more, one wants action so that help results. So it is necessary to follow up the original discussion, initially by reporting back to the supervisors in both departments.

This approach may seem trivial, or it may seem difficult. But it works. When the circumstances are right, it is well worth doing. It is recommended. In-house, we call this a Vonnegut meeting, because the author Kurt Vonnegut encapsulated the aim in one of his books when he wrote:[10]

> *We don't piss in your ashtrays,*
> *So please don't throw cigarettes in our urinal.*

This statement once, to our surprise and delight, actually appeared on the walls of a client.

Organization development – definition and background

It is not easy to define Organization Development. This is not because of semantic causes so much as a lack of agreement among practitioners as to exactly what the term encompasses. Most definitions offered are so abstruse as to defy understanding. One of the better ones was that coined by Richard Beckhard:[11]

> Organization Development is an effort planned, organization wide, managed from the top, to increase organization effectiveness and health, through planned interventions in the organization's processes using behavioural science knowledge.

The origins of Organization Development (OD) go back to the 1940s and the work of Kurt Lewin. Around 1945 he pioneered approaches that were used by the Survey Research Center and National Training Laboratories. Other behavioural scientists developed the approach for actual use in organizations, in the process often developing fresh tools. McGregor ('Theory X and Theory Y' initiator) and Beckhard worked at General Mills in 1956 and at Union Carbide in 1957.

Around the same time, Shepard and Blake were doing work at Esso which led Blake and Mouton to develop the Managerial Grid technique. Also around the same time, Rensis Likert and Floyd Mann were working at the Detroit Edison Company.

The actual term 'Organization Development' appeared in 1957. Who coined the term is a matter of some dispute; it may have been Beckhard or Herbert Shepard or Blake and Mouton. Thirty years later, the technique was being regarded somewhat dismissively by many managers. Currently, there are relatively few references to OD in management journals as compared with the coverage it received some years ago.

It is not easy to state categorically why this should be. It may be because OD is not a 'quick fix' or magic wand. It may even be a matter of fashion. It is regrettable but true that many management techniques are a matter of fashion – regrettable because many discarded techniques have about them some useful attributes even if some of the basics become out of date. It is all very well to throw out the baby, but some of the bathwater could still be useful.

To some extent the behavioural scientists themselves are to blame. Theories (such as the Needs Hierarchy) have just percolated into the thinking of managers when they are told that the theory is wrong. A friend of ours is an industrial psychologist; he often greets us with the question, 'What's new in motivation?' It is not easy to say that we do not care a lot, or that he should be telling us.

Many people would say that the whole of this chapter has been about OD. Others would feel that some of the basic techniques have been omitted or treated scantily. Our reply would be that an approach has been described that works, and that detailed descriptions of lots of techniques can actually get in the way. Another difference of opinion concerns what is known as 'contingency theory'. The contingency approach claims that there is not a 'one best way' of managing in all situations.

Adherents of the contingency approach believe that many aspects of management depend on circumstances. These include the technology used, size of the organization, location, type of industry, etc. Others dispute this belief, claiming that there is in fact one best way (in OD, Robert Blake would probably be counted in this category). Everybody has to decide for themselves whether they are contingencyites or not. Belief or not in the contingency approach probably depends on one's personality as much as on any possible proof. We tend to the contingency approach and so believe that the correct OD techniques that should be used depend on the prevailing circumstances.

Other OD techniques

The central core of OD (changing the culture) has remained largely unchanged over the past few years. Subsidiary techniques have changed rather more, especially those that are referred to as 'OD Productivity Interventions'. Some of these are described in brief below.

■ QUALITY OF WORK LIFE (QWL)

QWL is an attempt to improve the overall quality of life of employees. Its constituent parts are not widely agreed in the literature, but most definitions would include such matters as:

- proper compensation in monetary terms;
- healthy and safe working conditions;
- work that is designed to utilize to the full the skills, autonomy and aspirations of the staff;
- conditions that encourage a person's growth and security;
- freedom from racialism, sexism, ageism, together with real opportunities for upward progression;
- employees' rights embodied in a form of constitutionalism;
- an explicit and implicit right for all staff to lead their own lives outside the organization.

To some of us, this seems little more than what used to be known as 'good management practice'. Some practitioners would include in QWL a number of other approaches, including team-working, job design and workers' control.

C

■ JOB DESIGN

For the last two or three thousand years there has been disagreement on the relative benefits of specialization and generalization. Job design is a move towards more generalization, eschewing the extreme division of labour implicit in the scientific management approach.

One of the job design approaches is Job Enrichment. This aims to give staff greater responsibility and sense of achievement by making them responsible for a larger spread of tasks than would be the case with the division of labour concept. This is done by seeking to make the work itself more interesting, challenging and meaningful.

Another job design approach is Job Characteristics. This is based on the belief that job satisfaction and motivation are affected by five basic aspects: skill variety, task identity, task significance, autonomy and job feedback. A quasi-arithmetical formula for the motivational potential of a job is represented by:

$$\text{Motivating potential score (MPS)} = \left\{ \frac{\text{Skill variety} + \text{Task variety} + \text{Task significance}}{3} \right\} \times \text{Autonomy} \times \text{Job significance}$$

Skill variety is the extent to which a task or job needs a variety of different skills. Task variety is the extent that a job involves doing a complete and identifiable piece of work. Task significance is the extent that a task is perceived by the staff as having an impact on other people. Autonomy is the extent that the staff can control the work. Job feedback is the extent that there is feedback to the staff about how well the tasks are performed.

■ QUALITY CIRCLES (QC)

This approach uses the suggestions of small work groups to improve the quality of services or products in which the group is involved. It originated in Japan where it was a natural part of the organizational culture. It was adopted outside Japan in 1974 (by Lockheed in California). By 1982 it had spread in the USA so much that a study by the New York Stock Exchange suggested that 44 per cent of all American firms employing more than 500 people had a QC programme.[12]

There has been disagreement about how effective quality circles were. One commentator suggested that 90 per cent of all QC programmes were destined to become a failure.[13] Quality circles have been largely replaced by expanding the approach into such ideas as Total Quality Management (TQM) and Total Excellence (TE).

There has been much writing about Organizational Development. As a good primer, the book referred to in reference 6 is recommended. Another very interesting document is the brochure produced by Jan Carlzon after he was made chief executive of the Swedish SAS airline[14] with the task of turning it round. This brochure was aimed at all the staff. It starts off uncompromisingly: 'We have to fight competitors who are more efficient than we are. And who are at least as good as we are in figuring out the best deals. We can do it. But only if we are prepared to fight. Side by side. We are all in this together.' The brochure ends with a clear statement of philosophy which gives the aim of many OD and culture change programmes:

Bear in mind: The only really valuable asset we have is a truly satisfied customer.

References

1 Maslow, A. H., *Motivation and Personality*, New York: Harper, 1970.

2 Hall, D. T. and Nougaim, K. E., 'An examination of Maslow's need hierarchy in the organizational setting', *Organizational Behaviour and Human Performance*, Vol. 3, No. 1, 1968, p. 12.

3 Wahba, M. A. and Bridewell, L. G. in Steers, R. M. *et al.* (ed.), *Motivation and Work Behaviour*, New York: McGraw-Hill, 1979.

4 Robertson, I. T. and Smith, M., *Motivation and Job Design*, London: Institute of Personnel Management, 1985.

5 Markham, C., *Practical Consulting*, London: Institute of Chartered Accountants in England and Wales, 1987.

6 Harvey, D. F. and Brown, D. R., *An Experiential Approach to Organization Development*, Englewood Cliffs: Prentice-Hall, 1988.

7 Hawking, S. W., *A Brief History of Time*, New York: Bantam Books, 1988.

8 Lewin, K., 'Frontiers in group dynamics, concepts, methods and reality in social science', *Human Relations* 1, June 1974, p. 5.

9 Beckhard, R. and Harris, R. T., *Organization Transitions: Managing Complex Change*, Reading, Massachusetts: Addison-Wesley, 1977.

10 Vonnegut, K., *God Bless You, Mr Rosewater*, London: Jonathan Cape, 1965.

11 Beckhard, R., *Organizational Development: Strategies and Models*, Reading, Mass: Addison-Wesley, 1969.

12 Lawler, E. E. and Mohrman, S. A., 'Quality circles after the fad', *Harvard Business Review*, January/February 1985, p. 64.

13 Schwartz, H. S., 'A theory of deontic work motivation', *The Journal of Applied Behavioural Science*, Vol. 19, No. 2, 1983, p. 204.

14 Carlzon, J., *Let's Get In There and Fight!*, Scandinavian Airline Systems used by Nomme, R., *Economist* seminar, March 1988.

Further reading

Waterman, R. H., *The Renewal Factor*, London: Bantam Books (Transworld), 1989.

Schein, E. H., 'A general philosophy of helping: process consultation', *Sloan Management Review*, Vol. 31, No. 3, Spring 1990.

C

20

Management Accounting Aspects

Money will come when you are doing the right thing.
M. Philips, *The Seven Laws of Money* (1974)

[An accountant] is a man past middle age, spare, wrinkled ... minus
bowels, passion or a sense of humour. Happily they never
reproduce and all of them finally go to hell.
E. Hubbard (1856–1915), *The Note Book* (pub. 1927)

Management accounting is different from other forms of accounting such as financial
accounting. The difference has been succinctly put by one Professor of Accountancy
and Finance thus:[1]

- financial accounting and reporting is required by law or government bodies ... thus,
  it has to obey many rules and has to strive for objectivity;
- management accounting is designed specifically to serve the needs of managers ... to
  aid decision-making and planning.

Management accounting includes investment appraisal, cost accounting, budgets,
profitability analysis and long-range planning. It is on the first of these that this chapter
concentrates. However, first it is necessary to consider some aspects of cost accounting.

Costing

On the fact of it, 'costs' have a familiar, even cosy, feel. What could be more
straightforward than the idea of the cost of something? We can all feel at ease with the
cost of a television set or a house; it is the figure on the price tag.

This idea that the cost of something is the same as the price tag even extends to local
government, as can too frequently be observed. A local government authority decides
that it would be a good idea to build a new theatre or swimming pool. The capital is
raised and the building work completed. But this is not the end of the financial
implications. It is an almost universal truth that admission charges for a swimming
pool cannot cover the cost of running a swimming pool. Apart from the cost of the
capital (such as interest) there are the costs of heating, staff, water, purification,
building maintenance, tickets, promotion and so on. The bigger the swimming pool,
the larger the running costs.

Home-owners know that the cost of a house is not the purchase price. There are
additional initial costs such as taxes, lawyers' fees, mortgage start-up costs, furniture
removals. One may also have to buy light bulbs, curtains and curtain rails, electric
plugs. One may wish to enhance the house by buying floor-covering, heating, painting
the walls or buying some means of cleaning the house. These types of costs have
analogous costs when buying a computer or office technology.

A person, a local authority or a commercial firm must never forget the golden rule of life. This is:

Every capital cost brings with it revenue costs that last for the rest of the item's lifetime.

A corollary to this rule is that these extra costs are never less than one expects them to be.

The rule given above is not exactly a blinding revelation, but this does not prevent it from being ignored too often. Barclays Bank have a Business Advisory Service. A book written by Michael Pitcher[2] reveals that misconceptions about costs are the area that provides the most 'fruitful pastures' for this service to firms. Incidentally, although written basically for bank employees, this book is strongly recommended to anyone wishing to read a well-written primer for management accounting.

Accountants are therefore very careful about what the cost of something really means. They are careful for two reasons. First, because it is not a straightforward affair. Second, because costs matter.

A few definitions to clear the ground:

cost centre a location such as a department or section, or a group of people, or a piece of equipment or a group of pieces of equipment. A cost centre is chosen as such when it is a naturally discrete area, with its own identifiable cost to run it, and for which a person is identifiably responsible. Examples of cost centres might be the computer department, the mailroom, the export sales section.

cost unit a unit of a service, or product, or time (or some combination of these) that is the output of a cost centre. Cost units are often the same as the units used in work measurement (see Part E later in the book). Examples of cost units are the number of export orders, promissory notes, cars produced, tons of granite quarried.

absorption costing a system in which all the costs of all the cost centres are allocated to cost units in some way.

material costs the cost of commodities purchased by the organization.

labour costs the salaries, commissions, bonuses, etc. paid to staff.

expenses the cost of services and utilities purchased by the organization, such as electricity. Also includes intangibles such as depreciation.

direct cost a cost (material, labour or expense) that can be clearly recognized as being wholly allocatable to a cost unit (or a cost centre). An example of direct staff would be telesales staff. Supervisory staff can be more problematical.

indirect cost costs that are not clearly wholly allocatable to a cost unit (or cost centre). They therefore have to be allocated or apportioned in some way.

prime expenses direct material, direct labour and direct expenses.

prime cost the sum of all the prime expenses.

overheads indirect costs and the costs of selling, distribution, R & D, and administration.

fixed costs costs that occur with the passage of time and which are not dependent on the amount of output (e.g. rent, rates, insurance). Also known as period costs.

variable costs costs that vary, dependent on the amount of output (e.g. postage). Costs that have elements of time and output may be semi-variable. Few costs are entirely fixed over the long term, or variable over the very short term.

marginal cost   a system of costing in which only the variable costs are allocated to cost units.

Methods of costing

The main methods of costing are as follows:

■ ABSORPTION COSTING

This system (also known as total costing) is the commonest system. In it, all costs of the organization are allocated (or 'absorbed') to cost units, or a service or product, or groups of services or products. Advantages of absorption costing:

- decisions and pricing based on total costs ensures the complete recovery of costs, overheads and a profit margin. Failure to do this is a common failing of small businesses;
- allocation of total costs can provide a basis of overhead allocation that often seem fair and reasonable to the managers concerned;
- if a service or product cannot be sold at a profit under an absorption system, then many European and American firms would consider the probability of dropping it.

Disadvantages are:

- in practice, it is often very difficult indeed to allocate all indirect costs in a manner that is equally neutral for all possible decision-making situations. Inevitably, all allocations or apportionment must be arbitrary to some degree;
- this can lead to incorrect decisions being made, including the decision to drop specific services or products;
- the impact of change and decisions on working capital may be obscured.

■ MARGINAL COSTING

Marginal costing is mainly used as an aid to decision-making, and as such is not a substitute for other types of costing but rather an additional aid. Marginal costing (also known as variable costing) separates costs into fixed and variable, and concentrates on the variable cost part.

The marginal cost is thus the average variable cost of producing current services or goods. It is thence taken to be the variable cost of producing some extra services or goods. If one were to extrapolate this too far into the future or apply it to too large an increase, then one might not be quite accurate.

It should perhaps be pointed out that this is a different definition from the one used by economists when they speak of marginal costs. To an economist, marginal cost is the addition to total cost caused by the production of the last unit of goods or services.

The main advantage of marginal costing is that it provides a useful aid to decision-making by making it easier to assess the effect of changes in cost, volume or selling price. The main disadvantage of marginal costing is that people may start making too many decisions based on it, including many if not most pricing decisions. This can be seductive (especially if the market is ultracompetitive) but results in fixed costs not being covered in the selling price. A company can only do this for a short while, or bankruptcy surely beckons.

Another disadvantage lies in the difficulty of truly separating fixed and variable costs. In practice, the dividing line can be rather fuzzy. Moreover, this separation only remains valid within a range of output volume and of time. For example, increased volume will eventually need the rental or building of additional offices, warehouses, etc. Such increases are a 'step function' – the costs jump by a large amount at one time. One cannot increase office accommodation a square metre at a time as the demand increases.

■ DIRECT COSTING

This is the system in which as many costs that can be directly charged to an individual service or product are so charged. These costs can be either fixed or variable. In the past, Direct Costing was largely ignored (even worse, some textbooks actually combined it with marginal costing). The late 1980s showed a resurgence in interest since for long-term decision making it offers more help than other methods.

The main advantage of direct costing is that arbitrary allocation of costs is much reduced. So, the costs of services or products include direct costs including labour utilization.

The main disadvantage is that direct costing does not separate fixed and variable costs. It does not therefore show the effects of any change in volume.

■ STANDARD COSTING

This is the system commonly used when the major objective of the costing system is control of current operations. It consists of setting target costs and performances, known as standards. These standards are then compared with actual results achieved on a regular basis. These comparisons form the input for a system of reporting to management. The variances (the differences between standard and actual) then lead to action when they are adverse. Direct labour costs are preferably based on work quantification.

The main advantage of standard costing is that information is promptly made available for action. The use of variances can be further honed by only including them in the reporting system if they are significant. Variances (especially if reported on selectively) save management's time considerably.

The main disadvantage is that such systems can be complex, lengthy to install and need periodic revision. In addition, some managers using them do not take the time to understand fully their basis and so may use them blind, assuming that figures mean certain things that they do not.

Investment appraisal

The appraisal of capital investments is part of the wider concept of total capital budgeting. The nature of capital budgeting was spelt out by Joel Dean in a paper that has become a classic:[3]

- a continual search for good investment opportunities;
- long-range plans and projections;
- short-term budgets of cash and capital requirements;

- an accepted yardstick of economic worth;
- an estimate of the economic worth of different projects;
- standards for screening different investment projects;
- control of spending by comparing authorization with expenditure;
- carrying out a post mortem on actual project savings;
- analysis of facilities that are candidates for disposal;
- systems and procedures to ensure smooth administration.

The fact that senior management have to take this wider view may help to explain why so many people are disappointed if their pet project does not gain approval for expenditure. The point is that all capital expenditure is in competition with other possible projects. Management always has to choose, because no organization has access to unlimited funds. This choice is often between dissimilar projects, such as a new mainframe computer or taking over another company, or comparing new office technology with extending the product range to meet new competition. Even when no formal comparison is set up a choice has been made, though it may be by default.

When looking at capital expenditure, there are three important aspects that have to be remembered:

1 As already stated, all such expenditure is a choice between alternatives.
2 All measurements are made in terms of cash flows, whether cash coming in over the years as a result of spending exceeds cash going out. So the normal distinction between capital and revenue does not exist in appraising capital expenditure. It is all cash flow.
3 A comparison should be possible between the cash earned from a project and the cost of the capital used. There is little point in spending money on a project that will earn 5 per cent p.a. if the cost of the money to finance it is 10 per cent.

Different methods of appraisal

Just as there are various costing methods, so too there are different ways of appraising capital investments. The four main methods are known as pay-back, return on investment, net present value and internal rate of return. The final two (NPV and IRR) are two of the several methods that collectively are known as Discounted Cash Flow (DCF) methods. It should be pointed out that some of the methods quoted are sometimes referred to by other names.

In deciding which is the preferred approach, it has to be remembered that invest-ment appraisal may be concerned primarily with any one of three criteria:

- project profitability;
- effect on liquidity;
- change on the company's reported results.

If the main criterion is the project's inherent propensity to profitability, then the preferred approach would be one based on discounting such as Net Present Value (or perhaps Internal Rate of Return). If the main concern is liquidity, then one would use the pay-back method. If the main criterion is the change to the company accounts, then one would choose the Return on Investment methods since it uses conventions similar to those used in company accounts. These methods are shown below.

■ PAY-BACK METHOD

The pay-back method tests the effect of projects on liquidity. In effect, it indicates the number of years that a project will take to repay the original investment. The arithmetic is straightforward and this has led to the method's being widely used, especially for smaller projects, and for justifying changes in systems and procedures. An example is shown in Table 20.1. In this example, Project Y would be the preferred one although Project Z would eventually give a better return. The word 'earnings' is used, rather than savings, in order to emphasize the fact that even the spending of money to save money can be less attractive than spending money to make money. To repeat: all spending is a matter of choice.

Table 20.1 Pay-back example

	Project X	Project Y	Project Z
Original investment	£100,000	£100,000	£100,000
Earnings:			
Year 1	50,000	55,000	45,000
Year 2	50,000	50,000	50,000
Year 3	1,000	45,000	50,000
Year 4	1,000	1,000	50,000
Pay-back period	2 years	1.9 years	2.1 years
Ranking	2	1	3

The main advantage of this method is that it is easy to calculate and understand. It also ensures that every project 'washes its face'; that is, that it brings in as much money as it spends. It is self-liquidating. It thus shows how long is needed to turn a risky investment into profit.

The other side of this coin is also the method's main disadvantage, which is that it favours projects that offer high initial returns, and these can often be those that are the most risky. Other disadvantages are that no account is taken of earnings after the payback period; it does not show the return on investment (to compare with the cost of capital); and it may lead to underinvestment if too short a 'target' pay-back period is chosen. It also leads one to ignore outgoings which occur in most projects after the original investment has been made.

■ RETURN ON INVESTMENT (ROI)

This method uses concepts that are similar to those used in balance sheets and profit-and-loss accounts. In concept it is straightforward and an example is shown in Table 20.2 overleaf. In the example, Project Z moves into first place compared with last place in the pay-back method. The main advantages of this method are that it is easy to understand and that it provides a measure of being able to see the project as a financial affair. The main disadvantage is that (like the pay-back method) it does not take into account the time value of money.

The time value of money is an important matter for all organizations. A simple example may help to dispel the difficulty that some people have in understanding this concept. Which would you prefer – that I give you £1,000 now or £1,100 in five years' time? The correct response of course is to accept the £1,000 now. There are two reasons

Table 20.2 ROI example

	Project X	Project Y	Project Z
Original investment	£100,000	£100,000	£100,000
Earnings after depreciation:			
Year 1	50,000	55,000	45,000
Year 2	50,000	50,000	50,000
Year 3	1,000	45,000	50,000
Year 4	1,000	1,000	50,000
Average return p.a.	£25,500	£37,750	£48,750
Return on Investment	25½%	38%	49%
Ranking	3	2	1

for this. First, the £1,000 could be invested so that it would be worth more than £1,100 in five years' time. Second, there is a risk that I may not be around in five year's time to transfer the £1,100. The time value of money is taken into account by the two remaining methods of appraising capital expenditure.

■ NET PRESENT VALUE (NPV)

The concept of all Discounted Cash Flow (DCF) methods – of which NPV is one – is the idea of discounting. This can be shown by relating an example back to the idea of a transfer of £1,000 mentioned above. The capital sum of £1,000 is called the principal and if invested could earn interest of, let us say, 10 per cent p.a. So, over a period of three years, the picture would be as follows:

Start of Year 1	– Principal	1,000
End of Year 1	– Interest (10% × 1000)	100
End of Year 1	– Principal + interest	1,100
End of Year 2	– Interest (10% × 1100)	110
End of Year 2	– Principal + interest	1,210
End of Year 3	– Interest (10% × 1210)	121
End of Year 3	– Principal + interest	1,331

Investing £1,000 at 10 per cent would thus give £1,331 by the end of the third year. The interest would itself earn interest; since this means that the 10 per cent was compound interest, the process is known as compounding. Discounting is in effect the opposite of compounding. It tells us how much we would have to invest now, so that in three years' time we would have the £1,000. The answer is £751.3 because:

$$751.3 \times 1.10 \times 1.10 \times 1.10 = 1,000$$

The figure of 751.3 can be calculated from the formula:

$$\frac{1}{(1+i)^n}$$

where i is the rate of interest, and n is the number of years. To avoid having to calculate this formula, a table is given in the Appendix in chapter 49 for different rates of interest and numbers of years. It will also be found that most spreadsheet programs, except the very simplest, will have this formula as a standard entry.

It is now possible to repeat the example given in Tables 20.1 and 20.2, with three differences. First each figure for the earnings per year is multiplied by the Net Present Value factor from the Appendix; this tells us how much each year's earnings is worth now. This allows for the time value of money and enables one to get a figure that can be compared directly with the original investment amount.

Second, the figure for annual earnings is changed to 'net cash flows'. This means that we can allow for that spending which occurs after the original capital expenditure. To avoid confusion and complications, no such change has been made to the table in the example. Third, a figure has been added for 'residual value'. This acknowledges the fact that in most projects, an asset will have been acquired (such as an office computer) and that this will still be worth something at the end of the time in the table. Table 20.3 lays out the new calculation.

Table 20.3 Net present value example

	10% discount factor	Project X	Project Y	Project Z
Original investment	1.0000	£100,000	£100,000	£100,000
Net cash flows:				
Year I	0.9091	45,455	50,000	40,910
Year 2	0.8264	41,320	41,320	41,320
Year 3	0.7513	750	33,810	37,565
Year 4	0.6830	685	685	34,150
Residual value		20,390	–	15,265
Total Net Present Values		108,600	125,815	169,210
Ranking		3	2	1

The main advantage of the NPV method is that it takes account of the time value of money. It also approaches the concept of maximizing the present worth of the organization. It has the disadvantage of being superficially complex, and requiring an understanding of compound interest and discounts.

All the discounted cash flow methods have been the subject of considerable discussion and writing. Some of the controversy is rather technical, but it may be worth pointing out that the NPV method assumes that earnings inflows can be reinvested at the discount rate used (10 per cent in the example).

■ INTERNAL RATE OF RETURN (IRR)

The IRR method is the obverse of NPV. The aim is to calculate the actual discount rate which would make cash outlay equal to cash inflows. This is done by repeating the calculation in Table 20.3 at least twice for each project. For example, Project X is obviously slightly less than 10 per cent, so one would repeat the calculation, using a discount rate of 9 per cent. One would then have to interpolate between 9 per cent and 10 per cent to reach a closer approximation. Alternatively, one could use discount tables using decimal points or preferably use an office computer (manual calculations are lengthy, boring, and easy to get wrong).

The main advantage of the IRR method is that it enables a comparison to be made between the rate of return of a project and the rate for any borrowed money (or with the firm's average cost of capital). The main disadvantage is the length of time needed for calculations. There is also a problem when in any year there is a negative cash flow. The underlying equation can then give two answers (because the solution can have two roots – a fact that can be hidden when using an office computer, for example).

■ ADDITIONAL POINTS

As mentioned, there has been considerable discussion about capital appraisal over the years, especially about discounted cash flow methods such as NPV and IRR. Some points are:

1 As seen, not all methods give the same ranking for competing projects.
2 The methods as shown do not take account of the risks of competing projects. To do so requires additional calculations with the introduction of additional concepts.
3 In practice, of necessity, managerial decisions have to take account of factors other than just arithmetic ones, e.g. fending off the competition, gaining market share, etc.
4 Projects may be concerned with the acquisition of advanced technology. Acquisition is not the most important factor. This is what follows the acquisition – known as the Management of Technology.
5 Methods of capital appraisal depend on predicting the benefits over a period of time. This is notoriously difficult, especially in the hands of an enthusiast. Actually achieving the predicted benefits is also notoriously difficult.
6 The effects of taxation on both cost and benefits can be even more important than predicted costs and benefits.
7 Many project proposals omit the extra costs that inevitably occur in the years after the original expenditure. Some are mentioned in the simplified table given in Figure 39.1. This shortcoming led to the concept of 'lifetime costs'. This looks at the total costs that are involved during the lifetime of a major equipment acquisition. For example, it is common to find 50 per cent of the programmers in a computer department doing maintenance work on existing programs rather than on new projects. Another '50 per cent' figure is that later costs of advanced office technology are an additional 50 per cent of the original acquisition costs.
8 Much of the discussion about capital appraisal treats each project as being in isolation. The truth is that, in real life, many projects interlock. Not only do they happen at the same time, they also often build on one another. A simple example is the use of electronic mail. To justify this, should one include the cost of installing a network and additional terminals? Or was this going to happen anyway? Add to this the flexible nature of accounting,[4] and one can see that costing and capital appraisal is not necessarily the straightforwardly scientific matter that it seems at first.

Profits and cash flow

It is always possible for a company to report increasing profits and increasing capital expenditure, but to still go bankrupt. A notable example was Laker Airways (Table 20.4):[5] Here, the cash was going into additional investment (e.g. aircraft). This made it impossible to repay the ever-increasing debts.

Table 20.4 Reported profits and cash flow for Laker Airways for the years 1977–80

Year	1977	1978	1979	1980
Total reported profits (£m)	0.8	1.5	4.8	8.1
Cash flow in:				
Operating cash flow	4.5	12.1	10.7	17.6
Additional borrowing	–	11.2	27.3	52.0
Decrease in cash assets	2.4	–	2.0	0.8
Total cash flows	6.9	23.3	40.0	70.4
Cash flow out:				
Additional investment	3.5	19.1	40.0	70.4
Repayment of borrowings	3.4	–	–	–
Increase in cash assets	–	4.2	–	–

■ TWO TRENDS

There has been much criticism of the costing and accounting methods used by many firms. In particular, this criticism has been directed at putting a very large proportion of the costs into 'overheads' and then allocating them in proportion to direct labour. This can make all costing and decisions top-heavy. Overheads can be massive. For example, in one firm, a subsidiary was either profitable or a loss-maker depending entirely on its allocation of costs from the central computer department.

In addition, increased automation can effectively turn an organization from being labour intensive into being capital intensive. This can make a nonsense of using staff costs the basis for allocating overheads.

One of the reactions to this criticism has been to try to allocate costs much more closely to the cost unit or cost centre which gave rise to the cost. This is somewhat akin to the direct costing method described in this chapter (it is also another reason for not confusing direct costing with marginal costing). Such allocation is not always easy. For example, allocating the costs of a mainframe computer can be very complex if it is used for both batch and on-line processing.

The other trend could be viewed as being in some ways a contrary approach. Hitachi have the world's largest videocassette recorder factory.[6] This is highly automated, but Hitachi continue to allocate overheads to direct labour. This is because Hitachi regard reductions in direct labour as essential for cost reductions. Allocating overheads to direct labour, claim Hitachi, provides a strong incentive to the introduction of more automation – a strategic consideration. Another Hitachi factory allocates overheads to the number of parts in product models. This is because the number of parts (especially 'specials') affects directly the amount of overheads.

Some Japanese firms take matters further. Instead of starting with the cost of producing services or products and adding overheads and profit, they make their management accounting market driven. This means that the price (and hence total costs) are taken as being what the market will bear. They then work backwards from this figure until they arrive at what the costs of production and overheads *must* be, if not now then in the future. Everybody then has to work at making the costs equal to and then less than what the market says they should be.

References

1 Nobes, C., *Pocket Accountant*, London and Oxford: The Economist and Blackwell, 1985.
2 Pitcher, M. A., *Management Accounting for the Lending Banker*, London: The Institute of Bankers, 1979.
3 Dean, J., *Controls for Capital Expenditure*, Financial Management Series No. 105, New York: American Management Association, 1953.
4 Griffiths, I., *Creative Accounting*, London: Waterson, 1986.
5 Hindle, T., *Pocket Banker*, London and Oxford: The Economist and Blackwell, 1985.
6 Hiromoto, T., 'Another hidden edge – Japanese management accounting', *Harvard Business Review*, Vol. 66, No. 4, 1988, p. 22.

Further reading

Bierman, H., and Smidt, S., *The Capital Budgeting Decision*, New York: Macmillan, 1984.
Sizer, J., *An Insight into Management Accounting*, Harmondsworth: Penguin, 1969.

21

Management Information Systems

At this very moment the management of some company is devising
a means of going broke that I have not thought of. It may take a lot
of effort but they will do it.   Bill MacKay[1]

'It was a great loss, my Pharaoh', stated Rut-sekh ... 'ten bags of
grain, two large amphorae of oil, three amphorae of honey ... five
hundred forty-one loaves of bread, four amphorae of the wine of
Buto'.   **Norman Mailer**, *Ancient Evenings* (1983)

Most of us bring a rather blinkered approach to the subject of MIS (Management
Information Systems). This blinkered outlook results in the wide variation seen in the
MIS that exists in organizations. An accountant will see MIS as a natural extension of
management accounting. Since in the 1960s and 1970s (a period of rapid growth in
computer use) the computer department was often organizationally part of the financial director's division, this had practical effects. The type of information distributed
was often allied to balance sheet information. At times, considerable effort was
expended to line the two up so that MIS information for managers could be abstracted
to become financial data.

Where the setting up of an MIS was originally the responsibility of a head of
computing, it tended to take on a different appearance. In this case, it was common to
put the emphasis on a massive database. Access to this database could then be either
structured or free-form. This approach was reinforced during the 1970s when the idea
took root of 'unlimited data access'. This was the idea that everybody should have
access to all information − all information that was in the database, that is. The
response to this thought could be seen in the early 1980s when several computer
manufacturers used contrary ideas in their advertising. This advertising often referred
to 'filters' that would help to reduce the amount of information flow. This would lead to
greater managerial effectiveness, and hence greater profitability.

Even management consultants cannot always escape the accusation of taking a
blinkered approach. They will usually have a limited price (and hence time) in which
an MIS must be formulated and set up. This can lead one to taking a semi-packaged
approach. The aim may become safety by using a proven answer. Nobody thanks a
consultant for taking risks, especially if they do not succeed.

Another form of blinkered approach can arise from academia. Some academics see
MIS as an extension and reinforcer for a new theory of management or organization
structure.

Perhaps MIS is an area where we are all blinkered to some extent, first by a lack of
knowledge (none of us can know everything); secondly by a lack of experience (apart
from consultants and manufacturers, few people have installed more than three MIS
systems); thirdly, by the old enemy − lack of time.

So no MIS study is a trivial exercise. It takes time, for every stage. It is complex;

199

indeed for any study that is not for a small organization it can be quite difficult for the human brain to wrap itself round all the ramifications. This is particularly true for organizations that are effectively several businesses in one. A single-product organization (such as a car manufacturer or a hospital) may seem complex to the people who work there. From an MIS viewpoint, much more complex are those organizations that have a mix of, say, merchanting, manufacturing, retailing, plus an advertising agency.

This complexity often means that the only practical approach is seen as being to split the MIS up into suites of programs and to provide links between the suites. This reduces the problem to manageable proportions, but it brings other problems in its wake. First, the way the suites are allocated means that one is presented with a large part of the answer well before one has looked at the problem. This constraint can often be observed, and it is not easy to lose. The thought of the sheer time and effort needed to change or replace all the suites is enough to discourage all but the most determined. Second, the linkages between the discrete suites may hide what is known as 'gaps in the floorboards'. These gaps are the way things slip through the system. As each gap is revealed, it has to have a 'Band-Aid', a supplementary piece of software that covers the gap. Over a long enough period of time, the band-aids build up one on another. This makes unravelling (to mix the metaphors even further) an awe-inspiring task.

It might seem that there is little hope for us; that the perfect MIS must always remain a sort of Holy Grail. However, some organizations do have good MIS systems. Observation (for which no proof is offered) suggests that these organizations fall into certain categories:

- those who grew their MIS organically over a period of time, some parts being traceable back to non-computing ideas;
- those who are 'comfortable' with their MIS. Comfort can be due to widespread knowledge and understanding, or to the MIS remaining as a background non-intrusive aid;
- organizations that have metaphorically taken a deep breath and expended considerable time, effort, and money in installing a new MIS.

Principles of MIS

1 The introduction of sophisticated commercial computers revolutionized the whole concept of information for management. The computer has made it possible to do things that managers could only dream of previously. Having effected this revolution, the computer should be thought of as neither a servant or a master. It is something to be blended with our ideas and thoughts.

2 Management information that is made available does not have to be totally integrated with the financial accounts or the needs of the balance sheet. It can have an existence of its own.

3 An MIS should be based on the information needed to run an organization successfully now, and to help it prepare for the future.

4 An MIS should be tailored for individual organizations. This will depend on such factors as:
- the industry;
- the organization structure;

- the culture of the organization;
- corporate strategy.

5 To be successful, an MIS should not merely offer information on what is happening. It should also facilitate question answering and problem solving.

6 An MIS should be usable and used. It must therefore be part of each manager's normal life. For managers to be comfortable:

- the MIS must provide information that is useful;
- the MIS must provide information in a manner and format that makes it the best source of information in the eyes of the managers;
- users must be trained in using and exploiting the MIS;
- a reasonable level of user-friendliness should be aimed at.

7 No MIS can hope to provide the totality of information needed by managers. It must not therefore aim to do so.

Aspects affecting MIS development

C

1 *The culture of the organization.* No only does this affect the use that will be made of the MIS once it has been set up, it also affects whether the managers will accept a slow build up, or whether they need a 'big-bang' change which will need fewer changes later.

2 *The type of industry.* Of course, this affects the type of information that will be needed and the form in which it will be presented. But it affects other aspects as well. Different packages are more suitable for different industries. For example, IBM's MAAPICS was very good for firms manufacturing electronic parts. It would not be the first choice for an advertising agency, or even perhaps for a firm making cosmetics and pharmaceuticals.

The industry involved can even affect the programming language used, in those cases where an in-house package is written. For example, 4GL (fourth generation languages) started being used for database-type MIS in the mid-1970s. 4GLs (plus prototyping) are useful where there are rapid changes (quasi-governmental organizations), or where there is a need for many *ad hoc* reports (personnel). They may not be the first choice where real-time updating is needed or where there is an extremely high volume of transactions (banks).

3 *Legal requirements.* For example, information may be segmentally restricted in some banking firms.

4 *Audit requirements.* Apart from any financial considerations, there is a need for robustness in the systems especially for control and security points of view.

5 *The degree of integration.* There are a number of information flows in an organization at any time. These may include a management control system, financial/management accounting, balance sheet data, production/stock/marketing information systems and so on. If, how, and in what manner any of these are to be integrated with the MIS have to be considered.

6 *The organization structure.* The MIS for a single-product manufacturer will be very different from that suitable for a firm that uses the rapid formation and dissolution of teams; their structures will be different and so will be their MIS. The degree of centralization/decentralization will also have a marked impact.

7 *Technical considerations.* These will include database management, telecommunications involved and the hardware employed.

8 *Starting point.* Many observers agree that the MIS that is installed can depend on what it is replacing. A successful company may have grown so rapidly that the MIS may be replacing a largely manual system. In this situation, managers may have very high expectations from the new MIS and be unwilling to compromise. In another firm, the MIS may be replacing an existing MIS. In this situation, the managers may be more easily persuadable that perfection is not to be.

Data, information and knowledge

Data is infinite, information is what we want to use, knowledge is scarce. The aphorism hides a truism. There is no end to the data that is available; information is data that we wish to have – though there is no guarantee that either data or information are correct. For example, 10 per cent of men claim to share their bath with their wife, but only 6 per cent of women claim to share their bath with their husband. These two facts are data or information depending on whether or not you are a manufacturer of baths. If you know the reason for the discrepancy, then you have knowledge (if you can accept the discrepancy as natural, then perhaps you also have wisdom).[2]

Table 21.1 contains data. Depending on circumstances, it may or not be important. In a police murder investigation, the breakfasts column might matter if the people included a poison victim – or the activities column might if one of the people was a murder suspect. The breakfasts column might also matter if one were a breakfast cereal manufacturer. A personnel department might need to know that White was working overtime so that payment can be arranged.

Table 21.1 Data table

Clock No.	Name	Breakfast on Tuesday, 12 February	Times absent last year	Colour of eyes	What doing at 6 p.m. on Thursday, 14 February
1286	Smith	Black coffee	44	Brown	Drinking whisky
1297	Jones	Toast and jam	11	Blue	Watching TV
2014	Czernoci	Sausage	8	Blue	Praying
2155	Robinson	Eggs and bacon	9	Green	Watching TV
3038	White	Tea and toast	Nil	Blue	At work

What the table of data does not tell us is the sort of person that Smith is. She may be an alcoholic, often away from work through being incapable, and needing black coffee to try to get into shape to face a day's work. Or he may have had a daughter who had a bad pregnancy and took time off work to look after her, being unable to eat breakfast because of worry. The whisky may have been a celebration of a successful delivery.

So we can say that:

- data may not be infinite in quantity but it is close to infinite;
- data does not give us knowledge until it is bulked up, or compared with other data or filtered in some way. The table of data would not be the sort of material in an MIS. It would have to be worked on in some way before it would be of much use;

- different information will be of use to different managers at different times and in different circumstances;
- a database is not a management information system. A manager will normally need both;
- an MIS needs to produce reports of information that will help individual managers. Nearly always, it should also be able to produce *ad hoc* reports for special needs.

Revising old systems

Like old soldiers, many old MIS systems never die – they just need more and more Band-Aid. Or so it often seems. As has been rather cruelly pointed out, some MIS software is now effectively older than the people who are maintaining it. Another way of looking at it is to ask how old will one allow the software to get before revising it or replacing it? Thirty years? Forty years? Ridiculous? Well, some of it is already a quarter of a century old.

The basic problem is that an old system can become a snare. It may well contain thousands of old programs and data files. Since they are old, the documentation for them may be incomplete or in poor shape. They may even have been written in languages which new programmers are not familiar with. Where there is an old MIS system, the options are as follows:

1 Pretend that there is no MIS already in existence. Start again right from the beginning and install a completely new MIS. On the face of it, this sounds like an unthinkable solution to many organizations. But it does have advantages. It means that one can start afresh, with good documentation and little Band-Aiding. One can take advantage of the new packages that are more flexible than the old ones, or one can use a newer language if the software is to be written in-house. The firm may have changed since the concepts of the old MIS were formulated; certainly the firm will have more experience of MIS. The question of the data files must be considered carefully. Their complete replacement is a mammoth task, but transfer may be complex. The decisions are even more thought-provoking if the data files have been to some degree corrupted.

2 Install a new software package. This alternative can be attractive if the circumstances are suitable (e.g. changing the method of distribution). Some new software is more flexible than it was and so a package can be tailored more easily. Application generators can help where available (application generators generate the computer code for an application – though not everybody likes them).

3 Rewriting. It is possible to rewrite all the software, a solution that will be attractive if the old code has been continually patched or is over-convoluted. But this can be a massive task. One company had 50,000 COBOL programs (though, of course, not all were part of the MIS). These programs totalled over 37 million lines of code. To rewrite 20 per cent of this would take 2,000 work-years. Assuming that each line would cost $10 this amounted to $75 million.[3]

4 Enhancements. The old system may be capable of improvement. These improvements might be to improve the input process, the output process, the enquiry capabilities or the data manipulation. Irrespective of the original language, it may be possible to use a 4GL for many of the enhancements.

5 Restructuring. A system may still be doing what it should but be difficult to

maintain, or inefficient or not particularly robust. In such cases it may be attractive to restructure it. Restructuring cleans up the code. It highlights looping, removes dead code, reduces GOTOs, removes ALTER statements and so on. This is done automatically using special software. Some companies, such as Peat Marwick Catalyst Group, offer this service, which Peat call 'structured retrofit'.

Information for management

Since MIS is a management information system, the heart of any MIS study must be deciding what information should be available to user managers. This sentence is so obvious that it should be redundant. Unfortunately, it is not redundant. A surprisingly high number of MIS have been based on too little consideration of this basic matter. Some MIS are little more than a screen-based form of detailed management or labour controls. Some are an interrogatory system for database(s). A few are clearly driven by the accountant or the computer department. A few firms have renamed their computer department the MIS Department.

Deciding the information that should be made available is not a trivial matter. The first decision is – who should make the decisions? Any single person or group is likely to be biased, whether it be the accountants, the head of computing, the management consultants or even the managers themselves who may not have seen an MIS in action.

Our preferred choice is to base the information made available on the ideas of the managers themselves. But it is necessary to be careful how these ideas are collected, collated, integrated, added to, cut down and then turned into an MIS form. This should be the responsibility of one person or a small team, and treated as a specific study or project.

Who should lead this study? The preference must be for somebody who is respected as having knowledge about management in general, the actual industry, MIS and, where possible, the actual organization itself. This person might be a senior manager in the organization, a senior member of the auditors or an external management consultant.

The information needed by a manager will depend on a number of factors, including the seniority of the manager. As a generalization, the more senior the manager, the more that manager will need information from outside the organization. Middle managers are mainly concerned with how well the company is doing today, and thence improving that level of performance. Senior managers need to know how well the firm is doing in comparison with competitors, and laying down strategy and tactics.

The information and the facilities can be considered as falling into the following broad groupings:

1 *Information about internal operations*. This has to be tailored for each level in the organization. The chairman will want the balance sheet type of figures. The managing director will want key figures so that all managers will know that the MD has his finger on the pulse and that bad news will not go undetected. Junior managers may need the sort of information traditionally thought of as being the management control type.
2 *Problem information*. This includes figures derived from 'management by exception', figures that have fallen outside pre-set limits, reports on current major crises and controls on any major project.

3 *Access to data for 'end-user computing'.* End-user computing is the direct use of computing power by users instead of just using the output of the computer department. One often sees managers using a spreadsheet to investigate alternative courses of action. The 1970s saw an explosion in the growth of end-user computing. For example, during the 1970s in the Xerox Corporation end-user computing rose from almost nothing to nearly 40 per cent of the total computing power capacity.[4]

Nearly everyone agrees that the growth of end-user computing is a good thing. It may seem somewhat churlish, therefore, to point out that it is not an unmitigated blessing. It can lead to considerable duplication. It can lead managers to confuse sitting at a terminal with management. Worst of all, it can result in managers remaining ensconced in their offices in isolation when they should be out of the office and 'minding the shop'. The fact that we are something of a lone voice in making this warning does not necessarily mean that we are wrong.

4 *Comfort information.* This consists of a few figures each day, such as sales figures, etc. Managers do very little with this information but it gives a feeling of knowing what is going on. This can be expanded to a couple of paragraphs, giving extra information that will be of interest.

5 *External information.* This is information about the external environment. At one level, it can be just a subscription to external databases or information services (such as the Dow service, which gives considerable financial information). At another level, it may include various forms of analysis performed either in-house or externally. At the highest level, it may include the use of models. For example, one company built a model to predict price changes by competitors. No MIS should ignore the vast potential of external information.

Since an MIS screen may be an executive's main computer access, it can be useful to feed into it other services. These can include the manager's own data files, word processing facilities, electronic mail, private fax, and so on.

Study shape

All MIS studies are different, depending on the industry and the individual organization. However, the general shape of an MIS assignment will follow this pattern:

1 Obtain details of the organization structure, copy of the last balance sheets and chairman's reports (say, three) and inter-firm comparison and analysis. Study and learn.

2 Interview the top managers and discuss:
- how they view the company;
- how they see the current information flow and in what ways they want it improved;
- how they view the hierarchy in terms of centralization, allocation of responsibilities, budgetary formulation, autonomy of divisions;
- their views on computing power, facilities, availability, level of service and the computer department plus their attitudes to office automation and advanced office technology.

3 Prepare a seminar on the principles of MIS, computing power, etc.

4 Give the seminar to the top managers and selected middle managers. Try to get a good discussion going. This should include people's hopes and fears, as well as attitudes.

5 Repeat the seminar and discussion for middle managers.

6 Interview middle managers individually. In a large company, it may be necessary to interview only a sample. These interviews will cover:
   - a brief discussion of the seminar;
   - what information they need to do their job well, what they get currently, what they do not want, and what extra they wish to get and in what form;
   - what information is currently sent/received and to/from whom, and in what form.

7 Interview the head of computing and discuss his ideas, hopes and fears. Obtain details of:
   - hardware and software used;
   - current report generation and distribution;
   - any changes planned or in hand. Agree software to be used.

8 Interview the head of finance. Discuss the seminar, the current situation, its shortcomings, as well as the head's plans, hopes, fears and ideas.

9 If the organization feeds management information to external bodies, obtain details.

10 Prepare (initially for the analyst's own use) an overall picture of the current information flow, how prepared, the distribution logic.

11 It is usually necessary at this stage to split the information into its constituent data parts ('atomizing'), to discover the source of each piece of data, and to define data/information terms. Definitions are necessary since some items (such as 'sales' and 'staff numbers') will mean different things in different places. This atomizing stage can be lengthy and, frankly, rather boring for analysts who prefer action to desk-work.

12 Collate the non-data factors such as shortcomings of the current situation, and people's expectations. This collation may be a matrix, or just a series of lists.

13 The analyst now starts to prepare a paradigm of the proposed MIS. This will show broad headings of what information is needed by each level of the hierarchy (by divisions or major departments) to do their jobs well. This will be shown under the groupings given above under the heading information for management. Broad details will also be shown of the degree of integration and non-MIS uses of the managers' screens.

14 Discuss this paradigm with top managers. Amend as necessary.

15 Build up the information flow from its atoms – the reverse of Stage 11. This can be another lengthy stage.

16 Hold another interview with the head of computing to agree details of any programming work that is involved.

17 Finalize details of the new MIS in all aspects.

18 If prototyping is to be used, then this must be prepared. Prototyping is a working system which demonstrates the system. It is iterative – starting off with just a few basic functions and adding more as it evolves. Prototyping often uses applications generators to speed up the process. If prototyping is not to be used, then an alternative method of demonstration will normally need to be produced.

19 Discuss and demonstrate the new MIS to managers.

20 Write up the new system. Train managers in the use of the MIS.

The above description glosses over some of the software and installation stages to keep it to a reasonable length and to avoid overwhelming the mainstream of the study shape with too many details. In particular, some of the stages may have to be repeated as managers gain experience of using the MIS and improvements are introduced.

The incompleteness of MIS

MIS can be a powerful tool of management, but it is not a substitute for management. There is so much information that cannot appear on a screen – information gained from personal contact, by walking around, by having antennae. It cannot indicate politics, machinations or power playing.

It certainly cannot overcome deceit on even a major project. For example, President Kennedy was persuaded to authorize the invasion of Cuba in the operation known as the Bay of Pigs. He was given a considerable amount of information for the managerial decision, but not all the information available. Nobody in the CIA corrected Kennedy's belief that the invasion would be a 'quiet' affair, because, as Allen Dulles explained,

> We felt that when the chips were down – when the crisis arose in reality, any action required for success would be authorised rather than permit the enterprise to fail.[5]

Another view was that of Clarence Day: 'Information's pretty thin stuff, unless mixed with experience'.[6]

References

1 The official receiver appointed after the failure of Laker Airways.
2 Data from a BBC World Service news item, May 1988.
3 Lyons, M. J., 'Salvaging your software asset (tools-based maintenance)', *Proceedings of the 1981 National Computer Conference*, Reston: AFIPS Press, 1981, p. 337.
4 Benjamin, R. I., *MIS Quarterly*, June 1982, p. 11.
5 Vandenbroucke, L. S., *Diplomatic History*, Vol. 8, No. 4, Autumn 1984, p. 367.
6 Day, C. S., *The Crow's Nest*. 1921.

Further reading

Murdick, R. G. and Munson, J. C., *MIS Concepts and Design*, Englewood Cliffs: Prentice-Hall, 1986.
Sprague, R. H. and McNurlin, B. C. (eds), *Information Systems Management in Practice*, Englewood Cliffs: Prentice-Hall, 1986.

22

Levels of Service

> The pleasure we derive from doing favours is partly in the feeling it gives us that we are not altogether worthless.
> Eric Hoffer, *The Passionate State of Mind* (1954)

> In general, service in America stinks.
> Thomas Peters, *In Search of Excellence* (1982)

Service is a three-way process:

- service to customers, in any organization;
- service as the product, as in the service industries;
- service to other departments within the same organization.

Administration is a service; a service to the rest of the organization. When administration forgets that it is a service, it becomes a bureaucracy.

Basic considerations

There is considerable confusion about service. This may be because there is such a wide spectrum of attitudes to it. Moreover, people holding opposing attitudes can always find supporting examples and justification. Retailing is something that everybody is familiar with, even if only as a customer. Yet retailers vary widely in their attitude to service. The Nordstrom chain in the USA are well known for their level of service. Their 'money-back if not entirely satisfied' approach is quoted by many firms but there is an important difference: Nordstrom mean it. Stories about Nordstrom are legion, like the salesman who ironed a shirt for a customer who needed it for a meeting. Another well-esteemed American retailer is L. L. Bean, which has one shop in a town whose population is just 6,700. Mail order helps the turnover to reach $400 million p.a. Bean staff get forty hours of training before being allowed to talk to a customer. In Britain, Marks & Spencer also operate a 'the customer rules' attitude in much of their work.

So it may seem that giving top-notch service is the route to success in retailing. But not always. Some successful chains have based their success on promising to give almost no service. Discount stores may deliberately display a spartan appearance to show customers that they are a 'no frills' operation, and so by inference are offering good value for money.

In between are those firms that feel that they cannot afford to give a good level of service because they think that it is too expensive. Some such firms force themselves into a corner. As profitability sags, they cut back on the service level to save money. Customers perceive this and so profitability sags even further, and the downward spiral gains momentum. Even more annoying to deal with are the slash-and-burn firms. These are the firms that culturally do not care about customers. Some even have a siege mentality, regarding the customers as near-enemies. In Britain, these firms can often be recognized by the fact that the staff call the customers 'punters' or 'geese'.

So is good service a costly luxury to be indulged in by those with high profit margins? Is it a sign of weakness on the part of firms too weak to stand up to the punters? Or should it be an integral part of the overall search for excellence that is a moral duty?

Most books and academics are firmly on the side of the angels. Excellence and a high level of service are correct, desirable and non-negotiable. There does, however, have to be a limit to the level of service, or we have to start defining our terms carefully. This is because the question of cost often does arise. Nobody expects the same level of service in economy class of a cruise ship as is received in first class. Those in first class paid more in the expectation of better service.

Similarly, the queue length at supermarket checkouts or bank cashier counters is a function of the number of staff providing the service. More staff means shorter queues. It also means higher costs. This poses a stark choice to customers: pay less or wait less, though the starkness of the choice can often be ameliorated somewhat by improving the administration through better procedures. In some countries, banks use the system of double-queues. One waits at one counter, carries out the transaction when one reaches the head of the line of people, then one goes to another counter and waits again for the teller. In one bank people were waiting in the teller's line for over fifty minutes while other bank staff were sitting at their places with nothing to do, all because the bank did not know how to achieve a 'line of balance' solution.

Another example concerns a service to the service providers. This is the cleaning of offices. Most people would agree that the minimum level of service for cleaning offices is a daily emptying of the waste-paper baskets and removal of rubbish. But what about cleaning the windows, vacuuming the carpets, and polishing the desks? Should these be done? And if so, how frequently? How well? What would it cost? How do we ensure that it is done? Every office in the world has answered these questions, though the decisions may have been made by default rather than by a set procedure.

These basic considerations enable us to look more closely at the whole question of service, helping us to unravel the meaning of service. This is done by looking at service by dividing the concept into its constituent parts.

Aspects of service

Confusion about the provision of levels of service will continue until we look at service not as a whole but as what it is – a compound noun. Service is not just what is offered, it is also the way it is offered. A photoprocessor may have the idea of improving its service by offering a free voucher every time one has a film developed. Collecting four such vouchers may entitle one to a free album or an extra set of prints. This sounds like a good idea and is one that is often employed. The service aspect becomes degraded if the vouchers are offered with a grunt in a surly manner, instead of with a pleasant smile. Further degradation occurs if one has to demand the vouchers instead of being offered them.

If one's film is found to be badly processed, then the 'good service' seems less good. And if, finally, to get one's free gift one has to perform some bureaucratic chore like sending off for it then one ends up by cursing the poor office procedures rather than feeling a glow of satisfaction as was intended.

209

Service can be considered under four aspects:

- legal;
- procedural;
- tangibles;
- contact.

■ LEGAL

The impact of legal constraints on service levels should not be overlooked. Laws have been passed in most countries that affect the 'caveat emptor' adage. At the minimum level, it is illegal to sell food that will cause injury to the taker. Above the minimum level, the position varies widely from country to country, and from industry to industry. Thus in the USA and Britain, laws concerning food hygiene are reasonably drafted and are backed by the possibility of civil actions. In both countries, the basis of many laws is that if something is sold then it must be fit for its purpose, or that there is an element of product liability.

It is a mistake to think that all countries have the same attitude or similar laws. Dealing with countries that lack any concept of consumers' or workers' rights can be expensive. For example, a country that is short of hard currency may prevent the payment of penalty clauses if one of its organizations fails to live up to its international obligations.

■ PROCEDURAL

An organization's systems and procedures can affect the level of service that it is perceived as rendering. A firm made and sold a wide range of cakes and, although its customer base was only about 30,000, was well known. Any order placed by a customer by three o'clock in the afternoon would be despatched the next morning, although it was not always possible to fill the order completely since this could depend on the night shift's production schedule. So, although there were part orders, management thought that the company was offering a good level of service.

The problem was that the computer was unable to adjust the original order. So a customer would always get an invoice for the amount of the goods ordered – plus credit notes for every line that could not be filled. On occasions this would send the customers into near-paroxysms of anger and frustration, especially in the case of customers whose own computer treated invoices and credit notes by different paths. One day, the managing director of a customer strode into the firm's sales director's office and threw onto his desk an invoice for eighteen items – plus seventeen credit notes. The invoice should have been made out for only one item.

Like most true stories, the ending to this one is not entirely happy. The sales director reprimanded the production people in the strongest language for putting a sale at risk – mainly because the computer director managed to convince him that nothing could be done to improve the system.

Bad procedures and poor computer systems are often the root cause of bad service. Judging by the frequency of complaints, the Yugoslav customs authorities are not the most-loved group in the eyes of British tourists. An American importer bought glassware from Czechoslovakia and Yugoslavia. When the imports got to the USA, it was found that stoppers for wine decanters were the incorrect size, so they were returned to the manufacturer. The Yugoslav customs refused them admittance, claiming that 'Yugoslavia does not make sub-standard goods.' So in the eyes of the importer, the manufacturer was giving very poor service. One guess as to which country now exports the glassware.

On the other hand, good procedures and computer systems are often the route to giving good service. An obvious example is the ability of the computer to model stock changes so that stock-outs are reduced, stocks are used by age, and reordering is done to time. A less obvious example is the way the Manpower organization uses its computer to collect data and use it as part of their total service concept. This 'total service' concept enabled Manpower to grow from $400 million to $4 billion sales p.a. in just ten years.

Tangibles

The word tangibles is not really accurate, but some of the alternative terms used (e.g. 'commodities') are even less felicitous. By tangibles is meant the actual items that are offered by organizations as part of the service level. In a hotel, this might range from an after-dinner mint awaiting one on the bedside table to keeping details of one's personal preference for morning newspaper on its computer database.

C

In an office, items might include:

- backlog details (days of work outstanding);
- complaints (number/type/severity) from users and customers;
- delay in replying to letters from customers;
- percentage of letters of credit returned by the bank;
- calendar time taken in processing invoices;
- accuracy and timeliness of report and statistics production;
- error rate (e.g. in data prep);
- success rate in meeting deadlines, schedules and work flow milestones.

This list demonstrates both the way of thinking about service in the office, and also some of the pitfalls. These pitfalls are the same as those referred to in the chapter about controls (chapter 40), namely the danger of relating a tenuous concept like service to a single indicator.

Tangible service can, and must, be definable in every possible case. For example, ScotRail laid down the standard for answering phone queries as, 'answering all phone calls within 30 seconds'. Sometimes rigidity and over-emphasis can be self-defeating. Another organization set its standard as answering every telephone call before it had made five ringing tones, monitored the calls on the exchange and made this seem to the staff as being the most important object in life. So the staff, when under pressure, got into the habit of just raising the handset and then replacing it without actually talking to the caller.

Sometimes the service level cannot be measured – this is mostly in the area of trying to describe excellence as a concept or trying to describe the attitude of 'going the extra mile'. This particularly applies to the ideas discussed under 'Contact' below.

Tangible service items can slip over time just as any other aspect of good management. The film *Back to the Future* has its main character finding himself in a 1950s petrol station where the attendants are in pressed overalls and clean the window, polish the chrome and check the oil. This happens to few of us nowadays (except in Tokyo where the attendant will even hold up the passing traffic for one).

Undoubtedly, the best way of preventing service slippage is by having the right culture within the organization. This involves complete commitment from the top down. It also means avoiding a sense of inferiority among those staff who actually come into direct contact with the users or the customers. The sharp-end staff must never feel that everything is up to them, and that nobody else cares or will back them. This situation is one that most of us have suffered from in one form or another at some time. Since most of us have been on the receiving end, it is strange that the mirror-image cannot be understood by some organizations.

So it is not enough to believe that one is giving good service. Service needs constant monitoring. It is also important that the tangibles that are given are actually those that people want. An airline gathered together a group of business travellers for some market research. Would the customers be impressed with the new travellers' pack that was going to be given? The business travellers were almost unanimous: what they wanted was for the planes to arrive on time. The airline officials were taken back by the strength of feeling. What about special lounges to rest in before the flight? Unimpressed, the frequent travellers still insisted that what they wanted was prompt arrival. Special lounges were associated with delays. And so the meeting went on with growing bewilderment on the part of the airline officials. These business travellers did not seem to appreciate cosseting, free gifts or special offers. They just kept on repeating that they wanted prompt arrival.

British Airways also carried out a market study to find out how customers judged service. The customers came up with four quite sophisticated concepts. These are recommended to any managing director who is in the service industry. They could hardly be bettered:[1]

GOOD SERVICE

1 Care and concern (staff courtesy, warmth and friendliness).

2 Initiative (staff ability and willingness to manipulate the system for the benefit of the customer).

3 Problem solving (finding solutions to customers' difficulties, whether routine or not).

4 Recovery (going the extra mile when things go wrong. This can include the simple act of making an apology).

This box is not a technique. It is not arcane. It is not based on any theory. It is what customers want. So it seems like a good idea to try to follow it.

Sometimes attempts to ensure good service have amusing consequences.[2] K Mart tried to remind its check-out staff to say to their customers the catch-phrase, 'Thank you for shopping K-Mart'. So they put stickers on the cash registers with the reminder, 'TYFSOK'. It is reported that some harried clerks would blurt out 'Tyfsok' at the customers. And comedian Jay Leno says that when he reprimanded a clerk at a supermarket check-out for not saying thank you, she snapped, 'It's printed on your receipt'.

Contact

With some of the aspects mentioned above, we are moving into the fourth area of service, that of contact. This is the face to face interplay between the person giving the service and the recipient. The procedures can be nearly perfect, the tangibles correct but if there is a failure at the sharp end, then the result is still the same: failure.

This is true of all types of service. The aggressive colleague from accounts department can cause us to feel the same as the rude check-out clerk, or the unhelpful bank clerk. There are several reasons for bad service at the contact level:

- *geographical*. There are some places and some countries where courtesy is still thought of as being a form of weakness;
- *the culture of the organization*. This is the strongest cause. Some firms never attain good service because 'you cannot get good staff nowadays'. Strangely enough, other firms do not have the same trouble. Could it be because the staff one gets are self-selecting?;
- *personality problems of individual people*. It has to be admitted that there are people who are psychologically incapable of giving good service. Perhaps they confuse service with servility. It also has to be admitted that some people are resistant to receiving good service. Customers can have personality problems, too;
- *inadequate training*. If staff do not know the systems or do not have product knowledge then it may be impossible to give good service. The camera salesperson who does not understand photography, or the personnel clerk who does not know the rules about overtime are both at a serious disadvantage. And it is not their fault;
- *pressure of work*. When harried or over-stretched, the most equable of us may give way to flashes of bad temper.

It is even possible for success itself to be a contributory factor to poor service. The president of TGI Friday Inc. (a chain of restaurants) calls this the success syndrome.[3] When a business venture is new, everybody worries about its success. When a customer appears, 'you turn cartwheels to please. No request is impossible, no detail too small'. But success may bring more business than one can handle. If a customer is lost, one may slip into thinking that there are 'plenty more where that one came from'. Then service and standards drop. Soon the customers stop coming so readily. Turnover and profits decrease. To save money, the temptation is to employ fewer staff and to scrimp on some of the service. This brings one into a descending spiral that can end in disaster unless action is taken.

If success is no absolute guarantee of continuing good service, then nor is sloganizing. Some slogans are good, especially if they manage to encapsulate the central mores of an organization. They are not so good if they are merely cosmetic or, even worse, if they are a substitute for genuine service. Some of us consultants feel slightly uneasy when a managing director opens the conversation with us by saying, 'My door is always open.' Experience tells us that this is sometimes a sign that in fact that particular door is rarely open. Perhaps, in the words of the common misquotation, 'Methinks thou dost protest too much.'[4]

In the same way, seeing the sign on an office wall proclaiming, 'Here the customer is king' is not always to be entirely taken at face value. This well-known sign was seen on one assignment in a firm where the service left much to be desired, and the staff knew it.

213

Once we got to know the staff better, we tackled one of the managers about it. 'Oh, it's quite true. The customer is king.' he said, 'but you aren't allowed to work here unless you're a committed republican.'

A better example of sloganizing was the advertising copy used by KLM airlines after a survey showed that 98 per cent of KLM passengers voted the cabin crew as being 'first rate'. The advertising message was, 'Some airlines think good service is the smile on the face of a stewardess. For KLM, it's the smile on the face of the passenger.'

Aids to good service

As already stated, the best aid to good service is to ensure that the culture of the organization is right, and this means commitment from the top. And commitment is not just a matter of slogans. If good service is necessary for the firm, then it must be meant. Other aids to good service include:

1 The level of service to be attained must be spelt out and/or known by instinct. Knowing by instinct may appear odd to many firms since it may appear thence to be uncontrollable. It does not appear strange to many large Japanese companies nor to organizations like Nordstrom.
2 The work itself must be designed to facilitate service. Specialization is often a route to efficiency. Over-specialization can be a route to poor service if recovery or re-works are somebody else's job. Job design may have to be directed towards team building or group working.
3 Team building and group working are in many circumstances a key resource in improving service. A firm making chemicals had a bad problem with customers receiving burst and broken containers. At first, management were convinced that this was due to substandard plastic bags. Closer inspection revealed that it was due mainly to poor use of fork-lift trucks, especially when loading material on to the trains used for transportation. Even when bags burst during the loading operation they were just stuffed into the wagon. This all led to an incredible amount of work for the office: correspondence, investigation, monitoring goods return, computer re-work, rescheduling of part orders and so on. The only solution was to bring the loaders into group discussions with the office staff and a full explanation of the results of the poor loading.
4 Training of the staff must be recognized as part of the service. This may be product knowledge, knowledge of systems and procedures, and training in giving good service as part of the job.
5 When considering the service given by administration to the rest of the organization, the fact has to be faced that there will be times when conflicts will arise. It is not reasonable to assume that sweetness and light will prevail at all times. There must therefore be a procedure for conflict resolution.
6 Service has to be monitored. How this is done will depend on the circumstances and on the culture. A fast-food chain has a checklist which is used to assess how the staff do their job. In part, this is:

Greeting the customer.	Yes	No
1 There is a smile.		
2 It is a sincere greeting.		
3 There is eye contact.		

Thanking the customer.		
1 There is always a thank you.		
2 The thank you is sincere.		
3 There is eye contact.		
4 Return business was asked for.		

C

To some people, this may seem too much like, 'always be sincere, whether you mean it or not'. However, the company concerned is very successful, and finds it a natural extension of its philosophy.

7 Staff must know that they are doing a worthwhile job and that their efforts are appreciated. Again, this must be more than mere sloganizing. It is a multi-faceted thing. It certainly helps if people know that they belong to a group that is a success. It also helps if people feel that the organization is involved in doing something that is of worth in society. This does not necessarily mean being in some charitable work. Even management consultants can feel that their work is worthwhile. On the other hand, everyone agrees that hospital nurses are in a worthwhile job – but many nurses feel that management is so élitist that their efforts go unrecognized.

8 The systems and procedures must be in good shape. This involves the whole gamut from paperwork, forms, scheduling, timetabling, and back-ups.

The service assignment

In case this sounds rather tenuous, it is worth considering the shape of a typical assignment to improve service. Such assignments vary widely in scope, depending on circumstances, but usually follow the following pattern:

1 Exploratory talks with management – to gauge the situation and to discuss the intentions of management. This is sometimes a delicate matter since management may be suffering from a mixture of emotions. These can include a feeling of resentment, even anger. It is therefore necessary to try to prevent any allocation of blame arising during this initial stage and to concentrate on objectives of the study. This can be important since apparent causes may turn out not to be the real causes.

2 Clear the basics. This involves checking on quality control, scheduling, main procedures, backlogs, errors, re-work rates, etc.

3 At this stage one moves away from the centre, sometimes even leaving the premises. Discussions are held with user departments if the problem is interdepartmental. If the problem involves customers, then one has to see the customers. If the customers

are the general public, then market research may be needed. During this stage, which can take some time, it is necessary to maintain contact with senior management so that they do not feel that there is a lack of progress.

4 Defining the service, and the level of service. When interdepartmental this will include defining the outputs of the groups, deciding timetables and scheduling, and detailing how to deal with backlogs and re-works. If the provision of tangibles is involved, then it will usually be necessary to decide on the cost-effectiveness of optional alternatives. Defining the level of service will normally involve some aspect of measurement. It may also necessitate bringing providers and users together so that the groups can understand and appreciate the problems and difficulties faced by the other groups.

5 Formulate routes to achieving the level of service. This may involve changing the systems and procedures. It will certainly need staff training. Sometimes this training will approach organization development in its depth and impact.

6 Institution of methods of monitoring or control to ensure that service levels are maintained over a period of time. This monitoring has to be such that feedback continues to be received from users so that changes and improvements are incorporated as the need arises.

7 Institution of methods of conflict resolution, for when problems arise.

8 Installation of the changes. This is not just a matter of changing the methods. Changes have to be accompanied by advertising. When the service is directed to the general public, then actual media advertising is often used. If it is strictly an internal matter, then the advertising may be via meetings, discussions, articles in the internal newsletter – whatever communications channels are the most appropriate. But the change has to be built up into a major event in which top management are clearly seen to be part.

Of course, this has a possible downside and that is the possibility of failure. This would leave everybody in a worse condition than if nothing at all had been attempted – so failure must not be allowed, or even countenanced. In all events what has to be avoided is the attitude of 'well, let's try it and see if it's any good'.

For the final word on service we turn to Boyd Myers who, as a member of the top management at NASA, said:[5]

> Administration gives a service to the rest of the enterprise. A good administrator must know all sides of the business so that he can appreciate difficulties. Communication is the secret. All must really understand the total mission. To help each other, people must know about each other.
>
> The problem is never technology, it is people's attitude.

References

1 *Harvard Business Review*, Vol. 66, No. 4, July/August 1988, p. 57.
2 *Time*, 2 February, 1987, p. 28.
3 *Wall Street Journal*, 14 October, 1987, p. 9.
4 Shakespeare, 'The lady doth protest too much, methinks', *Hamlet*, III.ii.
5 During a private conversation.

Further reading

Jenkins, K. *et al.*, *Improving Management in Government: The Next Steps*, London: HMSO, 1988.

Hauser, J. R. and Clausing, D., *The House of Quality*, Harvard Business Review, Vol. 66, No. 3, May/June 1988, p. 63.

Mackay, H., *Swim with the Sharks*, New York: William Morrow, 1988.

OECD, *Administration as Service: The Public as Client*, Paris: OECD, 1987.

Peters, T., and Austin, N., *A Passion for Excellence*, New York: Random House, 1985.

Price, F., *Right First Time*, Aldershot: Gower, 1984, Wildwood House, 1986.

Setters, P., 'What customers really want', *Fortune*, 4 June, 1990.

'Serve them right', *The Economist*, Vol. 315, No. 7653, 5 May, 1990.

C

Method Design

23

ICICLES

All is change; all yields its place and goes.

Euripides, *Heracles*, c. 422 BC

It is best to do things systematically
Since we are only human,
and disorder is our worst enemy.

Hesiod, *Works and Days*, eighth century BC

There are three main stages in any methods design study where the aim is to improve the methods or procedure or system:

- planning;
- doing;
- implementing.

It is usual to expand this somewhat stark trio into a rather finer subdivision, and to use a mnemonic to help one remember the stages. When improving factory operations, it has become almost traditional to use the mnemonics SREDITIM or SREDIM (the latter was coined by Russell Currie of ICI). In office work for some years the mnemonic that was widely used was CREDITS, which stood for Choose/Record/Examine/ Develop/Install/Test/Stabilize. There are still many large organizations throughout the world that use CREDITS, especially when training new staff.

There was a certain amount of dissatisfaction with these early mnemonics. This was because of the first stage, described as either 'select' or 'choose'. It was felt that this did not reflect the true situation of modern life; nowadays one cannot just decide which department one would like to look at, and bowl in (if indeed one ever did). This first stage is not merely very important, it is also often a rather subtle affair needing an investigator to use his skills in a careful approach.

Any mnemonic is just that: an aid to memory so that one does not omit any stage of a study. It is not a talisman that ensures success any more than a rabbit's foot will. This may not be too obvious when one listens to a group of trainees lengthily dissecting a particular mnemonic.

The mnemonic that we use to describe the stages of improving the systems in an office is ICICLES, which has the virtue of being easy to remember. It also has the virtues of being accurate and useful. ICICLES stands for:

I – INITIATE   the methods design study

C – CHRONICLE   the current situation

I – INVESTIGATE	the current situation and systems
C – CREATE	a new method design
L – LAUNCH	the new systems, methods and procedures
E – ENHANCE	the new tested approach
S – STABILIZE	the new situation

Summary of the ICICLES stages

■ INITIATE

There are, of course, occasions (though they are few) when a study is so urgent or obvious or predictable that this first stage is glossed over. There are considerably more occasions when this first stage is glossed over, and people later wish that it had not been missed. This is because, at the very least, all parties involved must have a reasonably clear idea of what is to be done and how long it is going to take. Worst of all is when the company chairman calls one into his office and says, 'Would you mind having a look at the purchasing people?' One must avoid at all costs the temptation to reply, 'Yes sir, certainly sir, at once sir,' and then back out of the office in a warm glow induced by being asked by the chairman himself.

D

What did he mean? What does he think the problem is? Has he heard that the staff has been taking bribes? Does he think that they need retraining in something or other? Does he want the microcomputers put onto a network? Whichever it is, one must find out since each would mean a very different type of study. Also, when does he expect the answer? Next Wednesday? In four weeks, three months? Moreover, one really must know whether he has discussed it with the people in purchasing. If all this seems pretty obvious, then you have not had to do many methods design studies – because something similar has nearly happened to most of us. The activities that will usually be covered during the 'initiate' stage can be summarized as:

- broach the subject of the proposed study;
- obtain the concurrence of those who will be looked at;
- agree the area or problem that will be studied;
- agree the roles of the participants;
- agree the outer limits/parameters of the study (e.g. time);
- prepare a survey;
- finalize details of the assignment;
- prepare terms of reference (unless the survey is used);
- write and sign the contract (if working internationally).

■ CHRONICLE

To chronicle is to record events in the order of their happening. This is the major part of this stage – to get down on paper details of the work done in the order that it occurs. In this context, the phrase 'on paper' is used deliberately. Very few investigators eschew the use of paper in favour of exclusive use of their personal computer. The reason for this is purely practical. One may have to go at a moment's notice to a meeting in a warehouse, or to the company's lawyers, or to a director's office. It is much quicker and easier to pick up a file than to spend time booting up a computer and selecting the appropriate data.

The nature of exactly what is recorded will depend on the type of study being undertaken. The sort of items recorded will be:

- what people do;
- the systems used;
- the paperwork involved;
- the equipment employed;
- a plan of the offices (for office layout studies);
- what people feel (for attitude surveys);
- what people instinctively know (for expert systems).

Although this record preparation is the most visible part of this stage of the study, it is not the sole activity. It is not the first part. The first part is 'familiarization'. This is a two-way process. The investigator has to become familiar with a whole gamut of situational factors. These factors include people's names and foibles, hours of work and coffee breaks, where to sit and what to wear, non-smoking areas, personal relation-ships, jargon used, deadlines, security, social mores, location of toilets and tea machines, availability of rooms and items of stationery, and generally what one must/can/cannot do and say. If the list seems almost endless, this helps to explain a slight feeling of near panic that can assail one at the start of a study; one sometimes feels that one is not getting to grips with what is going on while trying to exude an air of confident professionalism. In fact, this flow of adrenalin is beneficial provided that it remains under control. It sharpens the senses and causes one to start the study at a higher work-rate. And one knows from experience that after a short while, one will become fully familiar with what is going on even to knowing which photocopier makes the best overhead transparencies.

Another part of this familiarization is the holding of initial meetings with a number of key personnel: managers, trade unions, staff, auditors, suppliers, etc. A danger of this part of the familiarization is that it can descend into a blur of handshaking with unremembered contacts. But earlier it was said that familiarization is a two-way process, and these initial meetings are part of this two-way aspect. While you are getting to know people, they are getting to know you. During the course of the study, you will be meeting these people time after time. They will of course always respond to your questions (people rarely lie to an investigator). But unless they feel that they know you and trust you then they will not tell you those extra details, those innermost emotions, those feelings that are so often vital for a really successful study.

This question of the attitude of an investigator during a study is at the heart of our work. We encapsulate this as being:

> **Courtesy with tenacity**

This is referred to elsewhere in this book but it is so important that no apology is made for repeating it.

Other information will be collected during the chronicle stage. It will almost always include the organization structure, copies of job descriptions, and, above all, detailed statistics of throughputs: the number of each form that is processed in a specific time period, number of enquiries answered, number of suppliers and customers, amounts of money, etc. The other items that will have to be collected and recorded will depend on circumstances. Examples are past balance sheets, staff turnover figures, advertising expenditure, train/plane/bus timetables, contacts' home telephone numbers. There is a temptation to collect every piece of information that might feasibly be useful, even to the extent of distributing vast over-detailed questionnaires. This temptation should be resisted. It wastes time, creates 'noise' in one's files, and will annoy people.

This introduction to the chronicle stage highlights another aspect of carrying out a study, namely that all the stages overlap to a quite considerable amount. Some of the 'initial meetings' will have taken place during the initiation stage, others will form part of the chronicle stage, while others may not take place until the investigate stage. Similarly, the fact-finding can in practice extend over all the stages. Many investigators will claim that one is (perhaps subconsciously) starting to develop a new system while one is nominally only collecting information. This shows again that ICICLES (or any other formula) is a guide to actions, not a set of watertight compartments.

■ INVESTIGATE

By this point in the study, one has a considerable quantity of information. One has collected details of volumes processed, the systems used, talked with people to get their opinions. The sheer volume of data can be quite impressive, especially if one has collected job descriptions, the accountants' costing figures or computer manuals. One also knows a lot of subtle material: people's hopes and biases, the culture present, staff morale, perhaps unspoken policies.

D

It is now necessary to examine this mass of data, knowledge and information. Here we come to two differences of opinion among experienced investigators. The first difference lies in the approach used to develop a new system. Some people believe that the examination of the existing situation must be done quite separately from the development of a new system. Others hold that the two happen inevitably at the same time. Our view lies between the two extremes. When examining the facts, one is looking at various possible alternatives. At such a time, it would need a saint-like devotion to pedantry to be able to avoid considering a new system (indeed, one of the common methods of analysis requires one to think of what 'should be done'). On the other hand, there is a real danger of having an early good idea for an improved method, and then obstinately sticking to it no matter what. In fact, while examining the facts that one has collected, two things will happen: one will realize that some further facts are needed and will start to move towards the general area of a preferred solution.

The second difference of opinion concerns the development of a new system that follows the examination phase. Some people use a strict, formal approach. Others prefer a more creative, brainstorming approach. Since both approaches work for different people and since both give good results, it is more a matter of personal preference rather than one of the approaches being the correct one.

Out of this examination, it is normal for a set of alternatives to be available out of which it is necessary to choose. This choice is not always as straightforward as one would like. To help in making this decision, a number of factors come into play, including:

- what are the effects and consequences of each alternative?
- do any of them shift a problem elsewhere rather than actually solving it?
- are we increasing productivity locally while reducing it globally?
- what do people think of the alternatives?

- are any of them beyond the capability of the organization to cope with, because of its culture?
- what are the financial costs?
- how long will it take to get each possibility up and running?

One must always remember the first alternative: to eliminate completely. This is sometimes called the 'zero option', and can be the answer in even the most unpromising situation. A national oil company asked a consultancy to investigate a department that provided a service to the rest of the organization. This service was the maintaining of a computer database and microfilming records. The alternatives seemed to be to change the organization structure, to improve the level of service being provided, to enhance the software, and to upgrade the technology. (These alternatives were not of course mutually exclusive.) On the face of it, the department represented that desirable feature: advanced information technology. The consultant concerned remained unhappy and undertook a further round of discussions with the user departments. This confirmed an earlier suspicion that users did not like the service, paid only lip-service to it, and had quietly substituted their own advanced technology in several cases. This in turn raised the problem of how the service could be upgraded so that it would satisfy users. The end result was a recommendation that the entire department should be dissolved. This recommendation was accepted and put into effect.

■ CREATE

This is the stage at which the new method of doing something is finalized. It might be thought to be the pinnacle of one's creative effort, the point at which all the hard work becomes real. In reality, it is not quite like that. If the previous stages have been done well, then it is rather more like putting flesh on a skeleton. At this stage one finalizes what has been done before and, in particular, prepares for the next stage. This is not to say that this stage is a purely mechanical one. It is not. But it is one that is less variable in nature than the other stages. It is also often the point when one really starts to feel the pressure of the completion deadline. A good investigator has to possess a number of skills. One of these is the ability to pace a study and oneself. It is assumed that one is working to a plan and keeping to it, but it is now that anything that was postponed catches up with one.

In addition, this stage often feels for some unaccountable reason to be slowing one down. This may be because some of its elements seem to be under the control of other people.

The elements of this stage are usually:

- finalize the development stage;
- build up the preferred method in detail;
- discuss it with colleagues and company staff;
- ensure the feasibility of the new system;
- gain acceptance of the new method;
- incorporate suggestions into the revised new method;
- make presentations to staff and management.

It is of little use inventing a revolutionary new way of doing things if people are unwilling to change to it. The matter of getting people to accept change can be a weighty one. It is rare that one is in a position of presenting a report which is read and results in immediate acceptance. That is why the creation of change extends over most of the stages of a study. It is not of itself a single separate stage. There are times when people do not need convincing of the need for change (ending an annoying bottleneck, for example). At other times (when working on organization development, for example), it may be the main part of a study, in calendar time.

Creating change is sometimes called 'persuasion' or 'selling'. The three things are somewhat different, however. They are far from being true synonyms. The approach used depends to some extent on a company's culture, the situation, the type of study, and personal preference. Sometimes it is just a matter of words. A few American firms have been observed where management have said that the staff 'must be happy with the change' and have then forced the staff to say that they are happy with it.

■ LAUNCH

Once a new method is agreed, it is then time to install it as standard practice. This stage often involves working at several tasks simultaneously. For example:

- arranging and then carrying out staff training;
- getting supplies of new forms;
- ordering new equipment;
- buying/writing/tweaking software;
- having walls knocked down and rebuilt;
- changing office layouts;
- liaising with interested parties (which at times can seem like everybody).

Quite often, when the change is affecting just one department, it is a matter of living for a while in the department – dealing with questions, encouraging people to try something new, ensuring that supplies do not run out and showing what a great success it is.

Perhaps the best thing about this stage is that the buck really does stop with you; if anything goes wrong, then it is clear to everybody that it is your fault. In the circumstances it is perhaps surprising how rarely anything does go disastrously wrong. It may be necessary to put in long hours but one does usually manage to overcome the difficulties. Even overcoming these difficulties can give a sense of achievement. Also, these difficulties remain in one's mind for a long time and add spice to life. Some of the difficulties that we have met have included a sudden influenza epidemic, a mainframe going down, a religious man going berserk, claiming that someone had stolen his prayer mat, a pregnant woman going into labour and a sudden dearth of Christmas puddings. In retrospect, one hopes that none of these was due to sabotage. How did the dearth of Christmas puddings affect us? It led to hundreds of letters of complaint, telephone calls, reorders, credit notes, ledger changes and so on. This upset our careful calculations of staff loading.

■ ENHANCE

Many of us have a fear of changing our mind when it concerns a new method that we have spent so much effort to bring to life. We find ourselves defending our baby in every smallest detail. Nothing must be altered.

But this is another example of turning a difficulty into an opportunity. Many of our best concepts can be further improved. So at this stage one listens to the staff carefully. They may have a problem with some aspect of the new situation. They may have some

D

suggestions for improvements that really are improvements (after all, they are doing the work). So now is the time to make the new system as perfect as possible. This is only a retreat if you make it one. Instead, make it an advance. Test the new system. Is it doing what you intended? If not, improve it.

There are times when there is an actual fault which has to be put right. A common cause for this is improving software which has a bug or shortcoming that had not been foreseen, or is not as user-friendly as wished. Whatever is the cause, it should be clear to all that you see your task as helping the staff to do the work, not as arguing with them or standing aloof.

■ STABILIZE

Once a new system is in place, one does not want the old one coming back again. Otherwise there will be confusion, even chaos, and all advantages will be lost. The commonest reason for an old system coming back is that if the workload increases for some reason, staff may be tempted to go back to what they know best. It may give a sense of security. Then again, it is common when installing a new computer system to run the old and the new in parallel for a while. During this time, hybrid extra procedures may be born.

Whatever the cause, if the new system works and is a proven improvement, then one wants it to be the one that is used. This is ensured by taking certain actions:

* remove all copies of old blank forms;
* remove and sell off old equipment;
* incorporate a new organization chart into staff manuals;
* write new job descriptions;
* install new control mechanisms;
* write new manuals;
* show everybody how much superior the new situation is.

A final report is then prepared and presented to management, relating what has been achieved.

This summary above shows the *what* is done on a methods design study. The *how* (or the 'techniques') is detailed in other chapters:

Initiate	– this chapter, below
Chronicle	– chapter 24
Investigate	– chapter 25
Create	– chapter 25
Launch	– chapter 38
Enhance	– chapter 38
Stabilize	– chapters 38 and 39.

I – Initiate

■ BROACH AND CONCUR

The two main factors in the initiate stage are known as 'broach and concur'. This phrase is used to describe the way in which a person or group will suggest that a particular study be undertaken, and another group or groups will agree to the study.

Broaching can come from a variety of sources, such as an external management consultant, an equipment supplier, trade union representatives, senior management, sales staff, computer staff, the board, departmental staff. Concurring can also come from a variety of sources such as middle management, trade union representatives, sales staff, computer staff, the board, departmental staff.

In theory, it might be thought that the Utopian situation would be for a group of people to be alternately broaching and concurring. On the face of it, this would be a most healthy situation. In practice, an investigator should be slightly wary when this happens. It is just possible that this is a sign that politics are the cause. For example, sometimes a manager or group will be trying to enhance their position in the hierarchy or establish hegemony. A study into themselves or another group may be seen as a means of furthering their aim. An example may illustrate this. A comptroller department in an international bank felt that it was receiving insufficient co-operation from the rest of the bank, particularly in the provision of statistical and financial information.

The comptrollers therefore made a strong request for external consultants to undertake a study into their procedures. They thought that this would result in the consultants' viewing their plight in a way similar to their own view of things. A report to head office would result which would reflect this. Head office would have a revelation, and would consequently give the comptrollers more 'power'. Problem solved.

D

As usual, the real situation was somewhat more complicated. The line departments were increasingly irritated by what they saw as high-handedness on the part of the comptrollers. The line staff just wanted to be left alone to get on with their day-to-day work, which they regarded as being paramount, and which was demanding enough anyway. Meanwhile, head office had heard about these rumblings and wanted them stopped.

The consultant had already started the study before he realized the situation that he was in (a not uncommon state of affairs). Rather than worry himself rigid, he followed the rule of 'doing what is best for the client'. He continued the study and soon realized that the difficulty was caused basically because the work of the comptrollers had just grown in an *ad hoc* manner, without any overall strategy. The end result was a recommendation for a new set of audit and control mechanisms. This did not satisfy the senior comptroller, who had mentally replaced his original desire for better figures with a wish for greater authority. He resigned to go to another bank. The rest of the staff, and head office, were more satisfied since the cause of their frustration had been eliminated.

This case study shows that it is sometimes important to try to understand the motives underlying a request for a study, but not to allow these motives completely to dictate the course of a resulting assignment.

The broach and concur period is sometimes complex, sometimes subtle. It can be frustrating. A large insurance company (tending to be somewhat self-satisfied and paternalistic) would have a study go round a department if the manager concerned did not agree initially to his group being included – without discussion. The position is very different when an organization is fighting for survival. Then the broach and concur step may disappear entirely, with the board insisting that everybody be studied. A board may also ignore the concur step when a firm has taken over another firm; in this case the investigator may be in the position of having to get concurrence as an integral part of the study. The broach and concur step becomes particularly important when the study concerns:

- organization development;
- introduction of advanced technology;
- organization structure;
- levels of service.

■ AGREE AREA OR PROBLEM FOR STUDY

The choice of subject for a study can arise for a number of reasons:

- a subject can be part of an overall corporate strategy (e.g. introducing office automation, cost reduction);
- an obvious problem (e.g. poor morale);
- a severe bottleneck;
- an area which is obviously going to yield a major improvement;
- an area employing a large amount of capital, especially if it is being used in a less than optimum manner (e.g. outstanding debtors);
- a group employing a large number of people on similar, repetitive work;
- a group of people with low output or high costs, when compared with similar groups;
- offices that are manned for peaks, that have a long backlog, or have frequent periods of waiting for work;
- departments where a major expansion is anticipated;
- anywhere open to the possibility of fraud or poor security, or over which management have insufficient control (e.g. high-value stores);
- offices with a high incidence of errors, overtime, absenteeism, labour turnover, or where working conditions are poor.

This list is not exhaustive, but it should be sufficient to encourage any internal investigatory department that cannot see the way ahead.

The choosing of the subject of a study is accompanied by discussions and by initial meetings with those involved. The aim of these is to gain a clearer idea of what will be involved in the study itself. This in turn leads to initial ideas concerning how the study will be carried out and the general shape of the study. If the study's aim is to solve a problem, then the nature of the problem is discussed and carefully defined. Many of the techniques of problem solving put considerable emphasis on this question of defining the problem, and hence these initial discussions will be of importance later.

It is also at this time that initial data is collected. This can include throughput volumes, the balance sheet, organization structures, primary contacts, previous history, costings, staffings, equipment, etc. This data will be expanded later, in the study itself, but at this stage it is needed as background and to gain a clearer idea of what the study will cover.

■ AGREE PARTICIPANTS' ROLES

Some studies are carried out by just one person, such as an external management consultant. Others will need a team drawn from several groups. The use of teams is very common, but it is necessary to agree this early so that the people concerned can be forewarned and clear their desks ready to take part. Preparatory specialized training may be needed. If extensive travel is involved then family arrangements have to be made with as much notice as possible. (Consultants' families have to adapt to the sudden disappearance of one of their members; for other families the event can be a major change to their habits.) When managers and technical staff are seconded to a team, then cover may be needed for what seems to them to be a long period.

'Staff representatives' are members of the staff of a department being studied who take part in the study itself. They have the advantage of knowing the work intimately. They act as a two-way communication channel for the rest of the staff. They know their colleagues' abilities and idiosyncrasies, and can even act as a useful brake on any impractical changes that the investigator may be tempted to consider. After the study, the staff representatives return to their former duties. Because of their increased knowledge and experience, they often find their promotion path enhanced. Where appropriate, the use of staff representatives is definitely recommended.

■ AGREE OUTER LIMITS/PARAMETERS

Every study has to have some limits. These limits can be obvious, such as formulating a new product range, or preparing a new office layout. However every study has within it the seed of proliferation. A child who is reading an interesting book as bedtime approaches will often make the plea of 'just one more chapter'. Similarly, an investigator may feel that the iteration of just a few more days' analysis of what-ifs on a spreadsheet would surely lead to a whole new area of investigation. He may be right, but a halt has to be called somewhere. As the old proverb says, if you keep throwing bread on the water you may just end up with more soggy bread.

So, agreement has to be reached on:

- how long the study will take to complete, in calendar time;
- how much time will be spent by the investigator and any teams;
- which departments will be studied;
- what data will be needed;
- what the outputs of the study will be (e.g. a report, a training course, a computer program);
- whether a pilot study or scheme will be performed, and if so, the parameters of the pilot.

In most cases, final agreement on some of these points will await the investigators own suggestions that he will put forward in a survey report.

■ PREPARE A SURVEY

A survey is written by the investigator or one of his colleagues in which a proposed study is put forward for discussion and agreement. Surveys tend to follow a traditional pattern which, while not mandatory, is recommended:

- an introductory section which sets the scene;
- a description of the current situation, including its history, selected figures, details of the groups involved;
- an outline of the proposed study;
- detailed steps of each stage of the proposed study;
- the participants who will take part;
- how long the study will take;
- the output(s) of the study;
- the costs and benefits of the study;

D

- appendices (e.g. a simple chart of the study showing planned progress deadlines, detailed figures, plans, charts).

Consultants will also include curricula vitae of the consultants being put forward for the study and a description of the consultancy firm's capabilities in the type of work. There may also be an explanation of the difference between calendar time (days and weeks on the calendar) and consultant time (days spent by a consultant on the study). Thus a consultant may spend ten days on a study that is spread over four calendar weeks, in which case the client will be invoiced for the ten days, not the four weeks.

The survey will end with a simple statement of future action, such as agreeing to a meeting to discuss the survey in detail.

Some people find writing surveys difficult. Advice that can be offered is:

- if in doubt, keep the survey simple and short rather than long and involved;
- do not put too many figures in the body of the survey. Keep them for the appendices;
- the survey may be read by a wide range of people. Unless it is aimed specifically at a technical group or problem, avoid jargon and over-technical language;
- keep the survey a professional-looking document (photocopies must be of high quality) but do not try to be too impressive, especially in writing style;
- the survey must be delivered on time.

■ FINALIZE DETAILS

After discussing the survey, it is possible to agree all the details about the study. The final details usually follow closely the proposals made in the survey (provided that the writer did his or her homework properly). Major changes are usually due to an important change in circumstances (such as the announcement of a forthcoming piece of legislation).

At the same time, arrangements will be agreed and put into motion. Examples are the start date, availability of staff, location of the investigator and making arrangements for early meetings.

■ PREPARE TERMS OF REFERENCE

Some organizations require terms of reference to be written for every study. Others would be baffled by such a concept, regarding them as being bureaucratic. There is little point in arguing one way or the other. Whatever an organization's habit is, one just has to live with it. If terms of reference have to be written, it can be sound practice for the writer of the survey to offer to write them. The writer will have been present at the preliminary meetings and will know what everyone wanted to happen, and what they understood to be agreed. It will also save time.

■ WRITE AND SIGN CONTRACT

Contracts are usually expected when working internationally. These could be troublesome and time-consuming to construct were it not for the fact that international management consultancies have a standard format for their contracts. Since these are based on previous experience, they are not changed extensively by clients. Such contracts have to take account of religious and political features of the country concerned. In socialist countries, they will have to be sanctioned by a centralized buying agency, including methods and currency of payment. In some Middle Eastern countries, the sale will have to go through an agency. In other countries (such as the

USA) working permits may be a difficulty. If the contract also involves an equipment supplier (such as a computer manufacturer or a supplier of factory machinery) keep the two contracts at arm's length. This may save complications later. It will more importantly show your independence.

There is one important point about a contract: namely, a contract is a contract. Whatever one says one will do, one has to do. It can be disastrous to agree to some clause in a contract, thinking that later discussion may be possible in order to change it. It is not.

Further reading

Markham, C., *Practical Consulting*, London: The Institute of Chartered Accountants (1987).

D

24

C – Chronicle

> I must create a system or be enslaved by another man's.
>
> William Blake, *Jerusalem* (1804/20)
>
> Things seen are mightier than things heard.
>
> Alfred, Lord Tennyson, *Enoch Arden* (1864)

The aim of this stage of methods design is to gain knowledge and information so that one is in a position to improve the current situation. Since memory is both finite and fallible, it is necessary to record the data in an orderly and convenient format. The main aspects of this are:

- fact finding;
- information relevance;
- information holding;
- recording some data in a semi-pictorial form (charts).

Fact finding

When a journalist writes an article, he has many sources of information. He will probably start with the journal's own library of cuttings held in a library and in a computer database (known as 'the morgue'). He can use reference books, his own files, the files of colleagues, his memory. He will then interview a number of people, both those connected with the subject personally and those who are reputed to be experts in the field. The article can then be written, during which it will often be necessary to recheck some facts. All this has to be done to meet a strict deadline. To be able to do all this, a journalist has to build up a particular skill so that it becomes second nature. (Cynics may refer to a well-known tabloid sports writer with the reputation of being able to write a piece on a boxing match without ever leaving the bar. But we are not concerned here with that particular skill.)

In a not dissimilar way, an investigator has to build up the ability to discover facts so that it becomes second nature. This is far from saying that one can ever become complacent or lazy. But it does mean that one has to learn the best sources of information, and the best way of extracting it. It also means that one has to learn how to plan and pace the work. Without this plan/pace ability, any investigator faces a rocky life; a management consultant faces an impossible one.

The sources of information used will depend on the particular type of study, and include:

- an organization's internally published material (e.g. the organization charts, costings, throughput volumes, job descriptions, admin. manuals);
- externally published material (e.g. books, magazines, inter-firm comparisons, analyses);
- reference material (e.g. standards of the Comité Consultatif International de Téléphonie et de Télégraphie);

230

- one's own files and those of one's colleagues;
- the records and files of one's department or consultancy;
- acknowledged experts in a particular field;
- institutes, international agencies, government departments.

In almost every study, however, the most important source of information is the knowledge and experience of the people who are doing the work itself. The primary method of discovering this is by interviewing the people themselves. This was covered in detail (in chapter 7) and so will not be repeated, except for yet a further reminder of the catch-phrase, 'courtesy with tenacity'.

There are other ways of getting some of this information, such as work diaries, electronic recorders and questionnaires. But the primary method remains the face-to-face interview. Questionnaires are useful in the right circumstances, but it must be remembered that they are only a one-way communication channel, lack subtle details, and can make the investigator seem like an aloof foreigner. They can, however, be very useful for collecting data quickly from a wide range of people, especially if the results will be used in a semi-statistical form.

While interviewing to follow the path of a procedure, some investigators make use of a pre-printed blank form called a procedure record sheet or a systems record sheet. These sheets have lines for writing the consecutive elements of work with spaces for additional data. These sheets are useful for:

D

- training new staff;
- when systems are extremely involved;
- when several phases of work are being studied simultaneously;
- if a team of people are looking at the work.

The primary aim of these interviews is to gain knowledge and to record each successive step of an overall procedure. The procedure may be 'order-to-invoice', 'obtaining items from stores', 'payroll' or any other administrative process. During the time of getting these facts, other facts will be recorded:

- volumes of throughput, plus details of peaks and troughs;
- details and examples of exceptions;
- blank and completed copies of all forms used;
- equipment used;
- software used, including changes to standard packages;
- inputs used (e.g. reference manuals);
- where the work comes from, and where it goes to;
- if relevant, office and workplace layout;
- any other information that is relevant.

One will also be listening to people: their comments, their opinions and, above all, their suggestions for improvements.

Information relevance

A balance has to be struck between obtaining too many facts and obtaining too few. Too many means taking too much time, and introducing 'noise' into the process. Too few means getting an incomplete picture and hence failing to produce a good new alternative.

Inevitably information will be gained that is not strictly relevant. This will include personal information about respondents and their families, and similar 'social' knowledge that is heard in any interaction between normal human beings. Other information will not be recorded because it is of a confidential nature. Apart from these cases, it is worthwhile to try to restrict efforts to pursuing the relevant rather than the merely interesting.

Information holding

There are people who can keep their work and notes without any order, in a randomized higgledy-piggledy mass. There are even people who can produce good results from this disordered mass. For the rest of us, a more systematic arrangement is a better approach. One arrangement is to divide the material into five separate files or section of a file. New material is then added to its preordained place:

Basics
> Background material, company-wide statistics, overall structure
> Reports prior to the start of the study
> *Aides-mémoire* on production processes
> Marketing and accounting information
> Product information

Working papers
> Notes on information flows
> Organization charts
> Personnel – standard levels, payroll
> Office layout
> Equipment
> Volumes, inputs, outputs, standards
> Procedures including charts
> Work quantification notes and calculations

Development
> Sales literature and notes of possible new equipment
> Copies of reports submitted
> Notes in preparation for future reports
> Notes for Investigation and Create stages

Launch
> Notes for the Launch stage
> Preparatory notes for training, job specifications, manuals

Finals
> Notes in preparation for Final Report
> Overall planning and progress charts
> Expenditure details

This suggested scheme is not inviolate; it can be easily adapted in any way that seems logical to a user. It is highly recommended if a study is being undertaken by a large team. Otherwise the result can be utter chaos followed by exasperation and acrimony.

Charts

There have been over the years quite a number of methods of recording systems data in a semi-pictorial form. Fortunately, most of them have died out, or almost died out. A few educational establishments still look back nostalgically to the 1950s and 1960s, which were the heydays of arcane charts. Professionals in the field cannot afford the luxury of making chart-drawing an end in itself.

Charting takes time. Charts should therefore be used to further a specific purpose. Charts are useful because they:

- assist in redesigning a method or procedure;
- highlight facts in an easily comprehensible form;
- reduce the amount of description needed;
- enable non-technical people (staff, unions, management) to understand somebody else's work.

The commonest chart used in administration is properly called a 'procedure flow-chart'. This is used for procedures and information flow. The method of charting described is not absolutely uniform everywhere. It is the one used in many countries, by at least five management consultancy firms, and in many large organizations.

D

■ PROCEDURE FLOWCHART

Like many charting methods, a set of stylized symbols is used:

Operation – an action that furthers the process. Work being carried out. Each activity is shown by a separate symbol.

Storage – the long-term filing of information or paperwork, e.g. data in a mainframe database, forms in a filing cabinet. If relevant, show whether storage is alphabetical, chronological, numerical, etc.

Delay – temporary storage or a pause in the flow of work, e.g. letters in an in-tray awaiting action, bytes in a buffer store between a word processor and printer.

Movement of paperwork or data, e.g. an invoice going to a customer, data being downloaded overnight from a terminal to head office. The first symbol is used if the movement is important, the second sign is used if it is trivial,

Check correctness (of information). If one form is being checked against another, then the dotted line is drawn between the two forms.

Transfer of information from one source to another, e.g. writing a passport number onto a duty-free invoice. The dotted line joins the two items.

Destruction of data or paperwork

Decision or conditional branch. The first symbol tends to be used for real decisions (e.g. when studying mental processes) and certainly never for anything which is merely a sorting operation. The second symbol is used for conditional branching. In some organizations, the two symbols are interchangeable.

Activities not relevant to a particular chart, e.g. activities that take place in a customer's office and which (it is presumed) cannot be changed.

233

New form or hard copy which appear in the chart for the first time at the place that this symbol appears.

 New form in triplicate or in more than three copies.

‾‾‾‾‾ Change in nature of an item being charted (for example, a pre-printed order form becoming an invoice).

Information stored in a permanent form, e.g. a price list, a thesaurus/spelling checker in a microcomputer.

The final two symbols are met with infrequently; perhaps they, too, are dying out as a further evolutionary stage of chart history. Stencils suitable for drawing the symbols are made by a number of manufacturers. An example in the UK is 'UNO stencil – reference no. D/T 302'.

The method of turning a procedure into a chart is shown in this example:

THE STOLEN CASH CARD

Background

A cash card is a plastic card with a magnetic stripe on it containing account details. In use, the owner presents the cash card to a cashier at any branch of his bank. The customer can collect up to $400 in any one day. A thief has stolen such a card and knows the password used for security, thus being able to use the card undetected. The thief is going from branch to branch, collecting money. The crime has been discovered and the police think that they know the pattern of the thief's visits to branches. They think that they know which branch he will visit next, but have few details about the thief's appearance.

Procedure

A policeman copies from the terminal in the police station onto a form 'C.7217' details of:

● reference number that is on the card (this has no relation to the password);
● outline physical description of the thief.

The policeman checks that he has written these details down correctly. He then takes the form to the bank branch in a police car (to save time). There the cashier writes down the contents of the form C.7217 onto a piece of scrap paper.

Each time a customer hands a cash card to the cashier, the cashier checks the card reference number and description of the thief against the notes on the scrap paper. He sees whether the card is the stolen one, and if the customer resembles the thief.

If not, then the transaction is processed in the normal manner. If it appears that the customer is the thief, then the cashier signals to the policeman who takes possession of the card.

Note

The procedure is the subject being charted, not the policeman or the cashier.

The resulting chart is shown in Figure 24.1.

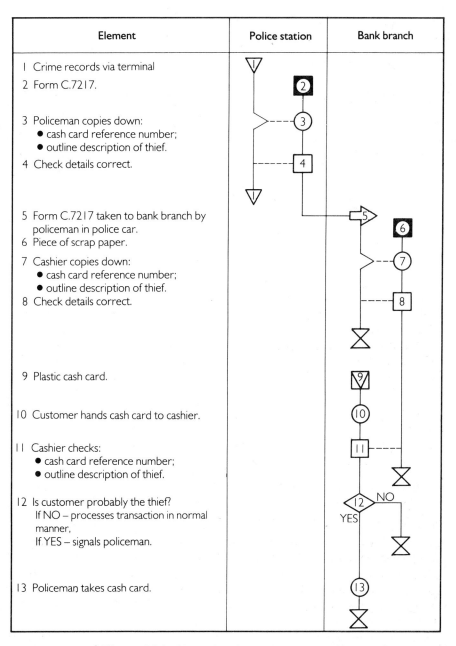

Element	Police station	Bank branch
1 Crime records via terminal		
2 Form C.7217.		
3 Policeman copies down: ● cash card reference number; ● outline description of thief.		
4 Check details correct.		
5 Form C.7217 taken to bank branch by policeman in police car.		
6 Piece of scrap paper.		
7 Cashier copies down: ● cash card reference number; ● outline description of thief.		
8 Check details correct.		
9 Plastic cash card.		
10 Customer hands cash card to cashier.		
11 Cashier checks: ● cash card reference number; ● outline description of thief.		
12 Is customer probably the thief? If NO – processes transaction in normal manner, If YES – signals policeman.		
13 Policeman takes cash card.		

Figure 24.1 Chart for the stolen cash card

D

A working example of a procedure flowchart is given in Figure 24.2. This is for a manufacturer of office technology, and shows the original method for 'order-to-delivery' (the part shown is about a third of the complete chart).

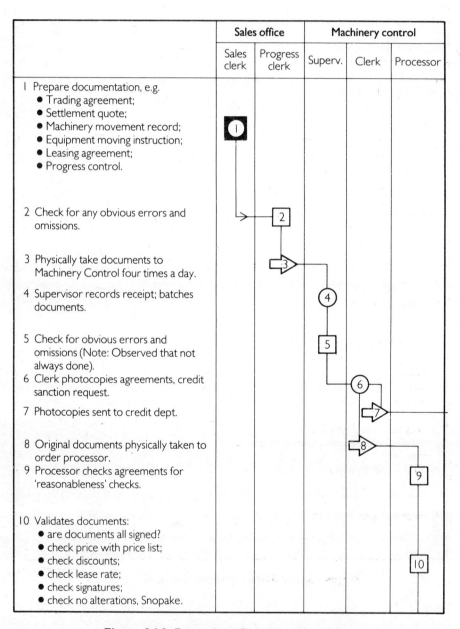

Figure 24.2 Procedure flowchart example

■ CHARTING GUIDELINES

Individual analysts have always demonstrated a certain independence when drawing charts, refusing to produce exactly uniform charts. It has to be assumed that this will continue to be so. In practice, slight differences do not seem to affect the final result too adversely, provided that a chart is clear, unambiguous, and can be understood by other people.

In spite of any slight variations, certain guidelines and conventions are accepted:

- the objective and subject of a chart must be known. For example, a single chart cannot follow both a procedure and the activities of a group of people. If this is attempted, the result is inevitably a muddle with a proliferation of branches going off in different directions;
- decide, and stick to, the level of detail to be used for individual elements of work or activities;
- charts proceed from top to bottom, and left to right;
- each chart needs a heading (specifying procedure/project or similar descriptor), a date (original and revisions), the name of the author, the people studied, a page number, plus any additional useful material such as explanatory notes and layout plans. When a project is large, a coding number may also be needed. These precautions do not take long to do, but can save frustrations at a later date;
- the standardized symbols should be employed (utilizing a stencil/template);
- if a chart is going to be unmanageably large, two alternative approaches can be used: (a) draw an outline summary chart which refers to a number of attached subsidiary charts; (b) draw a chart of the main procedure, plus other charts for the individual sub-systems;
- have as few lines crossing one another as possible;
- try to produce a neat chart. It is much easier to use for methods improvements, and is much easier for other people to understand.

Software is available for personal computers to help in drawing charts, but they do need a good microcomputer and a good plotter/printer to give acceptable results. 'Acceptable' means good enough to show other people or to use in a report; a number of them are good enough for purely personal use.

■ FLOW PROCESS CHART

Flow process charts are less common than procedure flowcharts, though some analysts prefer them. Usually, they are employed when it is wished to study work in greater detail than that in a procedure flowchart. They usually include details of distances moved and time taken. They are thus often used:

- when studying mailroom staff, messengers, internal mail and security staff;
- in the study of staff who work at computer terminals;
- to present differences (and hence improvements) between an original method and a proposed method.

Nowadays, flow process charts are usually pre-printed with a column of the five main symbols (for Operation, Movement, Delay, Check and Storage). Officially, a pre-printed form is called an 'OTIS' chart (OTIS being an acronym for Operation/Transport/Inspection/Storage).

D

The heading of a typical pre-printed flow process chart is given in Figure 24.3.

Flow Process Chart

JOB_____PRESENT/PROPOSED method

	Present		Proposed		Difference	
	No.	Time	No.	Time	No.	Time
Operations						
Movements						
Checks						
Storages						
Delays						
Distance						

Ref. No._____

Page_____of_____

Chart starts_____

Chart ends_____

Author_____

Date_____

Figure 24.3 Flow process chart – heading

■ COMPUTER SYSTEMS FLOWCHART

Investigators whose background is systems work for mainframe computers use a different set of symbols. The main symbols in this set are standard. Lesser symbols are used in practice in a variety of approaches. The main difference between these symbols and the set previously described is the convention that writing is inside the symbols rather than at the side. Most computer manufacturers produce a stencil or template for drawing the symbols, (e.g. IBM ref. X.20–8020).
Symbols used include:

Meaning/Use	Symbol	Example/Explanation
Computer process	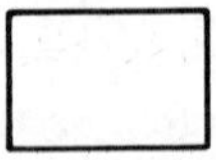	'Compute gross salary'
Predefined process	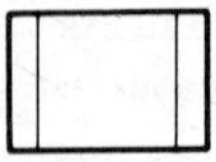	'Call input data'
Input/output	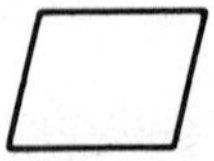	'Read employee's record'
Decision/conditional branch	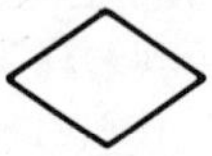	'Weekly paid/Piecework?'

Terminal/interrupt		Begin, end or interrupt a procedure
Connector		Exit to, or entry from another part of the chart
Manual process		'Log number of last invoice'
Document		'Students enrolled listing'
On-line storage		General symbol for any input/output on-line storage (e.g. disk, tape)
Off-line storage		General symbol for any off-line type of storage
Display		Any type of on-line display, (e.g. video, plotter). Also used for workstations
Manual input (on-line)		Keyboards, switches, pushbuttons, bar readers
Communication link		Information transmittal, usually by telecommunications
Magnetic disk		Input or output
Magnetic tape		

An example of a computer systems flowchart is shown in Figure 24.4. This was for a hospital payroll (simplified).

■ OTHER CHARTING METHODS

A number of other charts may be encountered, or utilized for special situations. These include:

Outline process chart

This chart shows an overall picture of a (usually large) procedure. It is useful:

- to help decide where more detailed analysis is indicated;
- to indicate key activities;

239

- in a large office where the analyst is unfamiliar with the activities of their sequence;
- where a large team of analysts are working, and separate areas have to be allocated to individuals for study.

This chart is built up using only two symbols and their activities: Operation and

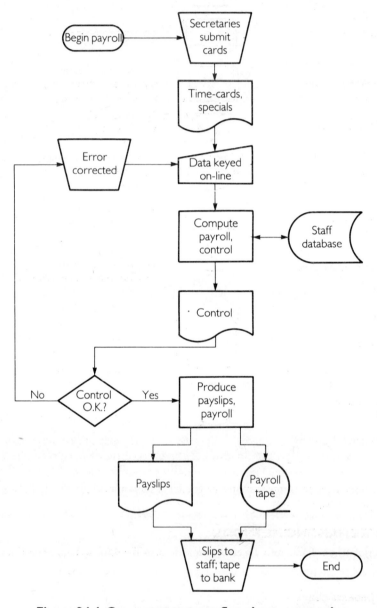

Figure 24.4 Computer systems flowchart – example

Check/Inspection. Part of a typical chart (for newspaper distribution) would use the following elements:

- newspapers bundled and labelled;
- quantity to each wholesaler checked;
- papers distributed;
- received quantity checked by wholesaler;
- papers sorted into newsagents' parcels;
- papers distributed.

Multiple activity time chart

The activities of a group of 'subjects' (which may be staff and/or equipment and/or facilities) are recorded against a common time scale. This enables one to examine (and thence to improve and plan) their interrelationships. Examples of use of this method include:

- utilization of lecture rooms at a management training centre,
- scheduling messengers' work,
- use of shared terminals,
- timetabling audio-conferencing.

Sundry charts

Other charts that will be met in books (even though rarely in real life, nowadays) are:

- simo charts (from 'simultaneous motion'), which offer a very detailed analysis of different parts of the body;
- therblig analysis (from 'Gilbreth' spelt backwards, nearly). Detailed motion analysis employing a special set of symbols and a set of eighteen different colours;
- actuality wallchart. Copies of actual forms are mounted on a spare wall and joined by tapes where related. Used for presentations and training;
- skill charts. Specialized pre-printed forms to facilitate the analysis of mental, physical and tactile skills;
- outline procedure charts (also called 'geo-operational'). Large block diagrams showing the flow of information or paperwork between offices in distant locations.

PMTS charts (chapter 35) are primarily used for work quantification but can also be used for methods design. It should also be remembered that algorithms (chapter 27), organization charts (chapter 17), and even networks are forms of charting.

■ OTHER RECORDING METHODS

These include:

- decision tables;
- office layouts, including string diagrams;
- graphs;
- various types of photography (still, ciné, video, time lapse);
- completed checklists.

There is one recording method which investigators virtually never get the opportunity to use (which is a pity since it can provide a welcome break from any sense of monotony). In spite of this rarity, it is widely referred to. This is the 'cyclegraph'. A small light source is attached to the hands or other limbs. Their path during an activity is recorded by a continuous exposure of a still camera. If the light source(s) are intermittent rather than continuous, then the resulting record is called a 'chronocyclegraph'. Cyclegraphs are used by sports coaches, by ergonomists, by research psychologists and in a few advertising campaigns. The rest of us, unfortunately, rarely have either the need or the time.

It can be seen that there is a very wide variety of recording and charting methods. But the basic premise remains: they are a means, not an end.

Further reading

Anderson, R. G., *Organisation and Methods*, Plymouth: Macdonald & Evans, 1980.

Bentley, T. J. (ed.), *The Management Services Handbook*, London: Holt, Rinehart & Winston, 1984.

BSI, *Work Study and Organization and Methods*, Part 2 (BS 3375/2), London: British Standards Institution, 1986.

Long, L., *Computers in Business*, Englewood Cliffs: Prentice-Hall, 1987.

Sprague, R. H. and McNurlin, B. C., *Information Systems Management in Practice*, Englewood Cliffs: Prentice-Hall, 1986.

25

I – Investigate and
C – Create

Better ask twice than lose your way once.
Danish proverb

The thoughts that come often unsought, and, as it were, drop into
the mind, are commonly the most valuable of any we have.
John Locke (in a letter), 1699

There are two aspects of 'Investigate and Create' that need to be referred to at the outset. First, there is no single approach that applies to all situations. This fact may be a disappointment to anybody seeking a single formula for success, and to those who have learnt only one approach from another book. But a single formula is not possible. This is because of the variety of studies that face one. These will include the organization structure of an entity that does not currently exist, the change of service in a value-adding partnership, the introduction of predetermined advanced technology, and straightforward cost reduction.

D

The second aspect is the question of whether Investigate and Create are quite separate steps, or whether they are almost simultaneous. Some analysts disagree that this is one step, claiming that the first step is critical and the second one is creative.[1] On the other hand, the International Labour Office guide to management consultancy says that there is 'no clear-cut limit between analysis and synthesis'.[2]

Without wishing to be accused of taking a typically pragmatic or compromise position, we feel that the truth lies in the middle. As stated previously, one must avoid the temptation of trying to think too early of some incredibly bright idea. On the other hand, when looking at the current situation, one inevitably thinks of possible alternatives. What is important is for one to be able always to retain the two abilities: both to be able to investigate critically and to synthesize creatively.

Investigate

■ GENERAL SCHEMA

Before looking at any specific technique for improving a current situation, it is worthwhile to get matters into perspective by considering what is done in rather general terms. In effect, we follow the same general path no matter what the subject under consideration. To take two extremes, it is what we do whether we are being asked to look at an aspect of government policy or planning the layout of a university lecture room. What is done is to answer the following questions shown in Figure 25.1. This process is always an iterative one: at any time it may become clear that more facts are needed. Or an option may have to be dropped. For example, the chosen option may be 'use a micro'. Developing this option may reveal that no machine on the market is suitable.

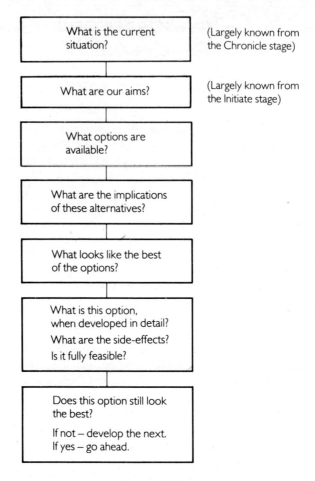

What is the current situation?	(Largely known from the Chronicle stage)
What are our aims?	(Largely known from the Initiate stage)
What options are available?	
What are the implications of these alternatives?	
What looks like the best of the options?	
What is this option, when developed in detail? What are the side-effects? Is it fully feasible?	
Does this option still look the best? If not – develop the next. If yes – go ahead.	

Figure 25.1

Superficially, this diagram may seem bland, even obvious, but it does highlight one important fact. Most of the special techniques that one hears about share a common aim: they are different ways of trying to help one to arrive at a range of options and then to select the best one. This diagram may therefore help to remove some of the mystique, the arguments and the problems of understanding some of the competing approaches. In fact, as it stands, the diagram itself is an approach.

■ FUNDAMENTAL STUDY

The so-called Fundamental Study is one that concerns itself with a basic commercial task, and develops a new system without considering overmuch the way things are done currently. For example, a financial institution paying out cash to its customers may at present use a 'pass-book'. A fundamental study would not allow this present approach to act as a constraint to inhibit the exploration of alternatives, e.g. a smart card. An interesting and challenging type of fundamental study is the greenfields study. A greenfields study is the development of a complete admin system in an office that has not yet been built or put into operation.

The approach to a fundamental study uses the mnemonic 'Fundamental':

F – find out the reasons for the study (e.g. expansion, office automation, a new law);
U – understand the basic aims of the new system (e.g. to take orders from television viewers and get them to a warehouse within eighteen hours);
N – name those aspects that are constraints (e.g. the law, company policy, techno-logy, costs);
D – determine all the possible alternatives. This is done under three group headings known as the M.3 heads – manual, mechanical and microprocessor;
A – assess the costs and side-effects of the most promising-looking of the alternatives;
M – modify the number of alternatives to a smaller number;
E – evaluate the feasibility and implications of this reduced list of alternatives;
N – nominate one alternative as the chosen, ideal one;
T – turn this ideal into a fully fleshed out one;
A – add to this ideal to allow for special needs, exceptions, secondary tasks and possible future changes;
L – lay this proposal out in detail for further discussion with interested parties.

D

■ GENERAL METHOD STUDY

One of the ways of improving methods in general is to use the 'critical examination' approach. This asks the questions:

What?   Why?   How?   When?   Where?   Who?

when investigating the aspects of:

Purpose	Means	Sequence	Time
Quality	Place	Person	Cost

The initial questioning leads on to a consideration of alternatives that may be possible, and thence to selecting the best of these alternatives. This approach is rather like an often quoted (and often misquoted) passage from a poem by Rudyard Kipling:[3]

> *I keep six honest serving-men*
> *(They taught me all I knew);*
> *Their names are What and Why and When*
> *And How and Where and Who.*

The critical examination approach is often expressed in the form of a matrix as an aid to investigation. An example of a critical examination matrix is given in Figure 25.2 overleaf. The title 'Subject' on the form can be used as referring to:

● an overall procedure, or method or problem;
● the most important Operation in a procedure chart;
● the most dominant Operations;
● all Operations in a procedure.

The final option seems somewhat extreme, but has been observed in two organizations. In the hands of people who are used to and like it, the matrix shown is very useful in a number of situations.

Critical Examination Matrix

Subject _____
Ref. No. _____

Author _____
Date _____

Current situation	Challenge	Alternatives	Selections
Purpose – WHAT is achieved? (Do not confuse with HOW?)	Is it NECESSARY? WHY is it necessary? (Discover the real reason)	What ELSE could be done? (Can the subject be eliminated, partly carried out, altered?)	What SHOULD be done? (Consider both long- and short-term implications)
Place – WHERE is it done? (Sketch, distances may be helpful. Location may be 'near power supply')	Why THERE? (If this is the original reason, is it still applicable?)	Where ELSE could it be done? (Locations can be near, far, or even 'anywhere'. Or combined)	Where SHOULD it be done? (If a compromise – record reason)
Means – HOW is it done? (Method, equipment, materials, forms, environment, hazards, 'specials')	Why THAT way? (Give reasons separately for each item covered in left-hand box)	How ELSE could it be done? (Consider alternatives for each item in left-hand box)	How SHOULD it be done? (Initially choose for each item. Bring together at 'Create' stage)
Time/Sequence – WHEN is it done? (i) Previous and subsequent activities (ii) Time factors (iii) Deadlines	Why THEN? (Give reasons separately for each item covered in left-hand box)	When ELSE could it be done? (Earlier? Later? Overlap? Change deadlines, frequency?)	When SHOULD it be done? (Initially choose for each item. Bring together at 'Create' stage)
Person – WHO does it? (Number of staff, titles, grades, shifts, overtime, special payments)	Why THAT person? (Give reasons separately for each item covered in left-hand box)	Who ELSE could do it? (Consider alternatives for each item in left-hand box)	Who SHOULD do it! (If a compromise – record reason)
Quality – how WELL is it done? (Levels of service, error levels, etc. How measured, use of controls)	Why THAT well? (Discover the real reason)	What quality COULD be used? (Consider alternatives for each item in left-hand box)	What quality SHOULD be used? (Define both quality and the method of measurement and control)
Cost – how MUCH does it cost? (Show direct + indirect + overheads separately. Quote sources)	Why THAT much? (Show main factors: staff, royalties, equipment, rent, etc.)	What ELSE could it cost? (Cost of alternatives)	What SHOULD it cost? (Target cost. Refined at later stage)

Figure 25.2 Critical examination matrix

There are people who do not like this approach. They prefer to use the general schema   (p. 244), using brainstorming to enable them to arrive at as many alternatives as possible. Both routes can be successful, and both have particular strengths. It is advisable to know both, try both, and then use both as circumstances dictate.

■ COMPUTER SYSTEMS

The initial stages of a computer systems study are similar to the standard approach given in Initiate and Chronicle – particularly broach and concur and charting. However, at the Investigate and Create stages, differences occur (though, with the development of new tools, computer systems studies are growing more like other studies).

The main stages of systems development that are equivalent to Investigate and Create can be categorized as:

- development of a prototype system;
- systems analysis and design;
- program writing.

The subsequent stages of systems development are again similar to other study forms.

The investigate and create stages of systems development can be subdivided into the following steps:

D

- discuss alternatives with users. Draw up a general systems design, showing the fundamental operation of the proposed system by means of a written description and a chart;
- define the system specification after talking to users. At one time changes to this were difficult (due to the nature of third-generation languages and file processing) so specs were sometimes rather ill-defined and incomplete. The use of fourth- and fifth-generation languages and database management have made things better. These made it feasible to make the prototype a subset of the proposed system;
- develop a prototype system. This can be tried out by a user. The trial will show up any shortcomings;
- specify the database requirements;
- develop controls for inputs, outputs, processing and procedures;
- define the detailed system design;
- discuss the system with other computer staff;
- describe the layouts of reports, screen displays and hardcopy;
- write, test and describe the computer programs.

Perhaps the main variability between analysts is the amount of interaction with users. Some analysts do not give enough weight to this aspect of their work. This is unfortunate – as those who have to live with the result can testify, complete with examples.

■ PROCEDURE IMPROVEMENT

Many procedures are in practice very complex and involved affairs. In such a situation, possible improvements may not be at all obvious. The procedure chart is investigated in a specific order, by looking at different symbols in turn:

1 The first two symbols to be investigated are those for transfer of information and new forms. These two symbols enable one to optimize the flow of information and to provide it in an optimum manner. Questions asked are:

- can the activity be eliminated?
- can the number of transfers and new forms be cut?
- which people really need information?
- what information do they really need?
- can activities be combined?
- can activities be changed or simplified?

If the answer to all questions is in the negative, try again.

2 The third symbol for investigation is the one for a decision. Every decision should be challenged, especially if it leads to a new branch of activities. Can the decision be eliminated by using algorithms, more precise rules, better information, better form design? Is a decision needed? Is more than one person making almost the same (or indeed the same) decision? If a decision can be removed, is mechanization then possible?

3 The next symbol for attention is that for an operation. If an operation can be eliminated, then other associated activities will automatically disappear. The operation activity can be eliminated, combined, simplified, changed or moved (in that order). If this is not successful, then it should be subjected to the full critical examination matrix described above.

4 The fifth symbol for investigation is the one for check. Here, one attempts to eliminate the need for checking. This may be done by ensuring that different databases contain exactly the same facts, or by the use of multi-part sets, or by using sample or restricted checks. An example of this last is in the banking world. At one time every fund transfer was checked for correct signature, right data, word-and-figure discrepancies, etc. But nowadays this checking is reserved usually only for payments in excess of £50.

If considered advisable, the remaining symbols can then be investigated, in turn.

■ ADVANCED TECHNOLOGY

It must be emphasized that we are not here considering office automation (where a major part of the operations are to be mechanized) – this is covered in a separate chapter. Here we are considering the introduction of a few pieces of technology, such as personal computers, which will leave much of the work of the office outside the scope of the microprocessor.

The introduction of advanced technology should come about quite naturally, as one of the alternatives for improving the current situation. The joker in the pack is that sometimes it is introduced as a non-strategic directive from management, who find the concept attractive. Worse still, this type of directive may come from a group who are technologically illiterate.

If this happens, then the plan of action depends on whether the directive is specific or general in nature. It can be quite specific, as in the case of the firm that decided to introduce video-conferencing for its secretaries in different countries to get to know one another better, or the multinational retail bank that distributed 400 personal computers to its branch managers to play with and so become better acquainted with new technology (presumably by some form of osmosis). In this sort of situation, one has to grit one's teeth and do the best one can. The more Machiavellian investigator may be able to turn the situation to the organization's benefit.

If the directive is general in nature, then one should be grateful. It can become the first step towards the formulation of a corporate strategy. Since the implication of such a decision is that capital will be made available, thoughts should be turned towards the question of – where will it be of best use? The first choice would be to tackle an area felt to be a problem, such as a bottleneck, a major source of customer complaints, or a high error-rate source. In the absence of a problem area then attention should be turned to whether selection should be a function (e.g. word processing) or a procedure (e.g. order taking).

When the introduction of advanced technology arises as a natural part of improvement (as an alternative), then the stages are similar to the general schema   (p. 244), with a few additions:

- discuss the needs of all users with them (e.g. the accountant may need spreadsheet help to produce forward budgets, 60-day unpaid bills may be needed every Thursday);
- ensure that all exceptions, 'specials', analyses, and all deadlines are known (this particular point is important when ledgers are involved);
- ensure that all volumes are known (e.g. for a sales ledger – number of live/dead accounts, lines per invoice, movements per month, invoices per month, general ledger/day book postings, changes, etc.);
- try to learn about advanced technology (books/magazines/courses/seminars/friends/colleagues) but do not become either overawed nor over-involved;
- write a user's specification in lay language, discuss it with the staff, translate it into more technical language;
- try to get a member of staff from a user department onto the team that is working on the study (not necessarily full time since this can cause problems with workloads of the other staff);
- list prospective manufacturers/suppliers of equipment, peripherals, software, supplies and maintenance;
- contact these suppliers and discuss the user's specification with them. Select a shortlist and ask those on it to submit their proposals. When these are received, inspect each one carefully and discuss with staff and colleagues;
- select the two proposals that seem most attractive. Visit locations that are using similar equipment and software. Talk to the staff and gauge their reactions;
- make the final selection. Prepare for the next stage.

D

If the organization has little experience of advanced technology, avoid anything described as 'the cutting edge of technology' or 'state of the art', and ensure that there are after-sales service and training schemes.

■ SPECIAL AREAS

Specialized forms of Investigate and Create will be found in the relevant chapters:

- organization structure (chapter 18);
- automating offices (chapter 15);
- Organization Development (chapter 19);
- office planning (chapter 28).

C – Create

As already indicated, the split between Investigate and Create depends on the type of study. However, the stages will normally be along the following lines:

- finalize the Investigate stage;
- build up the skeleton of the preferred option, if this has not already been done. In the case of a Fundamental study, the skeleton is built up from the basic essential requirements. If based on a procedure chart, then the skeleton is based on the essential 'information transfer', 'new form', and 'operation' elements;
- add flesh to this skeleton by adding the minimum of ancillary elements (such as check, movement) needed to make the method or procedure a feasible proposition;
- inspect carefully any 'delays' or awkward deadlines that have been introduced, or are implicit;
- ensure that all exceptions, specials and one-offs can be accommodated by the proposal;
- chart the new method/procedure as part of the checking process, to demonstrate the improvement, as an aid to discussions, and as a basis for the preparation of staff training;
- discuss the new system with colleagues and with the staff. This is partly to give everybody the opportunity of pointing out any obvious mistakes or omissions (better now than later on). It is also to gain an opportunity for further improvements, additions, amendments and refinement. Furthermore, it is a step towards gaining acceptance, as people start getting used to the new ideas and the prospect of change;
- check again that the proposal is feasible. Feasibility is of four kinds:
  - (a) economic (i.e. is the proposal cost-effective?),
  - (b) operational (i.e. will it work?),
  - (c) technical (i.e. is equipment available?),
  - (d) cultural (i.e. can the organization handle the change and the proposal?).
- check delivery dates for all equipment and supplies;
- check that any implications can be handled and/or are in hand (e.g. knocking down office walls, hiring temporary office accommodation, installing new power lines);
- make presentations to the staff and management who asked for the study and/or who have a power of veto;
- start preparations for the next stage (Launch – chapter 38).

It is at this time, during analysts' training, that a sense of trepidation fills some people. It all looks so straightforward in theory. What happens if an improvement is not made? Surely the shame would be unbearable? The answer is that firstly, the staff themselves will sometimes be better than you at making an improvement. Secondly, sometimes, just sometimes, an improvement is not possible. In this case, one has to remember the situation and remain determined that one will make the improvement one day, somehow – and be determined that the next study will be superb. Two mini case studies may demonstrate this.

A mailroom included the task of packing large parcels. This had been carefully studied in depth so that the task was precisely laid out. Two people stood on opposite sides of a bench on which the string and brown paper was laid. During packing, the people were trained to twist the parcel and to pass one another the string ends. It looked good – so good that the staff were put onto a piecework style of incentive. But they soon managed to beat the system. They did this by throwing the parcel up into the air and lassoing it in mid-air. Now, any analyst who had dared to suggest this (assuming that he had thought of it) would have been laughed at and told that it was impossible. The moral? Everybody can make improvements.

The second example concerns buying a new car. For most people, this involves the following steps:

- go to retailer, inspect car and make decision;
- pay with a cheque;
- receive a roadworthy car, complete with insurance and car plates;
- take the car home.

In one country, the steps are as follows:

- go to retailer; order car;
- wait for car to be manufactured and to be made available;
- receive telegram saying that car is ready;
- go to depot; queue; try to get desired colour and reserve a car without marks or rust;
- go to bank to get cash (low limit on cheque use); queue; show ID card and get cash;
- go to retailer; queue; paperwork prepared (show ID card);
- go to cashier; queue; pay for car; get receipt;
- return to clerk, queue; receive further paperwork;
- return to depot; queue; paperwork checked; show ID card;
- wait for car to be part-prepared;
- receive further paperwork;
- take car home;
- ensure/make car roadworthy;
- take car to test centre; queue; car tested; receive paperwork;
- go to car registration centre; queue; buy tax stamps; queue; carry out initial car registration; receive form and temporary car plates;
- take car to insurance office (for comprehensive insurance); queue; insure car; pay cash; receive form;
- return to car registration centre; queue; complete registration; receive permanent car plates;
- take car home;
- drill holes in car front and rear; affix car plates.

All this takes so long that it is normal practice for people to take a day off work to do it. To some extent this extended procedure is needed because cars are in short supply, but the fact remains that people dislike this procedure but nobody seems to know how to change it. The moral? Perhaps, as Mikhail Gorbachev once said, 'You cannot improve something without changing it.'[4]

The diagram in Figure 25.3 overleaf is a representation of the build-up of a proposal for an improvement. There are times when it is not obvious how to make the leap from what is known to what should be proposed. This gap (called the 'extrinsic gap') may be closed by:

- leaving the problem for a day or two and then returning to it;
- widening the circle of experience (by talking to people in other disciplines,

251

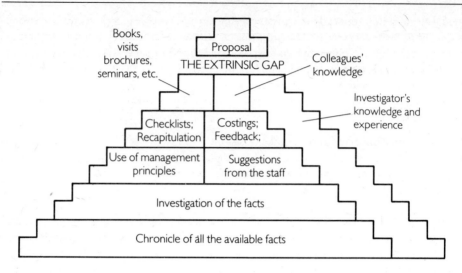

Figure 25.3 The extrinsic gap

approaching trade associations and professional institutes, holding further discussions, finding parallel situations);
- trying a different way of looking at the situation or restating a problem in a new way;
- imagine a slightly improved situation and then improve this imaginary solution;
- imagine that you have a completely greenfield position and develop a best means of doing the work;
- carry out a brainstorming session.

Before finally adopting the improvement, it may be necessary to set up a 'test-bed' to check its viability. This test-bed can take a number of forms. It may be just a dummy run, it may require a Monte Carlo statistical simulation, or it may be a computer simulation. Whatever form it takes, one is then ready for the next stage: the launching.

References

1 Gilbert, A. V., *Management Services*, May 1988, p. 38.
2 ILO, *Management Consulting*, Geneva: International Labour Office, 1977.
3 Rudyard Kipling, 'The Elephant's Child' , *Just-So Stories*, 1902.
4 Speech to the *27th Congress of the CPSU*, Moscow: Novosti Press, 1986.

Further reading

Hurndell, B. F., *Management Services*, March 1988, p. 14.
Plus books shown as further reading at the end of chapter 24.

26
Overhead Value Analysis

Everything is worth what its purchaser will pay for it.
Publilius Syrus, *Moral Sayings* (First century BC)

The value of a thing is the amount of labouring or work that its possession will save the possessor.
Henry George, *The Science of Political Economy* (1897)

Over the past few years, Overhead Value Analysis has moved down two paths which may seem to have resulted in two very different approaches. One path has been a semi-accounting route utilizing functional analysis and user requirements, often called by the acronym 'OVA'. This route generally leads to studies which include a definite cost reduction stage, in which case it may be called OCR: 'Overhead Cost Reduction'. The other path has been to emphasize the use of alternatives in a purer value analysis framework. In this case it may be called CBA: Cost–Benefit Administration.

D

In fact, both paths rely on the basic questions that value analysis asks:

- what are the admin activities and what do they cost?
- what benefits are gained by these activities?
- are these benefits necessary?
- how could the necessary benefits be obtained at less cost?

The 'OVA/OCR' approach has become particularly popular when a study concerns:

- an international organization which has offices in different countries performing basically similar activities (e.g. multinational banks with front and/or back offices in a number of countries); or
- an organization with a number of decentralized offices; or
- a department or function that has grown over the years without having had an investigation by management for some time; or
- where an organization has a large number of departments (in which case they will be providing services to one another).

The 'CBA' approach is particularly appropriate when:

- relatively inexperienced teams have been set up to make improvements (for, say, Management Development or Organization Development purposes); or
- people are having difficulty in thinking up new ideas for cost reduction exercises; or
- an organization knows that it has become 'fat' but has difficulty in focussing on a starting point.

OCR – Overhead cost reduction

The methodology for OCR can be summarized thus:

1 Functional Analysis of the work that is performed by the department(s) being studied.

2 User Analysis of users' perception of the services being provided.
3 Effectiveness Study of the work being performed. When the study is being carried out for an international organization, then this will include a comparison of the offices in different countries.
4 Formulation of proposals to improve efficiency and/or reduce costs.
5 Preparing and performing an Action Plan to achieve the proposed improvements.

■ FUNCTIONAL ANALYSIS

During the functional analysis stage, one is effectively asking:

- what tasks are actually carried out within each function?
- what services does this work lead to?
- how much time, etc. is spent on each service?
- who benefits from these services, and by how much?

Analysis of the answers to these questions enables one to answer two further questions:

- what inputs are devoted to each task, service and user?
- what is the cost to each user of each service?

Since much of the analysis work for OVA/OCR is normally computerized (an ordinary personal computer is adequate), use is made of pre-printed forms for recording responses. The first form that is used is the Key Task Sheet (if the investigator has carried out work previously on the functions, then it is just possible that the data for this form is already known). These forms are either sent to the departmental managers for completion, or are filled in by the investigator after interviews in the usual way. If the former, then they will have to be checked for relevance, consistency, etc. An example of a partially completed form is shown in Figure 26.1.

A key task is one of the basic reasons for the existence of a section. Generally, there should not be more than four key tasks to a section. These tasks are described briefly and specifically. Examples of key tasks are:

- provide a staff recruitment service;
- carry out market research.

If some sections carry out projects, they may need help in defining them.

The next step (and the next form) is to list the key tasks and to show individual steps (called 'activities' on the form) that are taken to perform each key task. In many cases the activities will amount to a description of the key task. Those completing the form should be reminded that it is important to include all activities necessary during the year – not just those that are being done at the time of filling in the form. They should also be asked to state the activity in what is known as 'action statement' mode; that is, verb/noun. Examples of activities in a personnel department are:

- interview job applicants;
- prepare monthly ABCD report;
- process visas and work permits.

It should be noted that 'management of a unit' is an activity in its own right and is listed (this may be a small detail and hardly worth mentioning – but it is surprising how often people ask). Individual tasks do not usually need more than six activities.

Functional Analysis		
Step 1		
Summary of Sections and Key Tasks		
Function: Controllers	**Prepared by:** J. Smith	**Date:** 3 March

Section			Key Tasks
A	Planning and Profit reporting	A1	Co-ordinate annual budget and plan.
		A2	Prepare management accounting information.
		A3	
		A4	
	Ref: 30/024	A5	
B	Policy and Systems control	B1	Provide accountancy policy guidance for MIS.
		B2	Develop accounting systems control.
		B3	Special projects.
		B4	
	Ref: 30/034	B5	

Figure 26.1 Key-task sheet

D

Functional Analysis						
Step 2						
Summary of services/end products						
Function: Controllers		**Key task No.:** A1				
Section: Planning and Profit Reporting		**Prepared by:** J. Smith				

Activities	Services/end products	Rating	Users			
Co-ordinate capital budgets	Capital Expenditure Plan	Mand.	San Fran. CONT-75%	London WWD-15%	London SEO-5%	London OPS-5%
Co-ordinate back-office budgets	HQ Corporate Plan	Mand.	San Fran. CONT-80%	London WWD-10%	London SEO-10%	

Figure 26.2 Summary of services/end products

The form (an example of which is shown in Figure 26.2) has considerably more information on it than just the activities. The column next to the one for activities is for the service or end product that are the result of the activity. These items could be used within the same function but will normally be those things that are delivered to users: in other words, outputs. The description has to say what is provided, not how. Even when the service is intangible, the service itself is still quoted, not the result of the service. For example, the activity of administering a grievance process will produce 'grievance procedure' and not 'happier staff'. Examples of entries are:

- shortlist of job applicants;
- a periodic report (shown by name);
- Aliens Regulations observed.

The next column is headed 'Rating'. Into this column, managers are asked to put a rating of how important they regard the completion of the activity. They may be asked to rate each activity on the usual 1–5 scale (with an 'M' for 'mandatory' to indicate tasks which have to be done by law, such as regulatory reporting, and for which a rating would be inappropriate). It may be thought odd to ask this of service producers, especially as later the users will be asked for their assessment. But this information can be of help in explaining incorrect priority setting, missed deadlines, backlogs, and friction between producers and users – especially if the two groups allot widely differing ratings to the same service.

The final columns on the form show the users of each service, and the relative use that each makes of the service. 'User' can mean a unit/section/function/department/group – but not an individual (except, perhaps, the chairman). Usually, a list of possible users is prepared and a copy given to every manager who is completing the form. As will be seen from the example, the relative usage is expressed in percentage terms. Some organizations have complex management accounting/management information systems. Such organizations will already have a method of allocating costs and overheads between functions. A decision will sometimes have to be made as to whether to use an existing system of allocation or whether to use a different basis. Discussions should be aimed at consistency and at ensuring that everybody is aware of the basis that is being used.

There is one final step in the functional analysis preparation. In this, we turn to the actions of individual members of staff. The aim is to estimate the time spent by the staff on each activity. Again, for ease of input, this is expressed as the percentage of time spent on each activity in a typical year. A typical example of a blank form used for this is shown in Figure 26.3 opposite. People sometimes need help with this. There are people who have considerable difficulty in indicating even approximate percentages. Others will insist on a form of extreme precision, using decimal points of a percentage. It will be found that this is one instance when people having difficulties will not ask their colleagues for advice – they will prefer to ask the investigator. A spot of patience without becoming pontifical has always been found to be all that is needed to give help to the small number of people who need it.

It may be helpful at this stage to recapitulate what information has been collected. Basically, one now knows:

- what goes on;
- who benefits; and
- what goes into the work (in person hours).

Functional Analysis Step 3 Summary of Time Allocation		
Division:	Prepared by:	
Section:		
Activities	Services/end products	Time spent – Name and %

Figure 26.3 Summary of time allocation

D

Expressed like that, it is fairly simple. What may not seem so simple is the thought of cross-analysing all this information and inverting it. This is the sort of task that accountants have been faced with for years.

Fortunately they (and we) can nowadays use a small computer and some basic software to carry out this sort of analysis.

It will be appreciated by now that OVA/OCR studies are considerably helped if an organization has a good management accounting system and/or work quantification/measurement. In their absence, there will probably have to be longer discussions on some aspects – the data collection may read as a complex process but in practice it is reasonably straightforward. There is one caveat. The data may be collected by an investigator. Or, as already suggested, it may be collected at arm's length by sending a packet of forms with detailed instructions to the managers. The basic reason for this is logistics and time. One may be comparing offices in London, San Francisco, Bahrain, Singapore and Sydney. The time and cost implications of an investigator spending time in each office can be a barrier.

In such a situation, the investigator may only visit the offices at the User Analysis stage, and such visits may be shortened. Even then, on one such study the cost of air fares, hotels and expenses increased the consultant's fees by 50 per cent. So careful planning and attention to detail can be even more important than usual.

■ CROSS-ANALYSIS AND INVERSION

The calculations are straightforward, though boring if done by hand:

- calculate hours per activity (percentages × hours per year);
- calculate cost per activity (hours × cost per hour);
- calculate activity cost per user (cost × percentages);
- sum the cost of services for each user.

This gives one the cost of each service to each user.

257

It is usual to use only clerical costs, ignoring subsidiary costs. But in this (and in the matter of the standard hourly costs) it is best just to follow established organization policy, unless there is obviously something amiss. The same approach should be used if one is concerned with the costs of a computer department. Otherwise one can become embroiled in that bane of the accountant's life: allocating computer costs where there is a mix of batch and on-line processing.

■ USERS' ANALYSIS

The focus of attention now moves from the producers of services to the users. During this stage, one is effectively asking users:

- how important are the services provided?
- how satisfactory is the level of service?
- what changes should be made?

Each manager is sent a list of the services/end products used by the staff for whom the manager is responsible. This list can just be a print-out of the user analysis. This list will show each service provided, together with its allocated cost. Many investigators will also include the percentage time allocation and the manpower (in years) involved.
   Managers are asked to rate each service, as it affects them, in three ways:

- the importance to the user of the service presently provided;
- how the user perceives the level of service received;
- the degree of reduction or increase in the service felt desirable by the user.

Importantly, there is also a column for comments. Respondents should be encouraged to use this space in any way whatsoever they wish. Time after time it has been found that this column provides valuable information, reinforced by discussions between the investigator and the manager.
   An example of the User Questionnaire is given in Figure 26.4.

Functional Analysis
Step 4

Response of Users

Division: World Sales – Asia   **Completed by:** D. Fong
Area/Office: Singapore

Key Task ID			Service ID	Importance	Service Level	Change Wanted	Comments
F5	Security	/01	Maintain security	4	1	4	
A1	General Services	/01	Stock control/Distribut.	3	5	3	
A1	General Services	/04	Control plant/Equipment	3	2	4	
A2	Reception	/02	Act as telephonist	3	5	3	
A4	Mail/Messenger	/01	External mess. service	2	5	2	

Figure 26.4 Response of users

■ EFFECTIVENESS STUDY

There are two aspects to the effectiveness study:

- the use of ratios to highlight the most efficient and the most inefficient offices;
- the use of high-level data for measuring the work.

Since the ratios will inevitably have a wide distribution, it is an idea to use pie charts and bar charts in their presentation. The use of these ratios is particularly useful for international organizations with offices in a number of different countries; without OVA/OCR it has traditionally been difficult to obtain agreed comparisons of such offices. It will be found that always and inevitably any office that scores as 'most inefficient' will quote special local circumstances as the cause. The other managers will deny this vigorously. The investigator should prevent any discussion from becoming too acrimonious, though a soupçon of acid has been known to galvanize into action an otherwise reluctant manager.

Examples of some ratios are given in Table 26.1.

Table 26.1 Sample ratios

D

Ratio	Minimum	AVERAGE	Maximum
1. General Services as % of total staff	18	24	37
2. No. of Admin Staff per £100m assets	3.2	4.5	6.9
3. Back-office staff per 10 front staff	7	19	30
4. No. of salesmen per £1m sales	2	3	5

The high-level data is used in response to certain parameters:

- the nature of the items of work performed by individuals, as shown in the summary of time allocation;
- the validity of the work done, as shown by the users' responses;
- the volumes of work done.

The resulting work quantifications will show:

- the work content of individuals' workloads;
- the work content of functions' workloads.

From this follows the calculation of staff numbers required for each function/office when performing agreed services at agreed levels of service.

The effectiveness study will also result in other proposals being made, such as:

- closing or setting up offices;
- changes in organization structure;
- changes in services being provided;
- changes in levels of service;
- cost reductions;
- purchase of equipment;
- changes in systems and methods.

The changes are turned into specific proposals that are then discussed and agreed. Finally, an action plan is prepared to turn these proposals as agreed into actions.

This description of OVA/OCR has been detailed, since it has been found that this is necessary for understanding it. It may therefore seem a lengthy process. In practice, however, this is not so.

CBA – Cost–benefit administration

The term cost–benefit administration has become something of a generic one for a variety of techniques. Here, we are concentrating on just one technique, the Cost–Benefit Matrix. This is based on the assumption that there are five options for action (pay less, use less, lose less, waste less or use alternatives) in four areas (money, assets, information, and people). This leads to the matrix shown in Table 26.2. The matrix can be used in three ways:

- brainstorming is carried out on each of the twenty boxes; or
- a team is set up to study a particular box, covering the entire organization; or
- a team studies a particular part of the organization, looking at every box.

Table 26.2 The cost–benefit matrix

Area \ Action	Assets/ Equipment	Information/ Paperwork	People	Money
Pay less	A1	I1	P1	M1
Use less	A2	I2	P2	M2
Lose less	A3	I3	P3	M3
Waste less	A4	I4	P4	M4
Use alternatives	A5	I5	P5	M5

Below are some typical ideas that have arisen from use of the matrix in a variety of situations and organizations:

A1
(i) Install feasibility studies for all acquisitions over £5,000 (buy v. hire v. lease).
(ii) Subscribe to a consumer magazine covering best buys for commerce.
(iii) Rent out excess capacity (e.g. mainframes) to other users.

A2
(i) Use a ratio analysis of space utilization per person (e.g. Personnel Dept. $= 11\,m^2$; Credit Control $= 6\,m^2$).
(ii) Increase asset utilization (e.g. COM output) by shift working.
(iii) Stop personal use of photocopiers.

A3
(i) Ensure that personal computers are not removable.

(ii)   Tighten stock-taking practices.

(iii) Centralize the issue of portable modems.

A4

(i)   Formalize preventive maintenance.

(ii)   Study optimum replacement times for office equipment.

(iii) Improve scheduling.

A5

(i)   Use bureaux/time-sharing.

(ii)   Stop microfilming.

(iii) Do not give salesmen dictating machines for use at home (additional benefit – it was claimed that the standard of reports improved).

I1

(i)   Use the Post Office EMS service instead of commercial couriers as they are often cheaper. The EMS is called Datapost in Britain, Chronopost in France (and Al-Barid al-Mumtaz in Saudi Arabia). Over 100 postal bodies are linked by this system.

(ii)   Examine in-house v. purchase for printing.

(iii) Use a cutting agency instead of the internal public relations for obtaining information.

D

I2

(i)   Use the Report Matrix to reduce reports and their distribution.

(ii)   Do not produce monthly balance sheets.

(iii) Use standard pre-printed forms instead of letters. A number of people in the public eye do this for responding to requests for their time – including a cabinet minister – and so, it is said, did Evelyn Waugh.

I3

(i)   Improve control of grandfather/father computer tapes.

(ii)   Institute disaster planning.

(iii) Introduce cross-index for information sources subscribed to.

I4

(i)   Overhaul printers so that computer stationery is accurately aligned. Poor alignment wastes paper, computer time, staff time and causes frustration.

(ii)   Filter material going into databases so that it is reduced.

(iii) Do not print excessive stocks of forms as they may have to be thrown away when a change is made (envelopes printed 'On *His* Majesty's Service' were still in use twenty years after the coronation of Queen Elizabeth II).

I5

(i)   Install terminals in the warehouse for direct input of receipts instead of paperwork.

(ii)   Use optical character readers/bar coding instead of writing.

(iii) Use fax instead of telex, and telephone instead of electronic mail – or vice versa.

P1

(i)   Move the head office out of the capital into a low-rent location.

(ii)   Eliminate overtime as soon as it becomes institutionalized.

(iii) Move tasks to Third World countries (this is very contentious – here we are reporting, not recommending). Non-English-speaking keypunchers in South Korea input complex legal documents into a database. American Airlines saved $3.5 million a year by transferring some computer work to a unit in Barbados.

P2
(i) Amalgamate small sections into larger groupings.
(ii) Ensure that all secretaries are either in pools or that their time is 'shared'. The president of a trade union had a personal secretary although he was only in the office for fifteen days a year. An international religious organization had seventy secretaries although a large number of its managers went on overseas secondment for periods of eighteen months to two years.
(iii) Ensure that no executive puts 'servants' on the organization's payroll.

P3
(i) Have a formal salary structure, the details of which are known to all.
(ii) Run training courses to improve two-way communication.
(iii) Introduce flexible working hours.

P4
(i) Improve staff training.
(ii) Stop secretaries being used as personal gofers (such as going out to buy cigarettes for a manager).
(iii) Arrange for early delivery and distribution of incoming morning mail.

P5
(i) Use pre-printed order forms that a customer fills in.
(ii) Use coffee-vending machines.
(iii) Allow secretaries to handle customer contacts instead of always sending out sales staff.

M1
(i) Replace preference shares with debentures.
(ii) Replace current accounts with high-interest accounts for sales staff who handle cash.
(iii) Arrange for nightly transfer of current account balances to deposit accounts.

M2
(i) Reduce stock levels.
(ii) Reduce debtors.
(iii) Improve the cash-flow analysis.

M3
(i) Reduce bad debts by improving credit control procedures.
(ii) Check the controls on cheque writing machines.
(iii) Use tokens instead of cash (vending machines, buses).

M4
(i) Tighten controls on travelling and entertainment expenses.
(ii) Invest cash balances overnight.
(iii) Disallow discounts claimed after the due date.

M5

(i)   Use bills of exchange.

(ii) Employ a factoring firm for invoices.

(iii) Allow time-off-in-lieu instead of cash for overtime.

Finally, the following is a reproduction of an internal memo.

INTERNATIONAL TRUST Inc.

To:
    Mail Department
	Date:
	    24th March

From:
    R. C. P. Johnson
	Re:
	    Postage stamp

Please provide one first-class stamp for a self-addressed envelope needed for company business concerned with obtaining a brochure.

Roger Johnson

One can only hope that the writer sent the memo with his tongue in his cheek.

D

27

Algorithms

'Begin at the beginning,' the King said, gravely, 'and go till you come
to the end; then stop.'

Lewis Carroll, *Alice's Adventures in Wonderland* (1865)

Care should be taken, not that the reader may understand, but that
he must understand.

Quintilian, *De Institutione Oratoria* (fl. AD 68)

Muhammed ibn Musa al-Khwarizmi (*c.* AD 780–*c.* 850) the Persian mathematician, is someone to whom we owe a lot. He introduced the Hindu decimal point and the use of zero into Arabic mathematics. The word algebra comes from the title of his book, *Al-Jabr*, and from his surname comes the word 'algorithm'. The word algorithm has long been used in mathematics to describe the set of steps used in a computation or to solve a problem (such as long division). The word has been borrowed now to describe a semi-graphic approach to learning, training and performing procedures.

Practical uses

Algorithms have been used for a number of practical purposes. These include:

- notes to companies from government departments, showing them what grants can be claimed and in what circumstances;
- an aid to doctors in diagnosis (e.g. peripheral vascular disorders);
- for self-tuition in product knowledge for salespeople;
- instructions for repairing machinery and for fault finding, including aid for stranded truck drivers;
- staff training in many organizations (e.g. car reservations);
- instructions to patrolmen on Canadian highways under varying conditions of snow and ice;
- as part of form design;
- as part of work quantification.

In fact, their use is as wide as people's imagination. There have even been occasions when it has been necessary to curb people's enthusiasm, when they first learn how to construct them.

Advantages

The main advantages of algorithms are:

- they present a series of small steps of action or information which are therefore much easier to comprehend, instead of the eye carrying on reading prose leading one on and on into ever more confusing areas;

- they are an aid to clarity since they force one to be clear;
- they are precise;
- they speed action since a user only has to read one route instead of reading everything;
- in practised hands, they can be quicker than writing prose;
- they are particularly useful for presenting information which would otherwise have many sentences starting with 'if', 'except', or 'unless';
- they can help prevent 'closed loops' in logical sequences.

An example of this last point was a government research programme into birth control. This included a lengthy interview based on a questionnaire which usually took over two hours to complete. Naturally this questionnaire was a branched interview: 'if the respondent says yes, turn to page 27: if she says no, turn to page 31'. After the research had been going on for some time, the inevitable happened: the survey was so complex that an interviewee was led round the branches back into the mainstream of questions and thence into a closed loop. The whole research had to be recast because no algorithm had been prepared of the outline branching system.

Initial examples

D

The best way to learn about algorithms is to study some examples and to do some of them. The first example arises from a European who was driving along Route 10 in California. There were a number of notices that said 'Please share your auto when going into Los Angeles.' This can be expressed as an algorithm:

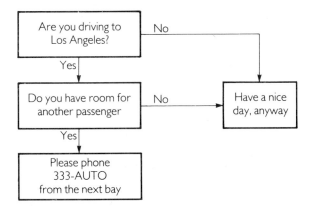

This is a rather trivial example. The one shown in Figure 27.1 overleaf is more complex. The originator of this algorithm is unknown. In various forms, it has been around since the early 1970s – it even surfaced once in a BBC television pop-science programme. If the originator were known, it would be possible to point out gently that the construction is not perfect. There are 'rules' for constructing algorithms. Most of these should be regarded with some reserve since otherwise construction becomes too restricted. Some people seem to have a natural ability at constructing algorithms, even when they take liberties with the rules. So instead of using the word 'rules', it may be preferable to refer to characteristics that good algorithms exhibit.

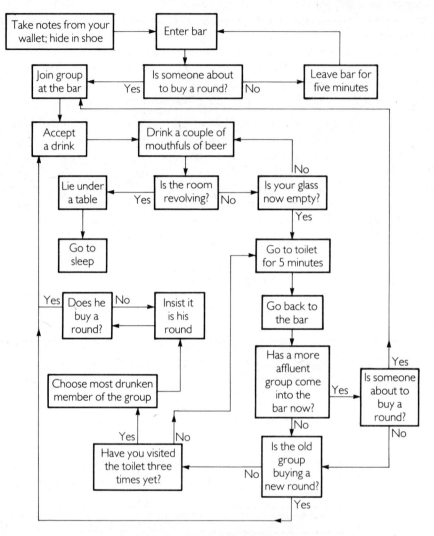

Figure 27.1 A free drink

Characteristics of good algorithms

Good algorithms exhibit the following characteristics:

- they should be neat and tidy. This is not a moralistic judgement: a neat-looking algorithm not only encourages people to use it, it is also quicker and easier to use;
- they should be clear and unambiguous. For example, the question, 'Is the patient overweight?' may be admissible in some circumstances. In others it may not be precise enough;
- controversy should be avoided. The question, 'Has the patient's liver condition been

aggravated by smoking marijuana?' will result in a range of responses which may depend on the respondent's general attitudes;

- questions offering two alternative answers should be incapable of prompting a further alternative. The commonest example is asking a member of the public, 'Are you married or single?' This causes difficulty for people who are widowed, divorced, separated or living-with-a-partner. The person asking the question may be clear about such distinctions, respondents may not;

- jargon should be avoided unless the target group will certainly understand it. In this case, jargon will save time and may aid clarity;

- they should be complete. In other words, they should cover every eventuality. This is to seek perfection which may not always be achievable. Still, any possibility that remains uncovered will inevitably cause a problem at some time in the future;

- they will normally only have one entry point (those that have several entry points are usually several algorithms in one chart). A single entry point makes both construction and usage easier;

- they have to cover 'contingencies' – events that may or may not happen. Common contingencies have to be covered individually. Those that occur only very rarely can often be covered in bulk. It may not be possible to cover absolutely every contingency that can arise (or even to think of them). This is one reason why algorithms cannot have a 100 per cent guarantee of success.

D

Constructing algorithms

The steps in building up an algorithm are as follows:

- obtain/write a prose edition of the subject matter;
- ensure that you have an understanding of the prose material and of the underlying background, including all technical terms or jargon;
- go through the prose and mark all the conditional steps (i.e. use or implied use of words like, 'if', 'unless', 'when', 'otherwise', 'or', 'but', 'except', 'only', 'however'). A tip is to use a pale-coloured 'highlighter' such as pink to mark each alternative; each mark will then have to become a branch in the final diagram;
- go through the prose again, this time making a mark for each separate action or step. If a highlighter was used in the previous step, it is useful to use a second one of a different colour (say, yellow);
- ensure that you know something about the target/potential group of users (e.g. the public, office staff, professional staff);
- select the first question or statement. This selection should be on a 'pareto' basis –it should cover or remove as large a section of the prose as possible in one step. Write this down in the top left-hand corner of a piece of paper and draw a box round it – you have started;
- go through the prose (keeping the first step in one's mind) and pencil in a first attempt at deciding the order that the steps will logically follow;
- draw a first draft of the algorithm. This will probably be untidy but this is not too important. Ensure that all steps are covered, all links in place, all branches shown and that there are no closed loops;
- check the language, etc. in the boxes;

- redraw the algorithm in a neat, open and tidy form. Try to avoid lines crossing;
- check the chart as though it were being used;
- get a colleague to check the chart;
- test the chart on a member of the target group of users;
- revise as necessary;
- use a pilot to test the proposed algorithm.

Practical examples

Some examples of algorithms that have been constructed for use in practice are given below. These have not been selected as perfect examples (indeed, some of them could be improved) but to show the range of tasks that the approach can be used for. In each case, the people involved felt that they were useful. The first one (Figure 27.2) was written by a Civil Service for use in a benefits office.

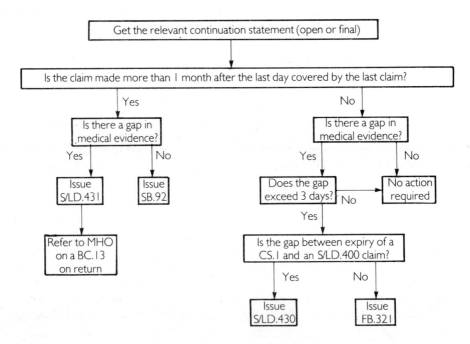

Figure 27.2 Benefit claim

The next example was introduced by a large organization that repaired domestic appliances. Difficulties were being experienced in getting the correct job numbers allocated to jobs. Job numbers can be important if they are used as the first step in a computer-controlled stock system for spare parts. The number of different spare parts for different equipment, manufacturers, models and year of manufacture is impressive in its level of magnitude (Figure 27.3).

The next example (Figure 27.4) comes from a despatch department which looks as though it is in need of a methods design study.

D

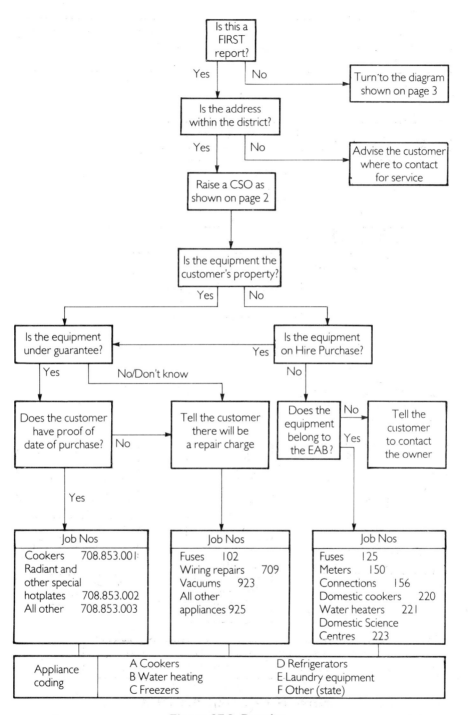

Figure 27.3 Repairs

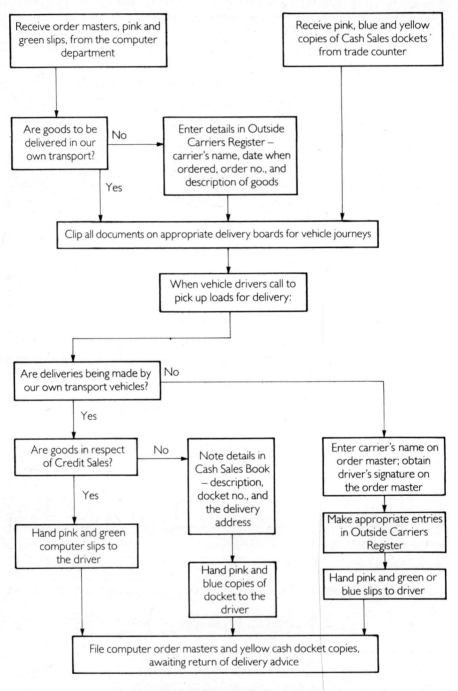

Figure 27.4 Despatch document

When an individual leaves a group pension scheme, it is necessary to calculate the results for both the individual and for the group scheme. The calculations would be performed by a pensions clerk and checked by an actuary. On the face of it, this seems like an ideal job for a microcomputer. For various reasons, an insurance company was unable to do this for two years or so. It was therefore in the position of having to do the calculations manually for two years while facing a shortage of suitably trained staff. The answer was a new form that was in effect a pre-printed algorithm. Part of this 'algorform' is shown in Figure 27.5.

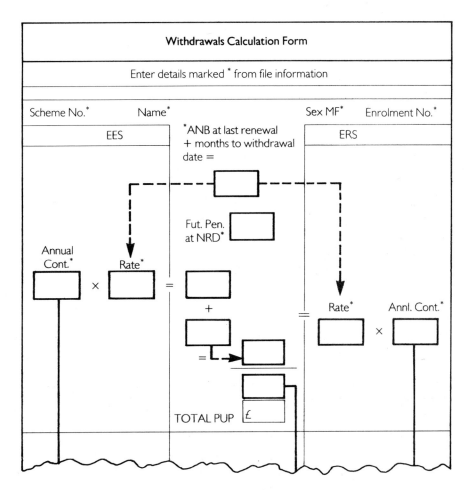

Figure 27.5 Pension algorform

These algorforms can have a formidable appearance to outsiders, but to people with specific industry knowledge they can be clarity itself. The form shown (about a quarter of the total form is shown) certainly worked. One pension clerk had received six weeks' training in carrying out the calculations in the old way, and two days after starting to use the algorform her output had increased to 400 per cent of the previous level.

Algorithm exercises

The best way to learn how to build algorithms is practice. Two exercises are given below that offer an opportunity for such practice. The first is unlikely to give much trouble, but the second may do.

Practical exercise No. 1 – The new pens

K. Ory & Sons are buying some beautiful new pens of a striking design, intended to be gifts for special customers. The first consignment has arrived, but this is a cause of some jealousy. Staff feel that if the sales staff get all the pens, then they will end up being given to the salesmen's families. And the computer staff have pointed out that the design would make the pens real time-savers for them.

After a special meeting, the board has decided that all employees will get two pens, unless they have been with Ory's for more than five years. In that case, they will get a bonus of 50 per cent extra, unless they are salesmen who receive the extra allocation irrespective of length of service. People who work in the Computer Centre are to receive an allocation of six pens, unless they are data clerks, in which case the allocation is reduced by one third.

Draw an algorithm that can be given to all staff so that they can discover their rights.

The answer is given in Figure 27.7 at the end of this chapter.

Practical exercise No. 2 – Pension rules

The following is an extract from a government leaflet setting out the rules for payment of a married woman's retirement pension:

The earliest age at which a woman can draw a retirement pension is 60. On her own insurance she can get a pension when she reaches that age, if she has then retired from regular employment. Otherwise she has to wait until she retires or reaches age 65. At age 65 a pension can be paid irrespective of retirement. To get a pension on her husband's insurance, however, she must be 60 or over and retired, and her husband must be 65 or over and retired from regular employment or 70 if he does not retire before reaching that age. A man over 70 or a woman over 65 is treated as retired whether working or not, and regardless of the amount of work done.

Draw an algorithm that can be given to a married woman so that she can see whether she is eligible for a pension yet.

An answer is shown in Figure 27.8 at the end of this chapter. It is not, of course, the only possible correct algorithm.

■ FINAL EXAMPLE

The final example of a practical use of an algorithm concerns a government department. The diagram shows the first few stages of a particular task. It is used for training
staff unacquainted with the task (it is in an area where tasks can change quickly owing
to changes in government policy). It is also a sort of flow chart of the work. In addition,
it is part of the calculation of work content of the task. Alongside each box is a figure of
the work content associated with that box. By studying and calculating the percentage
occurrence of each Yes/No alternative branch, the total work content for the whole task
can be stated.

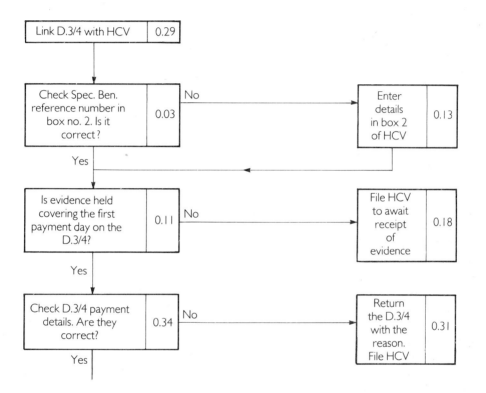

Figure 27.6 Task and time

Just as useful is the fact that if the chart changes (owing to policy changes) then the
new task time can be calculated easily and with certainty. This means that changes in
staffing levels can be found quickly. Even more useful, diagrams such as Figure 27.6
can be used actually to predict the effects of policy changes by the government. And the
predictions will be right – a claim that cannot be made by more traditional methods.

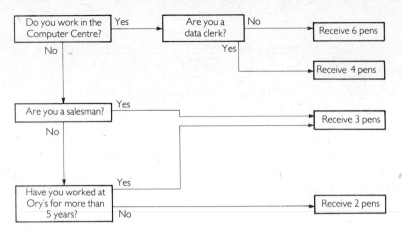

Figure 27.7 Answer to 'The new pens'

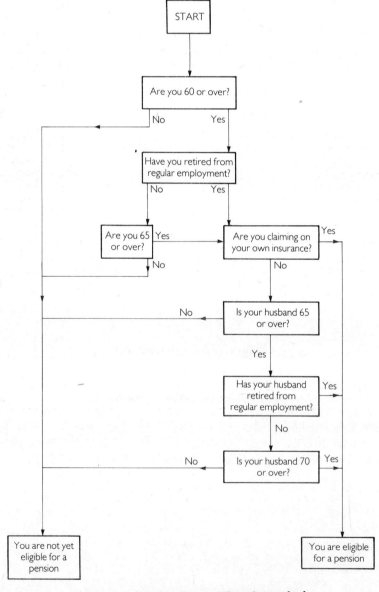

Figure 27.8 Answer to 'Pension rules'

274

28

Office Planning

A man who has no office to go to – I don't care who he is – is a trial
of which you can have no conception
George Bernard Shaw, *The Irrational Knot* (1887)

If the building is working beautifully, everyone has the furniture they
need, the storage they need, the right conditions to work in ... then
the Facilities Manager is doing his job superbly well.
George Young, in an interview (1987)[1]

People whose jobs take them into the offices of different organizations soon realize their great diversity, not just the chaos/order or manager/clerk spectra but also just in the offices' physical appearance. Some offices resemble a condemned building inhabited by short-stay squatters. Other offices exhibit a sybaritic luxury bordering on the palatial.

D

Moreover, before going to an office for the first time, it is not easy to predict accurately what it will be like. There is little correlation between the standard of the offices with either profitability or the type of industry (although advertising boutiques do tend to be rather better furnished than the clerical offices in the catering industry). On one occasion, a consultant was ceremoniously given the key to the executives' toilet. On using it for the first time, his mother's warnings from his childhood came flooding back and he felt like washing the soap before using it.

One international catering firm used to send new employees to its store of discarded desks to find the least bad one for their use – one got a better desk by grabbing that of a leaver. A large insurance firm used to have four different grades of toilet for its female employees, marked with the grade of staff for whom they were deemed appropriate (a practice now abandoned, it has to be said).

The reason for this diversity is that offices and their planning depend less on their relevance than on the culture of the organization. There are multinational firms with turnovers in the billions bracket to whom this entire chapter will be a complete irrelevancy. Others will have gone down the opposite path and will have in place an integrated system of facilities management.

Facilities management

Even the term 'facilities management' lacks a common definition in different organizations. To some firms it is largely a matter of repairs and maintenance. To one writer, it is 'a total approach to the supply of computing services. It involves subcontracting whole or part of a management services function to a computer service company'.[2]

One definition of facilities management is that it is:

1 Property selection and acquisition.
2 Design.
3 Interior design.

4 Space planning.
5 Office layout.
6 Space costs.
7 Furniture selection.
8 Maintenance – internal and external.
9 Repairs.
10 Working conditions.
11 Security systems.
12 Health and safety at work.

In a sense, this is a definition of perfection: very few organizations have a Facilities Manager who is in fact responsible for all of these aspects. However, most of these tasks have to be the responsibility of somebody – and many organizations find it administratively convenient to combine them in one person's job, whether the job is called Premises Manager, Facilities Manager or whatever.

Most organizations employ a mixture of internal and external people to provide this full range of office planning facets. There are a few external firms that appear to be offering unbiased advice but who in fact receive payments from manufacturers. This unpleasant practice does seem to be dying out, but one needs to be on one's guard. On the other hand, there are a number of consultancies – architectural/design/management – that produce some very impressive results. Some of these can be seen in the Office of the Year competition run by the Institute of Administrative Management. This competition has a consistently high standard of entrants covering a wide range of office needs. The same institute has a Facilities Management Group which acts as a focus for people working in this field. Membership of this group, and study of the competition, is recommended to anyone wishing to expand their knowledge and appreciation.

Property acquisition

Of the many questions raised by property acquisition, three are of particular importance:

- where;
- how; and
- how large?

The 'where' (location) question should be based on a number of factors, including an adequate supply of the kind of office staff needed, transport services, outside facilities, accessibility to business contacts, local facilities, housing, communications, prestige and availability of suitable offices at the right price.

In practice, other less quantifiable factors may come into play. One retail chain nearly moved its head office to Berkshire because that was where most of the board members lived. A trade union moved to the part of the country that its leader felt was his power base. In most instances, however, location is the product of considerable thought and planning.

In our experience, the two aspects that cause most thought are the staff and the communications. When W. H. Smith moved many head office functions from London to Swindon, they ran coach-loads of visits so that staff could inspect their new locality and liaised between the staff and the local council to arrange suitable housing. When J. Sainsbury moved from London to Basingstoke they were concerned about the need for telephone links between their buyers and the Covent Garden Market sellers. They were told at the time that they could have two telephone lines immediately for the entire office location. To which one senior manager replied, 'Well, that might be enough for the loaders to place their bets with the bookie. What about the rest of us?'

When relocating large offices, many organizations are over-optimistic about the number of staff who will actually eventually move with the organization to another part of the country. One director was heard to predict that 75–80 per cent of the staff would move house and stay with the firm. In the event, about 15 per cent did move – a figure that (for clerical staff) is typical. This fact means that careful planning is needed, both for the conditions for leavers (e.g. early retirement terms, if requested) and for the training of new staff.

The 'how' question usually revolves around three alternatives: ownership, rent or lease. The advantages of ownership are:

- capital is preserved in the form of a fixed asset which is currently likely to appreciate at a rate well in excess of inflation;
- the 'rent' aspect of costs of occupancy will not, in cash terms, increase or be unpredictable;
- alterations and extensions are not subject to any change in a landlord's dictates;
- property provides a ready security for a loan or debenture.

The disadvantages of ownership are:

- capital is tied up which might be put to more profitable use elsewhere in the organization;
- future moves are inhibited, since property disposal can be a lengthy process;
- ownership can set up an emotional block to change;
- large property assets can be a temptation to a predatory take-over;
- rent cannot be set off against revenues for tax purposes.

The 'how large' question is dealt with under 'Space planning', below.

Some idea of the relative costs of offices over their life may be given by a study which looked at the whole life cycle.[3] This study suggested that initial capital costs (construction, furniture) were only 2 per cent of the total. Operating expenses (rent, interest, utilities) were 6 per cent. The remaining 92 per cent of lifetime costs were for staff and their equipment. If nothing else, these figures show the importance of straightforward office efficiency.

After the first three basic questions have been addressed, there still remain a whole raft of second-level decisions. One of these is the alternative of moving into a new or old office that is basically a shell, or else moving into an office that has been refurbished speculatively. If the second choice is being considered, then certain needs should be satisfied:

- the speculative office should have been refurbished in line with the organization's preference for office layout, i.e. open plan or cellular;
- the distribution grid for electricity, communications and cabling should be generous, not adequate (expansion and technology will soon turn 'adequate' into 'headache');

- internal environment (lighting, heating, air conditioning) should not be set at average or background levels but be sufficient for the inevitable high-use areas (e.g. service rooms such as photocopying/word processing centres);
- external environment (noise, dust, smells) should not be at a level that they threaten to overcome the internal environment in a short time;
- ceilings should have acceptable acoustic properties; floors should have a non-static-inducing hard-wearing surface; plumbing should allow for enough toilets and vending machines.

If too many of these desirable attributes are absent, then it is probably better to consider taking on a shell and improving it oneself rather than committing oneself to a refurbished office that is going to cause difficulties in the fairly short term.

A problem that advanced technology has emphasized when moving into old buildings is the matter of the electricity supply. At one time, computers were housed in specially designed, air conditioned, separate areas. Now micros and modems are housed in the normal office. Here they may share a power point with a typewriter, a coffee machine, even a radio set. Radio-frequency emissions can also come from overhead power cables carrying the grid. A radio frequency interference filter will protect computers and other sensitive equipment from high-frequency power bursts in the mains. It will not protect a computer from 'spiking' (a sudden high in the power itself). For this, a constant-voltage transformer is indicated.

Symptoms such as random corruption of floppies or format corruptions on hard discs are signs of possible power problems. 'System hanging' is when the system stops operating, although information is still on the screen, and one has to switch off and then on again. This is caused by a mains spike which itself is likely to be caused by 'arcing' of an appliance switch. 'Self-destruct' is when the system stops operating and the screen goes dead, owing to the micro fuse having blown.[4]

Three brief examples may show the range of options available. Van Ommeren is a shipping company that was located in the City of London. Its lease was about to be renewed and the firm did not wish to pay the very high rents that were payable in the near locality. It found attractive the idea of having its brokers' office near the Baltic Exchange while its admin was housed somewhere else. A consultancy firm (Organised Office Designs) produced a feasibility study, which included a set of criteria for evaluating twenty possible alternatives for the existing buildings. After analysis, the head office was located near the Baltic Exchange with the rest of the firm at Barking, in Essex, to the east of London. This was done in such a way that the firm still had direct computer and telecommunications links with Amsterdam.[5]

The local government London Borough of Merton had a different circumstance. It had already decided on its new location (a twenty-year-old fourteen-floor building). But it was necessary to enhance the building, which suffered from strong winds, aircraft and vehicle noise, 'solar gain', and an inadequate power and communications grid. Doing so involved reaccommodating about 900 staff, establishing work patterns, installing ventilation, new ceilings, new lighting and a new power and communications grid. All this had to be done on time (one year) and within budget.

The States of Jersey (the governmental administration) had already planned its new centralized offices for its previously widely scattered office staffs. It then wished to improve the effectiveness of its administration before making the major move. This improvement would give a better level of service to the public, and would also make more effective use of the new office complex. It therefore commissioned a firm of management consultants (PA Consulting Services) to help it in these aims. The resulting series of studies looked at a variety of government departments such as computer services, income tax and car registration. At all stages, considerable emphasis was placed on the need to provide the public with an improving level of service stretching into the future.

Space planning

It is sometimes necessary to know how much office space is needed, either now or in the future. In talking about office space, it is necessary to differentiate between alternative definitions:

- 'gross floor area' is the total area of a floor, with no deductions whatsoever. Architects measure these dimensions from outside the external walls; thus gross floor areas includes the space occupied by the external walls themselves;
- 'net usable floor area' (sometimes called just 'net floor area') excludes the space taken by the external walls. It also excludes the space used for stairs, lifts, fire-fighting water tanks, boiler rooms, air ducting, etc. It usually includes corridors serving offices. The ratio of net : gross depends on the particular office. In a modern office block it will be about 70–75 per cent. In a very tall building, this may fall to 60–70 per cent (more lifts, ducting, etc.). Those modern offices which are very deep (50 m or more) and which use an artificial environment can have a ratio as high as 85 per cent;
- 'net-net floor area' (also known as 'carpeted area' whether or not it is actually carpeted) is the space occupied by the staff themselves plus their own furniture and immediate equipment. It excludes the main corridors or aisles and the corridors between individual offices. It includes the small spaces between desks. The ratio of carpeted : net usable is usually about 75–80 per cent in a modern office that has some partitions. In an open-plan or very deep office this may be more like 85–90 per cent. In old buildings, the ratio may fall to 65–75 per cent.

D

The methods of deciding how much space is needed include the use of indicators, calculation of ratios, a rule of thumb approach, the preparation of layout, and the use of calculations based on standards.

■ INDICATORS

By studying past records of space usage it is possible to correlate space and an indicator, such as number of customers, and then to draw a simple graph extrapolating the trend into the future. For this method, one needs records going back, say, ten years. This method can be useful for total space usage but is not always suitable for individual departments (mainly because the tasks of separate departments change over the years). Advantages of this approach are:

- since one has gone back several years for the underlying statistics and since one is producing global figures, the whole exercise can be carried out in an unemotional atmosphere. Ambitious managers jockeying for prestige will normally wait until later before making a move;

279

- the approach can be useful for predicting how far ahead a particular site will be sufficient, which in turn is useful for the entire planning cycle;
- the concept (especially when a simple graph is drawn) is very easy to understand and to use;
- it can be used for predicting the need for land (as opposed to actual office floor space). Any organization that bothers to predict office space twenty-five years ahead is being somewhat unrealistic. But a decision to buy adjacent empty land for the long term may be defensible.

The approach does have disadvantages:

- it is not easy to draw even a simple graph that is accurate. Each part of it introduces inaccuracies. Old office plans may not be available. Office space usage (both past and future) tends to follow a step function rather than a smooth curve. Over the long term, even the most conservative of offices will change the work done, so it becomes hard to compare apples with apples;
- meaningful accurate indicators are not easy to find in many industries. The most obvious (turnover) just does not work in many cases. Sometimes the answer is to admit from the outset that one is only trying to find an approximate picture;
- short-term fluctuations in office life mean that the approach is only suitable for long-term predictions. But it is in the long term that inaccuracies in the approach become most obvious.

For all its drawbacks, there are occasions when it is the only approach that is reasonably feasible. In such circumstances, one has to go ahead and use it – without letting anybody forget the limitations. There have been cases when an organization has performed the exercise and treated the result as sacrosanct long after the situation had obviously changed.

■ CALCULATION OF RATIOS

It is a straightforward matter to calculate 'square metres per person' for a group of staff. There can be slight problems when looking at large open-plan offices or at service areas but allocation can quickly follow the setting of some simple rules.

This ratio can be calculated for departments, sections, branches, subsidiaries, overseas representation, and any other discrete group. This figure can then be used for several purposes:

- to compare the space used by different groups of staff within a single set of offices. This comparison will seem a very rough sort of justice to the better-off. Every group can think of compelling reasons why they are a special case and need more space than their colleagues;
- to compare the space used by offices in different locations. This approach is highly applicable to this use. It can be used to compare branch offices in the same country, and to compare the offices in different countries;
- to predict future needs. This is done by using an indicator, or by assuming future numbers with a standard individual space, or by using different current branch sizes.

Advantages of this approach are:

- clear examples of unfairness can be eliminated;

- it can provide the basis for overhead allocation, which in turn can give an incentive for curbing empire building;
- 'figures is figures'. In other words, the approach does at least provide a factual basis for action;
- the figures can be quickly and easily calculated.

Disadvantages are:

- predictions for future needs are not easy if the office is monolithic, without separate branches of differing sizes;
- vacillating managements can find themselves in lengthy discussions with groups of staff claiming special circumstances;
- calculations only show what is, not what should be, in the sense that they only reflect current space allocations.

In spite of the disadvantages, this approach can be rewarding for the right purposes, especially in view of the ease of calculation.

■ RULE OF THUMB

In this approach, each departmental manager is asked to say by how much his office has too little or too much space either now or in the future. The responses are converted into a factor that is then applied to current space occupancy (e.g. 15 per cent more on $200\,m^2 = 230\,m^2$).

D

This approach is useful when one needs an answer extremely quickly. It can also be used where the managers possess a high degree of saintliness. In the absence of this quality, a better way of prediction is to factorize possible changes. To do this, one lists possible reasons for change and asks managers to put forward probable adjustments. Examples of such factors are:

- increase/decrease in throughput;
- impact of technology;
- effect of known planned changes;
- effect of starting/stopping shift working;
- change in space needs owing to improved efficiency.

The disadvantages of this approach are too obvious to warrant listing.

■ LAYOUT

Preparation of actual layouts can involve the use of floor plans, isometric drawings or three-dimensional models. Layouts can be of current needs, future predictions or greenfield studies. Since the purpose of such layouts is to calculate gross space needs and not to provide an accurate practical plan, one can use approximations and make assumptions.

This approach has several advantages. It provides a visual representation which is easy to comprehend and manipulate. It can be used as a check and a back-up to other methods. It can be used later when preparing accurate working layouts.

It also has disadvantages. Assumptions may be made that are not stated anywhere (e.g. the nature and numbers of equipment in the future). It can actually inhibit change by appearing to represent a final picture. It may result in substandard working layouts – these may be forced to comply with the rough layout for fear of making it look as though mistakes were made in the original work.

■ CALCULATIONS BASED ON STANDARDS

This approach is commonly used, perhaps because in essence it is easy to understand. A list of, say, ten different grades of staff is prepared. Against each grade of staff is written the number of staff in that grade. Each grade is alloted a standard area. The allotment multiplied by the number of staff gives the total space needed for each grade. Summing all the grades results in a total space requirement for people. To this must be added the space needed for major pieces of equipment such as photocopiers and mainframe computers.

Full details of standards are given in the section on 'Office layout' below. When using this approach, it is important to state whether the calculations refer to gross area, net usable or net-net. Advantages of this approach are:

- the results are accurate;
- it can handle the situation where the ratio of people to equipment is changing (e.g. doubling the number of programmers while the mainframe space only increases by a third);
- the standards and the results have a high acceptance rate (which means less bickering);
- office layouts are much much easier to draw.

The disadvantages are:

- recalculations resulting from changes are a chore and can introduce errors. For this reason, some people like to put the calculations onto a spreadsheet on a micro. This is advisable if the study is large or complex or people keep changing their minds. Otherwise it can become a sledgehammer to crack a nut;
- for predictive purposes, the system needs accurate manpower estimates;
- where offices are of the fixed cellular type, one has to deal with the problem of 'part-people' apparently sitting in an office;
- the standards themselves are subjective and may not always be accepted internationally.

In most situations, this is the preferred approach. It is consistent, easy to understand and gives good results.

Office layout

Before putting pen to paper to draw an actual layout, certain basic decisions have to be made. One of these is to set the parameters:

- what building are we planning?
- what are the time constraints (especially when must the staff be sitting in the new layout)?
- what is the budget and what does it cover?
- what changes have to be incorporated? (e.g. a new mainframe, shift working, organization structure changes, introduction of group working).

The next decision which impinges greatly is to decide on the type of office to be used. These may be:

- *cellular.* Cellular offices are individual enclosed offices, each office accommodating a small number of people, or even just one person. Partitions can be moveable or fixed, even made of brick in old offices. Cellular offices are good for security, privacy and dealing with the public and other visitors. They are poor for flexibility, change, space utilization, communications, co-operation, technology, equity and efficiency. An organization-wide adherence of everybody having their own individual office can be defended in the case of monasteries, but rarely otherwise;
- *half-height partition.* This can be a compromise between cells and open plan with proponents claiming advantages of both. When it is the result of selecting a half-way house between two opposing groups, then neither will be satisfied. It can be useful for group working, for performing discrete packets of work, for marking off senior or élite staff;
- *carrel.* A carrel is a workstation for one to four people, with an integrated working surface and semi-partitions and primary storage. It is strongly favoured by furniture suppliers. A private (and hence unpublished) study suggested that the carrel can be very poor for supervision and concentrated mental effort. In spite of this, carrels are sometimes found in research institutes and magazine publishers' offices;
- *open-plan.* An open-plan office consists of one room in which groups of people are seated together in small sets. One of the largest open-plan offices is at Solihull where one 'room' accommodates 1,700 staff. Open-plan is the traditional pattern for newspaper offices, as film buffs will be aware. The concept received a major boost in the 1930s when it was adopted by several large American insurance companies. Open plan is good for space utilization, communications, advanced technology, flexibility and work flow. It is poor for security. Privacy is poor unless special provisions are made. The odd thing about open plan is that people who are used to it prefer it, while people who are used to cells dislike the thought of adopting it;
- *landscaped offices.* These are open-plan offices plus. The desks are not set in rows or at right angles. Instead they have the appearance of being located in a random pattern. In fact, they rely on putting together groups of staff in an apparently unstructured way. Over the years the original concept of landscaping has to some extent disappeared. The difference between it and ordinary open plan has become blurred, with landscaping being used as a word to describe open plan of a high standard. Years ago, landscaped offices were also known as panoramic or 'bürolandschaft' but this last word is used much less often now.

D

The choice of type of office is rarely emotion free. People will buttress their preference by quoting 'evidence' which at times is little better than myths or old wives' tales. Thus cells may be described as a human right to dignity or an excuse for alcoholism. Landscaped offices may be cited as a cause for the spread of epidemics, or leading to a reduction in sickness absence of 15 per cent. Our own preference (which is quite unbiased, of course) is for well-planned, though not overly luxurious, landscaped offices.

After basic decisions have been made and parameters set, the next stage is to obtain and record information (it will be noted that the acronym ICICLES applies to office planning as to other studies). The information that is needed is:

- the flow of work. This may be obvious in the case of an office that uses paper exclusively as its medium of information flow. But it has been found that it also applies to those offices that have invested heavily in advanced technology. The

283

concept has even been found to apply to fully automated offices where it might be thought that flow does not exist. In most cases, it does;

- the organization structure, complete with staff levels in each part of the structure, together with their grades;
- a description of the work that is done in the office;
- a description of the communications systems, both internal and external;
- plans of the building, plus details of power trunking, power points, telephone and other connections, ventilation, air conditioning, doors, stanchions (very important), suspended floors and ceilings, stairs, lifts, emergency exits, fire points and any unusual features. Some features can be very unusual. A large insurance office in London has to protect the tiles on the walls and stanchions – the old GLC put a protection order on them;
- details of all powered or large equipment, together with any requirements such as high power, shielding. Noisy machinery should be listed. One sometimes has to watch out for very heavy items – these will entail checking that the floor loading is within safety limits. The same point often applies to storage of paper or magnetic tapes, especially if movable shelving is employed;
- details of planned changes, especially those connected with organization structure, staff levels, equipment acquisition, work organization and flows, service areas;
- type and amount of storage needed. A new office layout is a first-rate opportunity (one of the few such) to blitz all stored material with the intention of reducing it dramatically;
- type and amount of supervision;
- type and methods of information filing (cabinets, microfilm, floppy disks, old boxes);
- special working needs (e.g. large working surfaces, special lighting, darkrooms, soundproof rooms).

This list is not complete for every possible contingency and will have to be supplemented, depending on circumstances. For example, a charity needed double desks for counting and checking contributions. Tax offices in one country needed kiosks for self-employed 'char-wallahs' to come in and cook toasted sandwiches for the staff.

The next step is to produce a proximity matrix (though normally the information will have been collected during the previous stage). The proximity matrix is a simple diagram showing how near or far activities should be from one another. A blank diagram is shown in Figure 28.1 opposite. In appearance and use it resembles one of those distance charts that show the distances between various towns.

The information for the matrix will come from a number of possible sources – staff questionnaires, work and traffic flow analysis, discussions, and from much of the data collected in the previous stage. A further source will inevitably be the investigator's own knowledge and experience. A new layout should not merely replace an existing one, it must be an improvement.

On the chart are listed the 'activities', which can be in any order. Their relationship is marked in the box where the diagonals meet:

Relationship between items A and C

Proximity Matrix

Project ____________________ Item __________________________

Reference _____________ Date _____________ Author _______________

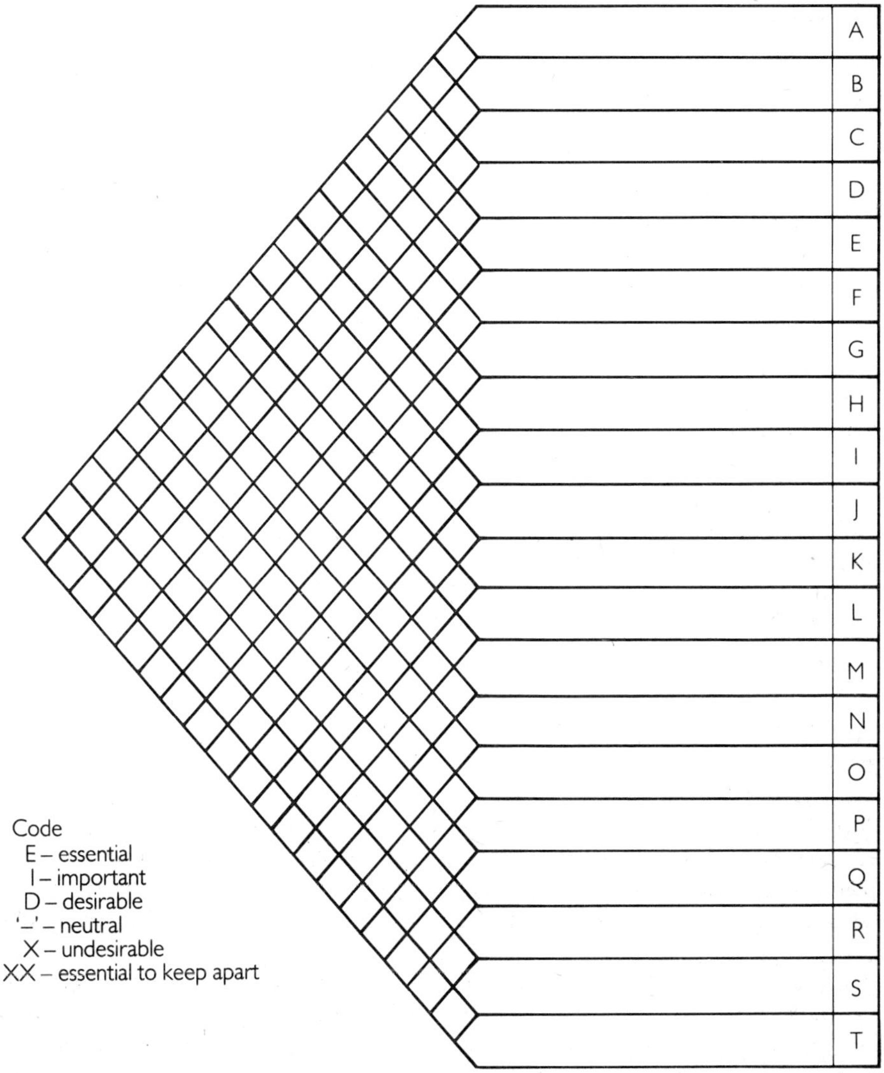
A
B
C
D
E
F
G
H
I
J
K
L
M
N
O
P
Q
R
S
T
Code
E – essential
I – important
D – desirable
'–' – neutral
X – undesirable
XX – essential to keep apart

Figure 28.1 Proximity matrix

Into each box goes a closeness rating;

    E – essential
     I – important
    D – desirable
    '–' – neutral
    X – undesirable
   XX – essential to keep apart

Some investigators split each box into two with a horizontal line:

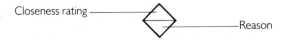

Closeness rating ——————⬦—————— Reason

This has the advantage of getting all the data onto one diagram. The disadvantage is that the chart becomes very crowded and can even cause one to miss a rating when inspecting the chart. The preferred alternative is to have a second piece of paper with a table/matrix on it showing reasons for any two items (e.g. A/F – 2). If this is done, it is then possible to array or group either items or reasons. Reasons for the closeness rating can include:

1 Traffic/paperwork/information flow.
2 Supervision (people/output/flow/deadlines).
3 Security.
4 External visitors (the public/messengers).
5 Expertise sourcing.
6 Equipment sharing/access.
7 Services (fax/photocopying/microfilm/storage/filing).
8 Environment (noise/hazards/light/fumes).

It is frequently necessary to produce more than one proximity chart. The first one would be for groups of staff such as sections and departments. Others would be for equipment, specialist groups, subdivisions of departments or to ensure deadline compliance. The temptation to list every member of staff on the matrix must be resisted; the sheer size of such a matrix means that it is only feasible for a very small office. And in that case, a proximity matrix is probably not needed, anyway.

It should be noted that a 'reason' may result in both nearness and separateness. Thus security may require a messenger to be near an entrance, but will require certain merchant bank staff to be kept away from specific files (to comply with Stock Exchange requirements).

By this time, a considerable volume of material will have been accumulated. This means that in a major or complex layout, it becomes easier to commit the sin of forgetting something vital. The next step is therefore to compile a constraint list, usually referred to as the *must do* list. This is just a list of items that will result in disaster if they are forgotten. This list must not be allowed to become too long, but may include:

● noisy or otherwise offensive equipment;
● public access;
● centralized/decentralized services;
● security (passes/locks);

- cabling (power/communications);
- very special items on the proximity matrix.

Provided that the layout study is a reasonably straightforward affair, the next step is to calculate the space needed, preferably based on space standards. Perusal of several modern textbooks revealed the odd fact that none of them gave actual figures to be used, presumably from a fear of causing disagreement. Since it is impossible to make calculations without having figures this is unfortunate. A guide to standards that can be used is:

Grade	m² each
Director	20–25
Senior executive	10–15
Departmental manager	9
Senior staff	7
Draughtsman	7
Secretary	6–7½
Terminal/micro operator	5½–7½
Clerk	5½
Data prep clerk	5

D

These figures are for a reasonably good office, and are for *net usable* calculations. A global figure (where needed) is to assume $10\,m^2$ per person as a net usable figure – in this case, the figure covers all office facilities. In the United Kingdom, there are legal minimum standards. The Offices, Shops and Railway Premises Act 1963 sets a minimum of $11.3\,m^3$ per person, the maximum ceiling height to be used in calculating minimum floor area to be 3 m. This means that each office worker must have at least $3.77\,m^2$, including furniture and fittings.

The width of aisles is slightly more subjective and often depends on the amount of traffic borne. Suggested standards are:

Type	Width (m)
Major aisles in large offices	1.6
Main aisles in small offices	1.2
Other aisles in large offices	1.2
Other aisles in small offices	0.9
Between desks (sideways)	0.8
Access to filing cabinets	1.1
Chair access to desks	0.9
Access to photocopiers, etc.	0.7
Access to fax, etc.	0.6
Access to vending machines (plus room for queue)	0.7

Where meals are to be provided, calculations can be based on:

Cooked meals	m² per diner
Dining space	1.1–1.9 per diner
Visitors restaurant	1.6–2.7 per diner
Food preparation, etc.	0.6–0.9 per diner
Snack service	
Dining space	0.7–1.1 per diner
Food preparation, etc.	0.3–0.6 per diner

These figures are based on a single 'sitting'. It must also be remembered that not all office staff will use eating facilities provided.

Ancillary space will depend on the nature of the office and the numbers of staff involved. For a medium-sized organization with a good profits record, the following is a guide (appropriate for an organization of say 250–400 total staff):

Boardroom	40 m²
Switchboard/reception	15 m²
Spare offices	15 m²
Maintenance stores	9 m²*
Stationery stores	9 m²
Showroom	12 m²
Mailroom	10 m²

*including small working area

Based on these standards (or variations thereon) it is now possible to start drawing up the actual layout. If the layout is complex or for a fair-sized open-plan office, then it is advisable first to draw up a block layout. This is just a series of rectangles to scale, sized in proportion to the office space needed for each group of people (e.g. departments). These are adjusted to conform to the proximity matrix and the constraint list. Each rectangle is moved until an approximation to a best fit is obtained.

This block layout should then be inspected carefully to look for any drawbacks or errors. There is an old saying in office layout circles: 'It is easier to use an eraser than a pneumatic drill.'

The detailed layout can now be based on the block layout. Many people will have laid out their house by cutting out pieces of card to scale to represent pieces of furniture. These pieces of card are then moved about a scale plan of the house until a good layout is obtained. Office layouts use the same system.

Once a good fit has been attained, the pieces of card are stuck onto the plan. The resulting layout is photocopied and discussed with management and staff. When agreement has been reached, the final layout can be drawn using either instant lettering or a template/stencil (such as the Rotring template no. 853 781 or 853 785).

Advanced technology and communications have introduced an extra problem: they produce large amounts of wire. Not only must this be provided for but their alteration can be expensive (e.g. moving a centralized word-processing centre). This has led to what is known as Wire Management. Wire management is the attempt to reduce the difficulties experienced in providing outlets for use by staff and equipment. The traditional approach used in computer rooms is to suspend the floor and take the cabling under the floor to where it is needed. Outlet points can be moved, covering the resulting gaps with a carpet square. This solution may not be perfect but it is far better than having trailing wires.

This solution is reasonable for one purpose-built room but may be unthinkable for an entire office block that was built some years ago. It has to be admitted that no one solution is ideal in every case. One answer is to imitate suspended flooring by cutting channels in the floor, inserting cables and then covering the ditches with metal plates before carpeting. Many furniture manufacturers have redesigned their desks and workstation carrels so that wiring can be carried up through the legs, etc. Some of this furniture is very attractive-looking. However, it does tend to command a premium price and can make it very time consuming to move the furniture even small distances.

For most of this century, offices have changed every twenty years or so in ways that have not been easy to predict. Presumably they will continue to do so, hence nobody can solve the wire management problem for ever. The best approach is to provide too much capacity rather than too little, and to try to retain a degree of flexibility for the future.

D

Working conditions

Staff wishes have combined with an appreciation of the effect of poor working conditions on efficiency to make people more aware of the office environment. This includes noise, fumes, lighting, heating, ventilation and cooling. Suggested standards are as follows:

Temperature	20–24°C
Humidity	35–60 per cent
Lighting	450–800 lux
Ventilation	25–35 m³ per person per hour
Noise average	35–55 dBA

Of these, the most persistently annoying is probably noise. Staff suffer from externally caused noise (aircraft, motorways, etc.) and noise generated internally. The traditional answers still apply: double glazing, curtains, acoustic screens, carpeting, absorbent ceilings and hoods. Sound is measured in dBAs; a quiet office is 35 dBA, a busy one has a sound level of 45 dBA. A word processing or typing centre is about 55 dBA. But people working say 60 cm away from a dot matrix printer will be subjected to a noise level of 61–78 dBA.[6]

The second major problem is what have come to be known as 'sick buildings', though this may be a misnomer, since it is the staff who feel sick. The Environmental Protection Agency (EPA) has its headquarters in Washington, DC, in a 'sealed' building. Some of its staff complained of sore throats, skin rashes, dizziness, even nausea – symptoms which seemed to decrease during the weekend when the staff were out of the office. So the EPA may have a sick building.[7] Putting a sick building right can take a lot of research and detective work. However, a lawsuit marked a turning point in making such research urgent. A Santa Barbara office worker sued 200 defendants (such as the building contractor, an architect, a ventilation engineer and manufacturers of floor tiles and glues). He claimed that his health had been injured by the air in the office. The lawsuit was settled for $700,000.

References

1 Interview in *Office Management International*, May 1987, p. 12.
2 'Facilities management', *IMC Handbook, 1987*, p. 265.
3 Study prepared by Buffalo Organization for Technological and Scientific Innovation.
4 'Old offices are problem sites for micros', *Management Services*, May 1986, p. 16.
5 'Planning the cost-effective office', *IMC Handbook, 1987*, p. 213.
6 *Byte*, Volume 13, No. 4, p. 118.
7 *The Economist*, 28 May, 1988, p. 44.

29

Filing and Finding

I write this to you, that it may serve as a witness between us, and
you must keep this letter, that in the future it may serve as a witness.

Letter from Ancient Egypt, c. 1300 BC

Good order is the foundation of all things.

Edmund Burke, *Reflections on the Revolution in France* (1790)

In 1882 Oscar Wilde paid a visit to the poet Walt Whitman, and was shown into Whitman's study. This was filled with dusty newspapers, retained because they referred somewhere to Walt Whitman. Wilde had to move a pile of these newspapers from a chair so that he could sit down.[1]

D

Seventy years later, the head office of a large bank was seen employing two men who spent their time inspecting microfilmed records searching for queried cheques. One hundred years after Oscar Wilde's discomforture, we were working in an automated paperless office that was in danger of collapsing because information held in the computer could not be located.

These three examples all point to the same lesson. Irrespective of the technology employed, the important factor remains the same:

> It is *finding*, not filing.
> It is access, not accumulation.
> It is retrieval, not retention.

The place (and, quite often, the perceived importance) of filing will vary widely depending on the organization. For example:

- filing is often not much of a problem in small and small-medium manufacturing concerns organized on functional lines (marketing/production/admin). If difficulties arise, they can usually be put right by installing a good indexing system, backed by some co-operation and self-discipline;
- in other concerns, filing may be important but (at least superficially) straightforward. A clinic may need to keep patients' files carefully but should have few problems provided agreement can be reached on how to deal with the names of people from different cultures;
- some organizations possess paperwork/data that is of great complexity, volume or importance. In such instances, the filing system has to be right;
- when an organization migrates from a manual/paperwork approach to a full-fledged 'paperless' or automated office, then it really does become a priority matter to install a first-rate filing system.

Similarly, the needs of organizations can vary widely at any time. A European investment bank found that it had three kilometres of paper files that were increasing at the rate of 29 per cent p.a. Rightly, it introduced a proper taxonomy, reduced duplication, and initiated an information destruction process. An oil company grew a collection of 300,000 drawings for oil exploration from subcontractors who all had individual styles, indexation, etc. Correctly, they saw a need for standard practices including a common indexing system.

This variability in organizations' needs and reliance on data retrieval means that there is no single standard pattern that can be applied to every investigation. It is as easy to over- as to underestimate the depth of study required. In the 1920s the function of records management (and records manager) started coming into prominence. Since that was a period of relatively cheap clerical staff and burgeoning bureaucracies, this had one historical and untoward effect. Records management became more concerned with security and permanence than with efficiency. This attitude still persists in some quarters today.

In case it be thought that we are underselling records management, it should be said that in larger organizations records are often becoming more important as time goes by. Reasons for this include:

- the increasing amount of information/paperwork in many organizations. For example, the civic authorities in cities such as Cairo and Calcutta find themselves in a position of increasing complexity as their cities grow;
- the increasing mobility of people. For example, a Yugoslav mental institution was asked to send copies of psychiatrists' reports covering a number of years to America to assist a decision to be made about a certain person's pension rights;
- litigation (e.g. the increasing importance of product liability in several countries);
- laws (e.g. control of drug research, laws on freedom of information, employment, safety, etc.);
- pressure groups (e.g. ecology, religious groups);
- technology (e.g. as drug manufacture becomes more complex, ever more drawings and plans for plant and equipment are needed).

So studies into records management may be a high priority. But one has to retain a proper sense of perspective.

Aspects of records management

The various aspects of records management that may be encountered are shown in Figure 29.1. These aspects are:

Strategy and policies

There are times, it must be admitted, when the topic 'the strategy of filing' is a sure-fire yawn inducer. In such cases, the best approach may be to go against the advice given in most textbooks. It is sometimes better to develop by oneself a coherent strategy and set of policies. These can be written up in the form of a summary ready for presentation to top management.

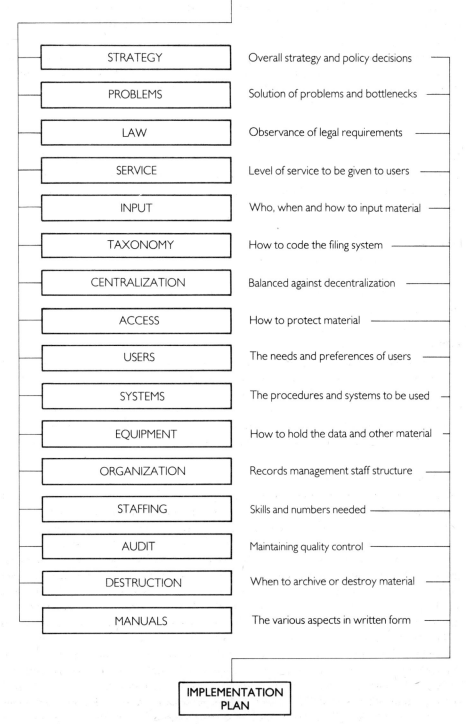

Figure 29.1 Aspects of data filing and retrieval

Problems

Problems should be handled by the normal methods design approaches, with one difference in emphasis. In 'filing' studies, one has to try to satisfy a wider than usual range of people's competing needs and wishes. The public relations department may feel strongly that they want some form of video discs. The personnel staff may want their records via an intelligent terminal linked to a specialist bureau. The legal department will want contracts, etc. kept on the original paper. This multi-media storage is sometimes unavoidable, though it can mean considerable complications in a large organization.

Law

Investigators who have spent a lot of time on records studies tend to know the legal implications as they relate to their own country. If inexperienced or working internationally, the rule is simple – check, do not guess.

Service

As always, it is important to consider, discuss, agree and set the level of service to be given to users. This affects most of the aspects shown in Figure 29.1. Attention is needed to timings, output quality, speed of retrieval, data security, and response to requests for material.

Input

As with other aspects of filing, the question of who, when, and how to input material may be straightforward or it can be complex. It can be as straightforward as spiking incoming delivery notes on a large nail in a warehouse. At other times it may be necessary to convince people as to who should have the passwords and authorization codes to alter a mainframe database. Many, if not most, computer departments will dislike the idea of unlimited decentralized input from remote terminals in real time.

Taxonomy

Some data specialists consider that taxonomy (the coding system) is by far the most important aspect of their work. It is certainly important enough to have its own chapter. Even simple coding systems can become complicated. For example, suppose we are going to keep records by using customer's names. Does McTavish come before or after 'M.3 Roadside Café'? (The solution is to utilize the same order as the telephone directory.) The marketing people may find it less easy when dealing with foreign customers. One may be known as Lionel Titman in one's own country but as Titman Lionel in others (and even as Mr George to one police force). Some countries have such a restricted number of names that one's mother's maiden name is used to try to differentiate between people. In Hungary, married women take a form of both their own and their husband's names, while in other countries many women keep their own names when marrying. In Sweden, everybody has a cradle-to-grave unique number; Greece was going to use the same approach until the Confederation of Industry pointed out that some older people had as many as four identity numbers. All these confusions lead to another simple rule: think the coding through before installation, not afterwards.

Centralization

Should one centralize all the records in one place? Believers in centralization can point out a number of advantages. Duplication is virtually eliminated. There is a saving in equipment and space. Staff can be more specialized, better trained, more knowledgeable, fewer in number. Systems, procedures, coding and indexing can be uniform. Record control is better. Reference to, and study of, a single subject is much easier and faster. On the other hand, there are also disadvantages to centralization. There are delays in accessing hardcopy files. There may be an unwillingness or delay in giving material to the centre. People will be tempted to make duplicates, anyway. Some departments may need continual access to material (e.g. drawing offices). The need for multimedia files (e.g. paper and optical discs) compounds the disadvantages.

In practice, most concerns compromise by using departmental filing. This is because most people do not see any great advantage in keeping together in one place the contracts for buying the office premises with a salesman's list of hot leads. One final comment. There have been attempts at full centralization of paper files. But we have yet to see one that operated effectively for very long.

Access

D

The right of access to information has to be balanced against security considerations. At the lowest level, it is inconvenient when records go missing. At a higher level, regulatory agencies have rules about open access to data (e.g. merchant banks).

Systems

Having got this far in an investigation, it should be possible to decide on the systems and procedures that will be installed. If any new equipment to be purchased is simple in nature, then it should also be possible to start staff training.

Equipment

Filing equipment can vary in complexity from the nail in a warehouse to an individually designed relational database on a mainframe supercomputer. Sometimes the nail is the best option. To reduce the range of options to 'thinkable' proportions, it is useful to think of storage in terms of just four storage alternatives: paper, electronic, microfilm and optical. These are considered in more detail below. Naturally, in many cases one is considering the equipment at the same time as the systems.

Organization

Decisions about organization structure arise from the decision about centralization. It is quite common to have centralized data handling (such as in-house microfilming) with decentralized storage. It is also not uncommon to have decentralized staff reporting, matrix-fashion, to a single records manager. Decisions about organization structure are not usually controversial. If a site is several hectares in size, or the need for security high (e.g. an Atomic Energy Agency), it is normally advisable to go for the obvious rather than strain after the novel.

There is one idea for centralized staff that is useful. That is to amalgamate the filing staff with those responsible for the mailroom, internal mail, messengers, 'walks' and reception. This often gives one a single department that can smooth out tasks that have peaks that occur at different times of the day.

Staffing

Decisions about skills and numbers needed can usually be based on normal work-measurement techniques. One must, however, take care over 'level of service' when balancing service levels against costs. It is easy to reduce costs centrally while simultaneously increasing costs downstream in user departments by introducing delays. It is equally easy to give such a high level of service that users do not bother to plan their work.

Audit

In some instances, it is advisable to introduce a form of quality control. This can take different forms. It may be schedule adherence (in a large mail-order firm). It may be sampled response delays at computer interrogatory terminals (in an insurance company answering telephone enquiries). As usual, such audit procedures must not become too bureaucratic.

Destruction

It is impressive to be taken into a large fire-proof safe to be shown rack after rack of stored magnetic tape. Impressive but not always heartening. Some concerns entered office automation by the word-processing route. Cases have been found where such firms now have permanently stored data which says, 'Dear Sir, Please reserve a hotel room for our Mr Robinson on the night of 17 May.' Much data is similarly ephemeral. This type of data clutters up the system and should be destroyed. However, to do this is fine in theory but can be difficult in practice. One way is the laborious (and difficult to maintain) coding of all documents at the time of initiation. Another system is to have somebody scan records periodically and decide what and when to destroy or achive. Such a person needs a wide span of knowledge, which has led to their being known as a 'cosmopolitan gate'. One computer manager convinced himself that it was cheaper to buy more tapes than to try to reduce the 'database'.

Filleting files is easier if they are on paper or if storage is departmental/functional. A suggested set of rules for retention periods for data is given in the Appendix at the end of this book.

Manuals

Many large organizations have manuals for records management. These are likely to be:

- a style book;
- a systems and procedures manual;
- a set of job descriptions, with organization chart;
- a manpower manual, with details of work schedules and manning levels.

Implementation plan

As with any other major change, a plan for installation is needed. This may be as simple as a bar chart. If the change is complex (such as full automation) then we move into the area of needing a fully detailed network plan.

Assignment pattern

These aspects of data filing and retrieval are likely to manifest themselves in the following, not untypical, study pattern:

- agree and communicate with employees an explanation of the purpose, nature and shape of the project;
- gain familiarization with the client's structure, business, locations, staff, plans, etc.;
- hold structured interviews/questionnaires to get detailed facts about policies, systems, procedures, equipment, experiences, etc. (details will include input, output, storage, hardware, retrieval, codes, indexes, volumes, security);
- hold user interviews/questionnaires to find details of problems, bottlenecks, needs, wishes (staff covered will include departmental heads plus up to 10 per cent of managers, professionals, secretaries/clerks);
- analyse critically the current situation. Prepare notes/discussion paper. Discuss. Agree imperative requirements and outline policies;
- develop a new scheme for records management, covering those aspects in Figure 29.1 that were included in the terms of reference. Agree this new scheme;
- develop and agree an implementation plan, covering responsibilities for actions, timescale, key events;
- write, agree and produce any manuals necessary.

D

Sundry statistics

Some figures which are widely believed in records circles are given below. Sources are largely undiscoverable:

- files usually grow by 10–15 per cent p.a.;
- 20 per cent of storage is for duplicates. Another 20 per cent is for material that need not have been stored at all;
- 90 per cent of references are to records which are less than three years old. Only 5–10 per cent of records that are more than five years old are ever referred to;
- 5 per cent of all insurance policies lack an individually identifiable audit trail.

On this last point, two interesting examples have been observed, both concerned with computer-based storage. One company omitted to record payments made by individual companies in a group pension scheme (a fact noticed by an employee who proceeded to defraud the firm). Another firm got its records into such confusion that it had to revert to manual methods. This change revealed that 30 per cent of policies had wrong payment records.

Equipment

It is assumed that most people are acquainted with the main methods of storing paperwork in offices. They will therefore be dealt with in a somewhat cursory manner:

■ VERTICAL FILING

Vertical filing is usually in the form of four-drawer cabinets. In use, papers to be filed are placed in a folder which is then put into a drawer with its face towards one. Advantages include flexibility of file size, easy access, protection from dirt, amenability to almost any coding and indexing system, facility of changes to systems and procedures, long archive life, inexpensiveness, low demand for specialized skills or knowledge. Disadvantages include the facts that folders can become hidden, removal is rather too easy, re-filing can be inaccurate, continual use (*in situ*) leads to deterioration of primary source material.

■ SUSPENSION/POCKET SUSPENSION

Suspension filing is similar to vertical filing but the folders are suspended from two metal rails in each drawer. The advantage is that the disadvantages of ordinary vertical filing are overcome. The disadvantages are the higher cost, lesser flexibility and about 25 per cent loss of capacity.

■ LATERAL FILING

Lateral filing is like suspension filing except that the files are turned through 90° (so that the edge of the folders face one) and the metal rails are mounted in special cupboards normally 1–1½ m wide. Advantages are a space saving of about 33 per cent compared with drawers (no room needed to pull out the drawers) and quicker visual checking on whether any files are missing. Disadvantages include the discomfort of locating folders (one's head has to be twisted sideways), the lengthy nature of the task of rearranging files as contents grow, and inflexibility when it becomes necessary to insert new files under many coding systems.

■ BOX FILES

Box files are basically a box (usually slightly larger than A4) with a hinged lid, capable of holding about 500 sheets of paper. Useful for bulky documents, and some special circumstances such as removal and return of material each day from a strongroom.

■ OTHER TYPES INCLUDE:

- plan chests (large, shallow drawers for drawings);
- plan cabinets (in which drawings are suspended unfolded from clips or spikes);
- cardboard tubes in pigeon holes (for bulky items);
- carousels (1 m diameter revolving metal discs on which ring binders can be stored). Carousel filing is very economical on space;
- filing for index cards (which can be held in books, on wheels, in shallow drawers and in special boxes);
- mobile trolleys and cabinets;
- powered pater nosters (these can be up to 3 m wide and extend through three floors of a building, so installation is likely to involve major structural work in an office. (Though they do look rather magnificent in a sort of 1930s baroque way.)

There is a similar range of equipment for filing video, audio and magnetic tapes and material. The computer equivalent of the pater noster is the powered MSD (mass storage device). In this, data cartridges are retrieved from a honeycomb of bins and loaded automatically into the read/write stations. An MSD holds 500,000 million characters.

Microfilm

Microfilm is used in several forms. For this reason it is sometimes referred to as microforms or micrographics. Microfilm has a long history: it was used by the besieged Parisians in 1870 to communicate with compatriots outside the city. But it was not until the 1920s that its use became commercially widespread when it was widely adopted by banks to record the passage of negotiable and other paper instruments.

Microfilming is the reduction of documentation by photographing onto film stock which then becomes the medium of storage and viewing. Viewing is usually done via an enlarging viewer or screen – rather like a photographer viewing transparencies. Typical reduction ratios are 20:1, 32:1, 40:1, and 50:1. The film stock is usually 16 mm, though 35 mm (and even 8 mm) is used by some systems. Images are usually white-on-black (i.e. negative film) though positive or colour film can be used at increased cost. The process is thus in four stages: photo-reducing the documents by photographing them, developing the film, filing the film, and retrieving/viewing the data.

There are four main methods of handling the film:

- *roll film*. Film is kept in a roll 30 m long. When needed, this roll can be loaded into the viewer (known as a 'reader') and projected on to a screen for inspection. Finding the correct frame of film can be excessively lengthy (and boring) unless a form of coding and/or automatic retrieval is used.
- *microfilm jackets*. Strips of film are inserted into pockets on a transparent polyester film sheet. Typically, a jacket of 150 × 100 mm contains up to 70 A4 sheets. In some industries, this is convenient for the correspondence for a single sale, or for a single report.
- *aperture cards*. These are like index cards with a transparent window into which a piece of film can be mounted. They are often used for drawings that will need copying.
- *microfiche*. This is a single sheet of film but one that contains a number of records arranged in rows. Different systems use different sizes of cards and records per card. Microfiche (like jackets and aperture cards) can be found in a standard of 150 × 100 mm but this is very far from being a universal standard. Such a microfiche sheet might contain, 80, 270 or even 690 records. The 690 are held in 23 rows of 30 records to a row. For some inexplicable reason, staff in offices that use microfilm jackets will often refer to them as 'microfiche'.

    Microfiche can be copied and then distributed at lower cost than paper. Most journals that state, 'This journal is available on microfilm' use it rather than in roll form. NASA's Scientific and Technical Information Facility (STIF) uses both microfiche and direct access remote terminals for distributing material to users. Microfiche can be used in portable readers. These readers use a small screen, are battery powered and enable field-service staff to carry and access the equivalent of 6,000 pages of manuals in a hand-held unit.

■ COMPUTER-ASSISTED RETRIEVAL (CAR)

Computers can be used in a variety of ways in conjunction with microfilm. At a fairly elementary level, the indexes can be held on a micro and searched there. The correct microfilm can be loaded into a reader when identified, and the required record found automatically for inspection or printing as a hard copy onto paper. It is possible to

299

build more and more automation into this process. A high level of automation means increased speed, and increased cost. But for some purposes this can be a very good system; American Express use it to process their credit card applications.

■ COMPUTER OUTPUT MICROFILM (COM)

If information is held on a computer medium such as magnetic tape then it can be printed onto microfilm without using paper as an intermediate stage. This can be done either by displaying the records onto a cathode ray tube and photographing the resulting image, or by recording directly onto film via laser. In either case, the resulting hard copy is unlikely to impress a fine art printer, but those dependent on computers have learnt to accept output of low quality. Conversationally, this is referred to as 'lo-fo' to distinguish it from 'hi-fi'.

High-speed mainframe printers are certainly fast, but most of them only give six copies of which the top copy is usually acceptable but the final two barely legible. So if one needs a report to go to, say, ten people one is faced with three alternatives: ten print runs of one copy each; one run plus photocopying; or two runs of five copies. Since high-speed printers are expensive, COM offers a useful alternative to big users. COM onto microfiche can produce masters at the rate of 100–200 per minute after which each copy takes a few seconds. This entails setting up a production line, which is not cheap. But a computer department in a large car manufacturer that did this saved £300,000 p.a.

Advanced filing

The methods other than paper and microfilm (such as computers and videodiscs) are discussed in the section on advanced technology.

However, effectiveness is not merely a matter of choosing a technology. To understand why, just ask yourself if you file your love letters in the same way and place as your overdue electricity bill. Studies of office workers show that they keep information in a similar range of alternatives. Customers' archives in old boxes, current files in a cabinet, old print-outs in a cupboard, reference material in the desk, current matter in heaps on top of the desk, a calendar and clock on the wall.[2] All this information can be held in a computer, using disk files and directories plus a memory-resident pop-up. Indeed, this is the approach of many paperless offices.

However, suppose a person needs to know the date. To glance at a calendar may take 17 milliseconds. To get the same information onto a computer screen may take 17 seconds, which is 1,000 times as long. This trivial example leads to the point that a number of factors have to be considered:

- location (the convenience, accuracy and speed with which information can be found);
- isolation (retrieving information that is needed without the 'noise' of unwanted extraneous or adjacent material);
- transfer (the speed with which information can be moved from where it is to where it is needed. For example, from a database on a disk to an applications software window);
- replacement (the convenience, accuracy and speed with which information can be returned to storage after it has been used);

300

- security (the restriction of access to information to those who have the right to do so).

These factors change priority depending on the situation. A clerk who is interrupted by a customer enquiry while searching a database wants fast relocation. If the same clerk wants to find a name in a lengthy report then he needs rapid isolation of the name. Some networking interactive systems are based on sequential records and name directories (such as Unix). Such systems may lack abilities or balance in the factors above. Those systems that do offer a choice of the factors often lack proper integration.

All this is leading to the use of multimedia filing. This may be mainframe + jacket microfilm, micros + paper, COM + fibreboard boxes, etc. Multi-media filing demands special care and accuracy with taxonomy, procedures and staff training. For many organizations, non-paper uni-medium filing must await one (perhaps two) new generations of hardware and software.

Microfilm pros and cons

The advantages of microfilm include:

- reduction by as much as 95 per cent in space requirements;
- easier record archiving and destruction;
- rapid search in many situations;
- low cost of record duplication and distribution;
- reduction in stationery costs;
- reduction in computer printing.

It should be noted that, firstly, most of these advantages depend on the situation and are not universally true. Secondly, the saving in space does not, as many people believe, automatically lead to a cost reduction. Accurate calculations of capital and revenue will reveal that a saving needs a very high office rent – so high that they may be met in Tokyo but rarely elsewhere. The real advantages (including cost saving) will be attained when microfilm is part of an overall effective and smart system.

The disadvantages of microfilm include:

- need for equipment compatibility across locations;
- cost of equipment, processing and supplies;
- difficulty of later systems migration;
- need for well-trained and self-disciplined staff;
- care needed in initial operations;
- storage life.

The last point is somewhat contentious. Manufacturers claim a long life for the materials. However, the experience of film-makers suggests that modern colour film stock can lose at least its colour-balance after about eight years.

Comments on procedures

On the next page are given some comments on various aspects of filing procedures:

Procedure	Commentary
Retrieval (a) Computer storage backed by computer indexing.	Retrieval is very flexible and effective. Success depends on good software. Many packages are very good at searches. Inspect other facilities carefully for suitability.
(b) Store multiple copies of paper under different headings.	Expensive (paper, space and equipment). In practice, seems to lead to user confusion.
(c) Print indexes with added cross references.	Difficult and costly to update while maintaining accuracy.
Control (a) Centralized automated system.	Often disliked by users. Can foster the 'them-and-us' feeling. Costly when dependent on telecommunications links – COM may be a better choice.
(b) Centralized paperwork control system.	Often disliked by users. Response can be slow.
(c) Local paperwork control system.	Often liked by users. But can easily fall into disuse when other work becomes urgent.
(d) Audited quality control.	Always advisable, though sometimes periodic 'blitzes' are more effective than continual monitoring if this is allowed by the culture to lose impact.
Cost reduction (a) Reduce quantity of records going into storage.	Sounds a good idea in theory. Just try it, though – user resistance will soon rise.
(b) Move away from using paper as the storage medium.	May save costs of space, copying and distribution. Can be expensive to convert to microfilm, videodisc or computer. Updating can be difficult.
(c) Use cheap off-site storage.	Good for archives. Would be good for material for which users will wait, say, 24 hours to get – if this can be predicted.
(d) Develop 'concordances' (indexes which give cross-references between different systems) to avoid migration to one new system.	Can be very useful provided there is a reasonable amount of overlap or compatibility of the systems. Manual creation and up-dating can be laborious, and fall into disuse.
(e) Use trainees for initial filing/storage of material.	Only advisable if quality control is strictly maintained and task is truly 'training', not just a dead-end job.

References

1 There are various references to the meeting of Wilde and Whitman, including:
   Ellmann, R., 'Oscar meets Walt', *The New York Review of Books*, Vol. XXXIV, No. 19, 1987.
2 One of the references to the way office staff work is:
   Malone, T., 'How do people organize their desks?', *ACM SIGOA Newsletter*, Vol. 3, 1982.

D

30

Forms and Paper

> Government defines the physical aspects of man by means of The
> Printed Form, so that for every man in the flesh there is an exactly
> corresponding man on paper.
>
> Jean Giraudoux, *The Enchanted* (1933)
>
> Simplify, simplify.   Henry Thoreau, *Walden* (1854)

Why does an up-to-date book on the effective office contain a chapter on 'forms and paper'? Surely computers and advanced technology are replacing paper and the need for forms? Or will do soon? In fact, the news about the death of paper has been greatly exaggerated. Not only is advanced technology failing to replace paper, it is actually increasing its usage.

The demise of paper has long been predicted. In 1895 two Frenchmen thought that cylinder gramophones (record players) meant the end of books. Jules Verne thought that novels would disappear possibly by 1950. In 1953 a group of us discussed the future of factories; cybernetics would replace most of the office though it might take until 1975 owing to conservatism.

Meanwhile, the use of paper continues to grow. Money transfers in the USA using cheques now total about 50 billion a year (up from 40 billion four years ago), with electronic funds transfers accounting for fewer than 5 per cent of transfers. Federal paperwork in the USA costs $100 billion a year. It has been estimated that Canadian firms spend \$C 500 million a year just to store 5 million m^3 of paper.[1] In Britain, it was estimated in a government report that over 2 billion government forms and leaflets are used each year by the public.[2] That is a lot of trees.

Equally disturbing is to go into a company and find it drowning in bureaucratic paper, with everybody apparently having the right to introduce a new form as they see fit. In one retail chain selling cakes and bread, a shop assistant complained that she could not move a cream puff from one side of the shop to the other side without filling in a form for head office.

Electronic technology is adding to the paper. Computer departments are notorious for producing mountains of hard-copy printout whether people want it or not. A busy supervisor received a control printout (among other printouts) every week that was 3 cm thick. One day he was seen bending under his desk deliberately scruffing up this control by twisting and creasing it. When tackled about this, he admitted sheepishly that he was just making the control look as though it had been used. He claimed that neither he nor his colleagues actually used the control because it was too bulky: 'How can I find anything in that lot?'

Electronic mail has started to lead to 'defensive printouts' for future reference, instead of the telephone calls that electronic mail replaced. Credit cards may be part of the 'cashless/chequeless society' but they are accompanied by up to ten pieces of paper when used to buy something. Airlines use massive computer-based reservation systems

– but every jumbo jet flying across the Atlantic still needs over 2,000 fax/telexes to get across. Meanwhile, photocopiers become faster.

In the face of such apparently overwhelming odds, the temptation is to ignore the problems in the hope that they will eventually solve themselves. Or set up a committee or a special group (the Internal Revenue Service has a staff of forty people for form design). Or accept the inevitable. As one journalist put it, 'the Micro Millennium is turning out to be the Cellulose Century'.[3]

Fortunately, something can be done about the situation. First, a real effort has to be made to ensure that computerization and advanced technology introduction is followed by cutting out manually prepared paperwork. Time after time after time, it is observed that manual methods are not stopped. This can be due to prolonged parallel running becoming dual running in time. It can be because the new system produces figures too late. It can be due to poor systems design or programming. It can be because of 'computer errors' (three quantity × price arithmetic errors per average A4 invoice, in one case seen).

However, the commonest reason observed is that the new system does not perform all necessary clerical tasks which then have to be continued manually – plus the ancillary tasks. Often the situation only needs relatively minor 'tweaking' to the system. But the computer department does not have time for the tweaking, and anyway has moved on to something else or cannot admit that the original work was imperfect. Meanwhile, there seems to be no communicating between the office and computer staffs for explanations – saying that this is what needs doing, that it would not take long, that we would like to help, and that this would be the payback in reduced frustration, boredom and costs.

This situation has been observed so many times that it is difficult to know why commerce does not cure it. It also makes one wonder whether this is a cause of the well-known phenomenon that computerization often leads to extra staff.

Secondly, straightforward method design is highly effective. The White Paper referred to above was followed by the Rayner Review to tackle the problem. The second progress report stated 125,000 government forms had been reviewed. With the result that 27,000 forms had been discontinued, 41,000 redesigned – and £14 million saved.[4]

One of the most frequently advanced techniques is that of Forms Management or Forms Control. This usually includes a system for ensuring that no new forms arise spontaneously, usually by ruling that requests for new forms must be channelled through a special department. This department will decide whether the new form is really needed and, if so, will design it. This certainly sounds like a good idea, especially for any forms that will be used by the public (e.g. those issued by civil services).

The same technique is widely recommended for all large companies. Textbooks nearly all praise it, experts in forms advocate it, magazine articles counsel it. It is even possible that some examinations insist on it. In response to this widespread acceptance, all we can reply is, 'We hear what you say.' In our experience, forms control is like fully centralized filing: it works fine at first, but it collapses in time. It may collapse after six months though it can last for two years, but collapse it does. It either becomes flooded with applications and cannot give a quality service, or else it loses its teeth and quietly becomes part of the bureaucracy.

If forms control does not control forms, then what will? The preferred approach is:

● instead of a continuous programme of reform, have a blitz to reduce forms every five

to eight years (and mean it);
- use advanced technology. But use it effectively and well;
- have a company culture that is anti-waste, anti-new forms and anti-bureaucratic;
- use normal method design to ensure that one has effective systems and procedures.

Form design

■ CORPORATE DESIGN

Before considering the actual design of forms, one has to remember the impact of corporate design. Many organizations take considerable care with this aspect of corporate identity. They will use a unique logo. They may emphasize the use of two specific colours. They may make extensive use of a particular typeface. These three (logo, colour, typeface) may then be employed for a number of purposes: on sales literature, advertising, lorries, cars, shop-fronts, office buildings, overalls, products, etc.

This design uniqueness will then usually be continued forward onto all forms and paperwork that will be seen by external contacts such as customers. It will almost always be used for letter-headings and compliments slips, probably for order forms and invoices, possibly for terms of business. Many firms will also use the house design on internal forms, believing that it both aids corporate togetherness and looks nice. If this is corporate policy, then all form design will have to take it into account. Also, it has to be admitted that it does give a pleasant, superficially professional appearance to all forms prepared in house.

■ PAPER

Knowledge of paper (and printing) helps one to design forms, and some technical terms will be used later. For this reason, some brief notes are included. Paper production was invented in China about AD 105 but the secret did not reach Europe until the mid-twelfth century. Making paper in continuous lengths was not possible until 1798. A further century went by before a Norwegian, in 1899, invented the paper-clip.

Before mechanization, paper was made by dipping a rectangle of material held on a wooden frame into a mix of water and fibres. The frame was taken from the mix, together with a quantity of water. By shaking the frame, the water drained through the material, leaving behind a sheet of fibres. This sheet was dried, and so became paper. The frames were not of a standard size: the stronger the papermaker, the larger the sheets of paper, since a strong man could lift more water. Individual papermakers would give individual names to their products which in time became associated with the size of paper (e.g. 'elephant').

In the last century, Germany started adopting a standard set of paper sizes. The basis was a large sheet whose side had the ratio of $1:\sqrt{2}$. This was a very ingenious idea: it meant that the sheet could be repeatedly cut in half and the resulting sheets would retain the original ratio. Moreover, when this is done, there is no waste. The basic sheet is 1 m^2, and the sides are 1,189 mm × 841 mm. The cut sheets are called A1, A2, A3 and so on, as in Figure 30.1 opposite.

The sheet used for forms is commonly A4 (297 mm × 210 mm), while smaller forms are put onto A5 (½ × A4). Associated with these standard sheets is a set of standard

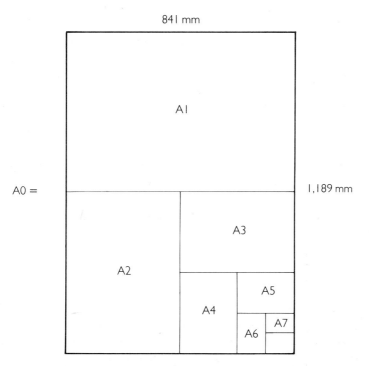

841 mm

A1

A0 =

1,189 mm

A3

A2

A5

A4

A7

A6

Figure 30.1 A0 cutting diagram

D

envelopes (see Figure 30.2 overleaf). The standard ratio of all the sheets makes them ideal for reduction and enlargement, such as microfilm and photocopying.

The advantages of the 'A' standards should have led to their automatic incorporation into computer printers when they were invented. However, it did not. This was because the original growth of computer printers was in the USA – the one major industrial power that has still not adopted the 'A' series. The resulting set of paper series is shown in the Appendix, towards the end of the book. Even the size known as American 'quarto' is not the same as other people's quarto.

One of the ways of describing paper is by its weight (which is also a measure of its 'thickness' to a large extent). The figure that is used is the weight in grams of a single A0 sheet. Airmail paper may be 40 gsm (grams per square metre). Flimsy paper used for multi-part sets is 45 gsm to 60 gsm. Photocopying paper is 70 gsm or 80 gsm. Letterheads are often 80 gsm, though good-quality prestige paper is 100 gsm. Manufacturers offer special paper for laser printers and ink-jet printers. Since a laser printer is only a copier in disguise, one can usually use ordinary photocopier paper for lasers. It may be necessary to use a good-quality photocopier paper, and some laser printers are still being manufactured that are choosy about the paper thickness. Ink-jet paper is still needed for some colour work on some printers. Most black-and-white ink-jet printers are now more tolerant of ordinary paper.

Irrespective of size, a 'quire' is usually 25 sheets of paper and a 'ream' is usually 500 sheets. One buys paper in packs of one ream each. The Americans also weigh paper this

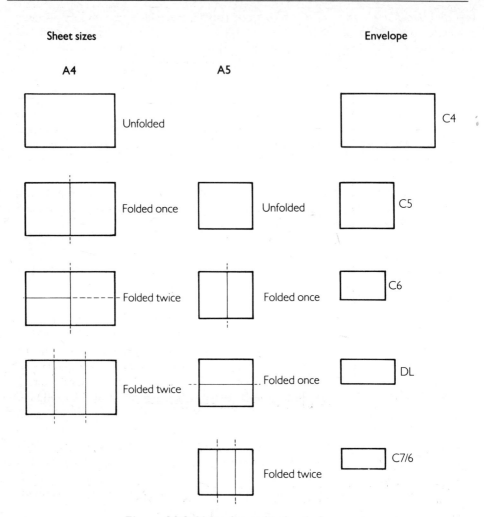

Figure 30.2 Use of standard envelopes

way. Imported special purpose computer paper may be described in 'pounds' instead of gsm. This is the weight in pounds of 500 sheets of paper each measuring 22 in × 17 in (559 mm × 432 mm). If the weight of such a ream is 20 lb (9 kg) then the paper is called '20-pound' paper. This is usually written on the packs as '20' or sometimes 'sub 20'. An added complication is that the weight of heavier paper is usually based on a different size of paper, so 30 may not be 50 per cent heavier than 20. If in doubt, buy 20 paper or 15 paper since most computer printers can use these satisfactorily. The alternative is to persuade the USA to change to international standards.

Another feature of paper is its texture. Some paper is very smooth (the term indicating this is 'calendered'), while other paper is given a sculptured or patterned finish (such as laid, wove or linen). Textured paper looks and feels more prestigious and is used for material that will go to customers. It can be used with daisywheel printers, typewriter-style impact printers, and some ink-jet printers (provided the ink is good quality and the texturing not too deep). Dot-matrix printers should be able to handle textured paper, but some of them (especially the portable varieties and line printers) can cause difficulties.

Smooth paper is needed for thermal transfer printers, especially for the multi-passing colour thermal transfer (colour thermal + linen can be used for special effects if you have the patience). Thermal transfer should not be confused with 'thermal' printers; these need their own special paper. Most page printers are laser printers and smooth paper is usually needed. Ink-jet printers need a non-absorbent paper as the ink tends to 'bleed' sideways into the paper before drying. Plastic ink printers are a type of ink-jet colour printers which do not bleed (nor do they suffer from jet clogging). The best tactics are to use smooth paper for everything except for prestige material, when one can use textured paper with a daisywheel.

All printing that is non-impact works best with paper that is free from fuzz or dust. If paper has been recycled several times, then the individual fibres become shorter, and some people believe that this can lead to more fuzz.

One final point about paper is that one should always shop around since prices vary for the same quality of paper. One photocopier manufacturer actually made more profit from selling paper than from selling photocopiers.

■ PRINTING PROCESSES

<u>**D**</u>

At one time, the training for forms designers included a number of ancillary subjects. For example, some of them would even have to produce hand-made paper. One subject that would always be covered would be the acquisition of knowledge about all the different methods of printing. This could range from rubber stamps to newspaper web offset. This was absolutely fascinating as one went round a whole range of printing establishments – fascinating but not always relevant since most of us never did get around to printing forms by such methods as photogravure or silk screens. Still, such knowledge can be very interesting and may provide useful background enabling one to make better decisions – which is another way of saying that this book does not include full details of all the possible processes. Anybody interested in reading about the basics of several printing processes should obtain a book published by Penguin Books and based on the work at the Islington Bus Company – a charity that has nothing to do with buses.[5]

The reason for not describing all the printing processes is that they will not normally be encountered. The majority of commercial printers are organized to provide two basic services, one suitable for printing forms, etc., and the other one for quality work. When accepting an order for printing forms, therefore, the average printer needs neither a discussion nor instructions about how he, or she, will perform the printing. What is needed is an indication about the paper, the quantity, the deadline and typefaces.

Some organizations print their own forms in-house. Even here, there is one predominant process: offset litho. Some organizations use a 'stencil' machine, but any commercial organization that is thinking of buying a stencil machine should consider carefully the running costs, especially paper and ink. In most cases a 'baby' litho will be cheaper than a stencil. A hand-operated stencil machine may be right for a boy scout troup or a gardening club, but in an office, the chosen operator would not welcome the task of producing forms on it – and the paper is not considered suitable for forms, anyway.

Litho is short for lithography. It was invented in 1798 by Aloys Senefelder after, so legend has it, trying to draw on wet stone with greasy chalk. This repulsion of grease and water is the principle on which the process depends. An image is made on a printing plate. The image can be produced photographically (a well-maintained electrostatic photocopier will do it) or by hand or transfer or from a typewriter. The plate can be paper (cheap), plastic coated (for longer runs) or metal (for even longer runs).

The non-image non-printing area is damped with water. This damped area repels the greasy ink when the ink is applied to the image. Thus only the image is printed. The 'offset' in offset litho indicates that the image is transferred from the plate to an intermediate rubber roller (called a 'blanket') before then being transferred to a piece of paper.

Where the 'filling-in' of a form can be performed by a computer, then it becomes possible to print both the form and the response material at the same time. Special high-speed machines have been developed to do this but are expensive.

■ TYPE

'Type' was the word given to a small block with a raised letter or numeral, though now it can be a character on an instant lettering sheet or on a sheet of film. Type (or printing of characters) is measured in 'points'. There are 72¼ points to an inch or 28½ to a centimetre. Length of print is measured in 'pica'. One pica is equal to 12 points.

Typical type size usage is:

7–9 point	minor information; blank forms
10–12 point	printed material such as books
12–18 point	headings
30–36 point	form titles

'Leading' is the space between lines of type. It is measured in points. The space is usually 1-pt (one point) or 2-pt. If space is short, then no leading is used. The type is then said to be 'solid' – which does not mean that one line touches the next, but that no extra space is added. Type of 12 pt with 2 points of leading would be described in writing as 12/14 pt and would be spoken of as being 'twelve on fourteen'.

The precise shape and style of characters used is the 'typeface'. There are hundreds of typefaces in use. Selection of a typeface can aid readability, clarity, emphasis and aesthetic appearance. Typeface selection is affected by fashion and personal preference. Most people have their favourites. Some examples, with possible attributes, are:

Clarity	Berling, Plantin Light
Official	Times Medium
Pleasant	Palatino

■ DESIGNING FORMS

Before putting pen to paper and actually starting to draw up a new form, it is assumed that the normal methods design approach will have been already used. This will have entailed asking questions such as:

- is the form necessary?
- can its design lead to other forms being eliminated?
- can the form combine other forms? Alternatively, can it be combined with another form with minor changes?
- is it possible to transfer the system to some form of advanced office technology?

The basic information that will be needed for the form design is collected on a pre-design checklist. An example of this is shown in Figure 30.3 overleaf. The main reason for having a checklist is to avoid having to repeatedly go back to staff to gain information that one forgot to ask. The steps are now:

1 Make an actual list of every piece of information that will have to go onto the form.
2 Renumber each item in the order that would be logical for completing the form. This may be dictated by the source of each item (group same-source items together), by calculations made (cost to the right of quantity and unit price), by degree of difficulty (easy points first) or by custom (name before date of birth).
3 Check that this order will also be logical for the person who will be using the information on the form. If completer and next user need different orders, decide if any changes should be made to the order.
4 Write the words that will prompt the response. In some cases this is obvious (e.g. date). In others, care will be needed to avoid ambiguity while at the same time being reasonably concise. If in doubt, err on the side of clarity.
5 For each item, calculate the amount of space that will be needed for prompt + response. This will be space vertically and horizontally. If the form is to be completed by hand indoors, allow at least 6 mm vertically for each line of response. If the form is to be completed by hand out of doors, allow at least 8 mm vertically for each line of response. For all hand-completed forms, allow 20 mm per word for lower-case words and 25 mm for capital words horizontally. If the form is to be completed on a typewriter or printer, allow 25 mm (1 inch) for every 10 characters horizontally. Vertically, allow for the standard line spacing on typewriters: for every 2.54 cm/1 inch allow 4 lines unless very short of space, in which case allow 6 lines. Use enclosed spaces, or boxes, or lines for handwritten use. Use open spaces or precisely measured vertical spaced boxes for typewriters and printers. Forms that are hand-completed for later data prep can employ rows of small vertical boxes (6 mm × 5 mm) if printed feint in a pale colour.
6 We now have a list of items numbered 1, 2, 3 ... n and for each item an imaginary space which can be thought of as imaginary rectangles. The next step is to take a piece of paper larger than the finished form will be – A3 if the form will be A4 but A4 if the form will be A5. On this paper is drawn an outline of the finished form. Because our piece of paper is larger than the finished form, we have a margin round the dummy form for our notes (type size, spacings, etc.).

This large piece of paper will have drawn on it our first draft of the completed form. We do this by deciding whether there have to be any special margins, etc. for future filing,

D

Form pre-design checklist

Title of form_____ Provisional ☐ Agreed ☐

    Reference number_____ Provisional ☐ Agreed ☐

Why is a new form needed?_____

For use in (Div/dept/sect/group)_____

Has a method design study been carried out?   Yes ☐ No ☐

    If 'No', reason:_____

Objective of form:_____

Sources of input information:_____

Main user of completed form:_____

    In what way will it be used?_____

    Spaces/pre-printed matter for main user?_____

Other distribution, and uses made of form:

Total number of copies:_____

Anticipated usage per annum: Single sheets _____ Sets _____ Pads _____

Form entries will be by: hand ☐ – indoors ☐ out of doors ☐

        typewriter ☐ printer ☐_____

        other ☐_____

Deadline for form to be up and running:_____

Special pre-set constraints: Reason

    Sets/pads/fanfold/etc._____

     details: _____

    Method of making copies:_____

    Filing methods: _____

    Non-standard size: _____

    Edge perfs, etc: _____

    Other: (+ Notes): _____

Completed by:_____ Date: _____

Figure 30.3 Form pre-design checklist

printer perforations, lawyers' annotations and so on. We then draw on the paper a series of rectangles, each one relating to our list of items taken in order. The order will have to be changed slightly, as will the sizes of the rectangles, to obtain a good fit. It is usually advisable, even though it takes time, to write in each rectangle the prompt that will appear on the finished form as pre-printed matter. We now have our first draft.

This first draft is now inspected from a number of viewpoints:

- can one improve the 'fit' by changing the order further?
- does the form have a pleasing appearance, and will it make a favourable impression on users?
- is the entry of data easy, especially for typing?
- are the printed prompts clear, unambiguous, suitable for probable users, and concise?
- for multi-part sets and printer use – is registration correct and not over-critical?
- if masking is to be used, check that it is correct.

If a separate set of instructions are needed, this should now be written, ready for a pilot run. The final draft can next be prepared. Depending on circumstances, this can be either a carefully drawn piece of artwork or something not much better than the first draft. If a pilot run or use of special equipment is indicated, then it may be necessary to prepare a draft to a high standard that can be copied as it is for experimental use. If the form is a run-of-the-mill item and the printer is accustomed to working with the designer, then prettification is a waste of effort and time.

D

For the final draft, many people use a form-design guide sheet or guide grid. This is a sheet of paper with an A4 rectangle in the middle, surrounded by spacing indicators and rules. These guides are usually printed feint in pale blue (the printing can then be lost when copied). These guides can be useful, especially if one has an in-house printer, for setting spacings. They can also be used for forms that are so simple that a first draft is not needed, and one can go directly to a final draft.

At this stage, one may have to consider some special factors. If masking is to be used, care must be taken with registration, with the method of use, and the need for training. One of the best examples of masking is the SITPRO set of documents for exports. A booklet on this was first published in 1976 and is a classic for form design.[6] Many firms make use of colour (paper and/or ink) for differentiating copies or usage, but it should be remembered that 15 per cent of males are colour-blind in some way. Where feasible, it may be better to use a large letter or number or sign (60 pt or more).

It is possible to buy packs of ready-printed forms, though these really need overprinting with the user's name and address. A better alternative for a small firm may be to buy a book of form masters.[7] These only need a piece of letterheading pasted on to give a reasonable master, which needs little expenditure of time. Larger organizations may find this route useful for internal forms, when in a hurry.

The final step is to prepare the 'printer's instructions' which tell the printer all the details that are not on the drawn draft. In fact, commercial printers can handle orders accompanied by the roughest of instructions. They often have to. But one does run the danger of not getting what one wanted or expected. One should therefore specify:

- the paper (weight, grade, colour, special characteristics);
- the size of the forms, and any special cutting instructions;
- the type (size, typeface, borders, cross-hatching and 'printers' ornaments' – a

jumble of print that obscures parts of some copies in a set);
- print colour, logos;
- details of registration;
- numbering of forms, sets and numbering within sets;
- whether forms are to be single sheets, sets, padded (along which edge), fanfolded, tumble printed (reverse printed head to toe), number of parts;
- any perforations, scoring, hole-drilling, glueing;
- method of copying (carbon sheets, 'one-time' carbon, impact, chemical male–female);
- deadline.

It is sometimes necessary to revamp forms that are not needed for immediate use, and a specific control needs to be set up for these. Examples are forms that are only used occasionally (e.g. financial institutions that are at times involved with large share/ Eurobond issues), and forms that are only used in an emergency (airlines need manual forms for use when their computers go down on reservation systems).

All forms change with the passage of time. The bar-coded European passport differs markedly from British passports used during the early part of this century.[8] These consisted of just one piece of paper, which stated simply that the bearer and, say, his (unnamed) niece were desirous of travelling in Europe and that His Britannic Majesty's Principal Secretary of State requested, etc. They were certainly simpler.

References
1 *Management Services*, March 1988, p. 18.
2 *Administrative Forms in Government*, HMSO, Cmnd 8504, February 1982.
3 Article in the *Khaleej Times*, United Arab Emirates, 19 March 1988.
4 Administrative forms in government – Progress Report to the Prime Minister, September 1987.
5 Treweek, C. and Zeitlyn, J., *The Alternative Printing Handbook*, Harmondsworth: Penguin Books, 1983.
6 SITPRO, *Systematic Export Documentation*, HMSO, 1976.
7 Pring, R., *The Instant Business Forms Book*, Harlow: Longman, 1985.
8 *Weekly Guardian*, 7 August, 1988, p. 22.

Other Method Design Aids

He had no problems. He solved everything in his imagination.
Gabriel Márquez, *One Hundred Years of Solitude* (1967)

The great pleasure of ignorance is the pleasure of asking questions.
The man who has lost this pleasure . . . is already beginning to stiffen.
Robert Lynd, *I Was Just Thinking* (1959)

There are several aspects of method design which, though not of universal application, are nevertheless of major impact in the right circumstances. The approaches described are:

D

- problem solving;
- the report matrix;
- time management;
- Q & Ds;
- photography;
- ergonomics.

Problem solving

It should perhaps be admitted that there are some analysts who use one of the problem-solving techniques as their main approach to method design. People who have had extensive training and experience in one of the techniques are certainly adept at getting results in this way. But the techniques are not, in our opinion and experience, an approach that should be used indiscriminately. It is another example of 'horses for courses'.

Most of the problem-solving techniques rely for their success on one's being able to define the problem in the correct (often new) format. Indeed, this very redefinition often leads one semi-automatically or inevitably to a correct solution.

This importance of problem solving has been quoted, for example, by apologists for the work of Sigmund Freud, some of whom emphasize Freud's problem-solving approach to psychoanalysis as opposed to any family, cultural or early belief patterns as a rebuttal to his critics.[1]

One of the most popular of the problem-solving techniques is the one developed by Charles Kepner and Benjamin Tregoe usually called, not unreasonably, the Kepner–Tregoe analysis. This argues that any problem is a deviation from what should be the situation. So any changes in the situation should be examined by comparing what has happened, where it happened, and to what extent matters are different. Having done this, one should have an idea about the cause of the deviation that caused the problem.

Since this may sound somewhat vague as a problem-solving technique, one has to consider the seven formal steps that enable one to arrive at the cause of the problem:

315

1 The analyst has an expected standard of performance, a 'should' against which actual performance may be compared.

2 A problem is a deviation from a standard of performance. Since several problems may exist at the same time, it is necessary to prioritize the problems by degrees of urgency.

3 A deviation from standard has to be precisely identified, located and described. This specification has four dimensions: identity, location, time and extent. At this stage, the analyst will also describe what the problem is not and so draws a boundary around the problem area.

4 There is always something distinguishing that which has been affected by the cause from that which has not. For example, if one is studying food that has gone bad, one has to separate out the characteristics of the bad food from those of the good food.

5 The cause of a problem is always a change that has occurred through a distinctive feature, condition or mechanism that has produced a new and unwanted effect.

6 The possible causes of a deviation are deduced from the relevant changes that are found when analysing the problem.

7 The most likely cause of a deviation is the one that exactly explains all the facts in the specification of the problem. For example, thunderstorms cannot be the reason for food going bad since the two events do not always coincide.

A diagram similar to the one in Figure 31.1 opposite is often used to show the seven steps.

An example of carefully redefining a problem is provided by the case of a new manager in a welfare services department of a large city in the north of England. His main job was the running of the local government's Homeless Family Unit, where wives and children of evicted families could stay until a new home was found. Previous managers had accepted that the problem was one of rehousing homeless families.

The new manager redefined the problem as one of preventing families from becoming homeless. Setting out to find why people became homeless, he found that the main reason was that they were evicted for failing to pay their rent, rather than overcrowding or damage to property. Further, he discovered that the main cause of getting behind with the rent was financial mismanagement.

Having redefined the problem, it was then possible to plan a course of action. In turn, this involved redefining the role of his team. Instead of looking after homeless families they became people who tried to ensure that people who were in danger of losing their home were helped to keep their existing home. This meant at times acting as unofficial rent collectors and as budget advisers. The results were most rewarding: within two years the number of homeless people was a small fraction of what it had been. This result was to everyone's advantage, especially in preventing families from being separated.

Another approach to problem solving is 'PABLA' (Problem Analysis By Logical Approach). This was an extension at the UK Atomic Energy Authority of FDM (Fundamental Design Method), which had been developed at Cranfield. As developed at UKAEA, PABLA was specifically aimed at systems and projects. Its visible result was a series of charts, one of which is shown (adapted) in Table 31.1 opposite.

The approach called 'Synectics' can be used by an individual or by very small groups, but for most people it is a system used for group discussion. The main features of such a discussion or meeting are:

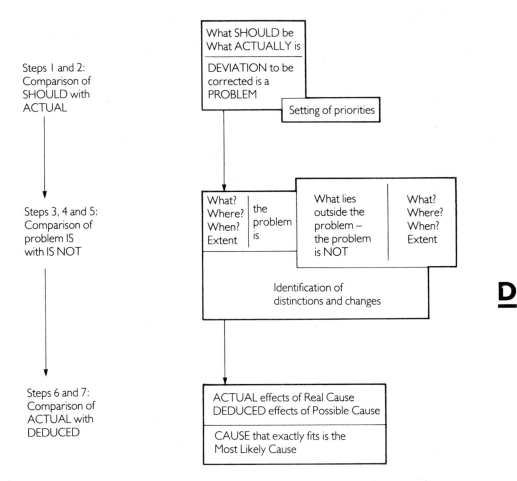

Steps 1 and 2:
Comparison of
SHOULD with
ACTUAL

What SHOULD be
What ACTUALLY is

DEVIATION to be
corrected is a
PROBLEM

Setting of priorities

Steps 3, 4 and 5:
Comparison of
problem IS
with IS NOT

| What?
Where?
When?
Extent | the
problem
is | What lies
outside the
problem –
the problem
is NOT | What?
Where?
When?
Extent |

Identification of
distinctions and changes

D

Steps 6 and 7:
Comparison of
ACTUAL with
DEDUCED

ACTUAL effects of Real Cause
DEDUCED effects of Possible Cause

CAUSE that exactly fits is the
Most Likely Cause

Figure 31.1 The seven steps of problem analysis

1 The meeting is specifically called to solve a problem, in the sense of inventing new solutions.

2 The control of the meeting is in the hands of a leader who does not take part in the discussion but who is there only to control the process.

3 A problem is considered from the point of view of the individual who has to deal with it. The entire meeting is geared towards helping this individual. Where several people are involved in different aspects of the same problem, then the role of 'client' is rotated.

4 Unlike Kepner–Tregoe, no attempt is made to redefine the problem, the 'client's' description of the problem is taken as the start point. The group instead restate the problem in a language of 'how to' statements (in the language of synectics, these 'how to' statements are called 'goals' but we prefer to reserve this word for its usual meaning). These statements can be as unrealistic or speculative as the group wishes. Their purpose is to open up the problem and give the 'client' a chance of getting away from the original way of looking at it.

Table 31.1 PABLA chart

Usage	Influences	Resources
Occasion When is it to be used? Special occasions? When something else is happening?	**Environment** Where might it be used in addition?	**Previous designs** Have we designed one before? Has someone else designed one?
Duration How long will it be in use/ last for? How short a use? Working life?	**Law and Security** Any legal constraints or requirements? Any security aspects to be considered?	**Existing Equipment** What existing equipment *can* we use? What existing equipment *must* we use?
Frequency How often?	**Policies** Are there fixed ideas? Standards to be maintained?	**Services** Power, data, information, databases, air, extract, input.
Sequence After something else has happened? Before something else has happened?	**Test and Install** Will it need testing? How do we install it? Who tests? Who installs?	**Experience** Who has done it before? Who might have to do it again? Who this time?
Operators Who will use it? What skills have they? Who must not use it? What skills must be taught?	**Time scale** Finish by a target date at all cost? Is it routine? Is it dependent on external influences?	
Maintenance Will maintenance need to be made automatic?	**Finance** Who controls it? How is it controlled? How much will it cost?	
Acceptability Will it cause difficulties? Will staff have faith in its accuracy, reliability, etc.?	**Completion** What facilities are required for completion? Will it have to go somewhere else for completion?	

5 Ideas are then sought of achieving the 'how to' statements. All ideas are allowed. Each one is paraphrased and developed. It is then evaluated by identifying its good points and then its deficiencies. Thus one does not dismiss an idea by saying that 'it is too expensive' but by asking 'How could we do this within our cost limits?' The sense may be the same, but the effect is different.

6 By evaluating ideas in this oblique way, good ideas are identified which can then be

processed by finding ways to overcome their deficiencies. A 'possible solution' is one that the 'client' accepts as being new and one that he is willing to pursue.

7 At any time (especially if the group is losing momentum) the leader can create an 'excursion'. An excursion is a deliberate move into the world of metaphor and fantasy. This creates fresh imaginative material which is then applied to the original problem by a process known as a 'force fit'. This may help to provide a solution.

The leader tries to ensure that everybody with something to contribute to the discussion makes the contribution. The leader also tries to discourage the over-talkative or time-hogger. But the leader is not a participant in the sense of putting forward ideas (not always easy). The leader is a referee, not a player.

A fourth problem-solving approach is the heuristic approach. This is an approach of some antiquity. The original aim of heuristics was to study the methods and ideas of discovery. Descartes (1598–1650) made a study of problem solving and wrote part of the result in *Rules for the Direction of the Mind*. Leibnitz (1646–1716) was interested in the heuristic and wrote the incomplete *Art of Invention*. In a treatise on logic, Bernard Bolzano (1781–1848) devoted nearly 300 pages on heuristic. To bring the concept rather more up to date, some people see heuristic as being the logical successor to expert systems when that technique has run its course. The heuristic approach follows the following pattern:

D

1 Decide and describe the sort of solution that is being sought (e.g. eliminating mailroom overtime).
2 Calculate a result from the existing data
   or
   Postulate a major change that seems to lead towards the goal.
3 Is the result of the calculation or the change 'anything like' the solution being sought?
4 Recalculate another result from the data
   or
   Add an additional change that seems to lead further towards the solution sought.
5 Are we nearer the solution sought?
6 Repeat steps 4 and 5 until the rate of improvement slows down.
7 Is it possible to take one final leap that takes us still further towards the solution sought?

As a technique, the heuristic may need considerable self-control. When carried out on a computer, it is often possible to go through a large number of iterations in a relatively short time. It is useful in situations where an analytical approach is not applicable, or where nobody has ever worked in a particular area and found a solution.

The report matrix

Managers and others often get reports that they do not use. Admittedly, this is sometimes because they need training in how to use the reports effectively, but more often it is because the reports are not doing their job properly of helping the recipients.

It is rather pointless to give reports to people that they do not want. And if there are reports that virtually nobody wants/needs, it is pointless to produce them at all. It is therefore a good plan to review the reports produced with the objectives of:

Review of Reports

Title of report	Value of report					Comments (Anything you like – e.g. appearance, size, frequency, duplication, timing, etc.)
	1	2	3	4	5	

In putting a value on the reports you
get, please ask yourself the question:

> Could I do my job effectively without
> getting this information in this way?

Figure 31.2 Review of reports

- ensuring that people get the information relevant to their needs and responsibilities;
- eliminating or reducing data collation, computation, report preparation and distribution;
- reducing 'noise' in the organization's systems – which is what unused reports are.

A list is prepared of reports that are distributed. To prevent the list becoming unmanageably long, it is usually advisable to use separate lists for each department (this also facilitates analysis and discussion). These lists are then transferred to a purpose-drawn form (Figure 31.2). A covering letter is prepared describing the study and also referring to a five-point scale that one wishes people to use.

This is the usual scale. For example:

| 1 = Report rarely used/information duplicated elsewhere. I would prefer not to receive it in the future. |
| 2 = Sometimes useful. Not essential to receive copies, provided I know where to access the data quickly. |
| 3 = Occasionally quite useful. I would prefer to continue receiving this report. |
| 4 = A good tool. I want to continue receiving this report. |
| 5 = A key document. It would be difficult to achieve my job objectives without it. |

D

A summary of the responses will show immediately which reports can be dropped and which ones need a change in frequency. The space for comments is particularly useful, since this may release many opinions that were previously dammed up for a long time.

An added sophistication is to put a price of production against each report; in effect, one is then asking, 'Is this report worth £50 a month to you?'

Advantages of this piece of work are:

- better information distribution;
- people are involved and can see their preferences and wishes translated quickly into positive action;
- money is saved quickly and at low cost;
- it can be used (when appropriate) as a good way of meeting managers or other groups that one does not know well, in a helpful non-emotional atmosphere.

When used in a European major oil company, this simple 'technique' resulted in the elimination of 36 per cent of all computer records circulated. It is definitely recommended for widespread use.

Executive time management

One often sees magazine articles or seminar advertisements that start with the words, 'Time is an executive's most important commodity', or something similar. In the face of this universal agreement it is surprising that, firstly, there has been little progress in improvements and, secondly, there is little agreement on what to do about it.

One book puts the emphasis on improving one's life style: 'Is it a waste of time to listen to your child's pop record collection?' One book wants busy managers to complete ten forms and keep them up-dated. A third book suggests that Zen Buddhism provides the right technique. In the early 1980s many executives could be seen lugging around 'personal organizers' – a sort of analytical diary that was too big to put into one's pocket. One can buy microcomputer software that promises much the same.

The fact is that many executives' style of working is a reflection of their personal characteristics and habits. These will not be changed easily. Moreover, many executives feel that pressure and strain is a necessary price to pay for being a success. They will only be receptive to taking action when they reach an insufferable level of pressure, or when a group of executives agree to take joint action.

Our own greatest successes in helping executives depended to a major degree on what can only be called counselling – by means of three or four fairly brief meetings. Since, of itself, that statement is of minimal practical help, three approaches are given below. The correct approach depends on how busy or pressured the executive is. A common phrase is 'The urgent drives out the important.' Or, in the words of the well-known notice, 'It is difficult to remember that one's primary objective is to drain the swamp when one is up to one's neck in alligators.'

The first approach is based on an analysis of how an executive actually spends his time. The most satisfactory way to do this is to use an electronic random analyser. One example is the 'Parameter' machine. This is a small box that sits on the executive's desk and which emits a buzz randomly, say five times an hour. When the machine buzzes, the executive touches the box with a plunger against a pre-agreed code, indicating what he was doing at the time. In our experience this machine has a very high degree of acceptability among executives, probably because it takes so little time to use each time.

The results from the Parameter can be analysed on a microcomputer in a multitude of ways, e.g., meetings with superior/telephone call initiated by customer/deciding overdraft increase. Other, though less satisfactory, ways of collecting information are to ask the executive to keep a diary-log, to mark a pre-printed form, to ask an analyst to do an activity sample, or even to get a secretary to record the manager's activities.

Whatever the method of collecting the data, at the end one has an analysis of the executive's activities usually expressed in percentage terms. For example:

Meetings – with superior	– just two of us	6%
	– departmental	4%
	– plus customer	3%
	– plus other department	5%
Meetings – with staff	– regular weekly	7%
	– personal	5%
	– projects	4%
	– training	3%

This analysis could be referred to by the number of analysis heads, and in the above example would be '1 × 2 × 4'. The maximum ever used is 12 × 12 × 12 and even this is only used for special purposes.

The analysis is then discussed with the executive, to see what changes and improvements should be made. Quite often, the analysis itself will be a revelation on its own. An action plan is prepared to help effect the changes that are seen to be needed. An alternative usage is to compare the analyses of a group of executives. This may reveal that certain factors are affecting sub-groups in different ways. For example, bank managers knew before such a study that managers of country branches had to work differently from those of town branches. What they did not know was exactly how the differences manifested themselves – though even in this case, the managers concerned were agreed in their opinion that management style of individual managers caused even more differences.

The analysis can also be used for a distinct group of executives to act as a peer group. In this approach, the print-outs are then inspected by all the participants. Discussions that follow act as powerful incentives to change, because of peer pressure (care must be taken to prevent the discussions becoming too personal or heated). This approach is popular in Sweden, where it has been used to great effect. Organizations in other parts of the world may find it too nerve-racking.

A very different approach is to use a simple-looking questionnaire which can be completed either by each executive, or by the consultant while discussing the situation with an executive. The first way is quicker but the second way gives more information and is much more supportive. The form lists just twelve of the commonest causes of time-management problems and asks the executive to rate each one for himself and his work. The rating is usually done by asking the executive to mark his personal response on a scale for each factor:

D

No problem

Overwhelming problem

The factors used (and their expansion) are:

Meetings	Too long; poorly chaired; too many; inconclusive; preparation time too short
Telephone calls	Too many; too long; technical difficulties
Interruptions	Too many people coming in unexpectedly; too lengthy
Too much reading	Too much paperwork; too many reports
Information	Unavailability of information when needed and/or in the form needed
Working hours	Too many hours spent working; too much work taken home in the evenings and at weekends
Over-reaching	Not allowing enough time to complete tasks/projects
Delegation	Doing work that should be done by subordinates
Procrastination	Not doing today's work today
Crises	Unexpected crises arising that prevent normal work being completed on time
Disorganization	Poor work organization within the firm
Own office	Poor information retrieval or filing; substandard secretarial help; poor self-organization and planning.

This approach is straightforward and appeals to many executives. There is no sense of criticism. However, it does need a good covering letter and/or an understanding and sympathetic consultant, otherwise it does not achieve impact. A discussion follows the questioning, and an action plan is prepared for improvement – accompanied by specific ideas that will help.

The third approach is to use a discussion at which one talks to the executive about his or her problems. Unless one knows the executive very well beforehand, one cannot just ask, 'Well, John, what are your problems?' Instead, one starts off with some general points about time management and its problems. One then asks if the executive has enough time for:

- long-term planning;
- dealing with staff personnel problems;
- studying all the reports;
- a home life;
- meetings, etc.

One tries not to make the meeting a question-and-answer affair. Instead one judges which matters are particularly hard and explores these with supplementary points. At the same time, one observes the 'style' of working – many visitors and telephone calls, leaping from one task to another, and so on. On the basis of two such meetings, a plan of action (plus practical ideas) can then be suggested.

Considerable research has been carried out on the work of executives. So we know that:

- executives spend a major part of their working lives in 'meetings'. Depending on the organization, this can vary from 25–70 per cent;
- many executives feel that they have too much reading but at the same time they feel that they need better information;
- executives suffer from many interruptions: on average they are likely to go only 12–19 minutes before there is another interruption;
- few executives think that they have enough time for strategic matters;
- most executives accept their hours of work (about fifty-five hours per week including weekends);
- most executives feel that they are reasonably good at their job, but would welcome some help to become better.

Better time management therefore often relies on doing two 'simple' things better. The first is improving the meetings in an organization. The second is ensuring that the Management Information System really does help people to do their job better. Neither of these improvements is revolutionary or novel – but their pay-back can be massive.

There are some other practical ideas that will help. The commonest one is also one of the simplest. This is the 'Priority 6 card'. One asks an executive to write down the (up to) six most important things that he or she must do the next day. The notes can be written on a small piece of card, or on a pre-printed form, or on a 3M 'Post-it' note, whatever the executive prefers; the important thing is to make it a habit. This piece of paper can either be written during the day or last thing. Next day, the executive crosses out the items as they are completed (some people like to put the six points in priority).

This simple habit has many advantages. It prevents some vital item from slipping out of one's memory. Crossing off the items gives a sense of achievement and activity. It helps prevent the urgent from driving out the important. Many years ago, a cabinet minister was prevailed upon to adopt this system. He claimed another advantage – it annoyed his adviser.

Other ideas will apply only in certain cases, namely when an executive feels able to live with them:

- ban portable telephones for all but junior staff;
- establish a 'safe house' – 'a room without a phone away from the office where the chief executive cannot be reached and where he can stay in peace for an hour (much longer than that and the system breaks down);
- learn the technique of 'rapid reading';
- move your microcomputer out of your office. Have it moved into the secretary's office and have the secretary trained to a high standard of competence in its use. If you cannot bear to part with your micro, take a course in touch-typing;
- institute a twelve-minute meeting scheduled for first thing every morning to sort out likely problems for the day;
- ban breakfast meetings. They are usually bad for both results and digestion.

Finally, remember that you are only here for seventy years and may not be coming back again – so be assertive with the professional time-waster.

D

Q & Ds

'Q&D' stands for 'quick and dirties' – actions that can be taken to improve the office but which do not take long. Examples of Q & Ds are:

- join together the mailroom/internal messengers/external messengers/internal mail/security into one unit, and schedule the individuals' work for optimum effectiveness;
- blitz the sales ledger. Reduce the outstanding debts, collect debts on the due date, do not allow discounts after the due date;
- reduce the stock levels (installing a completely new computerized stock control system definitely does not qualify as a Q & D);
- check the possibility of single sourcing for office supplies (lower stocks, faster service and better discounts – but watch the base price levels);
- reduce the overtime;
- if there are more than six secretaries, introduce a pool or else sharing;
- check the economics of in-house v. bought-in services, especially transport and printing;
- replace tea-persons with vending machines;
- reduce the number of restaurants;
- check the cost of paper and get it for less;
- use cash-in-hand better. A trade union had not revised its investments for five years, and had every branch maintain its own current account. Together, these two factors had led it to having one year's subscriptions in cash at the bank;
- install a telephone logging machine, known as a 'call-management system'.

At one time call management used to be for large organizations only. The introduction of machines for one- and two-line use tapped a large market for domestic use: middle-class parents hoping to encourage their teenage children from over-indulgence in making excessive use of the telephone. Whatever the reason, this brought the price of smaller machines down. Call logging does much more than just save money. It enables an organization to plan and fine-tune much of its telecommunications facilities.

Photography

Photography is not a 'technique' as such, but is used as an aid to a variety of techniques. The main forms of photography that are used are still, ciné and video.

■ STILL PHOTOGRAPHY

Uses of still photography in the office are:

- security passes. For this, it is usual to use instant photographs ('Polaroid'). These are much more expensive than conventional film but more convenient – issuing a security pass can be completed in a matter of minutes,
- as a way of showing present, proposed and alternative layouts, systems and methods. Such photographs can be used for comparison purposes. Even more frequently, they are used for showing to management and staff – both as an aid to making decisions and as an aid to the investigator when trying to persuade people of the value and correctness of the proposals;
- to improve and shorten staff training;
- to record standard layouts and methods. The photographs can be mounted on Standard Practice Instructions (SPIs). Similarly, they can show quality standards;
- as an aid to ergonomics studies;
- as a matter of record;
- as an aid to communicating ideas and information. The commonest use is still probably for staff newsletters.

Because of the format's convenience, cameras for office use should normally be 35 mm with interchangeable lenses. The equipment and ancillaries are easily obtainable, light in weight, relatively unobtrusive, and quick and easy to use. The camera should be auto-exposure and auto-focus, and used with a hot-shoe adjustable battery flash. These specifications would not be the choice of a professional photographer, whose aim may be to obtain high-quality results for advertising purposes. But that is not our aim here.

■ CINÉ AND VIDEO

Ciné (16 mm) and video can be used in the office for many purposes:

- training. Filming is very useful for training, especially for training in new methods and in using equipment. It demonstrates the ideal method without variability. The person being trained gets an excellent view, and does not get so flustered. It is often an ideal step between theoretical training and actually doing the task. When used for training, the film is often made into a continuous loop, so that it can be shown repeatedly;
- memomotion. Ciné film is shot at 16 or 24 pictures per second. Memomotion is shot at 1 or 2 frames per second. When viewed at normal speed of projection, the effect is of activities being speeded up by a factor of say 16 times. This reveals an overall view of movements and patterns of work. At even slower shooting speeds (typically one frame every 7½, 15, 30 or 60 seconds) filming is used for activity sampling. At 4

frames per second, film can be used in ergonomics studies;

- the opposite effect results from shooting at 64, 96 or even more frames per second. This slow-motion effect is used for analysing awkward movements, detecting faults in equipment, and setting standards in conjunction with existing standard time systems;
- split image. A task or situation is filmed on one half of the film only. A comparative situation is then filmed on the other half of the film. This enables a direct comparison to be made between two alternatives;
- straight recording. Ciné and video are an ideal way of making a record. This can be of anything from an old office layout to a retirement party;
- persuading. A well-made film can demonstrate with impact that a proposed method will really work in practice.

Films made in-house rarely compare favourably with those produced professionally, even when made on expensive equipment and facilities. For some purposes this does not matter (e.g. memomotion analysis). When used for more prestigious purposes, such as institutional advertising, the disparity matters – and it shows. Examples have been observed where enthusiasm has outrun ability.

For most purposes, video and ciné are equally appropriate. However, video can present problems of compatibility. One international company had to maintain banks of players for different systems. A multinational audit firm had to equip its offices in different countries with a single system. Even when made on the same system (NTSC/PAL/SECAM/DM) copies can give problems. Incompatibility is seen on the screen as multiple images, simultaneous loss of colour and sound, and by a bending distortion of the picture. A player with a variable tracking facility reduces but does not always completely eliminate these difficulties.

D

Ergonomics

Ergonomics is the study of work, environment and conditions related to the person doing the work. Perhaps a better description would be fitting the task to the person instead of fitting the person to the work. An example that is often given is the lathe in a factory that ideally needed a person to be 1.3 m tall with an arm span of 2.6 m. In the office we are mostly concerned with the environment (see chapter 28), and with the design of equipment and furniture.

Ergonomics is another of those techniques that after an active spell (in the 1950s and early 1960s) went into an unaccountable decline, only to be revived more recently. The revival may be due to advertising agencies, who rarely fail to call their clients' keyboards 'ergonomically designed'. Whether this is so or not, it has helped to demonstrate that the decline was unwarranted; few of us have escaped having to use chairs and desks that we soon realized were badly designed.

One of the best-known drawings in the world is Leonardo da Vinci's diagram of the relative dimensions of the human body, in which he drew a man with his arms outstretched contained within a circle. His study of human anatomy was profound (in 1510 he wrote, '. . . I think I will finish all this anatomy'). He also wrote on human effort, such as, 'Pushing and pulling can be done along diverse lines around the centre of the power of the mover . . .' (Codex M II). Five hundred years later we still have office desks that are too high. The working surface of an ordinary desk should be 71 cm from the floor. Desks for a keyboard should be 65–66 cm high. But some desks are still as much as 75 cm high. This leads many keyboard users to adopt what is called the 'crow' position for the hands.

Suggested standards are as follows (all dimensions in centimetres):

Office desks	
Working surface height	71
Working surface	110 × 70
Knee space: height	66 (min.)
width	60 (min.)
depth	60 at floor, 45 at top (min.)

Keyboard desks	
Working surface height	65
L-extension surface	75 × 40 (min.)
Working surface for microcomputer	120 × 85

Office chairs	
Seat height	40–50 adjustable (43 if fixed).
Seat width	40 (min.)
Seat depth	38 (min.)
Width of backrest	30 (min.)
Height of backrest	10–20
Backrest top to seat	40 (min.)
Backrest base to seat	20 (min.)
Backrest slope to seat	95°–105°
Backrest curvature	30–45 (radius)

The difference between seat height and office desk for normal working should be about 28 cm. For keyboard operation, the difference should be closer to 23 cm.

Keyboard chairs	
Seat height	38–48 adjustable (42 if fixed).
Width of backrest	30–36
Height of backrest	10–15
Arm rests	Never

Other dimensions as for ordinary office chairs.

Drafting stools	
Seat height	75
Height of footrest	30
Depth of footrest	8 (min.)
Seat tilt	30°

Other measurements

Ramps should be 15°, though up to 20° is reasonable.

Stairs should incline at 30°–45° (20°–50° is reasonable).
They should have a rise of 17–19 cm (20 cm max.), a tread depth of 24–28 cm and a nosing not exceeding 4 cm. Hand-rails should be 85 cm above the treads, with a maximum diameter of 4¾ cm.

In shelving, the top shelf should not be higher than 195 cm.

Counters should be 100 cm high with a 10 × 10 minimum kickroom.

A working surface for sorting mail into pigeonholes, etc. should be 100 cm high.

Using both arms and normal body bending, the arm reach for comfortable working is 140 cm wide by 100 cm high when standing (110 cm wide by 80 cm high when seated).

Further details can be found in additional publications. Office furniture is covered in a BSI publication,[2] equipment operation in a book by Woodson,[3] general matters in Murrell's classic.[4]

VDUs are covered in *Visual Display Terminals*[5] – a book that has provided a basis for several union–management agreements. Human body dimensions are given in the Appendix.

References

1 Gay, P., *Freud: A Life for Our Time*, New York: Norton, 1988.
2 BSI, *Specification for Office Desks, Tables and Seating* (B.S. 3893), London: British Standards Institution, 1965.
3 Woodson, W. E., *Human Engineering Guide for Equipment Designers*, Cambridge: Cambridge University Press.
4 Murrell, K. F. H., *Ergonomics, Man and His Working Environment*, London: Chapman & Hall, 1965.
5 Cakir, A., Hart and Stewart (based), *Visual Display Terminals*, Chichester: John Wiley & Sons, 1980.

D

Work Quantification

32

Introduction to Work Quantification

> Time is the measure of business, as money is of wares.
>
> **Francis Bacon, *Of Dispatch* (1625)**

> For tribal man space was the uncontrollable mystery. For
> technological man it is time that occupies the same role.
>
> **Marshall McLuhan, *The Mechanical Bridge* (1951)**

The basic aim of work quantification is to answer the straightforward question, 'How long should it take to do this task?' In offices, one usually takes this a stage further to answer the question, 'How many people are needed to do this group of tasks?' This is an important question. In every organization, an attempt is made (consciously or sub-consciously) to attain a balance between two objects:

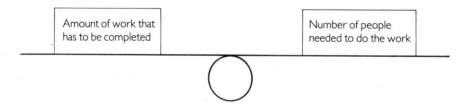

| Amount of work that has to be completed | Number of people needed to do the work |

This question has always been important – which is why there are so many historical references to it. The Bible refers to tasks to be done in a day, ancient Egypt and Rome had times for copying documents, armies all had standard marching times, the medieval church had project control times for building monasteries (though not for cathedrals, which may be why they often took centuries to complete). However, most of the historical references are of little use to us today. Firstly, the actual timings have rarely been handed down. Secondly, since offices in the modern sense did not arrive until the nineteenth and twentieth centuries, historical references do not apply to our current situation.

Nevertheless, the past can teach us some lessons and can also show us that the problems that we face have been faced before. One example comes from the Punic wars between Rome and Carthage for control of the Mediterranean (264–241 BC). Rome's newly built fleet was victorious at the battle of Mylae (260 BC). A question that long baffled historians was how the Roman fleet was built so quickly. On the face of it, some very advanced form of project control and administration had to be involved. It was not until the mid-1980s that the question was answered when a well-preserved ship was discovered (it can now be viewed in a museum in Sicily). It transpired that 'management' had introduced a major method design change before undertaking the project. Ships were normally built by first fabricating the ribcage (this needed skill and accuracy) and then adding the planking round the cage to make the shell. The Punic ship was built the other way round: a shell was built and the inside cage consisted of strengthening struts nailed into place. This was fast, though the resulting ships were not as strong. One is reminded of the Liberty ships built at speed by the Americans during the 1939–45 war.

One is also reminded of a common argument that is still unresolved. Should method design always precede work quantification? Purists insist that it should. They argue that there is no point in trying to measure work unless one first ensures that the work is being done in the best way. The purists are quite right; from a theoretical viewpoint, there is no doubt that work quantification should follow method improvements. In practice, however, it does not always happen. There are several reasons for this, some good and some bad. For example, it may be necessary to quantify work before deciding to introduce major new advanced technology – to get accurate costings and to help in the actual decision. At other times, management may want accurate management controls which are often impossible to install without work quantification. The dissatisfaction felt with traditional forms of management accounting in the 1980s needed work quantification studies to improve accuracy. Bad reasons for ignoring method improvement are impatience by management in achieving results and poor reputation of the internal 'O & M' department in improving methods. Purists may remain unconvinced, especially if they take a moral stand. The rest of us, while still maintaining that we are not immoral, will go along with the wishes of management – though if we think that they are wrong, we will do our best to convince them otherwise.

E

Like the Punic fleet builders, ships were the major concern of the Arsenal at Venice in the sixteenth century. The Venetian Arsenal is widely known to students of management since it brought together in one place so many of the techniques of management. The book-keeping and cost accounting resulted in good management accounts/management information system. Also present were merit rating, job specialization, assembly lines, standardization and the F. W. Taylor system of supervision and measurement. The use of measurement enabled the managers to achieve what is nowadays known as 'line of balance' – the balancing of groups of people in the right numbers so that the work progressed smoothly without bottlenecks. This is one of the aims of office work quantification. On one famous occasion, Henry III of France visited the Arsenal in 1574. A galley was prepared, launched and armed completely in one hour.[1] One writer, referring to the Arsenal, wrote, 'Underlying the problems of accounting were problems of observation and measurement, systems analysis, model construction, and decision theory – all necessitated by the early manager's quest for accurate records to be used in decision making.'[2] This is a quest we are still pursuing.

Like so many management techniques, work quantification reflects the state of society at the time. For example, in 1793 the person responsible for quantifying the work in a china manufacturer in Derby had to swear an oath of allegiance to the owner. He had to swear to be as accurate as possible (which is still necessary). But he also had to swear to do his best to prevent the employees from finding out that they were being measured or timed. Fortunately, the position is the opposite now. None of the techniques or results are kept hidden from the staff. Indeed, staff representatives or union representatives are usually invited to the same training courses that are used to train the people that will do the quantification. They receive the same training. (And we have trained people working for the Trades Union Congress at Congress House.) This openness is a gain, never a loss.

The turn of the eighteenth century saw work quantification being widely applied in manufacturing. The example most often quoted in the literature is pin-making, where competition made cost reduction imperative. The commonest route to cost reduction was 'division of labour' or specialization in tasks performed. This was described by Adam Smith in his book, *An Enquiry into the Nature and Causes of the Wealth of Nations*, first published in 1776:

> One man draws out the wire, another straights it, a third cuts it, a fourth points it, a fifth grinds it . . . it is even a trade by itself to put them into the paper.[3]

A picture of a pin-making assembly line was presented in Diderot's Encyclopaedia,[4] published 1751 to 1772, reproduced in a book by Professor Galbraith two hundred years later.[5] Pin-making efficiency depended on specialization – something that has exercised the minds of managers for thousands of years. It is still a problem in office work quantification today. How specialized should we ask people to become? On the face of it, extreme specialization should lead to greatest efficiency provided the measurements are accurate and we can attain a good line of balance. (It also makes the measurement itself easier in many cases.) Doubts about this approach were voiced by social researchers, who found that withdrawing from extreme specialization often actually increased productivity. Computers and new technology have tended to act as pressure towards more specialization. It may therefore need a certain amount of skill to strike the right balance.

By the 1840s, work quantification had become a technique used by the British government. During the famine in Ireland, public works were operated by the Board of Works under the direction of the Treasury. Work quantification was used in many cases to determine either wages or food allocation – in the circumstances a somewhat harrowing experience. This is shown by the Board of Works engineer who told the head of the Treasury, 'As an engineer I am ashamed of allotting so little task-work for a day's wages, while as a man I am ashamed of requiring so much.'[6] Today, we must still remember that work quantification concerns above all the people being studied.

That was during the 1846 winter. Meanwhile, Charles Babbage had been mentally bringing together those components of administration that were to lead to the movement known as 'scientific management'. Many people know about Charles Babbage, though for different reasons. Medical doctors know him as the inventor of an early and unsuccessful form of the ophthalmoscope. Techies know of his early work on a form of digital computer. But in commercial circles, he is best known for one of his books on management. This was *On the Economy of Machinery and Manufactures*, first published in 1832. Even during his lifetime, this book was an outstanding success: the first edition of 3,000 copies sold out in two months. Babbage proposed a number of means for attaining effective manufacturing and administration. These included:

1 Use time study (a work quantification technique).
2 Analyse processes and costs.
3 Use printed standard forms.

4 Use inter-firm comparisons.

5 Use various tints of paper and ink colours.

6 Determine how best to frame questions.

7 Use a suggestion scheme, for 'every person connected with it should derive more advantage from applying any improvement he might discover'.[7]

Time study usage spread to offices, though not everywhere. When F. W. Taylor wrote a series of articles for the *American Magazine* in 1911, readers sent in a large number of questions. These questions, with appropriate answers, were published in a book written by Frank B. Gilbreth in 1912. One of these questions was, 'Can Scientific Management be applied to office work, i.e. work that is mostly mental work?' Gilbreth's answer in the book was:

> Yes, there are many cases where it has been as effective as in the shop or on the job. On work of repetitive character we have, in several instances, doubled the amount of output per clerk, and shortened the working hours. We have never seen the case where higher wages, greater output, and lower costs have not resulted where an office force operated under Scientific Management.[8]

Nowadays, the position is slightly different. Work quantification in offices is widespread, especially in North America and in Western Europe. Most international financial institutions that one works for have a form of work quantification, nearly always based on work measurement. Management, staff and unions accept it as a normal part of everyday life and are often knowledgeable about it. This has two good effects. Work quantification is readily acceptable in offices (even more than twenty years ago) – and analysts must install it properly and accurately.

There are many reasons for the introduction of work quantification into an office, some of them highlighted by the brief historical notes given above. The reasons include:

1 To ensure a greater degree of equity and equality. Our society considers it wrong that one office worker should have too little to do while another has too much work. Such imbalances are usually historically based rather than a matter of deliberate policy and are not always easy to recognize or rectify without the use of some form of measurement.

2 As a basis for planning. For example, one of the world's main manufacturers of domestic appliances found that sales were cyclic with an upward trend, as shown in Figure 32.1. Extra office staff were required every two years or so. The precise

E

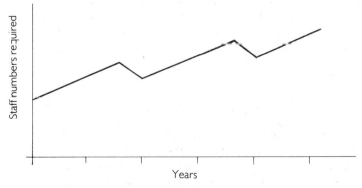

Figure 32.1 Cyclical staffing requirements

numbers required were difficult to state or predict until office work quantification was introduced throughout the offices.

3 As a basis for costing. Capital expenditure per person in offices still lags behind that in factories in most organizations. While this is so, people costs will remain an important component of costs, accounting systems and overhead allocations. Work quantification greatly increases the accuracy attained. This is of particular import-ance where the management accounting or management information system is felt to be lacking in the level of accuracy needed.

In a similar way, work quantification may be introduced as a basis for manage-ment controls and/or as one of the components of an executive information system.

4 As an aid to cost reduction. Cost effectiveness can often be improved by the better allocation of staff. And the only way of accurately allocating staff is by way of work quantification. In practice, cost reduction is probably the commonest initial reason for the introduction of the various work measurement programmes.

5 As an aid to method design. Many of the areas of method design are overwhelmingly enhanced by the use of work quantification. Examples are peaks and troughs, bottlenecks and the introduction of new technology. A unusual example concerned a company that wanted to introduce a new service to the market. This new service involved selling data from a large but changing databank. The company wished to know which would be cheaper: to use a computer interrogation system or to use a 'manual' approach. Work quantification was therefore carried out on the two competing approaches – both of which only existed in the imagination.

In a similar way, work quantification can be used for predictive purposes in any major systems changes.

Work quantification can be used for a number of other purposes, such as assisting job evaluation or training schemes. However, in practice such uses tend to be useful by-products rather than a primary reason. The primary reasons still tend to be planning staff levels or a route towards greater cost effectiveness.

A distinction is drawn between work quantification and work measurement. Work quantification tends to be used in the sense of any approach that enables one to define the quantity of work to be done. Work measurement implies actually being able to state the work content of a task or group of tasks accurately and objectively.

A common phrase that is used is to say that the time for tasks can be of two types: these are 'do-take' and 'should-take' times. The difference is important. For example, an insurance company may have a group of people concerned with new policies. These policies may be single premium, whole life or endowment with profits. The pattern shown in Table 32.1 has been recorded. A straightforward calculation shows that the number of people for 100,000 new policies is as follows:

Single premium	– 4
Whole life	– 6
Endowment with profit	– 16

In one sense, the staffing levels have been quantified. The manager of the department might even be congratulated for holding the staffing to the 'correct' level in the third year. But in fact all that has been done is to calculate how many staff are employed at varying mixes of work. The 'standards' are only 'do-take' standards. They may bear no resemblance to the numbers that should have been employed over the three-year

Table 32.1

Year	Number of policies initiated			Number of staff in department
	Single premiums	Whole Life	Endowment + profit	
1914	300,000	50,000	200,000	47
1915	115,000	40,000	250,000	47
1916	115,000	30,000	260,000	48

period. That can only be ascertained by actually measuring the work content of the three types of policy. Doing so would enable the firm to decide the 'should-take' times for the different policies and hence the correct staffing levels.

In case it is thought that no company would try to set standards on such arithmetic evidence, it should be pointed out that the above example is based on an historical event. The company concerned later turned to work measurement for standards setting. After a decade of work measurement (which was also a decade of growth in business) the company calculated the impact of measured standards. It calculated that the overall staffing was over a third less than it would have been if it had persisted in using the 'do-take' approach. The trade union involved was happy about the situation since its aim was well-paid staff with assured jobs. In this the union was most successful.

There are a number of approaches that may be encountered in offices that are used for quantifying the work and setting staff levels. These are described in outline below. The more important ones are described in greater detail in the next few chapters.

Historical records

The work that was in the past (or is currently being) performed can be studied by:

- analysing past records (e.g. number of invoices passed);
- analysing the work currently being produced (e.g. the work going through a word-processing centre);
- asking staff to diarize their work by self-recording their actions and work during the day.

It will be realized that the arithmetic example given above falls into this category. Being charitable, certain advantages for this approach are:

- results are achieved at relatively low cost;
- there is minimal staff disturbance;
- the results are acceptable to supervisors since they represent past achievements.

These advantages are greatly outweighed by the disadvantages:

- all existing ineffectiveness and inefficiencies are perpetuated and institutionalized;
- the results are 'do-take' and not 'should-take';
- adequate data is in practice rarely available to make calculations in a reasonable form;

- resulting standards lack precision;
- it is usually very difficult to change standards as and when the procedures change – which happens in every office.

Black book

The black book is a record kept by many supervisors to remind them how long different tasks should take in their section. This is an aid to supervision. Of course, often there is no actual black book; the supervisor may hold all the data mentally – but the phrase 'black book' is used anyway. Experienced supervisors are obviously a good source of information about their section, although some of them are reluctant to admit that they do actually keep a list of task timings.

Black book timings can be important for two reasons. Firstly, in some organizations they can become the *de facto* standards which, though useful, can be difficult to change. Secondly, if the supervisor is co-operative and forward-looking, they can be a useful source of checking an analyst's work measurement – a sort of belt-and-braces check that nothing has been forgotten and that the new standards are reasonable.

The value of black book timings often depends on how conscientious the supervisor is. Some supervisors will be found to have used their personal timings to increase effectiveness over a period of time. Other supervisors may have used them as a bulwark against management and to give themselves an easy life. Fortunately, the second type is rarely met nowadays. The majority of supervisors are knowledgeable and helpful, and will appreciate the fact that an accurate form of work quantification will assist them in their job. It is definitely better for the supervisors to be friends rather than obstructors.

The advantages and disadvantages of black book timings are in general the same as for historical records (above). How much better or worse they are depends on the individual supervisor. It also depends on whether the office treats the supervisor as being 'the senior person present' or whether the job is regarded as being genuinely supervisory in nature.

Short-interval scheduling

The basic idea behind short interval scheduling (SIS) is that the supervisor gives to each office worker a batch of work which should take a specific time to complete – commonly the period is two hours. When the work is completed, it is returned to the supervisor, who then hands over another batch. It is particularly found in offices where the work is repetitive; for example, it is commonly used for computer data preparation.

Clearly, short-interval scheduling depends on the degree of equity of the individual batches that are distributed. Each batch should be equally easy or difficult to complete in the time set. This is particularly important when the rate of batch completion affects the pay of the office employees. In this case, it is usual for individual employees to select for themselves the level at which they wish to work. Thus one person may aim at a 110 per cent target while another person may prefer a 90 per cent target. This does not involve any complex calculations. It is done by each person selecting his or her own level with the option of changing their level at the start of any month (in practice, people usually work up to a standard at which they feel comfortable and then they tend to stick with it for a long period of time). Depending on their level, people will go for the next batch of work at intervals of time that are greater or smaller than the two-hour standard. Thus a person on 109 per cent will complete each batch in 1 hour 50 minutes, while a person on a 92 per cent level will take 2 hours 10 minutes. In case this all sounds rather regimented, it has to be said that in those offices that use this approach the atmosphere is usually quite relaxed. This may be because people feel that they are controlling their own affairs.

Short-interval scheduling plus variable payments is fairly common in North America. Straight SIS has been observed in Australia, Asia and parts of Europe. It is less common in Britain, and has never been observed yet in Eastern Europe.

To be successful over a long period of time, the batches of work must be based on an accurate form of work measurement. This ensures that each batch is equal. The worst situation is where the batches are not equal and the supervisor gives the easier batches to personal favourites. Where this situation is discovered, the best advice is to abandon the SIS until proper measurement can be introduced.

Short-interval scheduling is often quoted as a form of work measurement. It is not. It is a form of work control or work progressing, but not measurement. The advantages of SIS are:

E

- the results are acceptable to supervision;
- it is relatively inexpensive in use;
- fine detail and complex record-keeping are eliminated;
- small variations in desirability of different types of task are averaged out;
- to a marked extent, the office staff feel that the flow of work is under their control.

The disadvantages of short-interval scheduling depend to some extent on how it is set up, but can include:

- to flourish successfully, it needs an open style of relationship between supervisor and staff;
- to avoid problems, it has to be based on accurate work measurement;
- unless the work is repetitive in nature, it can be difficult to install and use;
- differences in new procedures and outputs may not be detected or allowed for.

Time study

Time study is a long-established technique that involves timing a task at the time that it is performed by an office worker, using a stop-watch. Simultaneously with the timing, the analyst makes an assessment of the effective rate of working of the person being observed. This effective rate of working is compared with a standard scale of working. The time actually taken for the task is then converted to a calculated time by using the assessment. For example:

Time actually taken	= 10 minutes
Assessment of working performance	= 95%
Then:	
Calculated time that is set	= $10 \times \frac{95}{100}$
	= 9½ minutes

337

To this calculated time are added certain allowances to cover minor interruptions and personal needs such as rest.

The advantages of time study are:

- it is well-known, understood and well-established;
- it can be used for virtually all types of work, and can handle complexity of operations well;
- on simple, routine jobs the standards can be set relatively quickly;
- the results are precise, when installed by experienced and skilled analysts.

The disadvantages of time study in the office are:

- the analysts using it need to be well trained and skilled;
- it is not accurate for keyboard operations and mental calculations;
- changes in procedures and outputs can cause difficulties unless the original studies and documentation are clearly set out;
- some supervisors distrust what they regard as the subjective nature of the assessments of rate of working;
- in some offices there is an unfavourable reaction to the use of a stop-watch on the part of staff and trade unions.

The last of these disadvantages is one that is usually put forward in the literature. However, at least one piece of research (in Israel) suggested that time study could score higher in staff acceptability than some other approaches.[9]

Activity sampling

Activity sampling is the application of established sampling techniques to work in the office. In use, a number of 'snap-shot' observations are made of people and machines over an extended period of time. At each observation, a note is made of the nature of the activity that is taking place at the time (e.g. writing, calculating, speaking, awaiting work). When the observations have been completed, the percentage of times that a particular activity has been observed is a measure of how often it occurs in the office overall.

These percentages can then be converted into standard times for each task, from which standard staffing levels can be calculated. The mathematics of sampling enables the observer to know how many observations need to be made to attain a specific level of accuracy.

It will be realized that if one merely samples the work that is actually being performed, then we are again in the area of 'do-take' times rather than 'should-take' times. To achieve these, one must either use the time study assessment of rate of working or use predetermined standards as a cross-check (as explained in a later chapter).

The advantages of activity sampling are:

- the level of accuracy is known and can be stated;
- it can be used for both routine and non-routine work;
- it can be applied reasonably quickly;
- there is little interruption to staff activities and hence little unfavourable reaction to its use.

The disadvantages of activity sampling are:

- in practice it is difficult to apply in those situations where there are a large number of different activities going on in the office at the same time;
- unless the results are corrected, they represent 'do-take' times which are not accurate (even though statistically the correct number of observations have been made);
- the mathematical basis is not easy to explain to staff and supervisors;
- supervisors (rather than staff) sometimes find it difficult to accept the results of sampling.

Many organizations use activity sampling to quantify work in their offices. However, most of them use it in conjunction with another technique, especially predetermined standards.

Predetermined motion time systems

The phrase 'predetermined motion time systems' is such a mouthful that this technique is nearly always referred to by the initials 'PMTS'. The basis of PMTS is that in offices people use a restricted group of movements and actions. These include reaching for an object such as a pen, writing, reading, walking, etc. For each of these actions there is a pre-set time allowed as a standard time.

In use, an analyst studies a task and breaks it down into its basic actions such as reading, writing, etc. By applying the standard PMTS times to each of these actions, a total time for the whole task can be built up.

In the examples of times below, one 'MM' means one milliminute; that is a one-thousandth of a minute:

Read a single word silently	– 4 MM
Read 10 words out loud	– 55 MM
Walk one pace	– 9 MM
Type company name and address	– 155 MM
Open and close a zip fastener	– 77 MM

The advantages of PMTS are:

- it does not require an assessment of the rate of working as in time study (it is automatically built-in to the standard times);
- the results between different analysts are consistent. This consistency also holds between different offices which makes it very attractive to organizations that have offices in widespread locations, including internationally;
- there is little interruption to the office work;
- changes in procedures and outputs are handled effectively;
- it is widely held that the results from using PMTS have a high degree of accuracy.

The disadvantages of PMTS are:

- it needs trained and experienced analysts;
- for lengthy procedures, some PMTS systems are time-consuming to apply;

E

- a few types of work (such as dealing with the public) are difficult to cover;
- interruptions to the work flow are not accurately included, if PMTS is used by itself.

PMTS systems are widely used in offices; in fact currently PMTS is probably the most widely used technique for office work measurement.

Synthetics

Synthesis is the build-up of standard times for tasks by adding together times for parts of the task from various sources. The 'various sources' are collectively known as synthetics. In theory, synthetics are very useful for calculating times for office machinery such as photocopiers. In practice the situation is not straightforward. Synthetics have proved of considerable use in factories, for example in 'speed and feed' times for lathes, where they are the rule rather than the exception.

However, in offices they have had a less powerful impact. One reason is historic. At one time there were readily available tables of synthetics for a range of office equipment. Analysts found that many of them were inaccurate, usually because they were based on rather spurious speeds attained. For example, the theoretical speeds claimed for many computer printers in advertisements are difficult to achieve in practice (a common complaint by technical magazines carrying out test comparisons). This lack of robustness led to a lack of confidence, which in turn led to the synthetics' falling into disuse. This lack of confidence continues to this day. Analysts will still not use the synthetics if they know that they were issued by the manufacturers. Additionally, analysts will not use synthetics unless they know the source of the tables.

This lack of confidence has resulted in alternatives being used:

- a few large organizations build up their own synthetics for use within that organization;
- some analysts use time study on machine operations;
- most PMTS systems are proprietary, and the owners sometimes issue synthetics for machines to be used with their PMTS times. Generally, analysts have much more confidence in these synthetics since they know the source;
- most office equipment usage forms only a small part of an overall task, and so activity sampling can be used for that part of a task. Computer modems are sometimes an exception, and if this is so then analysts will use PMTS times that they have built up themselves.

The lack of confidence on the part of analysts is not misplaced. In factories, synthetics are fine. But in offices the rule is: do not use tables of synthetics unless you know their source or have checked them against practical results.

One final problem with synthetics is the wide range of models available for every type of office machine, and the frequent introduction of new models. This means that tables of synthetics can quickly become incomplete or out of date.

Categorized work values

The basis of the categorized work values technique is that the various tasks in an office are listed in ascending order of the approximate length of time that each task takes to complete. This list is then divided into a number of groups, usually four to eight groups. This division is done in such a way that the times for each item in the group do not differ excessively.

A time for one item in each group is then calculated accurately, usually employing PMTS. This time is called a 'benchmark' and is the time used for all the tasks in the group.

This approach is extremely useful for the situation where an individual office carries out a large number of tasks each month, say 70 to 100 typically. Many organizations have such an office, and setting standards by any other method is excessively time-consuming. It is a technique that will frequently be used, therefore, at least once in any organization that is applying work quantification. It is not a difficult technique to learn but a number of steps have to be followed carefully to be successful. Details are therefore given in a later chapter in this section.

Stages of a study

E

The approach to a work quantification study, like method design, follows the acronym ICICLES. Within this overall scheme, a study will normally include the following stages:

1 Design the system for optimum effectiveness:
- record and examine the existing systems;
- develop and install improved systems.
2 Develop a set of work standards:
- use the appropriate technique(s);
- balance precision needed against cost and time involved;
- calculate times for individual tasks;
- build up standards for jobs/departments;
- calculate staffing levels.
3 Change the organization structure:
- achieve a line of balance;
- eliminate duplication;
- optimize number of levels in the hierarchy.
4 Design a management reporting system:
- designed for specific reporting levels;
- based on work quantification results;
- show a productivity index (e.g. actual v. standard staffing levels);
- include other measures as appropriate (e.g. backlog, level of service).

Finally, install the new reporting system as standard practice and make arrangements for the entire work quantification scheme to be kept up to date and/or updated periodically.

References

1 Lane, F. C., *Venetian Ships and Shipbuilders of the Renaissance*, Baltimore: Johns Hopkins, 1934.
2 George, C. S., *The History of Management Thought*, Englewood Cliffs: Prentice-Hall, 1972.
3 Smith, A., *The Wealth of Nations*, London: Methuen, 1950 (originally published 1776).
4 Diderot, D., *Encyclopédie*, Paris: published in thirty-five volumes between 1751 and 1772.
5 Galbraith, J. K., *The Age of Uncertainty*, London: BBC/André Deutsch, 1977.
6 Woodham-Smith, C., *The Great Hunger*, London: Hamish Hamilton, 1962.
7 Babbage, C., *On the Economy of Machinery and Manufactures*, London: Charles Knight, 1832.
8 Gilbreth, F. B., *Primer of Scientific Management*, New York: Van Nostrand, 1912.
9 Wilde, E., 'An evaluation of alternative methods of clerical work measurement', *Management Services*, Vol. 32, No. 9, September 1988, p. 12.

Further reading

Bentley, T. J. (ed.), *The Management Services Handbook*, London: Holt, Rinehart & Winston, 1984.
BSI, *Glossary of Terms in Work Study and Organization and Methods (O & M)*, Ref. BS 3138:1979, London: British Standards Institution, 1979.
Currie, R. M., *The Measurement of Work*, London: Management Publications, 1965.
ILO, *Introduction to Work Study*, Geneva, International Labour Office, 1957.

33

Rating, Timing and Values

Dost thou love life, then do not squander time, for that's the stuff
life is made of.   Benjamin Franklin, *The Way to Wealth* (1757)

Those who make the worst use of their time are the first to
complain of its brevity.   La Bruyère, *Characters* (1688)

The long-established technique of time study is certainly not the commonest way of setting staffing levels in the office. However, it has been found in practice that even a superficial knowledge of it makes understanding of all the techniques much easier. Such basic knowledge also makes life easier when one is faced with a complex quantification job. It is like driving a car; knowing a little about how a car works helps when one is learning to drive and makes life easier when it dies on one.

For this reason this chapter deals briefly with rating, time studies and the build-up of work values. Almost everything dealt with occurs in some form or other when using any technique of measuring work in the office.

E

Rating

To many people there is a certain mystique surrounding rating. There is no good reason for this. Admittedly it is not easy to perform well, needing training and experience – but this is not the same as thinking that the underlying concepts are difficult to understand. They are not.

We all know how people do things in life at different speeds. People walk, talk, weed the garden, answer telephone enquiries, iron a shirt, type a memo, cut their toenails – all at different speeds. Sometimes, of course, this is because they are doing things in a different way. But even when they are using the same methods, speeds still vary.

Even more importantly, we will often say of somebody that 'she walks quickly' or 'he speaks slowly'. By saying this, we are unconsciously applying some sort of standard: there must be some speed of walking and speaking that we regard as normal. When we hear anybody speaking at 130 words or less per minute it strikes us as being very slow and deliberate (those who have heard Clement Freud speak think that he speaks slowly; his speed is 130 words/minute). A commentator on a horse race will, for the last exciting 100 metres, reach a speed of 300 words/minute or more. Similarly, a parent will grow exasperated when a child insists on walking through a departmental store in tow at 1–2 kph while the parent wants to do at least 5 kph. 'Don't dawdle' is a common admonishment.

'Rating' is merely a way of agreeing on a standard speed for activities and putting a number to various speeds. Putting numerical descriptions to varying speeds enables us to do away with descriptive words such as slow, very slow, fast, very fast, etc. This is the same as with temperatures. We could describe a day as being hot, cold, baking or freezing. Or we can describe it as being 33°C. What is 33°C? It is just an imaginary

343

point on a scale of 0 to 100, where 0 is the temperature at which water freezes and 100 the temperature at which it boils. And our 33°C is an imaginary point a third of the way along our scale of 0 to 100.

So all we need is an agreed scale, with a definition of what is meant by 0 and 100. This is in fact the scale that is used. The rating scale is usually referred to as the '0/100' scale, or sometimes the 'BS' scale. Since the scale is arithmetic, we can say that somebody is 'working at a hundred' or 'working at a 50' – where working at a 50 means half the speed of working at 100.

On the scale, 'standard rate' is the 100 point. It must be emphasized at once that this does not mean that one expects everybody in an office to work at this 100 rate of working. It is the standard that enables one to define the 0 to 100 scale. A verbal description of this 100, or standard, rate of working is provided in the British Standards Institution standard No. BS3138:1979 – 41025 which defines it as:

> ... the average rate at which qualified workers will naturally work, provided that they adhere to the specified method and that they are motivated to apply themselves to their work ...

A less formal demonstration of what is meant is given in Table 33.1, while Figure 33.1 compares rating of walking and typing.

Training in rating traditionally starts with learning to rate walking, typing, dealing a pack of cards, sorting and putting letters into envelopes. When proficiency has been attained in these activities, the next stage is to rate office tasks from a video or film. The third stage is to move into an office and learn to rate all the activities that are proceeding there. There is a tendency for trainees to be what is called 'flat' in their ratings. This means that the trainee does not rate fast staff high enough or slow staff low enough, tending to stay too close to the middle range of 75 to 100. The opposite of flat rating is being 'steep' – exaggerating fast and slow working.

Rating is done in steps of 5 points on the scale; that is, one uses 80, 85, 90, etc., and

Table 33.1

Rating (0–100)	How observed	Example – walking	
		kph	mph
150	Exceptionally fast. Needs intense effort and concentration. Only achieved for short periods of time or by gifted people.	9.7	6.0
125	Very fast. A high degree of assurance, co-ordination and dexterity is observed.	8.0	5.0
100	Quite brisk and business-like. Purposeful. Person seems to be motivated in his/her actions.	6.4	4.0
75	Unhurried but deliberate. May look slow but no too-obvious wasting of time.	4.8	3.0
50	Very slow. May appear clumsy or time-wasting. Person seems to have little interest in job.	3.2	2.0
0	At rest. Not working.	0	0

Words/minute	Typing	Rating	Walking	kph
216	One-minute record	270		
		260	World 3 km record	16.5
		240		
170	Simplified keyboard record	220	World 30 km record	14.2
		200		
149	World champion	180	British 50 km record	12.0
		160		
115	British champion	140		
96	Fast typing	120	Fast walking	8.0
80	'Standard'	100	'Standard'	6.4
		80		
50	Junior typist		Slow walk	4.8
		60		
40	Certificate 'pass'		Stroll	3.5
		40		
		20		
0	No movement	0	No movement	0

Figure 33.1 Rating of typing and walking

E

not 83, 86, 91, etc. A trainee who keeps rating too low on the scale is called 'tight' and one who rates too high on the scale is called 'loose'. So training aims to get people used to rating on the 0 to 100 scale in increments of 5 points, and continues until the trainee is neither flat or steep, and neither tight or loose.

Rating does make certain assumptions, particularly with regard to the concept of 'standard'. It is assumed that the person being rated has been trained and is of average skill and ability. It also has to be assumed that the correct method is being used (film analysis shows that when people work very slowly or very fast, they tend to change the pattern of working). So it is always advisable to pick an 'average' person to observe, not the super-skilled or the incapable. An example of this is reading. In medieval times, people read aloud, to savour the sounds (reading was sometimes referred to as 'ruminating'). In offices nowadays people read in silence. The 'standard' for reading aloud is 200 words/minute but for reading silently it is double this.

Reference has been made several times to the 0/100 scale that is used. This has not always been true. Just as there have been temperature scales other than the 0/100 Celsius (such as the Réamur and Fahrenheit scales) so there have been other rating scales, which may be seen in the literature. These all start at 0 for no movement but use other scales from 0 up. The table below gives their names and compares two points on the 0/100 scale (namely 75 and 100) with each of them:

0/100 (or BS)	60/80 (or Bedaux)	100/133	LMS (or Westinghouse)
100	80	133	120
75	60	100	90

One other item that may be seen in the literature or heard spoken by other analysts is the phrase 'day-rate'. This is the rate at which people are expected to work if there is no motivation. In most countries this is represented by 75 on the 100 scale, and this is used by the major international management consultancies. In some older American manufacturing companies, however, it is an 83 on the 0/100 scale. This confusion is slowly dying out but may still be encountered.

Performance

The term 'performance' is not the same as rating. Rating is the numerical value on a 0/100 scale used to define how fast a person is working during a short interval of time. Performance uses the same numerical description but is used to define the overall rate of output that is achieved over a longer period of time, such as a day or week or month. The term 'performance' is usually met when calculating how well people have done when compared with work values (see later in this chapter) rather than to indicate speed of working as such.

Time study

The basic concept of time study is straightforward. One times a task (using a stopwatch) and at the same time 'rates' the person being observed. Then, by using the rating, one converts the time actually taken to the time that would be taken if the person were working at a 100 rating.

In practice, there is more to it than that but the extra details do not affect this concept description; they merely facilitate the practical needs of the studies.

■ ELEMENTS

One does not time a complete task as a single unit. Instead, the overall task is broken down into smaller bits known as 'elements'. An element is a distinct part of a task and is selected for the convenience of timing and observation. Some elements do not occur every time that the task is performed. An example of an element in the task of 'man shaving in the morning' would be 'wet face'. Elements are usually expressed in this form: verb + object. Examples are 'load original into fax' or 'walk to modem'.

Elements should not be shorter than 0.10 minute (6 seconds), otherwise errors may occur, and one is spending so much time writing down the timings that something may be missed. Nor should they be longer than 0.50 minutes (30 seconds) – or the rate of working may vary undetected or one's attention wander. If an element is naturally longer than 0.50 minutes, then one splits it up into chunks of 0.50 minutes each. This is common in offices where we do not need the fine detail that is necessary in a factory.

It will have been noticed that the lengths of elements were described in the form '0.50' minutes, etc. This is another convention. Times are quoted in decimal parts of a minute, to two decimal places. Since this is always done, it means that when writing down the times one can omit the '0'. Thus 0.50 minutes would usually be recorded simply as '50'.

Elements should:

- be naturally distinct and easy to describe;
- have definite beginnings and endings. The point at which one element ends and the next starts is called a 'break-point';
- be between 0.10 and 0.50 minutes in length;
- show manual work separate from machine work;
- be convenient;
- separate out any time that is 'ineffective', e.g. lighting a cigarette, unwrapping a toffee.

Recognizing elements in a task or working cycle is not difficult and becomes second nature after taking a few studies.

■ EQUIPMENT

The equipment needed for taking time studies is not complicated. It consists of a stop-watch, some pre-printed forms, a pen, a wall clock or wristwatch, a board with a bulldog-type clip to rest the forms on while taking the study. For calculating the results one needs a ready-reckoner sheet or a calculator or some suitable software.

The stop-watch used is usually one that records decimal parts of a minute; that is, hundredths of a minute rather than seconds. It is also of the type known as 'fly-back' or 'snap-back'. When using a fly-back, one reads the timing and at the same instant zeroes the watch by pressing a button on the top of the watch. The hand flies back to zero and immediately starts again to record the next timing. The watch never stops, as it is continuously timing each successive element of work. Some of the cheaper electronic stop-watches lack this ability, in which case one has to take the stop-watch reading while it is running continuously. This then involves one in subtracting every reading from the next one in order to obtain the individual element times.

Perhaps surprisingly, it takes practice to be able to use a stop-watch accurately. At first, people tend to zero the watch before reading it or forget to release the zero button. Trainees must continue practising until they consistently do it accurately.

■ EXTENDING

So far, we have an element of work that we have rated and timed. The next stage is to convert this time to the time that the element would take if the person were working at a standard rate of 100. This is:

$$\text{Observed time} \times \frac{\text{Rating}}{100}$$

The resulting time is called 'basic time'. Basic time can be expressed as basic minutes ('BM') or basic hours. A reference to 5 BM means a task that takes 5 minutes to perform when working at a 100 rate.

One sometimes hears this calculation called 'normalizing' or 'converting'. However, the official terms are 'extending' and extension.

■ MAKE READY AND PUT AWAY

Many office tasks need preparatory work before actually carrying out the task. They also often involve ancillary work after the central task has been completed. For

Dept __Home__ Section __Bathroom__ No. __MS/161__

Name __A. Smith/C. Green__ No __1876/2131__ Taken by __JBF__ Date __1/4/1914__

Operation __Man shaving face.__ Start __06:30__

__Using shave foam from a can and safety razor.__ Finish __06:43__

Elapsed __13.00 minutes__

Working conditions __Water hot; lighting good.__ Ineffective __4.37 mins__

Net time __8.63 mins__

	TEBS – 2.17 minutes				
1	Get equipment from cupboard	85	29	25	
2	Wet face	100	25	25	
3	Apply shave foam, using fingers	100	50	50	
		90	44	40	Elapsed time = 13.00 mins
4	Shave face	100	50	50	Study time = 13.00 mins
		100	50	50	Error = 0%
		100	50	50	
		90	11	10	
5	Dry face	110	18	20	Average rating =
6	Apply aftershave	120	50	60	Basic minutes
7	Check result	100	10	10	—————————— × 100
8	Replace equipment in cupboard	85	24	20	Actual minutes
					= 8.20/8.63×100 =95
	Wait for C. Green	IT	—	80	
1		80	30	24	
2		95	26	25	
3		90	50	45	
		90	50	45	
4		90	50	45	
		90	50	45	
		90	50	45	
		90	29	26	
5		95	21	20	
6		100	50	50	
		100	10	10	
7		80	12	10	
8		85	24	20	
	TEAS – 1.40 minutes				

Figure 33.2 Time study – man shaving

example, the task may be to check on a customer's credit rating via a VDU. Before being able to do this it may be necessary to switch the screen on, wait, log on to the database, and go through a menu. Then one can check the credit rating by inputting the name, waiting briefly and then reading the data on the screen. One may then have to log off and switch the screen off.

The preparatory work is called 'make-ready'. The finishing-off work is called 'put-away'. This is a very useful concept. Analysts sometimes come across tasks in the office that seem complex to study. The answer is often to think of such tasks as consisting of three parts:

1 Make-ready.
2 Do.
3 Put-away.

This simple approach often works when confronted by a complex task. It also helps when trying to calculate a range of times. For example, the time to look up two credit ratings is not twice the time to obtain one. The make-ready and put-away components are a constant irrespective of how many enquiries are being made at one time. The only part that increases is the actual interrogation.

There is a further advantage. The time for make-ready and put-away for checking credit ratings may be exactly the same as that for other tasks, such as getting address or telephone number, in which case it does not have to be studied again since we can use the first time – and start to build up our own databank of synthetics, as mentioned previously.

E

■ EXAMPLE STUDY

In Figure 33.2 is shown an example of a study. It is an exercise that trainees are often set: how long does it take to shave. There are a number of points raised by this example.

The first point is that the study is not truly complete. It does not include the elements of walking to the bathroom, waiting for access, and walking from the bathroom. Whether or not these elements are included depends in large measure on the use for which the study is being taken. They are not needed if the aim is to establish bathroom utilization in a student's hostel. The 'waiting for access' time would be needed if one were trying to establish a schedule for users or deciding how many more bathrooms were required for a specific level of service.

Also missing are what are known as 'occasional elements'. Not unnaturally, these are elements that occur occasionally. They do not happen in every work cycle, and may be regular or irregular. However, if enough studywork is carried out, then it is possible to state how frequently they occur. An example of an occasional element would be 'replace razor blade'. It would not be easy to decide the frequency of such an element since people vary widely in how often they start a new blade. It can vary from every other day to once a month. Some elements occur very infrequently or very irregularly, so that they seem more like an interruption to the work. These are called 'contingencies'. An example of a contingency would be 'repair cut on face'. Sometimes one sees no contingencies during the studywork even though one is confident that they will occur at some time. In this case we make a special allowance (discussed below).

The study includes an item rated as 'IT'. IT stands for 'ineffective time', which is anything that is not a part of the specified task. Examples would be answering a friend's telephone call in the middle of actually shaving, or cleaning the floor after dropping a

349

bottle of aftershave on it. So – occasional elements and contingencies are genuinely part of the task being performed, ineffective time is not. In the office, a ballpoint pen running out of ink is a contingency; talking to a colleague about the latest football results is ineffective time.

Other points demonstrated by the example study are:

- the elements are written down once and numbered. In a later cycle, just the numbers are used. This saves time, increases attention and is common practice;
- the timing error has been calculated, and in this case is zero. If it had been higher than, say, 1½ per cent, then the study would have to be thrown away and not used;
- the method used has to be stated and checked that it is correct for the study purposes. In our example, one would not be able to include anybody that used a cutthroat razor or even a person using soap and brush. The time would be different. In the same way, the conditions must be constant (hot water and good light).

It will also be seen that the two people studied 'worked' at different rates, one at 100 and one at 91. But the basic number of minutes for both is the same, namely 4.10 minutes. This shows the effect of rating. If the rating and timing are correct, then for any element:

$$\text{Actual time taken} \times \text{Rating} = \text{a constant}$$

The other items on the example study are marked TEBS and TEAS. These are part of the check on the overall timing. The stop-watch is started against a clock or wristwatch when showing an exact minute (06:30 in the example). The time between this and the time at the start of the first element is TEBS – time elapsed before study. At the end of the study the stop-watch is left running and stopped when the same clock or watch shows an exact minute again. The time between the last element and stopping the stop-watch is TEAS – time elapsed after study. This means that all the time elapsed has been accounted for and can be checked for accuracy.

Taking a study

The actions taken when carrying out a study depend to a large extent on circumstances, especially whether it is the first time study in a section or whether it is the 50th in a series of 100. Before starting a study in a department it will be necessary to discuss the situation in detail with managers, staff, staff representatives and unions. Openness, clarity, reassurance and momentum are the objectives.

Relationships with the staff are of paramount importance. To an analyst, taking a study is a normal activity, one which has been done hundreds of times before. To the person being observed it may be a very unusual event. The sheer unusualness can result in different reactions. One person may be rather nervous. Another, especially if young, may be skittish or truculent. Some people will dress up for the occasion, others will come in late.

One person's reminiscence can be somebody else's boredom – but an event that occurred while we were studying in a newspaper office stays in the mind. It was inescapable that one particular elderly man had to be studied. The manager said that the man had been studied years before by another consultant – and had promptly had a heart attack. So the man was interviewed with great care and deliberation. It started with an enquiry about the health of his wife, who had once worked for the same newspaper. From there the discussion moved onto 'his' football team's efforts the previous Saturday. Then onto the world situation, that day's edition of the newspaper, the work of the department and his personal contribution over the years.

The conversation then turned to the current work and what the old man did at present. Finally, nearly two hours later, we eased into the study itself. This seemed to go well and we parted on good terms. But the next morning – no old man. Had he had another heart attack? If so, guess who would be held responsible. Imagination provided the next day's headline: 'Consultant held responsible for violent death of well-loved newsman'. The atmosphere in the newspaper was indescribable. It looked like the end to a once promising career.

By eleven o'clock the tension was unbearable and a friend was persuaded to phone the man's wife. The reply was that the man had 'flu and wished to apologize to that nice consultant for letting him down. The consultant was 'nice'? Wow. Smiles all round. Little whistle. On with the work.

Now this story may be trivial, but it points out the basic lesson: one has to treat the staff as human beings – and at the same time, one just has to do one's job. This balance is the basis of the rule:

> ## Courtesy with persistence

E

An abbreviated checklist for taking a study is given below. It assumes that it is not the first study in a department, and that initial discussions have already been held:

Make-ready:	Ensure background information known.
	Read Job Description.
	Ensure timetable known by interested parties.
	Telephone supervisor, as reminder.
	Collect equipment, notes, etc.
	Go to supervisor.
	Together select most suitable person to study.
	Supervisor introduces one to this person.
Study:	Interview staff member. Be:
	• informal;
	• enthusiastic;
	• tactful;
	• businesslike;
	• open;
	• non-technical;
	• a listener.
	Record all the relevant information.
	Get copies of paperwork.
	Get details of *volumes* and *frequencies*.
	Check the information.
	Thank interviewee and supervisor.

Put-away:	Check information (consistency, reasonableness).
	Review interview.
	Ensure no gaps or omissions.
	Complete studywork.
	Number study and file.
	Make a note of any ideas.

A 'memory card' for use at an initial interview with a staff member is:

Initial Talk with Job Holder
Introduction by supervisor. Initial greeting.
Explain procedure. Check Job Description correct.
Explain ● wish to go through each task broadly.
● then wish to go through each in detail.
● then wish to discuss problems, suggestions.
Talk through tasks, make notes. Check.
Discuss problems, e.g. peaks, bottlenecks. Get suggestions.
Get copies of paperwork, *volumes*, *frequencies*.
Thank interviewee.

Both the checklist and the memory card emphasize the importance of obtaining details of volumes and frequencies. The volume is how many (how many customers, letters, invoices, photocopies, fax, enquiries, VDUs). The frequency is how often (how often the photocopier needs loading, letters of credit are returned, insureds need a medical, goods are returned for a refund, the database is edited). Volumes and frequencies must never be forgotten; they are always important. Without them, one knows very little.

Each study is summarized individually as it is done, showing the results of the study. This summary is attached to the study as a top sheet. These summaries are then analysed on a separate sheet. An example of this analysis is shown in Table 33.2. Each element of each study is recorded as Total BMs/Number of times observed/BMs per occasion.

Allowances

The analysis for a man shaving suggests that it needs 4.10 Basic Minutes. This is not the time that would be quoted if it were a job in the office. To this basic time certain allowances have to be added. The two main allowances are Relaxation Allowance (RA) and Contingency Allowance (CA).

The idea behind relaxation allowance is that it allows for:

- attention to personal needs;
- recovery from fatigue caused by physical or mental effort;
- recovery from adverse environmental conditions.

The first of these ('personal needs') is a traditional phrase used on every training course and in every textbook. This strange coyness has led to generations of people wondering

Table 33.2 Analysis of study summaries

Man shaving							
Study No.	MS/	160	161	162	Total BMs	No.	BMs/ Occ.
Date	1914/	1/4	1/4	2/4			
by		HAE	JBF	KCG			
name		Smith	Jones	Brown			
		Green	White	Smith			
Average rating		98	95	91			
error		0%	0%	0.5%			
1 Get equipment from cupboard. T.BMs		0.50	0.49	0.51	1.50		
No.		2	2	2		6	
BM/							
Occ.		0.25	0.25	0.26			0.25
2. Wet face. T.BMs		0.24	0.50	0.52	1.26		
No.		1	2	2		5	
BM/							
Occ.		0.24	0.25	0.26			0.25
3. Apply shave foam, using fingers. T.BMs		1.82	1.80	1.78	5.40		
No.		2	2	2		6	
BM/							
Occ.		0.91	0.90	0.89			0.90
4. Shave face. T.BMs		3.18	3.21	3.19	9.58		
No.		2	2	2		6	
BM/							
Occ.		1.59	1.61	1.60			1.60
5. Dry face. T.BMs		0.40	0.40	0.38	1.18		
No.		2	2	2		6	
BM/							
Occ.		0.20	0.20	0.19			0.20
6. Apply aftershave. T.BMs		1.18	1.20	0.62	3.00		
No.		2	2	1		5	
BM/							
Occ.		0.59	0.60	0.62			0.60
7. Check result. T.BMs		0.18	0.20	0.11	0.49		
No.		2	2	1		5	
BM/							
Occ.		0.09	0.10	0.11			0.10
8. Replace equipment in cupboard. T.BMs		0.42	0.40	0.37	1.19		
No.		2	2	2		6	
BM/							
Occ.		0.21	0.20	0.19			0.20
Total BMs per occasion.							4.10
Contingencies Repair cut.				0.48	0.48		

E

what personal needs could be. Those who asked were often told, 'well, you know, personal needs'. With no small trepidation, therefore, it can be revealed that it includes – going to the lavatory. It is also meant to cover lighting up a cigarette, having a coffee, taking medication, etc. But it does *not* cover the main break for lunch which is taken around midday in most countries.

The fatigue recovery factor has been the subject of much research over the years; one university has spent twenty years studying it. The team has watched people on exercise bicycles, measuring their oxygen debt and the composition of their exhaled breath. Much of the work has been useful in factories though of less obvious application in offices. Similarly, the 'adverse environmental conditions' in offices are a whole quantum level below that seen in some factories.

The problems of precise quantification for office staff has led more and more organizations in different countries to adopt a standard of 10 per cent for relaxation allowance. A rationale for this (not a defence or proof, just a rationale) is that it is built up from:

Personal needs	– 6% to 7%
Fatigue recovery	– 2%
Concentration/monotony	– 1% to 2%

The figure of 10 per cent is particularly prevalent among consultancies, financial institutions, oil companies, multinationals and computer firms (though one bank has been heard of that was proposing to use 15 per cent – there were special circumstances). The figure of 10 per cent is the same for both sexes.

Where lifting weights is a regular part of a task, extra relaxation allowance should be given. The table below gives details. The percentages shown are additional to the standard 10 per cent, and are used only on those elements during which weights are actually involved and not for the whole task:

Weight (kg)	Percentage addition
3–5	1%
6–10	3%
11–15	6%
16–20	10%
21–25	15%

The second main allowance is the contingency allowance. As already stated, a contingency is something that prevents a person from working on the central task and which is not that person's fault. It is normal to calculate the percentage of time spent on contingencies observed during studywork. If this percentage is less than 1 per cent, then it is arbitrarily increased to the figure of 1 per cent. If it is more than 1 per cent, then the observed percentage is used as the allowance. If it is more than 3 per cent, then part of it may be treated as occasional elements or a separate allowance created (called ancillary work, with a definition of what it includes).

A less common allowance is one for Supervision and Training. This can be contentious, not to say philosophical. It is meant to cover time spent receiving instruction from the supervisor. When given, it is commonly 3 per cent.

354

The allowances are cumulative. In other words, relaxation time is allowed even when there is a contingency. This means that the percentages are multiplied together, not merely added up arithmetically. The time that results from adding the allowances to the basic time is called the Standard Time. This is the time that would be issued as a target to people doing the task, so it can be regarded as a work value. For this reason it is often called Standard Minute Value (SMV).

So, bringing all the jargon together in one place, we can say that:

$$SMV = BM + RA\% + CA\% + S\&T\%$$

Where an organization uses the common allowances of 10% (relaxation), 1% (contingencies) and 3% (supervisory) then since the allowances are cumulative, the total percentage allowance becomes:

$$\frac{110}{100} \times \frac{101}{100} \times \frac{103}{100} = 14.4\%$$

This is usually rounded up to 15 per cent. Another way of expressing this is to say that a factor of 1.15 is used to convert basic minutes to standard minutes. Returning to our shaving example, the Standard Minute Value for this would be:

$$4.10 \times 1.15 = 4.7 \text{ SMs.}$$

Presentation of values

A section receives requests from the salespeople for details of credit worthiness. These requests arrive on standard forms. A single form may have from one to three enquiries on it. A salesperson may send in several forms in a day. In use, the credit clerks interrogate a VDU by inputting the salesperson's name, followed by the names of the customers. The computer prints out the responses in another section once a day, bringing together the responses for each salesperson.

If one has to state a Standard Minute Value for the credit clerks, one is faced with a choice. One could express the time as being:

- per form;
- per request;
- per salesperson; or
- per computer log-on.

This is a common situation. One has to decide on the unit to be used – which is called the Control Unit. Usually the answer is obvious and natural. In a payroll section it will be the number of staff to be paid. In a data prep section it will probably be the number of keystrokes. In a word processing section it will often be number of reports + letters + memos. Usually one uses more than one control unit in a department. Where there is a choice, and no unit is obvious, then one has to consider:

- ease of counting the units in the future;
- ease of measurement and calculation;
- likelihood of the relationship between units changing.

In the example given, the answer will probably be to use the number of requests as the control unit. How this would be achieved in practice is shown in Table 33.3. Fortunately, few SMVs are this complex to calculate.

Table 33.3 Establishment of SM value

Department: Accounts. **Section:** Credit					Date: 10–7–14	
Operation: Get credit worthiness for Sales.					By: JBF	
Control unit: Enquiry request. **Allowance:** 15%					Page 1 of 1	

Operation/Element	Unit	BMs	Freq./ Control Unit	BM/ Control Unit	SM/ Control Unit
Register incoming forms	Enq. form	0.205	1 in 1.7	0.121	0.139
Sort by area	Enq. form	0.063	1 in 1.7	0.037	0.043
Batch enquiry forms	Batch	0.154	1 in 40	0.004	0.005
Log on to computer database	Batch	0.106	1 in 40	0.003	0.003
Input enquiry details	Enquiry	0.157	1	0.157	0.181
Sort by salesperson	Enq. form	0.063	1 in 1.7	0.037	0.043
Mark register for completion	Enquiry	0.126	1	0.126	0.145
Staple, put into pigeon hole	Salesperson	0.210	1 in 3.2	0.066	0.076
Total SMV					0.635
Select SMV					0.64

Production study

It may be necessary to 'prove' that SMVs are correct or to find out why people think them inaccurate. To do so, one carries out a Production Study. In this a study lasts for a whole day or shift. The analyst walks round the section, rating everybody once a minute. At the same time a note is made of what the person is doing – which control unit or if a contingency, IT relaxing, etc. This is similar to rated activity sampling (see next chapter).

By adding the ratings and dividing the answer by 100, one knows how many BMs were produced (because one was rating every minute). This can be compared with BMs earned (volumes × BMVs). This will highlight any differences. More detailed calculations are possible if required. Most people seem to call these studies Proof Studies but the official name is production studies.

34

Activity Sampling

I say, let your affairs be as two or three, and not a hundred or a thousand; instead of a million count half a dozen, and keep your accounts on your thumb-nail. **Thoreau, Walden (1854)**

A stander-by may sometimes, perhaps, see more of the game than he who plays it.
Swift, A Critical Essay Upon the Faculties of the Mind (1707)

The idea of taking a sample, and from it, assuming some knowledge about the whole picture is not uncommon. If while walking to work we pass a building site, we may see the same person every day and notice that he is reading a paper every time we see him. We may be tempted to think that the person is rather idle since he is 'always reading a paper'. In fact he may be the most energetic person on the project. It is just that we go to work at the same time every day, and the newspaper reader happens to get to work early every day so that he can read the paper before starting. A clearer picture of his working habits would only be gained if we were to pass by the site a number of times during the shift. In Activity Sampling, one does just this. The more times we were to pass by the building site, the more accurate our picture would become.

Sampling is used in offices for a number of purposes, such as:

- sampling correspondence to detect a pattern;
- asking a number of the staff about their opinions and their preferences;
- selectively checking work output for quality and accuracy.

Outside the office the best-known use of sampling is in opinion polls, often used to indicate the population's voting intentions or their opinions. The best-known poll is one that the pollsters would prefer people to forget. In 1936 in the USA the presidential election was between Roosevelt and Landon. The *Literary Digest* carried out a massive poll of ten million people to predict the result. This poll was based on the voting intentions of people who were subscribers to the magazine or who were listed in the telephone directories. The result of the poll was overwhelming: respondents assured the *Literary Digest* that Landon would be returned by a margin of more than 2 to 1. In fact, although the sample elected Landon, the voters elected Roosevelt. The failure of the poll was that in 1936 those who could afford a telephone or the magazine were not representative of the whole population.

Our two examples of the building site worker and the *Literary Digest* highlight important aspects of sampling, including activity sampling:

- there must be no bias in our observations;
- observations should be random and not regular;
- accuracy is not guaranteed by a large sample;
- sampling must be planned.

357

These aspects were very much in the mind of L. H. C. Tippett, who is usually given the credit for introducing activity sampling into industry and commerce. He was taking studies in a cotton mill in 1927 when he realized that a photograph of the looms would be very useful. This would indicate how many looms were active, how many were stopped, and the reasons for the stoppages. Furthermore, a series of photographs would give an approximate picture for the whole shift. A consideration of how many photographs would be needed for an acceptable degree of accuracy led to the development of activity sampling techniques. In case this sounds too much like a Newton-and-the-apple story, it should be said that Tippett himself confirmed in a conversation that the story was based on fact.

The 'series of photographs' concept describes quite well what is done during an activity sampling study. An observer walks round the office, noting the activity of people or machines at the time that they are passed. The phrase 'at the time that they are passed' is important. The relevant activity is the one at that instant: not what people are doing as they are approached, nor what they are about to do, but what is happening at the moment of passing – just like taking a photograph at that instant. The observations are repeated by continually making journeys around the office.

Provided that enough observations are made, and made correctly, then the proportion of times that an activity is seen is a good estimate of the actual incidence of the activity. If 2,500 observations are made of a modem and it was in use on 1,000 occasions, then we would estimate that the modem was in use for $1,000/2,500 \times 100 = 40$ per cent of the time.

If we wished to find out the percentage utilization of the modem, we could watch it all day, making a note of when it was active and when it was idle. In effect, this is what is done in a time study. Such a study would have certain disadvantages. It might not be accurate; the observations might all be made on a Monday and Monday may be the busiest or slackest day of the week. It would be rather expensive for just one machine, unless the purchase of further machines depended on it. It might not help a lot if we really wanted to cover ten modems. And it would be rather boring. Such a continuous study might result in the following:

- period of observation = 8 hours
- total time active = 3 hours 12 minutes

Hence active time as a percentage of total time

$$= 3.2/8 \times 100$$
$$= 40\%$$

Suppose that we dropped into the office 25 times during the day, and noticed that the modem was active on 9 of our visits. Then the active time as a percentage of total time would be calculated as being:

$$9/25 \times 100 = 36\%$$

The answer is not accurate; obviously, not enough observations were made. If all our calculations in the office were carried out in the same way, then we would not be 'confident' about the accuracy of the calculations. What is needed, therefore, is a way of stating how many observations we need to make, as well as a way of stating how confident we are in the accuracy of our results. To do this it is necessary to turn to the general theory of sampling.

In activity sampling there is one basic formula that is used. This is:

$$N = \frac{4p(100-p)}{L^2}$$

where N = number of observations
   p = percentage occurrence of the activity being observed
   L = accuracy limits $(+$ or $-)$ as a percentage.

The word 'confident' has been used twice. Like many words, this can be used in an ordinary conversational sense but can also be used in a technical sense. The formula given above is based on probabilities. That means that results obtained from using it are not absolutely correct 100 per cent of the time. In fact, it gives answers that are expected to be correct only 95 per cent of the time. So for 5 per cent of the time we can expect that the answers will be slightly different from the true answer. We can therefore say that we are 95 per cent confident that our answer is the true one. The technical phrase is that the formula has '95 per cent confidence limits'. Note that even when the answer is not absolutely correct, we would expect the true answer to be close to the one indicated.

To return to the example of the modem, we know that it is active 40 per cent of the time (this is 'p'). We may wish to use sampling, and want the answer to be correct to $\pm$ 4 per cent; that is, the answer would lie in the range of 40 ± 4, which is 36–44 per cent. This spread of 4 per cent is 'L'. Using the formula, we can say:

$$N = \frac{4p(100-p)}{L^2} = \frac{4 \times 40(100-40)}{4^2}$$

$$= \frac{160(60)}{16} = 600$$

If the spread of L at 4 per cent is not accurate enough for our purposes, then more readings or observations would be needed. If we decide that the answer should be correct to $\pm$ 2 per cent ('L'), then we can use the formula again to get the answer. This gives the number of readings ('N') as being 2,400. What does this mean? It means that if we took 2,400 observations, we can expect that 95 per cent of the time the answer we will get will lie between 38 and 42 per cent.

Incidentally, if we wished to get the answer even more accurately, to say $\pm$ 1 per cent, then the number of readings would be 9,600. Each time we double the accuracy, we have to quadruple the number of readings.

Using the formula all the time is a bit of a chore, and instead it is usual to use a nomogram – a pictorial presentation of the formula. A nomogram for our formula is given in Figure 34.1 overleaf. To use it we just lay a ruler on the chart so that it cuts two of the vertical lines at the two known values. The answer is shown by the position at which the ruler cuts the third vertical line.

For example, our modem has a 'p' of 40 per cent and an 'L' of 2 per cent. So we lay our ruler on the chart so that it cuts the left-hand line at 40 and the middle line at 2. It is then possible to read off the answer for 'N' on the right-hand line; it is 2,400. This is the same as that given by our formula. The formula is more accurate, of course, because of slight errors in printing and reading the ruler position. But for practical purposes, the chart is accurate enough and much quicker.

E

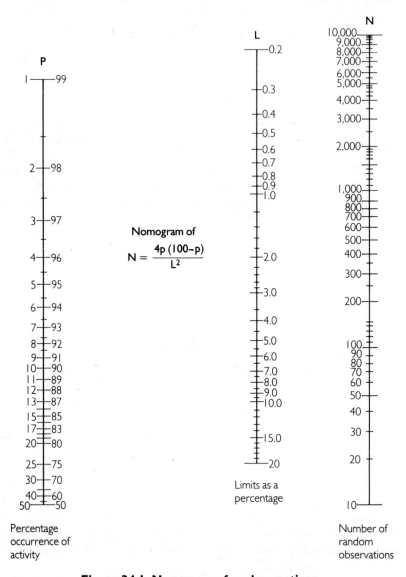

Figure 34.1 Nomogram for observations

As the chart shows, the maximum number of observations is needed when an activity occurs 50 per cent of the time. For an accuracy of ± 2 per cent, we would need 2,500 observations. So if we take 2,500 readings on an activity sampling study, we can be sure that we are within our accuracy limits for every activity that can occur. For this reason, many organizations have the habit of always taking 2,500 readings on every study. In case it be thought that ± 2 per cent is not very accurate, it should be said that (because of the way the sampling is used) it satisfies the statisticians of organizations in which it is used.

Possibilities of error

Apart from arithmetic considerations, there are other ways in which errors can arise in an activity sampling study:

1 The period of the study may not be representative of the work as a whole. A common example is that work can vary depending on the time of the month, such as month-end invoicing. There are three ways of dealing with this possibility. First, one always checks the situation before studying. Second, the length of studies is such that variations are usually covered. Third, one can stagger the days on which readings are taken. Thus one might take observations on Monday and Thursday in the first week, Wednesday and Friday in the second week and on Tuesday in the third week.

2 The fact that the analyst is present may affect the activities in some way. For example, in one study the staff were embarrassed at first at the poor quality of their fax machine. However, in practice, any changes usually become negligible after an initial period. This is because the staff being studied soon become accustomed to the analyst's presence and ignore him, especially as they soon have to concentrate on the work in hand. With experience, analysts seem to acquire a 'smell' for when things are not as they should be. If necessary, one can discard the readings that were taken during the first few journeys round the office.

3 It is always possible that the analyst is 'biased' in the sense that certain results are anticipated. This bias is reduced by the fact that it is normal for a number of analysts to share the taking of the observations; it is surprisingly fatiguing over a long period of time. The bias is eliminated by strict adherence to the technique of regarding the observations as being 'snap-shots', like a photograph as originally intended.

4 The observations might coincide with a cycle of an activity. For example, a messenger may leave the mailroom once an hour on the hour to do the internal mail rounds. On his return he sorts the mail for ten minutes before going off on his rounds again. If the observations were made every quarter of an hour then it would be quite easy to miss the sorting operations altogether. This possibility is eliminated by taking the readings at random intervals.

5 When going round the office taking observations, the analyst may notice that some people are not at their desk. The reason for the absence may not be obvious. One answer is to ask, but sometimes the person's colleagues may not be certain of the person's whereabouts or cause of absence, and the delay may upset the timing of the observations.

There is an alternative used by many organizations. This is the 'activity sampling triangle'. Strictly speaking this is not a triangle but a triangular prism, rather like the name plates often used at seminars. This has three faces, each about 3 cm × 15 cm. These three faces have written on them:

Absent.
Away working.
Personal.

E

Each member of staff being observed is given a prism/triangle before the study starts. When people leave their desk during the study, they leave the triangle on the desk with the relevant face showing. This can then be seen by the analyst when making an observation and recorded. In use, 'absent' includes such events as having lunch, visiting the dentist, buying a packet of cigarettes, etc.

The use of these triangles is not only useful, it also helps to show that the analyst is trying to be fair. Otherwise, staff may fear that they are not being 'credited' with those observations when they are not at their desk but are nevertheless still working productively.

Randomness

The formula, and indeed all of the theory of activity sampling, is based on the basic assumption that the observations are random; not interconnected in any way nor linked to an external facet such as time. The best way to achieve randomness is to make sure that the observations are taken at random times.

This is done by using random tables. These can be used in a variety of ways, of which the commonest is to say that five journeys round the office will be made very hour. The random numbers table is then read, using the numbers to indicate the minutes past the hour. The time thus generated becomes the time at which a journey starts.

A table of random numbers is given in the Appendix at the end of the book. The table headed '(b) 0–9' is divided into blocks of 25 two-digit numbers. The first line is:

08–38–54–24–18–58–37–31–06–56–(71)–44–40–(82)–13–(92)–20–(80)–33–36.

The figures in brackets are over 60 and are ignored because there are only 60 minutes in an hour. If it takes 4 minutes to make a round of the offices, it is usual to ignore also any time that would not allow this time. Going along the line we would get the following times to start each round:

09.08	10.58		09.08	10.06
09.38	10.37		09.18	10.31
09.54	10.31	Rearranging	09.24	10.37
09.24	10.06	these times	09.38	10.44
09.18	10.44	in order:	09.54	10.58

The numbers can be read in any direction: upwards, downwards, across, right to left, diagonally. One analyst used to read them using a chess knight's moves, which seems to be taking things a bit far. They can be started at any point; this prevents one from using the same times for every study, which some people would dislike. For those who would prefer to have the hours selected at random as well as the minutes, a second random numbers table is given in the Appendix.

The whole question of randomness can be a difficult one. The early proponents (including Tippett himself) were adamant that everything possible should be done to ensure that randomness was a state of grace. No deviation was allowed. More recently a number of people have shown that the numbers generated as random by computers are very far from being random and so should not be used. These analyses add to the oft-quoted remark of John von Neumann who in 1951 said, 'Anyone who considers arithmetic methods of producing random digits is, of course, in a state of sin.'

Table 34.1 Random observation times

Random Times—6 per hour 08.30 to 5.00									
	9.22	10.00	11.06	12.02	1.03	2.14	3.15	4.07	Monday
8.31	27	06	23	07	18	17	21	10	
36	30	22	30	17	27	28	24	23	
40	33	28	35	21	30	35	40	28	
45	42	50	38	26	46	45	44	37	
57	45	56	53	55	59	57	50	56	
	9.14	10.03	11.06	12.14	1.05	2.08	3.04	4.01	Tuesday
	23	31	15	21	16	15	07	07	
8.38	35	35	19	35	25	29	14	20	
45	48	46	30	54	35	42	36	27	
57	56	57	42	57	39	48	54	35	
59	58	59	51	59	42	52	59	54	
	9.01	10.00	11.19	12.11	1.16	2.11	3.32	4.01	Wednesday
	04	03	24	15	21	17	35	14	
	23	08	28	38	37	25	42	18	
8.30	38	12	33	43	41	30	48	32	
45	53	26	41	48	48	45	52	34	
50	56	29	49	54	57	50	58	54	
	9.00	10.03	11.00	12.04	1.14	2.03	3.20	4.22	Thursday
	03	10	05	14	30	14	31	27	
	22	30	13	28	34	37	36	30	
	33	36	30	33	45	41	40	33	
	40	51	33	40	48	48	47	42	
8.56	46	57	41	56	58	52	51	45	
	9.03	10.14	11.15	12.07	1.02	2.08	3.05	4.14	Friday
	18	17	21	10	13	18	23	24	
	27	28	24	23	29	30	38	35	
	30	35	40	28	32	35	45	48	
	46	45	44	37	39	45	56	55	
8.55	51	53	50	56	53	49	59	58	

E

Statisticians will argue hard and long about randomness in activity sampling. It can be important in factory operations, where one often encounters continually repeated short cycles. Many people who operate in offices take a rather more pragmatic line, claiming that the work in offices is of itself sufficiently random in its nature that no 'extra' randomness is needed. This is an area for the ultra-experts to dispute, and so no comment is offered – especially since long discussions have been sat through.

Having said that, the use of random times is always recommended. It may be of interest to note that the table of times in Table 34.1 is used by one well-known organization for all its activity sampling studies. Its use was sanctioned by its statisticians.

Shape of a study

The overall shape of a study is as follows:

1 Formulate the information that is needed.
2 Define a representative period.
3 Make initial arrangements for the study.
4 Select the people/equipment to be studied.
5 Decide the accuracy needed and hence the number of observations and the times for the observations.
6 Design the study sheet.
7 Hold talks with the staff.
8 Carry out the observations.
9 Analyse the results of the observations.

Some of these steps have already been covered in detail. Others are covered below.

Information sought

Formulating the information that is sought can often require great care. This fact may be surprising but it is so. Activity sampling can be used for a number of purposes, not just as an aid to work quantification. It can form part of Organization Development by showing people how they spend their time and then letting them modify their activities. It can be used for accounting purposes to increase activity in allocation and costing in professional partnerships. So it is sometimes necessary to go back to basics and agree on the objectives of the study.

Even when used in work quantification there is considerable scope for discussion about the information that is being sought. If it is being used to assist in the setting of staffing levels then it is usually easy to agree that the information that is needed is the relative time that is spent on the different tasks. Thus in a sales office the tasks may include phoning customers, explaining special offers, persuading, taking the orders, entering the order into the computer, telling the customer when delivery will be made. This split may be the one that is decided upon if that list represents the totality of work done in the office. However, if the same people deal with enquiries, chase bad debts, check invoices and liaise with lawyers, then the decision may be different.

One important point is that observers can only deal properly with a reasonably short list of alternatives. A list of thirty different activities is impossible; even if not impossible it is not recommended as errors will occur. Up to about fifteen is more manageable. If the work of a department is foreign to one, then it is a good idea either to carry out a pilot study and/or read the job specifications. Reading the job specifications will also help one to select a representative period of work.

Initial arrangements

As with all studies, it is necessary to lay some groundwork. If activity sampling is new to the organization then it will be necessary to explain to the managers and supervisors the technique that will be involved. This has to be an explanation, not a lecture. In other words, the technique has to be understood and not just listened to.

The reason for this is that the results will affect the managers and supervisors in their work – and they should be in a position to argue with one if they do not like the results.

Even where sampling studies are an everyday occurrence it is still necessary to arrange with the managers/supervisors for a study to take place. The desired dates may not be convenient for one of a number of valid reasons. At a basic level it is just well-mannered to give the people involved reasonable notice. It will be noticed that no reference has been made to discussions with the staff – these come later.

■ SELECT PEOPLE/EQUIPMENT

In most cases the people and equipment that will be covered select themselves when one is deciding what to study. For example, if a section is being work quantified, then the study will include all the staff in that section and the equipment that they use. At other times one may have to cut across departmental boundaries. For example, it is not unusual to cover all the machines in a building of a particular type, such as all the photocopiers.

■ DESIGN THE STUDY SHEET

Like most of the preparatory work, this is not difficult especially if one has done it before. But it has to be done. Once an activity sampling study is under way, it is too late to do anything that should have been done beforehand. There is no time – and that is a promise.

The study sheet is a piece of paper divided up into columns and rows. The columns are headed with the activities to be observed. Such as telephone queries, legal letters – do, legal letters – check, quotations – do, quotations – check, look at microfilm, check medical reports, and not working. The fact that 'not working' is recorded must be known to everybdy, as must the fact that everybody has a 'right' to spend a certain amount of time not working; since we are going to allow a relaxation allowance of 10 per cent it follows that in a sense we expect people to be 'idle' for 10 per cent of the time. Some supervisors have difficulty in grasping this aspect.

There is a choice about what is going to be written against the rows. Either one writes in the times that observations are going to be made, or one writes in the names of the people/equipment that will be covered. It depends on the objectives of the study and to some extent on the habit of the organization. Names are particularly useful if a department is split up into a number of small sections or if some people spend a high percentage of their time off the department. Times are useful if anonymity is desirable or if the study is mainly concerned with machine utilization.

Where the rows and columns meet there will be a series of boxes. Into these boxes the observations will be marked. Thus if Phoebe is checking a legal letter, a mark is made under 'legal letter-check' and opposite Phoebe. Marks are made using the five-bar gate system.

A refinement is to use a few letters instead of a mark. For example, under 'check medical report' one might put a letter 's' for a report written on a standard form. Although this is often done the habit should be resisted. One should either use a separate column or get the information some other way. Letters tend to lead to errors through not being distinguishable from marks, or from being forgotten in the heat of the moment.

Photocopies of the study sheet are made ready for the study. It is good practice to use

365

Activity Sampling Study Sheet

Department: Pensions
Analysts: John Clampton   Jane Bramley
Notes:

Section: ICF/2

Study No: MT/143
Date: 2 Oct 1914
Page: 1 **of** 10

Name	PMTS*		Related*		Phone query	Legals		Quotations		Micro film	Medicals	Absent working	Cont.	Not working
	Do	Check	Do	Check		Do	Check	Do	Check					
Phoebe Teagarten														
Jim Armstrong														
Jainee Johnson														
Peter Lyttleton														
Betty Bechet														
Chris Waller														
Jack Simone														
Nina Barber														
Bob Wilbur														
Doug Ory														
Cassietta Jackson														
Mahalia Dodds														
William Clapton														
Anne Brubeck														
David Beiderbecke														

*Explained in chapter 36

Figure 34.2 Example study sheet

a new sheet each day, which makes it possible to check on any suspected daily variation. Using a new sheet each day also makes analysis easier.

If the study is going to involve 15 people, then 15 observations will be recorded during each 'round' of the office. At 7 rounds per hour, one will be making $7 \times 15 = 105$ marks per hour, a number of marks that soon fills up a sheet of paper. There is no point in trying to cram too much onto one sheet, so the norm is – not more than one day to a sheet. A typical study sheet is shown in Figure 34.2.

■ HOLD TALKS WITH THE STAFF

A meeting is held with all those who are going to be involved in the study, including all the observers, all the staff who will be observed, the supervisor and other people who might be affected – such as the internal mail messengers. Sometimes the meeting will also include the manager, the trade union representative and the observers' manager. On the whole, the extra people are to be discouraged. A straight face-to-face between the observers and the observed is preferable. It results in greater freedom of expression, more openness by all, a sense of togetherness and greater informality, and it avoids building up the study into some fantastic event where everybody is on their best behaviour.

The items that will be covered include:

- a explanation of what the observers will be doing;
- the reason for the study;
- a brief explanation of activity sampling, avoiding any mathematics unless asked for;
- an explanation that one wants everybody to work normally, trying to ignore the observer;
- a demonstration of the study sheet. An explanation that everybody will be expected to take rest breaks and that being 'idle' is normal, not immoral;
- if used, an explanation of the triangles;
- check that the layout is correct with everybody sitting in their normal places;
- ask for details of anything unusual that may happen;
- answer all questions (there tend to be either none or many);
- a second request to work normally.

The meeting usually takes place on a Friday afternoon with the study itself starting on the next Monday morning. This is not to prevent any objections that may arise, but to ensure that the explanations are fresh in people's minds when the study takes place.

Carry out the observations

On the first morning of the actual study observations, one of the observers has to arrive early – before any of the staff. This is largely to show that the analysts are on the job and not taking things easy while the staff are having to slave away. Even more, it is to ensure that some initial activity is not being forgotten. Additionally, on many studies one needs to know the total number of hours that the staff have been present. If there is some method of recording attendance time then the existing method should be consulted. However, if there is no such record then some method of recording unlisted overtime may be needed. Finally, on the first morning a check must be made that all the staff have their triangles.

The first random time shown in the sheet in Figure 34.2 is 08.31. So if this sheet were being used, at 08.31 the observer starts on the first round. This consists of walking round the office, past each member of the staff. As each one is passed, a mark is made on the study sheet indicating the activity of that person at the instant of walking past them. This is repeated at the time indicated for the next round (08.36 in the example time sheet) and so on for the rest of the day.

It is usual for more than one observer to share the task of taking the observations, even if only to allow the analyst to have a lunch break; moreover, it can get tiring to carry out observations for a long period. As a young manager of an industrial engineering department, the author once unaided carried out an activity sampling study lasting thirty-six hours. This marathon study is not recommended practice.

On the example study sheet the column headed 'Not working' is anonymous in the sense that marks are not related to individuals. There seems little point to this but some organizations insist on it. One organization went further in asking that it be called 'Not wanted'.

If 15 people are observed on each round, then at 6 rounds per hour one will make 90 observations per hour. At 7 hours per day this is 630 in a day. So in a five-day week more than 3,000 readings will be taken. This would satisfy the statistical needs, but most firms study for two weeks to eliminate variations. The random times are such that there are periods of a quarter of an hour or more when the observer is not actually making a round. During these periods it is usual for the observer to analyse the previous day's results.

■ MEMORY CARD

An example of a memory card used in one organization for activity sampling is this:

Preparation for Activity Sampling
1 Check previous studies, charts, Job Descriptions.
2 Decide random times; draw up study sheet, copy.
3 Obtain office layout and names.
4 Learn work flow, forms, procedures.
5 Learn existing work measurement values.
6 Explain study to whole group of people.
7 Distribute triangles.
8 Plan work between study team.

Analyse observations

The exact way in which the study is analysed depends on the use to which the work is to be put. It always starts by adding up all the marks and then calculating the percentage of time spent on the different activities. In some Organization Development work these percentages will be separated out for each individual and the results printed and distributed to the staff for discussion.

In work quantification studies, it is normally necessary to know the total hours worked by the group and the volumes completed. For example, a group of 15 people may have worked a total of 550 hours in the week that an activity sampling study was proceeding. During this week a total of 238 medical reports were checked. During the study, 4.2 per cent of the observations were marked as being taken of checking the medical reports.

The time per report is calculated thus:

$$
\begin{aligned}
\text{Total number of hours} &= 550 \\
\text{Percentage of readings} & \\
\quad \text{for checking reports} &= 4.2\% \\
\text{Time on reports} &= 550 \times \tfrac{4.2}{100} \\
&= 23.1 \text{ hours } (= 1{,}386 \text{ minutes}) \\
\text{Number of reports} &= 238 \\
\text{Time per report} &= 1{,}386 \div 238 \\
&= 5.8 \text{ minutes}
\end{aligned}
$$

To this time must be added the allowances for relaxation, etc. Even then the time would still be a 'do-take' time and not a 'should-take' time. All that the activity sampling has done is to tell one how long people currently actually take to do a task. Ways of using activity sampling to obtain should-take work values are described in chapter 36.

The analysis can be performed on a spreadsheet, though since, as stated, most of the analysis is done during the study this is one case when the computer may take longer than a manual approach. There are occasions when the use of a computer is beneficial, as for example when the analysis is very complex, when studies from several locations are being combined, or when a running calculation of 'N' is needed to truncate the study when a desired accuracy has been reached. If readings are being collected on a hand-held terminal instead of on a study sheet, then computer analysis is the preferable option.

E

Further reading

Moore, P. G., *Reason by Numbers*, Harmondsworth: Penguin Books, 1982.

Murch, J. W. K., 'Activity sampling – monitoring by spreadsheet', *Management Services*, June 1986, p. 18.

Springer, C. H. *et al.*, *Mathematics for Management Series*, Vols I and III, Homewood: Richard D. Irwin, 1966.

35

PMTS

A race of hyperintelligent pan-dimensional beings once built
themselves a gigantic supercomputer called Deep Thought to
calculate once and for all the Answer to the Ultimate Question of
Life, the Universe, and Everything.

D. Adams, *The Restaurant at the End of the Universe* (1980)

Structure without life is dead. But life without structure is un-seen.

John Cage, *Silence* (1961)

The idea of being able to sit down at a screen and, by making a few keystrokes, obtain the standard time for an operation is very attractive to many people. We are certainly not at this stage yet, and claims to the contrary which appear every few years should be treated with reserve. If and when we do get reasonably close, it is likely that the path will have used a form of PMTS. The initials PMTS are the common abbreviation for the somewhat unwieldy phrase, Pre-determined Motion Time System.

In time study approaches, the answer is obtained by using a stop-watch and rating. PMTS frees one from both of these since the answer is obtained from pre-printed tables or from a databank held in a computer memory.

Principles

The basic principles upon which all PMTS systems are founded are:

- all the actions that a person in an office performs can be broken down into a limited list of fundamental smaller motions;
- the time to make each of these fundamental motions remains a constant, unless there is a change in the conditions;
- it is possible to set a standard time, therefore, for each of the fundamental motions;
- analysts can be trained to use these standard times so that their inherent accuracy is maintained.

To use the pre-set times, the analyst will:

- observe and understand the operation or task;
- break this down into a restricted list of fundamental motions;
- apply to each of the fundamental motions present, the pre-set time for that motion;
- add up all the pre-set times used to get the overall time for the operation or task.

While doing this, the analyst performs all the other items associated with all work quantification studies. These include proper preparation, treating the staff correctly, coding the studies, structuring the studywork and adding allowances for relaxation, etc.

History

The early PMTS systems were developed for factory use and were mostly designed for specific industries. Another attribute was that details were kept in strict secrecy and were never made available to the public. An example was one called Motion Time Analysis (MTA); this was developed by A. B. Segur in 1927 for the rubber industry. During the 1930s and 1940s other systems followed, still basically for industrial use and still not widely published. Examples were Basic Motion Timestudy and Work Factor. This latter became WOFAC; name-changing is a not uncommon feature of PMTS systems.

It was 1948 before a system was fully published. This was Methods Time Measurement (MTM), the work of Messrs Maynard, Stegemerten and Schwab, who became the central figures of Methods Engineering Council, an American firm of management consultants. MTM was destined to become one of the best-known systems and the basis of a number of other systems. Publication of its details made it the system most widely used for industrial PMTS work measurement.

MTM was developed by taking ciné films of a large number of common operations. These were then timed and rated by a large panel of experienced work measurement analysts. From the results, standard times were calculated for a set of fundamental motions.

E

Owing to the situation under which MTM was developed, it had certain unusual characteristics:

- because it was developed in America in the 1940s, the times in the MTM tables are at a rating that is often nowadays called 'American day-work rate'. On the standard 0/100 scale this is approximately equivalent to a rating of 83;
- the times were issued not in seconds or minutes but in units of one hundred-thousandth of an hour (0.00001). These units of time were called Time Measurement Units which were universally abbreviated to TMUs. Part of the mythology is that the original films were shot at 25 frames per second, which would mean 1 frame per 0.0000111 h, so 1 tmu = 1 frame. This is unlikely. Cameras and projectors operate at 16 (silent) or 24 (sound) frames per second. In fact, the size of the time unit meant that the tables could be expressed in digits without the use of decimal points;
- the system was very detailed, so the fundamental motions that were used were very small. In turn this meant that individual times in the tables were for very small values – and so analysis took a long time.

The original MTM is now referred to as MTM-1 since variations have been developed. Because of its characteristics, MTM-1 had and has certain disadvantages, but its appearance was a milestone and should not be underrated. Here, at last, was a good PMTS system that was widely publicized and implemented. It was well administered: training courses and testing meant that 'MTM-trained' gave reassurance to colleagues and employers.

MTM times are widely accepted as being accurate, a fact that led many other PMTS systems to lean heavily on MTM in their development. MTM-1 is still used in factories, where it is particularly applicable to short-cycle work. In offices it has been largely superseded by later systems. However, one can sometimes observe analysts reverting to

MTM in the office at moments of panic or forgetfulness.

MTM-1 and similar systems are known as 'first generation' systems. They led the field for more than a decade. But for use in the office, two improvements were needed:

- larger 'chunks' of work times would reduce the time needed for analysis;
- the common activities in offices are different from those in factories, so there was a demand for times for specific office use.

These considerations led to the development in the 1960s of 'second-generation' systems. Such systems proliferated during the next decade. Some were developed by management consultancy firms for use by their clients. Some were developed by business schools. Others were the result of co-operation within an industry, e.g. American banks. Still others were developed by large organizations. It is not easy to say how many second-generation systems were developed, especially since many of them have faded into insignificance. The figure is probably somewhere between 50 and 100. There are now about 20 main systems still in use.

These systems were themselves further developed during the 1960s and 1970s. The main development was the build-up of larger times for larger chunks of work. Indeed, for commercial survival, office PMTS systems needed times at two levels, one for small quasi-MTM motions and one for larger office tasks. The two levels enable organizations to build up their own specific task times, which can then be used in turn to obtain the times for operations.

The next development (during the mid-1980s) was to put the times into a computer databank. This development was accelerated by the increasing use in the office of microcomputers. Different approaches were used. Some people used a form of spreadsheet (quite quick and easy to get up and running). Others used a database management program (such as dBase plus Multimate Advantage). A few wrote specific specialized software.

Having the times in a micro is an advantage but not an enormous one. The real advantage comes from the ability it gives an organization in building up its own databank of times. This confers flexibility, consistency and accuracy, and it also saves a lot of time when operations and procedures change. It does need self-discipline and a well-thought-out structure to gain maximum benefits.

■ FIRST-GENERATION SYSTEMS

As already indicated, MTM is regarded as the grandfather of PMTS systems. The other best-known first-generation system is Work Factor. This was developed at RCA (by Messrs Quick, Shea and Kohler) between 1934 and 1938, so it actually pre-dates MTM. A book was published in 1945, but it did not go into full details as MTM did in 1948.

Work Factor became popular in the electronics industry, being used by Philips, for example. It later changed name to WOFAC and was sold by the WOFAC Corporation, which itself later became the Science Management Corporation.

The fine detail of first-generation systems means that one reckons on taking 100 to 300 minutes to analyse one minute of work.

■ SECOND-GENERATION SYSTEMS

Second-generation systems are faster to use: one can reckon on something like 50 to 120 minutes of analysis for each minute of work. They also require less practical experience in order to become proficient. Some of the systems that may be met are given in Table 35.1.

A common question is: which is the best PMTS system? This is not easy to answer. Most practitioners have their own preferences and favourites. It often seems that one likes best the system that one knows best – which is not surprising. With experience, one learns how to exploit a known system to best advantage and how to circumvent any inherent disadvantages.

Several PMTS systems are used by major management consultancies. None of them is felt by their clients to be wrong, in the sense that the times are incorrect, and clients are almost invariably pleased with the results. It can be quite time-consuming to compare the actual times because different systems have their own characteristics. For example, some have times based on the standard 100 rating on the 0/100 scale. Others use 83, and even 75. Some systems include allowances while others omit them. Even motion descriptions (e.g. 'stamp with rubber stamp') can have different interpretations

Table 35.1 Second-generation PMTS systems

Name	Notes
SPMTS (Simplified PMTS)	Developed in Britain by ICI. Really a sort of 1½ generation. Important feature was the use of milliminutes – 1/1000 minute.
BWD (Basic Work Data) and CWD (Clerical Work Data)	Based on SPMTS. Developed by ICI and British Rail. Useful for engineering maintenance work. CWD is the office version. CWD was purchased from British Rail by a new company, improved and relaunched in 1987.
GPD (General Purpose Data)	Published in 1962 by the American MTM Association. Faster than MTM-1 but with a complex coding.
MTM-2	Published in 1965. Based on research by the Swedish MTM Association.
MTM-3	Only four main categories (handle/transport/step/bend-and-arise). Useful for long-cycle maintenance work.
MODAPTS	Developed in Australia. Based on MTM-2.
PSD (Primary Standard Data)	Based on MTM-1. Developed by Urwick Orr. Later development led to PSD-2.
MCD (Master Clerical Data)	Based on MTM. Developed by Serge A. Birn Co. The non-office version is MSD (Master Standard Data).
UOC (Universal Office Controls)	Developed by Messrs. Maynard, Aiken and Lewis of H. B. Maynard & Co. Inc.
OSS (Office Staffing Standards)	Developed by Associated Industrial Consultants (AIC) which later became Inbucon and, still later, merged.
CSD (Clerical Standard Data)	Developed in Canada by Leetham Simpson & Associates.
SET (Sequence Element Technique) and SET-2	Developed by T. J. Davies of Berkswell Management Services. Based on MTM-1. Similarities to MTM-3. Basis for computerized work measurement.

E

(e.g. include or exclude opening/closing stamp pad).

A careful analysis was carried out (by Harvard Consultants Ltd) of common work elements of a number of the leading systems. This revealed a surprisingly large number of differences that could not be called trivial. Nevertheless, the fact remains that a skilled practitioner can achieve good results using any of the leading systems. Declaring our own bias, details of three systems that we like are given below. Commercially they could be regarded as competitors with one another – but all three were based on careful research and all three work in practice.

Three systems

■ MULLIGAN DATA

Paul B. Mulligan and Co. developed Mulligan Clerical Standards, usually referred to as 'Mulligan data'. Mulligan data was developed from independent films and was not based on existing first generation systems. It is widely used in Australia and Britain. It has had several names. It is the basis for CWIP (Clerical Work Improvement Programme) and was sold as such by W. D. Scott. It is also called Standard Time Data and SOS (Simplified Office Standards) at different levels. It is now sold by Coopers & Lybrand, after absorbing W. D. Scott in Britain.

The data has the following characteristics:

- times are issued in units of 0.00001 h. To most people this unit is a TMU but Mulligan calls it an STU (Standard Time Unit);
- times are issued at a rating of 83 on the 0/100 scale;
- the times include an allowance of 16.67 per cent. This covers relaxation, contingencies and a daily make-ready-and-put-away.

The system has the following plus points:

- the detailed level (Standard Time Data) has a very good coverage of office tasks. The tables of values are comprehensive and so reduce calculations;
- the simplified level (SOS) contains a number of useful generalized motion times that saves analyst time;
- an abstract of common SOS times is printed on a card that can be carried in the pocket.

Most PMTS systems use a coding system for their times. In analysing an operation, one writes down the element, its code and the time. An example of an SOS analysis is:

Pick up a box file from the floor, and put it on a desk 2½ m away:

Bend and arise	2 × MC	40
Get and put file	HG	55
Walk 4 paces	4 × MC	80
Total		175

374

■ MILLIMINUTE DATA/BASIC MINUTE DATA

In 1965, PA Consulting Services developed MMD (MilliMinute Data). This was based on a mix of GPD, MTM-2 and original times. One set of data was prepared for factory use and one for office use, but both are compatible, which is useful. MMD is at a detailed level (the motions and times are short), so subsequently a higher level system was developed for the office. This is BMD (Basic Minute Data), which has tables of standard times for longer items of work. BMD was developed from MMD in such a way that both are compatible – which is also very useful.

BMD is widely used in a number of countries, and seems particularly favoured in financial institutions where there is need for accuracy and flexibility. In the 1970s the American consultancy Arthur Andersen were comparing systems in various countries. They decided that BMD was the best available at the time for their purposes, and were licensed by PA to use it for their clients.

The characteristics of BMD are:

- times are issued in units of milliminutes (1/1000 minute);
- times are issued at a rating of 100 on the 0/100 scale;
- the times do not include any allowances for relaxation, etc.;
- these characteristics mean that times are already at the definition of Basic Minutes, without the need for any further calculations or manipulation.

The system has the following advantages:

E

- the times are in basic minutes, which facilitates the incorporation of any synthetics and makes most calculations straightforward;
- the way the times are built up means that changes in methods and procedures can be easily accommodated;
- the absolute compatibility of the two levels makes it easy for clients to build up their own databank;
- an abstract of common BMD times plus all the MMD times is printed on a well-produced card that can be carried in the pocket.

An example of a BMD analysis is:

Move chair, get up from desk, walk 4 paces to a filing cabinet, open a drawer, close it, return to the desk and sit down:

Move chair, stand, sit	SCM	86
To cabinet and return	8 × WO	72
Open and close drawer	30	35
Total		193

This total is 193 milliminutes, or 0.193 minutes (11.6 seconds).

■ OSIRIS

The third of our sample is OSIRIS. This was based on a wide mix of inputs: video films, empirical research at universities, time study orthometrics and an analysis of other systems. It arose out of meetings of practising analysts who knew the drawbacks of the systems that they used and who wanted a new system. The starting point was to avoid the inconsistencies and problems of existing systems, and to attain some high-level times. OSIRIS was developed by Berkeley Lion Ltd and Harvard Consultants; it was published in the 1980s.

The characteristics of OSIRIS are:

- times are issued in units of milliminutes (1/1000 minute);
- times are issued at a rating of 100 on the 0/100 scale;
- the times include an allowance of 15 per cent to cover relaxation, small contingencies, and supervision/training. Unlike Mulligan data, the allowance does not cover the daily make-ready-and-put-away.

The system has the following advantages:

- the times are at a true Standard Minute level. This makes calculations easier, and is easily understood by staff, management and unions;
- changes in methods and procedures can be well accommodated;
- the system has three levels (micro, macro and 'fast lane') that are fully compatible;
- an abstract of the micro and macro times is printed separately in a format that can be carried in the pocket.

It will be noticed that all three systems have certain similarities. They are reasonably consistent within themselves. They all have data at two or three levels. Their rating level and allowances are known. They all have an abstract that can be kept in the pocket. Any PMTS system meant for office use should possess these features.

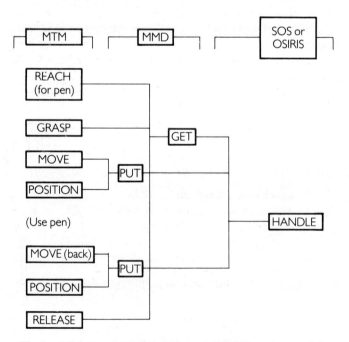

Figure 35.1 Analysis by different PMTS systems of the actions involved in using a pen

Levels of data

An understanding of the concept of levels of data is necessary for the efficient use of PMTS. Low levels of data are very detailed and are characterized by being short in duration (e.g. grasp a pen). Higher levels of data are progressively larger chunks of work and so are longer in duration. The use of low-level times is precise but time-consuming: in factory operations they are often appropriate but not in offices. Newly trained analysts frequently have a tendency to stick with low-level data, and have to be encouraged to move up the scale. Experienced analysts use high-level data, interspersed with the occasional use of low-level data.

The lowest level of data is represented by first-generation systems such as MTM-1. Analysts often refer to such times as 'Level 1' times. The second-generation systems all combined these times to Level 2 times. For example, getting a pen, using it and then replacing it on the desk is a common office task. This would be analysed by different systems as shown in Figure 35.1. Not surprisingly, Level 1 times are rarely used in the office. Further levels are shown in Table 35.2. In this table it will be seen that the time from one level is used in the build-up of the time in the next higher level. Also, the parts of each build-up get progressively larger. First-generation PMTS systems concentrated

E

Table 35.2 Levels of data

Level	Item	Build-up	Time
Level I	Reach towards micro		(8.7 tmu)
Level 2	Get screen	Reach towards screen Grasp Release	6 MM (MM = milliminute)
Level 3 (element)	Switch micro on	Get screen Apply force Move switch	16 MM
Level 4 (sub- operation)	Enter databank	Switch micro on Check screen Go to menu Go to entry Switch off	101 MM
Level 5 (operations)	Interrogate databank	Enter databank Log on to supplies-due Go to individual entry Exit databank	0.268 mins
Level 6 (task)	Sell supplies (per batch of 10 customers)	Interrogate databank Telephone customer Inform – supplies Inform – specials Improve order Key in order Inform – delivery	36.5 mins

on Level 1 times; Second-generation systems have times at Levels 2, 3, 4 and some at 5. Individual organizations build up their own specific Level 5 and 6 times.

Using PMTS in the office

No PMTS system can be learnt from a book. Training starts in a classroom and this theoretical training lasts from 1 to 3 weeks, depending on the system. Some courses end with an examination which may be formal or informal.

Many people are trained by management consultants as part of the introduction of PMTS into an organization. In this case, there will be a programme of work during which PMTS is scheduled to be introduced to departments a section at a time. Trainees will follow the classroom training by moving into the first office to be measured. They will start by learning to build up a few straightforward Level 3 times. Meanwhile the consultant will, in discussions, agree the ultimate shape of the databank that will be progressively built up.

In this way, newly trained analysts gain experience while the office work is measured and the high-level databank is built up. Initially there can be a problem at this early stage: the newly trained analysts have to gain confidence in their abilities while management may become impatient if progress seems to be falling behind schedule. It is part of the consultant's job to achieve a balance between the two needs.

Actual study-taking follows the normal pattern already described. The job of going from classroom seminar to a fully measured organization may appear a complex affair, but previous experience ensures that failure is avoided.

36

CWV and Other Notes

It is better to ask some of the questions than to know all of the
answers.   James Thurber, *The Thurber Carnival* (1945)

How much of life is lost in waiting.   Emerson, *Essays: First Series* (1841)

This chapter contains notes on three disparate areas:

- categorized work values;
- enhancements to PMTS-and-activity sampling;
- the use of hardware and software.

None of them is a work measurement technique as such but each is an aid to work
quantification studies.

Categorized work values (CWV)

E

Categorized work values are not uncommon in areas such as factories, nursing, hotels
and social work. For some reason, the approach is met with less often in offices. This is
unfortunate since there are many circumstances in offices when it should be the
preferred approach. It should perhaps be pointed out that the 'official' term for CWV is
Comparative Estimating; however, the number of office analysts who have been met
that use this term is approximately nil. So for once, the unofficial term will be used here.

■ SITUATIONS WHERE USEFUL

Categorized work values are particularly useful where:

- there are many different tasks, none of which accounts for a high proportion of the
total time of the office. It is not uncommon to find an office in an organization that is
responsible for seventy or more different tasks;
- the time taken for individual tasks varies widely for reasons that are both valid and
known. The overall time for a task may be 40 SMs. But if the spread of the work
content is 20–80 SMs, then issuing 40 SMs as the standard may imply an accuracy
that is unwarranted and resented;
- there may only be a very few people in a section, and lengthy measurement may be
uneconomic especially if no changes are anticipated;
- some tasks occur only infrequently and/or it proves very difficult to study the full
spectrum of tasks.

■ PRINCIPLES

The basic principles of the approach are:

- tasks are not given precise individual time values, but are allocated to predetermined ranges of time values known as categories;

- tasks are allocated to the correct categories by comparing them with specified tasks in each category. These tasks are known as benchmark tasks;
- the total work performed during a period, such as a month, can then be calculated by multiplying each category value by the number of items in that category. These totals are added together to give the grand total for the month.

■ ADVANTAGES AND DISADVANTAGES

The main advantages of the approach are:

- it is faster than full work measurement techniques, especially where there are a large number of tasks;
- where there are a significant number of new procedures or tasks introduced after quantification, results and management controls can be maintained. This is not at the cost of a sudden surge of measurement studies, or leaving a lot of work unmeasured;
- the approach is readily understood by the staff;
- results can be easily integrated with those obtained from other techniques;
- in one type of CWV, staff experience and contributions are incorporated in the build-up and the results.

The main disadvantage of the approach is a loss of precision as compared with full PMTS or time study. This is sometimes a matter of concern to the staff involved. Also, the type of CWV that incorporates staff contributions needs them to articulate their knowledge in a way that is likely to be new to them.

There are two main ways of operating CWV. The traditional one is designated the Arithmetic, while the newer is the Participatory.

■ ARITHMETIC CWV

The stages of the traditional CWV can be summarized as:

(a) The required level of accuracy is decided. So is the length of the control period. This will depend on the other control periods being used in the organization and on the type of work. For data prep, the control period may be one day while for creative and professional staff it is usually one month ($= 150$ hours, say).

(b) The number of staff involved is decided. This is normally the people in a section.

(c) Calculate 'x' from the formula, where x is the length of the first category. The formula used is:

$$x = 1.56\,NWP^2$$

where N = number of staff involved,
W = length of control period,
P = accuracy required.

This formula, like the activity sampling one, is for 95 per cent confidence limits.

If the section only has three people in it, then for a period of seven hours:

$x = 1.56(3)(7)(5/100)^2$

$= 0.082$ hours.

If the period is one month (150 hours), then:

$x = 1.56(3)(150)(5/100)^2$

$= 1.755$ hours.

(d) Calculate the time for the longest task to be categorized, using a relevant work measurement technique. This time is 'T_{max}'.

(e) Read the number of categories required from the chart given in Figure 36.1. People who favour the arithmetic approach do not like the number of categories to be more

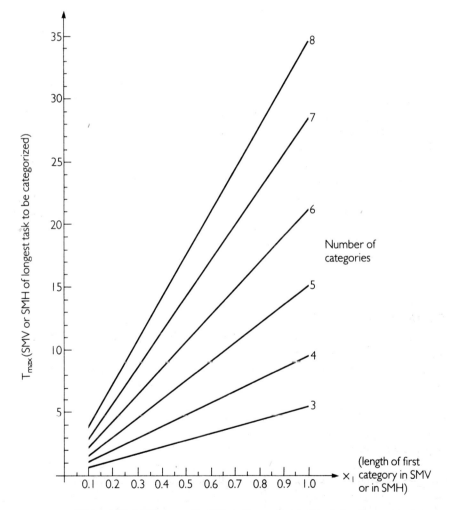

Figure 36.1 Determination of number of categories

than 6 in normal circumstances. If the number of categories is excessive, then consider changing N, W, P or T_{max}.

(f) Calculate the length of each category, and hence the ranges of each, that is the minimum and maximum. This is done by multiplying 'x' successively by 1, 2, 3, 4, and so on.

For example, assuming that the section size is 2, the control period is one week of 38 hours, the accuracy is ± 5 per cent and the longest job is 4 Standard Hours, then:

$$x = 1.56(2)(38)(5/100)^2$$

$$= 0.296 \text{ hours } (= \text{ say } 20\,\text{SMs})$$

The chart indicates 5 categories which would be:

Category	Category range
1	0–20 SMs
2	20–60 SMs
3	60–120 SMs
4	120–200 SMs
5	200–300 SMs

(g) Calculate the value for each category. Mathematically, this should be the weighted mean of each task in a category. This would imply changing the value every time a new job is introduced, and usually it is assumed that the mid-point of each range can be taken. However, for the first category a value 65 per cent along the range is taken. This is because no task actually takes nil time to complete and very small tasks would be included in contingencies.

So in the example in (f) above, the values would be 13, 40, 90, 160 and 250 SMs.

(h) A task at the upper and lower limit of each category is selected, measured accurately and comprehensively described. These tasks are known as the benchmark tasks. All the tasks can then be allocated to their correct category by comparing them with the benchmarks. In the arithmetic method, statisticians insist that the actual values of benchmark tasks should never be used as the standard averages.

■ PARTICIPATORY CWV

There is nothing intrinsically wrong with the traditional way of calculating categorized work values. However, some consultants and some clients' staff did not favour it. Somehow it seemed too remote and even mechanistic. This may be the reason that it became little used in offices, though it is unfortunate to lose its advantages. This is one reason why the participatory route to CWV was developed. It was developed within Harvard Consultants Ltd and is now used in large companies and by management consultants. It takes a very different route to getting categorized work values. The stages, with a simple worked example, are given below.

(a) Two or perhaps three (if a large group) members of staff are selected to help in the study. This selection may be done by the consultant, by the supervisor, or by the staff themselves, depending on circumstances. It is important that the people selected are experienced. They should know first-hand as many of the tasks performed in the section as possible.

(b) With the assistance of the two staff members the tasks done in the group are listed.

In the example shown, only ten tasks have been selected:

Tasks
Open morning mail
Sort morning mail and City Walks into pigeon holes
Take cuttings from daily newspapers
Take cuttings from Extel
Answer phone queries from public
Photocopy committees' agendas
Replenish stationery stores
Pack mail orders
Do accounts for staff restaurants
Send overseas telexes/fax

(c) These tasks are now arrayed – listed in order of size, with the shortest as '1'. This is done by the staff. A note is also made of the frequency of each. If possible, this should be factual. Otherwise, the staff are asked to make an estimate.

No.	Task	Freq.
1	Answer phone queries from public	Med.
2	Photocopy committees' agendas	High
3	Pack mail orders	High
4	Sort mail and City Walks	Med.
5	Send overseas telexes/fax	High
6	Take cuttings from Extel	Med.
7	Replenish stationery stores	Low
8	Open morning mail	Med.
9	Take cuttings from newspapers	Med.
10	Do accounts for staff restaurants	Med.

E

(d) Do a PMTS analysis on a task at the shorter end of the array, on a high-frequency job.

The task 'Photocopy committees' agendas' was selected. The result was that the time value was 1.5 minutes.

(e) Calculate the time for the longest task, using a relevant work measurement technique.

The task is 'Do accounts for staff restaurants'. The time for this task was 60 minutes.

(f) The staff members are asked to say how long they think each task in the list takes to perform.

Task 1 – 1 min	6 – 7 mins
2 – 2 mins	7 – 20 mins
3 – 2 mins	8 – 30 mins
4 – 5 mins	9 – 40 mins
5 – 5 mins	10 – 65 mins

383

(g) A first trial is made of splitting up the array into categories. Knowing frequencies assists this stage.

We have a spread of 1½–60 minutes. A possible split would be:

Category A:	0–3 minutes
Category B:	3–7 minutes
Category C:	7–20 minutes
Category D:	20–60 minutes

(h) A PMTS study is carried out in the item just below the first break-point. Also, if necessary, on the item just above the first break-point.

The item is 'Sort incoming mail'. For this the time was 3 minutes.

(i) Measure the items above and below the other break-points, as necessary.

Not necessary in our example. It would be done if there is any uncertainty or if the number of tasks were very large. To some extent, it depends on experience and staff feelings.

(j) Reinspect array. Check staff estimates with measured results. Finalize task, placing in categories.

Category A – 1	Category C – 7
2	Category D – 8
3	9
4	10
Category B – 5	
6	

(k) Finalize details and prepare a table of values. These are normally at the category mid-points (unless this conflicts with vital frequencies). For the first category, use a place 65 per cent in the range.

In the example, the resulting table is straightforward with no alterations:

Category	Range	Time
A	0–3	2 mins
B	3–7	5 mins
C	7–20	13½ mins
D	20–60	40 mins

(1) The final stage is to build up a dummy control period statement. This shows how the staff would have fared, using the CWV approach and values. This can then be discussed with all the staff involved. The example is:

Item	No.	Category	No.	Time	Time × No.
1	12				
2	60	A	102	2	204 mins
3	25				
4	5				
5	20	B	26	5	130 mins
6	6				
7	0.05	C	0.05	13.5	(0.7 mins)*
8	1				
9	1	D	3	40	120 mins
10	1				
Total minutes 'earned' per day					454 mins

*Once per month

In the particular example given, it is possible to compare the results obtained with CWV with that obtained from full calculations:

Item	No.	Time	Time × No.
1	12	1	12
2	60	1½	90
3	25	2	50
4	5	3	15
5	20	5	100
6	6	7	42
7	0·05	20	1
8	1	30	30
9	1	40	40
10	1	60	60
Total minutes per day			440

$$\text{Hence difference} = \frac{454 - 440}{454} \times 100 - 3\%$$

Note the following points on using the participatory route to CWV:

- in offices with a large number of tasks, the number of categories is usually 6–8 and should not be outside the spread of 4 to 10;
- if staff have difficulty in deciding how long they think a task takes them, ask for three estimates: minimum, medium and maximum. Then use the '1–4–1' formula:

$$\text{Normal} = \frac{(1 \times \text{min.}) + (4 \times \text{medium}) + (1 \times \text{max.})}{6}$$

385

Alternatively, agree with them on an example that is 'normal' and ask for a time for the example. If the staff find it difficult to array the tasks, pick out the frequent tasks and array these first. Then ask them to slot in the others;

- take care with jobs that are disliked or those recently introduced. Those disliked will be given a too-high frequency. New tasks may take a disproportionately long time;
- if tasks are completed intermittently over a period of time, then obtain separate estimates for each part and then sum. Alternatively, ask how many could be completed if there were no interruptions in say one hour or half a day;
- do not ask more than one person at a time for estimates, otherwise there is a danger of group discussions leading to an argument.

Building up the categories is largely a matter of practice. Inspect the tasks and look for clusters. Aim to get a natural look to the groupings, and watch out for the tasks with very high frequencies. The breakpoint for the shortest category usually lies between 4 and 10 minutes in offices; it is rarely more than 15 minutes.

For the first trial split it is usually useful to use a Fibonacci sequence. This is a sequence in which each number is the sum of the previous two. For example: 2, 3, 5 (3 + 2), 8 (5 + 3), 13 (8 + 5) and so on. Examples of other Fibonacci sequences are:

2	3	4	5
4	5	7	9
6	8	11	14
10	13	18	23
16	21	29	37
26	34	47	60
42	56	76	97

The standard for the second category should never be more than twice the standard for the first category. This would offend against a sense of natural justice, as well as probably being incorrect.

A useful property of CWV is its ability to incorporate new tasks and procedures as they arise, without the need to immediately carry out detailed work measurement. This is done by slotting the new procedure into the array as a temporary arrangement, in a position that the supervisor agrees is reasonable. Time is then allowed for the staff to become proficient at the new task, and to ensure that it is properly scheduled and flowing. The new procedure/task can then be allotted a permanent place in the array and hence allocated to its correct category.

Categorized work values can be a most useful technique in many office situations. When installed properly, its advantages can prove most satisfying.

Enhancements to PMTS-and-activity sampling

As already stated, a major disadvantage of activity sampling is that it only tells one the percentage of time currently being spent on different activities of tasks. Thus it can only tell one 'do-take' times and not 'should-take' times. It is, however, faster than full PMTS studies, which do tell one 'should-take' times.

This apparent dichotomy has led a number of organizations to combine the two techniques. First, as much work is timed by PMTS as seems economically justified; at least 40 per cent is normally insisted upon. Second, the rest of the work is studied using activity sampling.

Now, it is not possible to do an activity sampling study on just some of the work; a sample will include all the work being performed in an office. What is done, therefore, is to have some of the headings on the activity sampling study sheet reserved for PMTS-timed work and its related operations. Whenever an observer makes a reading of a job already timed by PMTS, the observer marks these in the columns headed 'PMTS' and 'PMTS related' of the study sheet in Figure 34.3. It might be thought that a disadvantage of the approach would be the difficulty of remembering which items had been PMTS-timed as one goes round the office taking readings. In practice this is not a problem. First, the people taking the sample are usually the same people who did the PMTS-timing, so they automatically remember which tasks they have been working on. Second, clients' staff who do the sampling are often quite experienced in the firm's work, so they tend to recognize the sort of work that will have been PMTS-timed.

Experience can be a two-edged sword, especially if, for some reason, the staff do not want their work measured. An example of this was met in a firm that had used PMTS/sampling for twelve years, in which there was one department that had never been studied. The staff felt that their work was too complex and professional to be studied. Inevitably the day came when their work was studied, although the staff felt that this would diminish their élitism. Since PMTS/sampling had been used in the firm for so many years, the staff were well acquainted with it. Instinctively they also were aware of the inherent weakness of sampling, namely that if used for setting standards, then 'do-take' times become the standards.

Thus the staff knew that the route to 'easy' standards was to work differently during the study period. They knew that they should build up a backlog and not be seen taking any rest periods. It happened that during the study period, there was in the department a temporary employee from a government-sponsored youth employment scheme. He was given the task of whistling loudly every time the analyst was seen approaching the department to start a round of readings (not the best introduction for him to life-after-school).

The textbook answer is that greater efforts should have been made beforehand to prepare the staff for work measurement. But life is not a textbook. Human beings are only human. Such incidents can happen at some time in any organization – and, in fact, staff relations were good in this particular organization. But the incident does highlight a weakness of using sampling for setting standards; it only gives 'do-take' times.

This fact remains true even when it is only used on 50 per cent of the work. In saying this, it is acknowledged that many organizations use this approach, that it has been used for years, that it has improved efficiency, and that thousands of people are working to its standards.

■ RATED ACTIVITY SAMPLING

Rated activity sampling is just that: sampling with rating. When the readings are taken during sampling, the pace of working is rated as already described. One therefore knows the proportion of time spent on the different activities, the volumes and frequences, and the rate of working. From this one can calculate the quantity of work done compared with Standard, and this in turn enables the standard times (SMVs) to be found.

There are different ways of doing this. One can take sampling readings in the normal

E

way and just add a rating at the instant of observation. Alternatively one can take a round of readings at intervals of one minute. Or one can study people for one minute each, rating for that minute, and noting activities during the minute. In each case, the calculations are slightly different.

The advantage of rating for one minute is that if the rating averages 105, then the amount of work done in the minute is 105/100 or 1.05 minutes. (One must still add the allowances, of course.) This makes the calculations much easier. But one can then lose the notion of randomness – and possibly have too few readings to satisfy statistical considerations. Also, in practice, it may be found difficult to handle a large number of both activities and people. However, rated activity sampling is often used to verify the correctness of already calculated work values. This is done by taking a study for a day. One can then calculate how many minutes of work were 'earned' in the day as indicated by the study. This can then be compared with that earned on the proposed or actual work values (quantity × value).

For use in setting work values, a formula is used:

$$T_1 = \frac{f \Sigma R_1}{100 N_1}$$

where T_1 = basic time for work activity 1
f = time interval between observations
ΣR_1 = sum of all the ratings of observations of 1
N_1 = number of occurrences of 1.

For example, it is wished to find the Basic time for inspecting a medical report. A study was taken of 500 observations, during which time 40 reports were inspected. Observations were at intervals of one minute each, during which 160 were seen to be of inspecting reports. The sum of the ratings of the observations was 15,000.

$$T = \frac{(1)(15000)}{(100)(40)} = \frac{15000}{4000} = 3.75 \text{ BMs.}$$

To this has to be added the allowances to get the SMV.

■ PMTS-RATED ACTIVITY SAMPLING

Rated activity sampling is not, in offices, the complete answer to the fact that sampling only gives do-take times. Quite apart from statistical considerations, there is the problem that comparatively few company analysts are sufficiently experienced in rating to attain accurate results. Moreover it is often difficult in practice to split out the PMTS and PMTS-related activities while taking one-minute readings.

What is needed is a method of rating a normal activity sampling study. Two factors enable us to achieve this desirable end:

● the rating level of times of PMTS systems is known;
● if we know the average rating of somebody for a large part of the day, then this will be that person's pace of working for the whole day (although research shows that this is not always true for new entrants).

These two factors can be applied to an activity sampling study that includes some PMTS-timed activities:

- we know how long was spent on work which has been subjected to PMTS analysis;
- we know the volumes processed during the sampling study;
- we know how long people would have been working on the PMTS work if they had been working at 100.

It is therefore possible to calculate the actual rate of working from:

$$\frac{\text{Time that should be taken at 100 on PMTS tasks}}{\text{Time that was actually taken}} \times 100$$

This rate can then be applied to the rest (non-PMTS) of the study. An example of this approach is:

Stage	Example
From the PMTS analysis, it is known how long certain items of work would take at a rating of 100.	180 minutes
From the sampling study, it is known how long these same items did actually take.	190 minutes
So it is straightforward to calculate the rate of working.	$180/190 \times 100 = 95$
This rate can then be applied to the rest of the sampling study time (say, 230 minutes).	$230 \times 95/100 = 218$ minutes
The total time is therefore:	$180 + 218 = 398$ minutes

Once the allowances have been added to these Basic Minutes, we have the Standard Minute Values. If the PMTS system used is based at a rating of 100 then the calculations are more straightforward than if it is not.

This approach was developed by Harvard Consultants, and has proved to be very effective. The first time that it was used was in an office that had hitherto used the common PMTS-plus-activity sampling mix described above. It showed that the standard staffing level of about 1,000 people was too large by 200.

Hardware and software

Electronic aids are used in work quantification for three main purposes:

- the collection of data;
- calculations;
- storing, accessing and manipulating data held in a databank.

The greater the degree of integration between these three, the easier life becomes.

■ DATA COLLECTION

Analysts need to be mobile, not to say peripatetic. Data collection equipment therefore needs to be portable. A number of units have been developed that can be used at the point of study. Some of these are similar to the units used for stocktaking in shops and stores, others are more like pocket calculators. A few are custom designed, though these

389

tend to be more expensive than the other two types. Although shapes vary somewhat, they mostly resemble 'pocket computers' with a reduced-size keyboard and a display window.

The major advantage of these machines is the facility to download the data to an office computer for later computation. There are occasions when this is a major aid to a study. Not least of the attractions is the reduction in manual calculations, with the possibility of error, although the major cause of error – getting volumes and frequencies wrong – still remains. Manufacturers also claim a saving in time, and that using the equipment means that one can concentrate more on what is going on.

The equipment has two main practical disadvantages. First, one often needs a piece of paper to write down notes, extra details and reminders. Scribbling these down on a form that one is using is faster than keying in with two fingers on a reduced keyboard while watching a poorly lit display window. Also, downloading the data may be inconvenient for these extra notes. The second practical disadvantage is the equipment's weight and cumbersome handling. Some units weigh in at as much as a half kilo, which can get tiring by the end of a day's studywork.

To some extent, the weight depends on the batteries. Extended use needs large batteries, which means weight. No unit should be bought unless it has a 'battery-low' indicator. Batteries running down in mid-study vie on the annoyance scale with losing one's data on a microcomputer.

The facility to download a megabyte of data to an office computer can be very useful. This facility has led to many of these units being called 'hand-held terminals'. The fact that more people do not use them must mean that such people think the disadvantages outweigh the advantages. Greater penetration will have to wait improved units.

■ CALCULATIONS

Certain tasks in work quantification are repetitive, manual and even, dare one say, boring. These are the tasks involved in going from time taken to SMVs. This involves continual rewriting. From study to study summary. From summary to study record. From study record to build-up. From build-up to SMV tables.

Not surprisingly, many people use an office computer to ease the burden. Commercial packages are available that will move, reasonably automatically, from actual times to complete work values. Such packages should have certain facilities:

- allowances should be changeable, but with default values;
- the intermediate stages should be printed out, to show to union representatives if needed;
- the software should be capable of handling input flexibly but must have the facility of by-passing menus;
- it is definitely advantageous to be able to drive high-quality printers/plotters, otherwise it may be necessary to retype the output for inclusion in a report.

An alternative to buying a commercial package is to evolve one's own software. The usual route for this is to use a simple spreadsheet, possibly in conjunction with a word processing program to get good output. Small companies with modest demands may like to approach the local secondary school and contact the teacher who is responsible for computing studies. Some such teachers will welcome the opportunity to move the pupils away from Moonlandings and Golf Courses for their programming practice (others will say, 'Not another one?').

■ DATABANKS

The use of office computers for use with databanks offers a high pay-back in convenience and saving of time and patience. At the same time, the software is more complex than those needed for calculating SMVs and will often need a hard disk at the sophisticated end.

The data must be held in a structured way (continual search by expert system approaches still takes too long). The data must be held in the 'levels of data' manner. This is so that one can enter at any level and then go up and down the levels as needed. A databank that tends to keep one at Level 2 may be worse than none at all.

Software is available that is all-singing and all-dancing, and that needs no skill or knowledge, or so the advertisement says. But unskilled singing and dancing is not much help when one is at the start of a 100 m sprint. Nevertheless, databanks on the office computer are destined to increase in penetration – they are needed and they are very useful.

■ PARAMETER

The Parameter system is based on a small (250 g) unit, one of which is used by each person involved. Thirty to forty times a day, it emits a beep at random intervals. When this happens, the user keys in the current activity, using a code. This entry is stored in the unit memory. At the end of the study, the data is downloaded to an office computer that analyses the results and prints them out.

The system is thus like activity sampling but with several advantages. The data is self-recorded and so is suitable for managers and others who are widely dispersed and/ or who at times perform confidential work that precludes interruption. The coding can be complex which enables analysis to be detailed. The cost per person studied is not high compared with other forms of sampling.

Parameter has been used for a number of interesting studies. These include Organization Development (especially in Sweden), Management Development, activity sampling of nursing staff, eliminating bottlenecks, and costing bank managers' time. Parameter was refined and developed by PA Consulting Services.

E

37

Special Problem Areas

I know of no enquiry which the impulses of man suggests, that is
forbidden to the resolution of man to pursue.

M. Fuller, *Summer on the Lakes* (1844)

On all the peaks lies peace.   Goethe, *Wanderers Nachtlied* (*c.* 1779)

There are three problem areas that cause considerable discussion, uncertainty and
difficulty. They are:

- dealing with peaks;
- handling staff reductions;
- controlling creative and professional work.

The first of these (peaks) causes the most uncertainty.

Dealing with peaks

In some offices, it is not possible to eliminate peaks completely. Nevertheless, they can
be greatly reduced. Such reduction needs some attention to detail, a precise (though
sometimes compact) study, knowledge of what one should do and – above all – a
willingness to act.

■ STUDY THE PEAKS

The first stage is to find out and be able to describe the peaks under consideration.
What exactly is the peak? What causes it? Why does it exist? When does it occur? How
big is it?

This last point is particularly important. If the peak is once a month, then the work
done during each day of the month should be ascertained. If this would take too long to
study, then it may be necessary just to use the weekly figures. If one does this, the result
will not be as accurate and one will probably miss those cases when there is a major
peak plus a minor peak in the work cycle.

In those offices where there is already a form of work quantification, then the task is
very much easier. One merely takes a count of the various outputs and then calculates,
say, the standard hours of work each day. Where there is no work quantification, then
even a crude measuring system will much enhance the accuracy. Alternatively, one can
use activity sampling, perhaps using fewer readings than one would use for full work
quantification purposes. In those rare offices with only one output (e.g. computer
inputting departments) then a straight count may suffice.

In every case, the amount of detail required depends on the size and severity of the
problem. As such, it is a matter of judgement at the time. One should also try to think
ahead. Exactly how is one going to use the information? Will it be possible to use the
information collected for another purpose?

Having tabulated the data, it is nearly always advantageous to draw a diagram. A table and a diagram should be prepared showing the number of staff required during the work cycle. Less good alternatives are diagrams showing straight output counts or percentage staff loading. Examples are shown in Table 37.1 and Figure 37.1.

Table 37.1 Tabulation of data

Day in monthly cycle	Workload-equivalent staffing	Day in monthly cycle	Workload-equivalent staffing	Day in monthly cycle	Workload-equivalent staffing
1	7.1	8	8.3	15	14.6
2	8.7	9	8.1	16	16.8
3	7.5	10	8.3	17	16.7
4	7.8	11	8.6	18	16.5
5	7.7	12	9.3	19	16.4
6	7.9	13	10.4	20	7.3
7	8.1	14	12.3		

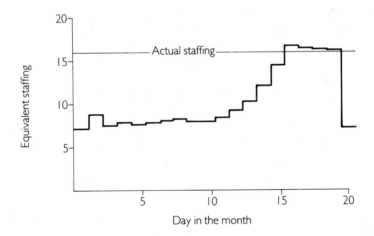

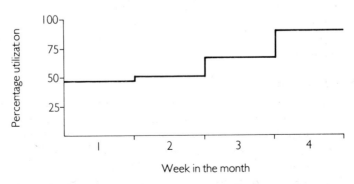

Figure 37.1 Presentation of the data shown in Table 37.1

393

The aim of this brief study is to know the nature of the peak, and be able to describe it. To this end, it will be necessary to discuss the problem with the staff concerned. Often, they will have pungent comments to make. Listen carefully to what or whom they blame, and what they would like to do about it. If a peak really disrupts their life, they will welcome the hope that at last something is going to be done. In particular, watch out for what the staff consider to be pseudo peaks – peaks that have been forced on them for no good reason. Once the peak has been described, it is then possible to consider the many ways of tackling the problem. It is difficult to think of a situation in which none of them can be used to advantage. In most cases, it will be found that more than one can be used.

■ STOP THE PEAK

The first approach is just that: stop the peak. It is remarkable how often unnecesary peaks are suffered. A graphic example from 1862 illustrates how it is not enough to know that a peak exists. Gloves were made on a cottage industry basis; the menfolk would prepare the gloves ready for the women and children to stitch and finish them. They had to be taken to town on Saturday. The problem was that the men left their work until as late as possible, leaving the women and children with a terrible peak at the end of the week:[1]

> Little children are kept up shamefully late if there is work, especially on Thursday and Friday nights when it is often till 11 or 12. . . . Mothers will pin them to their knee to keep them to their work, and if they are sleepy give them a slap on the head to keep them awake. . . . What makes the work come so heavy at the end of the week is that the men are slacking at the beginning. On St Monday they will go pigeoning or on some other amusement, and do but little on Tuesday . . . the work is always behind, and comes into the stitchers at all times on Friday night up to 12, and 1 and 2. They must sit up to do the work then as the gloves have to be finished and taken into Nottingham in the morning.

A less harrowing example occurred in a major bank which had a lot of work balancing all customers' accounts once a year. This was done on 31 December, New Year's Eve. Younger staff members wanted to finish everything quickly, early, so that they could go off to New Year parties. They were enraged by the habits of the older staff. These would work very slowly, chatting to one another. They would stop altogether during the evening, go out for a drink and a meal, returning later to finish the work very slowly. So there was a big peak, but it was a pseudo-peak.

In both of these examples the peak could have been almost eliminated easily, but in both cases, there was somebody who failed to be sufficiently motivated to act. So no action was taken.

■ STAFF TRANSFERS

A department can, during its peak periods, borrow staff from a department that does not have a peak at the same time. The many offices that use this system find it difficult to think of life without it. It seems quite natural. In other offices, to mention it causes surprise, even shock. Resistance does not usually come from the staff themselves: it can give them an extra interest in the work and opens up another personal promotion path. It is one of the ways in which job enrichment sometimes operates. Where there is resistance, it usually comes from supervisors and junior managers. To help them, it is necessary to discover the reason for their disapproval. It may be fear of losing control over 'their' staff. It may be fear that their own department will be faced with a suddenly increased workload just at the time that it is temporarily depleted. It may be a lack of commitment to the organization. Whatever the reason, it is worth persevering with this idea since in the right circumstances it can be most useful.

■ CHANGE THE DEADLINES

The majority of peaks are associated with a deadline of some sort. Careful inspection of these deadlines will often reveal the possibility of changing them. Sometimes it is possible to stagger the deadlines, sometimes to extend them. If they are part of a critical path, then it may be possible to change the allowances for slack.

An example of changing deadlines is the way that many, if not most, large organizations have stopped paying all their suppliers at the same time once a month. Instead, they have divided their purchase ledger into four; a quarter of their bills are paid each week. This system means that all of their suppliers are paid once a month, as before, but the monthly peak is spread more evenly over the month as a whole.

When changing the deadlines in a department it is vital to watch that one is not merely shifting a peak from one department on to another. If one does, then whole-hearted appreciation may be withheld from one.

■ COMPUTER DEADLINES

Many peaks are caused by deadlines imposed by the computer department. It is worthwhile looking at these quite strongly. Computer staff do not always realize the result of setting deadlines. One man's convenience can be another's millstone.

In a large insurance company the computer staff said that they had to have another department's output by 11.00 and 3.30 every day. This was complied with even though it frequently caused problems. It also meant that people had virtually nothing to do from 11.00 to lunchtime and from 3.30 to the end of the day. Close interrogation of the computer operation showed that the work was actually needed at 2.00 and at the end of the day. However, they had not trusted their non-computer colleagues to appreciate the importance of time and thought that delays would result if the true times were divulged. Fortunately for the consultant, the non-computer department had an excellent record of meeting their deadline, so the computer staff trusted them with the true timings.

To achieve success, it may be necessary to get the computer staff to reschedule their work. This is easy to say; it is less easy to convince them how worthwhile such an action would be. In many places, such work is not considered as being as 'sexy' as solving intricate graphic problems. When you succeed, your stock will rise considerably throughout the organization.

■ USE OTHER STAFF

The regular office staff can be reinforced with other staff during the peak periods. These other helpers can be of several types. Firstly, they can be part-timers. Retailers and fast-food outlets use this method as a matter of course. So can offices. Pensioners from the organization can be one such group since they already know the way the offices operate. They also tend to enjoy their work and are very willing to work unusual hours.

395

A second area of help is to use contract staff. In the majority of countries there are companies that will supply extra staff to work a set number of hours per week or per month. Their charges can be high, so it is necessary to cost the difference between staffing for peaks and using contract staff.

A third area of help is to employ home-workers, particularly in conjunction with electronic mail. Such people may have decided to become self-employed or be the heads of single-parent families. Whatever their situation, such staff are often of the highest calibre. One electronics company that followed this route found that it paid them to buy a microcomputer each for their home-workers.

In most towns there are also firms that will collect work (e.g. word processing), do it, and then return it overnight. Again, charges must be watched, although competition is such that they are not normally too exorbitant.

Whatever the source of this extra help, the result is the same. Effectively, the peak is removed from the regular office staff. This means that it is no longer necessary to set staffing levels to deal with the peak, and staffing can be reduced.

■ CHANGE THE PROCEDURES

Depending on circumstances, there are a number of attractive ways to reduce peaks by changing the procedures:

- use the method design techniques described earlier to install methods that have the avowed objective of reducing peaks;
- change the order in which the work is done, moving part of the work to the non-peak period;
- carry out pre- and post-working. This means doing some of the work content well before the peak and some after the peak. A common example is preparing wage packets well before payment, in those countries that still use cash for paying wages;
- schedule the total workload of a department to help its staff in pacing themselves and to recognize milestones.

Changing the procedures can result in a major improvement. When this is done, the proposed changes must not stay in a file in the investigator's office. Something more is needed to make the changes effective. This may take the form of a well-drawn schedule, special training of the staff and/or a round-table discussion.

■ OFFICE MECHANIZATION

Office mechanization or automation can, if handled intelligently, be a most potent way of reducing peaks. Such reduction is not, it should be noted, an automatic result as is sometimes thought. Unless care is taken, automation can actually increase peaking. In other cases, it may merely postpone the need for action. A commonly met case is replacing typewriters in a typing pool with word processors. At first, the increased productivity means that the pool can handle the workload easily. As the firm expands and the work increases, the original problems may reappear. For example, if dictaters have still continued to submit their work at 3.15 each day hoping for same-day completion, then the peak is still there. It never really went away. On the other hand, simple mechanization can have dramatic effects. An office had an electronic calculator that broke down. Their request for a replacement was refused (their manager was definitely one of the 'don't get involved with the staff' variety). The result was that the staff obstinately did their calculations mentally. Over a short period of time, the section was staffed for a peak. Work quantification, for another purpose, revealed that a new calculator would save sixty hours a month. At last, the section got its new calculator.

■ GIVE A HAND

It may be possible for other people to 'give a hand'. For example, supervisors who think that supervision means standing aloof from actual clerical work should be persuaded that they should help out with peaks. Some companies have found that it makes economic sense for them to switch technicians onto office work at peak periods. A confectionery wholesaler brought its salesmen into the office for two days a month. Not only did they help with the peak accounts work they could also discuss bad debts with the credit controllers and take the invoices with them for presenting to customers for payment on their next visit.

■ TEMPORARY INCREASE IN WORK RATE

As was mentioned in the section on work quantification, a number of organizations set their staffing levels not at 100 level but at some lower level such as 85 or 90. In such places, management may say to staff that they would like a higher work rate during peak periods, closer to 100 for a few days. If there is a definite slack period in the work cycle to compensate, then the staff are quite likely to agree. Even in offices without work quantification, it is a common understanding that staff work harder during peak periods.

E

Another use of work quantification occurred in an office that had three peaks in the year. These three peaks seemed to have a much greater effect than was expected from the working standards that had been set. Work quantification said no increase was needed, the staff said it was. The figures were rechecked. They seemed to be right. Then the consultant noticed something odd about the relationship between actual hours worked and standard hours produced. He carried out an analysis. This revealed an unusual situation. The staff were taking holidays and free days that coincided with the peaks – even the one in January. This was making the work even worse for the unfortunates left in the office. Discussions persuaded everybody that it would be better for all concerned if holidays were taken at more convenient times.

■ ORGANIZATION STRUCTURE

In any case, the best way to tackle peaks is through organization structure. An example may illustrate this. There was a small department of only seven people that was subdivided into sections each of which was housed in a separate room. Two sections consisted of two people each while three sections consisted of one person each – occupying five rooms. Such an idea may seem ridiculous, but in the country concerned it was not noteworthy. Each 'section' had its own peak with the result that the department was gossly overstaffed. The answer was obvious: do away with the separate sections and combine all the staff into a single-roomed department.

Now, the answer may be obvious. But it is worth recording that the concept was so alien to the culture that it required a considerable amount of time and effort to get it accepted. Similar proposals (but on a larger scale) may also be alien to an organization's culture in one's own country. Here, the diagram in Figure 37.1 comes into its own. The diagram showing the workload during the work cycle can be repeated for a number of groups. We then have a number of charts, each using the same scale. We turn them through 90° (for some reason, it works better this way). By putting the charts together, we can see for ourselves and demonstrate to others, the result of amalgamation: the peaks are reduced. This diagrammatical approach is most effective at explaining to others what we wish to do. An example is shown in Figure 37.2.

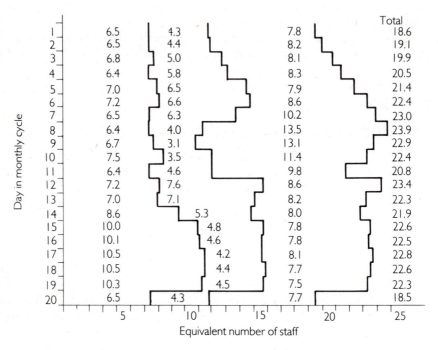

Day in monthly cycle				Total
1	6.5	4.3	7.8	18.6
2	6.5	4.4	8.2	19.1
3	6.8	5.0	8.1	19.9
4	6.4	5.8	8.3	20.5
5	7.0	6.5	7.9	21.4
6	7.2	6.6	8.6	22.4
7	6.5	6.3	10.2	23.0
8	6.4	4.0	13.5	23.9
9	6.7	3.1	13.1	22.9
10	7.5	3.5	11.4	22.4
11	6.4	4.6	9.8	20.8
12	7.2	7.6	8.6	23.4
13	7.0	7.1	8.2	22.3
14	8.6	5.3	8.0	21.9
15	10.0	4.8	7.8	22.6
16	10.1	4.6	7.8	22.5
17	10.5	4.2	8.1	22.8
18	10.5	4.4	7.7	22.6
19	10.3	4.5	7.5	22.3
20	6.5	4.3	7.7	18.5

Equivalent number of staff

Figure 37.2 Amalgamation of groups with different peaks.
Note: Without amalgamation the standard staffing would be 11 + 8 + 14 = 33. With amalgamation the standard staffing would be 24, a saving of 27 per cent

■ THE PENULTIMATE ALTERNATIVE

The last but one choice is to use overtime to deal with peaks. It is not, as some firms think, the first alternative. Firstly, overtime can become uneconomic. Secondly, it can become institutionalized, by which time payment is being made for little benefit. Thirdly, it may use up a valuable option, one that would be better reserved for dealing with emergencies.

■ THE FINAL ALTERNATIVE

It is possible that somewhere, somehow, somebody cannot use any of these alternatives. In such an unusual situation, the only alternative left may be to staff for peaks in the standard staffing levels. But such action needs a good excuse.

Handling staff reductions

There are a number of possible causes for staff reductions including:

- an inherent cyclic variability in operations (e.g. catering, retailing);
- a downturn in a particular activity (e.g. depletion of natural resources such as gas fields and quarries);
- a change in the direction of activities (e.g. a move from running lectures and seminars into the use of distance learning);
- a cost reduction exercise;
- the introduction of mechanization/automation;
- a threat to an organization's survival;
- changes to the organization structure;
- a merger of two or more organizations (e.g. governmental ministries);
- a change in the law or in public policy (e.g. a reduction in central state planning).

This variability of causation means that there is no one single solution that applies in every case. Another important factor is the question of time. How far in advance can an organization predict a future reduction? And over how long a period can a reduction be spread?

In all instances of staff reductions, there are two keys:

- care;
- flexibility.

Care has two facets: there is care for the people involved (who are one's colleagues), and care in how a reduction is carried out (which implies good planning). Caring for the people involved includes:

- acting properly, humanely and thoughtfully;
- never, never attacking someone's dignity;
- explaining the situation fully;
- taking people into your confidence;
- discussing the situation with the staff;
- asking for, and considering, staff suggestions;
- helping all leavers with their futures;
- remembering at all times that to be sacked is a traumatic exercise for anybody, no matter what the reason or circumstances.

The planning aspect of caring should also be part of caring for people. Most managers say that having to fire somebody is the most difficult aspect of their job (any manager who claims that he actually enjoys it has a psychological problem). This difficulty can actually lead to its being done badly: a manager may procrastinate or do it perfunctorily out of sheer fear of mishandling things. Good planning will help both the firer and the firee in what is admittedly a difficult situation.

The manner in which staff reductions are handled seems to depend on the culture of the organization. Instances have been observed where 'letting staff go' seems to be of little moment. Other cases have been seen where an organization will claim that they have never, ever, fired anybody for any reason. As usual, the middle path is preferred: if it has to be done, do it; but if it has to be done, do it properly.

E

399

Flexibility is another matter in which organizations vary greatly. Staff reductions are easier in an organization that:

- has a culture of change;
- has avoided overstaffing;
- has not manned for peaks;
- has withdrawn from the edge of over-specialization;
- has the ability to retrain staff;
- has a mix of staff types: full-time, part-time, temporaries, contract, self-employed, returned pensioners;
- buys in some services.

The first rule to follow can be expressed in the words, 'Reduce the reduction'. There are several ways in which this rule can be followed:

1 Do not make matters worse than they need be. An East European firm was computerizing its wages at a time when it had excess staff in various parts of the organization. Instead of training these people (or existing wages clerks), the firm took on a completely new group of dataprep staff. The result was that, when computerization was complete, the firm was faced with a problem largely of its own making: instead of having a few excess staff, virtually the whole of the old wages department was surplus to needs.
2 Sometimes it is better to increase revenues rather than reduce staff. The UK stockbroking subsidiary of Citicorp had poor profitability, which management assumed was because costs were too high. Consultants felt that for institutional equity sales, the firm had to retain its involvement in market-making, sales and research. It was felt that normal cost reduction would actually cause revenues to fail. The recommendation was to improve the quality of the research, and the inter-departmental communications.[2]
3 The fact of staff turnover is of major help. A firm with an annual staff turnover of say 20 per cent has an effective ready-made way to 'reduce the reductions'.

As can be seen, therefore, reducing the reductions need not be only a matter of morals and morale; it can sometimes make good economic sense. It should also be remembered that in many departments existing staff have a positive advantage over fresh staff: they already possess a level of knowledge of the organization that fresh staff have to take time to acquire.

■ CONCEPTS FOR ACTION

There are many ways and ideas of handling actual staff reductions, and a number of these are given below. In several instances, they represent a way of turning a problem into an opportunity. Of course, not every idea can apply to every organization on every occasion. On the other hand, action should not normally be restricted to just one idea.

Stop recruiting staff

This is the basic first action. A halt is put on engaging new staff and excess staff are transferred as vacancies arise in other departments. These vacancies arise quite naturally due to staff turnover. In many firms turnover can be 15–20 per cent because of people leaving, retirements, promotions, expansion, etc. The level of turnover varies greatly: it has been seen as low as 4 per cent and as high as over 300 per cent.

Of course, transfers are not always possible; a computer systems analyst cannot normally take over from a research physicist. But (with retraining) a great deal can be done, sometimes more than is realized. In one case, a firm (and the union) felt that a stores clerk would not be able to transfer to sales statistics since the work would be beyond his capabilities. The consultant's contrary feeling was reinforced when it transpired that the person concerned had in fact done very similar work for a previous firm.

The basic idea remains: 'retrain and retain'. In almost every example of major reductions, a stop should be put on engaging fresh staff.

Set up a 'pool'

Excess staff are transferred to a pool as their workload disappears. They are then transferred permanently to another department as vacancies occur, as before. While waiting, members of the pool are employed on temporary duties such as:

- assisting departments with short-term acute needs;
- getting the firm up to date by working on payments due, goods late, overdue deliveries, etc.;
- improving the stores;
- replacing staff undergoing training; this can allow the organization to undertake a major staff training scheme;
- carrying out those tasks that most firms would like to do if only they had the time (e.g. improving the files, preparation of special statistics, etc.).

Depending on circumstances, such a pool has been utilized for a variety of other purposes. In one firm, a pool volunteered to decorate the canteens, and paint the office and factories. In another, the firm brought forward the establishment of a new department.

Local contacts

Personnel staff contact local firms to discover if they are short of people, and if so, what type and grade. Staff can then be moved with little or no break in employment.

Emphasize in-house activities

A firm can reinforce in-house activities by:

- reducing or stopping the use of temporary staff;
- reducing or stopping the use of contract staff;
- temporarily not utilizing returned pensioners;
- reducing its reliance on bought-in services (e.g. purchasing, wages preparation, printing, transport, market research, audit preparation, etc.).

Such changes need not be permanent. Liaison and explanation to suppliers is needed to retain their goodwill.

Work sharing

A firm can introduce work sharing by:

- reducing overtime;
- asking staff to take some unpaid leave;

401

- asking staff to take their leave entitlement early;
- reducing the hours of work;
- closing the offices down to a skeleton service for say one week in five.

Such actions normally result in lower wages for all and most of us tend to live up to our income. It has to be admitted, therefore, that work sharing often becomes resented after a while even if it has been embraced with enthusiasm initially. It can work well if there is a strong community feeling. Otherwise, considerable thought should be given before its introduction.

Buy-outs and spin-offs

A buy-out occurs where a subsidiary or part of a firm (or even the whole firm) is sold to its staff. In Europe, the capital for the purchase usually comes from a bank, the government or the parent firm. There have been some notably successful buy-outs, where circumstances have been right. So far as job preservation is concerned, a staff buy-out is favoured over a management buy-out. Buy-outs are indicated where the industry is labour rather than capital intensive (e.g. road haulage) or where there are restrictive practices.

Spin-offs have tended to be found in technical or knowledge-based industries. France has introduced legislation to encourage spin-offs – they are put forward as stimulating entrepreneurial spirit as well as preserving jobs.

Intrapreneurship

An 'intrapreneur' is a firm's employee who exhibits some of the characteristics of an entrepreneur. He will have convinced the firm that they should allow him to follow up an idea – normally a new product or new market. He will then act as a product champion, in effect running a mini-company within the main company. Some firms have been successful at this approach, perhaps the best known being 3M. Some commentators have put forward the thought that intrapreneurs are able to run counter to the basic culture of the firm. Our own feeling is that the culture cannot be really inimical to the concept or it would never be able to get started. Intrapreneurship is sometimes put forward as a form of job creation. It is, however, no panacea: it can take time, and it must have potentially able product champions already working for a reasonably receptive culture.

New sales teams

Staff for whom there is little or no work available can be formed into new sales teams. This approach is particularly useful where a firm is convinced that a turn-down is temporary, or where a specific market has for some reason disappeared. Staff are trained in specific (and restricted) aspects of selling, such as finding leads or making contacts. The attitude of local union officials can be crucial: they can be most enthusiastic or just dismissive. Firms that have used this approach to the benefit of everybody include a package holiday firm, a word processing bureau, and even a management consultancy company in Italy. The benefits of this approach tend to be long lasting. It is good for morale, sales improve, people gain a better understanding of one another's work, and (after an initial wariness) it is enjoyed by the staff involved.

Self-employed home workers

A firm sets staff up to become self-employed, working from home. In some cases it has been found worthwhile to provide them with personal computers with modems. The firm guarantees to provide the homeworkers with a certain percentage of work which tapers off over time. Such a scheme needs careful planning, as does the selection of staff who will welcome and benefit from this style of working. Rank Xerox used this approach covering a wide range of work and staff, even including personnel staff – who might be thought to be one group who of necessity had to be on site.

Selling services

Selling services can be thought of as the reverse or extreme of bringing in-house those services that might be bought-in. A firm offers for sale to other organizations the work of its staff. Examples are word processing, printing, design, management services, project management, and computer time and software. When BOC's computer department sold its time, it did so well that the service took on a life of its own, becoming a profitable company in its own right. Companies undertaking this type of work need to cost the service accurately, control the inputs, and give responsibility for success to a named individual. It is also necessary to watch the question of priorities carefully. It is easy (and fatal to reputation) to use such a service to satisfy a firm's own priorities instead of those of external customers.

E

Internal expansion

A firm can set up a new department or a new subsidiary to exploit a new market or new activities. For example, a book publisher moved into children's books and paperbacks. For success, certain factors should be present:

- the new activity should be staffable by surplus people, without taking staff from existing work such that mainstream activities are weakened;
- the new activity should have a close affinity with the firm's existing activities;
- those taking part should be convinced that there is a reasonable chance of success, and be determined to achieve it;
- responsibility for success should be delegated to a named individual, so that the firm is not weakened by the new activity making heavy demands on the time of top management;
- a new activity set up in these circumstances will probably be undertaken with less preparation than would be the case if it were expansion as part of corporate strategy. It is therefore more important than usual to monitor costs and progress, and to have a definite date to achieve success.

A balance has to be achieved: participants should not feel either that they have been set an impossible task or that they are just charity cases.

Job creation

In the twenty years after 1970, more than thirty million new jobs were created in the USA. During the same period there was barely any increse in jobs in the main countries in Europe. Most of the increase was in small businesses and in self-employment (which increased by 50 per cent to 14 per cent of the labour force during this period). It is also interesting to note that most of the increase was in the service industries. It is estimated

403

that only 3 per cent of the new jobs were in the high-technology area. This is because these areas tend to be capital intensive rather than labour intensive, and that many of the jobs created there were for highly qualified personnel. An *OECD Observer* report[3] also comments that commercial venture capital only accounted for 15 per cent of the $45 billion invested annually in start-ups in the USA. The remaining 85 per cent came from what is called the 'FFA circuit' (Friends, Family and Associates) and the 'Love Network' (people who know and trust one).

In response to this situation, the OECD has been very supportive in Europe of ILEs (Initiatives for Local Employment). The first reaction in some European countries to the decline in large manufacturing industries was to inject large amounts of money into the worst areas. It is now realized that this is not necessarily the best approach. Instead, ILEs and other groups are putting the emphasis on local self-help.[4] The following lessons have been postulated:

- locally grown jobs may be more valuable than those arising by offering subsidies to large outside firms. Such jobs may wither when the subsidies cease – it is better to create a local climate of a dynamic work force;
- small and medium companies are important for job creation. Although new small firms can fail, large firms are more likely to move to an area with plenty of small firms;
- local partnerships between the public and private sectors can be a far better route then either of the two extremes of purely public investment or strict *laissez-faire*;
- poor local government is a problem in some countries. Spain has four levels of government that can get involved. In Britain, central government and local authorities often have different routes that they wish to follow;
- centralized decision making can work against local initiatives. In Europe, large companies are often reluctant to back local efforts while in America there is a stronger tradition of local philanthropy.

There have been a number of encouraging successes. In Sweden, the Kockums shipyard was closed but was split into three new parts: one to make Saab cars, one to make submarines and one for new businesses. Only 94 of the 2,000 employees had to be made redundant. In Britain, Lancashire Enterprise Ltd is a successful enterprise agency. In France, Elf Aquitaine has helped in setting up a large honey processor, a thermoplastics factory, a unit for electronic components, and a massive fish farm.

Creative and professional work

It is often said that all work can be measured. Without becoming involved in any arcane arguments about this statement, it can nevertheless be stated that most commercial work certainly can be measured. If Rembrandt could set standards for his studio painters, and if Albania can set output standards for its novelists, then the limits to what can be measured must be quite wide. In fact, the techniques have been used for people with widely varying occupations, including doctors, nurses, radiologists; lawyers; engravers; geologists; film directors; a cabinet minister.

Creative and professional work can be looked at in two ways: the type of work being undertaken and the nature of the work itself. These two aspects can then be further subdivided as shown in Figure 37.3.

Based on these subdivisions, an activity matrix can be built up as in Table 37.2.

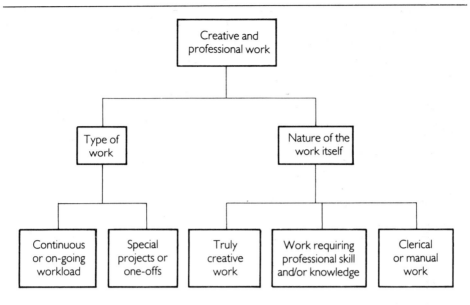

Figure 37.3 Creative and professional work

The activity matrix is then used in the following stages:

E

1 Calculate the time spent on the work in each box. This is usually done by means of Rated Activity Sampling. Care must be taken to choose a representative period; the first two rows in particular can vary widely over the year. It is possible, but not normally advisable, to get the split of time by means of a self-recording work diary or an electronic recorder such as a Parameter. In practice, however, this leads to a very low level of clerical/manual work being recorded. An accountant insisted that using an adder to total columns was creative work, not clerical; the resulting discussion became philosophical rather than fruitful.

2 If the total of the 'creative' column is more than 10 per cent, then the figures should be checked. A number of research studies, backed by practical experience, show that it is rare indeed for any job in commerce or industry to be consistently creative for more than 10 per cent of the time. This may surprise some staff but analysis shows it to be so.

3 The percentages in the individual boxes are for time actually working. They will not,

Table 37.2 Professional work activity matrix

	Truly creative work	Work needing professional abilities	Clerical or manual work	Other work
On-going work				
Special projects				
Ancillary work				

Notes:
(i)   'Ancillary work' includes time spent on travelling to clients, maintaining professional competence (how much is allowed during working hours is a matter of company policy).
(ii) 'Clerical and manual work' includes filing, typing, prolonged digging for samples, etc.
(iii) 'Other' includes attendance at meetings, etc. It will be found that much of this subdivision is also in the 'ancillary' box.

therefore, add up to 10 per cent since there is always a certain amount of ineffective time. Professional staff are often working under pressure; this means that they sometimes work long hours and may not take normal rest breaks. On the other hand, there may be a temptation to indulge in work that is not truly effective (e.g. too much technical reading, too many social E-mail messages, excessive 'what-ifing' of data-bases). These two opposing tendencies rarely cancel one another out in any single analysis. It is therefore necessary to be aware of these possibilities and to be ready for them. One should agree beforehand, for example, how much semi-socializing electronic mail is reasonable. A pilot study will highlight any abnormal working patterns.

4 The 'clerical/manual' work is quantified using the usual work measurement techniques, generally PMTS or time study.

5 The 'professional' work is quantified using the technique of categorized work values, previously described. Normally, these values are based on groups of staff (or groups of tasks). This both increases accuracy and saves time.

6 The act of quantifying the work in the clerical/manual and professional columns will slightly alter their percentages. These new percentages are added together. They are then increased by the observed percentage in the creative column. This means that the creative work is being taken as a 'do-take' time rather than a 'should-take' time. Any error in doing this is small, since the total creative percentage is not more than 10 per cent. Thus an error of as much as 15 per cent in the creative work will result in an overall error of only 10 per cent $\times$ 15 per cent = $1\frac{1}{2}$ per cent. It will also be found that with experience in an organization, it becomes feasible to set standard times for many creative tasks.

7 The 'other' work is then added as a percentage increase (it can be thought of as a kind of super-contingency allowance). Other allowances (rest allowance, etc.) are then added in the normal way.

8 Final work values are calculated in the usual way, their nature depending on the use that is to be made of them.

This approach to creative and professional work has been used in a wide variety of situations over the years. In the hands of an experienced practitioner, it gives accurate results. There are two types of job where problems have been encountered: senior computer programmers and social workers. Computer programming is better tackled by using project control (see below). Social workers in Europe (especially in Britain) are often rather resistant to all forms of work quantification. In North America, the approach that tends to be used is to use detailed and precisely worded job descriptions backed by a system of points-valued case loads based on a form of Management by Objectives.

Once the work of creative/professional staff has been quantified, method improvements can be undertaken.

■ MAKING IMPROVEMENTS

The recommended approach is as follows:

1 Inspect the causes of ineffective time and reduce or eliminate them. The commonest causes are waiting for work, waiting for shared resources, and poor scheduling. Improved pre-planning and scheduling is used to reduce travelling time, to reduce waiting time, and to plan the joint use of resources and facilities. Considerable

improvements can be made in this way in, for example, making films and performing research (a chemist may have to wait some hours for experimental equipment to achieve a steady state).

2 Reduce the clerical/manual work by assigning it to clerks, to semi-skilled workers or by mechanizing it. For example, radiologists in a clinic used to inspect X-rays in a viewing room, take notes while viewing, return to their office, write a report later and then have the reports typed for the patients (who may have been waiting the whole time). As an improvement, the doctors were given small portable dictating machines, so that they could dictate the reports while viewing the X-rays. This increased productivity by over 100 per cent, increased the accuracy of the reports, and greatly reduced the patients' waiting time.

3 Reduce the creative-professional work by using trained assistants or trainees to carry out part of the work (like Rembrandt again). For example, one person can perform certain test procedures for a number of geologists; post-graduate students can carry out IQ tests for a research psychologist.

4 Inspect the work done in all three rows. Is it necessary? Can it be eliminated, reduced, combined, or improved? In other words, carry out the normal method design technique.

5 Introduce project control for the 'special projects and one-off' work.

■ SIMPLIFIED PROJECT CONTROL

E

A simplified form of project control has these stages:

- treat all non-continuous work as projects;
- give to every project before commencement:
    (a) objectives and agreed outputs;
    (b) inputs (time, money, resources, facilities);
    (c) deadlines;
    (d) a target completion date.

Some projects will be very small, taking just a few days of work spread over a few weeks. In such cases, the project control will be extremely simple. This may be thought so obvious that it is not worth mentioning. But one sophisticated organization has been observed using the same project control methods for every project that was undertaken. These could vary from preparing a training course to building an oil refinery. In each case, computerized control was used including automated drawing of a critical path scheme. The result was that some projects were completed well before the control was in place;

- projects will often be split between several people (especially if some projects are effectively being used to eliminate waiting time). In such cases, it is necessary to appoint a project leader who is responsible for time allocation, progress and the production of the final outputs;
- a weekly Work Sheet is introduced for everybody working on the project, showing work done and any expenditure made;
- for major projects a '1:1 Chart' is introduced. This chart has two axes:

$$x\text{-axis:} \frac{\text{Spent to date}}{\text{Total original estimate}}$$

$$y\text{-axis:} \frac{\text{Estimated balance to do}}{\text{Total original estimate}}$$

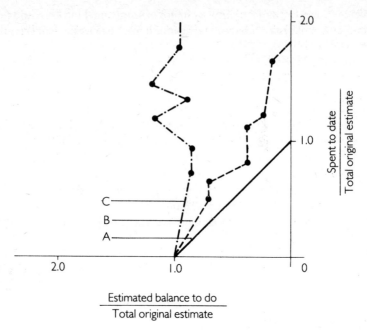

Figure 37.4 Sample 1:1 chart

1:1 charts are usually used to show overall time progress on a project. They can also be used to show expenditure made where this is important. Comparison of the two ratios on the two axes gives an immediate picture of how well a project is progressing. Comparing successive charts shows progress made since the previous chart (or the previous period if only one chart is maintained). A not untypical 1:1 chart is shown in Figure 37.4. As can be seen, it is set in the fourth quadrant, not the first as is usual. If actual results follow line A then progress is exactly on schedule. Line B shows a project well behind schedule but not out of control. Line C shows a project that is out of control and which at some stage should be abandoned as a failure. With practice, it is possible to obtain a useful quick picture of progress very easily. The 1:1 chart may seem simple, even crude. In appropriate circumstances, however, it is highly effective.

The reaction of creative and professional staff to work quantification and improvement has been found to vary greatly. Some of them have requested (almost demanded) a study. The reasons for such a request vary from utter frustration with colleagues to a wish for greater funding. Other people resent what they see as interference. In the end, it usually comes down to a mixture of the personalities involved and the culture of the organization. As ever, the investigator must be mindful of the people involved. An accountant was trying to get a film director to use a very simple costing form, an example of which the accountant had brought to a meeting. The film director took the form and without looking at it tore it up into small pieces, finally throwing it theatrically into the air. 'I leave that sort of thing to you figurepushers,' he said. It was quite some time before the two men would speak to one another again.

References

1 Evidence from Mary Thorpe of Bulwell to the Children's Employment Commission, 1862.
2 *The Economist*, Vol. 308, No. 7558, p. 62.
3 *The OECD Observer*, No. 152, p. 9.
4 *The Economist*, Vol. 307, No. 7552, p. 30.

Further reading

The Mechanisms of Employment Creation, Paris: OECD, 1988.

E

Support Techniques

38

L – Launch and E – Enhance

Action is the proper fruit of knowledge.

Thomas Fuller, *Gnomologia* (1732)

It is not the going out of port, but the coming in, that determines the success of a voyage.

Henry Ward Beecher, *Proverbs from Plymouth Pulpit* (1887)

L – Launch

No investigator escapes a *frisson* of excitement when the time approaches to launch 'The Change' – a change which the investigator has developed and even created. This excitement has two components. First, there is the undoubted pleasure that comes from having created something new, and then seeing it take practical shape. But the second component is a slight sense of anxiety: will the launch go well, has anything been overlooked, are Murphy and his law waiting to ambush?

Launches cover a very wide spectrum. At times, the change involved is quite straightforward, as in the case of a slightly improved procedure. At times it can be complex, such as the introduction of new technology throughout an organization. And at times it can be almost traumatic – such as moving an entire organization to a new location several hundred kilometres away.

The route to a smooth launch is good preparation. To assist in this preparation, the mnemonic is 'P – PLOTTING'. This is short for:

P – Proselytize
P – Plan
L – Liaise
O – Order new items
T – Train
T – Transmit momentum
I – Install the changes
N – Nurse
G – Get out

In this case, the order of performing the stages does not always follow the letters of the mnemonic. For example, equipment may have to be ordered early if it has a long lead time.

■ PROSELYTIZE

During the course of the study, it will have been necessary to convince and persuade people of the correctness of proposed changes. It is offering a hostage to fortune to wait until the last moment before suddenly producing proposals. It also increases the likelihood of failure. One of the commonest mistakes made by the tyro analyst is to keep his proposals secret until suddenly revealing them in a final report, rather like a conjuror producing the white rabbit out of a hat. Like the conjuror, the tyro analyst is then disappointed if the white rabbit's appearance is not met by a burst of wild applause.

However, it is very common for a certain amount of explanation/persuasion to be needed at this stage of a study. There is also a need to discuss the plans for the launch itself.

The proselytizing is aimed at three groups: management, supervision and staff. As major changes have been developed they will have been discussed with managers and their agreement and co-operation obtained. But it is normal for the finalized and detailed proposals to be presented in the form of a formal report. This report will also include calculations of financial implications and a plan of action for implementation. The report will usually be presented at a meeting with management, discussed and agreed. Some organizations like a draft report first, which is then amended before a formal presentation (local government councils often prefer this system). A few organizations like to write the report jointly with the consultant; lawyers are inclined to this approach, which can be a most pleasing experience.

Supervisors have a different view of life from management. Their main concern is likely to be the launch itself. Since they are responsible for ensuring that output is produced on time, they may be worried about how the change-over will interrupt the flow of work. They will therefore want to make sure that they really understand the details of the launch. This should be thought of as a positive aspect, not a negative one. In effect, management are vetting the strategy, and supervisors the tactics. Together the two viewpoints help make the launch a smooth one, so it is always worth listening to any observations or objections made by the supervisors.

F

Discussions with staff can take many forms at this stage, and can even provide a few surprises. A really major change (such as moving to a far-off location) will already have been discussed at such length that there is little left to say. But a change that seems minor (such as the introduction of flexible working hours) may need considerable explanation. Sometimes, managements in foreign countries have insisted on mass meetings at which one has to address hundreds of people through an interpreter. On one such occasion, the head of the organization announced that no employees were going to lose their jobs. This was fine except that the word that he used for 'job' implied that there would be no change in any activities – a mistake that haunted the assignment for two years. Immediately after this mass meeting, private meetings were held with the union representative and the Party secretary. Both said that it was all right to talk with the staff but the real problem was management – they were too conservative and would not really change anything.

On another occasion, the union representative complained that the report had understated staff reductions and that this must have been because of management interference. How was he going to increase his members' standard of living if the firm was not made efficient? It proved necessary to go through the study with him in great detail to demonstrate that the staff reduction could not be greater.

411

One sometimes meets people who are genuinely afraid of change – all change of any kind. Twice people have been encountered whose fear seemed to border on the pathological. This is a difficult situation, especially when the person's colleagues have too little sympathy for them. In both cases the answer used was the same. A separate enclosed office was taken over. Over a perid of time, the person was schooled in the new ways, taking everything very slowly and changing a piece at a time. Of course, some changes are not of a type to make this approach possible.

■ PLAN

The amount and type of planning needed is dictated by the nature of the change involved. A simple *aide-mémoire* list sometimes satisfies. At other times, a full-blown critical path network is needed. Usually a bar or Gantt chart will suffice; this can be drawn in a simple way but may have to be detailed in the sense of having many entries.

Some people have difficulty in planning effectively. The answer is to imagine oneself in the situation of working after the change. Then go through the activities slowly and in detail in one's imagination. While doing this, list everything that is used, looked at, listened to, received or sent. Then look at the list and check whether every item is currently in the right place at the right time. If not, then planning becomes a matter of arranging for it to be there.

No check list could hope to be complete, but some of the items that often have to be covered are:

- a timetable and programme of work;
- individual responsibilities for implementation assigned;
- a check on layouts. Availability of services, power;
- availability of equipment, machinery, materials, supplies;
- design of all new forms. Dummies for practice runs;
- arrangements and material for training;
- staff recruitment and transfers;
- arrangements for disposal of unwanted items and stocks;
- arrangement for double running (e.g. computer/manual);
- arrangements for overtime, temporary staff while changing;
- special arrangements with suppliers and customers;
- changes in schedules, work flow and timings;
- knock-on effects on other departments;
- likely absence/availability of key personnel;
- anticipation of possible problems.

It may also be necessary to have a rehearsal of either the change or the new working methods.

■ LIAISE

Liaison and setting up paths of communication with interested parties has to be arranged. This can extend to people outside the organization. Major changes will benefit from the introduction of a newsletter for the staff. Such a newsletter will be separate from existing newsletters and will cease soon after the change is complete. It should be informative about other parts of the organization but not become the way people learn about their own area. It must not become turgid, nor be insensitive. Insensitivity is easy to achieve. We all act insensitively at times in spite of good intentions. One large organization undertook a cost-reduction exercise. A 'newsletter' was printed showing a breakdown of costs. The items that were noticed and remembered by the staff were two pictures and figures – of the consumption of string and toilet paper. Then a video was produced. In this the chairman explained that as part of the cost-reduction he had undertaken visits to subsidiaries in Australia, South Africa and Canada. This was done with the best of intentions – to show that even the chairman had been making sacrifices – but it was not how the staff saw it.

■ ORDER NEW ITEMS

Writing out an order for equipment is easy. What needs planning is ensuring that the right items are received at the right time and that they are satisfactory. This is particularly true of computer software, which may need rewrites or extensive tweaking. It will certainly need some dummy rums.

Lead times can catch one unawares by their length, even for staple items like office furniture. When working in countries with centrally planned economies one can shake one's head in disbelief. In one case, the printing of packaging had a lead time of twelve months.

Ordering new items also includes changing buildings and having new ones built. And then one really is into planning.

■ TRAIN

Unless training is arranged for the staff, their performance in the new situation after a change will be below par. This leads to backlogs, bottlenecks and a feeling of pressure to get the work through. Also, if people have not been trained, they do not feel confident and errors increase. This is all so obvious that it may not seem worth stating.

F

What makes it worth stating is the simple fact that it often is not done. First, there is a feeling that time spent on training will interfere with the current work. Second, the need for training coincides with a period when the analyst is pressed for time. Third, too many offices are accustomed to neglecting training in general. So it is possible for all parties to back off from training: management, supervision, staff and analyst.

An added complication is that training may have to be varied for the needs of different groups. The introduction of a new Management Information System may require training in data collection for some clerks, training in software use for office staff, education in control mechanisms for supervisors, training in MIS for the managers, and education for the internal accountants.

So training can present difficulties. But this does not mean that it should be avoided. The basic principles of training are:

- training should be in small steps that are then combined for the overall action;
- response by the people being trained has to be active, not passive;
- there has to be feedback of how well the training is succeeding;
- a final test of the trainees' understanding and skill is needed.

Training can be in the office, in a classroom, or in separate premises. In each case, training usually starts with an overall description of the new situation and the changes involved. The instructor can then show the various steps in the operation. Each step is then taken one at a time in detail, building up expertise and speed and skill before moving on to the next step. The steps are then put together. For a while, the trainee carries out the operation with the instructor looking on to give help and encourage-

413

ment. The trainee then practises the whole operation with the instructor available to give help if needed, by staying nearby. Follow-up practice ensures that the learning is retained and reinforced.

The precepts for a training session are:

1 Decide what one wants the trainees to know.

There is a great temptation to put in too much extraneous matter. For example, to learn how to use a spreadsheet it is quite unnecessary to understand basic electronics or the nature of a transistor; excess training can actually cause confusion or act as a barrier. In spite of this, too many software instruction courses include such unwanted matter.

2 Find out what the trainees already know.

Training has to be tailored to the needs of the trainees. With a group of trainees, it is nearly always true that individuals will have varying levels of knowledge, so some overlap cannot be avoided.

3 Relate the new to what the trainees already know.

For the initial stages, it is worthwhile to cover briefly the knowledge that it is assumed people know. Provided detail is avoided, this has a number of advantages: it inspires some confidence; it gives people a chance to get acclimatized to the training role; it gives them a chance to ask questions to refresh their memory; and it provides a common foundation for the next few stages. Later stages are somewhat easier since these lead on from stages that everybody has covered together during the training.

4 Use the familiar to lead to the unknown.

Major or unfamiliar ideas are easier to absorb if they follow on from minor or familiar ones. Many of us tend to use analogies which are clear-cut to us, but they may not be so obvious to others. This is often true when one is training people from another country, especially if we are going through an interpreter. Some analogies have become clichés but still do not work. In 1951, a medical student met a computer trainee. The latter mentioned that he was being taught about computers, cybernetic feedback and artificial intelligence by reference to the workings of the brain – but that it did not really help much. This interested the medical student. He was learning about the brain with references to computers, cybernetics and artificial intelligence – but it was not helping much either.

5 Go from the concrete to the abstract.

It is easy (and therefore common) to state a new principle or idea and then to illustrate it with examples. Indeed this is the normal format for scientific papers and for books. For actual training, however, this is the wrong way round. In training it is more effective to go from examples to the conclusion. This involves thinking through a logical path to avoid untidiness.

6 Do not cover too much too quickly.

Nobody can absorb too many new ideas quickly. When training is going well, there is a tendency to leap ahead to maintain interest. In doing this, there may be a loss of understanding of what had already been covered. A good instructor has 'antennae' to gauge the correct pace. In addition, about 40–45 minutes is long enough on a new subject for one session.

7 A picture is worth a thousand words.

An old cliché – but still true. Unending talk will eventually and inevitably lead to poor absorption. Diagrams, examples, dummy forms and pictures all help. So do videos, films and role-playing. Even having more than one instructor can be a help – though sometimes the trainees and the instructor feel a real rapport; in this case one has to be prepared to stay with just the one. The main reason for using these aids is not to introduce some levity (though that can also help). It is to make things clearer, to show another angle to aid understanding, and to act as a change of pace from continual talk.

8 Repeat for reinforcement.

Repetition by just saying the same words several times is not what is meant. Nor what is wanted. What has to be repeated is the ideas, concepts and actions. This can be effected by using different examples. For example, learning to interrogate a databank needs a stock of different examples and problems, each one being similar but each showing a new facet.

9 Get the trainees to work.

Most people enjoy learning a new skill. It is also true that most people do not want to go on a training course as a holiday. They will resent it – after all, their time is valuable too. They want, and expect, to work and to be stretched. This does not mean that the instructor has to be a termagant or over-didactic. As in everything else in life, the aim should be to achieve a balance. The best training courses are enjoyed by both instructor and learners – and they result in something positive being achieved.

10 Obtain feedback.

By some means, it is necessary to check on whether the trainees have learnt what they came to learn. This may be a questionnaire, a special worked example, a case study, even a test. If a test, then it should be in the form of ensuring comprehension rather than a formal examination that nominates failures.

When new machinery is being introduced, then manufacturers or suppliers will normally offer to arrange the training. Such training is often done well and can be done in a neutral atmosphere that some staff will find reassuring.

■ TRANSMIT MOMENTUM

If the investigator is unsure about the changes, is diffident or seems to be living more in hope than in confidence, then difficulties beckon. Every politician knows that the smell of defeat brings defeat. The analyst has to achieve a sense of inevitability, of momentum becoming irresistible, and of success being certain. This is not acting or a confidence trick. The analyst must not fake confidence, he must feel it. How does the analyst feel confident? By being right, and by careful planning. In other words, by doing a good assignment.

■ INSTALL THE CHANGES

Having prepared carefully, and having had a rehearsal, the first day of the change can be faced with confidence and even pleasure:

● get to the office bright and early, ready to greet the staff as they arrive. They will

415

bring with them mixed emotions. For major changes, there may be a buzz of excitement. This is fine so long as it does not feel like panic (that should be reserved for when there is something really to panic about);

- avoid any dislocation to the service. Ensure that all timetables are met and schedules adhered to;
- anticipate anything going wrong and keep the antennae on;
- deal with all difficulties as soon as possible, like at once;
- keep the momentum going.

If possible, the day of the change should coincide with a slack work period. This enables staff to build up confidence and speed before meeting a peak, and to avoid a backlog occurring. Some changes should coincide with the start of an accounting period, though not as many as accountants claim. If possible, major changes should be introduced one department at a time. Otherwise the study team becomes too thinly stretched.

■ NURSE

The term 'nursing' is not one of our favourite words; it implies illness or childishness. But it is a term that is widely used. Nursing means being present in the office, helping until the changes have become established. The first few days after a change are important. It is during this period that any difficulties are most likely to surface.

During this period, the investigator spends his or her time in the office affected by the changes. Queries are dealt with quickly and thoroughly. Immediate assistance is given if there are any problems. Encouragement is given to the staff and an optimistic, friendly but effective ambiance is attained. Extra training is arranged for any staff who are struggling. If snags arise, the cause is traced back to their source and rectified; the way that this is done can set the tone in the office. Reasons are sought and offered, not excuses.

Over a period of time, the new situation stabilizes and is no longer new. Staff adjust to the new situation. The work flows well. The problems dissolve. The investigator's presence is no longer required.

■ GET OUT

The investigator must always beware of *de facto* taking over a department in the role of helping the installation stage. Otherwise withdrawal is inhibited. But there soon comes a time when the new operations are running well, staff are confident, there is no backlog. It is said that this moment can be recognized quite easily – it is when the investigator has time to sit down for longer than thirty seconds.

When all is smooth, there is only one thing for the investigator to do – and that is to get out.

E – Enhance

It is sometimes necessary to improve the solution to a problem. Enhancement can be more difficult than the original solution-finding. There is always the situation that one has expended considerable effort in attaining a solution and so defends it against any whiff of alteration. Perversely, this is most often the reaction when the solution arrived in a burst of inspiration in the guise of a 'bright idea'.

We are all prone to this defensive action. Thomas Edison produced his first experimental cylinder recording in 1877. Earlier music reproduction of the 'music box' origination had used either flat disks or cylinders. But Edison solved the problems of sound reproduction with a cylinder. He soon showed his commercial acumen. Thus although anything approaching 'jazz' was not to his personal taste, he realized that there was a market for it and so in 1913 released a recording of 'Hungarian Rag' played by the New York Military Band (when the BBC played this famous record, the presenter managed to get both the title and the band wrong).[1]

But Edison's commercial acumen did not extend to his basic solution: the cylinder recording. He stuck with this doggedly. His company still produced cylinders through the 1920s although the competition had long been using disks. In spite of the evidence to the contrary, Edison continued to believe in the cylinder recording right to the time in 1929 when he closed his recording business.

One of the best sources for enhancement is the staff. Their ideas may come at the investigation stage, during pre-installation discussions or during the actual nursing stage. As already stated, it is always worth listening to the staff because they really do know the work.

There are times when a solution has faults which only come to light during rehearsals or even actual installation. Fortunately, these occasions are very rare. The commonest cause is a failure on the part of new technology hardware (not attaining specification) or software (hidden bugs or shortcomings). When this happens, there is inevitably a need for fast decisions. In the extreme, there may even be a need for postponement. This is very rare indeed. Usually, there is a much more pleasant alternative (like working through the night).

F

Enhancements always have to be controlled – in two senses. First, they must be the result of reasoned thought and not the product of panic. Second, they often have a knock-on effect by affecting other parts of the solution. These knock-on effects have to be carefully monitored and documented. It is rather like watching somebody photo-copying a 20-page report and realizing that pages 3 and 9 have copied badly and that pages 5 and 10 are in the wrong order. What is wrong may be obvious but putting it right is a messy affair.

Enhancements are a way of trying to achieve the perfect solution, which all of us are trying to attain but never quite achieve. Fortunately, few of us are as unhappy with great works as Leonardo da Vinci. His dying words are said to have been, 'I have offended against God and mankind because my work did not reach the quality it should have.'

References

1 'Hungarian Rag' (Julius Lenzberg), The New York Military Band, July 1913, on Edison Blue Amberol 2089. Reproduced (1982) on Saydisc SDL 334.

39

S – Stabilize

> The toughest thing about success is that you've got to keep on being
> a success.
> Irving Berlin, *Theatre Arts* (1958)
>
> Since 'tis Nature's law to change,
> Constancy alone is strange.
> John Wilmot, Earl of Rochester (1647–1680), *A Dialogue XXXI*

The benefits gained from the introduction of a new situation can be lost unless there is a measure of stabilization. This loss can occur from a number of causes:

1 A new computer system frequently involves running the old system for a while in parallel. There are times when the two become mixed. This can be because of habit, because the new system omitted some outputs that are still needed, or because the computer department do not have time to make required enhancements. This is not as infrequent as may be thought. All analysts know the result. One goes into a department only to be faced with the sight of people busily filling in reams of paper by hand although one is assured that the system 'is computerized'. Everyone in authority is struck with a form of paralysis and is fearful of what might happen if it were stopped. It should never happen, but it does.

2 A supervisor may ask for extra staff on a temporary basis and the request is granted. These extra staff may not be moved after the need for them has ceased. Ghost activities then arise to give them something to do.

3 New staff may not be properly trained and then non-standard practices creep in, with an added possibility of errors.

4 People may find it difficult not to use pieces of paper after office automation has been installed, or may become impatient when it seems slow. This can lead to manual methods being introduced, and thereby a hybrid system.

Stabilization is effected as the cumulation of a number of steps:

- firstly, many of the stages that were carried out in the ICICLES study inherently lay the foundations for stabilization (e.g. training);
- preparing a savings report that details capital expenditure and other ongoing costs;
- carrying out an assessment of the new situation;
- writing specific manuals, and standard instructions.

There is always the possibility that so much stabilization will carve the new procedures in stone and strangle any future improvements. This can only happen if people let it happen which, truth to tell, probably means that people are quite content to let it happen.

Savings report

A statement of benefits and costs can arise at a number of points. If the study is undertaken by management consultants, then their initial survey of the situation will have contained an assessment of likely costs and benefits. If a proposed change involves major expenditure, then this will require an analysis to show cash flow implications. If a study includes a project control input, then there will be regular cost reports. Finally, if a change appears not to have delivered savings, then there may be a post-operational report.

Thus a savings report can occur before, during or after a change has been initiated. In all events, it is an agent for stabilization in showing how much more expensive the old ways are/were compared with the new.

The basic idea behind savings reports is simplicity itself. It is to compare four things:

	Old	New
Costs		
Benefits		

We have slipped from using the word 'savings' to referring to 'benefits'. This is because some benefits may not represent a saving. For example, widening the gross profit margin by 1 per cent is a financial benefit but not a saving in the ordinary sense of the word. Although the basic idea of savings reports is so simple, it is when we move away from the basic idea to actually preparing one that the complications start. Each of the four boxes of Old/New, Costs/Benefits offers plenty of scope for argument and general fuzziness.

F

In offices, the capital investment per person is still less than in factories. So one usually starts by calculating the staff costs for the old and the new situations, though even here one does not use the 'actual-actual' cost but a 'standard-actual'. A department may have a higher or lower incidence of absenteeism or trainees that can affect its costs but these are usually ignored. It is usual to use a standard cost per person. For this, one uses the standard figure that the internal accountants have calculated for such situations. But not always.

The internal accountants will have included in the salary costs certain extras: the overheads, such as the taxes and insurance that have to be paid for every employee. This is fine. What is not so fine is that 'staff costs' standards may also include such things as the cost of the Personnel Department and Sports and Recreation facilities. These costs may be unchanged by the changes that are being made and so should be excluded. So it is normal practice first to find out what is meant by the figure of staff costs, and amend as necessary. But not always.

A change may involve a whole division or a subsidiary that has its accounts consolidated with those of the parent company. In this case it may be necessary to include those overheads that are specific and wholly incurred by the group under inspection.

The position for capital items can be equally thought-provoking. When one replaces a telephone exchange in an organization, the old one will not have been written off in

419

the books and will have almost no second-hand value. Its replacement therefore is a capital cost. It is usual in such circumstances to take the written down value in the books as being the capital cost of scrapping it. But not always.

Many large equipment items are the subject of contractual payments, or may be leased or hired. Contracts covering such items may specify penalty payments for revoking the agreement. It is a common failing to assume that these payments will be forgiven because the supplier wishes to maintain 'goodwill'. They may be. But definitely not always.

The benefits of the current system may be glossed over or even omitted, especially if the aim of the savings report is to convince people that a change should be made. However, some organizations like to see quoted here the inverse of the disadvantages of the proposal. For example, documents from a new fax may take longer to read because of quality degradation, compared with typed reports. In this case, some organizations like to see 'faster reading due to clarity' as a benefit of the present system.

If there is scope for discussion when one is calculating current costs, it is nothing compared with that when looking at future costs and benefits. There is often a fuzziness when looking at future costs of staff, equipment, software and on-costs. Costs of materials, services and supplies are often thought of as being more straightforward. But not always.

In 1974 it was decided by Bramber Parish Council to forego street lighting for three days to save some money. The result was that £11.59's worth of electricity was saved. However, it cost £18.48 to switch the electricity off and £12.00 to switch it on again. So an anticipated saving of £11.59 became a cost of £18.89.

Similarly, it is too easy to assume staff savings that do not in fact happen. Even equipment costs can be a trap. A word processing manufacturer actually underestimated the number of stations required by 50 per cent – and the analyst had accepted the figure unchecked and had incorporated it in the savings report.

Two types of costs are often underestimated. One is the cost of migrating from the old to the new. This cost can include the cost of investigating the change (analysts + management), project control, implementing the change, installation costs (structural changes, loss of profits during the change-over), training, loss of profits during the familiarization phase. Organizations vary widely as to which costs they expect to see in a savings report.

The second type of cost that is often underestimated is the costs that a change will bring in its train and that are inescapable. These include software enhancements, technology maintenance (frequently 10 per cent of capital cost per year), extended training, computer air-conditioning. Again, organizations vary widely in their treatment of such costs.

Some organizations lump everything into 'overheads' and let it go at that, with some form of allocation. But even this does not help with the fact that new technology may attract a much faster rate of depreciation in real terms than the internal accountants are accustomed to handling. Some equipment has a rapid obsolescence, though the rate may be difficult to estimate.

This brings us to the concept of lifetime costs or life-cycle costing. This is part of capital investment appraisal which was dealt with earlier in the book. At this point, it is enough to say that many organizations pay too little attention to true costs. Sometimes this seems to be almost deliberate policy – as though the costs of new technology are so high that it would never get introduced in the face of full calculations. Rather like the

420

chairman of a very successful chain of retail shops who is reputed to have said, 'If I listened to my accountants, I'd never open a new branch.'

A major problem is that many of the benefits of new equipment are either intangible or extremely difficult to put a financial benefit to. For example, how would one put a financial benefit on having telephones? Even worse, what is the financial benefit of a new Management Information System? There are two common approaches to this, neither of which is satisfactory. One is to give a dummy estimated benefit of such items as, 'Improved management understanding of the business'. The other approach is to state the costs, and then to give a laundry list of intangible benefits. Management can then make a decision as to whether it is worth paying the cost of achieving the intangibles.

In both cases, the savings report or cost–benefit analysis has moved considerably away from its role of assisting decisions by putting parameters around them. In the early 1980s we had the heyday in many organizations of new 'information technology' installations. Since information technology was clearly a Good Thing, many organizations lowered their defences and allowed poorly argued savings reports through. These savings reports were full of intangible benefits. Some effectively abandoned any attempt at financial justification.

There were even a few people who openly claimed that financial benefits did not really matter as much as installing new information technology. The reaction to this was inevitable. Management insisted on better reports and more information. The results were healthy. The result was not, as the 'techies' feared, a cutback on new technology. Instead, the results were better thought-through proposals. As one manager put it, 'We want results, not all this blue sky and motherhood-is-good stuff.'

F

Better proposals meant fewer errors, better planning, lower costs and, above all, more robust solutions. They did not mean less advanced office technology; they meant better, more suitable advanced office technology. The new technology is still a Good Thing – for some firms it is a necessity – but now a higher level of proof is needed, as well as careful proposals.

This does not mean that we have yet got good ways of proving the value of some proposals, such as MIS, which is still problematical. But at least we no longer pretend that it does not matter.

A savings report will usually follow the pattern:

- introduction to area under discussion;
- brief summary of costs and benefits;
- description of the current situation;
- description of the proposed situation;
- description of the migration from current to proposed;
- costs and benefits calculations;
- caveats and other notes;
- an action plan for implementation;
- appendices giving detailed reasoning behind the proposals such as cash flow discounting, and basis of intangible benefits.

Some organizations have pre-printed formats for the justification of the purchase of small items of equipment and software enhancements. These are useful since they ensure a commonality of approach and hence speed managerial decision-making. They cannot normally be used for major capital expenditure projects.

A typical evaluation sheet for an MIS proposal is shown in Figure 39.1. Since the capital costs are not high, there is no discounting of cash flow (the main equipment is leased).

Apart from those savings reports that contain an arithmetic error which materially affects the final outcome, probably the worst ones are those that do not really show any savings at all. In April 1983, the US Pentagon promised a savings report. This showed a saving of $11.3 billions on the Trident nuclear submarine programme. This was because there would be eight, instead of fifteen, submarines. This interested the journalists. Did this mean that part of the nuclear deterrent was to be reduced by almost half? No, said the Pentagon, the remaining seven had been renamed Trident II and would be part of a new programme. Further questions revealed that Trident II submarines were to be the same as Trident I submarines. In fact the cost of building the

MIS Project title Department Author		Ref. Date	
Start-up Costs	1914	1915	Total
1 Consultancy study costs	20,000		20,000
2 Project planning	6,000		6,000
3 Design	3,000		3,000
4 Software plus enhancements	18,000	14,000	32,000
5 Implementation		6,000	6,000
6 Testing		5,000	5,000
7 Management training		10,000	10,000
8 Structural alterations		4,000	4,000
Total start-up costs	47,000	39,000	£86,000
Capital Costs			
9 Computer centre equipment	3,000	28,000	31,000
10 Additional facilities and modems		18,000	18,000
Total capital costs	3,000	46,000	£49,000
Annual Operating Costs			
11 Personnel costs			120,000
12 Computer and equipment lease			30,000
13 Supplies and services			6,000
Total annual operating costs			£156,000
Annual Benefits			
14 Personnel costs			22,000
15 Equipment lease			2,000
16 Reduced management committee meetings			3,000
17 Reduced time on capital budgets			2,000
Total annual benefits			£29,000
Annual Intangible Benefits			
18 Improved strategic decision-making			70,000
19 Net profit from orders not lost due to stock-outs			60,000
20 Interest saved on reduced stock-holding			46,000
Total annual intangible benefits			£176,000

Figure 39.1 Example cost–benefit sheet

fifteen submarines would not be reduced by \$11.3 billions. It would be increased by \$2.7 billions. Not the best savings report ever.

Test assessment

A test assessment is the second of our ways of stabilizing a change. This can be carried out some while after the changes have been made. It provides a final feedback for enhancing the methods still further, ensuring that the changes are operating satisfactorily, and that the changes have not themselves been changed.

The new situation is tested in several ways:

- is the level of service satisfactory and being maintained?
- is the output being produced in the correct format, as specified, and is the quality satisfactory?
- have all remains of the old operations been removed (old blank forms discarded, old equipment removed)?
- are the new methods, systems, equipment, procedures, forms and software being used, and used as specified? If not, why not and what should be done?
- are deadlines and schedules being met?
- is there a backlog, and if so is it increasing or reducing?
- are levels of output satisfactory and the error rate? If not, why not and what should be done?
- are the users of the outputs satisfied?
- have any unforeseen problems or exceptions arisen and, if so, have they been solved? Have any unforseen expenses or costs been incurred?
- are the anticipated savings being attained?
- are the anticipated intangible benefits being attained and, if so, at what level? Can the connection be shown?
- is morale high among the staff? Is management enthusiastic?

An important aspect of the test assessment is that it should not become a whitewash exercise, nor should problems be hidden. It is an opportunity – an opportunity to get everything as near perfect as possible. Any problems that are hidden will return later to haunt the organization – and solving them later will definitely take longer.

Written manuals

The third way of stabilizing is to write new manuals, etc. This writing may be of:

- job descriptions;
- Standard Practice Instructions (SPIs);
- Admin manuals.

One sometimes has a slight feeling of unease when writing these manuals. They feel bureaucratic, an inhibiting influence. They feel antipathetic to the notion of 'The Effective Office', which should somehow be more active, more positive. However, that being said, it must be admitted that they have a place in the scheme of things; they have advantages and large multinationals would find life more difficult without them. They are not an end in themselves, nor do they directly assist us in making offices more effective. Their effectiveness is indirect.

Job descriptions describe a job, a position within the office structure. They are concerned with the work itself, and not with the persona of the staff doing the work. If a member of staff leaves and is replaced, the job description stays the same. Most organizations have a standard format for job descriptions and their own way of completing them. A sample job description is given in Figure 39.2.

Standard Practice Instructions (SPIs) detail the procedures. They are usually a step-by-step description, and are very useful for training new staff. The language used should be straightforward, and should be accompanied by examples of forms involved. The addition of methods flow charts can aid clarity. The most difficult aspect of SPIs in practice is keeping them up to date.

Some organizations have detailed multi-volume admin manuals. These will cover many points from how to lay out letters to company policy on making charitable contributions. Other organizations would not dream of using admin manuals. They appear to be yet another facet of organizational culture. As such, it is a surprisingly large step for an organization to install admin manuals – especially since by 'install' is meant to use, not just have them in the manager's office. For organizations with offices in a number of countries, admin manuals ensure a degree of universality for items as

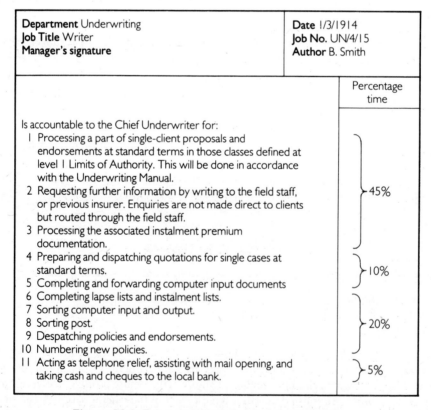

Figure 39.2 Extract from sample job description

diverse as systems, procedures, house style and policy decisions. For government offices and audit firms, admin manuals take on an even more serious role – as shown by their common nickname of the office 'Bible'.

A final way of stabilization is the use of management controls, and this is dealt with in the next chapter.

Further reading

BIM, *Job Evaluation*, London: Management Publications, 1970.

F

40

Controls

How can a man learn navigation
Where there's no rudder?

Christopher Fry, *A Sleep of Prisoners* (1951)

A good system of control provides against undesirable surprises,
capable of degenerating into catastrophes . . . it demands constant
and sustained attention and often a good deal of art.

Henri Fayol, *General and Industrial Management* (1916)

Control is one of the fundamental aspects of effective management, whether it be control of budgets, projects, action plans or office work. Without controls, one stays in the dark. Because of the widespread impact of controls, their nature varies widely. They also vary in the detail involved: they can be concerned with minutes of work (in factories) or in broad organization-wide ratios such as inter-firm comparisons. As an example of this latter, one can consider how many soldiers an army has for every senior officer:[1]

Name of country	Soldiers per senior officer
USA	2,300
France	1,900
W. Germany	1,900
Britain	495

Does this mean that Britain has too many brigadiers and generals? It may look like it, but we cannot be certain without knowing what the 'standard' should be or knowing the position in more armies.

A more complex example is Table 40.1, which compares the results for some commercial banks (chosen because their names happen to start with B or C). No inter-firm comparison is perfect. For example, in Table 40.1, wholesale and retail banks are mixed, balance sheets and the definition of assets differ between countries, and some banks have hidden assets. So we cannot be absolutely certain when we are comparing like with like. Thus one bank (Continental Illinois) has a profit per branch of $125 million – but then, it only has one branch.

And yet, in spite of all our reservations, the table remains of interest. It shows what was happening as Citicorp toppled Bank of America from the position of biggest bank in the USA. The poor profits at Commerzbank led it to a sale-and-leaseback of its head office. And Banque Nationale de Paris became a possible candidate for privatization.

The table still does not tell us what the 'standard' should be. Nor does it tell us what should be done about poor comparative figures. Should a bank move out of retail banking into wholesale banking, changing their nature? (Some banks have in fact done this.)

Table 40.1 Number of staff and profits for various commercial banks

Bank	No. of staff	Profits in $ per		
		Employee	$1000 assets	Branch
Bank of America	91,068	5,500	4.4	370,000
Barclays Bank	67,700	11,900	8.6	280,000
Citicorp	63,700	25,200	12.8	620,000
Banque Nationale de Paris	60,615	5,500	3.3	130,000
Commerzbank	22,047	7,400	4.0	200,000
Bank of Tokyo	14,736	19,700	4.5	1,060,000
Credit Suisse	12,260	18,600	6.5	1,270,000

(Source data: Pocket Banker, *The Economist*)

There certainly does seem to be a strong correlation between profitability and global labour productivity (such as sales per person). A well-known British life insurance company had used work measurement, 'O & M' and computerization for some years. A representative from an overseas company that did not came to visit it. He found that the British company needed one member of staff for every 6,000 policies; his own needed many more – one member of staff for every 3,500 policies.

A third example of comparison and control is highlighted by a favourite question. This is to ask a manager, 'Are you doing your job better now than you were a year ago?' The answer is nearly always yes. To this the response is, 'If I asked you to demonstrate this to me, to prove it, what would you reply?' It is surprising how many managers cannot give a good proof.

F

■ CONTROL SYSTEM REQUIREMENTS

These three examples help us to state the requirements of a control system:

- it should have a standard, to use as a comparison;
- comparisons should be between like and like;
- variations from standard should be known, be capable of explanation, and lead to action to rectify;
- controls should cover as large a portion of the staff as possible;
- feedback needs to be soon after the event.

■ CONTROL SYSTEM STEPS

From these requirements can be stated the five steps in any control system:

- measurement of the item(s) to be controlled;
- the establishment of standards, based on this measurement;
- comparison of actual results with these standards;
- feedback of this comparison to those held responsible;
- the correction of deviations from standard.

A domestic example of a control system is the kitchen oven when baking a cake. The initial measurement process will have been carried out by the manufacturer and incorporated in a thermostat. The cook will set the standard as 210°C. The oven continually checks the temperature for deviations from 210°C, and deviations are fed back to the input of gas or electricity. Energy inputs are increased or decreased until the temperature returns to the standard.

This type of automatic control system uses information and results that arise only from within the system. It is therefore known as a 'closed-loop' system. Management controls are not like this and are known as 'open-loop' systems. This is because they are affected by the world outside the system. The manager handling the deviations from standard may introduce new inputs, data and decisions into the process. Even the causes of the deviations may lie outside the system. Computer utilization in a mail order firm will drop during a postal strike, not because of deficiencies within the system (in this case the computer department), but because the level of input (postal orders) has fallen.

The fact that management controls take the form of an open loop has practical effects. The impact of outside influences leads us to understand why Henry Fayol called controls an 'art'. As one external influence is dealt with, another one arises. So a manager is correcting one deviation at the same time that another one is starting. Thus they will overlap. This makes it more difficult to be able to state unequivocally why a deviation exists.

In poorly managed organizations this inability is then turned into the finding of excuses for deviations rather than reasons. In turn, this leads to inaction. This, in its turn, leads to ignoring the controls. In a large Project Management company, a manager was overheard talking earnestly to a member of staff before a progress meeting. This went along the lines of, 'Remember that the important thing is not falling behind on this project. What is important is to have an excuse. If you've got an excuse, then it's OK.'

■ OFFICE CONTROLS

In offices, the items that can be included in controls may be:

- quality (e.g. data prep error rate);
- performance (e.g. productivity of staff);
- backlogs;
- attainment of schedules and deadlines;
- costs;
- volume of throughput;
- cross-boundary (e.g. effects of shortcomings in one department on another).

■ CONTROL DESIGN

In designing a control process, it is important that the controls are:

- tailor-made for their purpose;
- understood and accepted;
- at the correct level of accuracy and complexity;
- not too time-consuming in data collection;
- clear.

This is very easy to say, but less easy to achieve in practice. The first item on this list is for the controls to be tailor-made. This is because different information is needed at the various levels in the hierarchy. The chairman of a company will concentrate his or her attention on what may be called 'balance sheet items', and will not be concerned that this month 11,254 invoices were passed compared with the usual 10,987. The general

428

rule is that each recipient gets information related to the direct responsibilities of the recipient and immediate subordinates. But this rule will have to be broken when it inhibits effectiveness.

It will be realized that management control can often edge into the Management Information System. In an ideal world, one would carefully balance the five information systems: Financial Accounting, Strategic Planning, Management Accounting, Management Information System and the Management Controls. In practice, it is never possible to set all of them up simultaneously and integrate them since each of them is a moving target. Some people would claim that it does not really matter, anyway. Certainly the 1970s idea of a Total Information System is less fashionable now.

The second item on the design list was that the controls should be 'understood and accepted'. Acceptability is largely another facet of the culture. So is the level of comprehension. Some control documents are dauntingly complex to an outsider at first glance, but users seem able to learn how to use them. Nevertheless, the rule is the usual one – keep it simple.

The question of the 'correct level of accuracy' can be a vexing one. There is a strong tendency to pursue accuracy too far. It is not uncommon to see controls of staff time where the SMVs are quoted to too many places of decimals, in spite of the fact that they are used to calculate whole numbers of people, not whole numbers of minutes. Such controls imply a degree of accuracy that is spurious and unwarranted. Many places of decimal may make an answer more precise, but they cannot make it more accurate.

Accuracy pursuit is better aimed at obtaining correct volumes than at using many decimal places. However, there are times when even volumes at not needed accurately. A Chicago client performed computer bureau services for its customers, offering a twenty-four hour turnround. To achieve this, it was often necessary to work overtime. Since this was variable, the staff wished to know before the end of the day whether they would be needed to work late. A ruler was made on which each mark indicated an hour's work when placed against a pile of work input forms. In use, every day at 3.30 the remaining work was piled on the supervisor's desk. It was then measured using the special ruler, and from this the hours of work remaining were read. If overtime was indicated, the staff then decided among themselves who wanted to do it and how much. This simple procedure was quite accurate enough for its purpose. It was also much liked by the staff.

F

Work controls in the office

To many people, the word controls means a form of control for the time spent by the office staff. This form of control is very common – few work quantification investigations do not result in the adoption of such controls. These controls usually show the number of SMVs 'earned' in a month. This is calculated from Volume × SMV for each item. The SMVs earned are then divided by the time 'paid' for. The result is a productivity index or, if multiplied by 100, a productivity percentage. An extract from a typical control is shown in Figure 40.1.

■ POLICY ALLOWANCE

Many PMTS and other work measurement studies result in the staff productivity reports being based on a 100 level on the 0/100 scale. There may be reasons why

Productivity Report

Department Money market support   **Date** April, 1914

Item	Volume	SMV	Hours earned	Backlog
Brokerage	956	4.96	79	17
Book transfer	915	2.49	38	–
Confirmations	1,784	4.98	148	414
Merchant bank confirmations	2,592	4.98	215	–
Interest exception queries	301	34.9	175	13
Interest payments	132	12.3	27	–
£ reconciliations	472	22.4	176	59
$ reconciliations	47	23.0	18	–
Merchant bank reconciliations	2,790	2.5	116	–
Reconciliation queries	133	22.6	50	43
Rate changes	4	150	10	–
Other queries	430	29.9	214	–
			1,266	

Total hours earned (A)   = 1,266
Total hours paid (B)   = 1,229
PERFORMANCE (A ÷ B) = 103
Last month's performance = 110

Figure 40.1 Productivity report extract

management and unions agree that the level should not be 100, at any rate not for a while. This may be because the office is new, or because people are not yet used to the new technology, or because productivity has in the past been low.

Whatever the reason, it may be decided that for, say, nine months, the target will not be 100 performance. It may be decided that the target performance will be 90, or even 85. There are two ways of doing this. One is just to accept that a performance figure of 90 or 85 is the target, changing this later to 100.

However, many people (both staff and management) prefer the idea of always working towards the figure of 100. It may somehow seem more 'natural'. To do this, it is necessary to multiply the productivity or performance figure by a factor. For example, if it is decided that the target performance should be 80, then the actual performance has to be increased by a quarter. In Figure 40.1, the calculation would then become:

Total hours earned (A)   = 1,266
Total hours paid (B)   = 1,229
Policy factor is: 1.25
PERFORMANCE (A ÷ B) × 1.25 = 129
Last month's performance   = 138

It is important that when a policy allowance is used, the resulting performance is never, ever, referred to as being '100 per cent'. One major bank installed its controls at an 83 level and called them '100 per cent'. When later the bank wished to increase the level, it caused surprise. The staff felt, understandably, that since they were already working at 100 per cent, they should not be asked to work harder. The factors that have to be used to increase performance to an apparent 100 level are:

Performance	Factor
80	1.25
85	1.18
90	1.11
95	1.05

■ INDICATORS

An indicator is an isolated figure chosen so that as it varies it indicates how the whole varies. For example, a department may handle a variety of items of work of which the main one is invoices. It may be decided to choose the number of invoices handled as an indicator of the total workload of the department. This figure may even be used as a form of control for the department.

Indicators are often used to compare whole companies. Thus airlines may be compared by calculating the figure of number of staff per million passenger miles. A similar approach can be used to compare companies within any industry, such as car manufacturers (people per thousand cars per year), railways, hospitals, insurance companies, etc. Care has to be used when applying this approach (certainly, organizations at the bottom of any such league can always see reasons for their apparent inefficiency). A common ratio used in restaurants is the number of covers (seats) per waiter. But this ratio will be lower at lunchtime when one wants customers in and out within 30 minutes than at evening dinners. Then 60 minutes per sitting may be fine – because there will be a higher consumption of drinks, which have a higher profit margin.

So, again – care with indicators. In offices, some analysts regularly use as an indicator the single most common item. It has to be said that we do not like this approach:

- staff mistrust it (perhaps because they can instinctively see the disadvantages);
- the ratio of the single most common item to the total workload does not stay constant month by month. So variations are hidden by the variability of the ratio;
- the most common item may account for a minority of the work in an office, and an indicator based on say 30–40 per cent of the total workload is a poor control;
- these indicators (known as 'single indicators') have a short life since work in offices changes. Unfortunately, they may stay in place a long time, certainly long after they have any relevance;
- single indicators cannot handle changes in procedures and departmental boundary changes.

Indicators, especially single indicators, can actually have an effect opposite to the one intended. A well-known example occurred during the 1939–45 war. The British Coastal Command used as an indicator for control at each airfield the percentage of

F

planes ready to fly operationally. This was meant to monitor efficiency, but it did not take people long to realize how to attain a high rating – which was not to fly any operations. All the planes were then ready to fly.

It may appear that indicators are no use, but this is not so: they can be very useful but they must be set up properly and with thought. A department may be small but unlikely to yield reductions. A programme of work measurement may be lengthy but controls wanted quickly, even if these are not permanent. Some areas may provide a service that is getting expensive and is out of control. Some departments may not justify accurate work measurement. In all these cases, indicators may be useful.

To use indicators effectively, they need to be harnessed to a measure that reflects their level of cost. For example, it is often possible to use 'number of staff' as an indicator for the workload of a personnel department. This can be used even after accurate work quantification. Other possible indicators that can prove useful are turnover, number of customers on the sales ledger, number of suppliers, capital assets, etc.

■ BEATING THE CONTROLS

It is said that management controls, like rules, are made to be broken. Or, if not broken, at least bent a little. If controls are thought to be too constrictive, people are very adept at finding ways of evading them or circumventing them, especially if the bending causes amusement or affects people's pay packets. A few cautionary tales (out of many encountered) may illustrate this:

1 A company had its offices fitted out with carpet squares. The financial director thought that a good way of allocating overheads to departments would be to base the allocation on the number of carpet squares in each department. This would accurately reflect square metres occupied, was quick to ascertain as partitions were moved, and would be a practical means of persuading people not to have too-large offices. Quickly, one manager succeeded in getting hold of larger carpet squares for his office.

2 A manufacturer of photocopiers wanted to ensure a high level of service for the largest machines. To do this, a control was instituted whereby head office had to be informed of all instances where a call-out for service was answered in more than 40 minutes. Local staff realized that the easiest way to reduce the over-40-minutes incidents was to let some customers wait three or four hours. This made it possible to service more call-outs in less than 40 minutes. So a control that was designed to improve the service actually resulted in a poorer service for customers.

3 Some years ago, a candidate for mayor of New York promised that if elected he would improve the productivity of city employees. After being elected, it was decided that one of the places for improvement would be the rate at which asphalt was laid on the pavements. Sure enough, over a period of 18 months productivity increased steadily but surely until it reached an increase of 100 per cent. How was this praiseworthy increase achieved? Well, productivity was measured by the weight of asphalt applied. So the employees gradually increased the thickness applied from 5 cm to 10 cm.

Perhaps the oddest example of controls being evaded concerned the attempt by some companies to reduce the incidence of engaging drug takers. To do this, some companies asked for urine samples to be provided. Whereupon one J. Nightbyrd from Austin,

432

Texas, came upon the scene. He obtained clean urine samples from a Bible study group and sold them for $49.95 each.

Reference

1 Kitson, Sir F., *Warfare as a Whole*, London: Faber & Faber, 1987.

Further reading

Locke, E. A. and Latham, G. P., *Goal Setting*, Englewood Cliffs: Prentice-Hall, 1984.
NASA, *A Framework for Action*, Washington: NASA, 1984.

F

41

Trees and Taxonomy

There's no limit to how complicated things can get, on account of
one thing always leading to another.

E. B. White, *Quo Vadimus* (1939)

Science is the attempt to make the chaotic diversity of our sense-
experience correspond to a logically uniform system of thought.

Einstein, *Out of My Later Years* (1950)

Introduction

There are many occasions when it is necessary to think up a structure, when we need a
logical framework to hold information, ideas or physical objects. This is so when we
have to think up a system for filing correspondence, keeping manufacturers' brochures
or setting up the root directory on a hard disk. The same logical approach is needed for
a number of office techniques such as algorithms, decision trees and expert systems.
Some of these uses are covered elsewhere (chapters 16 and 27) but many people have
difficulty in grasping the process: one frequently sees examples of coding which are
based on elementary errors.

All such systems automatically bring in their train certain problems. First is that all
division creates grey areas of uncertainty. A store may hold voltmeters and ammeters –
where should one store multimeters? A tobacconist may keep cigarettes separately from
cigars – where would 'whiffs' in white wrappers go? Second, most divisions create items
that should go into more than one division. A consultant may keep sample balance
sheets by industry – where does he put conglomerates? Third, all divisions are made in
ignorance of future changes or inventions. One may have kept software by function
such as word processing and desk-top publishing – what did one do when software was
produced which combined both features?

So the aim has to be to avoid the problems so far as possible, while admitting that
they can never be completely eliminated, only ameliorated. The word 'tree' is used to
denote any diagram in which successive layers follow on logically from the previous
layer, thus:

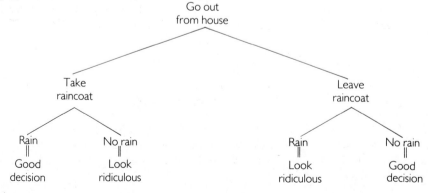

A 'decision tree' would have the probability of each alternative branch against it plus the financial outcome of each final result. A 'shred-out' is a tree in which the first item is successively divided into its constituent parts:

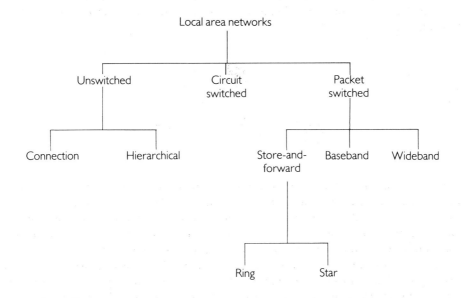

F

Even this simple example of a shred-out raises some practical problems. It omits some types (such as token), it omits some concepts (such as polling) and uses a non-universal term (wideband, also known a broadband). It could also cause difficulty if one wanted to insert 'loop', which might be part of wideband or could be used as an alternative to 'ring'.

It will be noticed that two different methods of drawing lines between the items has been used in the examples. This is a convention that is commonly used, though a reason for the two types is not easy to imagine. Trees, including decision trees, usually have angled lines; shred-outs usually have lines at right angles.

The word 'taxonomy', originally reserved for the classification and descriptions of organisms, was adopted to describe general systems of coding and classification, including those used in offices. It has been seen used as a synonym for trees, but it is felt that that is stretching its meaning too far. A coding system for classification is often accompanied by a shred-out diagram, and this may be where the confusion arose. But taxonomy refers to the classification and coding itself rather than to a diagram.

Historical background

Apart from various classification systems proposed by the ancients, one of the earliest was the Amera Cosha prepared by Amera Sinha in Sanscrit around AD 1000. One section included Gods, Demons, Velocity and Much while another covered Sin, Virtue, Tastes and Odours.

In 1668 Bishop Wilkins published an essay which was intended to lead to a universal language based on symbols. This was based on 'a scheme of analysis of the things or notions to which names were to be assigned'. As an aside, another universal language based on symbols was Paleneo,[1] invented by Leslie Charteris, the writer of thriller stories such as the 'Saint' series. In Paleneo, the ideogram for 'organization' is a basic shred-out, thus:

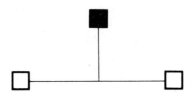

In the eighteenth century, Carolus Linnaeus put forward a system for the classification and naming of plants and animals. His three works (1735, 1737 and 1753) are superb examples of the taxonomist's art. Linnaeus is credited with producing the first major attempt at bringing a logical order to the field of living objects. Even more, his work laid the foundation for much later work on classification.

One example of later work was that of Baron Cuvier. He published his classification system for animals, including extinct fossils, in *Le Règne Animal* in 1817. Thirty-five years later came the publication of a work with which most people are familiar. This was *Roget's Thesaurus of English Words and Phrases* (1853). This is now usually referred to just as *Roget's Thesaurus*. In this Peter Roget divided the language into thirty-nine subdivisions. The first level of his shred-out has just six divisions:

- abstract relations (such as resemblance and number);
- space (including motion and dimensions);
- matter (the properties of matter and its perceptions);
- intellect (the acquisition, retention and communication of ideas);
- volition (including choice and action);
- affections (such as feelings and religious sentiments).

Roget's Thesaurus has been a success for over a century for several reasons. Firstly, it is of course extremely useful. Secondly, the classification system has proved able to absorb additions without changing the underlying system (current editions include such items as spacecraft, bulldozer and juke-box, all of which were unknown to Roget). Thirdly, all current editions have an excellent indexing system which speeds their use.

Further examples

The most straightforward type of tree is the one that shows pedigree. This may be one showing the evolution of the intelligent photocopier or the progeny of Queen Victoria. The main problems associated with such trees lie in the discovery of all the entries and good draughtsmanship to make it clear. The example opposite shows the relationship of Hercules and Perseus:

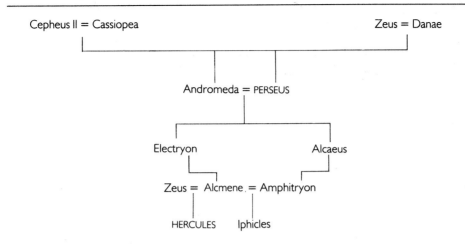

The second example is the classification of the over one million species of animals. The main (initial) groupings are known as phyla. There are about thirty phyla – but authorities differ to some extent on what these phyla should be. Therefore classifications differ. In the extract shred-out below, the first row are phyla, the second classes and the third are examples:

F

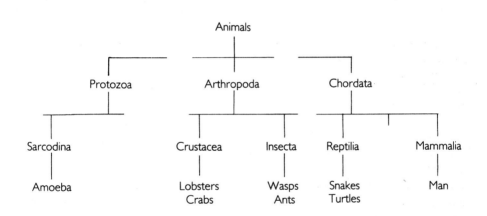

The third example is the classification of languages. Here, classifiers have a choice of different approaches to the method of analysis. Languages can be grouped by the continents and countries in which they are found. They can also be grouped by their grammar and construction. Thus English and Chinese would be grouped together since word forms vary little but word order is important (in English 'The dog bit the man' is not the same as 'The man bit the dog'). A third approach is to group languages by their development. Thus Celtic languages would be Gaullish, Goidelic (Manx, Gaelic) or Brythonic (Cornish, Welsh, Breton).

None of these approaches is watertight. For example, the third approach is troubled by Basque, which has uncertain relationships. The shred-out overleaf shows the relationships of the West Germanic languages:

437

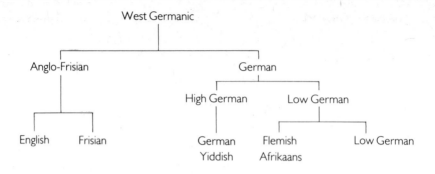

Even this grouping would not satisfy some French academics who claim English is not a real language at all but a mongrel mixture, like Esperanto.

Our next example concerns holding material on a hard disk. A hard disk can hold at least 20–760 MBytes of data. That is a lot of data and it needs organizing, otherwise looking for and finding something on it will take a very long time – like putting all the office correspondence in one pile. The DOS software locates the data, but it does not organize it in the 'tree' sense.

The hard disk will slowly be filled with files as it is used. Some files will be computer programs (such as graphics software), others will be text or data that has been produced. Each file is given a name to identify it. The files are grouped together, and each group is known as a directory – rather as animals were grouped together in phyla in the example already considered.

When a disk is first formatted using DOS, a top-level directory is created. This is the root directory. A hard disk will hold at least 512 entries in its root directory. However, it is good practice to limit the contents of the root directory to a relatively few files. This facilitates the visualization of the whole shred-out and will thus make it easier to keep track of the large number of files on the disk.

Each directory can hold not only files but also subdirectories. These subdirectories can also hold files and further subdirectories – thus building up our tree. DOS identifies each file by its 'path name'. Referring again to the chart of animal classification, the root directory would contain a directory named 'Chordata'. This would contain a subdirectory named 'Reptilia' which would contain a file named 'Turtles'. So if we keep our hard disk in drive C of our computer, the path name of the file telling us all about turtles would then be 'C:\Chordata\Reptilia\Turtles' (directories can have names up to eight characters).

Setting up the tree is similar to the examples already given of classifying animals or languages plus a dash of the Perseus–Hercules chart. Files may be grouped by office departments (Marketing, Personnel, Audit and so on) – or they can be grouped by type of data (such as balance sheet figures, costing standards, experimentation results). It depends on the use to which the hard disk is being put.

People with computers at home will tend to hold the data according to the different packages that they have bought. Subdirectories will then logically hold the files that are associated with each particular package. It is usual to maintain a separate directory for the DOS software itself in order to avoid complications. The names of the other directories could then be by type, such as BASE for one's database program. In fact, most people use instead a contraction of the name of the actual package, such as 'Fox' for Foxbase. So the tree for a domestic computer might be, in part, as shown below:

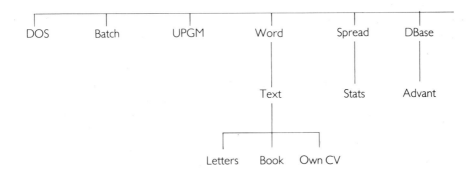

In this tree 'DOS' is just the DOS files. 'Batch' would be frequently used batch files plus their associated files. 'UPGM' would be utility programs, plus programs for the batch files. The other directories would be for one's word processing, spreadsheet and database software.

Some people never seem to get their directories organized. Others will actually have a tree diagram of a sort. As the hard disk fills up, it is the latter group who can feel satisfied with themselves.

Our final example concerns coding without a tree. When this is being formulated, one has to use enough digits and letters to cover all the existing needs, plus some spaces to allow for expansion in the future. Some coding will also include further information about what is coded (the codes used for car number plates also include, in many countries, an indication of the town where the car was registered).

The codes used to identify airlines were originally kept to just two letters, such as DL for Delta Airlines and BA for British Airways. This saved money on the more than ten billion messages generated by airlines round the world each year. But by 1984 the number of airlines registered reached 600. This meant that the number of possible two-letter combinations would soon be exceeded ($26 \times 26 = 676$), so it was necessary to introduce three-letter codes. The change-over (during 1987–1993) to all the computer databases, etc., was estimated to cost £150 million. Some airlines were quite pleased with their new codes: Sierra Vista Aviation managed to get FLY as its prefix. Others were not so lucky. Tarom from Romania got ROT, while Mid-West Aviation pondered its NIT prefix.

Coding principles

Some guidelines from our examples that will at least help to avoid a few mistakes are:

- when preparing a shred-out, cover the entire field, so that the whole equals the sum of the parts;
- use a miscellaneous classification for small items, not for anything which may get much bigger in the future;
- try to keep groupings 'natural' with no obvious kinship between the items;

- try very hard to think of the future. Some developments will be missed, but it is certainly possible to anticipate others;
- classification can start at the bottom and work up, or can start at the top and work down. In office use the top-and-down is usually the quicker. Sometimes one has to start at the bottom, move up, and then restart at the top;
- an alternative approach is to look for a special reason for the groupings into divisions rather than at the objects themselves. Bases can be form or nature of the items, numerical, statistical, historical, functions or relationships;
- many codings use the digits 0–9 at each layer. Do *not* use all ten digits, especially for the first layer. Ever. This must be one of the commonest reasons for badly-thought out codings failing. Another division will arise at some stage in the future. Instead try to use only seven digits, leaving 8 and 9 for future expansion. If one of the divisions is 'miscellaneous', then use 9 for it, and leave 7 and 8 blank;
- try to keep it obvious where items will fall in the system. If necessary, prepare a comprehensive index. If users will have to employ an alphabetical order of names, follow the same scheme as is used in the telephone directory to decide the order;
- sometimes one has to scrap a classification system that one is developing and start again. In the long run, this is better than trying to force items into impossible places.

No taxonomy is fail-safe, even those that are in widespread use. For example, books are frequently misplaced in libraries and these errors are often quoted in the trade press. Hastings Public Library had Kafka's *The Trial* under detective fiction. Grays Thurrock library had *Time Study* under philosophy. A more bizarre case concerned the book *Alive*, which is about survivors of a Peru air crash, some of whom kept themselves alive by resorting to cannibalism. This was found in a New York bookshop under cookery books.

Decision trees

Decision trees are a particular type of tree with their own conventions and uses, though over time some of the conventions have become somewhat bent. At one time decision trees were learnt on many management training courses; for example, they were an important aspect of the Managerial Economics analysis at Harvard Business School.[2] They fell slightly out of favour, for reasons which may become clearer as we look at them. They should not be forgotten completely, though, as they do have uses. In particular, they are easier for most of us to visualize than tables like a pay-off matrix.

The tree branches at either a decision or at events over which one has no control. The former is shown by a small box, and the latter by a small circle. A tree is thus different from a critical path chart, which is not considered to be a tree by most people.

The tree is drawn by thinking of what will happen after each event or decision. As an example, consider a software house that is considering launching a new book-plus-video that will explain modelling on small office computers. The first decision is whether to launch the product or to abort. It is considered that to abort now will not involve the company in any further expenditure.

To launch will mean certain costs: tooling up, production, stocks, and a major advertising campaign, not to mention the time of staff and of management. This means that if the launch is a flop, then it will cost the company £400,000. But if the launch is a success, then the company expects to make an extra profit of £2,000,000. The final

calculation is that the probability of success is put at 20 per cent.
   A tree-ing of this situation will be:

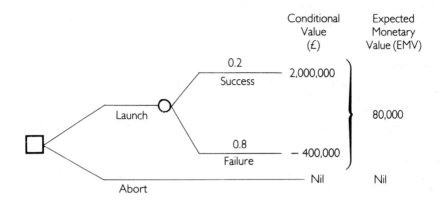

	Conditional Value (£)	Expected Monetary Value (EMV)

0.2 Success — 2,000,000

Launch — 80,000

0.8 Failure — − 400,000

Abort — Nil — Nil

The Expected Monetary Value (EMV) is the sum of all the conditional values times
their probability, of all the branches that followed the decision. Thus, in this simple
example:

$$\text{EMV} = (0{\cdot}2)(2{,}000{,}000) - (0{\cdot}8)(400{,}000)$$
$$= 400{,}000 - 320{,}000$$
$$= £80{,}000.$$

F

This, then, is the probabilistic outcome of a launch – which does not look very attractive
when compared with the heady prospect of making £2,000,000. It is also obvious that
the result depends very much on the probability of success. If this is really only 15 per
cent then the EMV becomes minus (− £40,000). Different values would give different
results, and finding the point at which the launch EMV equals the abort EMV is
known as 'sensitivity analysis'. In our example it is roughly 16½ per cent. Thus our
probabilities had better be right, whether obtained by market research or however.
   The decision tree approach has evolved to include a large number of associated
techniques. There are different ways of carrying out a sensitivity analysis. There are
many approaches to forecasting the probabilities. There is even a way of incorporating
the regret one may experience on finding that one has made the wrong decision – the
Savage criterion of minimax regret.[3]
   Points to be kept in mind when constructing a decision tree include:

- all monetary values must be either pre-tax or post-tax (usually the latter);
- all outcome values should be based on the value of money with respect to time (e.g.
  discounted cashflows);
- alternatives must be mutually exclusive;
- all possible alternatives have to be considered;
- events and decisions have to be drawn in chronological order, from left to right;
- decisions taken may trigger off a reaction by competitors, and so cannot be considered in a vacuum.

   Decision trees are not perfect. Many branches are not true alternatives: for example,
product launches are not always successes or failures but can be somewhere in between.

In complex trees, the opportunities for action can be very much a reflection of the drafter's assessment. It is easy for trees to incorporate subjective assessments. Probabilities of probabilities of probabilities can get somewhat complicated. Branches can depend on resource allocation which may be diffuse. To help with some of these points, computer assistance may be used, probably incorporating forms of simulation modelling and linear programming.

References

1 Charteris, L., *Paleneo*, London: Hodder & Stoughton, 1972.
2 Kelly, F. J. and Kelly, H. M., *What They Really Teach You at the Harvard Business School*, New York: Warner Books, 1986.
3 Peppers, L. C. and Bails, D. G., *Managerial Economics*, Englewood Cliffs: Prentice-Hall, 1987.

Further reading

Magee, J. F., 'Decision trees for decision making,' *Business Classics*, Harvard Business Review, 1986, originally in HBR July 1964.

<table>
<tr><td>42</td></tr>
</table>

Security

Nothing is as good as holding on to safety.

Euripedes, *The Phoenician Women* (c. 410 BC)

To keep oneself safe does not mean to bury oneself.

Seneca, *Moral Issues* (first century)

By their nature, offices are not secure. They are under threat from natural sources (fire, flood), competitors (industrial espionage), suppliers (shortages), customers (bribery), staff (theft, sabotage), the post office (mail non-delivery) and credit card companies (mysterious charges) – to say nothing of errors and mistakes, the efforts of vandals and hackers, and even in some countries the ability of the censors to mislay important documents. The endless list is exploited by firms offering security services, which have a multitude of horror stories.

These horror stories are reinforced by the popular press, to whom disasters are obvious items of news. There are certainly examples of firms going bankrupt through poor security. This being so, it is remarkable how organizations vary in their approach to security. Management consultants are aware of this in their day-to-day activities. Some offices allow virtually unrestricted access and exit, while others are rigorous in their application of security measures.

F

The road to good security is based on four aspects:

- *culture*. The attitude of an organization can determine where it lies on the spectrum of rogues' paradise to angels' delight. Clear guidelines on ethical conduct need to be issued, with the consequences of improper actions spelt out;
- *systems*. All systems contain within them the seed of insecurity. Good systems minimize the prospect of errors, collusion and leakages;
- *internal controls*. These are even more necessary for computerized operations. Generally speaking, computer staff are insufficiently concerned with security aspects. Rather like documentation, security is regarded as an add-on job that delays one from getting on with something more interesting;
- *universality*. Security measures must apply to everybody, from the lavatory cleaner to the chairman. Passes must be shown by all: in some companies the showing of passes is a natural act while in others avoidance is a badge of rank and importance.

■ CULTURE AND ETHICS

Talk of ethics still embarrasses some people. Others regard an ethical outlook as being inimical to competitiveness and success. A few see its ramifications as being an attack on their personal freedom. Most staff see little wrong in taking pencils or pens from the office for home use.

Ethics is a major subject and certainly transcends the single aspect of security. But it is part of the culture of an organization, and is a contributary factor in security.

443

■ PHYSICAL SECURITY

Safeguarding assets involves maintenance, storage, control, stock levels – and just plain looking after the stuff. For some reason, this seems to be a special problem in socialist countries. It may be due to the system of book-keeping. Whatever the cause, stocks often cause one to think twice. Assets well past any possible usefulness will be found in a field, overgrown with vegetation and slowly sinking into the ground. One can imagine the organization in a hundred years' time doing the stocktaking. A handful of rust will be ticked off as a giant turbine blade. Not that capitalist firms are immune. A printing firm had a large stock of heavy old metal engraved plates, including some 'By Appointment' engravings for monarchs no longer around to appoint anything.

Where a firm's assets can disappear, so can the staff's: each year in London there are 15,000 instances of walk-in theft. One large London bank was encouraged to tighten up its security practices when it found that it had become the target for vendors of books, etc. These strangers were just wandering around the offices unhindered.

■ PAPERWORK

Paper is such a commonplace object that it is not given a second thought. But in the wrong hands it can be dangerous, especially given the ubiquitous nature of photo-copiers. It was not until 1988 that permission was given in Moscow for unfettered photocopying by allowing a chain of copy-shops to be started (an example not immediately followed by Romania). And cheque-writers were originally invented for security reasons, not for convenience.

Many firms find it difficult to enforce paper security, even after the introduction of paper shredders. Other firms find it no problem at all – another example of the culture of the organization, and the habits that become second nature. At the same time, some paper just has to be left unshredded – as shown in the retention schedule in the Appendix. One may also have to have a system of paper back-up for a microfilm procedure.

■ SYSTEMS

Where the handling of cash is involved, the need for security-conscious systems is obvious. What is not so obvious is the ways that other systems can be manipulated. Here the main problem is collusion. A world-famous retailer employed a clerk in the accounts department who had an uncle who owned a small firm that supplied sundries (wrapping, string, timber, etc.). The uncle sent in invoices for goods that were never delivered. The accounts clerk initialled the goods-received note (in the space meant for the loading bay supervisor) and passed the invoice for payment. Peanuts? In a few years, the two of them cleared over £1,000,000.

The need for good accounting systems can be highlighted by considering two aspects of life that many of us take for granted: airline tickets and credit cards.

A major headache for airlines is the matter of stolen tickets. The number of tickets on the list of those stolen or missing is 200,000. (About 60 per cent of stolen tickets are used within two years.) A stolen airline ticket is like a blank cheque, only better from the thief's point of view. It becomes worth whatever is written on it, which can be £3,000. Organized gangs are responsible for much of the trouble. Accounting systems that act after the theft are of limited use; the airlines therefore have tight controls at the centre. The difficulty is that controls are not enforced downstream, where people become careless or are dishonest. This downstream carelessness can be a headache in any office.

An outright fraud is the trick of making out the airline's copy of a ticket for a cheap flight such as Rome to Zurich. The part of the ticket that is used by the passenger is made out for a flight worth, say, £2,000. Not only does this provide enough profit for all concerned, it is also not easy to detect with normal accounting systems.

An added complication is that, in practice, a stolen or fraudulent ticket can be exchanged for a perfectly respectable ticket. It is presented by someone who says that they want to change the routing. A new ticket is then made out.

Organized criminals have other approaches. One is to set up a travel agency, get blank tickets from as many airlines as are willing to trust them, use them to get cash and then liquidate the travel agency. The setting up of dummy firms to get goods without payment and then disappearing is done in many trades. The answer for most offices is to insist on proper credit control clearance, in spite of any objections from one's sales force. Airlines have the special problem that if a dummy travel agent can get hold of as few as 200 blank tickets, these can be worth £500,000, which makes it an attractive proposition.

These three examples all have parallels in ordinary commercial life. Our fourth example may be less applicable but also has lessons. At any point in time, certain countries will be having problems with foreign currency and will have tight exchange controls. A way round this is to use airline tickets. These are made out in the local currency, bundled up, taken to a country such as the USA where they are sold or exchanged. The result is that the criminals have got dollars while the airline cannot get its money out of the country of origin because of the exchange controls. This got so bad that at least one airline closed down its operations in one country and stopped flying there. Other (non-airline) companies have long faced problems in obtaining payment from certain countries. The traditional answer is to use hard currency denominated Letters of Credit, or even barter. Even this may not help if foreign governments change the rules (currently, one country has effectively stopped all penalty clause payments). When dealing with such countries one tries to get advance payments and staged payments – until one's competitors do not.

F

Now that so many corporate credit card accounts are around, fraudulent usage is even more attractive than it is for personal accounts. Most people can recognize the signs of possible incipient fraud: the garage or hotel where the cashier has to go into a 'back office' to run off the card impression on the form set, or the shop where a second set is run off because the first set 'was not clear' but which is not given to the card holder. If two sets are run off, then the second one can be filled in for any amount and the signature copied from the first one. A hotel can double your bill quite easily this way – which can be several hundred pounds. The two sets are presented for payment in two consecutive calendar months. In many companies, this will slip through the accounting checks since the actual amount will be on the expense sheet. A phone call from the accounts department to the employee may only serve to jog the memory that the amount shown was indeed the hotel bill. A few companies (and individuals) do not bother to check every item on the credit company's listing.

More valuable in the eyes of organized criminals is the set of carbons used in many credit card form sets. From the carbon sheets it is possible to make a counterfeit card – all the necessary details are there, including the signature. This gives all the advantages of a stolen card, plus extra time before discovery. This is such an attractive and well-organized type of crime that it is normal practice in many countries (such as the USA) for the carbons to be given to the customer. In Britain, at the time of writing, one still has to ask for them for some reason.

There are still in Britain some hotels that ask for your credit card when booking in, run off a form set and keep the set until you check out. A few will actually ask for it to be signed. It is then a simple matter to photocopy the sets of several customers. Counterfeit cards can then again be made as before. If any hotel clerk tries to get a signed form set from one, then in theory one should just walk out. But this is not so easy when one checks in late at night in a strange town.

The answer to many credit card frauds is a strict accounting system that reconciles the figures and that scrutinizes the expense sheets. If this sounds like too much bother, then it is unreasonable to complain about being defrauded. Extra defence is afforded if employees can be trained to demand the carbons. And, of course, any hotel that asks for signed impressed form sets should be put on to the corporate black list.

Credit card fraud amounts to nearly $1 billion in the USA and over £50,000,000 in Britain. Twenty per cent of lost cards are used for fraud. During the 1980s card counterfeiting worldwide of just Visa cards rose by a factor of about seven, to reach nearly $50 million by 1989. And all these figures are each year.

Computers

The media often refer to 'computer fraud'. In many cases, this is a slight misnomer since the reference is to a fraud that happened to involve a computer but which could have taken place almost as easily with a quill pen. For example, one of the best-known frauds was the creation of 64,000 fake insurance policies involving $2 billion at Equity Funding Corporation – the computer just made it easier. But a Los Angeles bank was defrauded of $10 million by manipulating the computer system.[1]

Fraud is not the only computer concern for management. Equally important is the security of the data against theft, and security against tampering with the data or computer system. This was brought home in 1986 when a Dutch engineer gave a demonstration that appeared in a number of television programmes and was reported in several magazines.[2] He showed how an ordinary television set could be modified for a few pounds so that it could recreate outside an office building the computer displays that there were inside the building. This led embassies and other sensitive users to screen their computers and display screens.

A number of audit firms have issued reports highlighting the dangers (e.g. Coopers & Lybrand, Arthur Young). These reports show that too many firms are lax over the first line of defence: passwords.

■ PASSWORDS

A password is a group of (say) five characters that has to be keyed into a computer before it will operate a program. This protects the computer system from use by unauthorized users – that is, until the unauthorized user learns or guesses the password. We are all trusting by nature and it is rare to see anybody at a terminal with his or her shoulders hunched round the display so that it cannot be read by passers-by. As consultants, we are often offered the passwords in a client's computer department. It sometimes causes amusement when we ask not to be given a password and ask to be logged on.

Passwords matter. Without them, an employee can tamper with the payroll and add a few fictitious names, later collecting the salaries of these 'ghost' employees. Even large organizations can suffer from ghost staff – the British Airports Authority seems to have had this jolt in the past. An example of password insufficiency concerned a small builders' merchant. Sales were over the counter to firms whose employees took the goods with them. A small computer was installed with terminals at the counters. Data was keyed at the terminals which then produced the invoices. But the price list was not password protected, so prices could be reduced and then returned to the correct level. So, although stock levels were correct, invoices were made out for smaller amounts than they should have been.

In the year after installing the small office computer, an annual profit of £1 million was turned into a loss of £1 million. The lost money was not recovered and the firm went into liquidation.

Passwords need to be changed at intervals (yes, a nuisance), need to define the area of data to which access is obtained, and should not be easily guessable. That means not using the main user's name or nickname, or the job title (SYSOP is a favourite), or the name of spouse or dog – and definitely not 'FRED'. This is another favourite (look at a qwerty keyboard to see why) and is likely to be an early guess by an unauthorized user. The terminal should shut down automatically if three wrong attempts are made at keying in a password (yes, another nuisance).

Passwords do not give security, they just help a bit by slowing down access. A programmer can find out passwords given time. It is just necessary to insert a few lines of code that will record the passwords as they are used for later use. For example, a programmer can make a terminal look as though it is ready for use, with the instruction displayed to 'Enter password'. A user complies with this instruction. The program records the password and displays the message 'Terminal error, start again', whereupon the user does as instructed. The program stays quiet until the next password is used and then records that one as well. A lot of passwords can be stored until the programmer calls up the results. So passwords are never perfect but they do help.

F

■ OPERATING SYSTEMS

The first weak point is the most basic, the operating system itself, which is the software used to control all the flow of data within the computer. Operating systems are graded from A to D. Grade D will do little except not deleting files when asked to, waiting to be overwritten. Grade C still allows a user to transfer data (e.g. to another computer). Grade B identifies the user of each transfer and monitors the files in their travels. It will stop unauthorized transfers such as those out of office hours or onto terminals outside the main department. A mainframe operating system can contain several million lines of code so it is a long job ensuring that there are no errors or holes (known as 'trapdoors') in it. As the operating system becomes more secure, so it moves towards an A grading.

Most operating systems are Grade C, even D. The first Grade A operating system was developed by Honeywell (SKOMP). The same company produced an early grade C/B Unix called Multix – in general, systems that have networking capabilities are less easy to make secure. One has to pay a price for having a secure operating system. SKOMP is good on security but not on productivity or on user-friendliness.

■ NETWORKS

Networks, whether LANs or wide area networks, are very prone to being insecure. The growth of external users and machinery meant to make communications easier increases the insecurity. Some LANs effectively send all messages to all points; they may carry different types of signal, and they may even have spare points for future requirements. All this makes it easy to eavesdrop.

The commonest security measure is probably the dial-back system. In this, the early models needed a password from a user who would hang up. The modem would then call the user on the (secret) telephone number before access was granted. This did not work for long. People found that all they needed was the password. After dialling up the modem number they did not hang up – so they were already on the line from the modem when it tried to phone the correct number.

The next stage was dynamic or one-time passwords. These were passwords that were generated by a calculating device and were used for just one message before being changed. So an unauthorized user of call-up networks needed both the first password and a copy of the calculating device. By now, things were getting complicated – but not complicated enough, because a call-back plus one-time passwords (together known as 'front-end security')[3] may only stop entry or access to the entire system. They will not stop a major insecurity – people who are authorized access to only parts of the system. To stop them moving into no-go areas further passwords must be used, or careful monitoring by the dynamic system.

Another approach is coding, or 'encryption'. Most of us, as children, sent secret messages to our friends, usually by substituting one letter for another, from a secret alphabet. Substitution is easy to code, but it is also easy to uncode. This type of coding is known as 'monoalphabetic' coding. If the coding alphabet is still in normal alphabetic order (F for A, G for B, H for C, and so on) then it is the simplest of all: a Caesar cipher. If one uses several monoalphabets in a cycle, then the coding becomes 'polyalphabetic'. If each bit of data is individually coded with a key, then the result is a 'stream' cipher. If a block of, say, eight characters are encrypted together then the result is a 'block' cipher.

In 1917, G. S. Vernam invented a stream cipher that was the first not to need a coding clerk. It was on-line, involving no delay. It was based on exclusive–or logic and was such that as usual plaintext + key = ciphertext but also ciphertext + key = plaintext. During development, the key tapes were based on characters drawn at random, literally, out of a hat; these key tapes were then formed into short endless loops. It was realized that the resulting polyalphabetic ciphers could be solved, as a first stage to decoding, by what is known as the Kasinsky method, so two endless loops were used to provide a sort of double coding. If one loop has 1001 characters and the second has 999, then the cipher effectively is based on 999,999 alphabets. The Vernam system is still the basis for most stream-encryption.

Systems for block-encryption include the DES, Lucifer and RSA systems. DES (from 'data encryption standard') is complex and needs either a medium-size computer or a small one plus a dedicated VLSI logic chip. Lucifer is similar to DES as a system. RSA comes from the intials of the three people (Messrs Rivest, Shamir and Adleman) who developed it at MIT in 1977. RSA is copyrighted and involves large-integer arithmetic. It is also called a 'public key' system.

Encryption voids a security leakage that other approaches suffer, known as 'clamping'. This is a system used by eavesdroppers and is very simple. It involves putting a clamp onto a cable carrying data and thereby detecting the magnetic changes and hence the data. Optical fibres discourage clamping (so far). Anybody interested in building a data encryptor is referred to an excellent article by the well-known electronics engineer and author, Steve Ciarcia.[4]

■ VIRUSES AND VACCINES

One of the most unpleasant security problems is that of viruses. A virus is a short program that is hidden in a host program, awaiting a trigger such as a particular date. It then comes to life. What it does when it comes to life depends on the person who put it there. A few viruses will just display a jokey message. Most are more unpleasant: they will delete all your files, or scramble all the data or attack the FAT table. FAT is the file allocation table. It tells the operating system where each segment of each file is located. Without it, the computer does not know where anything is on the disks.

The trouble with a virus is that it can be transmitted from computer to computer every time that a disk is used or copied onto another computer, so it lies in a lot of computers just waiting to strike. It has been estimated that in 1988 viruses had infected over a quarter of a million computers.[5]

The basis of viral infection can be traced back to about 1960 when three computer programmers at AT&T Bell started to play a game called Core Wars. Two of them would write self-replicating programs whose task was to attack their opponent's program. The winner was the one whose program was the more intact after a pre-set time. This game spread to other places such as Xerox's PARC and the MIT artificial intelligence group. The dangers of such activities were recognized if used on interconnected machines and so were kept quiet. The secret was let out in a speech by the originator of Unix, K. Thompson. (To this day, some people are chary of using Unix for fear of a virus suddenly appearing. We know of no reason for this fear.) This act was compounded shortly afterwards when in May 1984 *Scientific American* published an article by A. K. Dewdney. This gave details of Core Wars and offered a handout for $2.

Viruses can spread at an incredible pace. One called SCORES was first seen in Apple Macintoshes at a computer services organization called EDS, in the USA. It has since spread to Boeing, NASA, the Internal Revenue Service and the US House of Representatives.[5] Another virus infected an estimated 100,000 IBM PC disks, including back-up disks. One bulletin board stopped upload capabilities.

One of the cleverest viruses is the Lahore virus, so-called from the originators, two brothers who run a shop in Lahore in Pakistan selling cut-price bootleg software. If Pakistanis came into the shop they were sold clean copies. But if foreigners (often students) came into the shop they received disks with the Lahore or Pakistan virus. This spread to an estimated 100,000 floppies by 1987, at which time the brothers claim that they stopped selling infected copies. But of course, it may still be lurking somewhere.

Some public domain software is very useful and has been donated by altruistic individuals. But some of this, too, has been infected. Software that may be infected includes:

ARC513.EXE	MAP	STRIPES.EXE
CDIR.COM	PACKDIR	VDIR.COM
EGABTR		

Some vaccine programs have been developed that help to prevent infection. These include Vaccine, Mace Vaccine, Viru-Safe and Disk Defender. But it is not easy to stay ahead of the virus writers. The best defence is to stop all non-work use of the computers by the staff, though this is difficult in many organizations, and it does not stop in-house programmers from planting a virus. One programmer left a virus when he left a company that wiped out 168,000 records of sales commissions.

■ HACKERS

The word 'hacker' used to be used to describe a computer-obsessive enthusiast. This sense of the word has been replaced by 'techie'. Hacker is now used to describe somebody who gains unauthorized access to a network or computer. Once access has been gained, some hackers may do nothing (the game was to gain access). Others may change the data or destroy some of it.

Much has been written in the press about the successes of hackers,[6-8] and details need not be repeated. But groups such as the West German Kaos Klub and the Data Travellers have penetrated parts of NASA, the DEC Vax computers, Prestel and, of course, the Duke of Edinburgh's electronic mailbox.

Hackers will spend six months or more trying to penetrate a target. They will obtain computer manuals, use auto-diallers with a utility program, impersonate 'super-users', guess passwords, tap lines, or rummage through dustbins.[9] In all this, the law may provide little protection or redress, or punishment. The House of Lords dismissed an appeal by the Crown in *Regina* v. *Gold and another* for various offences alleged against the Forgery and Counterfeiting Act.[10] An OECD report tells how other countries are grappling with this problem.[11] In the meantime, it is up to individual organizations to defend themselves.

References

1 McWhirter, N. D., *The Guinness Book of Records*, Enfield: Guinness Superlatives, annually.
2 Microbytes, *Byte*, March 1986, p. 9.
3 *Communicate*, April 1988, p. 38.
4 Ciarcia, S., 'Build a hardware data encryptor', *Byte*, Vol. 11, No. 9, September 1986, p. 97.
5 *Time*, Vol. 132, No. 13, September 1988, p. 40.
6 *The Economist*, 9 July, 1988.
7 *The Khaleej Times*, 17 March, 1988.
8 *The Guardian Weekly*, 20 September, 1987.
9 Cornwall, H., *The Hacker's Handbok*, London: Century Communications, 1985.
10 *The Times* Law Report, 22 April, 1988.
11 OECD, *Computer-related Crime: Analysis of Legal Policy*, 1986; 'Computer crime', *OECD Observer*, No. 142, September 1986.

Further reading

Comer, M. J., *Corporate Fraud*, Maidenhead: McGraw-Hill, 1986.
Williams, C. A. and Heins, R. M., *Risk Management and Insurance*, Singapore: McGraw-Hill, 1985.

43

Report Writing

What is conceived well is expressed clearly,
And the words to say it will arrive with ease.
Nicolas Boileau, *L'Art Poetique* (1674)

Every man speaks and writes with intent to be understood; and it
can seldom happen but he that understands himself might convey
his notions if, content to be understood, he did not seek to be
admired.
Samuel Johnson, *The Idler* (1758–60)

Writing reports is rather like giving after-dinner speeches or responding to a toast at a wedding. Some people seem to have a natural facility for them and even enjoy the experience. Others dread them and put off all preparation until the last minute.

Like after-dinner speeches, too many reports are:

- boring and/or difficult to understand;
- too long;
- self-justifying (even an attempt to settle old scores);
- full of jargon;
- their own worst enemy.

F

The main problem with advising new analysts on how to write reports is the wide spread of recipients' expectations and preferences. Sir Terence Beckett, as Director-General of the CBI, received many reports. Reviewing a Frederick Forsyth novel on the BBC in 1986, he said, 'Forsyth's novels are really reports. They have pace. They are easy to read. I wish other reports were like it.' Other people have different preferences. One client was a well-educated, rather donnish, senior civil servant. He was never really happy with a consultancy report unless it contained a Latin or Greek tag and a couple of classical allusions. Since some reports will be read by a number of people, all with different preferences, we often feel forced to take refuge in safety, blandness and boredom.

Types of report

Reports that one may be called upon to write can be classified as being (a) regular (b) occasional and (c) special. Examples of these three are:

Regular	Occasional	Special
Progress report	Accident report	Market research report
Sales report	Committee reports	Strategy report
Costings report	Backlogs report	Competitors report

The reports that analysts and consultants are likely to write are:

- survey reports that propose that a particular investigatory study be undertaken;
- assignment reports that give details of a study undertaken;
- an adjunct to or part of a presentation;
- a technical assessment of equipment;
- a SitRep (or situation report), which is a review of the current situation within an organization or of progress made to date on a study or project;
- a staff operating manual, including job descriptions, admin manuals and standards;
- an annual report on the activities and successes of an internal management services department.

It is with the first two of these that we are mainly concerned in this chapter: survey and assignment reports.

Style

The word 'style' has two distinct meanings. One is the layout of written communications, here called house style. The other is the contents (e.g. not using slang), which is called 'writing style'.

■ HOUSE STYLE

Many organizations have their own house style for writing reports. This is often illustrated in the admin manuals, and may even be incorporated in the centralized word processing service. So, although house styles vary, within an individual organization house style can be quite rigid. Unless one feels strongly about the matter, it is therefore difficult to go against accepted rules. Of course, when one changes employers, one may have to accustom oneself to a new house style.

Individual house styles are quite likely to lay down rules for report structures, page layout, covers and numbering. Some organizations insist on having every paragraph consecutively numbered along quasi-decimal lines. This has the advantage that a paragraph can be referred to at a meeting as 'paragraph 3.11.1.7' instead of 'the second paragraph on page 16'. To those of us who regard the system with distaste, this seems a minor advantage compared with the disadvantages of ugliness, loss of clarity, the interrupting of flow and logical thought, and an encouragement to pedantic over-dissection.

A few management consultants consciously try to follow a client's internal house style in their reports to that client. The larger consultancies, however, have their own house style which they follow.

■ WRITING STYLE

There is certainly no shortage of advice about style and how to effect good writing. Some of it is contradictory, much of it is based on the preferences of one person, all of it has to be ignored at some time.

Perhaps the commonest piece of advice that is offered for writing reports is, 'keep it simple; use short Anglo-Saxon words and not long Latin words'. This seems like sound advice. But do the people that give this advice really mean it? There are in Britain two newspapers of widely varying nature: the *Sun* and the *Independent*. The *Sun* is written in simple language, and uses short sentences. It has an outstandingly good Fog Index (see later). But the very people who enjoin one to write reports in the same vein do not enjoy reading the *Sun*. It feels to them as though it were written by the poorly educated for the uneducated. They miss the stimulus and interest that they can get from the writing style to be found in British newspapers like the *Independent*, *The Times* or the *Financial Times*.

Reports written by management consultants for their clients are written and read by a group who share a way of speaking and expressing themselves. This group know that there is no such thing as a true synonym, and instinctively know the subtle shades of differences in meaning of words. Should one use the language of the primary school if one thereby insults the reader, loses the reader's interest and loses the richness of subtlety in the language?

This subtlety exists in many languages. The richness of English derives largely because it contains words that came from three major sources and many minor sources. Chinese pictograms are built up from components that have delighted their philosophers over the years. Hungarian has a bewildering use of prefixes and suffixes that enables subtlety of expression. Slovene has forty dialects for fewer than three million speakers.

In spite of instructions to the contrary, therefore, many of us will continue to refuse to bring all our reports down to the, 'The cat sat on the mat' level. Instead of simplicity, the aim should be clarity and ease of understanding.

Even clarity and comprehensibility are not just a matter of the language used. Equally important are the logical progression of the ideas that are being put forward, and the avoidance of clutter in the report. For this reason, there are two things that should be done. The first is to exploit the use of appendices. Large and/or complex tables of figures should be made into an appendix. So should complex proofs, statistical back-up data, copies of supporting documents – anything that interrupts the flow of the report and which is not an integral part of the logic. Sometimes, appendices can become very bulky. At such times, it can be better to bind all the appendices as a separate entity.

F

The second aid to clarity is to have the report read by a colleague. It is then important not to get defensive about one's writing, or to try to explain what one meant. The rule is quite simple: if a colleague finds something unclear then other readers will, too. The only response is to change or completely rewrite the offending section.

Another aspect of clarity is the use of jargon. Most advisers tell one to avoid jargon. But this is too simple. Every trade, profession and industry uses technical words and jargon. It is a sort of shorthand of communication. If a report is being written for a person or a group that habitually uses these special words, then they should be used, not avoided. This is still true even when words have different meanings to different clients. One would use 'average' to ship insurers, 'through-the-wall' to a bank, 'dram' to a computer manufacturer. In these and similar instances, jargon becomes an aid to clarity, not a hindrance.

A useful book on style is the *Pocket Style Book* published by *The Economist*,[1] which gives some general advice on writing. In an opening note, this states, 'The first requirement of *The Economist* is that it should be readily understandable.' That is true of reports, as well. This same book puts forward a few basic rules to follow:

- do not be pompous;
- do not be hectoring or arrogant;
- do not be too pleased with yourself;

- do not be too chatty (e.g. avoid 'Ho, ho');
- do not be too free with slang;
- be careful in the construction of sentences and paragraphs.

The advantage of a style book is that it increases consistency, not that it is somehow engraved in stone and based on unviolable laws. *The Economist Style Book* tells us that titles are not necessary for dead people 'except, perhaps . . . Mr. Gladstone'. Then on the same page it states, 'Avoid the American habit of joining office and name' as in 'Chancellor Kohl'. However, a textbook was written during Gladstone's lifetime about writing certain reports. This book was strictly British Establishment and so presumably free from any alien influence. A clear injunction in it is, 'In the case of great men use their names only, e.g., Mr. Gladstone, but in the case of obscure men state their office as well, e.g. Administrator Kortright'.[2]

So it is always a hazardous affair to give advice about style. Should one obey Aristotle's well-known injunction, 'To write well, express yourself like the common people but think like a wise man'? Or should one accept Somerset Maugham's, 'Good prose should resemble the conversation of a well-bred man'?[3]

Of course, if one is a skilled enough writer one can break all the rules. In *The Craft of Novel-Writing*[4] the usual advice against the over-use of adjectives is countered with an example from Margaret Drabble's *The Realms of Gold*: '. . . the dead bracken, with its lovely, special, eccentric cold burnished leafy metallic dead but promising beauty'. And of course it is a permanent reproach to think how Charles Dickens could write so prolifically but nearly always against the clock. So often he had to scribble away to meet the demand of monthly or weeky periodicals – and produce masterpieces while doing so.

Few of us are in this elevated company. We have to write naturally, as well as we can, aiming always to be clear and to avoid anything that jars too badly on the readers of our reports. Our in-house set of principles has been adapted from a set that appeared in the International Labour Office book on management consultancy.[5] This is:

PRINCIPLES OF WRITING REPORTS
1 Only write a report if it is necessary and timely.
2 Aim the report at the readers.
3 Make the report look good and deliver it on time.
4 Keep it clear. Keep it logical. Keep it short.
5 Write to express, not to impress.
6 Write naturally and keep the report flowing smoothly.
7 Avoid complex sentences. Vary their length but keep the average less than 25 words.
8 Blend short and long words. Avoid slang. Restrict clichés and very unusual words to no more than once in every twenty reports.
9 Use jargon only if it will be familiar to all readers and you are certain of its meaning.
10 Do not pad. Use the appendices for all subsidiary material including tables and statistics.
11 Make most of the verbs active, using the passive form for variation. Use the imperative for action plans.
12 Reports should be businesslike and serious, never jocular. Euphemisms and a delicacy of phrasing are occasionally needed but do not ask readers to read between the lines. They may read something that is not meant to be there.

13 Use graphics if they help but not to pad.
14 Check and improve every first draft.
15 Ask a colleague to read the report if it is unusual, complex or especially important. If a colleague finds something baffling or jarring, then so will the client.
16 Break any of these principles rather than write anything outright barbarous.

The avoidance of anything 'outright barbarous' was a writing rule of George Orwell.[6] In practical terms, it is more important than many people realize. One may be able to rescue the situation if a report is too long, too boring, contains sesquipedalia, or is unbalanced. However, trouble looms if it contains a bad gaffe, a gross arithmetical error or a grotesque turn of phrase. A few examples of the type of phrase one should try to avoid:[7]

We were unanimous – in fact everyone was unanimous. (Eric Heffer)

. . . and Hare kicked 19 of the 17 points. (David Coleman)

Of course Kirkpatrick will serve nowhere near the 900 years to which he has been sentenced because the system in Northern Ireland allows for up to 50 per cent remission for good behaviour. (N.I. correspondent)

Football's a game of skill. We kicked them a bit and they kicked us a bit.
(Graham Roberts)

F

■ THE FOG INDEX

People often refer to the 'fog index' without being sure what it is. As a formula, it is:

$$FI = 0.4 \, (S + N)$$

where S = average number of words of three syllables or more in a sentence,
N = average number of words per sentence.

In use, it is common to take a number of samples each of about 100 consecutive words. In counting the multi-syllable words, words with capital letters (such as company names) are ignored. When the Fog Index (FI) is calculated in this manner, it is said to indicate the number of years of full-time education needed to understand the writing. However, the index is usually just expressed as a number.

The fog index is a measure of the complexity of the language used. One should not strain artificially to lower the index of one's writing too much, or allow oneself to become dominated by it. For those who are determined to pursue it, the easiest route is to use one of the several pieces of software that can be used with word processing programs.

Structure

All reports should have a structure within which one can express ideas. Reports written after the completion of a study can vary in scope: a market research report is dissimilar from one following a work quantification study. The first stage in writing such a report may be to sketch out the overall structure.

Other reports, such as a survey report recommending that a study be undertaken, tend to follow a more consistent pattern. In such cases, with experience one can use the structure as a beneficial aid to writing.

A typical survey report written by external management consultants will follow the pattern of:

General introduction
A statement of the current situation and the problems
Objectives and scope of the study
Methodology to be used
The programme of work
Resources that will be involved
Costs and benefits
Experience of the consultancy firm
Appendices – timetable and/or programme chart
           – CVs of probable consultants
           – terms of business

■ PREPARATION

Unless one is gifted with total recall and has ample time, it is advisable to prepare for most reports well before they have to be written. For example, during a study, one should collect together material that is likely to be needed for a report and keep it separate from the actual working papers. This material will include:

- data for the appendices;
- reminders of how calculations were made;
- important facts and figures;
- a diary of important meetings held with non-client contacts, such as auditors or a merchant bank;
- a reminder of points to be made.

■ WRITING THE REPORT

Before writing the first sentence of the report, one should ask oneself three questions:

- is a report necessary at this time?
- what are the objectives of the report?
- who will read the report, and why?

If the report is a major one, then one should still not start on that first sentence. First, one has to plan the report. There are several approaches used by the major consultancies, with at least one using a rigid pyramid structure. Our own in-house approach is based on a shred-out tree which is drawn on an A3 sheet of paper. In use, one considers a number of aspects:

- problems or questions tackled;
- methodology used in the study;
- the findings of the study;
- conclusions, based on the findings;
- recommendations, based on the conclusions.

For each of these aspects, a key or bullet point is selected and written in a box on the chart. A further four or five points are then made and also written in boxes on the chart.

Appendices that will be needed are also noted, under the relevant aspect.

An action plan, or programme of work, to attain the recommendations is then outlined. Finally, the main points of a management summary can now be prepared. Completion of this tree is not a lengthy process. Any time spent is more than recouped in the actual writing of the report.

A partially completed chart of a report plan is shown in Figure 43.1. Advantages of this approach include:

- the report concentrates on the important points and so avoids dilution by trivia;
- it ensures a balanced, well-structured and logical report,
- it is a very considerable help in writing the report;
- it provides the basis for the preparation of visual aids for a presentation;
- it enables one to check back with the original terms of reference and the survey, to make absolutely certain that all matters have indeed been covered.

Having completed the chart, one then writes the report itself. As each point on the chart is covered, the relevant box can be ticked to show that it has been incorporated.

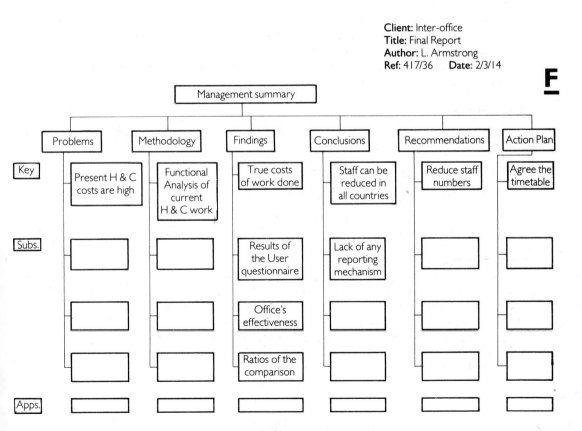

Figure 43.1 Report plan

■ REPORT PRODUCTION

The final production of the report covers:

- ordering and production of special binders;
- preparation of any special artwork;
- typing;
- proof-reading and correcting;
- approval of final product;
- printing, collation and addition of any extra material such as externally prepared artwork;
- binding;
- distribution.

When listed out in this way, one point is obvious: it takes time. Since a date for a presentation has usually been set in advance, it needs proper organization. Large organizations usually have a specialist group that can assist in the actual production work, but the ultimate responsibility always rests with the individual consultant.

■ PRESENTATION

The final stage of a report is the presentation. Many consultants would say that the report is merely an adjunct to the presentation, and that it is the presentation (and definitely not the report) that is the end of a study.

The presentation must be on time, never late. It must be rehearsed. It must be convincing. It must be prepared. It must be good.

References

1 Grimond, J., *The Economist Pocket Style Book*, London: Economist Publications, 1986.
2 Johnston, R. and Anderson, J. H., *Civil Service and Army Précis and Indexing*, London: Longman, Green, 1898.
3 Maugham, W. S., *The Summing Up*, 1938.
4 Doubtfire, D., *The Craft of Novel-Writing*, London: Allison & Busby, 1978.
5 ILO, *Management Consulting*, Geneva: International Labour Office, 1976.
6 Orwell, G., *Politics and the English Language*, 1966.
7 Fantoni, B. (ed.), *Private Eye's Colemanballs 2*, London: Private Eye Publications, 1984.

Further reading

Burchfield, R. W., *The Spoken Word*, London: British Broadcasting Corporation, 1981.
Fowler, H. W., *A Dictionary of Modern English Usage*, Oxford: Oxford University Press, 1926 (second edition 1965).
Franklin, J., *Which Witch?*, London: Hamish Hamilton, 1966.
Gowers, Sir E., *The Complete Plain Words*, London: Her Majesty's Stationery Office, 1954.
Gunning, R., *The Technique of Clear Writing*, New York: McGraw-Hill, 1952.
Partridge, E., *Usage and Abusage*, London: Hamish Hamilton, 1947.

44

Mathematics Review

Arithmetic is where the answer is right and everything is nice and
you can look out of the window and see the blue sky – or the
answer is wrong and you have to start all over and try again and see
how it comes out this time.   **Carl Sandburg, *Complete Poems* (1950)**

In a Symbol there is concealment and yet revelation; here,
therefore, by Silence and by Speech acting together, comes a
double significance.   **Thomas Carlyle, *Sartor Resartus* (1834)**

The sight of an equation or a mathematical proof has different effects on people. Some
greet them with pleasurable anticipation, others hurriedly turn the page. A few aspects
of mathematics have therefore been collected together here for reference and for the
pleasure of those who enjoy them.

The ability to remember some of the basic ideas of mathematics is to some extent
affected by how long it is since one was at school. This is not the definition of 'distance
learning', so a few basic definitions to clear the ground are:

F

integer   the numbers 0, 1, 2, 3, 4 . . . and so on are known as integers or whole
numbers. Hence 28 is an integer but 3½ is not. So is −6 but not −4¼.

digit   written characters that are numbers. In everyday life we use ten: 0, 1, 2, 3, 4, 5,
6, 7, 8 and 9. These are the decimal digits. Because the basis of this system is ten
decimal digits, it is called the base-10 notation. This is not the only possible way of
counting. The Sumerians had a base-60 system that was adopted by the Babylonians –
which is how we came to have 60 minutes in an hour instead of 100. Certain aboriginal
tribes and most computers use a base-2 or binary method of counting. The binary digits
are the two numbers 0 and 1.

rational numbers   numbers that are integers. Also fractions with integers both above
and below the line. In decimal notation, a rational number is a number that can be
expressed as the ratio of two integers, such as 3/4.

irrational number   a real number that is not rational. Examples of irrational
numbers are $\sqrt{2}$, 'pi' and 'e'.

real numbers   all numbers that are not imaginary. $\sqrt{-1}$ is imaginary.

prime   an integer (other than 0, 1 and −1) that cannot be divided by any integer
except itself or 1 without leaving a 'remainder'. The smallest primes are 2, 3, 5, 7, 11,
13. . . . The largest primes so far discovered are $2^{11213}-1$ and $2^{19937}-1$. The latter
integer has 6002 digits, was discovered in 1971, and was displayed at one time on the
letterhead of the IBM Watson Centre.

e   a special irrational number. It is the limit of the expression $(1 + 1/n)^n$ as n increases
to infinity. It is the base for 'natural' logarithms.

set   a collection of objects, numbers – just about anything that has something in common. Examples would be animals with feathers, positive integers, the jet set, prime numbers, plants with red flowers, radios with in-built clocks, etc.

exponent   in an expression such as 4^3, 4 is the base while 3 is the exponent. The exponent in x^y is y. Exponents can be negative. 4^{-1} is the same as $\frac{1}{4}$, and x^{-y} is the same as $\frac{1}{x^y}$.

Sets and Venn

As already stated, a set is a collection of things. These things can be tangible, such as all the cars in Sicily that were made by Renault, or they can be intangible, such as the rules for deciding what objects can be accepted for display by the Nether Wallop Agricultural Museum.

The branch of mathematics that deals with sets is known as set theory. This has its own symbols and rules for the relationships between the symbols, which led the area to being loosely known as symbolic logic. A system of symbolic logic was devised by George Boole (1815–64) which became known as Boolean algebra. In his book *The Investigation of Thought* (1854), Boole described a way of handling sets and the propositions of non-arithmetic objects. From their earliest days, computers have used Boolean algebra in their logic, and still do. In the 1950s, training courses for O & M staff and Industrial Engineers started to include Boolean algebra. It then started to be taught in schools. By the 1970s, aspects of set theory (and Venn diagrams) were being taught to the very young – well before they were introduced to ordinary algebra. For a while this therefore became another area where parents had difficulty helping their children with their homework.

Venn diagrams are named after John Venn (1834–1923), who developed a graphical way of representing sets and sub-sets. A sub-set is a set of objects that is completely contained within the first set. Thus if the set is all the books in the local library, a sub-set might be all the poetry books. It must be emphasized that the set of books is not the same as the books themselves. It is an idea or concept, rather like the idea of the jet set, a stamp collection or a football crowd.

One other concept to consider before looking at Venn diagrams is the idea of universe. A universe is a super-set which contains all the set and sub-sets that are being considered. A universe is usually called U or E. Sets are given capital letters while sub-sets are given lower case letters.

So we can draw a rectangle which is meant to represent all the items that we are looking at:

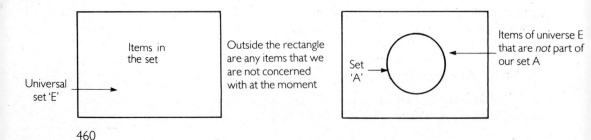

Universal set 'E'

Items in the set

Outside the rectangle are any items that we are not concerned with at the moment

Set 'A'

Items of universe E that are *not* part of our set A

If we use two circles, then we can express further ideas. First, if we put one circle inside another, we show that everything in one set is contained within another. Using the library example again, we might want to show the set of poetry books (B) as being part of the totality of books that are in the local library (A):

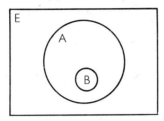

If we follow a convention of using shading to highlight those items that we are concerned with, we can show two alternatives. The first (on the left) is the 'union' of sets A and B; that is, all the items that are covered in the two sets. Since some items are in both sets, the union of A and B is not the same as 'A + B', which would give us double counting of those items that are in both sets. The diagram on the right shows those items that are indeed in both sets and only those items that are in both. This is known as the 'intersection' of A and B. If set A is 'all Ford cars' and B 'all black cars', then the first diagram indicates all Ford and/or black cars, while the second indicates all black Fords:

F

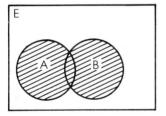
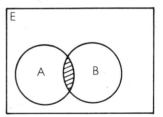

A fourth diagram shows a way of indicating the 'complement of A'. This is all those items that are in the universal set E – *except* for those that are in set A:

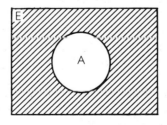

Venn diagrams are used by analysts in a number of ways. Perhaps the commonest is in reports and presentations, especially in conjunction with other graphics such as pie charts. They are a useful way to show overlaps in particular. For example, one might want to show a set of those departments with a major backlog and a set of those

461

departments with high absenteeism. In presentations it is common to leave out any indication of a universal set E. It is 'understood' to be there. In this case the universal set would be all departments in the organization:

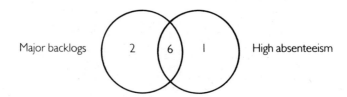

Of course this does not in any way prove that high absenteeism is the cause of major backlogs. The logic of Venn diagrams and Boolean algebra can be used to prove many things but not this type of relationship.

Another use of a Venn diagram is to demonstrate an answer to a logic problem to someone who is unsure of an arithmetic approach. As an example, an office of 90 people is laid out in such a way that 40 of them have access to both Taxan and Tatung monitors, although some people have access to only one type of monitor. If 60 people can get access to a Taxan, how many people have access only to a Tatung?

We have two sets – people with access to a Taxan is one, while the other is people with access to a Tatung. Since some staff are in both sets, we can represent the situation with two overlapping circles thus:

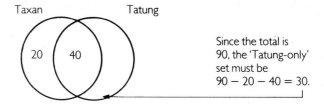

Since the total is 90, the 'Tatung-only' set must be 90 − 20 − 40 = 30.

Venn diagrams can also be used for actually solving problems, whether or not these involve quantification. An example concerns some rules that have been laid down:

The computer department managers must select from among their number a group who will be told the top-level computer passwords. No computer department managers can be told how to alter the door access codes unless they also know the top-level computer codes. Nobody who knows how to alter the door access codes may also know the top-level passwords. The problem is, can a computer manager be told how to alter the door access codes?

Here we have three sets which we can refer to as M (computer department managers), P (people who will be told the top-level passwords) and D (those who can be told how to alter the door access codes).

The first sentence prohibits anyone being in set P unless in set M. The second sentence prohibits anyone from being in both M and D who is not in P. The third prohibits anyone from being in both P and D. This can be shown by a Venn diagram, shading in the three prohibitions:

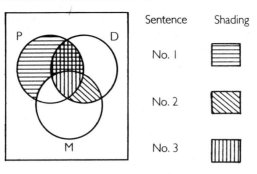

Sentence	Shading
No. 1	
No. 2	
No. 3	

The question is, can a member of set M be a member of set D? Inspection of the diagram shows that the whole area is shaded – so it is prohibited. This is a fairly easy problem. A more complex one is as follows.

A computer department splits its staff into two grades, officer and clerk. In the department are 8 male clerks, 9 female non-programmers, 7 clerical programmers, 4 male officer programmers, 7 male programmers, 9 male officers and 14 programmers. How many females are there and what is the total number of staff in the department?

Again, we have three sets. Thesé we can call P (programmers), O (officers) and M (males). The complements are then non-programmers, non-officers (clerks) and non-males (females). We could of course have chosen females as the set relating to sex. In this case the complement would have been non-females (males). The reason for choosing males as the set instead of females is that the data gives us four references to males and only one to females. In using Venn solutions, it makes the solution easier if one relates the sets to the most often quoted items. We can draw a Venn diagram with our three sets shown thus:

F

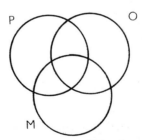

The total number of staff in the department will be the sum of all seven segments, the number of females will be the total of the three non-M segments. It is now possible to fill in each segment from the data. '4 male officer programmers' enables us to put a '4' in the segment that is part of all three sets. The segments are filled in as follows, in the order indicated:

Data	Segment	Amount
4 male officer programmers	(i)	4
9 male officers	(ii)	9–4 = 5
7 male programmers	(iii)	7–4 = 3
8 male non-officers	(iv)	8–3 = 5
7 non-officer programmers	(v)	7–3 = 4
14 programmers	(vi)	14–11 = 3
9 female non-programmers	(vii)	9

463

The size of the three sets is thus:

$$P \ \text{(programmers)} = 14$$
$$O \ \text{(officers)} \qquad = 21$$
$$M \ \text{(males)} \qquad = 17$$

The total number of staff is the sum of all seven segments and is 33. The total number of females is the total staff less the number of males. This is 33 minus 17 which is 16:

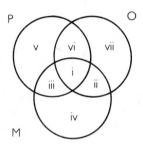 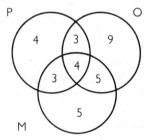

Solving this problem by using a Venn diagram is faster than other approaches. It is also easy to check both during the solving and at the conclusion of the exercise.

Least squares

Moving away from pictorial representations for a while we consider the general formula or equation for a straight line on a graph. This is in the form of:

$$y = a + bx$$

where $a =$ the place where the straight line cuts the y-axis,

$\qquad b =$ the slope of the line,

$\qquad y =$ a variable that is to be predicted (known as the dependent variable because it depends on the way in which x moves about),

$\qquad x =$ a variable that is independent (it does not depend on the way in which y changes).

This line is usually represented as in Figure 44.1.

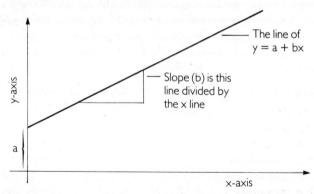

Figure 44.1 Graphical representation of a straight line

The sign '$\sum$' means the sum of similar items. So '$\sum a$' means the sum of all a's. We can have two equations that are of the form of our straight line, thus:

$$\sum y = Na + b\sum x \tag{1}$$

$$\sum xy = a\sum x + b\sum x^2 \tag{2}$$

Changing (1) around, we get:

$$a = \frac{\sum y - b\sum x}{N} = \frac{\sum y}{N} - \frac{b\sum x}{N}$$

Replacing a in equation (2) we get:

$$\sum xy = \sum x\left(\frac{\sum y - b\sum x}{N}\right) + b\sum x^2$$

Then: $N\sum xy = \sum x\sum y - b(\sum x)^2 + Nb\sum x^2$

And: $N\sum xy - \sum x\sum y = b[N\sum x^2 - (\sum x)^2]$

So: $b = \dfrac{N\sum xy - \sum x\sum y}{N\sum x^2 - (\sum x)^2}$

The two equations that have been solved above are known as 'normal equations'. If equations have the same variables, their values affect one another and have to be solved simultaneously. So the above equations are also 'simultaneous equations'.

We often draw points on a graph that we wish to draw a straight line through, being as accurate as we can. The common way of doing this is to place a transparent ruler on the points and move it around until it looks as though the edge is making a reasonably good fit to the points. In 1795 the German mathematician Karl Gauss was eighteen years old. He decided that the best fit of a straight line to a number of points could be defined more precisely. It is the line that minimizes the sum of the squares of the vertical distances from each point to the line.

This line is known as the least square line, or the line of best fit, or the regression line (see Figure 44.2). The best-fit line can be described as $y = a + bx$. The line is calculated

F

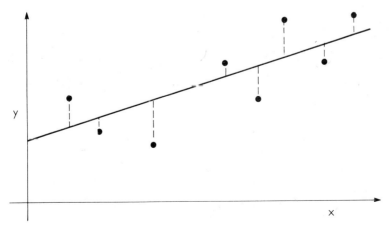

Figure 44.2 Gaussian best fit for $y = a + bx$

by substituting values for $\sum y, \sum x, \sum xy$ and $\sum x^2$ in the two equations (1) and (2) above. As an example of the use of these two formulae, let us assume that we wish to fit a regression line to the following data:

x	y
2	3
4	5
6	6
8	7
10	8
12	10

To use the equations, we need just two more columns: xy and x^2:

	x	y	xy	x^2
	2	3	6	4
	4	5	20	16
	6	6	36	36
	8	7	56	64
	10	8	80	100
	12	10	120	144
$\sum$	42	39	318	364

We can now substitute these values in our two equations:

$$b = \frac{N\sum xy - \sum x \sum y}{N\sum x^2 - (\sum x)^2} = \frac{6(318) - (42)(39)}{6(364) - (42)(42)}$$

$$= \frac{1908 - 1638}{2184 - 1764} = \frac{270}{420} = 0.64$$

$$a = \frac{\sum y}{N} - b\frac{\sum x}{N} = \frac{39}{6} - 0.64\frac{42}{6}$$

$$= 6.5 - 4.48 = 2.02$$

We can now say that $y = 2.02 + 0.64x$

To draw our regression line, we just need two points that we can then join together. When $x = 0$, then $y = 2.02$. And when $y = 10$, then $x = \dfrac{10 - 2.02}{0.64}$ which is 12.5 (Figure 44.3).

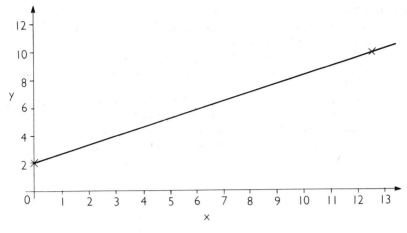

Figure 44.3

Regression analysis

Some people refer to this calculation of the line of regression by the term 'regression analysis'. This is incorrect. Regression analysis has a number of other aspects to it, in addition to just the line of regression. For this reason, to avoid confusion, we tend not to use the term 'line of regression' in ordinary conversation.

Even the term 'goodness of fit' has a much wider implication than just calculating the line shown above. The preferred term for this operation is therefore the 'least squares line'. This has the added advantage of being understood by more people than the other two terms.

Even worse, the least squares line has been heard referred to as 'multiple regression analysis'. This it most certainly is not. Firstly, as the name suggests, multiple regression analysis is concerned with multiple variables. For example, success of students on a computer literacy course was in one study found to depend on a number of variables. These included: simultaneous attendance on an accelerated maths class, sex of students, access to a computer outside the classroom. Other variables (such as asking the lecturer for help and playing computer games) had less correlation with success.

Expressing say four variables graphically would require a five-dimensional graph, so it would not be possible to draw a line on a scatter diagram on a graph on a two-dimensional piece of paper. The second reason for not calling a least squares line 'multiple regression analysis' is that it too is much more complex and much wider than its use in solving some variables. For this reason some people are not entirely happy with the way computer software is used for solving variables, feeling that the software encourages a mechanistic approach to what is a complex area and so may lead to errors of concept. However, for those that understand the complexities of the subject, the software is extremely useful since it is much, much faster than the tedium of other methods.

F

Further reading

Becker, W. E. and Harnett, D. L., *Business and Economics Statistics with Computer Applications*, Reading, Massachusetts: Addison-Wesley, 1987.

Draper, N. R. and Smith, H., *Applied Regression Analysis*, New York: John Wiley, 1981.

Gallagher, C. A. and Watson, H. J., *Quantitative Methods for Business Decisions*, New York: McGraw-Hill, 1980.

Hamburg, M., *Basic Statistics: A Modern Approach*, San Diego: Harcourt Brace Jovanovich, 1985.

Moore, P. G., *Reason by Numbers*, Harmondsworth: Penguin Books.

Sage University Paper series on *Quantitative Applications in the Social Services*, Beverly Hills and London: Sage Publications (a useful series of paperback monographs).

Final Notes

45
Technique Miscellany

Nothing can be loved or hated unless it is first known.
Leonardo da Vinci, *Notebooks* (c. 1500)

Zeal without knowledge is fire without light.
Thomas Fuller, *Gnomologia* (1732)

A number of techniques have not been covered in this book. The reason for this is that attaining the effective office has to be a positive and incisive affair. Some techniques (such as Job Evaluation) are usually utilized in a non-incisive way – more as part of administration itself rather than in making that administration a sharper tool.

Some other techniques are included. The ones covered briefly below are:

- Group research (Nominal Group Technique, the Delphi approach, Ideawriting and Interpretive Structural Modelling);
- Decision support systems;
- Expert systems.

G

Group researching

The value of group working has already been emphasized. A committee is a group, but committees tend to have a bad reputation for attaining results when they are concerned with looking at a new or difficult area of knowledge. Better group working in such circumstances can use some subsidiary techniques. Four of these are:

- Nominal Group Technique ('NGT');
- the Delphi approach;
- Ideawriting;
- Interpretive Structural Modelling ('ISM').

These four techniques are described below.

■ NOMINAL GROUP TECHNIQUE

Nominal Group Technique or NGT is an approach that aims to bring a structure to the meetings of small groups. It is particularly useful where there is a measure of disagreement about the very nature of the problem that is under consideration. Some adherents of the approach prefer it to brainstorming. It is often very popular with participants, though overexposure to NGT can lead to 'NGT fatigue' – a sort of blocking of the creative and participative process.

469

Success at NGT needs:

- a small group. The ideal is probably 5 to 9 people, though some adherents prefer 4 members. Large groups (say, more than 12) should be subdivided;
- members who are motivated towards finding a solution, and who are not the type that insist on having their own way all the time;
- members who have a background knowledge about the subject under consideration;
- a group leader who has taken part before in NGT and who is willing to act as a progress-effecter rather than as an active participant;
- a well thought out opening start point, known as the 'NGT question'.

Before an NGT meeting, it is necessary to formulate the NGT question. This question decides what will be discussed; it will also be found that the wording of the question decides the level at which it will be answered. Only one question and one area is tackled at an NGT session. So a question such as, 'What are the objectives of the present British government?' is not suitable for NGT; it is too diffuse and open-ended. A better question (and subject matter) would be, 'What difficulties are expected for the staff in implementing office automation?'

This question is then put at the top of a piece of A4 paper with a box drawn round it. Copies of this paper are then distributed to everybody at the meeting. The four steps of an NGT meeting are then explained to the meeting. These are:

GENERATION

ROUND-ROBIN RECORD

SERIAL DISCUSSION

VOTE

For the first step, people work individually, writing on their pieces of paper ideas for responding to the NGT question. People think, write and work independently – in silence. The leader tries not to lead, in the sense that if somebody does not understand the question, no attempt is made to lead people into a particular area of response. People should answer the question as they understand it. For this first step, a time of 5 to 10 minutes is allowed.

The second step is for the leader to go round the people at the meeting. Each person in turn reads out one of the items on their list. This should be expressed in the form of a short sentence or phrase. Each item as it is read out is written on a flip-chart size piece of paper. When each such sheet is full it is taped to the wall. This writing and the giving of items should be fairly rapid, but not at the high speed associated with brainstorming. Nor are we after sheer volume of ideas as an objective. Indeed, people may be encouraged to put forward their 'best' ideas. If the group is large, it can be a good practice to announce that the leader will only go round the room, say, three times.

The third step is to clarify each of the items that has been written on the large sheets. Each item is read out loud and comments are invited. These comments can be explanatory, or can be assenting or disagreeing, but long discussions or arguments should be stopped short. They are not necessary anyway, since everybody will have an opportunity to vote for their preference in the fourth step. With experience, a leader soon gets to know what sort of comments to encourage and which to discourage. It is important that the leader does not express any preference for any items nor exhibit disapproval for any of them. The advantage of NGT is that participants know that the outcome is theirs, and was not the leader's (who may be an outsider). The group is solving its own problems. Within reason, items can be changed, enlarged, combined or edited – provided that the leader feels that this is not making an item so broad as to be too fuzzy, lacking precision.

The fourth step is voting for the items that have been put forward. It is normal *not* to present the list and take a straight vote. A slightly involved ranking system is usually employed; this facilitates further discussion which a straight vote could inhibit. Each member is given five 125 mm × 75 mm 'index' cards or something similar. Members mentally select their five most important suggestions from the large sheets on the wall. They write (without care) these five selected items on their cards, one item to a card. In the top left-hand corner they write the reference number (this is to help the leader later).

When everybody has written down their selections, the leader gets them to rank-order their preferences. This is done by giving instructions as they do it. The cards are spread out in front of each person. Each person decides the most important card and writes a figure '1' in the bottom right-hand corner, putting a circle round the figure (this is to prevent confusion between the ranking figures and the reference figure). This card is then turned over so that it is face down. Members are then asked to select the *least* important card remaining. This is marked with a circled '5'. Next, the most important card remaining is selected and marked '2'. These two cards are turned over also. Of the two cards remaining, the less important card is marked with '4'. The remaining single card is marked with a '3'.

All the cards are now collected and the rankings marked off against a previously prepared list, e.g.

> 1. 3, 4, 1, 2
> 2. 1, 2
> 3.
> 4. 5, 3, 5, 4
> 5.
> 6. 4, 5, 3, 2, 3, 3   and so on.

A discussion then follows on the voting pattern. This pattern is not always simple. It is good practice (if there is enough time) to have a second round of voting after this discussion; a much stronger pattern will then often arise. The precise method of presenting the results of an NGT session will depend on the circumstances. Where it arose because of a difficulty within a group, it may be possible just to agree to adopt some of the ideas as standard practice.

In fairness, it should be pointed out that some people much prefer the ranking to be done in a contrary fashion (i.e. calling the most important item '5' and the least '1'). This can, however, lead one to mentally add up the ranking as points (rather in the fashion of the 'Eurovision Song Contest') which is not wanted. NGT was evolved in 1968 by A. Delbecq and A. van de Ven. They published a book with fuller details in 1975.[1]

G

■ THE DELPHI APPROACH

The Delphi approach first came into prominence as a way of 'predicting' future events. Some of the well-publicized results seemed to suggest that either the millennium of perfect technology or the end of the world through disaster were about to engulf us all very shortly. When the 'predicted' time for the events passed without their occurrence, many people turned away from the approach, some even mocking it humorously. It has now been changed somewhat in emphasis, and is useful when one wants to have an indication of a joint or pooled judgement.

The basis of the Delphi is the use of questionnaires. These are completed by people who are knowledgeable in the field of enquiry. The questionnaires usually present a list to people who are asked to rate the importance or relevance of each item on the list. Examples might be, 'What are the priorities in going global in our provision of financial services?', or 'What are the dangers we face in the short term from our competitors?', or 'What specific technical objectives should we set for automating our branch offices?'

An initial questionnaire is sent out to respondents; this may seek opinions, information, data or judgements. The items on this initial questionnaire may be 'invented' by those who are running the study. Alternatively, they may be based on an NGT (Nominal Group Technique) session(s) as described above. Sometimes, by the nature of the study, the items select themselves to a large extent. When these initial questionnaires are returned, they are analysed to show the initial results.

On the basis of these results a second questionnaire is prepared. Depending on the responses, this may expand certain points to give more detail, or it may introduce additional alternatives grouped around the points that respondents felt were the most important. Or it may have to explore completely new areas. This second questionnaire is then sent out – to the same people who completed the first one. At the same time, the results of the first questionnaire are communicated to the participants. This second questionnaire, when it is returned, is analysed in the same way as the first one. It is common practice to use a third questionnaire; social researchers often use four, even five, still on an iterative route.

Apart from this conventional Delphi approach (which will take 6–8 weeks to complete), it is also possible to carry out a study at a meeting by using terminals. Either the questionnaires are completed by hand and the responses data-prepared by a third party, or the responses are made direct to a terminal in reply to displayed questionnaires. This method is known, with a slight disregard for veracity, as Real-Time Delphi. The advantage of the method is a considerable reduction in calendar time. The disadvantage is that the people running the study may find themselves under time pressure to prepare good subsequent questionnaires.

A third type is the Policy Delphi approach. The aim of this is to make sure that all alternative ideas or options are uncovered, rather than making consensus the primary objective. It is often used by social researchers. Details may be found in a book by M. Turoff et al.[2]

The Delphi approach is particularly useful for areas of subjective judgements, and/or where face-to-face meetings are contra-indicated (because respondents are widely dispersed or too numerous or in considerable disagreement).

■ IDEAWRITING

Ideawriting was first published by J. N. Warfield, who called it 'brainwriting'.[3] It can be an aid to idea generation, but it is of greater use in turning a generalized concept into

472

something more specific. The basic idea is simple (though a brief explanation may make it sound like the game of 'Consequences' that used to be played at children's parties).

Ideawriting is usually performed using pads of pre-printed forms. These forms have a vertical line drawn the whole length of the form about a quarter of the way across. At the top of the form are two boxes. One is large enough to write a person's name in. The second box takes up the right-hand three-quarters of the page and is deep enough to take three lines of handwriting (about 25 mm deep). An example is shown in Figure 45.1. The rest of the form is feint ruled.

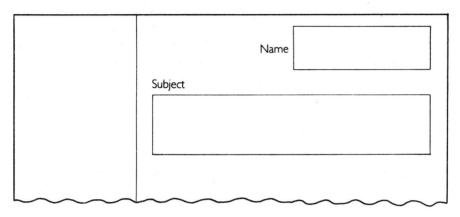

Figure 45.1 Idea writing form

G

Ideawriting works best with small groups (say, 4–7) so large groups have to be divided into smaller groups. One person writes the subject in the box, plus his or her name. A group can have just one subject or as many as one subject per person. The person then writes a response or answer on the page under the box – each participant will have a form.

About five minutes is allowed for thinking and writing; participants should be discouraged from writing at length. Their response should ideally be about 3–8 lines long. After these initial responses have been written down, all the forms are put into the middle of a table or desk. Each participant then takes another form, reads what was written on it, and adds to it. This addition may be an expansion, an alternative, an answer, or even a riposte (these are written in the left-hand column). This process is repeated until everybody has written on every form.

It is usual for a discussion on the forms to follow. If a large group has been divided, then the whole group is brought together for this. Alternatively, a monitoring team may assemble the forms and feedback the results to the participants. It depends on the purpose of the session – which takes about forty-five minutes unless there is a lengthy group discussion. The sort of question that might be answered by an ideawriting session is, 'What is the best strategy for improving technology awareness among the staff?'

■ INTERPRETIVE STRUCTURAL MODELLING (ISM)

To many of us, Interpretive Structural Modelling (ISM) is no different from the paired comparison method used for many years in Job Evaluation, etc. However, the literature[3] presents it as a specific technique, so it is mentioned here.

There are occasions when we wish to array a number of items, or to decide the relationships between a large number of items. Examples are:

- the relationships between items in a decision tree;
- the relative importance/feasibility/chronology of a set of proposed cost-cutting measures;
- building a Decision Support System model;
- deciding the base cause of a long chain of effects.

The first step is to list all the items under consideration. In a cost-cutting situation these might be, for example, sell 90 per cent of company-owned cars, stop canteen subsidies, stop all bonus payments, cut charitable contributions by 80 per cent, etc.

Each item on the list is then compared with every other item on the list in a specific way, e.g.:

- is less important than;
- is caused by;
- helps to achieve;
- should be done before.

From this completed pairs-comparison an array or pseudo-network is prepared. This could be done manually though it is normal to use a computer. Any pairs-comparison software could be used, although there are specific ISM programs.

The pairs-comparison session can be fatiguing and, since there is usually considerable discussion, can be lengthy. A list of twenty-five items can take a day to complete; in Job Evaluation it can take $1\frac{1}{2}$–2 days. A straight majority vote is usually employed to make decisions, although it is sometimes advisable to try for, say, 60/40 as a minimum for decisions.

When the final result is printed out, it is a good plan to discuss it and allow the group to amend it slightly if they feel that it contains nonsenses or something that offends equity. 'Odd' relationships are by no means unusual.

Decision support systems

When trying to decide between alternative configurations of office technology, an office manager might list some desirable features. The manager might then mark two competitors (out of, say, ten maximum marks) for each feature. If each feature is then given a weighting to reflect the relative importance of each feature, the result might be something like that shown in Table 45.1.

If the office manager truly believes the marking and the weighting, then the 737 system will be purchased. Of course, it is always possible that the total marks, when weighted, seem too close together to make the decision automatic. This example is a somewhat trivial example of the value of trying to use arithmetic to help the decision-making process – and the fact that many managers are wary of relying completely on the results of such arithmetic.

Other decisions are more complex. An example might be the decision as to whether or not to build a new head office. In such cases building a Decision Support System

Table 45.1 Weighted markings as used in decision making

Feature	System 737	System 310	Weight	Weighted marks 737	Weighted marks 310
1 Price of system	10	6	1.0	10	6
2 Number installed	8	6	0.9	7.2	5.4
3 Suitability for us	5	8	0.8	4.8	6.4
4 Training given	8	5	0.7	5.6	3.5
5 Ease of use	2	6	0.7	1.4	4.2
6 Vendor commitment	7	4	0.7	4.9	2.8
7 Quality of manuals	3	6	0.4	1.2	2.0
8 Network capability	2	8	0.1	0.2	0.8
9 Ease of upgrading	3	7	0.1	0.3	0.7
10 Maintenance	7	5	0.1	0.7	0.5
			Total	36.3	32.3

(DSS) model will be of considerable assistance. A DSS model will incorporate forecasts, variables, relationships within an arithmetic framework. Putting this model on to a computer reduces the chore of calculations and enables one to change the variables in a 'what-if' manner. Indeed, a spreadsheet or equation solver software may be good enough for many models, although complex models will need more sophisticated programs.

A model will help the decision-making process because it can encompass a greater amount of complexity than a person can. Putting it on to a computer speeds the whole process up, especially if one wants to use a complicated relationship between two variables, though of course one must always remember that a model is not an end in itself; it just helps one to make a decision – a truism that escapes the grasp of some model builders.

There are three roles in building a model: the analyst (who builds the model), the user (who starts the process) and the client (who obtains the benefit from the model). Sometimes all three roles are vested in a single person. This can be useful since a model can give an insight into a particular problem. On the other hand, many managers lack the time or the experience to fulfil all three roles.

The first step in building a model is to consider the variables and objective(s). Like many techniques, DSS has its own jargon. So a 'decision' variable is one that is under the control of the decision-maker (e.g. which computer?). An 'outcome' variable is one that measures performance (we prefer the term 'measure'). An 'intermediate' variable is one that links a decision to a measurement (e.g. working capital).

Variables may be binary, discrete or continuous. A 'binary' variable (0 or 1) is often of the yes/no or go/no go type, e.g. do or do not move to a new office. A 'discrete' variable is one of a finite set (e.g. five word processors). A 'continuous' variable is one that can have an infinite number of possibilities within a set range (e.g. number of square metres of new office space).

Finally, variables may be random or exogenous. A 'random' variable is one that varies and which will be described in terms of probability (e.g. expenses will be £1

G

million with a probability of 50 per cent ± 2 per cent and £2 million with a probability of 5 per cent ± 2 per cent). An 'exogenous' variable is one that is external and which cannot be affected by one of our decisions (e.g. the state of the country's economy).

In most models it is also necessary to state objectives – in the form of minimizing or maximizing. Such objectives can be in opposition to one another: minimize office space and maximize productivity, for example, might involve one in a trade-off. Discussions by a group or with colleagues will always result in a better set of variables and objectives, though it has to be said that such discussions can become quite protracted, because different people will often regard different factors as being outstandingly important, depending on their work.

A good example of setting objectives and their measures is the building of a model for an information system.[4] The primary objective might be to maximize the value of the information system. This primary objective might lead to three more concrete objectives:

- maximize the ability to get the job done ('productivity');
- maximize the soundness of the system ('integrity'); and
- maximize the response to future unknowns ('flexibility').

Each of these three would then be subdivided. Thus flexibility could be divided, and described as 'adaptability' and 'generality'. These two would then be further subdivided. Generality might be divided into comprehensiveness of applications and of users. User comprehensiveness could be measured by counting the percentage of users serviced in any one month.

One has to beware of going too far in either direction – either missing out something that is important or thinking up too many objectives and variables in the expectation that one is gaining greater 'accuracy'. Four testing questions are:

- have all the really important factors been covered?
- are any of them redundant?
- are any of them ambiguous?
- can they be properly measured?

Having listed the variables and objectives, with the relevant measures, one can move on to the next step. This is the building up of an influence diagram. This step is more important than may at first appear. An influence diagram is a simple chart in which the links are shown between the decisions, the intermediate variables and the measured variables. The nature of these links is also shown.

The symbols used are not universal, but one set is:[5]

A decision

An intermediate variable (including those that are defined as 'random')

A measurable variable

The influence of one variable on another, if this influence nature is known or can be positively identified

The influence of one variable on another, if the influence nature is uncertain

The influence of one variable on another, if this is a 'preference' rather than an arithmetic dependency

A simplified influence diagram is shown in Figure 45.2. This was prepared for an organization that carried out computer data-prep work for customers.

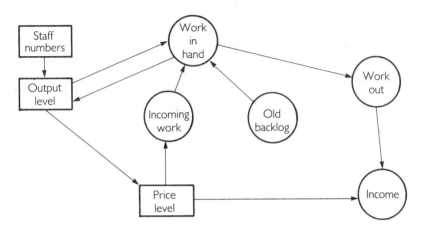

Figure 45.2 Influence diagram

G

The influence diagram should be studied carefully and (unless trivial) should be the subject of discussion. To some extent this is to make sure that it has been correctly drawn. Even more, it is a final check on the variables, objectives and dependencies. As a general rule, models should err on the side of simplicity, rather than straining after completeness. Completeness as a measure of likely accuracy can be an illusion. The rule is to ask, 'Would the inclusion of a further variable affect the ultimate outcome materially?'

Once an agreed influence diagram has been drawn, the next step is to define and specify each of the links, or dependencies, on the diagram. These are specified in arithmetic terms. This requires a knowledge of the subject being studied and of different mathematical functions. The simplest relationship is usually the well-known one of:

$$y = a + b.x$$

For example:

Profit after tax $= (1 - \text{Tax rate}) \times (\text{Profit before tax})$.
Total cost $= \text{Overhead} + b.(\text{Staff numbers})$.

477

Other relationships that may be used include:

- power curves (e.g. $y = x^3$);
- exponential;
- logarithmic;
- S-shaped logistic (useful for product life-cycle growth);
- Poisson or Gaussian curves;
- step function (e.g. discounts for quantity).

As previously stated, random variables involve probabilistic relationships. Modelling software will include facilities for 'goodness of fit' curve fitting. For probabilistic uncertainties, many of them use Monte Carlo simulations.

Modelling software will also include what-if facilities, and the ability to perform sensitivity analysis. Sensitivity analysis is a form of what-if in which the variable(s) are changed automatically by incremental steps within pre-set ranges, and the effects of successive changes are shown.

The final step is to load the completed model into a computer using suitable software. An ordinary spreadsheet will sometimes suffice, provided it can handle the relationships of the dependencies. For more complex models or mathematics, then a program specifically meant for modelling will be needed.

There are certainly occasions when the usefulness of a model depends on identifying the variables and their relationships, and where the influence diagram is more important than any subsequent arithmetic. For example a manufacturer of razor blades wanted a model of its administration processes. The influence diagram in this particular case was almost the end product since it could reveal where problems were taking place; mathematical analysis was just a refinement.

Influence diagrams have also been used for strategic planning where the important value of the work was in defining relationship between parts of the strategic plan. It is useful to be able to draw good, accurate influence diagrams even if one lacks the mathematical knowledge to exploit fully a modelling program. They can be useful in a wide variety of unexpected situations. This ability can best be built up by trying a few simple examples, based on one's own experience and knowledge of a subject.

Expert systems

There are two ways of looking at the human brain and intelligence. One is to say that a human being can be reduced to a fairly low-level, mechanistic, on/off (binary) system that can be replicated if we have a large enough computer and sophisticated software. The other way is to say that human judgement transcends mere logic, that it learns from cases, not from rules. Those interested in pursuing this dichotomy further may like to read a book by Fischler and Firschlein.[6]

The mechanistic approach provided the impetus for Artificial Intelligence (AI). This attempted to build a computer that could see, think and respond like a human being. In the 1940s the mathematician Alan Turing proposed a way of knowing when such a machine had been built. This 'Turing Test' was to place a computer behind a curtain and see if a human would know whether behind the curtain was another human or a computer.

Artificial Intelligence has been called 'a field where scientific objectivity seems to get trampled underfoot more often than in others'.[7] It has, however, provided the spur for a number of computer languages. One of the earliest (in the mid-1950s) was Logic Theorist, written by Drs Newell, Simon and Shaw, designed to prove theorems in mathematics. Another was LISP (short for 'list processing'). This was developed by Dr John McCarthy, and was published in 1962 in the book, *The LISP 1.5 Programmer's Manual*. It attracted little attention for a quarter of a century, but then became part of the world of what is now called 'expert systems'. LISP is not an easy language, nor is it helped by some of the published books which claim to teach it. Those who have tried to learn it without success may like to try a book by Friedman and Felleisen.[8] A simpler, but still elegant, language – really a LISP dialect – was SCHEME, which was introduced in 1975 by Sussman and Steele.

LISP is still widely used in expert systems. So is PROLOG, a language developed at the University of Marseilles in 1972 (purists claim that PROLOG is a declarative language rather than a solver like LISP but that need not concern us here). There are two main dialect streams of PROLOG: the Marseilles and the Edinburgh, named for the universities where development took place. A book on the 'core' language was written by Clocksin and Mellish[9], though the typeface and printing certainly defy any attempt at rapid reading.

An expert system is a piece of hardware–software. It has two main components, a reasoning facility and a large 'database' of knowledge. The reasoning facility can draw inferences from rules and relationships between facts that have been fed in. This component is known as an 'inference engine'. The other component – the database of knowledge – is known as a 'knowledge base'. This is built up by analysts who, in the past, were called 'knowledge engineers'. These analysts build up the knowledge base by lengthy quizzing of experts. This enables them to create thousands of cause-and-effect relationships. This is done by asking the experts exactly how they solve problems; the steps taken, the signs looked for, the observations made, the possible branches. These factors are then all fed into the computer in a list ready for processing (which explains why LISP means list processing).

An example of using an expert system is a doctor with a personal computer in his surgery. A patient comes in with certain symptoms which the doctor keys in: male, age 12, mouth dry, tongue furred, temperature 39.5°C, swollen and painful lymph nodes. On the screen questions or instructions will lead the doctor through a series of logical steps which aim at reducing the area of alternatives. In the example, the doctor would be told to inspect certain glands, including the parotid gland. If this is swollen the computer would ask if the child had been immunized against mumps, or had already had that disease. If the reply is negative, then the screen would indicate that the child has mumps, or parotitis, possibly with an indication of probability (95 per cent). It might also indicate treatment – which in the case of mumps is not very much: rest and an aspirin, unless the testicles were inflamed, when an intramuscular injection of serum or gamma-globulin would be suggested.

This example shows both the strengths and weaknesses of expert systems. It uses the expertise of doctors to enable one to identify a disease, which is extremely useful where the disease is rare or complex. (One of the early successes was CASNET, a system for diagnosing glaucoma.) The information can be updated to take account of recent advances in knowledge. The system can 'learn' to some extent: if there is an epidemic, it will start to concentrate on a smaller area by changing the order in which questions are posed. Above all, it enables branches to be explored or discarded quickly without

G

forgetting. This attribute means that the knowledge of experts is stored for anyone to use.

On the other hand there are disadvantages. Building up a knowledge base is a lengthy process. Use of advanced expert systems needs a reasonable level of knowledge on the part of the user and may itself be a lengthy process. Inevitably, some of the inference results are trivial, and these dilute the complex results. (Most doctors and many parents can recognize mumps in less time than it takes to boot up a system.) Also, expert systems need a lot of computing power to be effective; an inference engine can handle about 1,000 rules before its responses become annoyingly slow with present methods of electronics.

A rather more basic problem is that many researchers would like to imitate the human brain. But we still do not know how people can use analogies, how they learn, how memory works. Considerable work is being done on overcoming the disadvantages, either by increasing our knowledge or by finding ways round the problems.

The problems have had another effect: expert systems have had a somewhat chequered career. After it had lain ignored for a quarter of a century, the exploitation of LISP raised expectations, especially after some early, much-publicized successes with expert systems. As late as 1985, some venture capital was still chasing new firms that were selling expert systems. They were widely tipped as being a future profit maker. However, insiders were already sounding caution (*Electronics*, 7 August, 1986, p. 56). A high percentage of the early high-flying expert-systems companies disappeared or hit deep trouble. By 1988 the same magazine (*Electronics*, June) had two articles entitled 'Can expert systems survive? Some say yes' and 'Surprisingly, a new AI crop may be making it'.

Why did expert systems hit a bad patch? First, many of the early LISP systems ran on expensive stand-alone machines that did not integrate easily with conventional computers. In turn this also meant that firms selling development tools had a much smaller market than had been hoped. Second, too many of the systems seemed to work in the laboratory but were not robust enough for practical commercial use. Third, they were oversold. Fourth, too many people tried to get on the bandwagon by selling as 'expert systems' software that was not – at best some were decision support systems, at worst a few were little more than windowed databases.

This downturn in the mid-1980s led to some positive actions. First, rule-based expert systems were developed (known as 'dumb systems') that were very useful for a number of tasks such as bank tellers and aircraft reservations. These may not be 'expert systems' but they are useful. Second, simpler languages were used that could be used on normal computers. Third, some firms retreated into writing custom software instead of general systems; special applications are still worthwhile and economic in the right situations. Fourth, expert systems became a transparent part of a larger applications program (such as model building).

Where does this leave us? First, one has to ask if one really does need an expert system. If so, then there is sufficient knowledge around to provide some useful tools. If not, then one has to use an alternative. Some of the expert systems written for administration cover personnel selection, clerical instruction, job evaluation, etc. As alternatives one may be able to use algorithms, a decisions support system (DSS) or even a well-written manual.

In the 1940s, Turing thought that a machine that could fully pass the Turing test would be built within fifty years. Some experts now think that we are still about fifty years behind this event. Similarly, the next quarter of a century will show whether expert systems become part of everyday life, or whether firms like Tecknowledge become a Harvard Business School case study.

References

1 Delbecq, A. L. *et al.*, *Group Techniques for Program Planning*, Glenview: Scott-Foresman, 1975.
2 Linstone, H. A. and Turoff, M. (eds), *The Delphi Method: Techniques and Applications*, Reading, Massachusetts: Addison-Wesley, 1975.
3 Warfield, J. N., *Societal Systems: Planning, Policy and Complexity*, New York: John Wiley, 1976.
4 Bodily, S. E., *Modern Decision Making*, Singapore: McGraw-Hill, 1985.
5 Bodily, S. E., op. cit.
6 Fischler, M. A. and Firschlein, O., *Intelligence: The Eye, the Brain, and the Computer*, Reading, Massachusetts: Addison-Wesley, 1987.
7 *Byte*, Vol. 12, No. 9, August 1987, p. 90.
8 Friedman, D. P. and Felleisen, M., *The Little Lisper, Trade Edition*, Cambridge, Massachusetts: MIT Press, 1987.
9 Clocksin, W. F. and Mellish, C. S., *Programming in Prolog*, Berlin: Springer-Verlag, 1987.

Further reading

Murray, J. T. and Murray, M. J., *Expert Systems in Data Processing*, New York: McGraw-Hill, 1988.

G

46

It Can't Be Done . . .

Skill and confidence are an unconquered army.

George Herbert, *Jacula Prudentum* (1651)

The mind of a bigot is like the pupil of the eye; the more light you pour upon it, the more it will contract.

Justice Oliver Wendell Holmes (1841–1935)

Investigators are often told, when presenting a proposal, that 'It can't be done.' This can be a disheartening response. It is particularly upsetting when the response comes from somebody who is a definite expert on the matter under discussion. But investigators must remember that experts can be wrong, too. For example, Thomas Edison said in 1926:

> Talking on the screen destroys the illusion. Devices for projecting the film actor's speech can be perfected, but the idea is not practical.

This was twenty years after the Lauste patent and just before the success of *The Jazz Singer, Broadway Melody* and Greta Garbo in *Anna Christie* (which really was advertised with the words, 'Hear her talk'). Also mistaken was the UK Astronomer Royal (Dr Wooley) in 1956 when he said:

> Space travel is utter bilge.

These expert responses are far from being unique. A professor (Dr D. Lardner) made some calculations as a result of which he pointed out the impossibility of a steamship ever crossing the Atlantic. The calculations proved that a steamship could not carry enough coal for its weight; building a larger ship to carry more coal merely resulted in more coal being needed for the extra weight. The careful calculations were made shortly before the *Great Western* crossed the Atlantic. Professor Lardner also claimed that there was no point in building a train capable of 190 km/h. At high speeds passengers would be unable to breathe and so would die of asphyxiation.

Simon Newcomb (1835–1909) was a brilliant man. His calculations of the motions of heavenly bodies advanced scientific knowledge. Perhaps encouraged by this success, he published a number of articles stating that flights by heavier-than-air machines were impossible. Even the flights of the Wright Brothers (1903–5) did not change his mind that such things were impractical, insignificant if not utterly impossible. History does not record when, or even if, he changed his mind.

William Thomson is better known as Lord Kelvin, one of Britain's foremost scientists. But he held the idea that light could exert pressure as not being tenable, calling it merely 'curious and ingenious'. Ernst Mach had the Mach number named after him and earned the admiration of Einstein. But he just could not accept the idea of atomic structures. Nor, in spite of Einstein's admiration, could he accept the idea of relativity.

Nikola Tesla was the brilliant Yugoslav who was largely responsible for inventing electric generation for street lighting. But in the early 1940s he asserted that atomic power was an impossibility – shortly before the explosion of the first atomic bomb. The nuclear physicist Ernest Rutherford similarly scoffed at the idea of releasing the power of the atomic nucleus. Moreover, he was reluctant to accept Einstein's idea of relativity.

Alexander Graham Bell had difficulty getting people to accept his idea of the telephone. He offered it to Western Union at the time when they were the dominant force in the telegraph business. Western Union set up a committee to look at the new invention. After an investigation, the committee's report included the following points:

- Mr Bell's profession is that of a voice teacher. Yet he claims to have discovered [a] communication which has been overlooked by thousands of workers who have spent years in this field.
- His proposal to place his instrument in almost every home and business is fantastic.
- In conclusion, the committee feels that it must advise against any investment in Mr Bell's scheme. We do not doubt that it will find users in special circumstances, but any development of the kind and scale that Bell so fondly imagines is utterly out of the question.

In view of these examples, next time an expert tells you that something cannot be done it might be advisable to get a second opinion – or try to find some way in which your idea can be fulfilled.

It seems that almost every new idea, every attempt at change, has caused somebody to feel that it cannot be done. Some more examples:

- the prospect of making ships of iron was widely condemned. They could not float, they would rust away, they would damage more easily than wooden ships when they grounded, and the iron would make the compass useless;
- similarly, the cast-iron plough was rejected by farmers at first because it would poison the land and would stimulate the growth of weeds;
- when a patent was taken out for building steel-framed skyscrapers, *Architectural News* predicted that the expansion and contraction of the metal would crack all the plaster, thus eventually leaving just the shell;
- a priest declared that the introduction of railways would require the building of many insane asylums – people would go mad with fright at the sight of locomotives moving across the countryside;
- when the YWCA in New York announced that it proposed giving typing lessons for women, the result was vigorous protestations, on the grounds that the female constitution would break down under the strain.

G

To bring this whole problem nearer home, here is a partial list of reasons for not making the office more effective:

1 We're just coming up to the holiday period.
2 Will the staff be happy with any change?
3 Perhaps I could help you rewrite your report, putting things into perspective.
4 We've tried that before.
5 It's not in the budget.
6 There isn't the manpower to handle this right now.
7 We're too busy with the new management information system.
8 It's never been part of our job to do that.
9 It won't work.

10 It's much too expensive to buy that equipment.

11 The staff don't understand this new technology.

12 How many extra staff will we get to do that?

13 We're not ready for it yet.

14 Certainly seems like a good idea for some companies, but we're different here.

15 It's all right in theory, but not in practice.

16 It will be too complicated to administer.

17 We don't have the room.

18 The approach is too academic.

19 You will go on to the next project, but we will have to live with the changes.

20 It will result in too much paperwork.

21 A pity – you are too early.

22 A pity – you are too late.

23 There must be a better idea than this – leave it with me.

24 The customers will object – and here the customer is king.

25 The union will never agree to this.

26 It's against company policy.

27 It's against the law.

28 The auditors will definitely veto it.

29 It would have been introduced already if it were any good.

30 I've only just taken over this department so I'll need a few months to find out what goes on around here.

31 You don't seem to have grasped our real problem.

32 Headquarters are just about to start a pilot scheme for a similar problem in Brazil, so let's see how that turns out.

33 We're too small for something as complicated as this.

34 We have a high percentage of physically disabled staff in this office, and it wouldn't be fair to them.

35 The new mainframe will make this idea redundant.

36 All our work depends on the Finance Department so there's no point in changing us until you've improved things there.

37 You don't seem to have considered the new Smudgeworthy Turbo Micro 486 with an optical hard card interfacing network.

38 But we've only just changed all our procedures.

39 Could we see this working in some of your other clients first?

40 I see you've fallen into the same trap as all the others.

41 Ah, what you are really proposing is . . .

42 I can't understand a word of your report.

43 We have been successful doing it our way for fifteen years, so why change a winning formula?

44 Which of your idiot colleagues thought that up?

45 OK. We'll form a committee to look at this.

46 It needs a lot more fact-finding and study before thinking about a possible solution.

47 We had a full meeting to discuss this and we decided against it.

48 We'll discuss this when you've written new job descriptions for everybody, so that people can judge how it will affect them.

49 How much fee have you got left? Enough to fly back here a few times next month?

50 As I said to the Chairman this morning – over my dead body.

Experienced investigators will be able to add to this list from their own past studies. Objections can come from any quarter. A firm in Eastern Europe was observed where a boring job had to be performed by a clerk. This consisted of writing down in a column details of every one of the firm's products (over 2,000). This had to be done every month, by copying the details from the previous month's list. Inevitably, the hand-writing became substandard, items were missed off, errors crept in. Several alternatives were possible, such as printing out from a word processing record. However, for specific reasons, it seemed that the best solution would be to type the list once, and to take a photocopy of this each month.

The conversation between the consultant and the objector went like this:

Con: We can type the list in a column on an A3 sheet . . .

Obj: But the sheet is larger than A3.

Con: Yes, but we can use an A3 sheet.

Obj: No we can't – it's bigger than A3; which is why we can't photocopy it as our copier will only take A3.

Con: Yes, but the new sheets will be reduced to A3.

Obj: But our copier cannot reduce.

Con: It won't have to if we use A3 sheets to type on.

Obj: Well, we can't use a photocopier.

Con: Why not?

Obj: (triumphantly) Because the form is filled in with blue ballpoint pens which won't copy.

Con: We can use black ballpoints.

Obj: But we don't have any.

Con: I'll buy some tomorrow. OK?

Obj: We'll see.

G

The point of this example is that the Objector was a member of the Systems and Procedures team whose job it was to improve procedures.

The examples given above may lead one to imagine that raising objections is the normal reaction which may seem a daunting prospect. In practice objections are the exception rather than the rule, especially when the study has been carried out properly.

When objections arise there are two possible causes. It is either because of the investigator or the objector. There is no doubt that sometimes it is because of the investigator, who has committed a sin of omission or commission. Points to watch have already been covered (some of them in considerable detail) in this book. But some of them are repeated here:

1 Care and attention must be observed in all aspects. Quoted facts must be right. Calculations must be correct. The problems must be understood thoroughly. Opinions and attitudes must be heeded. Savings claimed must be real and attainable. Solutions must be possible for the organization involved.

2 The investigator has to pace the study so that it does not become necessary to hurry over the later stages, otherwise mistakes seem to become inevitable. And one of the things that gets cut to save time may be a vital one – namely, keeping people in the picture.

3 In most instances, it is a great mistake to present a report in such a way that it represents the first time people have heard about the proposed improvements.

485

Remember, Improvements = Change. During the course of the study, people should be kept aware of the route that the investigator is thinking of going. In our experience, the rabbit-out-of-the-hat style of report presentation is the commonest single mistake that internal investigators make in their work.

4 Investigators carry with them their own 'culture'. This is a culture of continuous change. It is very easy to forget that this culture is not shared by everybody else. At times, this can cause an investigator to be surprised when staff are wary of a change to their way of doing things.

5 One of the major aids that an investigator has is to create momentum – a sense of inevitability. Yes, we can and will make this office more effective. Yes, we can and will make changes. Yes, we can and will succeed.

6 The appearance and impact of the investigator matters. Some of us are naturally scruffy in appearance and manage to get away with it – but it is a barrier that we ourselves erect and whose effect we have to overcome. An investigator must be knowledgeable about the specialism for which fees are being paid. Poor body language can be distracting. An investigator must be confident about the study. Above all, an investigator must be honest.

7 Advanced office technology can bring its own problems, especially in terms of compatibility and quality. It is one area where sometimes 'it [really] can't be done'. Computer magazines such as *Byte* continually print letters from readers along the lines of, 'Why will my Toshiba P1340 printer not work with my Macintosh SE?' The lack of compatibility between processor/software/ancillaries is a constant headache. So is the level of 'hype' or overselling of the abilities of hardware and software.

Another problem is copy protection, and systems needs of software. Dongles cease to be transparent when they develop a fault. Software is often sold where one has to buy it and remove the shrink-wrap before one can make sure what one needs to make it work (it may need DOS 4.0+ while one only has version 3.2). So – do not recommend unknown equipment or software. Do not believe advertised claims. Try to avoid copy-protected software.

8 The final point is the most important: treat the staff well. Our slogan is still:

> **Courtesy with tenacity**

As previously stated, there are times when objections are caused by the objector. The objector may feel threatened by the proposed changes, may not understand the proposals, may genuinely have reasons to feel that the proposals will not work, may have an unfortunate personality trait, may distrust the investigator, or may be overworked and so feel the proposal is not worth the time expenditure involved.

Whatever the reason, the best cure is to carry out the study properly so that the objections do not occur. Otherwise, it is necessary to answer the objections in such a way that they dissolve.

The last few paragraphs read rather like a sermon. So, to finish this chapter, a few more examples of mistaken responses.

Allowing for inflation, the most successful movie film of all time is *Gone with the Wind*, which took over $300 million. Director Victor Fleming rejected David Selznick's offer of a percentage of the profits rather than a straight salary with the words, 'Don't be a damned fool, David, *Gone with the Wind* is going to be one of the biggest white elephants of all time'. The actor Gary Cooper said, '*Gone with the Wind* is going to be the biggest flop in Hollywood history. I'm just glad it'll be Clark Gable who's falling flat on his face and not me.'

The most successful pop group, The Beatles, were turned down by the Decca company with the words, 'We do not like their sound. Groups with guitars are on the way out.' The Beatles were also turned down by other companies: HMV, Pye and Columbia. In his diary, Tchaikovsky wrote, 'I played over the music of that scoundrel Brahms. What a giftless bastard! It annoys me that this self-inflated mediocrity is hailed as a genius. Why, in comparison with him, Raff is a genius.' Albert Einstein's schoolmaster said of him, 'You will never amount to very much.'

The final words of this book (apart from the glossary, etc.) should act as an incentive to every investigator to carry on no matter what others may say. They are the last words of General J. Sedgwick at the battle of Spotsylvania. Looking at the enemy he said, 'They couldn't hit an elephant at this dist. . . .'

G

47

Glossary

Definitions are a kind of scratching and generally leave a sore place more sore than it was before.

Samuel Butler (d. 1902), *Note-Books* (1912)

Who is this that darkeneth counsel by words without knowledge?

Job 38:2

absorption costing   the allocation of fixed as well as variable costs when calculating the overall cost of products and services.

abstinence   the concept that by not using something that is available (e.g. a fast fax) or by failing to make a decision, an organization incurs a cost.

accepted batch listing   a listing of monetary amounts that has been accepted by a computer department on one specific day for processing on that day.

accountability   the implied or stated obligation to be answerable to a higher authority for the results achieved in the execution of delegated duties.

acoustic coupler   device attached to an ordinary telephone handset, enabling a (portable) terminal to be connected to a remote processor for transmitting data over a telephone network, by converting digital data into sound waves. Now largely replaced by direct coupling.

active   in continual and/or frequent use.

activity   (1) a specific work task; (2) in a critical path, a task using time and resources when moving from one event to another; (3) in computing, a read or write operation on a file.

activity ratio   (1) the percentages of time spent by a person on different tasks; (2) the percentage of records in a computer file that have been processed or moved during a specific time period.

activity sampling   a technique in which a number of sampling observations are made of people/equipment/processes to ascertain the percentages of time spent on different activities or delays.

Administrative Support Centre   a centralized office which provides typing, copying, mail handling, filing, microfilming, telephone answering, fax, and other clerical and personal services.

algorithm   a set of procedures or instructions to be followed when carrying out a specific task, especially a mathematical calculation or when solving a problem. Originally 'algorism' from al-Khwarizmi, the ninth-century Persian mathematician. Changed during the seventeenth century through the influence of the Greek 'arithmos', a number.

alphageometric   see *alphamosaic.*

alphamosaic   a method leading to the display on screens of pictures formed from small rectangles. Used mainly for videotex and teletext. Enables an inexpensive decoder to be used but leads to irregular shapes such as the staircase appearance of diagonal lines. Smoother outlines and infilling are obtained by using an alphageometric display. Better still is alphaphotographic coding but this needs more time for transmission and a more complex decoder. Alphamosaic is widely used in Europe; alphageometric is used by the Canadian Telidon and the American A T & T systems.

alphaphotographic   see *alphamosaic.*

amplitude modulation   a transmission technique in which the amplitude of a signal is the characteristic that is changed to transmit information.

analgesic   a system or computer program that carries out a long boring task with little human attention or activity.

analog(ue)   (1) a thing similar to something else in certain characteristics; (2) a machine using one type of movement to show some other type of change or movement (e.g. a clock, a car tachometer); (3) in computing, the use of electrical quantities (usually voltages) to represent the magnitude of numbers.

applications software   programs used for specific tasks (e.g. payroll) as opposed to general-purpose software that manages the working of the computer.

architecture   the overall design of a computer or communications network and the way in which the components relate to one another.

array   a list of numerical amounts, arranged in order of size (smallest to largest or vice versa).

assembler   a device or a program which translates a high-level language into machine language code that can be run on a particular computer.

asynchronous transmission   transmission of individual characters where each character has a start and a stop signal. The start signal switches on the receiver so that it is ready to receive the character. The stop signal at the end of each character switches the receiver off momentarily until it gets the start signal for the next character.

attenuation   a decrease in the magnitude of the power of a signal during transmission. This can lead to fading or signal loss. The attenuation of spurious signals assists communication.

attribute lists   a list of qualities of a system or object which can be compared with those qualities considered desirable.

automation   the use of equipment possessing feedback, to replace human mental and manual effort. Word first used in 1935 by D. S. Harder.

autonomous work group   a group of people to whom responsibility has been delegated for achieving certain objectives or performing certain tasks. Since some constraints are always present, the degree of autonomy is variable.

availability of service   the cost of a service must be balanced against the level of user satisfaction or expectation. A measure of quality of service is how often the service will be unavailable. A target, based on probabilities, can be set.

average traffic   a technical term for the average (mean) amount of traffic (E) in a communications system in a given period of time (T):

$$E = (nh)/T$$

where n = number of calls and h = mean holding time per call. In this sense 'holding' means taking place, not waiting.

489

back-end processing   computer processing of local, group, or in-house matter without passing the data outside a prescribed group or to outsiders.

back-office crunch   failure of a computer department or a service office to keep up with its workload, leading to a backlog.

bandwidth   the range of frequencies that can be handled by a communications channel. Nowadays usually used in the sense of the difference between the highest and lowest frequencies. Thus a voice channel has a bandwidth of 2700 Hz – the difference between the lowest (taken as 300 Hz) and the highest (taken as 3,000 Hz).

batch processing   the processing of transactions a group at a time instead of as they arise. Useful for control purposes but involves a delay between an event (e.g. removing an item from a store) and its appearance in the computer records.

baud rate   the number of pulses per second which can be transmitted in a communications system. Named after J. M. Emile Baudot.

Bildschirmtext   the West German public videotex service.

bit stream   the continuous transfer of binary digits along a communications channel.

boot   to get the initial instructions into computer memory when a program is loaded. Hence, to start a computer working on a routine. The word is an abbreviation of 'bootstrap'.

brainstorming   a technique utilizing the free use of creative thinking, in which a group of people interact to produce alternatives leading to solutions to problems.

breakpoint   the instant of time at which one element of a work cycle ends and the next one starts.

broadband channel   a channel with a wide bandwidth. For example, a domestic TV channel needs a bandwidth of 5.5 megahertz – about 1,500 times greater than that of a telephone system. Sometimes used for any channel wider than a voice channel. Also called 'wideband'.

broadband multiplexing channel   a channel with a bandwidth wide enough to accommodate a number of message signals, utilizing multiplexing. Thus a 2-gigahertz channel could accept half a million telephone channels, even allowing as much as 4,000 hertz for each telephone channel.

buffering   (1) copying the data on the usage magnetic stripe on a credit card, etc., then fraudulently using the card, and finally restoring the original data; (2) a similar computer misuse for personal gain; (3) using a temporary storage between two devices with different operating speeds.

bug   a program error or computer malfunction that interferes with the smooth running of a computer routine.

buy-out   the purchase of the shares of a company by its employees.

byte   a cluster of 8 bits used to represent one character in most computer systems. Hence usually used as a synonym for character when defining capacity of storage.

Captains   the Japanese public videotex system.

cats and dogs   products or services with low current sales or usage but with high stocks or costs.

CCITT (Comité Consultatif International de Téléphonie et de Télégraphie) an international body best known for setting and promulgating a group of series of telecommunications standards.

cellular radio a mobile telephone and data transmission service. A locality such as a town is divided into zones ('cells') each 3–15 km wide. Each zone has its own transmitter/receiver and handles users who are within the zone.

channel a link between two terminals over which communication can take place. A channel can be simple (such as two intercoms connected by a piece of wire) or complex (such as a broadband multiplexed channel).

character (1) distinguishing qualities of an object; (2) a symbol used in writing, such as a letter or digit, that can be uniquely represented in binary code; (3) such a symbol that is part of a standard data communications code.

chart of accounts a standardized system of account codes for assets, liabilities, capital, income and expenditures. The system can be expressed as a decimal code. The uniform code and definitions are mandatory in France as part of the 'plan comptable général' (general accountancy plan). The system is voluntary in Germany, where it originated.

check bit/digit/character a bit/digit/character that is added to a character or a block to assist error detection.

check study a relatively short time study taken with the aim of checking a proposed (or an existing) standard time value.

collision the event when two or more users try to transmit (usually in a local loop) at the same time.

Comité Consultatif International de Téléphonie et de Télégraphie see CCITT above.

common carrier a public or private company that provides the telecommunications services in a country or part of a country. In some countries this is the PTT or Post Office; in others it is kept separate.

communications satellite an artificial body placed in space in orbit above the earth that provides communications channels between users. Originally designed for audio communications only, they are now also used for television, fax, and other data.

compile to convert computer program instructions into machine language code.

cost–benefit analysis the measurement in monetary terms of resources required for an activity or purchase, which is then compared with the value of the benefit to be obtained from the activity or purchase.

cost effectiveness a measure of the resources needed to obtain a stated result compared with the level of resources needed to obtain similar types of results. The measurement is usually in monetary terms but may also include non-financial considerations.

critical examination a formal, systematic analysis of the current situation concerning an activity or problem with a view to later improvement.

crosstalk the situation when signals in one channel are accidentally picked up by another channel (e.g. the well-known telephone nuisance known as 'crossed lines').

G

cybernetics   the science of communication and control in animals and in machines and organizations. Word coined by Norbert Wiener (from the Greek for 'steersman'), an American mathematician (1894–1964) who was the pioneer of the science.

cyberphobia   an extreme fear of computers.

database   (1) a general term for any large body of data, usually relating to a specific area of interest; (2) a file of data held in a computer and structured in such a way that applications can access the data and update it without constraining its design.

database management   a system of file organization enabling data to be retrieved in the manner, style and format desired.

Datex   a group of public data transmission services in West Germany.

decision table   a matrix used to illustrate appropriate actions or results when certain conditions occur. Based on 'if . . . then' logic. An example would be '*if* student sits examination . . . *then* distribute results notification'.

decision tree   a diagram showing successive alternative decisions with results and probabilities associated with each alternative.

decoder   (1) a device which receives coded data and generates output in a form required for processing; (2) a device which receives electrical signals and generates output in a form required by the receiving terminal.

demodulator   a device that removes a carrier wave from a signal and then reconstructs the message.

dibit   two bits.

discounted cash flow   a technique of relating anticipated future income and expenditure of a project or purchase to a present value based on compounded rates of interest.

dumb terminal   a visual display unit on which information can be displayed but which has little or no processing capability.

dump   (1) an office of an unacceptably low standard; (2) to transfer responsibility for a mistaken action from a guilty to an innocent person; (3) to transfer or copy the contents of a computer store. This can be of various types, e.g. from internal memory to external store, from local micro to a central mainframe.

duplex   transmission between two terminals in both directions simultaneously.

effective time   time spent in the proper performance of a prescribed task. When spoken of in relation to a work quantification study, it is often expressed in percentage terms.

elapsed time   the total clock time between the start and the finish of a work quantification study (especially a time study or a rated activity sample).

element   a distinctive portion of a working activity. Often delineated by being between two stated break-points. The element and the breakpoints are selected so as to assist description, observation, measurement, calculation, analysis and synthesis.

electromagnetic wave   a wave of energy propagated in an electromagnetic field. Examples of electromagnetic waves are X-rays, visible light, radar and radio.

electronic funds transfer system (EFTS)   a generic term for computer systems that effect financial transactions (or data about such transactions). Such transfers usually involve more than one separate organization, especially more than one financial institution.

electronic mail   a system of point-to-point or person-to-person messages via terminals. Messages are entered (usually at a keyboard) by the sender, transmitted electronically and read when convenient by the recipient on a visual display unit.

email
E-mail }   two abbreviations for *electronic mail* (see above).

encoder   (1) a device that generates characters or bits to a defined code; (2) a device that translates signals into a bit-stream for transmission.

ergonomics   the science of the relationship of people and equipment/activities/ environment. Utilizes physiological and psychological knowledge. In some countries the term 'human factors engineering' is used instead. Word derived from the Greek 'ergon' (work) plus 'economics'.

Euronet   A European packet switching service, originally developed within the European Economic Community (EEC).

facsimile telegraphy   a method of sending and receiving graphics and text over a telecommunications network, by converting visual images into electrical signals and then converting them back again into a copy of the original.

fast cash   notes pre-counted and banded or bagged in specific amounts for rapid cash handling. Idea based on a copyrighted system originally called 'Fas-Cash'.

fax   abbreviation for *facsimile telegraphy* (see above).

feedback   the extraction of information from one part of a situation/process/equipment to modify the same situation/process/equipment so as to produce a desired result. Examples are using the temperature of an oven to increase or decrease the flow of electricity to achieve a desired temperature, or using students' comments to change a lecture to increase its effectiveness.

G

field   (1) an area of human activity, knowledge or interest; (2) a place away from an office (especially a head office) that is the normal place of work; (3) a group of one or more characters that comprise a piece of information (such as a job number, sale price) held in computer storage.

file   (1) a holder or cover for keeping papers together for future reference; (2) its contents; (3) a group of records in computer storage that can be used according to the contents of fields within the records.

financial instrument   any written document that is formal evidence of a legal financial agreement or action, or a document possessing monetary value.

first in, first out (FIFO)   (1) a convention that assumes that the first items received as part of inventory are the first ones used or sold; (2) the sequence in which messages are stored and retrieved in an electronic mail system.

frame   (1) the outlined limits of a project; (2) the amount of information that fills a screen; (3) in data transmission, the amount of information between error checks.

fugleman   (1) (formerly) a soldier used as an example for those recruits learning drill to follow; (2) any person who acts as a leader or example.

ghosting   the appearance of a second, shadow image on a screen.

ghosts   imaginary non-existent employees whose names appear on a payroll and whose 'salaries' are fraudulently collected. A fraud known to have existed in ancient Egypt, and one that still surfaces today.

GIGO (garbage in, garbage out)   a phrase used to illustrate the fact that if poor data is used as input to a system, then the resulting output will also be poor.

half-duplex   two-way data transmission which can only take place one way at a time.

handshaking   the process of establishing a link between a source and a destination for information communication.

hard copy   output in a permanent physical form (such as printing on paper).

hertz   cycles per second. Named after H. R. Hertz (1857–94), who did much early work on electromagnetic waves. The first letter of the word should be in lower case. Because the symbol for hertz is 'Hz', some people mistakenly write 'Hertz'. However, this only refers to waves with a wavelength of less than 2,000 m, or to a car-hire company started by John D. Hertz.

heuristic   problem solving by a step-by-step procedure based on previous experience or knowledge since no algorithm exists or is relevant. Word comes from the Greek 'heuriskein' (to discover).

high-level language   a programming language that in appearance resembles a normal spoken language such as English rather than the code used by computers.

holding time   the period of time that a particular call occupies a communication link or system.

holdover   work not completed in normal office hours, but which is processed by an evening or night shift. For work such as word processing this may have no ramifications, but legal considerations may follow for some accounting and financial work.

horizontal specialization   a form of work organization in which one person performs a few specialized tasks for a number of other people. For example, one person in an office may be responsible for checking all letters of credit, waybills and negotiable instruments for the whole office staff.

hypertext   a linking of related information so that one can leap from topic to topic and find related material in a database (unlike, say, word processors which use information in a linear manner). Hypertext creates a 'network' enabling cross-references and other related material to be accessed automatically. Access can be to any digitized material: text, graphics, video, audio. Concept originally initiated in 1965 by Ted Nelson.

icon   a representational picture of an object used instead of words on video displays.

inchoate   not fully developed or completed; recently begun.

ineffective time   time spent on any activity that is not part of or does not further a specified task, or time spent on no activity at all. When spoken of in relation to a work quantification study, it is often expressed in percentage terms.

information provider   an organization or person who supplies information for a videotex service.

information theory   the theoretical mathematics concerned with transmissions in a network.

in-plant communications   synonymous with *intra-locality communications* (see below).

inside work   activities or elements of work that can be carried out by a person while a machine is operating (e.g. loading paper into the hopper of a word processor while it is printing).

494

integrated digital exchange   an exchange based on digital technology (speech is converted from analog to digital for handling). Such exchanges are called 'integrated' because, being digital, they can be built to handle the full range of basic services (e.g. data, voice, telex, fax, videotex) in one trunk network. A less unwieldy phrase would be preferable.

intelligent terminal   a terminal that possesses storage and processing abilities, as well as transmission capability.

International Alphabet No. 2 (IA2)   a data communications code used mainly for telex communications.

International Alphabet No. 5 (IA5)   a data communications code for telegraphic and data transmission. It originated from a standard known as ASCII (American Standard Code for Information Interchange). This standard was then developed by the ISO (International Organization for Standardization) and by the CCITT, and ratified by them in 1968.

interpellator   (formerly) one who questions a member of the government on an aspect of government policy, even if this means interrupting the business of the day. Now used as an up-market alternative to 'investigator' or 'analyst'.

intralocality communications   communications by means of a private network within a specific location such as a group of offices. Such a network would not normally use public service facilities.

jitter   the condition in which the timing of bits in a digital signal is advanced or retarded.

job description   a written outline of the activities associated with the performance of a job. It may include targets, desirable levels of output, and levels of service to be attained.

G

job enrichment   an increase in the 'vertical' components of a job to make it more interesting, responsible and challenging.

job evaluation   analysing the components of a job with a view to ranking the relative value of different jobs, and ensuring that people have proper training and equipment for the performance of their jobs.

job specification   a written description of the essential qualities of a job and its holder (such as qualifications, duties, responsibilities, authority, knowledge requirements).

judder   (1) the condition of a printer when it moves slightly when printing successive characters; (2) the condition in fax when parts of the picture overlap owing to irregular picture scanning.

justification   (1) the rationale behind or defence of a past or proposed course of action; (2) typing or printing a document so that the left and right edges of written material are flush; (3) altering a signal bit rate so that it conforms with some other specific rate.

keypad   a device for entering a restricted group of characters and functions into a terminal or computer. A sort of mini-keyboard.

large-scale integration (LSI)   the combining of hundreds/thousands of electrical components onto a single piece ('chip') of material of small size.

last in, last out   opposite of *first in, first out* (see above).

lateral thinking   a method of thought based on trying to find new standpoints from which to view a problem, rather than by following the dictates of conventional logic.

local area network   a network providing communications between users within a defined locality. Such a network may be independent of public services.

local loop   a local area network using a broad bandwidth channel for communications between a large number of users. Often used for intralocality communications.

low-level language   a programming language that resembles the code used by computers rather than a recognizable normal spoken language, such as English.

marginal cost   the extra cost incurred from producing one extra unit of a product or service.

merit rating   the assessment of the performance or ability of people in the carrying out of their work, usually based on a pre-set system of factor comparison.

modem   a device that both modulates and demodulates transmitted messages.

modulator   a device that adds a carrier wave and converts a message into a form suitable for onward transmission.

motherboard   a circuit board containing a microprocessor, memory chip, and circuitry for handling basic tasks such as handling input/output signals.

multiple regression analysis   a mathematical calculation of the relationship between a set of values and those other sets of values which are thought to affect it.

multiplexing   the process whereby separate signal channels are combined into one composite stream.

multi-variate analysis   a generic term for those analytical techniques used to identify or to show the effect of a number of variables that interact.

multi-variate analysis, participation and structure (MAPS)   a management development tool in which participants define their tasks and groupings, and select preferred staff for working in these groups.

network   an interconnection of computer-based devices and systems to provide information services and transmissions covering a number of locations.

on-line   a device is on-line if it is directly connected to and hence under the control of the central processor.

on-line off-host   terminals operating without direct access to the central processor or database, but that can access an intermediate processor.

oops facility   the ability of some programs to undo changes just made to a record.

Open Systems Interconnection (OSI)   a standardized set of procedures for the exchange of information between computers, terminals, networks, etc.

operating system   a program permanently resident in a computer or communications system which controls the use of the hardware and facilitates the operating of other software.

opportunity cost   the cost of using a service, asset or effort in a less than optimum fashion; the cost of not changing or improving.

orphan   the last line of a paragraph which is printed as the first isolated line on a new page.

496

packet switching in network data transmission, the division of data into blocks of data ('packets'), routing these blocks along different arms of the network, and reassembling the packets into the correct sequence at their destination.

password a word, phrase or group of letters or digits that enable a user to gain access to a location, system, computer or data.

payback period the time that elapses before savings equals expenditure on a project or purchase.

philoxenic a definitely up-market word for 'user-friendly'. Derived from the Greek 'philos' (loving) and 'xenos' (strange).

pitch the number of characters printed per inch (per 2½ cm). The commonest ones are pica (10) and élite (12). Others include matrix condensed (16½) and proportional (11–17).

predetermined motion time system (PMTS) a work qualification technique in which pre-set times have been established for classified human physical movements and mental activities.

Prestel the British videotex service.

protocol a set of rules. In particular, a set of rules governing the way that information can flow in a system. Such rules cover 'syntax' (the structure of commands and responses), 'semantics' (the requests, responses and actions that users can perform), and 'timing' (the sequence and ordering of events).

public domain published work that is not subject to copyright or patents. Often used as a term for software donated by the author to the computer fraternity. Some of this is trivial (e.g. poorly constructed games) but some is very good. Interesting examples are PD PROLOG (for use with MS-DOS) and Abundance – a language originally designed for charities but which evolved for business use.

G

queuing theory the use of mathematical calculations and models in the analysis of service provision under conditions of varying demand and supply, where a waiting-line for service is involved. Examples are staffing of pay-toll booths, patient health care, the processing of court cases, and deciding how many tellers should be present at different times to service bank customers.

raster the pattern of lines formed by the movement of an electron beam inside a screen or camera when scanning a picture.

Regulation E the American regulation implementing the Electronic Fund Transfer Act 1978. This, plus later amendments, covers transfer documentation, error processing, pre authorized credits, debit and credit card issuance, etc.

return on investment (ROI) the net proceeds, profits or savings of a project or purchase compared with the amount of money spent. Usually expressed as a percentage.

Rule of 72 a quick approximation to calculate how long it takes for monetary or project investments to double in value, based on compound interest. If 72 is divided by the rate of interest or return, then the result is the number of years to double in value (e.g. $72 \div 12$ per cent = 6 years).

skimming (1) fraudulently removing small amounts of money from a large number of transactions or accounts and accumulating the results, usually in a false account; (2) fraudulently duplicating the encoded data on a plastic card (credit/debit/ID/smart).

smart card   a plastic card with an embedded microprocessor.

spooling   loading computer input or output temporarily into secondary storage ready for later transmission (e.g. between a computer and a printer).

Stakhanovism   a system designed to raise output by offering incentives to high-producing workers. Originated in the USSR. Named after A. G. Stakhanov, a Russian coalminer who in 1935 was the first to be awarded benefits under the system.

string diagram   a plan or model, to scale, of an office upon which a thread is used to trace and measure the path of staff or materials during a particular procedure or sequence of activities.

Strowger selectors   electromechanical devices used in early telephone exchanges to connect incoming and outgoing lines. Still used in a few countries where they have not yet been replaced by electronic methods. Named after A. Strowger, who developed an early mechanical relay in 1891.

synchronous transmission   a method of data transmission in which the transmitting and receiving points are kept in step with one another by means of a timing device. This allows the data to flow at a fixed rate without stopping and starting between each character.

techie   a person overly concerned with technical matters in the field of computers and advanced technology. An abbreviation of 'technician'. Usually used as a term of disparagement.

Telepac   the packet-switching service in Switzerland.

teletex   a standard for text and message transmission originating from the CCITT.

teletext   a broadcast service in which text and graphics can be received on a suitably adapted television set. The teletext signals are broadcast during the blank intervals of the normal television service unless using a dedicated channel.

terminal   any device able to send and/or receive data via a communications channel.

transceiver   a device that can both send (transmit) and receive information.

Transpac   the packet-switching service in France.

Universal Product Code   a machine-readable code consisting of a set of vertical lines ('bars').

user-friendly   refers to computer hardware or software designed for use by people who may lack computer knowledge and experience in depth. In the hands of advertisers, this has become a rather meaningless cliché.

value analysis   the examination of factors that make up the cost of a product or service with the aim of reducing the cost while still maintaining the ability to achieve the purpose of the product or service.

very large-scale integration (VLSI)   the combining of tens of thousands of electrical components onto a single piece ('chip') of material of small size.

videotex   a generic term for all forms of viewdata and teletext.

viewdata   a public information service in which users can access information stored in a particular computer via a suitably adapted television and their telephone.

virtual memory   the use of secondary storage devices which, in conjunction with a computer's primary storage, can give the appearance of effectively increasing the computer's storage capacity.

widow   in printing, a short line at the end of a paragraph, especially one that occurs as the top line of a page or column. To be avoided.

window   a rectangle within a display screen in which part of an application can be viewed and worked on independently. In appearance, rather like the small boxes on a television screen in which some producers still show secondary pictures.

work quantification   a generic term for techniques and models used in measuring the work content of working activities.

work measurement   the use of techniques to establish the time to carry out a task by a qualified person at a defined rate of working.

xerography   a photocopying process in which an electrostatic image of an original is formed on a selenium surface. A resinous powder is then cascaded over this surface, adhering to the charged area; this powder is transferred to paper, card or film where it is fixed by heat fusing. Word derived from the Greek 'xeros' (dry) and 'graphein' (to write).

x-height   in printing, the depth of a lower-case letter, ignoring any ascenders or descenders.

X-series   sets of telecommunications standards set by the CCITT. (See appendix.)

zero-base budgeting   a system of budgeting which starts from scratch without building on previous budgets.

G

48

Acronyms

It is one thing to abbreviate by contracting, another by cutting off.

Francis Bacon, *Of Dispatch* (1625)

ABC	automatic binary computer
ABL	accepted batch listing
ABRACADABRA	Abbreviations and Related Acronyms Associated with Defense, Astronautics, Business and Radio-electronics
ACD	automatic call distribution
ACH	automated clearing house
ACK/ack	acknowledge
ACSS	automated colour separation system
ACU	acknowledgement signal unit; automatic calling unit
ACV	actual cash value
ACWP	actual cost of work performed
A/D	analog to digital
adc	analog to digital converter
ADCP	advanced data communication protocol
ADS	accurately defined system
ADX	automatic digital/data exchange
AFT	automatic fund transfer
AFTN	aeronautical fixed telecommunications network
AG	Aktiengesellschaft
AGC	automatic gain control
AI	artificial intelligence
ALF	automatic letter facer
ALGOL	algorithmic language
ALPURCOMS	all-purpose communications system
ALU	arithmetic and logic unit
AM	amplitude modulation
AMI	alternative mark inversion
AML	amplitude modulation with noise limiter
AMW	average monthly wage
AN	account number
ANS	artificial neural system
ANSI	American National Standards Institute
AOCR	advanced optical character reader
AOT	advanced office technology
A/P	authority to pay
API	application program interface
APL	a programming language
APOTA	automatic positioning telemetering antenna
APSE	Ada programming support environment

AQL	acceptable quality level
ARIEL	automated real-time investments exchange
ARP	address resolution protocol
ARPA	Advanced Research Projects Agency
ARPANET	advanced research projects agency network
ARQ	answer-return query; automatic repeat request
ARR	average rate of return
AS	activity sampling
ASC	administrative support centre
ASCII	American Standard Code for Information Interchange
ASIC	application-specific integrated circuit
ASME	American Society of Mechanical Engineers
ASR	automatic send and receive
AT&T	American Telephone and Telegraph Company
ATC	average total cost
ATE	automatic test equipment
ATM	automatic teller machine
AVL	Adelson, Velskin and Landis
BAC	budget at completion
BAM	bidirectional associative memory
BAR	base address register
BASIC	Beginners' All-purpose Symbolic Instruction Code
BC	budgeted cost
BCD	binary coded decimal
BCH	bids per circuit per hour
BCWP	budget/budgeted cost of work performed
BCWS	budget/budgeted cost of work scheduled
BFO	beat-frequency oscillator
BGC	bank giro credit
BIN	bank identification number
BIOS	basic input–output system
bit	binary digit
BIU	bus interface unit
BLT	bit boundary block transfer
blit	(verb) to BLT
BM	basic minute
BMD	basic minute data
BMV	basic minute value
BNF	Backus Naur form
BOMP	bills of material processor
bps	bits per second
BS	backspace
BSC	binary synchronous communications
CA	contingency allowance
CAD	cash against documents; computer-aided design; computer-aided despatch/dispatch

G

CADE	computer-assisted data evaluation
CAI	computer-assisted/aided instruction
CAL	computer-aided learning
CAM	computer-aided manufacture/manufacturing
CAMMU	cache-memory management unit
C&D	cats and dogs
CAP	computer-aided print and production
Captains	character and pattern telephone access information network system
CATV	community antenna/aerial television
CBA	cost benefit analysis
CBCT	customer–bank communication channel
CBD	cash before delivery
CBI	computer-based instruction
CBMS	computer-based message system
CCA	current cost accounting
CCD	charge-coupled device
CCIR	Comité Consultatif International de Radio-communication
CCITT	Comité Consultatif International de Téléphonie et de Télégraphie
CCSA	common controlled switching arrangement
CDROM	compact disk read-only memory
CED	capacitance electronic disk
CEDEL	Centrale de Livraison de Valeurs Mobilières
CEM	cost and effectiveness method
CF	certainty factor
CGA	colour graphics adapter
CGI	computer-generated image
CHILL	CCITT high-level language
CIL	call identification line
CIM	computer-integrated manufacturing; computers in manufacturing
CIRC	cross-interleaved Reed–Solomon code
CISC	complex instruction set computer
CISCOBOL	compact interactive standard COBOL
CLP	constraint logic program/programming
CLUT	colour look-up table
CMCS	computer-mediated communication system
CMOS	complementary metal oxide semiconductor
CMY	cyan, magenta, yellow
CNC	computer numerically control/controlled
COBOL	common business oriented language
CoCoA	continuously contemporary accounting
CODASYL	Conference for Data Systems Languages
COLS	communications for on-line systems
COM	computer output (onto) microfilm
COV	computer output on video
CPA	critical path analysis

CPE	customer premises equipment
cpi	characters per inch
CPM	critical path method
CP/M	control program for microcomputers
cpm	cards per minute
cps	centimetres per second; characters per second; cycles per second
CPU	central processing unit
CR	carriage return
CRAG	control and row address group
CRC	current replacement cost; cyclic/cyclical redundancy check
CSDN	circuit switched data network
CSF	critical success factor
CSMA	carrier sense multiple access
CSMA/CD	CSMA with collision detection
CT	computerized tomography
CUG	closed user group
CV	cost variance
CVP	cost–volume–profit (analysis)
cw	carrier wave
D/A	documents against acceptance; digital to analog
DAC	data analysis and control
dac	digital to analog converter
DAR	direct access register
DASD	direct access storage device
DASS	digital access signalling standard
DAT	digital audio tape
DATEL	data telecommunications
DAVFU	direct access vertical format unit
dB	decibel
DBA	database administrator
DBMS	database management system
DBS	direct broadcast satellite
DCE	data circuit terminating equipment
DCF	discounted cash flow
DCO	digitally controlled oscillator
DDD	direct distance dialling
DDE	direct data entry
DDL	data description language
DDP	direct deposit of payroll
DDS	digital data service
DEA	data encryption algorithm
DEL	delete
DES	data encryption standard
DEUCE	digital electronic universal computing engine
DFC	data flow control
DFD	data flow diagram
DFG	diode function generator

G

DI	disable interrupt
diac	diode alternating current
DI/CMOS	dielectrically isolated CMOS
DID	direct inward dialling
DIF	data interchange format
DIL	dual in-line package (usually DIP)
DIP	dual in-line package
DLC	data link control
DLE	data link escape
DLI	display-list interpreter
DMA	direct memory access
DMI	dot matrix impact
DMMU	discrete memory management unit
DOS	disk operating system
D/P	documents against payment
DPNSS	digital private networks signalling system
DPS	distributed processing system; document preparation system
dpx	duplex
DRAM	dynamic random access memory
DRAW	direct read after write
DRCS	dynamically redefinable character set
DSB	direct satellite broadcasting
dsb	double sideband
DSI	digital speech interpolation
DSL	data sub-language
DSO	digital storage oscilloscope
DSS	decision support systems
DSU	data service unit
DTA	direct tape access
DTE	data terminal equipment
DTL	diode transistor logic
DUART	dual universal asynchronous receiver-transmitter
DUT	device under test
EAC	estimate at completion
EAN	European article numbering
E&OE	errors and omissions excepted
EAR	employee attitude research
EAROM	electrically alterable read-only memory
EAX	electronic automatic exchange
EBCDIC	extended binary coded decimal interchange code
EBR	electron beam recording
ECC	error correction coding
ECL	emitter coupled logic
ECMA	European Computer Manufacturers' Association
ECR	electronic cash register; embossed character reader
ECS	European communications satellite
EDP	electronic data processing

EDS	exchangeable disk store
EEPLD	electrically erasable programmable logic device
EEPROM	electrically erasable programmable read-only memory
EFS	external file system
EFT(S)	electronic funds transfer (system)
EFTPOS	electronic funds transfer at the point of sale
EGA	enhanced graphics adapter
EI	enable interrupt
EIA	Electronic Industries' Association
EIRP	equivalent isotropically radiated power
EIS	executive information system
EIT	extended intelligent terminal
ELD	electroluminescent display
EM	electronic mail; end of medium
EMAIL	electronic mail
EMS	electronic message system; expanded memory specification
ENIAC	electronic numerical integrator and calculator
ENQ	enquiry
EOB	end of block
EOC	end of conversion signal
EOF	end of file
EOM	end of message
EOQ	economic order quantity
EOR	end of run
EOT	end of transmission
EPLD	erasable programmable logic device
EPM	equivalent protection margin
EPOS	electronic point-of-sale
EPR	executive performance review
EPROM	erasable programmable read-only memory
EPS	electronic publishing system
ERNIE	electronic random number indicator equipment
ERP	effective radiated power
ES	economic study
ESC	escape
ESDI	enhanced small-device interface
ESPRIT	European Strategic Program on Research in Information Technology
ETB	end of transmission block
ETC	estimate to complete
ETH	Eidgenossische Technische Hochschule
ETX	end of text
EUC	end-user computing
EUTELSAT	European Telecommunications Satellite (Organization)
EV	economic value
4GL	fourth-generation language
FAC	forecast at completion

G

fax	facsimile
FCC	Federal Communications Commission
FCS	frame check sequence
FDC	floppy disk controller
FDM	frequency division multiplexing
FDMA	frequency division multiple access
FEP	front-end processor
FET	field effect transistor
FF	form feed
FGL	forms-generation language
FIFO	first in, first out
FILO	first in, last out
FIR	finite impulse response
FLSS	forms length select switch
FM	facilities management; frequency modulation
FOL	first-order logic
FORTRAN	formula translator
FOSDIC	film optical sensing device
FP	floating-point
FPD	full-page display
FPP	fixed path protocol; floating-point processor
FPU	floating-point unit
FS	feasibility study; file separator
FSK	frequency shift keying
FTC	forecast to complete
GAAP	generally accepted accounting principles
GADS	gate array design system
GCOS	general comprehensive operating system
GEOS	graphic environment operating system
GIGO	garbage in, garbage out
GKS	graphical kernel system
GmbH	Gesellschaft mit beschränkter Haftung
GMD	Gesellschaft für Mathematik und Datenverarbeitung
GOOF	general on-line oriented function
GPS	general problem solver
GRN	goods received note
GS	group separator
GSS	geo-stationery satellite
GTS	global telecommunication system; Greenwich time signal
HBR	Harvard Business Review
HDL	hardware description language
HDLC	high-level data link control
HDTV	high-definition television
HF/hf	high frequency
HIPO	hierarchical plus input processing output
HLDA	hold acknowledge

HORUS	higher OSIRIS ranges and unlinked specials
HSF	High Sierra format
hsp	high-speed printer
hsr	high-speed reader
HT	horizontal tabulation
Hz	hertz
IA	investment appraisal
IAB	indirect address buffer
IAL	international algebraic language
IAR	indirect address register
ias	immediate access storage
IBG	inter-block gap
IBI	International Bureau for Information
IBM	International Business Machines
IC/ic	integrated circuit
ICAM	integrated computer-aided manufacturing
ICOT	Institute for New Generation Computer Technology
IDA	integrated digital access
IDIMS	interactive digital image manipulation system
IDMS	integrated database management system
IDP	integrated data processing
IE	industrial engineering
IEC	International Electrotechnical Commission
IFP	Illinois functional programming
IGES	initial graphics exchange specification
IGFET	insulated gate field effect transistor
IIL/I^{2}L	integrated injection logic
IKBS	intelligent knowledge-based system
ILO	International Labour Office
IMIS	integrated management information system
IMS	information management system
INMARSAT	international maritime satellite
INRIA	Institut National de Recherche en Informatique et en Automatique
INTELSAT	international telecommunications satellite
i/o	input/output
IOCS	input/output control system
IOL	interactive on-line
IP	information provider
IPC	inter-process communications
IPOT	inductive potential divider
IPSS	international packet switching service
IR	instruction register
IRM	information resource management
IRR	internal rate of return
ISAM	index sequential-access method
ISB	independent side-band

G

ISDN	integrated services digital network
ISO	International Organization for Standardization
ISPABX	integrated services PABX
ISPC	international sound programme centre
ISR	interrupt service routine
IT	information technology; ineffective time
it	information theory
ITC	international television centre
ITDM	intelligent time division multiplexor
ITU	International Telecommunications Union (now UIT)
IW	inside work
JAJO	January, April, July, October
JCL	job control language
JD	job description
JE	job evaluation
JFET	junction field-effect transistor
JIT	job instruction training; just-in-time
k	kilo
kb/kB/KB	kilobytes
kc	kilocycle
kcs	kilocharacters per second; kilocycles per second
kHz	kilohertz
KSR	keyboard send and receive
KWIC	keyword in context
KWOC	keyword out of context
LAN	local area network
LAP	link access procedure
LAPB	link access procedure B
laser	light amplification by stimulated emission of radiation
lbs	*lectori benevolo salutem*
LCC	leadless chip carrier
LCD	liquid crystal display
LCGN	logical channel group number
LCS	least-cost scheduling; liquid-crystal shutter
LE	local exchange
LED/led	light-emitting diode
LF	line feed; low frequency
LIFO	last in, first out
LIM	Lotus-Intel-Microsoft
LIS	linear image sensor
LISP	list processing
LNA	low-noise amplifier
LOC/loc	lines of code
LP	linear programming
LPC	linear predictive coding

lpi	lines per inch
LPM	lines per minute
LRC	longitudinal redundancy checking
LRP	long-range planning
LRU	least recently used
LSB	least significant bit; lower side band
LSD	least significant digit
LSI	large-scale integration
LTM	long-term memory
MA	management accounting
MAC	multi-access computing
MAP	manpower allocation procedure; manufacturing automation protocol
MAPS	multi-variate analysis, participation and structure
MARECS	maritime European communications satellite
Mb/MB	megabyte
MBMS	model base management system
MBO/MbO	management by objectives
MC	machine control/controlled
MCCD	message cryptographic check digit
MCGA	multicolour graphics adapter
MCS	maritime communications service
MD	management development
MDNS	managed data network service
MDT	mobile digital terminal
MFLOPS	million floating-point operations per second
MF	multi-frequency
MHz	megahertz
MICR	magnetic ink character recognition
MIDI	musical instrument digital interface
mips	million instructions per second
MIS	management information system; marketing information system
MIT	miniature inquiry terminal
MITI	Ministry of International Trade and Industry
MM	materials management; milli-minute
mm	milli-minute
MMD	milli-minute data
MML	man–machine language
MMU	memory management unit
modem	modulator–demodulator
MOS	metal oxide semiconductor
MOSFET	MOS field effect transistor
MPFI	multi-purpose financial institution
MR	market research; merit rating
MRA	multiple regression analysis
MRI	magnetic resonance imaging
MRP	materials requirements planning

G

MS	management services; method study
MSB	most significant bit
MSD	most significant digit
MS/DOS	Microsoft disk operating system
MSI	medium-scale integration
MST	methods, skills, time
MT	management training
MTBF	mean time between failures
MTM	methods time measurement
MTTR	mean time to repair
MUM	methodology for unmarked manufacturing
MUX	multiplexer/multiplexor
MVS	multiple virtual storage
MWCA	monetary working capital adjustment
NAK	negative acknowledge
NAPLPS	North American presentation level protocol standard
NCR	no carbon required; National Cash Register
NF	noise factor
NIMBY	not in my back yard
NLP	natural language program/processing
NLQ	near letter quality
NMC	network management centre
NMR	nuclear magnetic resonance
NPV	net present value
NRV	net realizable value
NRZ	non-return to zero
NRZI	non-return to zero inverted
NTSC	National Television Systems Committee
NUA	network user address
NUI	network user identity/identifier
NW	not working/wanted
OA	office automation
O&M	organization and methods
OBC	on-board computer
OCR	optical character recognition/reader; overhead cost reduction
OCS	optical character scanner
OD	optical disc/disk; organization development
OEM	original equipment manufacturer
Oftel	Office of Telecommunications
OGC	office group capability
OJT	on-the-job training
OLRT	on-line real-time
OLTT	on-line teller terminal
OOPL	object-oriented programming language
OOPS	object-oriented programs/programming
oso	one sheet of paper

510

OPROM	optical programmable read-only memory
OR	operational research
OROM	optical read-only memory
OS	organization structure/study; operating system
OSA	open systems architecture
OSI	open systems interface/interconnection
OSIRIS	office standards including rest, incidentals, and supervision
OT	office technology; operative training
OTIS	operation, transport, inspection, storage
OVA	overhead/office value analysis
OW	outside work
OWM	office work measurement
PABX	private automatic branch exchange
PAD	packet assembler–disassembler/assembly–disassembly
PAL	phase alternation by line; programmable array logic
PAM	pulse amplitude modulation
PAR	participation–achievement–reward
PBR	payment by results
PBT	push-button telephone
PBX	private branch exchange
PC	personal computer; production control; program counter
%C	percentage complete
PCB	printed circuit board
PCC	personal computer co-processor
PCM	plug-compatible manufacturer; pulse code modulation
PCMI	photochromic micro image
PDE	portable data entry
PDI	picture description instruction
PDL	page description language
PDN	public data network
PEP	paperless electronic payment
PERT	project evaluation and review technique
PFO	program-forming operations
PGA	pin grid array
PHIGS	programmers hierarchical interactive graphics standard
PIA	peripheral interface adapter
PIN	personal identity/identification number
PIP	path independent protocol; profit improvement programme
PIPS	paperless item processing system
PISO	parallel in, serial out
PL/1	programming language one
PLA	programmable logic array
PLC	product life cycle; programmable logic controller
PLD	programmable logic device
PLE	programmable logic element
PLS	programmable logic sequencer(s)
PM	personnel management

G

PMBX	private manual branch exchange
PMTS	predetermined motion time system
p–n	positive–negative
PNA	project network analysis
PNT	project network techniques
POACH	personal computer on a chip
POS	point-of-sale
POSDCORB	planning, organizing, staffing, directing, co-ordinating, reporting and budgeting
POTS	plain old telephone system
PP	project planning
pp	*per procurationem*
PPS	page printing system
PRESS	Prolog equation solving system
PRF	pulse repetition frequency
PROLOG	programming logic
PROM	programmable read-only memory
PS	personal system; production study
PSE	packet switching exchange
PSK	phase shift keying
PSS	packet switching service; packet switch stream
PSTN	public switched telephone network
PTT	postes, télégraphes et télécommunications; postes, téléphones et télégraphes; post, telephone, telecommunications
Pty	proprietary
PUT	programmable unijunction transistor
PVC	permanent virtual circuit
PWR	power
QA	quality assurance
QAM	quadrative/quadrature amplitude modulation
QC	quality control
QPSK	quadrature phase shift keying
RA	relaxation/rest allowance
RADAR	radio detection and ranging
RAM	random access memory
RAMPS	resource allocation in multi-project scheduling
R&D	research and development
RAP	remote access point
RAS	rated activity sampling
RBP	remote batch printer
RBT	remote batch terminal
RCN	remote computing network
RDOS	real-time disk operating system
RDS	radio data system
rf	radio-frequency
RFP	request for proposal

RGB	red, green, blue
RIP	raster image processor
RISC	reduced instruction set computer
RIU	ring interface unit
RJE	remote job entry
RLL	run length limit/limited
RNG	random number generator
RO	receive only
ROC	recommended operating conditions
ROCE	return on capital employed
ROI	return on investment
ROM	read-only memory
RPN	reverse Polish notation
RS	record separator; requirement specification
RSI	repetitive strain injury
RTL	resistor transistor logic
RTOS	real-time operating system
RTTY	radio teletype
SA	société anonyme; società anonima
Sarl	société à responsabilité limitée
SBS	small business system
SC	stock control
SCL	supervisory/system control language
SCPC	single channel per carrier
SCR	silicon controlled rectifier
SCU	system control (signal) unit
SD	space division
SDL	specification and description language
SDLC	synchronous data link control
SECAM	séquentiel couleur à mémoire
SFA	success factor analysis
SI	shift in
SIMO	simultaneous motions
SIP	single in-line package
SIPO	serial in, parallel out
SITA	Société Internationale de Télécommunication Aéronautique
SITREP	situation report
SM	standard minute
SMD	surface mount/mounted device
SMV	standard minute value
SNA	systems network architecture
SO	shift out
SOH	start of heading
SOM	start of message
SPC	stored program control
SPRS	signal processing router-scheduler
SQL	structured query language

G

SR&CC	strikes, riots and civil commotion
SS	satellite switched
SSB/ssb	single sideband
SSI	small-scale integration
SSU	subsequent signal unit
STD	subscriber trunk dialling
STDM	synchronous time division multiplexing
S–T–S	space–time–space
STX	start text
SU	signal unit
SV	schedule variance
SVC	switched virtual cell
SWIFT	Society for World-wide Inter-bank Financial Telecommunications
SWOT	strengths, weaknesses, opportunities, threats
SYN	synchronous idle
SYU	synchronization signal unit
TACS	total access communications system
TASI	time-assigned speech interpolation
TC	transmission control code
TCU	transmission control unit
TD	time division
TDM	time division multiplexing/multiplexor
TDMA	time division multiple access
TF	technological forecasting
TFP	total factor productivity
TLU	table look-up
TM	Turing machine
TMS	text message system
TOF	top of form
TOP	technical and office protocol
TP	transaction processing
TPIN	true personal identification number
TPM	teleprocessing monitor
triac	triode alternating current
TRT	text retrieval terminal
TS	time study
TTL	transistor–transistor logic
TTW/ttw	through the wall
TTY	teletype
TU	temps universel
TWT	travelling wave tube
TWX	two-way exchange/transmission
UCSD	University of California, San Diego
UDP	user datagram protocol

UEC	Union Européenne des Experts Comptables Économiques et Financiers
UHF	ultra high frequency
UIT	Union Internationale des Télécommunications
UJT	unijunction transistor
ULA	uncommitted logic array
UNIVAC	universal automatic computer
UPC	universal product code
UPS	uninterruptible power source/supply
US	unit separator
UT	universal time; unoccupied time
UVEPROM	ultraviolet erasable programmable read-only memory
VA	value added
VAN(S)	value added network (service)
VAT	value added tax
VCO	voltage-controlled oscillator
VDT	video/visual display terminal
VDU	video/visual display unit
VFM	value for money
VFT	voice frequency telegraph
VGA	video graphics array
VGC	video graphics controller
VHD	very high-density disks
VHF	very high frequency
VHSIC	very high-speed integrated circuits
VLSI	very large-scale integration
VM	virtual memory
VMS	voice messaging system
VRC	visible record computer
VRS	voice recognition system
VRT	volume-rendering technique
VSB	vestigial sideband modulation
VS/DOS	virtual storage disk operating system
VT	vertical tabulation
VVLSI	very very large-scale integration
VX	videotex
WA	with average
WAN	wide area network
WATS	wide area telephone service
WCS	write-controlled storage
WDV	written-down value
WISC	writable instruction set computer
WM	work measurement
WMO	World Meteorological Office
WORM	write once, read many
WP	word processing/processor

G

WPA	with particular average
WS	work study
WYSIWYG	what you see is what you get
XACT	X automatic code translation
x'd	crossed out
XMIT	transmit
XS/xs	excess; expenses
xtran	experimental language
YP	year's purchase
ZB	zero beat
ZBB	zero-base budgeting
ZD	zero defect(s)
zd	zener diode
ZIF	zero insertion force
ZIP/zip	zoning improvement plan
ZKP	zero-knowledge proof
ZPT	zero power test

49

APPENDICES

For reference purposes, certain material has been assembled in this final chapter as a group of appendices. These are:

I   Random numbers
      (a) 01–25
      (b) 0–9
II   Measurement
      (a) Measurement prefixes
      (b) Radio frequencies
      (c) Conversion factors
III   Paper sizes
IV   Retention periods
V   Body dimensions
VI   The electromagnetic system
VII CCITT standards series
VIII Present value factors

G

Appendix I

■ RANDOM NUMBERS

(a) 01–25

12 25 07 18 13	06 21 17 05 11	20 02 19 14 08
03 16 01 22 24	09 15 04 10 23	04 21 16 13 24
20 22 19 02 17	06 16 11 25 15	13 08 22 02 20
23 10 01 12 08	12 17 06 09 07	03 10 05 24 11
15 21 07 19 14	01 18 23 25 05	03 14 18 04 09
06 09 19 14 24	24 08 17 21 04	25 18 13 12 02
20 05 01 09 07	23 08 01 19 15	10 15 04 17 25
16 05 03 11 13	16 02 20 07 14	03 10 22 12 22
18 06 23 11 21	23 17 19 25 13	02 23 09 05 17
13 07 25 02 06	19 03 23 06 16	25 13 25 20 11
16 12 18 08 11	24 21 09 04 20	16 19 23 04 12
18 24 06 07 17	23 20 07 03 06	13 11 05 16 01
25 02 20 17 04	22 23 06 10 21	11 10 09 25 08
18 21 17 22 02	02 12 06 24 14	04 13 06 21 21
11 05 10 15 12	05 14 15 08 09	02 19 02 13 11
21 25 10 04 24	19 01 07 02 12	24 12 04 12 15
09 24 07 10 20	17 14 20 05 18	05 23 16 12 25
15 02 20 11 04	01 10 23 20 08	05 16 08 04 22
19 11 21 19 05	22 18 02 16 10	04 22 13 03 22
13 21 04 21 12	02 03 11 02 23	12 19 05 08 19
12 12 10 11 04	11 17 01 16 10	06 02 06 01 10
22 17 08 16 17	08 02 20 12 03	03 22 07 14 19
05 09 07 04 01	15 03 13 07 08	01 22 12 13 15
11 18 12 08 06	16 05 11 17 02	16 22 09 13 17
05 01 16 11 01	19 06 08 16 02	21 01 08 02 13
15 10 25 03 17	14 20 04 21 07	18 03 14 13 15
19 15 06 10 18	16 07 22 01 11	03 23 19 09 14
22 06 18 14 22	04 15 25 07 08	25 01 20 24 05
03 24 14 09 20	20 14 04 24 21	05 25 13 03 18
23 08 15 03 17	14 14 09 13 01	25 06 10 18 03
23 01 15 07 18	15 21 10 24 09	01 12 24 10 19
18 03 22 07 21	20 17 08 23 15	16 22 14 23 09
01 24 06 20 14	13 23 07 18 05	15 24 19 14 17
18 04 21 24 09	14 01 05 25 10	03 17 12 25 02
07 21 05 17 24	09 23 01 16 06	12 08 19 02 25
20 10 16 03 18	10 23 04 08 21	20 01 12 13 07
04 14 18 11 24	17 04 13 21 11	11 21 06 08 25
22 18 09 20 15	14 23 14 22 02	22 15 05 19 02
09 24 06 15 07	21 16 15 19 02	14 01 22 13 04
03 17 06 16 19	13 07 12 10 17	20 15 03 18 23

518

(b) 0–9

```
08 38 54 24 18    58 37 31 06 56    71 44 40 82 13    92 20 80 33 36
03 79 89 98 70    43 60 23 26 66    24 22 28 13 19    51 45 60 37 57
61 51 01 48 71    01 65 06 99 61    22 46 97 36 74    02 79 57 28 20
32 91 80 88 05    79 02 03 98 01    73 24 64 93 10    89 20 22 63 06
02 01 40 52 11    10 44 21 75 99    48 54 10 22 50    91 51 72 00 32

23 82 20 59 72    39 81 75 81 14    76 14 81 33 00    64 44 54 74 20
52 31 58 35 23    94 72 30 75 58    94 11 19 53 58    19 75 75 41 16
64 44 07 28 80    82 18 17 65 28    71 68 56 87 00    37 53 95 39 82
95 88 30 69 41    64 95 07 66 71    16 66 89 08 98    36 93 88 41 05
08 94 72 94 49    34 13 46 66 96    56 82 82 06 89    81 37 10 26 69

77 72 95 38 18    67 74 80 38 11    62 47 37 96 84    72 94 27 99 34
56 56 75 86 05    45 48 57 99 62    63 25 12 53 26    88 90 91 48 56
26 00 04 00 56    46 88 94 84 67    91 32 15 96 38    42 73 51 62 74
87 89 34 72 93    28 64 96 40 62    00 21 83 99 85    56 98 95 58 68
38 71 25 75 50    15 24 98 86 30    90 62 59 61 38    74 61 25 02 94

01 14 74 35 79    10 24 97 25 21    54 23 39 36 07    54 85 94 14 33
53 48 85 29 11    69 57 67 42 15    32 96 12 45 11    84 94 77 97 33
18 61 63 54 15    71 38 21 82 62    93 82 80 53 58    14 16 02 06 97
22 30 23 04 54    96 04 78 71 74    55 24 62 76 34    47 07 47 36 54
36 16 74 69 17    97 96 27 80 72    48 65 69 13 70    12 44 31 90 67

20 99 08 89 69    20 10 74 84 90    58 63 05 19 72    53 05 32 94 82
90 06 27 29 76    07 23 29 72 35    66 16 75 30 17    19 61 85 61 46
13 04 36 43 11    94 12 75 23 86    49 70 32 35 69    92 33 77 63 65
40 15 38 76 59    84 72 66 59 14    27 93 89 81 60    41 69 83 24 02
02 88 67 96 76    75 02 42 45 22    26 69 03 91 48    97 45 96 07 24

82 26 16 96 81    15 52 76 61 96    92 56 25 47 21    48 01 50 45 53
33 91 30 46 76    90 65 94 58 42    68 69 60 73 86    12 57 28 23 84
37 38 69 83 42    24 32 49 79 98    96 60 46 35 76    55 83 15 29 42
54 34 15 45 50    14 32 95 94 73    42 98 14 34 48    22 95 69 37 35
36 64 40 89 31    76 55 88 53 64    70 18 11 78 40    02 92 28 62 33

59 47 70 23 80    23 90 48 08 68    01 20 35 15 57    52 90 52 19 69
29 94 78 91 45    91 39 40 52 48    38 36 60 65 57    39 66 61 04 38
15 65 15 12 45    71 85 24 67 41    26 18 50 79 26    42 94 49 93 63
75 47 71 18 09    98 76 74 38 09    38 05 56 58 34    07 69 06 18 96
25 74 81 70 20    43 83 08 01 56    42 18 83 23 86    37 88 00 80 19

94 82 80 18 92    45 76 44 67 86    25 89 30 60 77    94 14 33 81 03
87 49 27 93 60    12 58 07 51 32    39 45 19 31 18    78 15 84 63 98
57 97 80 29 98    07 65 49 60 95    66 63 89 05 82    54 70 18 04 74
43 99 88 82 19    56 53 13 14 84    22 01 86 63 65    78 56 18 03 14
40 19 21 99 95    61 73 69 45 93    65 85 13 06 21    03 54 55 75 47

39 49 72 98 80    96 47 55 32 54    11 82 12 11 48    07 89 80 44 54
13 47 63 14 64    35 80 16 37 52    03 58 62 17 60    63 42 62 76 01
65 72 29 66 83    92 34 65 91 53    67 30 16 90 84    09 14 63 92 13
71 93 57 08 56    93 74 55 99 29    88 59 59 13 18    34 30 36 18 41
45 50 19 43 78    91 37 03 08 30    80 13 54 24 26    18 81 79 12 53

98 21 42 07 25    11 54 77 08 26    99 24 21 95 27    89 60 62 81 56
83 38 80 32 39    08 19 78 39 52    15 88 61 48 46    08 11 42 64 98
39 49 19 12 91    66 85 78 81 38    60 30 79 35 39    06 36 09 09 94
31 98 77 97 44    30 41 54 07 93    34 00 02 52 96    72 44 86 11 48
22 92 16 76 75    25 61 73 27 64    07 21 28 27 03    75 35 07 19 09
```

G

Appendix II

■ MEASUREMENT

(a) Measurement prefixes

International units of measurement are initially based on the second, the kilogram and the metre. These SI units (Système International d'Unités) use prefixes to show magnitude, such as millimetre, decagram, nanosecond. The prefixes are:

Multiple	Prefix	Multiple	Prefix		Submultiple	Prefix	Submultiple	Prefix
10	deca-	10^9	giga-		10^{-1}	deci-	10^{-9}	nano-
10^2	hecto-	10^{12}	tera-		10^{-2}	centi-	10^{-12}	pico-
10^3	kilo-	10^{15}	peta-		10^{-3}	milli-	10^{-15}	femto-
10^6	mega-	10^{18}	exa-		10^{-6}	micro-	10^{-18}	atto-

(b) Radio frequencies

In communications, the following terms are frequently met:

LF	low frequency	30 kilohertz to 300 kilohertz
MF	medium frequency	300 kilohertz to 3 megahertz
HF	high frequency	3 megahertz to 30 megahertz
VHF	very high frequency	30 megahertz to 300 megahertz
UHF	ultra high frequency	300 megahertz to 3 gigahertz
SHF	super high frequency	3 gigahertz to 30 gigahertz

(c) Conversion factors

To convert Imperial measures to metric, quantities should be **multiplied** by the factors shown:

From	To	Factor	From	To	Factor
inches	millimetres	25.4	miles	kilometres	1.6093
	centimetres	2.54	sq. miles	sq. kilometres	2.59
sq. inches	sq. millimetres	645.16	nautical miles	kilometres	1.852
	sq. centimetres	6.4516	acres	sq. metres	4046.9
cu. inches	cu. millimetres	1638.71		hectares	0.40469
	cu. centimetres	16.3871	UK pints	litres	0.5683
feet	centimetres	30.48	UK gallons	litres	4.5461
	metres	0.3048	US gallons	litres	3.785
sq. feet	sq. centimetres	929.03	ounces	grams	28.3495
	sq. metres	0.092903	pounds	grams	453.59
cu. feet	cu. metres	0.028317		kilograms	0.45359
yards	metres	0.9144	miles/hour	kilometres/hour	1.6093
sq. yards	sq. metres	0.83613	knots	kilometres/hour	1.852
cu. yards	cu. metres	0.76456	°F	°C	0.55556, after subtracting 32.

To convert from metric to Imperial, **divide** by the factors shown above.

Appendix III

■ PAPER SIZES

The International Standard Paper sizes are based on a sheet of paper known as 'A0' and which measures 1,189 mm × 841 mm. By successively cutting this and folding sheets into half, a standard set of paper sizes is obtained. This standard set has the following dimensions:

Name	Size in mm	Name	Size in mm
A0	1189 × 841	A4	297 × 210
A1	841 × 594	A5	210 × 148
A2	594 × 420	A6	148 × 105
A3	420 × 297	A7	105 × 74

These sizes are all 'trimmed' sizes – guillotined, ready for use.

The standard set of envelope sizes is as follows:

Name	Size in mm	Name	Size in mm
C3	458 × 324	B6	176 × 125
B4	353 × 250	C6	162 × 114
C4	324 × 229	DL	220 × 110
B5	250 × 176	C7/6	162 × 81
C5	229 × 162	C7	114 × 81
B6/C4	324 × 125		

G

Paper for computer printers can be either cut-sheet or in the format of continuous paper. Sizes of paper available are:

Cut-sheet paper

Size in mm	Quoted size (in inches)
216 × 279	8½ × 11
216 × 356	8½ × 14
279 × 432	11 × 17

Continuous paper

Size in mm	Quoted size (in inches)	Size in mm	Quoted size (in inches)	Size in mm	Quoted size (in inches)
Friction feed		Sprocket feed		Word processing	
216 × 279	8½ × 11	216 × 279	8½ × 11	241 × 89	9½ × 3½
352 × 279	13⅞ × 11	216 × 89	8½ × 3½	241 × 140	9½ × 5½
		241 × 279	9½ × 11	241 × 178	9½ × 7
		251 × 279	9⅞ × 11	241 × 279	9½ × 11
		298 × 216	11¾ × 8½	241 × 356	9½ × 14
		378 × 216	14⅞ × 8½	305 × 216	12 × 8½
		378 × 279	14⅞ × 11	378 × 279	14⅞ × 11

521

Appendix IV

■ RETENTION PERIODS

Suggested retention periods for data are as follows:

Contracts/agreements	Under seal – 12 years after expiry. Others – 6 years after expiry
Title deeds and other property documents	12 years after connection with property ceases
Trade mark documents	Indefinitely
Corporate documents	Indefinitely

    (Balance sheets, P&L accounts, Minutes, Registers, Powers of Attorney, Investments, Share registration, Pension Fund)

Insurance:

Policies	3 years after lapse
Schedules	10 years
Radiation claims	31 years
Common law claims	7 years after claim completion
Claims correspondence	3 years after settlement
Accident books	Indefinitely

Medical records:

Record cards, X-rays	30 years after employment ends
Radioactive exposure	31 years
Accident reports	Indefinitely

Superannuation:

Pensioners' records	6 years after benefit cessation
Certs. of Existence	6 years

Salaries/wages:

Payroll	7 years
Annual earnings	13 years
Income tax records	6 years after end of tax year
Clock cards	2 years

Assets:

Ledgers	10 years
Asset disposal	Indefinitely
Consolidated a/c's	Indefinitely

Ledgers:

Nominal/general	Indefinitely
Sales/receivables	10 years
Purchases/payables	10 years
Journal	10 years

Cash records:

Paying-in records	6 years
Bank statements	6 years
Bank reconciliation	6 years
Remittance advices	6 years
Daily cash book	10 years
Petty cash records	6 years
Main cash book	Indefinitely

Suppliers:

Invoices – capital	10 years
– revenue	6 years
Quotations – capital	Indefinitely
– revenue	2 years
Purchase orders	3 years after receipt
Shipping documents	3 years
Customs & Excise	5 years

Sales:

Orders	6 years after supply
Quotations – capital	Indefinitely
– other	6 years after supply
Customers' complaints	4 years (for tax)
Sales invoices	6 years
Credit notes	6 years
Consignment notes	6 years
Statements	2 years

Stores:

Goods received notes	2 years
Goods in/out books	3 years
Stock inventories	6 years
Stock changes	2 years

G

Some organizations like to retain 'historically interesting' records indefinitely.

Appendix V

■ BODY DIMENSIONS

The dimensions below (in centimetres) cover 90 per cent of the population of Western industrialized countries.

Dimension	Men Average	Men Range ±	Women Average	Women Range ±
Height	174	14	162½	11½
Crown to eye	13	1½	10	1½
Eye to shoulder joint	19	1½	16½	1½
Shoulder to hip joint	48	2½	46	2½
Hip joint to knee joint	46	2½	43	2½
Knee joint to ankle joint	39½	2½	37	2½
Ankle joint to floor	9	1½	9	1½
Shoulder joint to elbow joint	29	2½	29	2½
Elbow joint to wrist joint	25½	2½	20½	2½
Wrist joint to middle finger tip	19	1½	16½	1½
Arm bent – rear of elbow to tip of middle finger	46	2½	37	2½
Arm extended – back to tip of middle finger	85	7½	76	7½
Seated				
Crown to buttock	90	7½	85	7½
Buttock to front of knee	58½	4	56	4
Leg extended – buttock to sole of foot	105½	9	100½	9
Top of knee to floor	53	2½	51	2½

Appendix VI

■ THE ELECTROMAGNETIC SYSTEM

Type of emission	*Approximate wavelength (metres)*
Gamma rays	10^{-12}
X-rays	10^{-10}
Ultraviolet	10^{-9}
Visible light	$10^{-7}-10^{-6}$
Infra-red	10^{-5}
Heat	10^{-3}
Radar	10^{-2}
Radio	$10^{1}-10^{3}$

Examples

kHz	*Waveband allocation (Europe)*
15010–14990	Standard frequency and time (15000 kHz/20 m)
14990–14350	Fixed
14350–14000	Amateur band
14000–13800	Fixed
13800–13600	Broadcasting ('22 metre short-wave band')
13600–13410	Fixed
13410–13360	Fixed/Radio astronomy
13360–13200	Aeronautical mobile

Examples

13770 kHz	Moscow/Netherlands	21.79 m
13759 kHz	Iceland	21.80 m
13755 kHz	Moscow	21.81 m
13750 kHz	Voice of Israel/Pyongyang	21.82 m
13715 kHz	Prague	21.87 m
13680 kHz	Baghdad	21.93 m
13670 kHz	Korea	21.95 m

Notes

1 The 'standard frequency and time' is a signal issuing on a wavelength of 20 m (15,000 kHz). This signal can be used for setting up and calibrating equipment.
2 Most radio-teletype and radio-data equipment in the office equipment field uses the 'fixed' bands. Though regrettably it does spill over into the amateur and maritime (and even broadcasting) bands.
3 The broadcasting bands are those used mainly by countries broadcasting to other countries. Like all the allocated bands, there is not enough room for everybody.

G

Appendix VII

■ CCITT STANDARDS SERIES

The CCITT set and promulgate a series of standards that are widely recognized. The main series (grouped within an initial identifying letter) are as follows:

D — tariff principles
E — international telephone
F — telegraph and telematic operations and quality
G — general characteristics of certain services
H — non-telephonic services
J — television and sound programmes
K — interference protection
L — cable and pole protection
M ⎫
N ⎭ — maintenance
O — measuring equipment
P — telephone quality.
Q — signalling
R — telegraph transmission
S — telegraph terminals
T — telematic services
V — telephone data communications
X — data communications networks
Z — languages (SDL, CHILL, MML)

The most often quoted series (in magazines and by manufacturers) are the V-series and the X-series. Of these, the two most often referred to are the X–24 and X–25 standards. These are concerned with connecting modems to data terminals on a public data network. X–25 is concerned with packet switching services.

Appendix VIII

■ PRESENT VALUE FACTORS

Formula: $(1 + i)^{-n}$ (i = interest rate, n = no. of years)

Years	2%	4%	6%	8%	10%	12%	14%	16%	18%	20%	25%	30%	50%
1	0.9804	0.9615	0.9434	0.9259	0.9091	0.8929	0.8772	0.8621	0.8475	0.8333	0.8000	0.7692	0.6667
2	0.9612	0.9246	0.8900	0.8573	0.8264	0.7972	0.7695	0.7432	0.7182	0.6944	0.6400	0.5917	0.4444
3	0.9423	0.8890	0.8396	0.7938	0.7513	0.7118	0.6750	0.6407	0.6086	0.5787	0.5120	0.4552	0.2963
4	0.9238	0.8548	0.7921	0.7350	0.6830	0.6355	0.5921	0.5523	0.5158	0.4823	0.4096	0.3501	0.1975
5	0.9057	0.8219	0.7473	0.6806	0.6209	0.5674	0.5194	0.4761	0.4371	0.4019	0.3277	0.2693	0.1317
6	0.8880	0.7903	0.7050	0.6302	0.5645	0.5066	0.4556	0.4104	0.3704	0.3349	0.2621	0.2072	0.0878
7	0.8706	0.7599	0.6651	0.5835	0.5132	0.4523	0.3996	0.3538	0.3139	0.2791	0.2097	0.1594	0.0585
8	0.8535	0.7307	0.6274	0.5403	0.4665	0.4039	0.3506	0.3050	0.2660	0.2326	0.1678	0.1226	0.0390
9	0.8368	0.7026	0.5919	0.5002	0.4241	0.3606	0.3075	0.2630	0.2255	0.1938	0.1342	0.0943	0.0260
10	0.8203	0.6756	0.5584	0.4632	0.3855	0.3220	0.2679	0.2267	0.1911	0.1615	0.1074	0.0725	0.0173
11	0.8043	0.6496	0.5268	0.4289	0.3505	0.2875	0.2366	0.1954	0.1619	0.1346	0.0859	0.0558	0.0116
12	0.7885	0.6246	0.4970	0.3971	0.3186	0.2567	0.2076	0.1685	0.1372	0.1122	0.0687	0.0429	0.0077
13	0.7730	0.6006	0.4688	0.3677	0.2897	0.2292	0.1821	0.1452	0.1163	0.0935	0.0550	0.0330	0.0051
14	0.7579	0.5775	0.4423	0.3405	0.2633	0.2046	0.1597	0.1252	0.0985	0.0779	0.0440	0.0254	0.0034
15	0.7430	0.5553	0.4173	0.3152	0.2394	0.1827	0.1401	0.1079	0.0835	0.0649	0.0352	0.0195	0.0023
16	0.7284	0.5339	0.3936	0.2919	0.2176	0.1631	0.1229	0.0930	0.0708	0.0541	0.0281	0.0150	0.0015
17	0.7142	0.5134	0.3714	0.2703	0.1978	0.1456	0.1078	0.0802	0.0600	0.0451	0.0225	0.0116	0.0010
18	0.7002	0.4936	0.3503	0.2502	0.1799	0.1300	0.0946	0.0691	0.0508	0.0376	0.0180	0.0089	0.0007
19	0.6864	0.4746	0.3305	0.2317	0.1635	0.1161	0.0829	0.0596	0.0431	0.0313	0.0144	0.0068	0.0005
20	0.6730	0.4564	0.3118	0.2145	0.1486	0.1037	0.0728	0.0514	0.0365	0.0261	0.0115	0.0053	0.0003

G

NAME INDEX

Numbers in *italics* refer to names occurring in reference lists and lists of further reading.